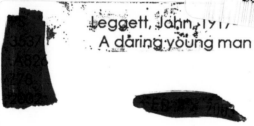

A

ALSO BY JOHN LEGGETT

Wilder Stone

The Gloucester Branch

Who Took the Gold Away

Ross and Tom: Two American Tragedies

Storytelling

Gulliver House

Making Believe

A DARING
YOUNG MAN

A DARING
YOUNG MAN

A Biography of William Saroyan

JOHN
LEGGETT

ALFRED A. KNOPF
NEW YORK
2002

THIS IS A BORZOI BOOK
PUBLISHED BY ALFRED A. KNOPF

Copyright © 2002 by John Leggett
All rights reserved under International and Pan-American Copyright
Conventions. Published in the United States by Alfred A. Knopf,
a division of Random House, Inc., New York, and simultaneously
in Canada by Random House of Canada Limited, Toronto.
Distributed by Random House, Inc., New York.
www.aaknopf.com

Knopf, Borzoi Books, and the colophon are registered trademarks
of Random House, Inc.

Library of Congress Cataloging-in-Publication Data
Leggett, John, [date]
A daring young man : a biography of William
Saroyan / by John Leggett. — 1st ed.
p.   cm.
ISBN 0-375-41301-4 (alk. paper)
1. Saroyan, William, 1908–1981 2. Authors, American—20th century—
Biography. 3. Armenian Americans—Biography. I. Title.
PS3537.A826 Z78 2002
818'.5209—dc21
[B]   2002067149

Manufactured in the United States of America
First Edition

For Alice Adams

Contents

Acknowledgments

I am especially grateful to the late William Abrahams for proposing this project, to the late James D. Hart, director of the Bancroft Library at the University of California, for encouraging me in it, and to Bonnie Hardwick, also of the Bancroft, for knowledge and kindness during my many years in its reading room.

I am also grateful to Patricia Perez-Arce for psychological guidelines, to the late Alan Williams for editorial overview, to Fred Hill, my literary agent, for sound judgment and timely counsel, to Robert Powsner for expert piloting in legal waters, and to Frances Kiernan for her encouragement at a time when it was critical. Further thanks to Ben Amirkhanian for being a good friend and trusting there would be virtue to my portrait of William Saroyan, and, finally, to my editor, Victoria Wilson, whose instinct for what a writing person means is a joy to share.

Introduction

I REMEMBER WHEN SAROYAN was the rage, when plays spilled from his beloved Underwood like bucketfuls from a swollen springtime stream. In the year 1939 three of them were on Broadway, one a Pulitzer and Drama Critics prizewinner for best play of the year. College and community theaters staged his latest fantasies, and audiences across the nation rejoiced in the escape into a latter-day Forest of Arden.

The Saroyan assault on the theater was no surprise to the publishing world, where, four years earlier, he had arrived in a similar whirlwind of marvels and adulation. His publisher, Bennett Cerf, had dubbed him "the Wonder Boy from Fresno."

Today he is out of fashion. Young people have never heard of him. "Styron?" they ask, or "Steinbeck, you mean?" He used to be taught in the schools, read on the beach, talked of earnestly among aspiring writers. In five high school English classes where I inquired, only one hand was raised. It belonged to a bookish teenager who claimed to have read everything Saroyan had written.

Why has Saroyan lost the enthusiasm of the young? "Sentimentality" is the usual reply. With his saintly whores and generous grocers, he is too maudlin for a generation bred to expect evil and pestilence. If that were entirely true Saroyan would be doomed to eternal forgettery, but despite the amiable voice, the real Saroyan is not a sentimental man. He is an angry one, and most of his work is openly so. He is angry at a world so misguided as to make poverty and war. He is angry at authority, *anyone* who tells him what, or what not, to do.

There is a small but thriving Saroyan industry built on a solemn devotion to the author, to his exaltation of society's outcasts and denunciation of their oppressors.

One division is academic. In universities that attract ethnic students, Saroyan and his work make a centerpiece of graduate study. Even his obscure work is a favorite subject for doctoral dissertation, psychological analysis, and scholarly debate.

Another division is made up of the collectors. Rare-book dealers find a lively market in the multitude of Saroyan titles. A self-respecting collector would have a hundred of them. A good copy of *Three Times Three* brings $250.

The third division is that of the zealots. There are Saroyan fans who find a gemlike perfection in one or another Saroyan work. Some actors feel that way about his one-act play *Hello Out There.* I know a fine-press printer who believes in *Five Ripe Pears* as gospel of the short-story form and has set an edition by hand to prove it.

There is no denying Saroyan's bountiful gift. At its core was the great gusher of his energy. It burst from him when he sat down to his typewriter as if it were the compressed spirit of generations of martyred Armenians, suddenly released by the Bill of Rights.

An equal blessing was his innate sense of language. He had an ear for the rhythm, sonority, and sensuality of colloquial speech. He had an eye for the precisely right detail that revealed an emotion, a desire, an anxiety. Although a man stoutly opposed to his own formal education, his aim for the bull's-eye word was a marksman's.

Also, he had an instinct for subject. It led him off the trodden paths in search of cause and hero, and instead of the nation's victors and swells, he chose its rejects and losers. He recognized them as important from his own mirror. This was a kind of man he really knew.

For a fellow who lacked the patience to read a book to its end, he made remarkably good use of the public library. He was drawn to the best writers there, who rewarded him with a sense of literary form and the importance of an authoritative narrative voice.

He was fearless in pursuit of honesty, the telling of his personal truth, which alternated between belief in his insignificance, the accuracy of society's contempt for him, and in his greatness, that he had been created a special creature, talented and perceptive enough to lead the world to essential truth and purpose.

This was the force that brought forth five lasting achievements: his first story collection, *The Daring Young Man on the Flying Trapeze;* his one-act play *My Heart's in the Highlands;* his full-length play *The Time of Your Life;* his collection of boyhood stories *My Name Is Aram;* and the screenplay and novel *The Human Comedy.*

But for all the promise and brilliance of Saroyan's launching of a literary career, and his half century of struggle to reach the place he believed was being held for him in the pantheon of American writers, his gift was not large enough. More accurately, his gift came with a powerful curb, the nature of which can be seen in the revelations of Saroyan's huge, candid journal, which he kept from 1934 until his death, in the spring of 1981.

It is a cautionary tale that lies within the classic American success story of an immigrant boy's rise from the loneliness and misery of an orphanage to the peculiar grandeur of international celebrity and prominence in what was known as café society.

This ascent culminated in a stormy marriage, a yearned-for family life shattered in a sensational divorce, a reprise of both events, and a lifetime of tormented relations with his children.

While Saroyan was the only member of his own family born in America, his roots were wholly Armenian. His father, Armenak, died when Bill was an infant, but the boy mourned him throughout his life, which he often thought of as atonement for the gyp of Armenak's emigration and humiliating failure in California, and for the pitiful, unfinished scraps of his writing.

For a three-year-old, the Fred Finch orphanage in Oakland was a chilling place to be left, and his years there planted a bitterness toward institutional life that he carried with him when, at eight, he left. As a schoolboy in Fresno he continued to feel his nobodiness as an Armenian kid, too unsavory and perverse for any respect at all. It would cause him to drop out of school entirely and forego further education.

He had no firsthand knowledge of Armenia, nor of the genocide his family had fled, but I like to think he carried a racial gene from his ancestral home of Bitlis, a tribal memory of massacre by the bloody and perfidious Turks.

By adolescence, Saroyan had anesthetized his heart to such painful feelings as loss, scorn, and unrequited love. He substituted a force of self-reliance strong enough to dismiss the outcast he had been. Belief in himself as a writer became a characteristic cockiness. When threatened, it grew into a hubris, a denial of his limitations, and an indifference to the feelings of others, making him the kind of man we might cross a busy street to avoid.

Why do I identify with this bitter and ultimately lonely human being? Because he found that being a writer lifted him out of obscurity and the scorn of his family and friends. He also found that self-reliance, the dependence on his own mind and heart to find his way, was the only reliable compass.

It was a pretty good compass, too, guiding him to fame, front pages, front tables, and acquaintance with the principal literary, theater, and film figures of his times. However, it was not true enough to see him through the perversity, humiliation, and hardship he made of going to war. World War II did put an end to his extraordinary run of luck, and yet he managed to press on toward acknowledged achievement even when he knew he had lost his way.

Although Saroyan's later years provided him some professional satisfactions, further triumphs in the short story, and a new facility with the memoir, time only multiplied his resentments, deepened his failures at friendship and love for those he loved most, and sped him along his vertiginous course.

The Saroyan story, so gallantly begun, becomes a tragedy of rage and rejection. We can feel pity and fear for him and the catharsis these are said to bring—in gratitude for being spared ourselves.

A DARING
YOUNG MAN

ROOTS

WILLIAM SAROYAN was wholly a writer, a man with a gift for communicating emotion through language and an extravagant ambition to put it to use, to tell the world about his feelings and be embraced, made famous and rich for it. He was equally a *new* American, a tribal escapee from the bloody slaughters of his ancestral Armenia, miraculously afloat in New World promise.

His story, with its dizzying ascents of literary success followed by plunges into humiliating failure, suggests that he was manipulated by a capricious, Dickensian creator, but it leaves us in no doubt of the virtues and vices that propelled his errant course. In his life as well as in his most successful work, Saroyan reveals a powerful inner conflict between those traditional values brought through Ellis Island with his family's threadbare clothing and those new ones that beckoned from American billboards and movie screens.

In fact, Saroyan was born in Fresno, California, on August 31, 1908, and had no firsthand knowledge of his Armenian homeland and the massacre of his people, but the brutality of it was in his Armenian soul and consciousness. So it is fair to say that an element of William Saroyan's life began before his birth, as early as 1896, when "the Great Assassin," Sultan Abdul Hamid, concluded that he could cure the Ottoman Empire's many ills by destroying the Christian Armenian nation.

The massacre of three hundred thousand Armenians during the sultan's reign was continued during World War I by the Young Turks, who destroyed a million more. Among the civilized voices raised against these Turkish atrocities was that of the American Presbyterian Church. One of its missionaries, Dr. William Stonehill, took an interest in Armenak Saroyan, a young Armenian with a likable earnestness and an aptitude for English.

Stonehill felt he could find work for Armenak if he would come to his parish in metropolitan New Jersey.

Thus Armenak, a strikingly handsome fellow with huge, sympathetic eyes, a steep brow, and an imposing sweep of mustache, arrived in Jersey City in 1905. Under the sponsorship of Dr. Stonehill and his wife, he began ministering, in English and Armenian, to congregations in Paterson and New York City.

The continuing Turkish oppression made Armenak's family follow him as soon as it could. As Saroyan recalls in *The Bicycle Rider in Beverly Hills*, it took his mother, Takoohi, then in her twenties; her two daughters, Cosette and Zabel; her mother, Lucy Garoghlanian; her sister Verkine; and her brother Aram nearly two years to complete their journey to the New World. They had to bivouac along the way to gather enough money to proceed. During their first layover, in the Armenian town of Erzurum, Takoohi increased the party with a first son, Henry. They stayed in Marseille for several months and spent six more in Le Havre, the women knitting stockings that Aram peddled to the shops.

The transatlantic journey in steerage was a nightmare, and Takoohi always recalled the kindness of a fellow passenger, an Assyrian woman, who looked after her children when she was too ill to do so. The worst of their passage came when they reached the crowded halls of the U.S. immigration service on Ellis Island. The health inspectors found Grandmother Lucy's eyes were infected. She could not be admitted and would have to return to France.

They were told there was no recourse, and the Saroyan family waited in despair, not knowing what to do. Fortunately, Lucy did know. She prayed throughout the night for help, and in the morning the doctors approved her entry into the United States.

Armenak, delighted at the first sight of his son, took his family to Mrs. Stonehill for indoctrination. The womenfolk were wearing the clothes in which they had left Bitlis two years earlier, and Mrs. Stonehill felt finding replacements for these would be a good place to begin. She set out to find more conventional dresses for the ladies and laid out corsets for them, all of which the Saroyan women spurned. They were happy in their familiar garments.

Takoohi was equally determined about lifestyle. She did not care for what she had seen of New Jersey, and she had heard that Fresno was a paradise where fruit grew in unbelievable flavor and profusion and where an Armenian colony prospered. She felt a brighter future awaited them in California, so the Saroyans went west.

Although Armenak was promised a church assignment at Yettem, near Fresno, its congregation was Turkish-speaking, and he did not get along with it. As the family found a ramshackle house on H Street in Fresno and struggled to establish itself there, poor Armenak's luck ran thin. He turned to whatever agricultural jobs he could find.

On the night of August 31, 1908, while Armenak was working at his cousins' the Mouradians' vineyard in Sanger, Takoohi bore him another child. The next morning Armenak bicycled the eleven miles to Fresno to greet his second son and give him the name William, after his friend and patron Dr. Stonehill, who had died three months earlier.

Neither Grandmother Lucy, not yet forty, nor Takoohi, not yet twenty-five, were pleased at yet another mouth to feed nor with Armenak's hesitancy at finding his place in this land of boundless promise. Although Armenak's mother, Hripsime, had come to live nearby, Takoohi held her responsible for Armenak's fecklessness and would not have her in the house.

Over the next several years, Armenak searched for better work, moving his family first to San Bruno, then to San Francisco for a job with the Salvation Army, and finally to Campbell, a small town forty miles south of San Francisco, where he hoped to make a living by raising chickens.

But his luck had run out entirely. The price of eggs declined. The chickens died. Then, on one hot afternoon in July 1911, he came home complaining of a stomachache and a great thirst. All the water he drank would not quench that thirst. His final plea to Takoohi was not to beat the kids. Then he died of a burst appendix. He was thirty-six; his son William was three.

Faced with raising four children alone, Takoohi decided to put them in the Fred Finch orphanage, in Oakland, and to take a job in San Francisco as a domestic. Young Willie, as he was known then, was a round-faced three-year-old with a mop of dark hair, challenging eyes, and a sulky lower lip. At the orphanage, Takoohi told him that she had to leave him but he must not cry for he was a big boy. She gave him a toy, a windup, a dancing black man called "the Coon Jigger." Willie did cry, and although he knew that the brightly painted toy was a flimsy substitute for his mother and didn't want it, he kept it for a long time and remembered it for the rest of his life.

The orphanage superintendent, John Wesley Hagen, congratulated Willie on his manly behavior and took him to the dormitory for small boys, a place that became somewhat less dismal when Willie was visited by Henry, who would be living nearby, and when he learned that his sisters would be living in the girls' dormitory.

Takoohi found work as cook and housekeeper for a family in San Francisco, and she was able to visit her children on occasional Sundays. She would bring a picnic lunch and spread it on the grass, where there was a view of the bay. She spoke mostly to her eldest daughter, Cosette, softly, in Armenian.

Willie asked six-year-old Henry why their mother did not come *every* afternoon, and while he did not understand the reason, he gathered there was one, and that it was possible she might never return. When Henry assured him she would, Willie asked why they never saw their father. Henry explained the difference. Their father was dead. But Willie did not understand. When their mother was away, was she not dead too?

The Fred Finch orphanage made much of Christmas, and Saroyan would never forget its central feature, a visit from the Shriners' Santa Claus. With his red suit and plainly false beard, he looked suspect to Willie, but Willie still got into line for an interview.

Reading the boy's name tag, Santa greeted him heartily and tried to take him onto his lap. Willie resisted, standing his ground until he was asked, as the others had been, what Santa could bring him.

His response was immediate: "My father."

A perplexed Santa replied that he would see what he could do.

Over the next several days, Willie wondered if Santa would, or could, deliver, if he were a man of such powers. Santa was onstage for the presentation, and when their names were called the children rose from their seats in the auditorium to queue up at his sleigh.

When Willie reached Santa he heard his name mispronounced, and Santa's helper handed him a package with his name on it. It was the size of a shoebox, and heavy. When Willie asked Santa what it was, he got no answer. In spite of pressure from behind, he stood, tearing off the wrapping. Finding a set of blocks, he protested that it wasn't what he wanted.

Back in his seat among the others, he felt he had been fooled, that his expectancy had been encouraged and then mocked. It was a feeling he was to reexperience every Christmas of his life.

At the next Christmas, when he was four, he contracted a contagious illness and was put to bed alone in an attic room. He could hear the distant voices of the others singing "Silent Night" while a fever raged in his bones, and he knew that something inside was trying to burn him up.

In *Sons Come and Go, Mothers Go on Forever,* Saroyan remembers summoning the image of his mother, with her womanly cushioning and the peculiarly comforting scents of her sweat and her dime-store perfume. He imagined she would know he was fighting a hard fight and would hurry from Laguna Street in San Francisco, come by ferry boat to Oakland, and walk up the stairs to open the door and be beside him.

No one came. Although he knew something deadly was happening to him, he was determined to look after himself and refused to believe that anything could kill him. He passed through a delirium that seemed to threaten his being but endured it and, at dawn, knew he had survived a terrifying crisis and been restored to life stronger, surer of himself than before the ordeal.

Thirty years later, at Christmastime when he was settling into a midtown Manhattan apartment with his wife and two children, he wrote a story, "Third Day After Christmas," that echoes these infant experiences. It is a curiously bitter, poignant account of six-year-old Donald Efaw, who, on the third day after Christmas, is abandoned by his father outside a Third Avenue saloon. The bartender ignores the weeping boy throughout the cold day but at nightfall admits him, feeds him, and takes him home. There Donald resolves that he has finished crying, quite likely for life.

Although Saroyan described "Third Day After Christmas" as a tour de force, he infused it with the unmistakable power of self-revelation. Donald Efaw is clearly a depiction of the very young William.

Seven of the smallest boys at Fred Finch lived in a dormitory presided over by Miss Winchester, a woman of thirty or so who wore perfume. She used the nearby lavatory, and they all laughed at the sounds she made in there. Willie dreaded Saturday night, when Miss Winchester knelt at the big bathtub to bathe the children, one by one. Some in the small boys' ward cried every night. Some were rockers, some were criers. They began as soon as Miss Winchester turned out the lights.

The criers cried softly most of the time but occasionally burst forth. The rockers rocked slowly most of the time, but sometimes they rocked swiftly, making much noise, and one child would bang his head against his crib's headboard. In the darkness it was impossible to know who was doing what, and as soon as the door opened all was quiet. The seven boys knew that it was weak to rock or cry, but they didn't stop. In the morning, however, there would be accusations and taunts about it.

Listening, Willie decided he was lucky, since he didn't want to cry, or didn't need to, and the crying suggested that the orphanage was even more hateful to the other boys than it was to him. He particularly liked a staff member named Blanche Fulton. She was a volunteer who came to the orphanage to look after the smaller kids and teach them about art. Said to be a rich woman, she brought them paper, crayons, and paint. Willie annoyed her by whistling while he drew and painted.

One day she took eight of the small boys by streetcar and ferryboat to the 1915 San Francisco Fair, the Panama Pacific International Exposition. Willie was impressed by a magnificent Oriental building from which two camels appeared, followed by four Arabs in bright costume, one of them making strange music on a pipe.

Then, in 1916, when Willie was eight, there was a change in the family fortunes. After five years of separation, Takoohi was able to reunite her family. Cosette, who had been working in the orphanage office, had a final argument with orphanage management, and all four children boarded the train for Fresno. It was a journey of wonderful expectation. They were going *home*, back to Fresno, in the San Joaquin Valley.

At the Fresno station they were met by Uncle Dickran Bagdasarian, husband of Takoohi's sister Verkine. He drove them to their grandmother Lucy's house, where they stayed until they were able to find one of their own. This was at 2226 San Benito Avenue, near the Southern Pacific tracks. The rent was $20 a month, and the house was no more than a porous-roofed shack that they shared with a variety of bugs and rodents. But it was the first Saroyan home Willie would remember, and it was the center of his boyhood world.

They all worked to keep the family together. Takoohi packed figs and grapes at Roeding's. Cosette went to Heald's Business College and got a job in a law office. Zabel clerked at Woolworth's. Henry sold papers and later worked as a messenger for Postal Telegraph, while Willie followed, as closely as he could, in his brother's tracks.

Willie's first encounter with his mother's younger brother Aram came soon after their arrival at the San Benito house. Although Aram was still in his twenties, to Willie he was an elder, entitled to full honors. Uncle Aram spoke rapidly, colorfully, to a spellbound family audience. He paused suddenly to tell Willie, in Armenian, to shut the door.

Leaning on orphanage custom and his meager Armenian, Willie replied that he hadn't opened the door. Uncle Aram replied quickly that this was no obstacle to his shutting it. Then, convulsed by the boy's garbled defense and his own brilliant parry, Aram roared.

Willie shut the door amid the laughter of everyone in the kitchen—his mother, his sisters, his brother, and this strange man. In the end, his embarrassment gave way to satisfaction that he had been taken for a comic. While he knew he was no such thing, he had a new respect for clowning.

Uncle Aram had some training in law and spoke an accented English interlarded with legal cliches that were intended to provide professional authority but that added a further droll aspect to his performance. He told stories with style, control, and timing, and they were the funniest Willie had ever heard.

On one hand, Willie found his uncle the most arrogant and unreasonable of men. On the other, he knew that, during his nine years in the New World, Uncle Aram had learned about growing and shipping grapes and had moved from poverty to wealth. In terms of making out in the world, Aram was the greatest man in his family.

Aram went to meetings and spoke on behalf of Armenian causes. Like others of the Armenian community in Fresno he felt the weight of Armenian history. While the allied victory of 1918 had ended the Turkish horror, its systematic genocide had slaughtered over half the Armenian population. The Armenia that was proclaimed a Soviet republic in 1921 was one tenth the size of the historic nation. It had lost all independence and could look only to its diaspora for pride.

For Willie, of course, the bloody history of the Armenian people lacked the immediacy of Fresno, the city that was to be his forge. He would rise before daybreak to walk to the San Joaquin Baking Company, redolent with the aroma of newly baked loaves. Here he would search out the important man in the fine suit to inquire if there was any "chicken bread." The man understood what kind he meant and picked out the best flawed loaves to drop into the sack Willie held open. The chicken bread was not good enough for the rich and too good for chickens. But there were many people at Willie's house, and none were ashamed to eat it. Later he would think of chicken bread as what made him solid, what allowed him to move through the city and shout. It was bread to nourish his anger.

Grandmother Lucy presided over the weekly baths, heating water on the sawdust-fueled kitchen stove and pouring it over the protesting Willie, seated in a laundry tub on the crumbling, often freezing, back porch. She scrubbed him with a coarse cloth and strong laundry soap, and in a comic acknowledgment of his maleness she handed him the soap to deal with that equipment while she applied the cloth to his back.

Takoohi was a fine Armenian cook, and the four children were happiest while feasting at the kitchen table, but they took great care not to spill sugar on the kitchen floor, for that infuriated their mother. When she stepped in just a few grains of it she would curse them violently. Her rages were terrible, ending in her going off to be by herself for hours or even days, leading Henry to believe she was insane. This was not so, but at thirty-six her hands were gnarled from hard work, she was eight years a widow, and she knew she would be one for the rest of her life.

She was also perceptive about the people she met, saw them clearly enough to mimic them. From the fruit-packing houses and canneries where she worked she brought home the news of her day in a performance that kept Willie rapt with wonder and admiration.

Even the earliest Saroyan stories are autobiographical enough to provide a reliable portrait of the artist as a boy, to show Willie the child enveloped by his fatherless family. In "The Broken Wheel" he learns the strength of the clan. An older brother introduces him to the joy that he has found in the countryside and in a battered horn; an uncle, owner of the only red Apperson roadster in America, shows him the delicious pride of lifestyle. The

Saroyan family: Mihran (Armenak's younger brother), Takoohi,
and Armenak Saroyan holding two-year-old Bill, Fresno, 1910

story's climax comes in the collapse of an overburdened bicycle, comic enough to elicit the whole family's laughter and an early understanding that this chorus is the antidote to grief, and to death.

The force of his mother, Takoohi, is here in her momentary sorrow but mainly in her assurance that while tragedy and pain are the substance of life, as a family they always survive them, and always will. Although Willie's father, Armenak, is dead, he is here as well. In "The Moment of Life" and "Summertime" Armenak is reconstructed from a photograph, from family recollections of his self-education in Armenia, his plans for the American adventure, his journey, his subsequent hard times, and his premature death. In Willie's uncle's mourning for Armenak, Willie finds a certainty that his father is not dead, but alive, in nature and in himself.

Willie went to nearby Emerson School and soon developed strong feelings about his several teachers. Although the school was in the heart of Fresno's Armenian town, he sensed that one particular teacher, Miss Clifford, disliked Armenian children. Not only was she open and persistent about this, but she centered her dislike on him. He felt she had marked him as her personal enemy and began each day with sarcasm about his appearance, his clothing, his manners, his intelligence, and his impatience with her teaching. She had chosen a determined adversary. The more she reprimanded him for his arrogance and his refusal to accept anything she said, the more he resented and rebelled against her. He never forgave Miss Clifford for her rudeness and hostility toward him nor for her indifference to his own lesson, that any sarcasm from her would be answered in kind by him.

Another teacher, Miss Brockington, was thin, prim, and older than the others, but he respected her. He felt she was wrong about whom to emulate in the world and what to aspire to in life. He felt her heroes were frauds, and the goal she held out to the children, the finding and keeping of a job, was too limiting and belittling. But she didn't hold his nationality or his personality against him, and he was always courteous toward her.

As for his teacher Miss Chambers, he developed an instant crush. She was a soft-voiced beauty in her mid-twenties. She had a gravity and poise and a kind of pathos he suspected was the result of a lost love. There was a pleasing, womanly fragrance about her.

When he spoke she often encouraged him with her smile, and that smile was a matter of complicity between them. It gave him a sense of importance that stayed with him when he went into the street and then home to supper and bed. He dreamed of her, and it seemed that he loved her forever afterward.

It was the teacher Miss Carmichael who kept him after school one day, not for punishment, as he had suspected, but to tell him that she knew he was somebody and to urge him to go to college. He had always believed that he was important, but she was the first teacher to acknowledge it. She made him think that he had a responsibility toward this matter of being somebody, and he was grateful to her. He sensed that the intentions of all his teachers, even Miss Clifford's, were excellent, but that whatever education he acquired would be *in spite of,* and not on account of, them.

He was under the illusion that there wasn't a course in which he didn't excel, but each week one or another of his teachers told him that he was failing, and unless he improved he would be kept back. This frightened him, for if anything filled his young heart with terror it was the notion of not moving on. But he hated school. He was hugely bored by it. He responded by ridiculing the principal, the teachers, the subjects, and the students.

When he was not criticizing some part of the school system he grew depressed and fell to dreaming. When one of his teachers requested that he pay attention instead of dreaming, he told her he was not *dreaming,* he was *thinking.*

During the ten-minute recesses, morning and afternoon, he would race to the playground and tell himself that school was so boring, so useless, so everlastingly slow that he didn't know what to do.

The early stories reveal a boy who feels physically vulnerable, such as "Fifty Yard Dash," in which the boy sends off for the Lionel Strongfort bodybuilding course in vain hopes of winning a race. Although he still comes in last, he takes comfort from his philosopher uncle's belief in family spiritual powers.

In "A Fistfight for Armenia," he is cowed by schoolyard bullies who want to punish him for being a "dirty Armenian." Although he takes wrestling lessons in order to retaliate, he understands that *real* victory lies elsewhere.

This fictional Willie sympathizes with another victim of persecution in the story "War." He is a German boy spurned by his playmates because it is 1918, and World War I. The young narrator, like young Saroyan, sees that it is not Germans who make the war—for Germans are just like us—but the evil that is in everyone.

When Willie was eight he asked his mother if he could sell papers as Henry did, and she said he was too young to go into the streets. As he would recall for the piece "Daily News," his brother confirmed this, saying he had to be at least ten, but finally agreed to talk to his boss about it.

When Henry took his younger brother to visit the *Evening Herald* building, Willie was awed by everything he saw. The press itself was a huge black machine giving off an odor of ink and paper and warm oil. The pressmen's arms and faces were smeared with ink, and they wore square caps made of old newspapers. They were amiable fellows, telling stories and singing, until they went to work in a kind of frenzy. Rushing in with chases of type, they climbed onto the press to loosen screws, remove parts and insert others, and pour ink onto the platen and spread it. Then the press would stir, slowly gathering speed until it was making a thunderous noise, and from its mouth the papers spewed—folded, stacked, and ready for the street. Outside, thirty or forty boys were waiting for their papers, and the crowd of them was a daunting sight.

Henry introduced Willie to the boss, a moon-faced, kindly sort of man. The boss studied Willie carefully and asked him how old he was. Primed for the question, Willie replied that he was ten, and he understood at once that the man knew he was not telling the truth. He was as sure the man would deny him the newsboy job as he was that he wanted it desperately, and he was stunned to be told that he could go to work.

Henry and Bill with a neighbor's dog, just after their
father's death, in Campbell, California, 1911

He was soon on Fresno's streets, holding a half-dozen newspapers under his arm, trying his voice on the city's people. He shouted with all his might. He felt it a privilege and an honor to stand in the center of Fresno and shout.

On his first day he sold four papers and earned only ten cents, but he felt it had been a success, since he had learned how to shout and what to expect from the world around him. A policeman had looked him over suspiciously, and an older newsboy had told him to get away from his corner and stay away. The boy's manner had been unfriendly. Nevertheless, walking home with Henry that evening, Willie felt newly important.

Henceforth he prowled Fresno with his armload of papers. He slipped into the saloons and gambling joints and up the stairs of whorehouses, curious to see the faces of those who shared the city with him. He was fascinated by the appearance of the old whores and by the way they spoke to him, and by the ugliness and foul smells of the old buildings.

As the fictional Saroyan adolescent becomes aware of girls, he is particularly susceptible to the pretty, well-dressed ones from the *right* side of the railroad tracks, and to his family's amusement he roams the town in his moonstruck state. In "And Man," his feelings of ugliness are intensified by his family's jokes about his big nose and its indication of having genitals to match. But at school he feels the sting, real or imagined, of prejudice. In class he is ridiculed by his teacher for being Armenian, and among his laughing classmates he finds the girl whom he secretly loves.

In "Seventeen," another portrayal of his vulnerable adolescence, Saroyan's ethnic hero is powerfully attracted to girls and concedes it is "the female shape" that bewitches him. However, he is made to feel "unworthy," and becomes a hardened boy, the terror of his teachers. He persuades himself that women are evil, that the tenderness he sees in movies is fake and only lust is real. This belief takes him to a whorehouse to find out about women, and in the discovery's aftermath he despises himself.

He made a friend of Charley Willie, a ticket taker at the Hippodrome. He would give Charley a free paper, and Charley would let him into the theater. The day the dance team of Reno and Mary came to the Hippodrome, Saroyan sat down in the auditorium with no idea he was about to have a revelation.

He had learned how it was in the adult world with no work in the packing houses and people dying by the thousands in the flu epidemic. Then this young Italian, Reno, came out onto the stage. With a derby cocked on his head and a cigar in his mouth, he looked tough. He didn't speak and seemed indifferent to the audience as he tapped his way around the stage, smiling in a way that was both resentful and accepting. He began to sing, and he seemed to be saying that, however bad things were, a fellow could still move around in his best style and prove he was alive.

When the song and dance routine ended, Reno did not bow. He just smiled as if he really felt sorry for everybody, and Willie recognized himself. This was how he would be in years ahead—sore, but wanting to get all he could. He'd bust his neck getting it. He knew there wasn't much to get, but he'd keep right on trying till he died.

By the time he entered Fresno High School, Willie had taken a job, as Henry had, as a Postal Telegraph messenger. He worked the night shift, from four in the afternoon until midnight, and, as a result, often fell asleep in class. His teachers caught him, warned him, and in the end despaired of him. This didn't matter to Willie. He wouldn't have given up his job at the telegraph office for all the sleep or all the schooling in the world. He took pride in being the best messenger at the office. The job came first.

One day Takoohi brought out a packet of Armenak's writing, notebooks he had made out of wrapping paper, and explained to Willie that some of the notebooks had been lost and this was all that remained. For an hour Willie puzzled over the scraps. Some were in English, but most of them were in Armenian, which he could not read. There were fragments of prose and poetry, some written while Armenak was in New York. The penmanship was careful, but what Willie could understand of the content disappointed him. He was left with a sense of his father's failure. He felt his father should have done better in his short, tragic life.

Tying up the bundle, Takoohi told him that his father had run out of time. Willie resolved that he would have the time. Where his father had failed, he would succeed. Although his days were crowded with work, school, and play, he sought out the Fresno Public Library. Its displays of newspapers and magazines, and its stacks of books, seemed a depot of life's possibilities, and he became a regular browser.

When he was twelve he came across Guy de Maupassant's story "Bell," about a cripple, an outcast, who was turned from every door, starving and beaten. Willie had found a hero with whom he could identify, and he was moved. He would always recall that moment as the one in which he resolved to be a writer.

In the early story "Baby," another fictional Willie sublimates his attraction to a fourteen-year-old new girl in his vast writing ambitions. His ambitions are on the scale of Genesis, cosmological, sure to command attention—as the whale rolling in the fathomless sea—and he intends them to reveal *everything* about embracing life and death. In endearing self-mockery, he reminds himself he is just a small boy, always in trouble, but still, he sings the glory of being alive.

In 1921, Willie's thirteenth year, he hoped to transfer from Longfellow Junior High to Tech High so that he could learn typing. He felt it unwise to admit that he thought typing would improve his chances of becoming a great writer, so he told the woman in charge that in looking for work he would need to know how to type. She let him have the transfer slip, and he went to typing class faithfully. Within two months he became an expert. If he thought a word or sentence, his fingers typed it. When he brought to mind a paragraph, his fingers kept pace with his thinking. He knew this was an achievement, and he felt nothing could stop him now.

Nor was the young fictional Saroyan always on the wistful end of desire. In the story "Sweetheart, Sweetheart," his emergent masculinity has seized the attention of the sexy next-door neighbor, and her crush on him brings more teasing from the women in his family. Just as he felt despised for his appearance, clumsiness, and Armenianness, Saroyan also knew he was attractive to women, from his first awareness of himself as a boy becoming a man.

In 1925, when he was eighteen, Saroyan—now called Bill—dropped out

Eleven-year-old Bill in Fresno, 1919

of high school altogether. Through family connections he found work in the vineyards and offices, but none interested him nor kept him long. When Henry left Fresno for San Francisco, in 1926, Bill followed him there but could find no satisfactory job. He hitchhiked to Los Angeles, hoping to sell a story to a motion-picture company, but no one was willing to read unsolicited manuscripts.

He found temporary jobs at the ACLU office and as a clerk at Bullock's department store. Want of a regular paycheck and of treatment for a persistent fever made him join the National Guard. He was assigned to the Presidio at Monterey, where his fever developed into pneumonia, and he served most of his time in the infirmary.

Henry had established himself in San Francisco. Encouraged by this, his mother and two sisters had joined him there. So it was Bill's home too, and he returned there to take various jobs in the city's markets, warehouses, and a cemetery. He and Henry went into business together, as Saroyan Brothers, selling flowers for all occasions. They rented a little shop on Geary Street, and Bill, who had been reading the Thackeray novel at the library, named it Vanity Fair Florists. But it did not flourish, and after four months the Saroyan Brothers were evicted for not paying their rent.

Although he put in regular hours at the library and wrote when he could, Bill's goal seemed ever distant. In the summer of 1928, he decided that he must go it alone, and do so in New York. He chose New York because he was an immigrant like his father, who had begun his naturalization there, and because it was where one went to succeed as a writer. Although he lacked even the $38 for his bus fare, his father's younger brother, Mihran, loaned him $200, which his grandmother Lucy sewed into his sweater.

The trip took ten days and brought him to Manhattan on an August night, which was when he discovered his suitcase, with his precious sweater, was missing. He had only a dollar and some change, and he knew no one and had no letter of introduction, nor any idea where he would sleep. As he set off into the city's dark streets he was tired, angry, and anxious. He ran for two blocks, then walked downtown until, at Twenty-third Street, he saw the lighted sign of the YMCA.

A room required his dollar in advance. The cafeteria was closed, but a man there made him a ham and cheese sandwich for a dime. Up in his room Bill ate the sandwich and drank cold water, four glasses of it, and then told himself that, lost suitcase or not, he was going to make it here.

But New York was a desolate city. Penniless and hungry, Bill wandered the crowded streets and understood that here, in the press and jostle of a multitude of strangers, he was as alone as he could be. There were too many people. He could not believe so many were alive. There was too much noise.

The furnished room he found on Forty-third Street had no window, and its only light was a sputtering gas jet. While he moved on to others, none suited him. The sight of a million windows glowing at night brought him sadness and a longing for home, and he felt deceived by the city.

But he soon found a job at Postal Telegraph, in the Warren Street branch in the wholesale-produce district. His shift began at five in the morning, so he was off at three in the afternoon and free to explore the city.

He crossed the bridge to Brooklyn and called on Mrs. Stonehill. Although unwarned, she recognized him at once as Armenak Saroyan's son and invited him in for tea. In her cozy parlor, Bill nibbled little cakes while she recalled that his father had been content with plans for a ministry here in New York until Bill's mother and grandmother arrived. They had other plans. The women seemed to scorn her kind of good works, as well as the corsets she had tried to give them. The two were determined that Armenak should drop his promising career in New York in favor of a life in California, which, they had heard, was a paradise. She spoke of the "notes" she and her husband had held from so many of the Armenian immigrants, and when Bill asked, she explained they were for the loans they made to them. Not one was ever repaid. When she tried to reassure him that the Saroyans had been exceptions, Bill was unconvinced.

In the city, Bill was discovering the poor man's sanctuaries. The best of these was the public library at Fifth Avenue and Forty-second Street, and next best were the cheap restaurants, like Hoetzer's, on Fortieth Street, where an eight-course meal could be had for fifty-five cents. It was Bill's first experience with pig knuckles and sauerkraut, which he thought were delicious.

Waiting for sleep at night, he would recall a school friend who had died and then would congratulate himself on being alive and in New York, where he had yearned to be for so long. In these reveries it occurred to him that life itself was a dream, and he was not the dreamer, but the dreamed—by which he surely meant that his ambition had no more limit than his imagination.

Most afternoons he went "home" to the library, where he carefully selected six or seven books, sat down at a table, and "read around" in them, believing he would learn from their pages how, and what, to write.

With his first wages he bought a portable typewriter, on which he intended to write something so right it would take him straight to fame and riches. He saw several plays, among them Eugene O'Neill's *Strange Interlude,* and felt sure he could write better ones. He did write an essay about the people of New York, titled it "The Mentality of Apes," and sent it to the *Brooklynite,* which failed to accept, or even return, it.

Then, as winter came and first snow fell on the public library, Saroyan saw himself as a writer who had spent three and a half months in New York without achieving success. His loneliness became unbearable. A sense of desertion and grief he associated with his earliest years at the Fred Finch orphanage stole over him. In December, Bill swallowed his humiliation and returned to San Francisco.

The reception of his family was chilly. Henry's first question was about what he now intended to do. Although he resented this, Bill knew that if he was to stay he must help with the expenses, and he agreed to look for a job.

Henry urged him to apply at Postal Telegraph, still his own employer, and Bill did. The job he was offered was in a noisy department and had him working among thirty-five girls. He protested to Henry that he would not be able to stand it. Henry insisted he do so, but when Henry came by to see how his brother was getting along, Bill told him the job could go to hell. He was not going to do anything that was no good for him. They parted in anger. Bill could not understand how anyone could put up with the boredom of office work, with the files, the adding machines, and the superintendents with their sharp eyes and self-importance.

There were four of them at home now, living in a small flat, at 348 Carl Street, whose kitchen windows overlooked the Kezar Stadium and the treetops of Golden Gate Park. Six years before, when they had moved here from Fresno, Henry had been full of hopes. He was planning to finish college at Berkeley. Instead, he had settled for a dreary job at the main office of the Postal Telegraph Company on Market Street. Cosette, Bill's older sister, had a part-time job as a clerk in a law office. She spent the rest of her time doing the dishes and cleaning the flat, ever mindful of her mother's rages. These were known to spring from anxiety over the rent or the Pacific Gas & Electric bill, but they were still painful to endure.

Takoohi's worst storms fell upon Bill now. There would be screams and curses over his listless job searches, and then she would not speak to him for a day. But eventually she would soften and bake him the biscuits she knew were his favorite. He thought his mother was a small, handsome woman. Although she spoke poor English and could not write it at all, he felt that if she had not lost a young husband, roughened her hands on a million packing boxes, and coarsened her voice with men's oaths, she would have had a distinctive, even aristocratic, style. He saw her face as a perfect one and sometimes thought of her sexually. He felt she often provoked him, confronting him with a smile he recognized as a womanly challenge of his masculinity.

The worst of it was that he was finding it hard to write at the Carl Street flat. He could read contempt in the eyes of each member of his family. They recognized only one form of success—a weekly salary. He was determined that as soon as he could make his stake he would leave them once and for all.

Meanwhile, he had been given the front room in which to sleep and write. From its bay window he could gaze onto Carl Street, where streetcars passed on their way through the Sunset District to the ocean. Sometimes he walked there, to stroll the beach, look out across the Pacific, and think about the places he would go. He picked up stones that had been shaped by the sea. He thought they were beautiful, works of art, and he brought them home to polish and save.

On his desk stood his beloved old Underwood typewriter. It was a rare day when it failed to bring forth a new story. He had been writing stories for twelve years now, since he began substituting them for high school homework. Recently he had begun a novel and written seven chapters before losing heart for it.

He read the literary magazines, studied the taste of their editors, and took a particular interest in their contributors. In 1930 he wrote fan letters to two women whose published work he liked. He had discovered Goldie Weisberg of Phoenix, Arizona, in *The American Mercury*, and he told her that he admired both her writing and biographical note. She was a schoolteacher interested in community theater. He described himself whimsically, as a young Armenian at work on six novels, innumerable stories, and three plays. They were soon exchanging flatteries, photographs, and literary judgments. Bill gave approval to Cummings, Hemingway, Lardner, Mencken, and Dreiser.

Their correspondence flourished, both parties complaining when it faltered. Bill admitted to a stockpile of thirty stories, only a few of which had been published, and that for a time he was abandoning fiction in order to express himself in "the treatise, or essay." Incidentally, he felt that Edward O'Brien had included some good stories in his collection of the year's best. Katherine Anne Porter was certainly competent. And yet he had omitted many good ones—some thirty of his own.

In the same year, Bill courted the good will of another schoolteacher, Grace Stone Coates of Martindale, Montana. He had found her story "Wild Plums" in the O'Brien collection, but it had first appeared in *The Frontier*, a magazine published in Missoula of which she had the additional virtue of being assistant editor. When she returned a Saroyan story marked with suggestions for its improvement, Bill wrote that in view of her generous interest and encouragement he had had no better friend in all his life. He would be satisfied to go unpublished if only he could count on her reading his work.

He confessed that he had been intending a novel for years and recently become jealous of Thomas Wolfe's *Look Homeward Angel*, for he had found its first page much the same as a story of his own, one he had just sent to *Prairie Schooner*.

Bill was soon exchanging poems with Grace Stone Coates, rejoicing further in her editorial advice and guidance on how best to submit his stories to *The Frontier* and to its Iowa rival, *Midland*.

Overland Monthly accepted a story but collapsed before using it. Through a family acquaintance he had been urged to submit material to the Armenian daily newspaper *Hairenik*, published by the Armenian Revolutionary Federation, in Boston. Its name meant "fatherland," and its read-

Bill at nineteen, 1927

ership was wholly Armenian, but it had an English-language section, and to this Bill had sent seven chapters of his novel about Armenia, *Home Is Hayastan.*

The novel proved not to *Hairenik's* liking, but Bill responded with four of his poems and then some stories under the pen name Sirak Goryan. Although *Hairenik* paid no fee, it accepted the whole batch. The poems appeared in January 1933; a first story, "A Fist Fight for Armenia," in April; "The Broken Wheel," in three installments, during June; "The Baker's Apprentice" in October; and "The Moment of Life" in November.

From that time onward, *Hairenik* took and printed everything that Bill sent. Since he wrote swiftly, conceiving and writing a story in a few hours, often turning out two in a day, he was glad to have a showcase, to know that they would appear and be read by many people.

He was unshaken in his belief that what he wrote was good. It had been confirmed by the editor of the now defunct literary magazine *Gyroscope,* published at Stanford. Yvor Winters had written that he liked three of the stories Bill had sent him, and that he should send them to *Hound & Horn* and *The New Republic*.

Winters, well known as a Stanford English professor and caretaker of young poets, now invited Bill to several of his "Sunday afternoons," when he would gather students in his living room to read their work. He met Bill at the station and drove him to his house in Los Altos, feeling correctly that Bill would liven things up.

Bill had never encountered anyone with Winters's erudition. This would normally have alienated him, but the man's liking for his work made him listen to the professorial advice. Clearly, the scholarly man knew what he was talking about. Winters proposed that for starters Bill read Joyce's *Dubliners* and *Portrait of the Artist,* postponing *Ulysses* until he had a better knowledge of English prose.

He provided Bill a first reading list, with William Carlos Williams's *In the American Grain,* Elizabeth Madox Roberts's *The Time of Man* and *My Heart and My Flesh,* Kenneth Burke's *White Oxen,* Katherine Anne Porter's *Flowering Judas,* all of Virginia Woolf, and Henry James's *The Wings of the Dove* and *The Golden Bowl.* Bill protested that he was not after a Ph.D. but was only trying to express his feelings. Winters said that was the trouble, all these kids believing self-expression was enough, that technique and thought itself were sterile. He said they were deceiving themselves by glorifying contemporary notions of decency without knowing their intellectual tradition and its masters. In advising Bill to read Jane Austen, especially *Pride and Prejudice,* Winters urged him to be tougher on himself and revise a story once he'd finished it. He should beware a girlish tendency for self-expression. Writing was damned hard work.

Bill enjoyed his Sunday nights at the Winterses'. He got along well with Winters's lively wife, the writer Janet Lewis, and the students who circled the Winterses' living room ready to read and make up a critical audience.

He put up with Winters's scolding over his blighted education and even carried away the daunting reading lists, promising to pursue them. He was learning from Winters, and he thought the "ironbound academic" would help him publish. But in spite of Winters's praise, Bill knew the man did not understand his purpose, nor was there any way he could be made into a Wintersian.

There was never a time in his long apprenticeship that Bill Saroyan lost belief in himself as a writer. As 1933 drew to a close, he told himself that his stories were getting better and better. They were already superior to those he read in the literary quarterlies and in such slicks as the *Saturday Evening Post* and *Collier's.* He was certain that, very soon, the best magazines in the country would be publishing him.

LAND OF PROMISE

1933–1934

ON THE MORNING of December 14, 1933, when he was twenty-four and living at home in San Francisco, Bill Saroyan opened a letter from New York for which he had been waiting for a dozen years and which he knew was going to change the disheartening slope of his life.

On the letterhead of *Story* magazine, edited by Whit Burnett and Martha Foley, he read, "Dear Mr. Saroyan: We have finally found room for 'The Daring Young Man on the Flying Trapeze' which is a nicely handled piece of work. A check for $15 will be sent to you in a week or ten days and we should greatly appreciate your sending us by return mail a brief biography of yourself and your writing. Sincerely yours, Whit Burnett."

Bill Saroyan read and reread Whit Burnett's letter. He knew *Story* was the touchstone. He was joining a roll of contributors that included Sherwood Anderson, Erskine Caldwell, Malcolm Lowry, James T. Farrell, William Faulkner, Nelson Algren, and Gertrude Stein. *Story* and its readers knew and cared about short fiction. This was the breakthrough in that high wall of indifference, a first experience with approval that opened the gate on every delicious prospect. He did not distinguish between possibility and realization, and felt sure that from now on, gradually but certainly, he would be in the money, that he stood on the threshold of a literary career that was going to be all he had ever yearned for, and more.

Just before Christmas, *Story*'s check for $15 arrived with a letter from Martha Foley saying that "Trapeze" would appear in the February issue, due out January 15. She thought it excellent and expected much good news about it.

"The Daring Young Man on the Flying Trapeze" is a curious, stream-of-consciousness story. The narrator is a down-and-out writer in San Francisco. At first he is asleep, dreaming of doom. The dream is apocalyptic, galactic, literary, historical, that of a man who has learned to soar in the stacks of libraries. Then he is awake, shaving, preparing for the day, with its search for work and food, for he is lightheaded with starvation. He is alone, a stranger, as much an outcast as the crippled, starving hero of Saroyan's favorite story, de Maupassant's "Bell."

Although the narrator knows death is near, his only regret is not having read the books he intended to read. Indeed, he is inexplicably exuberant, delighted to find a penny in the street and polish it. He sings the popular song "The Daring Young Man on the Flying Trapeze" and laughs aloud at his plight, a writer starving in the midst of the city's plenty. After being refused a job, drinking water, and reading Proust in the library, he returns to his room, and, lying upon his bed, fades into nothingness, death's perfection.

The story has power, an ironic humor, and no self-pity at all. Saroyan had turned his resentment at being an outsider, at being discriminated against and denied, into a celebration of being alive. Writing in the Depression's darkest year, 1933, he had transformed hunger and the want of a job into rapture. It was a literary conjuring that would often inspire his work.

Bill's exuberant response to *Story's* acceptance letter was to tuck the current issue under his arm and visit San Francisco's newsstands, urging each to carry the magazine. He also rode the streetcar while turning *Story's* pages with an expression of delighted absorption.

He reported these promotional efforts to Whit Burnett and Martha Foley in what became a fervent and nearly daily directive. *Story,* he told them, was the best fiction magazine in the country, and he offered suggestions for making it even better. He wanted them to know he was no one-timer but the writer who would prove central to *Story's* future.

Young Saroyan was a spouting Vesuvius of the short story. He could write one in a few hours and did so daily. Some were as good, or better than, "Trapeze." Now a stream of them threatened to swamp *Story's* editorial desks. They were accompanied by the author's enthusiastic assurances that he would be central to the magazine's future.

Whit Burnett conceded that many were original, exceptional tales, but he took a firm, helpful hand with the pile of Saroyan stories accumulating on his desk and wrote Bill that he was turning down a dozen inferior ones. Others were good, and he would see what he could do with them. He was sending two to Eugene Jolas in Paris for his *Transition,* four to O'Brien in Oxford to see if he could place them in the British magazines. He felt Bill should try two of them on Arnold Gingrich, at *Esquire,* which paid as much as $100 for a story. He was holding four for *Story* and planned to use "Seventy Thousand Assyrians" soon. He thought it owed much to Sherwood

Anderson, but it was the best of the lot. It would probably appear in the April issue, and he would be paying $20 for it.

When Whit offered Bill his first editorial suggestion, it was about his narrative voice: "Keep the cockiness a little bit humble in the stories as you did so beautifully in the Assyrian piece. Otherwise you have nothing to worry about."

Bill replied by explaining that his cockiness was irrepressible. He was always trying to curb it, and yet it was ever plainer to him that all the big shots were frauds.

The cockiness, so apparent in both his writing and his behavior, was becoming his trademark, and it was rooted in a newfound self-assertion and dismissal of competitors. The field awaited him, *needed* him. The acknowledged champs would soon be giving way to him. He was convinced of his superiority and spoke of it so openly and lightheartedly that at first his associates took it as playful flamboyance, not the hubris it was.

Some earlier stories, written under the pseudonym Sirak Goryan, had suffered multiple rejections before appearing in the Armenian periodical *Hairenik*. He submitted them to the short-story annuals, hoping for further exposure, and early in 1934 Bill had a letter of surprising good news. It was from Edward J. O'Brien, editor of *The Best Short Stories*, informing Sirak Goryan that his tragicomic story "The Broken Wheel," which had appeared in *Hairenik*, would be included in the new volume. Confirming that acceptance by the *Best Short Stories* anthology was no accident, the competitive O'Henry collection reported that it too was selecting a Sirak Goryan story for its annual edition.

Bill did not hesitate to introduce his pseudonymous counterpart to Whit and Martha, writing them as Goryan, describing himself as a cousin of the William Saroyan whose story they had just bought and much under his literary influence. He reported his own acceptance into the O'Brien collection, and said that at its editor's suggestion he was submitting several of his *Hairenik* pieces to *Story.*

As Sirak Goryan, Bill heard from Martha Foley that, while *Hairenik* was undoubtedly little read by *Story*'s readers, they preferred unpublished material. As Bill Saroyan, he did not immediately reveal the deception, for his had been an earnest effort at self-multiplication.

When asked to supply biographical details about Sirak Goryan for the O'Brien and O'Henry collections, Bill turned to Whit for advice and thus unmasked his pseudonymous cousin. Whit was more amused than offended by the misrepresentation and proposed that they explain it all in *Story*'s notes on contributors.

Bill wrote Whit that he had a novel and asked his advice about getting an

Story magazine's editor, Whit Burnett, who was first to
find and publish Bill's extraordinary early stories

agent to find a publisher for it. Whit reminded Bill that he was doing as much for him as any agent could. He had just sent "Aspirin Is a Member of the NRA" to Bruce Bliven at *The New Republic.* There was a stir about Saroyan, and he would soon be hearing from many editors, but there was no need for further representation.

But Bill would not be put off about his novel. He told Whit he had several, and one would soon be ready. There was already a lively competition for it, which included a conspiracy in Whit's own staff. He confided that the magazine's business manager had tipped friends at Covici-Friede about *Story*'s lucky strike in Saroyan, then had written Bill that the firm would be making him a book offer. He advised asking a healthy advance of $150.

An indignant Martha Foley reminded Bill that she and Whit were hard at work on his launching, not only publishing his stories but urging them on other editors. They had further plans for him. She had a particular warning against Covici-Friede, a publisher of limited resources. He must not become "tangled with the wrong sort."

Bill was aware of his debt to Whit and Martha, yet he was curiously oblivious of an obligation to accept their guidance and see the consequence of defying it. So, flouting Martha's advice, he sent Covici-Friede *Trapeze Over the Universe,* a novel he had written the previous year and from which he had distilled "Trapeze."

On learning that Bill had done this, Whit was furious and wrote him so. He had heard that Covici-Friede's opinion of the novel was unfavorable, and Bill would be lucky if they turned it down. Whit's own plan for Saroyan book publication lay with Random House. He had already passed along some of the stories, and when Bill had a book to show, Random would want to look at it.

When Covici-Friede rebuffed the novel, a somewhat chastened Bill replied that the matter was now closed, and a somewhat appeased Whit questioned whether Bill understood their belief in him. They knew him to be an unusual writer, and as time went by he would be more important. They were proud of helping him and wanted to see him get off on the right foot when he had "important long stuff" to publish. Few publishers could be worse for him to become entangled with than Covici-Friede. Was that clear? All was forgiven. He should sit down and turn to deeper concerns.

The sense that the editors had a "discovery" in Saroyan was now burgeoning in the *Story* office—which, incidentally, had been provided by Random House. Bennett Cerf and Donald Klopfer, owners of the fledgling book publisher, had bought *Story* in 1933 in hopes of finding writers of promise through its panning of the literary streams.

In February, Bill heard from Cerf that he had read the stories Whit had passed along and become interested in publishing him. He explained that Klopfer and he were part owners of the magazine, and it was housed in their office. Although they had published James Joyce's *Ulysses,* they had so far done little fiction, but they were about to develop the trade end of their business and would be glad to look at any novel he had written or planned.

Bill replied at once that he liked the idea of Random House as his publisher and was now trying to write a good novel. If he succeeded, he wanted Random House to have a first look at it. Cerf told him to take his time with the novel and make it as good as he could. If he became hard up while working on it, Cerf urged him to call upon them to pay him an advance.

When the *Mercury* paid Bill the substantial sum of $45 for his story "Aspirin Is a Member of the NRA," he decided to blow the money on a visit to Hollywood. The motion-picture capital had awed him since childhood and no longer seemed unassailable.

He was drawn to Stanley Rose's bookstore on Vine Street, where writers and publishers' representatives gathered in the back room for orange wine and talk about the book and movie businesses. Stanley Rose was a raffish man with a slow, Texas drawl and a love of drink, books, and mischief of all kinds.

Rose encouraged Bill to autograph the half-dozen copies of *Story* he had on hand and to learn more about Hollywood opportunity. He pointed out that James Cain had just gotten $25,000 for his *Postman Always Rings Twice,* and that an *idea* for a movie could be sold for as much as $5,000. Stanley Rose would be Bill's closest Hollywood friend for twenty years.

In March, Bill wrote Bennett Cerf from Hollywood to thank him for the offer of an advance on a novel and admitted that his was not the only attractive proposal he had had. Covici-Friede, Harrison Smith, and Alfred Knopf were wooing him, and he expected to hear from other publishers soon.

Now Bill got down to business, saying he would rather have Bennett Cerf for a publisher than anyone else because he was backing *Story.* His short stories had won him some attention, and he had enough to publish a collection. This is what he wanted published now, *before* the novel. He wanted no advance, but he did want Random House to do the stories—and everything else he wrote.

For a title he proposed simply *27 Stories* by William Saroyan. He had already written a preface for the first edition and would write a new one for each successive edition. He was ready to sign a contract for novels or other books and assured Cerf that the result would never disappoint him.

Cerf promptly agreed to the book of short stories. Whit Burnett would help prepare it, and Random House would publish it within the year. Cerf insisted on Bill's accepting an advance of $100 and that he call on them if he needed funds while working on the novel.

He did not care for Bill's title suggestion. The book needed a name they could impress on the minds of bookstore owners and book buyers. Both he and Whit felt the general title might be *The Daring Young Man on the Flying Trapeze and Other Stories.*

Finally, Cerf warned Bill that books of short stories usually fare very badly, but after the fanfare that had accompanied the appearance of some of his tales, he thought they might be able to work up a great deal of interest in his first book. Cerf further assured him, "We look forward to publishing everything that you write from now on, with the greatest enthusiasm."

In April, Cerf sent Bill the contract for *The Daring Young Man on the Flying Trapeze.* Cerf was off on a trip to Russia, and, until his return, Donald Klopfer would be overseeing publication of the book. Bill immediately wrote Klopfer to say that Michael Arlen's stories *These Charming People* had sold well, which encouraged him to think his book might do even better and, in translation, find readers throughout the world.

Alarmed by Bill's ambitious notions about the sales of *Trapeze,* Klopfer set about curbing them. Klopfer hoped the collection would make enough money to allow Bill to get to the country and finish his novel, but he warned that sales of anything over $2,000 on a book of short stories was unusual. Klopfer assured Bill that the collection would be submitted to book clubs and that Random House was going to make a handsome volume of it.

At Random House, editor Saxe Commins was assigned to coedit the Saroyan collection with Whit Burnett. Once again, Bill tried Whit's considerable patience with directives about the book's design and manufacture and by urging the addition of recent stories. Whit wrote him that these were no help, that the book was shaping up beautifully and would surely please him when he saw it. Meanwhile, he should keep busy at something else.

Donald Klopfer became aware of the new author's demands, and while Cerf was abroad, took on the task of explaining to the irrepressible Saroyan their separate roles. As his publisher, they would attend to the launching of the book, to advertising it, and to getting it into libraries. There was no need for him to worry about all that. His job was as a writer.

What did worry him, Klopfer admitted, was that Bill would want to rewrite some of the stories in galleys. He further cautioned Bill against his inclination to spill forth language impulsively, to get every feeling and thought down on paper, and noted that if he did some rewriting before submitting the stories he would turn out more satisfying prose. He noted that Flaubert had worked for a week over one paragraph; then he quickly urged Bill not to respond to that, for he knew what the response would be.

Bill responded anyway, pointing out that Flaubert's method was that of an old man, and he himself would be one of those soon enough. Besides, he had labored over a paragraph for a month only to have it turn sick, just as he had written another in two hours which broke the rules and sang with life. He went on to question whether any writers today—excepting Joyce and possibly Cummings—were saying anything. He thought most writers, the big shots included, were dabbling, repeating the past in slick and conventional ways.

They decided to publish the book in October and selected twenty-six stories. The first would be "The Daring Young Man on the Flying Trapeze," followed by "Seventy Thousand Assyrians," a meditation on the writing of innovative stories, the dignity of poor immigrants, and the survival of immigrants' ancient cultures.

The editors agreed to include Bill's introduction, in which he confided his writing rules. These were to forget rules, to be yourself and write what you pleased, to spurn adjectives that killed words with kindness, to learn typing for speed, and, above all, to live life to its emotional peaks, to be alive, for you would be dead soon enough.

This was the essence of Saroyan's belief in himself. While he never credited Emerson as its source, it surely parallels the urgings in "Self-Reliance" to toss "the laws, the books, idolatries and customs out the window," and the warnings that "society everywhere is in conspiracy against the manhood of every one of its members."

Bill clung to the idea that an agent could do more for him than Whit, and although Donald Klopfer urged him to get along without one for the present, he decided to let Ann Watkins represent him. On learning this, Whit told him it was a wise choice. With a book on the way, an agent could prove useful, and both Watkins and her assistant, Harold Matson, were excellent. Whit would turn over to them a recent inquiry from *Vanity Fair.*

Saxe Commins's admiration for the *Trapeze* collection was reflected in the flap copy, which described Bill as an unusually gifted writer of short stories who had arrived without any cautious apprenticeship but by the shortest possible route, taking "a headlong plunge into the vivid life around him, recording it with wonder and compassion and conviction as they reflect his own nimble curiosity and his insatiable demand for new affirmations of life."

And indeed *Trapeze* was an arresting book, its twenty-six stories quite unlike the customary "well-made" ones. They were more essay than story, each one marked by Saroyan's sweepingly confident, brash, yet compassionate voice. He wrote about being Armenian, about being young, innocent, and left out, and, if somewhat puzzled about the future, anticipating it. Under the sense of man's tragedy lay a big joy.

Increasingly aware that the stairway to literary eminence led from the short story to the novel, Bill announced to Random House that he was busy on a long work, and, unless something went wrong, he would complete it by the end of May. It would be a novel fit to follow a book of short stories.

When Bill asked Donald Klopfer's advice about what kind of novel he should write, Klopfer whimsically proposed he write a classic, one of enough popular appeal to sell a million copies and still be critically acknowledged as the long-awaited great American one.

Bill promised his publisher a full-length work about the American experience, as significant as Thomas Wolfe's *Look Homeward, Angel.* He called it *Twentieth Century Blues* and planned to assemble it from the introspective short pieces he had first offered as stories.

He worked at it, expecting to finish by the end of May, but by midmonth he suspected he had overreached his strengths. He wrote Klopfer that he would not be sure *Twentieth Century Blues* deserved publication until he had written its last word, and then sounded a further uncertain note that he was going through with it as discipline. By the month's end he gave it its coup de grâce.

In mid-July, Bill sent off to Donald Klopfer what he described as "a book." It was of three parts, and he admitted that the first two were worthless, but he felt the third, "Untitled Work with Drawings," had something. It was not the promised novel, but he had just read it for the first time and found it odd but appealing. He explained that the pencil drawings were no more expensive to print than a page of writing, and if Random House would do an edition of five hundred to a thousand copies made to sell for a dollar, it would not lose money. Klopfer thought otherwise. In self-acquittal and recovery of aplomb, Bill told Klopfer that he would take some time to discover what his novel was about and what, if anything, he meant to say.

Bennett Cerf returned from his Russian trip in July, reporting that he had been touting Saroyan to the English publishers and had sold "Seventy Thousand Assyrians" to Lovat Dickson's *London Literary Magazine*. Bill told him he was now over his shame at not producing the novel. If his book of stories went over well, he would not want to follow it with poor stuff. Sometime soon he would write a good one. He needed more leisure. He had been looking at *The Magic Mountain* and felt he could do something of that sort if he were in the right place and didn't have to rush.

There had been many promises that *Trapeze* would be a beautiful book, and when, on August 1, two advance copies arrived at 348 Carl Street, Bill found it so. The design was imaginative, long and narrow in shape, handsomely bound in natural linen with a black spine and girded with a broad band of gold foil. The paper was rich. The jacket type, with letters formed of acrobats, suggested a circus poster.

Bill wrote Bennett Cerf that it was a swell job of bookmaking and that the writing was such that it was a far better choice for the buyer than most current novels. At the same time he complained about what appeared to be some flaws and alterations in the text and soon heard from Saxe Commins that these were either in accordance with requirements of fine printing or of standard English usage.

With publication set for October 15, just two and a half months off, Bill undertook to learn all he could about book marketing. He knew Paul Elder's shop at 239 Post Street as the classiest in San Francisco. Indeed, Elder had turned him away when he had applied for a job there four years before, and Bill had been to a few of the shop's Saturday-afternoon salons with famous writers, and had found them a waste of everyone's time.

But now, with a copy of *Trapeze* under his arm, Bill got a more cordial reception. Elder invited him to be the honored guest at one of his gallery sessions. He would send out a notice to his ten thousand customers and would expect Bill to give an informal talk about his book.

Bill wrote Bennett Cerf that this put him in a nice fix, for he could not

The Daring Young Man on the Flying Trapeze, the story collection
published by Random House in October 1934, which launched
Bill's writing career

and would not speak. His father had been one of the best extemporaneous
speakers in Armenia, but it had brought him no fame in the United States.
He doubted Elder's would sell as many copies as Stanley Rose's little shop in
Hollywood, because the rich San Franciscans didn't buy books; they came
only to kill time and see the writer's performance. His book would succeed
or fail on its own merits.

Cerf replied that Elder could sell books, so Bill should let him down as
easy as possible. As for book signing, he shouldn't neglect that either. So Bill
made the rounds of the bookstores with Ray Healy, the Random House

Bennett Cerf, cofounder of Random House and Bill's early
sponsor, who dubbed him "The wonder boy from Fresno"

salesman, who took him to lunch with the principal book reviewer on the
West Coast, the *San Francisco Chronicle*'s Joseph Henry Jackson. Perversely,
Bill had begun telling everyone he met that his book wasn't worth a damn,
and he bet Healy a five-dollar hat it wouldn't sell two thousand copies—
hoping, of course, that he would lose.

Cerf had placed a prepublication ad for *Trapeze* in the current issue of
Story, and forty orders had already come in; also, Stanley Rose had confirmed his order for one hundred copies. On the last day of August—his
birthday—Bill went to the Railway Express Company's freight shed and
signed a hundred copies Cerf had sent him for presentation to buyers for
the major accounts. It took him three and a half hours, and he reported that
he was pretty sure he had signed them on the proper page, since it was the
one Yvor Winters had signed when he had given Bill a copy of *The Bare
Hills.*

In spite of earlier scorn for the "big shots" and their resistance to change,
Bill now asked Cerf to send copies of *Trapeze* to William Carlos Williams,
Ezra Pound, T. S. Eliot, Gertrude Stein, James Joyce, Ford Madox Ford, and
E. E. Cummings. He wanted to pay for these copies and to say that the

book came with his compliments, then wondered if that was an impertinence.

Cerf gave Bill the addresses of the writers but urged him not to send the
books until at least after publication date, when the reviews had made him
better known. These authors were always getting books from people they
didn't know, and Cerf was sure they didn't read them.

Bill agreed, saying he understood that the best way to be known to one's
contemporaries was to write well enough to become known. Still, his admiration for these writers was such that he would like to be known to them
humbly. He would always regret not having met and talked to D. H.
Lawrence, simply because he wanted to know the minds of his times and to
have some understanding of their texture and movement. He would let the
matter ride for the present, but he had *wanted* to knock at the doors of the
greatest of his contemporaries. Meanwhile, if one or another of them died
without hearing about him, it would be lamentable. Clearly he felt that he
was arriving on Parnassus and needed to meet his neighbors.

In New York, the surge of interest in *Trapeze* was still rising. "Great news,
my lad—great news indeed!" Cerf wrote Bill, reporting that he had persuaded T. S. Eliot and Frank Morley, "the presiding geniuses at Faber &
Faber in England, to publish *The Daring Young Man*."

Cerf explained that Faber's was one of the finest British publishing
houses. Bill could not be in better hands. The terms were generous, and,
moreover, Random House would take only one third of the British rights,
instead of the half to which it was entitled. Cerf wanted Bill to get as much
as possible on this first book.

It seemed that Eliot wanted to rearrange the contents, omitting Bill's
preface and the story "Love," and Cerf urged Bill to approve, pointing out
that these "boys know their own market," and there was much prestige in
appearing on so distinguished a list, "for which many a young writer would
gladly exchange his left whoozis." Jonathan Cape was considering the book,
and Cerf was looking forward to "telling that pompous old dodo that he
was too late." Bill lost no time in wiring his affirmative response.

Cerf himself was selling the book to some accounts in the New York area,
finding the handsome binding a big help and the title an inspiration. Everyone smiled at the sight of *The Daring Young Man on the Flying Trapeze*. He
was also touting the book with the editors of the book reviews. At lunch
with the *Herald Tribune*'s Irita Van Doren, he deduced that she was asking
the *Mercury*'s editor Charles Angoff to do the review. To this he soon added
an enthusiastic letter from Michael March, of the *Brooklyn Citizen*, who had
decided that this Saroyan was "greater than Lawrence." Sending Bill a copy
of March's tribute, Cerf hoped Bill would still be able to get his hat on after
reading it.

The first printing had been a sensible two thousand copies, but by mid-September Random House had an advance sale of fourteen hundred, with the big New York stores still to be heard from. As Cerf ordered a second printing, he wrote Bill that at lunch, when he had bragged about these figures to the heads of Viking and Scribner's, "they both thought I was handing them some of the old bologna."

Cerf was also placing prepublication ads in the *Times* and *Tribune* Sunday book reviews and the *Saturday Review of Literature*. He urged Bill to watch for them, suggesting he could find the papers at the San Francisco library.

When Joseph Henry Jackson invited Bill to appear on his radio program, he asked him to set down beforehand what he intended to say about the short-story form and his own work in particular. Bill did so, saying that the main reason he wrote stories was that he was unhappy, and since he didn't care for door-to-door salesmanship, he didn't know what else to do. As for *The Daring Young Man on the Flying Trapeze,* he believed it was a very unimportant book and that very few people would enjoy reading it. In fact, he said, he had written it principally for his own pleasure and that of his relations in the San Joaquin Valley. Jackson was not amused by this Saroyan facetiousness, which was to mark Bill's public speaking henceforth, and refused to let him read it on the program.

But in New York, as the month of *Trapeze's* publication began, the favorable signs were multiplying. The book columnist Harry Hansen noted that first editions were so sought after that they looked to be "a better buy than U.S. Steel."

At Bill's suggestion, Kay Boyle had received an advance copy, and she wrote from Austria, "What a book. It has everything." She was a little disappointed in the title story, "But my God what a story is '1,2,3 etc.' It's a new kind of writing. 'And Man,' and 'Snake,' and 'Laughter,' and 'Fight Your Own War.' I have read them with my eyes, ears, nose." She thought Saroyan "terribly, marvelously good . . . more alive and funnier than anyone else."

On October 11, three days before publication, Bennett had a letter from author Christopher Morley, a Book-of-the-Month Club judge and widely respected literary arbiter. He had found *Trapeze* both tender and subtle and had not enjoyed such unexpected pleasure since *Winesburg, Ohio.* He thought Saroyan's theme—a celebration of being alive—was a noble one, and his voice, whether in humor or bitterness, a rich one. He felt that older writers should read Saroyan's book to rediscover their own clear youth. He sent Saroyan a warning against the coming praise, along with his own hearty congratulation.

In his front room overlooking the car tracks on Carl Street, October 15 struck Bill as disturbingly routine. There were two telegrams of congratula-

Bill in 1934, the year of his first book's publication,
fedora set at a suitably rakish angle

tion, one from Hal Matson and Ann Watkins, another from Whit and Martha in Croton, saying "SAROYAN TRAPEZE SWINGING HIGH MAR-VELOUS REVIEWS," but his phone was still, and the mail was disappointing.

He wrote Cerf that all local fronts were quiet. There were no crowds in pursuit of his book. Nevertheless, he knew Random House was giving *Trapeze* every possible break and claimed to be giddy with gratitude. His one problem was not having done any writing in two days.

In New York, however, Saroyan was getting plenty of attention. Louis Kronenberger told the *Times Book Review* readers that while William Saroyan's ego was his undoing, "there can be no question of his talent. He writes with an ease and dexterity and, at times with a freshness that one seldom encounters in a first book by a 26 year old author; he is bursting with personality; and he reveals enough cleverness to startle both the stodgy and the hard-boiled. But unfortunately he doesn't possess a lot of humility or, what is more important in literary matters, of restraint."

At Random House the editors now knew they had a hit. A second edition of a thousand copies had sold out, a third of a thousand copies was on press, and a fourth of two thousand was now ordered. Enclosing the enthusiastic Hansen and Gannett reviews, Cerf told Bill to "play them over on your pianola and let me know if the melody is indeed not a magnificent one."

Cerf was proud of the ads Random House was running for *The Daring Young Man.* "The New Big Name in Short Stories—SAROYAN," they proclaimed. "No short story writer in years has caused so much excitement and interest. . . . [He is] the most talked of and sought after young writer in America. He has a talent as distinctive as that of Faulkner, Dreiser or Lardner."

With copies of these, Cerf enclosed John Chamberlain's captious vote from the *Daily Times.* Chamberlain had found a freshness in Saroyan, but said "his virtues do not include a sense of architecture. He is getting by at present on his personality. . . . His conception of writing is simply Sherwood Anderson's repeated in a new dress. It is simply to 'express yourself.' "

Cerf assured Bill that "On the whole, however, reviews have been simply marvelous and everybody around town has been roaring for first edition copies of the book. There isn't another one of them left in the office. Current quotation, 5 bucks for a first!"

Bill's publication-day feeling of neglect in San Francisco was soon swept away. He was asked across the bay to Oakland and Berkeley. Signing books in Capwell's, Mitchell's, and the Sather Gate bookstores, he found the clerks genuinely enthusiastic. He wrote Cerf that once a person read the book he couldn't keep quiet about it. *Trapeze* was selling everywhere.

Success did change Saroyan's world, wholly, reenforcing a precarious belief that he *was* somebody of importance. Once the family ne'er-do-well, he had suddenly become its prince. It had been a miraculously short trip from worthlessness to worthiness, and he was heady with it. From the start he had believed in his gift. The praise had convinced him that as a writer he was without a peer.

He was peeved that Joseph Henry Jackson had so far not reviewed him in the *Chronicle,* San Francisco's major newspaper. A friend named John Woodburn, who occasionally reviewed for Jackson, explained that his boss was bewildered by the book and doubtless was waiting to see what the eastern reviewers said.

When Bill received a batch of fine reviews from Cerf with the warning that one of them—that of the *Akron Beacon-Journal*—was bad, he replied that it wouldn't bother him at all. Reviews, whether good or bad, didn't affect him. He couldn't be got down by this one. It would just sell more books in Akron.

While it was not true that he ignored his reviews, he did feel that no critic was on equal footing with him, nor entitled to pass significant judgment on his work.

He told Cerf that he had gone to his favorite bookie joint, Number One Opera Alley, and had found a horse named Resurrection running at the Laurel, Maryland, track. Since he had written a story called "Resurrection of a Life," he bet a dollar on the horse to win and felt he was betting on his book at the same time. Although Resurrection ran in third place most of the way, he won the race. Bill was a happy man—too happy to care what critics said about *Trapeze*.

Before the month was out, Cerf replied, "Your hunch that all would be well when Resurrection won that race has worked out. *The Daring Young Man* has climbed onto the best-seller list in New York City, the first time in I don't know how long that a book of short stories has done so. We're well over 4000 now and I should say we can count on another 2000 before the fervor dies down."

III

THE FLAW

1935–1937

A N ELEMENT of William Saroyan's nature, one that would persist throughout his life, was wanderlust. It was in part his boyhood need to move on, a dread of being in the "rut" that had trapped most of his family and friends. It was also a reward for hard work, an example set by his peripatetic uncle Aram. Later, it would be an escape from frustration and unhappiness. But here, at the greenest time of his life, it was a search for his roots, for the source of his always surprising energy.

In the summer of 1935, with the substantial accomplishment of *The Daring Young Man on the Flying Trapeze* behind him, he decided to go on a long journey. It was to be a grand tour of Europe, with the final goal a visit to the land of his ancestors, an Armenia now deep within the Soviet Union.

He had grown up hearing the retelling of his people's tragic history, and consciousness of it was in his bones, a source of both pride and anger. He was a "Hai"—the term all Armenians used to describe themselves—and his home was "Haigastan," the mountainous Armenian plateau that lies between the Black and Caspian Seas. But he wanted no part of the quarrel that divided Hais wherever they lived. The Ramgavar was the party of the status quo, accepting Armenia's shrunken borders and limited aspirations under Soviet rule as preferable to the Turks' bloody oppression. The Tashnag was the party of bitter opposition, determined to wrest the homeland from Russia and regain the nation's lost pride.

Indeed, Bill had leapt fearlessly into this fray at the height of *Trapeze's* success. In November 1934, he had written the editor of the Armenian newspaper *Hairenik,* whose staff and readership were markedly Tashnag, about his success as an American writer. He believed his success was important to every Armenian in America, particularly those young Armenians who hoped for a career in the arts. As for his political views, they were revealed in his work. In short, he questioned the importance of politics, opposed all groups, and believed racial growth took place only in the man who walks a lonely path.

In "My Armenia," a piece for *Hairenik* that must have stretched the editor's tolerance and riled a few subscribers, Bill wrote that he had no use for mobs or gangs of any kind, and he included what he saw as the many befuddled Armenian societies in America, whether they be political, social, or religious. He found political oratory false, social events a disgusting waste of time, and communities of prayer blasphemous.

His devotion was to a greater Armenia, one that knew its folk songs to be superior to its oratory and its laughter the only medicine for the bitterness that divided them. The Armenian spirit was the greatness of their race. It made the brotherhood that he did embrace.

This was his manifesto as an antinationalist. *All* governments were evil. He could see no virtue in militant patriotism, nor could he admit to the complex political issues that divided Armenians and were beginning to envelop the world. As a statement, this was as cheeky as it was questionable, and it leaves one to wonder if he wrote it to provoke Armenian outrage or if he was simply indifferent to it.

Bill Saroyan's lifelong distaste for governments of all sorts was surely confirmed by what he knew about Armenian history, and his anarchic leanings made no exception of the Soviet Union. However, he was pleased to learn that word of his *Trapeze* had penetrated Russia, and he was to be published there.

When he inquired of the Intourist office in New York he was soon assured of a welcome, not just in Soviet Armenia but in Moscow as well. Although skeptical of Marxist ideas, the current Soviet leaders, and the new society of which they boasted, he wanted to see it all for himself.

In May 1935, Intourist announced to the American press that this "brightest meteor in the literary sky" would spend a month among his people and then proceed to Moscow. He was quoted as wanting to know how Armenians felt about the "New Order." He said he would know if they laughed loudly, like the Armenians of central California did.

Armed with letters of introduction from Bennett Cerf and a plan to interview such literary eminences as Rebecca West, H. G. Wells, and George Bernard Shaw for the North American Newspaper Alliance, he sailed from New York on May 29, aboard the *Berengaria.*

Crossing the Atlantic, he was struck by the sea's immensity. He stood at the ship's rail for hours, awed by the sight of such a huge expanse of water. At the *Berengaria*'s Carnival Night, he was given a toy whistle, which made a shrill, ridiculous sound. He decided the whistle had rounded out his vocabulary and was just what he needed to answer political questions.

In London he was welcomed at his British publisher by the proprietor, Geoffrey Faber. Bill found the interviews he had planned too difficult to arrange and abandoned them. He went on to Paris, and while he could not understand a word of French and the Parisians shrugged away his English, he rejoiced in the city's wonders. Not the least of these was a bordello that was in a class by itself. His erotic fantasies were fulfilled when he was confronted with a circle of two dozen beautiful girls, naked except for jewelry and shoes. He chose a small one with a face full of amorous amusement and a mirrored bedroom. His reflected experience there left him with a new understanding of joie de vivre.

He headed for Armenia by train, crossing into the Soviet Union at the Polish border. The more he saw of central Europe, the less he liked it. In the Polish city of Lemberg, he found the sky low and black, its air stagnant, its people walking in misery.

But it was here in a restaurant that he heard a blind violinist play, and the man's little daughter sing a beautiful song. It seemed to spring from the bleak heart of a sorrowful people, but, like an Armenian folk song, it was buoyant with longing for life. When the little girl passed her tambourine, Bill asked the song's name, but she didn't understand, nor did the musician, nor anyone in the restaurant, including the cook. As he crossed into Russia he heard many Poles and even a Russian soldier singing this song, but he could not learn its name.

Then in Kharkov, where his guide spoke English—so perfectly, in fact, that he had difficulty understanding her—he hummed the song to her, and she said it was a Polish song called "Malenka Manon," "Little Manon." The title made it his, part of a folk-song repertoire that would provide one of his exceptional lucky strikes.

He found Kiev, the capital of Ukraine, a beautiful city. In its parks he saw people behaving just as they did in New York's Central Park and decided that human beings were the same everywhere and always.

He found one exception. While drawn to an orchestra of proletarians playing American jazz, he noticed that the drummer, a Russian of seventeen or so, was going about his drumming without joy. The Russians, Bill decided, could never play jazz, since it requires freedom. It was the tragicomic utterance of the poor in a capitalist society, a music that rejoices in its despair. It had nothing whatever to do with the dour, fateful Marxist mood, and the sooner the Russians found that out, the better off they would be.

He traveled eastward toward his ancestral town of Bitlis, but on crossing into the Republic of Armenia, he learned that Bitlis now lay outside the nation's new borders, and he lacked the visa to travel there. He did reach the Armenian capital, Yerevan, and treated himself to a hotel room with a balcony overlooking a park. Roaming the city he found a near-famine shortage of food and faces that reflected despair. He met several Armenian writers, and, while they were fearful of expressing any political opinion, their resentment of Soviet rule was obvious.

In the lobby of his hotel he told a curious eleven-year-old boy that he was a visitor from America. The boy replied that his country, Armenia, was greater than Bill's. When Bill asked him why, the boy said it was because he lived here. The boy, his father, and Bill laughed boisterously together, and Bill delighted in these sudden high spirits, which he read as assurance that Armenian joy in life and confidence in the future was intact.

On his return journey, Bill paused in a beer parlor in Rostov on the Don and recognized that his waiter, dark-skinned, hairy, curve-nosed, was Armenian. He bought two glasses of deplorable Russian beer, and they drank together, agreeing they didn't care about the rotten quality of the beer, nor, for that matter, the Soviet dictatorship, since some things were impossible to change. Although they mourned the million Armenians who had been killed, they shared the heartening thought that their people would endure.

While he had been denied Bitlis, Bill felt he had gotten what he had come for. No matter that his country's history was finished, its literature unread, its music unheard, its prayers unanswered—his race was indestructible.

In Moscow he found a room at the modest New Moscow Hotel and suffered the obligatory tour of Red Square and Lenin's tomb, but then he managed to dismiss his Intourist guide so he could prowl the city on his own. Standing in line to buy vodka, Bill found himself beside the American critic Edmund Wilson and learned he was in Russia on a Guggenheim travel grant, studying the Russian language and the Stalinist government for a book that would be called *To the Finland Station*. In the course of an evening spent together, Wilson cautioned Bill about his scoffing views of Marxism, pointing out an interested bystander he felt sure was an informer. Saroyan's blooming literary career would not escape Wilson's sharp, critical eye. He would soon have an assessment and some stern advice to offer him.

While Bill had never read a word of the Armenian poet Yegishe Charentz, he had been told at *Hairenik* of the man's eminence and asked Intourist to arrange an introduction. His guide took him to Charentz's suite, in Moscow's best hotel, and left the two writers alone. Bill thought Charentz was a small, ugly man with a huge hooked nose, but his warmth and intelligence soon beguiled Bill, and he felt the man's greatness.

Although now sanctioned by the Soviet regime, Charentz candidly admitted that he was opposed to it. He was ashamed of pretending to be one of them and of repudiating his earlier writing. Bill assured him this did not matter, for that writing had a life of its own that could not be ended. This clearly pleased Charentz. At one point in their interview, Charentz asked Bill to step onto the balcony while he injected himself with a drug he did not identify. From that moment Bill had a sense of the pain and the bitterness the man had endured and the laughter with which he mastered it. He saw him as a symbol of the indestructible Armenian spirit and culture. He was his brother.

Miraculously, Bill could write as he traveled. One of his Russian stories described a little dog that lived near the Kremlin and could be heard howling in misery. In spite of a sullen expression, the dog's eyes revealed a wisdom and a capacity for laughter. When Bill argued that the social system was not so bad, the dog laughed at him and ridiculed communism for keeping its people in an equality of poverty and mediocrity, and then it returned to its howling.

A long story Bill wrote at the New Moscow Hotel, "Moscow in Tears," he entrusted to the hotel manager for mailing to Ann Watkins in New York. He never saw the story again and never forgave the manager—nor the Soviet Union—for this carelessness.

Bill was wearying of Stalinist ways. He saw the same dumb, heartbreaking agony in the streets of each new city. He left Russia at Leningrad, stopping for a day in Helsinki, where he felt a marked improvement and decided it had to do with the Finns' owning things. The girl in a music store was different from the Russian girls. She was polite, handsome, and lacked the dialectical odor common to young Soviets. Moreover, she let him listen to a record of Sibelius's *Finlandia* and even provided him with the composer's address.

Bill was soon on his way to Järvenpää by taxi to do an interview. The seventy-year old Sibelius received him. But Bill's questions about art and its sources seemed to bewilder, and then anger, Sibelius. He waved off an interview and called for whiskey and cigars. Silence, he told Bill, is everything. Music is like life. It begins and ends in silence.

Bill came home at the end of July. There would be many more European journeys, but this first one was the most influential of his life. He would later learn that the writers he had met in Yerevan had disappeared—no one knew how or where—and that Charentz had committed suicide in a Yerevan prison. He would forever keep this first impression of his poor Armenia. He had found it a place of natural beauty, although its earth was still red from the blood of his countrymen.

From his travels Bill had brought a propitiatory gift for Ernest Hemingway, a Russian edition of *Death in the Afternoon.* The need for it sprang from an impertinence he had planted in "The Daring Young Man on the Flying Trapeze." It was a jibe at *Death in the Afternoon,* combined with a dubious compliment for its author, which went, "Even when Hemingway is a fool, he is at least an accurate fool. He tells you what actually takes place."

Soon after *Trapeze's* publication, Bill received, from Arnold Gingrich, *Esquire's* editor, the lead piece for the January issue. It was by Ernest Hemingway, who clearly *had* taken offense at Bill's disparagements. In his most bullying manner Hemingway told *Esquire* readers that he had had enough of the flying trapeze. He was particularly annoyed with Saroyan's claim that, if he wanted to, he could write like, or better than, Dos Passos, Joyce, and Faulkner. Anybody could write like somebody else, he agreed; the hard thing was to write like yourself and then to have something to say. Saroyan had not been around as his elders and betters had, and so had only himself to write about. "You're not that bright," he told Bill. "You don't know what you're up against. You've only got one new trick and that is that you're an Armenian."

"And we've seen them come and go, Mr. Saroyan," he went on. "Better ones than you, Mr. Saroyan. . . . You want to watch yourself, Mr. S., that you don't get so bright that you don't learn. . . . Also your ear isn't so good. And a good ear in a writer is like a good left hand in a fighter. Do I make myself clear? Or would you like me to push your puss in?"

Bill's sense of having overmatched himself led him to decline Gingrich's offer of space in *Esquire* for a reply. Instead, he wrote Hemingway a letter explaining that his intent had been playful and innocent. A mollified Hemingway replied that they could drop it. The use of the names had irritated him. Also, anybody who could really write bettered his ability only by writing, not by talking about it.

Then he told Bill that being an Armenian was good. He believed imagination was nothing but racial experience, what his people had done in the past. A writer did learn imagination through observation and experience, did learn to reject what wouldn't happen and know, truly, what would. Actual recall was likely to be flatter than what was imagined, for that could have several dimensions. The lecture complete, he wished him lots of luck and warned that this was a private letter, not the second exhibit in a publishable correspondence.

On receiving the Russian translation of his book, Hemingway wrote from Key West thanking Bill for it, regretting that he could not read Russian. He wished him luck in his writing and in "every other way." With this cordial exchange Bill felt, mistakenly as it would later turn out, that he had not only atoned for past damage but established a useful bond with the famous author.

Anxious to get on with his career, Bill returned to San Francisco and began to assemble a second story collection. On hearing of it, Donald Klopfer discouraged him, advising him to write a good novel instead. It would be much harder than batting out short stories, but Klopfer felt it would demand a discipline that would be just the schooling for a writer on his way.

Cerf had a more acceptable idea. He thought Bill might be one of those writers who can do superlative short stories but can't write a novel. In any case, the coming fall was too soon after *Trapeze* for another story collection. But the following year would be another matter; Bill should, with due deliberation, submit the stories for Random House publication at that time.

Cerf decided to share his pleasure over bringing some other fiction writers—William Faulkner, André Malraux, and Isak Dinesen—onto his list, and Bill responded with a facetious reminder of Random House's good fortune in publishing his own work. Cerf enjoyed Bill's cheek, and read it as the mark of a gifted, exuberant young man. He replied that as long as Bill was willing to tell him what a great author he was, he felt no shame in admitting that he expected Random House to be the foremost publisher in America almost any minute now, and that lo, the name of Saroyan would head the list—unless some other author learned to yell louder than he did. Which, he felt, was a very remote possibility.

On August 15, Bill sent in his plan for *Inhale & Exhale*. It was to have four parts: the great stuff; the comic stuff, for the fun of it; the experimental stuff and his own evaluation of it; and prose of the traveler. He assured his publishers that the title was great. It would be a new kind of book. Cerf replied that Bill's plan sounded elegant, and he offered an advance of a thousand dollars.

In accepting the advance, Bill urged Random House to make a handsome package. He wanted the best paper, the best print, and the best binding, with each story having generous titles, as in the *Trapeze* book. The jacket should have either the very best illustration or none at all. The cover should be red and black. They should plan on February or March publication and on making a fuss with the book, both as a job of bookmaking and as a job of writing. They should spare no expense. In this imperative tone, he assured his publishers that they could not lose.

If there had been any deference to the wisdom and dignity of his editors, Bill Saroyan's belief in his own newfound importance took precedence. Success had given him an insensitivity to professional relationships that his associates would endure—up to a point.

Bill found an office on Sutter Street for $15 a month, and here he began assembling the stories for *Inhale*. One Saturday, while feeling particularly deprived over want of money, he turned the grievance into a story about a failed poet who survives on the charity of his grocer. The poet's son, Johnny, does the procuring of food, and a wandering, possibly crazy horn player arrives to share in the free lunch. The theme, put forth by the poet, is that society owes the artist a living. On reading it, Bill suddenly felt ill and decided it must be a terrible story.

The pain in his stomach grew worse, and the next day, when in such agony he could no longer walk, he took a cab to the hospital. He was operated on immediately. Waking from the anesthetic, he learned from the doctor that if he had come in ten minutes later, his appendix would have burst. He told the doctor that although his father had died in this way, he felt sure he himself would have survived it. The doctor disagreed.

When Bill reread the story that had prefaced his attack, he decided that, although goofy, it was comic, tragic, and a classic. He called the story "The Man with the Heart in the Highlands."

In New York, Donald Klopfer and Saxe Commins confronted the manuscript of *Inhale & Exhale* and were appalled at its length and uneven quality. Klopfer wrote Bill that they had decided the book should not be published as it stood. Klopfer urged Bill not to fly off the handle at this news, arguing that the public and the critics were expectant about the next Saroyan book and would surely see this one as no more than a receptacle into which Bill had thrown all the odds and ends a self-respecting writer would have dumped. Publication would do his reputation great harm. However, among the finger exercises and duds there were some good stories, and he proposed to select no more than thirty of these for a second collection of real merit.

When Bill complained that Max Perkins had not approached the work of Thomas Wolfe bent on cutting him down to size, Klopfer told him that Maxwell Perkins had not only cut *Of Time and the River* by 25 percent, he had also confided that it would have been a better book if he had cut another 25 percent. Klopfer went on to remind Bill that he had been yelling at him ever since *Trapeze* that he lacked discipline and selectivity about his writing, and he knew he was right about this.

Reluctantly, Bill yielded to the Random House shears, which now cut away all of the material the editors had decided was second-rate. When Bennett Cerf turned up in San Francisco in late October, he assured Bill that this was all for the best. After lunch and a tour of the bookstores, Cerf dismissed the idea that theirs was merely an author-publisher relationship; he felt they were great friends.

Bill did not share this feeling. He was uncomfortable with Cerf's erudition, and it was also not his nature to confuse business dealings with friendship. Instinct warned him that affection was appropriate within a family but not in the marketplace. Even a partner could so easily become a rival.

Bill insisted on additions to the *Inhale* manuscript, which swelled it from the promised 175,000 to 292,000 words and, in spite of further cuts, left Random House with a 450-page book to publish. As *Inhale* went to press, Bill sensed it was the moment to call on his Hemingway easement and asked him for a quote on the new book. Hemingway declined graciously. He said he would have been glad to help, but it was too late now for Bill's publication—and in any case the critics had disliked him since his Africa book, so any praise from him might incense them. He urged Bill to go to work and write a novel that would dazzle them.

In reply, Bill admitted that his hesitancy about a novel stemmed from a poor memory. He had started several novels, only to fail along the way because he had forgotten his purpose. Such facetiousness would not have amused so expert a storyteller as Hemingway. Bill's failure to provide himself a structure suggested he did not respect or understand the need.

In spite of previous experience with the Hemingway pique, Bill couldn't leave well enough alone. He now asked the man who had threatened him with facial damage to contribute to a book he was planning. Would Hemingway write him something about himself and his critics? Hemingway did not reply. However, the snub was not to be the end of their relationship, or of the ill will that had flared between them.

When *Inhale & Exhale* appeared, in February 1936, the buyers liked the format and placed orders enough for a second printing, but the reviews were diffident, and Cerf's survey of the stores showed the book wasn't catching on as *Trapeze* had two years earlier.

Inhale's sales reached only three thousand copies. Bill claimed it was because of the dust jacket. Bennett disagreed. *Inhale* had suffered from too much trivial stuff. They had tried to tell him, but he had objected every time they wanted to cut a word. Cerf hoped Bill was not discouraged by the outcome; it was nothing to be ashamed of. They were all headed for big things, and this would take time.

Bill's dismaying response to this counsel was to submit a third collection of stories. He called it *American Glory,* and proposed that if Cerf were reluctant to publish it, other publishers would be less so.

Cerf explained that under any imprint, another book of Saroyan stories in 1936 would be a great mistake. He urged him to put the *American Glory* manuscript aside and to try again to write a novel. He should also go ahead writing short stories. But Cerf *did* want a new Saroyan book for sometime in *1937,* and he wanted the book to be so much better than the first two that they could publish it in a big way. He was willing to help Bill out financially when needed, but urged him to learn patience.

In the belief that need was the spur to his creativity, Bill was being unusually careless with money, and he repeatedly turned to Random House for more. So he was stunned when Cerf refused him another hundred-dollar loan and warned that with the $200 they had wired to him the previous week, he was more than $600 in debt to them. Cerf felt Bill should draw no more against future books until he had something to show.

Thus, Bill offered him a collection of humorous stories. Cerf replied with a scolding for such a risk to his reputation. He felt Bill had been kidding around long enough, and urged him to sit down—now—and write a novel. It was time to deliver the goods, if he had them in him.

Curiously forgetful of the enthusiasm with which Bennett Cerf had launched *Trapeze*—to say nothing of the likelihood that Cerf would be instrumental in his future success—Bill wrote him loftily that his failure to provide the hundred dollars had been a misdemeanor. Moreover, Cerf had fumbled with *Inhale & Exhale,* which was an excellent second book and would take its place in American literature.

He lectured Cerf for taking the critics far too seriously. The reviews for *Inhale,* good and bad, had been excellent publicity and worthless criticism. While there had been no first-rate criticism of him so far, it would be coming in the next five years. By which time, he felt, any discussion of American writing of this decade would have to be pretty much a discussion of his own.

As for writing a novel, it would be a waste of his time. Short prose was his natural form. The only novel he proposed to do was a great one, and this would require a year, a place to write, and the money for both, which were all beyond reach at present. In any case, his third collection was now ready to be published. When he finished a book—which was to say about every six months—it must be published. He didn't mind if the book didn't earn a nickel. The important thing was to be in print, and available. Thus, if Cerf didn't want it, would he consent to Bill's publishing it elsewhere?

Cerf responded amiably, saying he did not want to sound like a schoolteacher addressing an unruly scholar, but it did rile him that Bill continued to flout the critics, wave aside all their objections, and keep on that he must have the book printed. He conceded that Bill might find a publisher for *American Glory,* but that anyone who took it on would not have Bill's best interests at heart, and he, Cerf, would be bitterly disappointed.

He pleaded that Bill give them credit for knowing something about what they were doing. He was taking it for granted that Random House would go on publishing Saroyan, and nothing had altered his feelings of deep friendship and admiration for him.

Within a few days of writing this, Cerf learned that Bill had submitted *American Glory* to Alfred Knopf. He wired his author angrily, demanding an explanation. Although Bill explained that he had lost at poker and on the horses and owed a thousand dollars, he was far from contrite, and he chided Bennett again for his lack of generosity and faith in him. There was going to be a Saroyan bonanza.

Cerf responded with gracious resignation, noting he could not prevent Bill from submitting *American Glory* elsewhere but trusting Bill would continue to regard Random House as his regular publisher and not let their differences interfere with their friendship. Bill continued to urge a new book on Random House, proposing a "juvenile" book, to be called *Little Children.* He added an ultimatum: if Cerf did not publish him by December, he could consider their relationship ended.

Cerf proposed that Bill send him *Little Children* and stop picking on him, as he was giving him an inferiority complex. Then, while awaiting the manuscript's arrival, he learned from his friend Dick Simon that Bill had just offered *Little Children* to Simon & Schuster.

Angrily, Cerf wrote Bill that he could find no excuse whatever for his action. Putting aside all questions of ethics and common decency for the moment, he wanted to point out that Random had an option on his next book and therefore it *must* be submitted to them before it went to another publisher. If he insisted on writing to other publishers behind Random's back, Cerf advised him to acquaint others with this fact, because if Bill didn't, he would. It would not enhance Bill's reputation. He signed the letter, "Disgustedly, Bennett."

In late August, when Random House did see *Little Children,* there was no cheer to offer. Cerf wrote that the decision on the stories submitted under the title *Little Children* was "thumbs down." He had never approached a manuscript more eagerly, but, once more, Bill had presented them with a pile of odds and ends. His suggestion that they publish this book as a juvenile had to be a prank, for it was no different from his previous collections, except that here the startling originality of the early Saroyan was running thin.

Thwarted in his publishing plans, Bill set out on another exploratory trip to Hollywood, thinking he might strike some good luck there. He hung out at Stanley Rose's Hollywood Bookshop, autographed a hundred copies of *Inhale & Exhale,* and further befriended the proprietor.

Bill was fascinated with Stanley's background as con man, bootlegger, and pornographer, his shrewdness about the books in his shop, and the salty, sleazy good humor with which he kept his precarious business afloat. Every afternoon Stanley would fill a satchel with new books and visit the studios to sell them to the producers, directors, writers, and actors, whom he mischievously called "people in the *industry.*" It was clear that Stanley

Rose knew everybody, and the truth about everybody, in town. In Stanley's famous back room, Bill listened to the tales of fortunes made at the studios, but none came his way.

Hollywood swarmed with pretty, ambitious girls, and Bill enjoyed fleeting relationships with many, but then, in an act of unusual constancy, he settled on a particularly sweet and lovely one. Pat Winter came to live with him.

In September, Bill wrote to Cerf somewhat contritely. He understood their contract was terminated and hoped it was without hard feelings. He accepted some of the blame but felt he had done what he had had to do. He was grateful for the swell work Random House had done in introducing him to the public, was honored to be on its list, and was sure that within ten years it would be the number one publisher in America. If Cerf would give him a little time, and he could get an advance from another publisher, he would pay off his debt.

Cerf replied that it was one of the nicest letters Bill had ever sent him. He certainly wouldn't insist on immediate payment, but if he did get a good advance urged him to make a partial settlement. Also, if the third book didn't work out elsewhere, he hoped Bill would continue as a Random House author.

Two years earlier, Budd Schulberg and his wife had called on Bill in San Francisco. They had read him in *Story* and wanted to tell him how much they admired his work. They had all spent some happy times together. Now, in Hollywood, Bill found that Budd was a part of the literary community surrounding Stanley Rose's bookshop. When Bill described his difficulty in publishing a third volume of stories, Budd proposed that he and Stanley bring it out, a first offering of the Stanley Rose Press.

When Budd undertook the editing job, he was soon as discouraged by the mass and unevenness of the Saroyan material as the Random House editors had been. He abandoned the plan to publish the book, but toward the end of the summer of 1936, he persuaded his father, the independent producer B. P. Schulberg, to take Bill on as a writer.

In October, Bill wrote Cerf that he had found a job in Hollywood. He would be working for B. P. Schulberg at $250 a week. He asked Cerf to send him twelve copies of each of his two Random House books. Cerf responded with congratulations—$250 might be chicken feed in Hollywood, but elsewhere it was a fortune. He and Schulberg had not hit it off, but Schulberg was one of the most competent men in the film business, and Bill should learn much from him.

Now that Bill was making some real money, Cerf urged him to bury the story collection in his cupboard. Also, Cerf declined to send the requested books; there was no reason for his Random House debt to grow bigger. He felt that a starving young Armenian artist was one thing, and a bloated Hollywood capitalist was quite another.

Bill was put to work on a picture called *A Doctor's Diary*. He provided the doctor with a memorable line for completing a delivery. Holding up the newborn, the doctor says, "Okay, Baby, this is the world." Bill liked it well enough to use as a title of a short story, and it contributed to his reputation as a contract writer who could add brilliant bits to the work of others rather than conceive an entire screenplay.

In November 1936, while he was working, with growing reluctance, for Ben Schulberg, four UCLA students—Edward Babigian, Gilbert Harrison, William Okie, and Hal Levy—called on him. In the course of a rambling conversation about the difficulty of publishing, even for an established author, the quartet offered to publish Bill's third collection. Within ten minutes they had founded a publishing company, decided on black for the book's cover, and selected a publication date, December 10, 1936.

A week later, Bill presented a manuscript of nine pieces, titled *Three Times Three*. An editorial dispute arose over Bill's decision to include his play *Subway Circus*. Over Bill's protests that it was a great play and had to be in the book, his board of directors, who felt just as strongly otherwise, unanimously overruled him. *Three Times Three* was published on schedule in an edition of one thousand copies by the Conference Press, in Westwood Village, Los Angeles, and it contained some of Saroyan's most vivid and significant work.

"The Man with His Heart in the Highlands," the story of the welfare poet, would, with minor changes, become his first Broadway play. "The Living and the Dead" contains an affectionate portrait of Bill's grandmother Lucy, which is a triumph of characterization and family comedy. It also has a scene wherein a drunk, calling a wrong number from a bar, finds romance, a situation central to his second Broadway play, *The Time of Your Life*. In "Baby" there is a scene of a telegraph messenger bringing a mother news of her son's death, the situation on which his novel and motion picture *The Human Comedy* would turn.

When a complimentary copy of *Three Times Three* reached Bennett Cerf, he wrote to congratulate Bill and wish him a happy new year. He was enjoying an irony that he was happy to share: despite Bill's complaints about *Inhale & Exhale*'s appearance, the American Institute of Graphic Arts had just singled it out as one of the most beautifully produced books of the year.

When a better job—one that paid $300 a week, at Harry Cohn's Columbia Pictures—came along, Bill took it. He was to work with Dalton Trumbo on a comedy, but collaboration proved agonizing. On February 5, he wrote

Budd Schulberg, an early admirer of Bill's stories, who got
him a job as a Hollywood screenwriter

Cerf that he had just gotten fed up with his Columbia job and was returning to San Francisco. Unfortunately, the $300 check he had mailed to Cerf
was going to bounce. He was disgusted with his luck and the town. Everybody, even people like himself, who were all right elsewhere, behaved like
idiots in Hollywood. He had only $40 to his name. Would Cerf get his
bank to pull the check and forget it?

Understanding that they were parting ways, Bennett wished him well,
and gave him a dose of fatherly advice. He urged him to stop blaming
Inhale's failure on the critics, the publishers, and the ignorance of the reading public. The disappointment in his second book had been real, and picking quarrels with critics was no longer amusing. He must get down to some
real work. When he thought about what Bill *could* do, and looked at the
stuff he had been submitting in the past year, he felt like screaming.

This advice had absolutely no effect. There was far too much evidence in
Bill's daily mail that his readers were plentiful and ready for more.

His ignoring the counsel of so experienced a publisher as Bennett Cerf is baffling. How could he have been so insensitive to the man's feelings and to the consequences for himself? This Saroyan gall is evident as well in his scuffle with Ernest Hemingway. Why did he feel no deference to these dynamic, influential men? Why didn't he listen and learn? Saroyan could not bear the short end of the master-apprentice relationship. His resistance to conventional learning went back to Emerson School, where he had shunned his teachers and their classroom instruction. It was all too slow and irrelevant for him. He already knew what was important. In addition, gratitude and deference were alien emotions; they looked to him like weakness.

Saroyan gives the clue to this disposition in his fiction, notably in the 1949 story "The Parsley Garden." It tells of a boy from a poor, immigrant family who steals a hammer from a shop. He is caught and humiliated by a clerk but is let off with a warning by the owner, allowed to work off his debt, and then offered a permanent job. The boy responds to this clemency by refusing the job. He does so out of a pride that ties hatred for the clerk to the establishment that has the power to employ—and so control—him.

Thus, gratitude is evidence of inferiority and therefore unwelcome. Its opposite is the hubris that now fired Saroyan and gave him license to be demanding and to ignore the feelings of others, even those to whom he was indebted. It was a state of mind far removed from an orphanage sickbed. He felt entitled to his arrogance, and it was all the tragic flaw an ambitious man could handle.

IV

THE TIME OF HIS LIFE

1939–1940

Iɴ ᴛʜᴇ sᴘʀɪɴɢ of 1937, as he drifted clear of Bennett Cerf and Random House, Bill was confident that their sponsorship would soon be replaced. Charles A. "Cap" Pearce, an experienced editor at Harcourt Brace, had been an admirer since first reading Saroyan in *Story*. Bill felt sure Pearce would want to publish him now, and he offered Pearce the *American Glory* collection Cerf had spurned, now retitled *The Tiger and Other Stories*.

Instead, Pearce turned the book down. Like Cerf, Pearce scolded Bill for dividing his writerly need to publish from his readers' appetite for his work. He felt *Inhale & Exhale* had been too long, too uneven in quality, as a follow-up to *Trapeze*. *The Tiger and Other Stories* was a similar, catchall kind of book. While they might sell enough to make it profitable, as Bill had suggested, it would not enhance his reputation, nor theirs.

Among the seventeen stories they had found six good ones, four indifferent ones, and seven "lousy" ones. They preferred his witty, objective, less pretentious stories over the oracular ones—what one reader had called Bill's "streak of Whitmania." Pearce felt this lot was so disparate as to reveal that Saroyan was unable to judge his own work. He wished him the best of luck and hoped that "some day we'll get together. I'd like that."

As ever, Bill was deaf to editorial advice, saw no reason to deny his market, and argued the case for every story on Pearce's "lousy" list.

Home in California, Bill was writing as profusely as ever, turning out some fine stories and finding a ready market for them. Such editors as Ted Weeks, at the *Atlantic Monthly*, and Kyle Crighton, at *Collier's*, were seeking him out, and he was getting checks in the mail. Nevertheless, it was ever clearer that climbing the literary ladder required a novel of him. If he stayed here at his desk overlooking the car tracks on San Francisco's Carl Street, he would never make it into the big league. That would always be in New York.

If he were in New York, with the resourceful Harold Matson to make the arrangements, he saw nothing to prevent his producing that novel within the year—before he turned thirty.

Two years earlier, Hal Matson had quit Ann Watkins to open his own agency, and Bill had joined him to become one of the original Matson clients. Bill admired Hal's familiarity with the marketplace and expertise in placing Saroyan stories. But at the same time, Bill enjoyed the speculation and barter over his own work. It was exciting, and he saw no reason to pay someone else for this pleasure. So Bill had kept Hal clear of his dealings with Random House.

But now, in early July 1937, ready for another assault on New York, he needed the full Matson stewardship. As soon as Bill had arrived and found a reasonable room, at the Great Northern Hotel on Fifty-seventh Street, he called on Hal and was made welcome. For the balance of the summer, the Matson office was his hangout. Each day he dropped by to dally with Tommy, Hal's loyal secretary, and with Pat Duggan, his partner, who dealt in dramatic rights. At day's end Hal would take him out for drinks and a game at the pool parlor across Sixth Avenue. When Bill was broke, Hal loaned him a few dollars against future income.

Hal was reassuring about prospects for a Saroyan novel. He thought Cap Pearce's enthusiasm was most promising and felt sure he could persuade him to contract for a book and provide the money for Bill to survive while writing it. When Hal brought the two men together, Bill assured Pearce that his novel was underway, and the editor agreed to publish it. There would be an advance of a thousand dollars, payable over the next ten weeks, with the balance due on seeing what he had accomplished by early October.

Throughout the summer Bill worked intermittently on the promised novel, but by August he was mired in it. Even as he was determined to complete it, and assured Harcourt that they would have it by the end of September and should announce it for next year, he was doubtful. In the end he had to admit that another novel had sunk beneath him.

As before, he wasted no time in self-reproach and attributed the project's collapse to bad luck rather than artistic overreaching. Hal Matson stood by him and proposed that Harcourt accept a story collection in its place.

Hoping to salvage some of his Saroyan investment, Cap Pearce agreed to the substitution of the collection *Little Children,* which Random House had rejected so indignantly. Harcourt published it that same fall, and Bill enjoyed calling on Bennett Cerf with a presentation copy. He explained that Cap Pearce had proved a fine editor, omitting certain stories and changing others so that the book was now excellent, and he thought it might sell handsomely.

Cerf was glad to see him and had some good news. He had sold the reprint rights of *Trapeze* to Modern Age Books for $500, half of which was Bill's. However, Bill's indebtedness was such that Cerf was keeping all but $125, which left Bill with a $113 debt to Random House. All this ended in an argument, during which Cerf asked Bill if he intended to pay the $113. Bill took offense at the suggestion that he failed to pay his debts, and it was rankling as they parted.

To Bill's delight, the reviews of *Little Children* were good. *Newsweek* said these were first-rate short stories, the best yet. *The New Yorker* admired Saroyan's artful way with the short story and found his characters "funny, pathetic, exasperating and unfailingly interesting." In this climate, Harcourt agreed to publish yet another collection. It was *The Trouble with Tigers,* which both Cerf and Pearce had earlier refused.

The Trouble with Tigers, published in the fall of 1938, encountered a market that was at last saturated with Saroyan stories. When it failed to find readers, Harcourt blamed its author—much as Random House had over *Inhale*—for having urged publication of an inferior book.

All Hal Matson's arguments were no match for Cap Pearce's annoyance at being offered another Saroyan story collection, *Take It or Leave It.* Rejecting the collection, Pearce wrote Bill that it was unworthy of him, and that he should not allow its publication. Pearce was further aggrieved to discover that Matson had sold yet another Saroyan story collection, *Love, Here Is My Hat,* to the paperback publisher Modern Age and that Bill had arranged to publish a fifth, *A Native American.*

This last was a limited edition, five hundred copies of a volume of eight Saroyan stories to be done by George Fields, a local publisher in San Francisco. Fields agreed on an advance of $50 and fifty copies of the book.

These stories were new ones he had written early the previous year, and they included "The Summer of the Beautiful White Horse." The story described the adventures of Aram Garoghlanian, whose lighthearted Fresno boyhood Bill would have preferred to his own bleak one. Bill sensed *A Native American* deserved a wider audience than George Fields could provide, but he did not want to overburden Harcourt.

Cap Pearce was not persuaded by Bill's assurance that *A Native American* was "merely a Christmas gift for friends," nor that his editorial gamble on Saroyan had been wise. With the dwindling of Pearce's enthusiasm and the author's own sense of failing the make-or-break challenge he had set himself in coming to New York, the final months of 1938 had a terminal pallor. A publishing relationship seemed to have sputtered out, and a promising author's career spent like a wastrel's legacy.

It was to be otherwise. With publication of these two widely ignored collections, which Random House had shunned, Bill began a quarter century's publishing relationship with Harcourt Brace. The publisher would be the roving Saroyan's home, bank, lifeboat, and sponsor of two of his most conspicuous publishing successes.

It was here at the end of 1938 that Saroyan's volatile fortunes took a surprising upward turn. The theater had enchanted him since childhood. On his first visit to New York, in 1928, he had tried in vain to write a play. Now, ten years later, he made a simple stage adaptation of his story "The Man with His Heart in the Highlands" and sent it off to *One Act Play* magazine. The magazine's editor, William Kozlenko, not only accepted it but suggested he expand it for possible production.

Bill did this, retitled it *My Heart's in the Highlands,* and entrusted it to Matson's adroit, theatrical partner, Pat Duggan. This fanciful story about a penniless poet and his kindness to an aging, bugle-bearing actor named Jasper MacGregor is also about the loyalty of his six-year-old son, Johnny. When sent to the corner grocer to coerce further credit, the boy proves a master of persuasion, but the aggregate hunger is not wholly satisfied until Jasper offers a neighborhood concert. In the story, the ending is whimsical, with Jasper's keepers restoring him to the Old People's Home. But the dramatization provided a tragic end, with the death of MacGregor and the eviction of the poet's family.

Like "Trapeze," the story sprang from Bill's hungry apprenticeship and a belief that the world owes the artist a living. The language has a poetic innocence that brings to the play a sense of fantasy like that of a fairy tale.

Pat Duggan found some enthusiasm for the play with Harold Clurman's innovative Group Theatre and the possibility of an early presentation. He soon confirmed that the Group had accepted *Highlands.* It was paying an advance of $300, and production was planned for the following spring. Bill added some finishing touches to the play and confidently awaited his debut in the theater.

Home in San Francisco, he enjoyed wandering his neighborhood's once-wild Sunset District. He was fascinated by the construction that was turning it into a new community. He remembered its sand dunes and view of the sea from earlier years. Introducing *The Agony of Little Nations,* a play he set there, he explained that he had named the place Red Rock Hill because of the rosy promontory and its meadow of grasses, gophers, and slim, agile snakes.

He took a particular liking to a half-finished house facing Red Rock Hill. Its rear windows would command a sweeping view of the Pacific. He learned that with an FHA loan and a small down payment, the house could be his. Carl Street, with its streetcars and the noise from the adjoining school playground, was no longer suitable for him or his family. He was determined that they should move here, and he put down $100 as a deposit, but he feared that might be the end of it.

The state of his royalty account at Harcourt Brace and the chill of the publisher's response to further stories left no doubt that he must look elsewhere for home finance. The theater offered an enticing new market. Just as he had felt fully arrived as a fiction writer when *Story* accepted "Trapeze," he now felt himself a playwright and wrote new plays briskly and profusely. He urged Pat Duggan to turn his stage efforts into the income he so sorely needed. Most of these plays were short, abstract, and more enigmatic than *Highlands,* and Pat Duggan could find no market for them. Bill could not accept that verdict, and as the year ended with no word, he accused his agents of neglect.

Duggan's unruffled response was that there was plenty of energy at the office ready to work for him, and it would, if he provided the means. Duggan had asked for a play idea to discuss with the producer Jed Harris and another for radio. Duggan would never be able to send him more money if all he could do was *say* that Bill Saroyan was a great playwright.

In response, Bill did, grudgingly, offer a play idea for Jed Harris. It would be called *The Man Who Talked Back,* and would portray a heroic skeptic who not only recognizes the propaganda with which politicians are misleading the nation but protests it. For his pains, his sanity is questioned. He is jailed and murdered but not before his revolution is taken up by the people and his immortality is assured.

In retrospect, *The Man Who Talked Back* can be seen as Saroyan's own messianic fantasy, but Pat Duggan thought it a negotiable idea and promised to try it on Harris as well as Herman Shumlin and the Group.

When Duggan did interest Jed Harris in the Saroyan play, Bill did not pursue it but continued to goad Pat Duggan, with heavy irony, about the pace of his agentry: it was too fast for him. His Group Theatre check was overdue, as was another from *Story.* He wanted them now, and wanted Duggan to oversee the Group's *Highlands* production and mend his diffident way of representation.

When Hal Matson proposed to visit him in San Francisco, Bill answered with a complaint about his services and set him a model of professional behavior in his London agent, Laurence Pollinger. Pollinger, Bill maintained, sold his stuff widely, sent royalties promptly, and answered his questions before he forgot what they were. As a result Bill was regarded abroad as a major writer.

Matson explained patiently that his monthly Group check was usually a couple of days late and that the Theatre Guild added more time for bookkeeping and clearing the bank, so it arrived at the Matson office in midmonth. Hal urged Bill not to go around thinking bad thoughts about them.

But Bill did not change his mind about his agents, and in spite of their constancy decided to end his connection with Matson and Duggan. He thought about opening an office of his own in New York and finding a young man, possibly an Armenian, possibly a lawyer, to put in charge of it, someone who could represent him in all things.

On March 9, 1939, Pat Duggan wrote that rehearsals of *Highlands* had begun and the cast was excellent. The boy would be played by Sidney Lumet, who, for a kid, had a remarkable record. There was slight picture interest in the play. April 12 had been set as the opening date for *Highlands,* and he hoped Bill would come to New York for it. Bill assured Duggan that the picture interest in *Highlands* would soon be tremendous. It was sure to suit a producer-director like Frank Capra.

There was further good news. *Collier's* bought a story and paid $500 for it. He added this to his deposit and told the bank he hoped to have more soon. The house was being completed as he left for New York.

Accord was rare within the Group, as with its parent company, the Theatre Guild, and *Highlands* proved no exception. Robert Lewis had been chosen as director, and his reading of the script to the company had elicited widespread groans. Elia Kazan had likened it to "a flute's complaint," and the stage manager had called it "a piece of cheese." Only one Group actor, Art Smith, had volunteered for it, and he had been given the role of MacGregor.

However, Lewis saw it as a "libretto on which to build a poetic production by adding music, sound, color and movement to the enchanting dialogue." He commissioned a fanciful set by Herbert Andrews and a score by Paul Bowles. When the Group's Franchot Tone turned down the lead, Lewis cast Philip Loeb in it and filled out the cast with his students and friends, Nick Conte and Harry Bratsburg among them.

Bill arrived in New York on April 12, 1939, and that night turned up for the *Highlands* dress rehearsal. He was enthralled by the sound of his own words uttered by these clearly talented actors, and was enchanted by the fanciful set and Bowles's exotic incidental music.

Afterward he walked about the stage in a daze, touching the props, the scenery, and all the machinery of theatrical illusion. He admitted to Lewis that this was his first produced play, and he found its presentation far more fascinating and complex than he had imagined. In this mood of childlike wonder, he noted with surprise that his initials were the same as Shakespeare's.

Over coffee he praised the work Lewis and the others had done to bring his play to the stage. He felt his own contribution was lacking and promised some new dialogue. When Lewis protested that the opening would take place the following night and there was no time for actors to learn new

The Group Theatre's production of Bill's first play, *My Heart's in the Highlands*,
with Sidney Lumet, Philip Loeb, and Harry Bratsburg, April 1939

lines, Bill insisted on making a few improvements. Back at the Great Northern, he made a number of revisions. The next day, when Lewis balked at
most of them, significant friction grew between the two men.

This month would be the beginning of what Bill Saroyan would always
regard as his miraculous year. Five years earlier, when Saroyan's fresh voice
was first heard in New York, doldrums lingered over the close of the Depression era. His message had been the importance of self and of rejoicing in it,
and of understanding that poverty was really nothing compared to the wonder of being alive. It had made a heartening sound.

Now, in the closing year of the decade, the nation faced new anxieties. In
January, President Roosevelt had warned that the world stood at the threshold of World War II, and the newspapers were black with news of Germany's ambitions. Nevertheless, the amiable Saroyan voice was no less ready
to speak to theater audiences about the decency and kindliness of common
people, whatever their nationality, and of their capacity to stand up to the
institutionalized, authorized hatreds of the social order. Again, that optimistic, playful, otherworldly voice would be heard.

Through its earnestly elfin characters, *My Heart's in the Highlands* seemed to say that in spite of hardship, ordinary people have a powerful need for poetry, and for other expressions of their spirit. However zany they may seem, theirs is an admirable way, deserving of praise and support.

Word of *Highlands* had spread through the theatrical community, and Laurence Olivier, Margalo Gilmore, Irwin Shaw, and Alfred Stieglitz were all in the opening-night audience. The response was spirited. No one could recall anything so fanciful and imaginative on the contemporary stage.

The reviewers were sharply divided. As Wolcott Gibbs told the readers of *The New Yorker,* "This collision between the most completely undisciplined talent in American letters and the actors of the Group Theatre bored me nearly to distraction and I would advise you to stay away from it." Burns Mantle, in the *Daily News,* decided the play had been put on simply to aggravate its audience. Sidney Whipple, in the *World Telegram,* found it a painful experiment and advised the Group "to pay no further attention to Mr. Saroyan's babbling."

Never easily resigned to bad reviews, Bill turned to the telegraph office. The next morning, Burns Mantle found Bill's telegram on his desk, telling him that *Highlands* was not goofy at all but a good and great play that would haunt him. If he were to see it again he might change his mind.

On the other hand, the more influential Brooks Atkinson, in the *New York Times,* found *Highlands* "wholly enchanting," and its production one "that the Moscow Art Theatre would be glad to accept as worthy of the Stanislavski standard." In the *New York Post,* John Mason Brown praised *Highlands* for its rejection of realism in favor of a skillful and poignant fantasy. He found the play more moving than most of the season's offerings.

George Jean Nathan's *Newsweek* review described *Highlands* as "a fascinating, sentimental work, lit with the gleam of fancy, humor and compassion." He compared it favorably to the previous year's entry from California, John Steinbeck's *Of Mice and Men.*

Nathan asked Bill to join him for lunch at Jack and Charlie's "21" Club. Bill was immediately at home there. The rising voices of the rich and beautiful, and the aroma of liquor, food, and cigars, brought forth his easy laugh, his role as the charming, flamboyant genius. Nathan decided that this supremely confident young man from California was every bit as rare and gifted a dramatist as he claimed to be.

Nathan, at fifty-seven, had been writing theater criticism since 1908 and was author of a score of books on the American theater. He was H. L. Mencken's friend, and with him had founded and edited the *American Mercury.* He was among the earliest champions of the plays of Eugene O'Neill and was now president of the New York Drama Critics Circle. While

Bill with his ardent Broadway sponsor, George Jean Nathan,
head of the Drama Critics Circle, 1940

Saroyan certainly sensed that he had made an influential friend in Nathan, he could not have imagined what a force the man's sponsorship would be in his career.

So much of the praise for *Highlands* had gone to the production itself that Bill forgave Bobby Lewis his reluctance to make the last-minute changes. He inscribed a book for Lewis with thanks for directing his first play and hopes to have more directed so ably.

Theresa Helburn, codirector of the Theatre Guild with Lawrence Langner, thought *Highlands* sentimental but agreed to extend its run by making it the fifth play of the Guild's season. She was not surprised when it stumbled at the box office. "Everybody loved it," she later remembered, "but nobody bought a ticket. I think it did two hundred dollars a night."

She was less than enthusiastic about Saroyan, too. When he called on her for the first time she found him "an attractive young man, hearty-looking, strong and sturdy, outspoken and direct—not a smoothie as theatre people sometimes tend to be. He's a natural with no pose to him. He means what he says and he is not hampered by conventional ideas. The first day I had to keep him waiting five minutes. After we had talked for a while I asked him to lunch with me but he refused. Bill was not a man to waste time. He had spent that five minutes dating the telephone operator."

The *Highlands* reception was at least as glamorous as Bill's arrival in the literary world had been five years earlier. In Sardi's and Lindy's theater people spoke of Saroyan, this new young playwright, and they knew him when he came in. However, when he was shown to George Jean Nathan's table at "21," *Highlands* had posted its closing notice. He was broke. His sister Cosette had written from San Francisco that unless he sent more money they would be unable to make the payment on the new house. They had put all their hopes on the $1,000 from Harcourt and some weekly income from the play. They had no intention of borrowing from anyone. Everyone believed Bill was making a lot of money in New York, and they must not be disenchanted.

It was Bill's intention to return to San Francisco at once and, one way or another, to secure the house on Fifteenth Avenue. When he told Nathan that he did have an idea for another play and might write it at home, the critic urged him to stay in New York, where the theater was. Bill replied that it would be impossible without a commitment from a producer. Nathan thought that was a reasonable request and assigned himself the arranging of it.

He had proposed to the Drama Critics Circle, of which he was president, that they give Saroyan a citation as the most promising playwright of the season. This done, he was able to see that Saroyan sat across from Eddie Dowling at the awards dinner in the Algonquin Hotel. In the course of the evening, Dowling told Bill how much he admired *Highlands,* and that if Bill ever wrote another play, he would buy it. This promise sent Bill to work at once. On Monday morning, May 8, 1939, he sat down at his typewriter in the Great Northern Hotel, determined to write a second play within the week. By Saturday, May 13, he had done just that.

He had set it in a favorite San Francisco hangout, Izzy Gomez's bar, renaming it Nick's Pacific Street Saloon. It became the scene for a parade of comic vaudeville turns—the hoofer, the braggart, the funny drunk—portraying Bill Saroyan's world, a heaven where the raffish and disenfranchised rejoiced in the boozy atmosphere and where Joe, the playwright's alter ego, managed the progression of events from his bar-side table.

Joe has a "gofer," slow-witted, dependent, grateful Tom, and there is a heroine, Kitty, a sweet-natured whore with whom Joe can reward Tom for his loyalty. There is a villain, Blick, the plainclothes cop who threatens the idyllic world of Nick's bar. Blick is slain by Kit Carson, one of the oddball barflies, which provides the play's climax and completes its message—that you should live your brief life to its fullest, and drink deep, for it is precious, perishable stuff, and if anyone should try to stop you, you may kill him without regret.

Like its author, *The Time of Your Life* seemed to be an amiable, larky play. In affirming the decency and lovableness of society's dropouts, it falls into the romantic category the French call *nostalgie de la boue*—nostalgia for the gutter. Yet the play has a dark side. Nick's is only a dream factory, a temporary refuge from the bleakness outside. Kitty remembers Ohio as a scene of trouble, loss, and death. Krupp, the good cop, sees his beat as hopeless, a world of bad kids selling themselves. The mysterious, God-like Joe lives his own contradictory fantasy of success and guilt. In fact, Joe is Saroyan's adolescent image of himself in heaven, where at the adjacent horse parlor his bets are always winners, where the girls are sweet-natured, redeemable whores, and the barflies are talented entertainers gathered to amuse him and affirm his reign over them. It makes a striking self-portrait of a man who sees himself as spectator and manipulator, a vessel of knowledge, wealth, and power, a benevolent despot to his dependents, a man who sees friendship as dominance.

The Time of Your Life was to be Saroyan's major theatrical statement, a wistful dream of human decency, an endorsement of anarchy and that innocence about to be lost forever in the political complexities of World War II.

On Monday, May 15, a week after he had begun the play, Bill sent Dowling a finished script, along with a note on Matson and Duggan letterhead saying that he had enclosed the new play and hoped to hear from him soon. He wrote that he would be at the Guild that evening and proposed they go for a drink after the performance.

He also offered the play to the Group Theatre's brilliant head, Harold Clurman. Clurman approved some of its fantasies, but found the whole too sentimental and self-indulgent for his taste. Although Clurman was ready to explain all this, Bill would have none of it. Clurman's judgment was an affront; Bill could scorn but certainly not learn from it.

Dowling, however, liked the play. He saw in the leading role of Joe a good part for himself and believed he could get the backing to produce it. Pleased with the way the plans for his new protégé were taking shape, Nathan gathered Dowling and Bill around his lunch table at "21." At Nathan's side was his constant girl, Julie Haydon. As they discussed casting

Bobby Lewis, director of both the Group's *Highlands* and early phases of the Theatre Guild's *Time of Your Life*. Lewis was founder of the Actor's Studio and is shown here with Eli Wallach and Joanne Woodward.

the play, Nathan turned to Julie, and, to everyone's surprise, said, "and here's your Kitty Duval." While there were to be some doubts about the wisdom of this choice, Bill agreed at once, and the two principal roles were cast.

Dowling assured Bill there would be money forthcoming from *The Time of Your Life* and guaranteed it with an immediate $885 of his own. Harcourt now agreed to publish *Highlands,* providing a $400 advance, while Samuel French paid $750 for the play's amateur rights. Matson sold a story, "Presbyterian Choir," to *Harper's* magazine for $225, and Pat Duggan negotiated a $250 fee from CBS for an experimental radio play.

In June, Saroyan went back to San Francisco with enough money to make the house on Red Rock Hill a certainty. He found that Takoohi and Cosette had left Carl Street for the upstairs quarters of 1821 Fifteenth Avenue and moved his belongings into the ground-floor apartment.

Now all that was needed was more and better furniture, and he set that as his next goal. He was determined to keep up the flow of his plays. He was becoming as facile with the form as he was with stories and could turn one out in a single day. Soon after his arrival in San Francisco, he was urging Pat Duggan to get a copy of his play *Noonday Dark Enfolding Texas* to Beatrice Straight at the Chekhov Theatre Studio, in Ridgefield, Connecticut, and his play *Subway Circus* to the American Lyric Theatre.

He would miss the broadcast of the CBS radio play, since he was going abroad, but he told Duggan to see that CBS did it right. By this he meant in his style, casually, energetically, the laughter and the seriousness combined. He continued to chide Duggan for failing to sell *The Several Ways of Looking at Everything* and *Subway Circus*. If Duggan were going to represent him on easy stuff, he must make himself valuable by putting over more difficult deals. Bill wanted a sale of both movie and British rights to *Highlands*. The main thing was to make Bill some money, to figure that out some way. If Duggan failed, Bill felt it only proper that he look elsewhere for representation.

Just as Bill had rewarded himself with a long, European holiday after *Trapeze*, now, on completing *The Time of Your Life*, the self-congratulatory voyage became ritual. He returned to New York in early June, stayed long enough to spur the efforts of Matson, Duggan, and Eddie Dowling, and on the fourteenth sailed for England.

He went to Dublin, as he had long planned to do, and there sought out the city's young poets and writers. They gave him an enthusiastic welcome. Bill particularly liked Flann O'Brien, who revealed that the original title of his first novel, *At Swim-Two-Birds,* had been *Sweeney in the Trees.* Bill admired O'Brien's cast-off title enough to borrow it from him later.

Still enjoying Dublin, Bill received a cable from Pat Duggan, who had been busy with the Saroyan cause. It told him that Vincente Minelli and Bela Blau were ready to sponsor an all-negro surrealist revue, with a book by Saroyan, a possible score by Rodgers and Hart, and an early fall opening. It was likely to be a big Broadway hit and required his immediate return.

Although Bill had planned to go on to Europe, he agreed, asking only for his return boat fare. He cut short his holiday, except for a trip to Paris.

On June 29 he flew there, where his new love of Ireland led him to telephone James Joyce and ask to see him. Joyce agreed to meet him later in the week, and made a point of pronouncing his name very accurately, as Armenians do. But Bill was irked by the delay and returned to London at once. On July 5 he sailed for home on the *Normandie.*

He returned to New York to find Dowling preparing *The Time of Your Life* for production, and impresarios seeking his attention, urging new entertainments upon him. His theatrical future seemed like spring itself, with possibilities sprouting in every direction. Each one held promise and fostered his belief that anything he turned his hand to would succeed.

Over several evenings, Bill and Minelli made subway excursions to Harlem. They would start with the show at the Apollo Theatre and move on to the Savoy Ballroom to watch the exuberant dance-floor outbursts of the boys and girls and later to hear the laughter of young men cake-walking, as if heaven-bound, on early-morning Lenox Avenue. They wanted to capture this innocence and energy, so their own show would burst with that kind of laughter.

Bill set to work on some sketches for the revue and then decided to return to San Francisco, where there would be less distraction and fewer ways to spend money. As he settled into his new office in the house on Fifteenth Avenue, he heard from an excited Pat Duggan that Broadway's foremost acting couple, Alfred Lunt and Lynn Fontanne, wanted a Saroyan play, and would pay money for an option on an idea that suited them. Pat explained that it should include parts not only for the two stars but for their company, which boasted the actors Richard Whorf and Sidney Greenstreet.

Bill replied that he had just begun a play, *The Hero of the World,* which he thought was his best so far. While he didn't know enough about the Lunts or their company to be sure it would suit them, he saw no reason why it wouldn't. He promised it by the end of the month.

This was prospect enough for Duggan to persuade the Lunts to advance a thousand dollars, payable immediately. The play was to be delivered in September for production early the following year. The royalty would be generous.

The Hero of the World had become a multifamily, multigenerational epic. The central figures in its cast of twenty-four are a father and his illegitimate son. Both lead confused, unhappy lives, allowing Saroyan to deplore the war, heroism, and the hollow marriages that befall the characters and to endorse the love that eludes them. It was Saroyan's reach for profundity, and it brought forth a sprawling, unearned grievance against life itself.

On finishing the play, Bill sent Nathan a copy and promptly heard from him that he did not like it. This time, Nathan felt, Bill had failed the mark by dramatizing psychic confusion in terms of dramatic confusion. The result was unintentional chaos. It certainly was not the play for the Lunts. They would simply reject it.

Reaffirming his faith in the Saroyan talent, Nathan urged Bill to write slower and with more self-criticism. He urged Bill to let him read the next one, for he had a grand scheme for it.

Sobered by this news, Bill wrote a humble letter to Pat Duggan accepting the Nathan verdict on *Hero.* However, with the Lunts his likeliest source of income, Bill inquired about their company, what plays they had done, what roles they preferred. He admitted to being broke and urged Duggan to find him money wherever he could, and to look around midtown New York for a suitable apartment at about $125 a month.

When Duggan replied that the Lunts had already agreed to a thousand-dollar advance for an unwritten play, Bill reacted with surprising reluctance.

A scene from *The Time of Your Life*, with Charles de Sheim, Gene Kelly,
Julie Haydon, and Eddie Dowling

He was not sure he could write a play in which one or two characters were
more important than the others, and he didn't want to swindle anybody.

Feeling that Bill was ignoring a main chance, Pat reminded him of the
crisis abroad and the certainty of its devastating effect on the theatrical season. He told Bill he should accept the Guild-Lunt offer immediately.

Saroyan was curiously oblivious, or perhaps blindered, to the gravity of
the times. Although Hitler had signed a nonaggression pact with the Soviets
and the German army stood poised on the Polish border, Bill assured his
acquaintances there would be no war over Poland, because, sooner or later,
Germany would have all its demands met. Within the week, Germany
invaded Poland, while Britain and France declared war against Germany.
On September 3, President Franklin D. Roosevelt spoke to the nation
through a radio "fireside chat," proclaiming a U.S. neutrality that would
prevail until November.

In New York, Eddie Dowling had been busy with *The Time of Your Life.* He had approached the Theatre Guild and found that both Lawrence Langner and Theresa Helburn liked the play and were willing to coproduce it for their subscribers in the forthcoming season. Recalling that Bobby Lewis had been so successful in catching the Saroyan mood in *Highlands,* they selected him as director.

Lewis soon bridled under Langner's pragmatic approach to the production, in particular his insistence on casting the play from the standpoint of actors' salaries. Nor was he pleased at the choice of Julie Haydon, George Jean Nathan's protégé, to play Kitty Duval. However, he was cheered by an endorsement from the playwright.

Bill wrote that he was delighted to find Lewis directing a second Saroyan play and felt he would do it superbly. He knew Bobby would recognize it for the great, even miraculous, play it was, and expand its virtues. The gadgets, the telephone and the marble game, were important. He must take pains to get the kind he had written about, to make sure that their effect was zany and bigger than life. He urged the director to be a poet.

With this mandate Lewis chose as designer the imaginative Boris Aronson, who made plans for a wild pinball machine and costumes as fanciful as Bill wanted. He put Lehman Engel in charge of both music and sound effects. As rehearsals began, Lewis found Lawrence Langner's suggestions insensitive and his cast in a rebellious mood. Julie Haydon seemed particularly resentful of him. When Aronson brought her costume sketches, she showed her disapproval by ripping them in two. Aware of Miss Haydon's connections, the horrified director kept a silence he would later regret as cowardice.

Hortense Alden, cast as Elsie, a nurse, refused to play against an offstage voice Lewis planned as counterpoint, while Dowling, in the leading role of Joe, insisted that his own ideas on characterization prevail over the director's.

In Fresno, Bill had talked to his cousin Ross Bagdasarian about playing in the forthcoming show, and on August 26 Bill wrote Duggan that although Ross had only amateur experience he felt he was absolutely right for the part of Willie, the marble-game maniac. He asked Duggan to look after him.

In mid-September Ross Bagdasarian arrived in New York ready to join the cast. He soon wrote Bill that although the role of Willie had already been assigned, he would have a part. Julie Haydon, who struck him as "a very nice girl," had taken him to lunch at Jack Dempsey's, where she was besieged for her autograph. Everyone spoke highly of the play, so he knew it would be a big hit.

He assured Bill that he was being discreet about their relationship, not socializing with the cast and in general behaving himself. He found the New

York women phony. He kept to himself and a few old people he had met at the hotel. On the twentieth, he wrote Bill that he was understudying the role of Willie and playing one of the musicians that came in before the show and came in again at its close. He was joining Actors' Equity and would be paid $40 a week. He thought Len Doyle as Kit Carson was as good as W. C. Fields, and that Bobby Lewis was a great director who understood the play. Lewis had taken Bill's letter from his pocket and read it to the cast.

Ross explained how Lewis was staging the play as a symphony. The band of four musicians made a prologue. They came on as if hurrying to a concert, could be heard tuning up, then a tapping of the conductor's baton was heard as the play began, the spot falling on Eddie Dowling. Similarly, the musicians closed the play, reentering to a record of applause, whereupon, Ross explained, they went to the bar, got a drink, congratulated each other, tipped hats, and shook hands as the light faded. And then, blackout.

Ross Bagdasarian's view that all was well with the play was not shared by Lawrence Langner, whose distrust of Lewis's direction had increased with every rehearsal. Langner felt some drastic remedies were needed. Lewis noticed strangers in the theater balcony and sent the stage manager to inquire about them. He was dismayed to learn they were cast replacements sent by the Theatre Guild for changes of which Lewis had no knowledge.

Bill decided to accept the Lunts' offer to write another play, and signed the contract, which was with the Theatre Guild as well. As he started east to join the *Time of Your Life* company on the road, Bill wrote Pat Duggan that Duggan should plan to go to New Haven and Boston with him. He would not want to argue this time but rather would give him the necessary changes and have him see that they were made. This was to be his new blitzkrieg technique, similar to Hitler's tactic of surrounding Warsaw and then demanding peace. Bill assured Duggan it was going to be some year.

Arriving in New York in the first week of October, Bill learned of Lawrence Langner's misgivings and persuaded George Jean Nathan to come to the New Haven opening. There they found Bobby Lewis in despair, feeling that through inexperience and weakness he had allowed Lawrence Langner and Eddie Dowling to undermine his fanciful, imaginative plan for Saroyan's poetic play. He was further dismayed to find that Saroyan had turned against him and now wanted to scrap the artistry and stylization they had agreed on, for realism.

After the New Haven performance there was agreement on one thing: the show had been a disaster. Langner described it as "incredible chaos. Nobody, including the actors, seemed to know what the play was about. A bewildered audience left the theatre and learned from the papers next day that the drama critics were equally bewildered."

Bill joined Nathan in putting the blame on both Lewis's misguided direction and Theatre Guild meddling. But in his *Newsweek* account, Nathan sounded a hopeful note. He had detected "the rich essences and uncommon beauties which are deep within the play." He felt that the play "brings to the American drama, as its author's 'My Heart's in the Highlands' did before it . . . a new and noteworthy originality, life, force, freshness, and humor."

Langner's recent history of firing directors when a play was in trouble convinced Lewis that he was next. When he realized that the Guild, with the assent of Dowling and Saroyan, was about to drop the curtain on him, he locked himself in his room and stayed there until he could figure out what to do. He decided to quit and go back to New York. He would always recall Lawrence Langner's last words to him: "After you and Orson Welles, no more geniuses."

Saroyan and Dowling decided they could bring the play into Boston and New York without help, and Langner agreed to give them billing as codirectors. Lehman Engel's score was cast out. Aronson's fanciful set was junked for a realistic one by Watson Barratt, and hasty casting call was issued in New York for the replacement of eight actors. Celeste Holm, then a teenager without professional experience, was chosen as the new Mary L. William Bendix was chosen to replace Karl Malden and Gene Kelly to replace Martin Ritt. These new members of the cast arrived at the Plymouth Theatre in Boston to find it empty. The survivors, in fear of further firings, were in hiding.

The Saroyan directing style was unorthodox. He sat onstage, making occasional outcries but offering few suggestions. He was conspicuous in his consumption of pears. Although he complained that they were not good pears, he munched them to the cores, which he flung into the footlights.

Lawrence Langner saw Saroyan as "a man of varying amiability," at one moment displaying "the charm of an Eastern potentate," in the next, the sensitivity of a truck driver. Langner learned that Saroyan lacked any directing experience and had no idea how to talk to actors. Saroyan tried to show what he wanted by clumsy demonstration—and, when that failed, by bellowing.

The play opened at the Plymouth Theatre on October 14, and, just as in New Haven, it flopped. The critics, with the single exception of the *Boston Herald*'s Elliot Norton, found little to admire in it. In the week remaining before the New York opening, Langner, Dowling, and Saroyan redoubled their efforts, but the actors had lost all confidence and the play grew steadily worse.

When Saroyan confronted Langner in the theater lobby demanding to know what the matter was with the actors, Langner replied, "Do you really want to know? *You* are what is the matter with the actors. If you'll keep out of the theater the next three days, we will be able to bring this play into good condition." When Saroyan appeared in Eddie Dowling's dressing room to ask if Langner could keep him out of the theater, the actor tactfully suggested that he relinquish his onstage seat for one in the orchestra.

The quarrel between Saroyan and Langner continued as the company journeyed to New York. Bill complained that the Booth Theatre's stage was too confining for his cast, and he wanted the set widened. He turned up with an Armenian girl from Fresno, ready to add a part for her. Then, at George Jean Nathan's suggestion, he proposed to move a Julie Haydon scene from her bedroom to the saloon. With a day left before the opening, Langner denied all these requests and urged that Nathan mind his own business.

To the surprise of everyone—save for Bill Saroyan—the play was an immediate Broadway hit. On the evening of October 25, 1939, when Eddie Dowling rose from the chair upon which he had sat as Joe throughout the play and waved farewell to the first-night audience, the applause was immense. There were twenty-seven curtain calls, and the next day the critical praise was widespread.

" 'The Time of Your Life' is something worth cherishing," Brooks Atkinson wrote in the *New York Times,* "a prose poem in ragtime with a humorous and lovable point of view. . . . Some of the warmest and heartiest comedy in the modern drama comes bubbling up through Mr. Saroyan's pungent dialogue." He concluded that in spite of "the waywardness of Mr. Saroyan's genius," the writer is "creative, which is the most precious thing in art, and he has rubbed his elbows in life without soiling his spirit."

Time magazine found Saroyan's world "cockeyed and alcoholic and all its outcasts childlike and starry eyed," but admitted that "Out of a warm heart and a lively fancy, Saroyan has written a paean to the essential goodness in life and people, a chant of love for the scorned and rejected." In *Newsweek,* George Jean Nathan called it "the season's first new play of definite quality. It has a truth of character, a diggingly rich humor, an overtone of vibrant human music and a bright and gleaming freshness that lift it high above the general. . . . In its young author the American stage has uncovered someone eminently worthwhile."

It was to be the play of William Saroyan's life. It portrayed the fantasies and dreams of an innocent America about to perish in World War II. While it lacked a conventional plot, it had a frame, a barroom full of outcasts beset by an Emersonian repressive society. Saroyan's comic touch brought these caricatures of braggart drunks, whores—life's failures—alive, and revealed them as amusing, talented, and lovable in their rowdy ways. With the onset

Bill during his "miracle year," 1939

of new, complex values and ideologies, the play's charitable message would be ever clearer.

With the play running to full and enthusiastic audiences, Bill's royalties would be bringing him about $750 a week. There was talk of forming a road company. Bela Blau and Vincente Minelli had engaged E. Y. Harburg to do the score for the Harlem musical and had paid Bill a $200 advance for its script. Eugene Loring, of the Ballet Theatre, was preparing to stage Saroyan's ballet, *The Great American Goof.*

Best of all, Bill had a new play, which he had titled *Love's Old Sweet Song* and believed to be a vehicle for the Lunts. Nathan had given it enthusiastic approval, as had Eddie Dowling, with a $250 advance for rights to it. The Guild was interested in producing it, and the Guild-Lunt advance of a thousand dollars had arrived.

Bill's financial worries appeared to be over. He did several things he had wanted to do all his life. He sent substantial sums of money to his relatives. He remembered his uncle Mihran particularly, for the financing of his first New York trip, in 1928. Then he bought a car, a Buick, and persuaded Ross to quit his role as the newsboy and drive back to California with him. It was Bill's hope to intercept the Lunts, who were touring in *The Taming of the Shrew,* and convince them to undertake *Love's Old Sweet Song.*

The two cousins were united by a lusty, Armenian exuberance. They laughed at one another's jokes and sang for the joy of life and its possibility. Just being together was hilarious good fun. Their cross-country ride was a celebration. They had pulled it off, a big Broadway smash, and they were headed for more and more of the same.

On their way through Arizona they composed a song. Bill wrote Pat Duggan that its music was Armenian, while the words, composed mainly by himself, were American. They called it "Come on My House (I'm Gonna Give You Candy)." It was funny, sad, and beautiful, sure to be popular. He asked Duggan to find a publisher for it and arrange for Ross to sing the vocal.

Through a telegram from his brother Henry, Bill learned that their grandmother Hripsime, Mrs. Bedros Saroyan, had died, at the age of eighty-two. He was glad that she had received the check he had sent her a few days earlier, and had departed life painlessly—she had simply gone to sleep and dreamed into eternity. He would miss the childlike woman.

Promising to be on hand for the funeral, on Monday, Bill and Ross drove on to San Diego to see the Lunts perform in *The Taming of the Shrew*. Bill thought the famous actors were everything he had heard about them, putting on a good, high-spirited show. He wrote Pat Duggan that Lynn Fontanne had looked and acted like sheer fairy madness. When he went backstage, he was cordially received by Alfred Lunt in his dressing room. Lynn Fontanne joined them briefly, left to change from her costume, and returned for an hour's talk, from which he concluded they would *not* be doing *Love's Old Sweet Song*.

He had a similar feeling that *The Time of Your Life* was not going to sell to the movies, but he assured Duggan he would make no compromise with his demands for it: he must have approval of the script, the director, the cast, and the billing. He didn't expect Hollywood to agree, which was fine, since he no longer needed money.

In the final months of 1939 and the early ones of 1940, Bill had his share of disappointments. There was the waning enthusiasm of the Lunts for a Saroyan play, and of Minelli and Blau for a Harlem musical.

As Christmas approached, *The Time of Your Life* was playing to ever-dwindling audiences, and Bill was dismayed to find it not included in the ten most sought-after plays of the holiday season. His resentment was undiluted by the thought that it was competing with such monuments as Robert Sherwood's *Abe Lincoln in Illinois*, Lillian Hellman's *Little Foxes*, George Kaufman's *Man Who Came to Dinner*, and Philip Barry's *Philadelphia Story*.

He wanted another play on Broadway at once and decided on the one the Lunts had spurned, *Love's Old Sweet Song*. It was a story about the pathetic love of a forty-four-year-old California woman for a fifty-one-year-old traveling pitchman. Their attraction is generated by a false telegram delivered by a Postal Telegraph messenger. By introducing a homeless family of sixteen that camps on the heroine's lawn and ultimately destroys her house, Bill lampooned the Okies of his friend John Steinbeck's best-selling novel *The Grapes of Wrath*. With the character of the magazine salesman, he had more satiric fun, at the expense of Henry Luce's ubiquitous *Time* magazine. Although *Love's Old Sweet Song* had a full quota of the whimsy that had characterized *Highlands* and *Time of Your Life*, it lacked its predecessors' roots in Bill's own experience, and, with it, an element of credibility.

The Theatre Guild liked the new play well enough to overcome its irritation with Saroyan and agreed to coproduce it with Dowling. Similarly, Bill was accepted by Langner and Helburn as codirector with Dowling. In addition to his royalties, Bill was to receive a codirector's salary of $1,000, payable in $250 installments at the end of each week of rehearsal.

The play had only two acts, but since it was to be a full evening's entertainment, Bill decided to add a third act, and he turned up with this in New York, early enough to take part in the casting. To Langner's dismay, Bill not only insisted on hiring eccentric actors he encountered by accident, but on writing in new scenes for them. Nevertheless, the cast turned out to be a fine one, headed by Walter Huston, Jessie Royce Landis, and Arthur Hunnicutt.

It was at this time that Theresa Helburn wrote to her friend George Bernard Shaw, describing the playwright as "The erratic young genius Saroyan. . . . He is as independent of any conventional structure as the later GBS and I might as well admit that so far none of his plays have even paid their production cost. His characterization is fresh and inventive but I am afraid he is a sentimentalist and lacks the intellectual clarity or drive. Nevertheless his plays bring a fresh breeze into a stale theatre so we continue to do our best with them."

On the road, Bill resisted all criticism of the three-act play until the lackluster Philadelphia opening, on April 8, 1940, when it became clear to all that the play's climax was in the middle of the second act, after which point the tedium multiplied. Bill capitulated, agreeing to omit the recently added third act. In Baltimore, reaction to the two-act play was enthusiastic.

Langner and Dowling now believed they were coming into New York with a hit. However, two days before the opening there, Saroyan argued for a return to the three-act version. Although they believed he was acting on Nathan's doubtful advice that the playwright knows best, they conceded, and it was this version that opened at the Plymouth Theatre in New York to an indifferent audience and apathetic reviews. Brooks Atkinson saw *Love's Old Sweet Song* as "an ambling stage diversion that comes to a platitudinous

On the set of *Love's Old Sweet Song*, its two lead players, Jessie Royce Landis and Walter Huston, talk about the play with its author, Saroyan, and its director, Eddie Dowling. In spite of Theatre Guild hopes, it closed after only forty-four performances.

conclusion," and warned, "Sooner or later, Mr. Saroyan will have to put his mind to work."

Langner, who felt they had thus " 'lost' one of the most delightful plays Saroyan has ever written," later recalled that the next day Saroyan called him to say "you had better put the curtain back the way it was in Baltimore." It was already too late. The show closed on June 8, and the Theatre Guild had lost again on Saroyan, this time a total of $31,248.96.

On May 3, the day after the opening, the Drama Critics Circle met to decide on honors for the current Broadway season. Nathan, as its head, was determined that a Saroyan play be their choice and argued that they should celebrate art rather than the commercial success favored by the Pulitzer Prize committee. The vote went to *The Time of Your Life*. The citation praised the play for its "exhilarating demonstration of the fresh original and imaginative talent [Saroyan] has brought into our theatre" and "the depth of its honest joy."

At its annual meeting, the Pulitzer committee dismissed the 1940 theater season as a mediocre one lacking a frontrunner, but agreed that Saroyan's play held promise for the playwright's future. Thus, on behalf of the trustees of Columbia University, it awarded the drama prize to *The Time of Your Life*.

It fell to Robert Giroux, then a new editor at Harcourt, to telephone the news to Bill in San Francisco. He was astonished to be told by Bill that he would refuse it, explaining that "they should have given it to me for *My Heart's in the Highlands*."

The prize for fiction had gone to Bill's fellow Californian and onetime drinking companion, John Steinbeck, for his monumental novel *The Grapes of Wrath*. Steinbeck's gracious response was that he was flattered to be chosen along with Saroyan: "It was good company."

In reporting his refusal of the prize to the Pulitzer committee, Bill offered a second reason: he disliked institutional patronage of the arts.

While Bill was mindful of the publicity gained in rejecting the prize—and he would often be accused of that motivation—his response to the committee was perfectly in character. It was his "Parsley Garden" principle at work. He did resent institutions. He did bridle at honors and the gratitude expected in exchange. They were transactions in which he seemed to lose some precious independence and to catch an offensive whiff of servility.

Columbia's provost responded with regret at Bill's decision and told him the check for $1,000 was already on its way. Bill noted that he could hardly deny his play whatever distinction the Pulitzer committee had given it, but he did return Columbia University's check.

V

IN THE MOGUL'S PALACE

1940–1941

In 1940, REFLECTING on his previous year's siege of the theater, Bill Saroyan saw himself on the threshold of a major dramatist's career. Since the opening of *Highlands* a year and a half before, three of his plays had appeared on Broadway, one an acclaimed masterpiece, and he had written a dozen more. Three of these stood ready for the stage, and Pat Duggan had arranged for their presentation at three different summer theaters.

But the season proved a cheerless one. After *Something About a Soldier*'s week-long run at the Bucks County Playhouse, Jose Ferrer decided against bringing it to Broadway in the fall. Then tryouts of *The Hero of the World,* at Roslyn, Long Island, and of Bill's favorite, *Sweeney in the Trees,* at the Cape May Playhouse, in New Jersey, were unredeemable disasters.

In September 1940, Brooks Atkinson gave Saroyan sharp warning in the *New York Times*. Reviewing the Harcourt collection *Three Plays,* which included *Highlands, Time of Your Life,* and *Love's Old Sweet Song,* the critic bridled at Bill's self-praising introduction and wrote that artistically Saroyan was showing no progress. *Highlands* was the best of his plays. His bent was for hospitality and goodwill, which he portrayed very well. When he got to ideas, however, Saroyan had written "some of the worst nonsense that ever clattered out of a typewriter."

Atkinson concluded that while Saroyan's central concern was love, he failed to grasp its essence. Nowhere in Saroyan's plays had he found an "instance of a love that is a union and represents a surrender of self. As an egoist Mr. Saroyan may not know that such a thing exists but as an artist he ought to take it on faith." Bill replied that Atkinson had less "mind" than he, and he *did* know all about love, which he felt to be extreme selfishness.

But Brooks Atkinson had identified Saroyan's misconception and told him how grave a disability it was for a playwright. In the stories, he had portrayed love as eros: it is the mission of the whores in "Sleep in Unheavenly Peace"; the burden of adolescent Sam in "Seventeen," who decides that tenderness is movie fakery, and that only lust is real; and the mystery of "Snake," wherein the narrator draws a parallel between his girlfriend and a snake, which he recognizes as beautiful, but very likely evil. Nowhere had he portrayed love as a union, a sharing and a self-sacrifice.

Broadway's lights were dimming for playwright Saroyan, yet he seemed oblivious. He believed he could bring *Sweeney* to Broadway himself and spent the autumn in New York trying to arrange its financing. Although *Time of Your Life* began its national tour in September, reopening to widely favorable reviews and reinforcing Bill's belief in his directing abilities, producers were wary. These men who had seemed to be mere facilitators, as replaceable as publishers, were now a wall before him. They persuaded him that he needed enough money to be his own producer, and he vowed to have it.

It is a fine irony that during this anticlimactic year of 1940, while Saroyan's attention was wholly absorbed with plays, he published his most accomplished book of fiction. His Harcourt editors had noted that the Garoghlanian stories of *A Native American,* his "Christmas gift for friends," were better than those he had offered them. Thus Bill agreed to add six Garoghlanian stories to *A Native American's* eight to make a new Harcourt collection. This book, which he titled *My Name Is Aram,* would be his eighth collection of short fiction, and he saw no reason for expectations beyond those of its predecessors.

But *My Name Is Aram* was a very different book. In Aram Garoghlanian, an Armenian-American boy growing up in Fresno in the years prior to World War I, Bill had found a winsome narrator. The book's incidents, which were full of Aram's boyish mischief and clear insights into the conflicts between old-country and new-country values, were not those of Saroyan's own painful experience, but rather those of a happy childhood he felt denied. This act of "positive tropism," which converted bitter memory into youth's exuberance, was a virtuosity he could not always summon, but when he did, he brought his gift for characterization, his amiable, risible voice, to the top of its form. It was a wellspring of his talent that would freshen, again and again, and it gave this book a novel-like unity.

To Bill's surprise, *My Name Is Aram* won him the long-sought approval of the Book-of-the-Month Club judges. When the book was published, in December 1940, it immediately became a best-seller, and took on a life that would outlast its author's.

While the year had spread unexpected gloom over Bill Saroyan's theatri-

My Name Is Aram, Bill's short-story collection about
growing up in Fresno, published in 1940, stands as his
most enduring work of fiction.

cal prospects, a second, even more menacing, shadow darkened his path:
the growing war in Europe and the likelihood that the United States would
be drawn into it. The surge of nationalism was threatening Bill's world of
the self. Although he tried, he could neither deny nor ignore it.

The most infuriating charge the critics had made against *Love's Old Sweet
Song* was that Saroyan was unwilling to address the reality of a world at war.
He took this as a challenge, and countered with a new play, *Across the Board
on Tomorrow Morning.* As in *Time of Your Life,* the bar setting is a refuge
from an evil world. Saroyan is there again as the customer, Harry Mallory.
The tone of the play is the facetious one with which Saroyan often addressed
serious questions.

Harry delivers the play's message—that the world outside is running
amok, fraught with a lying radio, shellfire, and mass murder. Man must find
refuge in the self until the world ends—and this will not be long in coming.
A look outside the bar reveals there is no longer anything there. Salvation
too is soon at hand, in the birth of a child. Its mother is known to us as a

telephone number, and Harry is its father. The baby grows to manhood in another instant, and it is he who carries the shaky hopes for all men's futures. Again, Saroyan had ignored experience to root his play in abstraction, his indignation toward the war. For lack of a persuasive solution or story, he turned to baffling surrealism.

Bill believed he could bring this play into New York, producing and directing it himself, but when the opportunity of a West Coast tryout came along, he took it.

Across the Board on Tomorrow Morning was presented at the Pasadena Playhouse on February 11, 1941, and it was an undeniable flop. Saroyan faced the failure with candor, acknowledging that nobody seemed to know what it was all about, yet he continued to believe the play was important.

The powerful emotion and gift for lyrical speech that had carried him so well through his stories and his first two plays were no longer enough to supplant structure. Speed, his onetime ally, was also against him now. He lacked the discipline to develop an idea for a full-length play through character and narrative, so he took refuge in facetiousness and deliberate obscurity.

But he was determined on a Broadway entry in 1941, and turned his attention to another recently completed play, *The Beautiful People.* It was set on Red Rock Hill in San Francisco, the site of his recently acquired homestead. Just as *Across the Board* had derived from *Time of Your Life,* so *The Beautiful People* owed a debt of fey zaniness to *Highlands.* It depicted a family of three: the gentle, addled, philosophizing patriarch, Jonah; his enterprising, poet-gambler son, Owen; and his saintly, mouse-protecting daughter, Agnes.

Jonah delivers the play's message, his worship of the universe itself and belief in the significance of all its beings, even its mice. Thus he encourages his daughter's devotion to the creatures and believes this to be the source of her wondrous virtue. Jonah's revelations are recognizable as the playwright's understanding of the world and his credentials for addressing it.

Meanwhile, the national company of *Time of Your Life,* starring Eddie Dowling and Julie Haydon, was enjoying a twenty-eight-week tour playing to full houses. Saroyan saw its triumphant San Francisco performance in early March, and then he left for New York to bring *The Beautiful People* to Broadway by himself.

He exulted in producing and directing his play unencumbered with bosses, fancy theories, and pressure from investors. He set about casting in his characteristic haphazard manner. For the role of Owen Webster, the young poet-gambler, he chose the choreographer Eugene Loring; for Owen's father, Jonah, the veteran actor Curtis Cooksey; and for Agnes, his friend Gene Kelly's teenage girlfriend, Betsy Blair, a dancer in the chorus of *Panama Hattie.*

His direction was permissive. Customarily he perched on the back of a chair, listened attentively, and rarely corrected or even interrupted the actors. At the end of a scene he was likely to applaud and declare it was time for lunch. He often treated the whole cast. Saroyan's budget for the play was only $10,000. There was no money for a road tour, and as the New York opening approached, the cast members grew anxious over whether they were ready. They welcomed Bill's plan for a "free week" of audience previews and the opportunity to work out performance flaws.

Bill's classified ad in the *Herald Tribune* urged 750 persons who had never seen a Broadway play to be his guests at a rehearsal. The result was desirable publicity, a line at the box office, and further previews, with one specifically for children.

The Beautiful People opened at the Lyceum Theatre on Monday, April 21, 1941, to generally favorable reviews. In the *Herald Tribune,* Richard Watts told his readers that "There is so much humor, beauty and imagination and emotional richness about the play that its frailty, its slightness and its moments of excessive sentimentality seem of strange unimportance." In the *Times,* Brooks Atkinson found "there is about as much plot as you can crowd on the point of a pin," but it is "a beguiling and tender little comedy with an ingratiating spirit of general good will." Later, Mr. Atkinson would observe that *"The Beautiful People* was only about half-staged," and that "Mr. Saroyan's direction is little more than stage-managing."

Nevertheless, when the New York Drama Critics Circle made its choice for the year's best play, *The Beautiful People* ran second only to Lillian Hellman's *Watch on the Rhine.* At the awards dinner in May, Bill was a gracious loser. Although he scarcely knew Miss Hellman, he put an affectionate arm around her to say that her play deserved to win out over his. Nevertheless, he insisted that her plays would be improved by the addition of songs such as those he always included. He went on to sing her several.

Saroyan returned to California believing his play was out of the red and that he would have the money to produce another one when the new season began. If that play did as well, he would produce another. It was the origin of his idea for a Saroyan Theatre, a perpetual showing of the plays that emerged so swiftly and easily from his typewriter.

He felt sure that *The Beautiful People* would survive the summer doldrums, but it did not. On June 28 he learned from Pat Duggan that a heat wave had been punishing, and the box office was a lonely place; a weekly loss of $1,300 compelled a closing notice.

Bill felt otherwise and wired Duggan to place an ad in the four principal

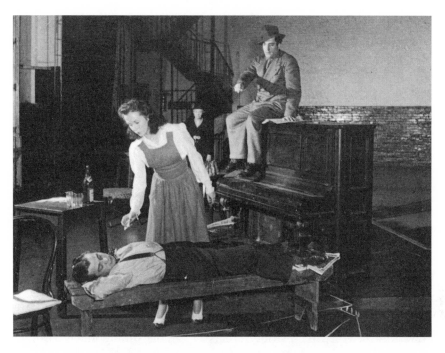

Bill Saroyan directing Betsy Blair from on top of the piano
in *The Beautiful People,* New York, 1941 . . . and in the same
rehearsal, explaining the play's whimsical mood to his cast

Gene Kelly, Betsy Blair, and Bill Saroyan

New York newspapers, inviting readers to gamble with William Saroyan. The text described his belief in *The Beautiful People* and his willingness to bet on it. He would refund the ticket price of anyone who felt they hadn't had their money's worth, no questions asked.

The ads caused some controversy and though there was a brief upturn in business, the cast had to take voluntary salary cuts, and attendance dwindled. The play closed on August 2 after 120 performances, by which time its loss had increased to $12,000.

A midsummer audit confirmed that Bill owed the Matson office $4,000. In denying his responsibility he blamed his agents' mismanagement and added it to his list of grievances, which included their failure, despite the play's success on the road, to sell the movie rights to *Time of Your Life.*

Bill had taken an ad in *Variety* offering the rights free to any motion-picture company that would turn over its profits to the national defense. The industry response—that the play lacked the necessary plot for a film—added to Bill's sense of neglect. When he turned indignantly to Matson and Duggan, they asked how he could have been so perverse as to offer, in that ill-conceived *Variety* ad, to give away motion-picture rights without consulting them.

Bill offered no explanation, but warned Pat Duggan that he should do the work for which he was receiving a commission; that if he was incapable of arranging *The Beautiful People*'s reopening in New York or on tour, he must place the set and props in storage and waive all rights to the play.

Duggan replied that he was following Bill's instructions in storing the play's props and scenery, but Bill needed to understand that they were waiving no agency rights in this or any other Saroyan work. He told Bill that he was confused about the function of manager and agent. The office would continue as his agent for all properties in which it was so named.

Now Bill replied that he did not trust their bookkeeping and wanted a full accounting of the money due him from Harcourt and expended on *The Beautiful People*. If they were to continue as his agent, he wanted all incoming checks made out and sent directly to him. He would return their 10-percent commission. Then, in an outburst of rancor, he told Duggan it was his job to listen to the Saroyan wishes and see them carried out. If he couldn't do that, or didn't want to, they should end the relationship.

A horrified Pat Duggan and Hal Matson replied that he had surely lost his grip on reason, for his letter was not only wrongheaded but oblivious of the faith and trust with which they had been working on his behalf. If they were to continue representing him, they would want a written agency contract that would prevent loaning him money he had not earned, bookkeeping his personal business, paying for his telephone and telegraph expenses, and performing such extra-agency services as acting as his producer, as in the case of *The Beautiful People*. Moreover, they would need to represent him exclusively and wholly—which was to say, in Hollywood too.

To Duggan and Matson's astonishment, Bill now ordered an end to all their efforts on his stage and film rights. He would draw future contracts himself, notably for *Jim Dandy, Sweeney,* and *Across the Board,* which they had failed to sell. When he got no reply, Bill wrote again instructing them to waive all rights to his work and to provide an itemized statement of his account for the five years in which they had been representing him. Bill's relations with Matson and Duggan would remain in this standoff for nine months.

Jim Dandy stood ready for presentation this year. Bill had written it on his return from New York in May, with Eddie Dowling in mind. *Jim Dandy* is an adventure in abstractions, in *subjective* correlatives. The scene is an eggshell filled with civilization's wreckage and assorted castaways. Jim Dandy is an enormous fat man who serves as mouthpiece for the Saroyan philosophy—how the vast brotherhood of misfortune is redeemed through the simple joys of love and living, which are always at hand. This optimistic belief in hope itself as man's salvation finds its adversary in Fishkin, the doubter, the man whose mind is in charge and so denies himself both illusion and faith.

The mood is surreal, the narrative negligible. Characters waken from a kind of eternal coma to speak, do their turn, and sleep again. But, surprising in a Saroyan play, *Jim Dandy* has a Christian theme. The gloomy Fishkin is helped into a positive enlightenment by both Jim Dandy and readings in the Bible. Moreover, the play finds its climax in a symbolic sacrament, a sharing of bread and a miracle of water becoming wine.

Although the Theatre Guild had taken an option on this play, it decided against a presentation. So when Gilman Brown of the National Theatre Conference, which supplied plays to college and community theaters, inquired about a new play, Bill offered him *Jim Dandy*. It appeared during the latter months of 1941 at fifteen theaters in such cities as Minneapolis and Terre Haute, and there were university productions at Fordham and Princeton, but none of these sparked the Broadway interest for which Saroyan had hoped.

Bill wrote the one-act play *Hello Out There* during his summer sojourn in Fresno. The title came from the mouth of Stanley Rose—to Bill's amusement, Stanley had uttered the phrase into the darkness from a Fresno streetcorner. The play is a striking departure from the half-dozen more ambitious plays he wrote during this striving year. It has two strong characters and a sound, simple structure. The principals are a condemned man in jail and a girl who brings his meals and falls in love with him. The couple's plans to go away together are thwarted by the gun of an angry vigilante.

John Houseman was in San Francisco during August, directing the play *Anna Christie,* and when he inquired about Saroyan one-acts, Bill sent him a copy of *Hello Out There.* Houseman telephoned that he liked the play and wanted to produce it in Santa Barbara in early September. It was to be a curtain-raiser for Shaw's *Devil's Disciple.* Bill agreed. Whereupon Nathan wrote Bill that he liked *Hello Out There* and was urging Dowling to produce it immediately. Bill did not see the Santa Barbara production, but he was pleased by a review of it that reported that "it stole the night" from the Shaw play.

Hello Out There did not seem to him a significant achievement. In fact, he would later renounce it for its violence and presentation of evil force in the vigilante. Nevertheless, the play would endure as the best of his one-acts and a standard exercise for actors' studios.

It was late in this summer of looking for some new, hopeful direction that he came upon Robert Burns's poem "Afton Water," in *Songs of Scotland,* beginning, "Flow gently, sweet Afton, among thy green braes," a lament for the poet's dead love, "My Mary's asleep by thy murmuring stream." Bill was so moved that he shouted the lines aloud.

The concept prompted him to conceive of a simple play, like *Playboy of the Western World,* about a girl not dead but asleep, dreaming of love, and of a lover who would come to her. He called it *Afton Water* and saw the setting as a shabby farmhouse in a little town in Vermont. He put it on the Mad

River and gave it the name Moretown. He saw the curtain opening on beautiful, eighteen-year-old Mary McKenna, who is asleep on the couch. There would be an old stove and an old-fashioned organ in the room. Also there would be several lambs present, along with a young half-wit, Willie Murray, who does the chores.

Before the day was out he had written the first scene and half of act 1. It became his own version of *Sleeping Beauty*, the innocent girl comatose in the midst of her simple, anxious family. Her awakening comes from her brother Douglas's gambling. He has lost a big bet on a horse, can't cover it, and is on the run. The "prince" appears as Nick the bookie, come to collect his debt. Instead, Nick falls for and wakes sleeping Mary. *Afton Water*'s theme thus emerged from Bill's belief that a certain weakness for gambling was the unlikely but blessed source of his art, which healed and justified all.

When a letter from Theresa Helburn urged Bill to write a full-length play for the Theatre Guild and possibly the Lunts, he replied that he was working on one, *Afton Water*, which might be exactly what they wanted. His terms would be demanding ones. On November 12, he finished the play and felt he could look forward to some income from it, whether or not the Guild was its producer.

Now, in the fall of 1941, he wanted some major change in his life and again considered Hollywood. He decided to go there to see Onslow Stevens's production of *Jim Dandy* at the Pasadena Playhouse and to discover what kind of place he could make for himself in the motion-picture business.

On arrival at the Hollywood Knickerbocker Hotel, he put in a call to Louis B. Mayer at MGM, hoping to interest him in the several of his plays that he felt were ready for the screen. Mayer's secretary told him that she would bring this to Mr. Mayer's attention, and Bill was sure he would hear no more of it.

He made a date to see a *Jim Dandy* rehearsal on Sunday, November 16, and another with the actress Phyllis Brooks, a favorite girlfriend and good-natured regular at film colony parties. With her help, he immersed himself in the town's hectic social life. If he was dazzled by the glamour of Hollywood, he was also repelled, deciding it was a town of fabulous phonies. He got along with them well enough, was probably thought to be a phony himself, and decided he would write about them someday.

His talks with the agents Chuck Daggett and Ben Medford about working in Hollywood were encouraging, and he decided to pay a call on MGM. As he had supposed, Mayer was unavailable, but he was cordially received by some of the studio's principal figures. Arthur Freed, whom Bill had met at Stanley Rose's, was a particular admirer. He also knew Bernie Hyman, Stella Adler, and George Cukor.

Bill felt himself regarded as an impressive, legendary sort of person. The amiable executive Eddie Mannix was surprised to find that Bill was smaller than he had expected. Mannix had imagined a heavyset man, over six feet, and older, too, but Bill was just a kid. Bill liked Mannix for his Irish heartiness. He bristled, not thinking of himself as small, but then he realized they all thought of him as physically big because of their respect for the name Saroyan. Hyman thought Bill might want to start with some work for them on troublesome scenarios. He promised to send Bill a couple for an opinion.

Bill had the impression he could have whatever sort of deal he wanted, one that might allow him to write, produce, and direct with no bosses. He decided that if he were going to make the Hollywood mistake at some point, now was the time for it.

Bill returned to San Francisco to share Thanksgiving dinner with his family. He told them his visit to Hollywood had paid off; the big shots at MGM had offered him the possibility of a fine job and a huge income. But when two scenarios that might have become projects for him arrived from Bernie Hyman, Bill was not so sure. One was for John Steinbeck's *Tortilla Flat,* and both were written as screenplays, complete with instructions for director and cameraman. He could not interest himself in either long enough to finish reading them.

He had no inclination to work on other writers' material when his own was in such plenty. Although George Jean Nathan had just turned his thumbs down on *Afton Water,* Bill consoled himself with thoughts of salvaging it, and on reading a freshly typed copy decided it would appeal to the Theatre Guild as it stood and also serve as a key to the front gate at MGM.

The copy he sent to the Theatre Guild brought a telephone call from Lawrence Langner in New York to say the Guild was interested but wanted revisions that would reveal more of sleeping Mary and Nick. The idea of revisions had no appeal for Bill, but he encouraged Langner to make a substantial offer.

He admitted to Arthur Freed at MGM that Nathan had not liked *Afton Water,* but he had to disagree. He saw it as a big picture, with Mickey Rooney playing Willie Murray, and went on to cast the other parts from MGM's players. Freed consented to read the play.

On his return to Hollywood, Bill sought out his favorite drinking and gambling companion, Stanley Rose. Stanley brimmed with confidence about Bill's future here, guaranteed him a fat writer's salary, and then, in his Texas drawl, confided that if, one way or another, he didn't find $10,000, he would soon lose his bookshop. In agreeing to let Stanley represent him, Bill reasoned that *somebody* had to be his agent. Why not Stanley Rose?

Bill believed in a Broadway future for *Jim Dandy.* At the end of November, when it was presented at the Pasadena Playhouse, he took along a party of friends that included Stanley, the producer Jed Harris, the film director George Stevens, and the writer John Fante.

The response to *Jim Dandy* was no more than polite, and Bill blamed it on Onslow Stevens's stoic direction. As for the widespread bewilderment about the play, he thought it a shortcoming of the audience itself.

Hard on this disappointment came word from MGM that both Freed and Bernie Hyman had read *Afton Water* but were noncommital. Further interest depended on Mayer, who had not yet read it, but an appointment with the studio head was fixed. Meanwhile, Bill and Stanley Rose went to the Mexicali track, where their horses ran out of the money. They returned to find the appointment with Mayer had been canceled. Since MGM had no further use for the *Afton Water* script, they could call for it whenever they chose.

Bill read this as the slam of MGM's door and turned his anger on the loyal Stanley, blaming him and his drinking for collapse of the negotiation. But the outcome would be miraculously different. When Stanley went to pick up the unwanted script, he learned that the appointment with Mayer had not been canceled, but rescheduled. He wanted to see them on December 1.

Bill's first impression of MGM's awesome studio head was of power. His plumpness was that of an Oriental potentate. A photograph of Mayer with his good friend Franklin Roosevelt was prominently displayed. The deference shown him by his executive staff confirmed his reputation for ruthlessness. He rewarded the faithful, and demolished any he thought to be wise guys.

While Saroyan was determined not to have a subordinate role here, he listened while Mayer told him that because of Bill's literary and dramatic reputation he was willing to hire him as an MGM writer. Bill replied, with some force, that he did not want to be hired as just another contract writer. He had special plans and lots of ideas.

As Bill began to describe those plans, Mayer said he could hear perfectly well, and there was no need for Bill to shout. Bill explained that a slight deafness accounted for his volume, to which Mayer replied that he didn't mind a man's being loud, so long as he was courteous.

In a more moderate voice, Bill asked what the studio had in mind for him. Mayer proposed a "test drive," in which Bill would spend a few weeks at the studio and try out some of his ideas. Instead of a salary, he would receive an expense account of $300 a week. At the end of this trial period they would decide whether to make a permanent arrangement. Bill liked the sound of it, and agreed.

The next day, Bill checked out of the Knickerbocker and moved into the more costly Beverly Wilshire. Then he went out to MGM, where he was welcomed and assigned temporary workspace. He called home to tell his family that he was phoning from his office at MGM.

He rented a typewriter and a phonograph and dined with Gene Kelly and Betsy Blair, glowing with the prospect of going to work at MGM with a mandate to create his own kind of motion picture. On his first morning at work, he found he had been so eager to avoid studio assignments that he had no idea what to do. Stanley Rose brought Chuck Daggett for a visit to Bill's office, and all three drank from Stanley's bottle. Otherwise, the first day was uneventful.

The following days were little busier. He found no reason to arrive at his office until afternoon. On one of these he saw the rushes of *Mrs. Miniver* and watched the sound dubbing of *Burma Road,* but no plan was forthcoming. Walking around the lot, he had a glimpse of Greta Garbo, and one evening Vincente Minelli took him to a party at Ira Gershwin's. When Bill saw Irwin Shaw driving an open convertible, he was reminded of the automotive hierarchy, and he confirmed his order for a Cadillac convertible.

He liked dropping in on Arthur Freed. Freed's girth had earned him the nickname "the Tank," but his musical knowledge was vast, and he was the unquestioned maestro at MGM. Bill had once found Duke Ellington in his office, trying out some ideas on Freed's piano. More importantly, Freed was an admirer of Bill and his work and had become his particular counselor at MGM.

One day, as he was coming out the MGM gate, Bill found a crowd surrounding Mickey Rooney's open car. Arthur Freed introduced Bill to the young actor and his sister and to the orchestra leader Paul Whiteman. Bill was pleased that Whiteman doffed his hat.

John Garfield took him onto the set for Steinbeck's *Tortilla Flat,* where Stella Adler, the acting teacher who had studied with Stanislavsky, joked that Bill was going to come in and ruin the picture industry just as he had ruined the Broadway theater. Her comment assumed a comradeliness, a willingness to play the good-natured victim of show-business gossip, but Bill was far too thin-skinned for it. He was not amused.

His first week at MGM ended on December 7, 1941, the day of the Japanese attack on Pearl Harbor. In the Brown Derby, Bill listened to a broadcast from the battle zone and was puzzled by the outrage of others. Although he was a native-born U.S. citizen, the only one in his family, he felt no patriotic response. Walter Winchell's evening broadcast struck him as needlessly melodramatic.

Although he heard President Roosevelt's "day of infamy" speech on Monday, he was unmoved. His country's full-scale entry into World War II only confirmed his view that the world was mismanaged and that the fault lay with incompetent world leaders. He included Hitler, Mussolini, Stalin, Churchill, Roosevelt, and LaGuardia in this charge. The surge of patriotism overwhelming the nation simply increased his skepticism toward it.

As the new week began on December 8 his thoughts were only of what his film project might be about. So far he had no idea how to describe it, nor how it might be both a play and a movie at the same time. He decided that he would write a play, then have a movie writer break it down into scenario form. He would then alter this and simply cast it and shoot it.

He did know that this was no place for him to write, and he needed to go home to San Francisco to get to work. He wanted to be home for Christmas, in any case. In the New Year he would return to MGM and set up his organization, his unit for the making of the movie.

Bill left for home, and there, on December 20, with the fire going in his basement workroom, he sized up the job before him. Writing and producing his own MGM movie was a challenge, and he didn't want to fumble it. His picture must be truly great, must appeal to every kind of person. It needed to have movement, since movement, even when not fully understood, delights the eye. He wanted laughter too, throughout.

He began by sketching a hero, a man who never stops, who keeps going even when he stumbles—which was to say, his view of himself. Although he gave this man a son and imagined them arguing, he could find no story, nor even any circumstances for them. As Christmas approached, he dreaded working on the project and decided that coming home had been a mistake.

Although he dismissed thoughts about his country at war, he knew that his movie needed to deal with it. He had no idea in what way, but he believed the Axis was doomed and that its defeat would begin the real war—between communism and capitalism.

On Christmas Day he went to his sister Zabe's house for a family dinner and was entertained, as always, by his grandmother Lucy. She was eighty-two and mourning the loss of her youngest daughter, Verkine, but she was in good spirits. She told stories of an Armenian girlhood that rejoiced in life.

Still without inclination to write, Bill did conceive of a situation, a family such as his own enduring the war. It would include a widowed mother who provides for her four children by working at a packing plant. Her oldest son would be in the army. His younger brother would be a rebel at school but a whiz of a telegraph messenger. Early in the story he would deliver to a woman a telegram that reports the death of her son, and later he would deliver such a telegram to his own mother. That news might be both true and untrue.

Without knowing it, Bill had broken through the wall to what he needed, a cast (in his own family), a story (in its endurance of the war), even a plot device, that fatal telegram, salvaged from his 1934 story "Baby."

He gave himself fifteen days to write the scenario but then found himself stuck. He had some good characters, and things for them to do, but no strong central situation, nothing eventful happening. He had lost all relish for the job.

A day later he resumed work on the story, letting it go along carelessly with lots of talk, which he planned to cut later. In a burst of optimism he saw himself with a good title, *The Human Comedy,* some swell characters, and, in the fourteen-year-old telegraph messenger, Homer Macauley, a great point of view. Once again he was performing a positive tropism on his own bleak boyhood. He now recognized that he had in hand the makings of an outstandingly funny and heartbreaking picture.

On January 7, with only eight days left before his self-imposed deadline, he was stuck again. He found himself killing time, listening to the news as if it were important. He quieted his alarm with the thought that MGM could put a scenario writer with him, someone who could listen and turn this idea into a scenario that he would then correct. But the days passed with no progress.

With three days left, Bill began to work in earnest on *The Human Comedy,* and his confidence returned. Marcus, the eldest brother, would be killed in the war, and it would fall to his younger brother, Homer, to deliver the War Department telegram to his home. Marcus's army buddy Tobey would return in his stead.

Bill decided that if he didn't finish on time it would be all right. He was only midway, but in spite of a bad cold, fever, and sleeplessness, he was confident of *The Human Comedy*'s outcome.

He worked on a scene about the youngest brother, Ulysses-in-the-trap, and found that the story was getting him, that it was on its own now and going strong. Tired or not, he liked to keep writing.

On January 17 he shaved off several days' growth of beard. He left the mustache to be shaved when he finished *The Human Comedy.* He was so sure of it as a story that he now saw it as a book as well as a movie, each episode with a title: "Ulysses in the Trap," "Tom Spangler and Diana Steed," and "The Running of the 220 Low Hurdles."

He told himself that *The Human Comedy* was very likely the greatest story ever written specifically for motion pictures. He felt he must insist on selling it for a one-time-only filming, so that he could have it remade later.

During this time, he was distracted by the notices of Samson Raphaelson's play *Jason,* which was said to be a satire about Saroyan himself, a role played by Nicholas Conte, who had been the real estate man in *Highlands.*

One theater column described *Jason* as better than anything of Saroyan's, and the Saroyan character as "the loud, adolescent-mind playwright." He felt the columnists got much pleasure from this kind of mayhem but consoled himself with the thought that Raphaelson was keeping the Saroyan name in the news, which would soon be enlivened by MGM's wanting *The Human Comedy.*

On January 20, Bill telephoned Stanley Rose to try out the title on him, and Stanley did not care for it. The following day Bill thought *O Ithaca* might be a better title, but almost at once returned to *The Human Comedy,* thinking that if Mickey Rooney played Homer Macauley and Clark Gable played Spangler, the office manager, it would be a good title.

He was especially pleased with the Marcus-Tobey troop train episode wherein they pray that God will let them survive and return to Ithaca and told himself he had the story whole now. Its success depended on keeping his own faith in the contest with possibility.

The apricots were ripe as the Macauleys went to church. Diana Steed and Spangler at last would be talking of marriage. An injured Tobey was coming home from the war to Ithaca, and he would speak to the Macauleys as if Marcus were alive and all right.

Bill finished *The Human Comedy* on January 23. At 158 pages, it was the longest work he had ever done. He celebrated by telling his mother and Cosette about the story, over fresh *bagharch.* It was about a small-town American family enduring the war. Some of the episodes were comic, but the theme was an earnest one, about how, in spite of death, both father and brother live on in their survivors.

When Bill described his plan to direct and produce the film, both Takoohi and Cosette warned against it. Their advice, delivered partly in Armenian, was to rub his screenplay in MGM's face and get out of the place. But Bill was undeterred. He would ask $250,000 for the story and for producing and directing it. He deserved it, he thought, and, considering the profits they would make, they could afford it.

On reading *The Human Comedy,* just come from the typist, he thought it sounded somewhat preachy, but he sent a copy off to Stanley Rose and another to Arthur Freed. Stanley responded in a telegram, congratulating his client on "the greatest story ever written for moving pictures." Studying this, Bill decided Stanley wouldn't bluff just because of his interest in the project—but even if it was bluff, it was good to hear.

On the last day of the month, Arthur Freed called from MGM to tell Bill that *The Human Comedy* was the best thing he had ever written. When asked what the others thought, Freed said that Jack McGowan was sitting with him and he was equally enthusiastic.

Bill managed to contain his joy at this first sign of his victory at MGM and thanked Arthur Freed in the most casual way. A half hour later, Stanley Rose called, unable to control his emotion. Stanley had shown *The Human Comedy* to his friend Chuck Daggett, and now they were both weeping over it.

Bill agreed to return to Hollywood the following week so that they could lay siege to MGM. Meanwhile, he warned himself to lay low and let the response build on its own. Before Bill's departure, Arthur Freed telephoned again to say that he liked *The Human Comedy* even better than he had the last time and then put Sam Katz on to tell Bill that he had read the story to his wife last night and he was crazy about it. It was American; it was timely; it showed the effect of war on an American family; it simply had everything. They would be seeing him at eleven the following morning.

As he headed for Hollywood, Bill reasoned that the studio seemed to be sold absolutely, but he must sit easy, unimpressed, and wait for their proposal. He must not let himself get excited.

Stanley Rose met him at Glendale station on the morning of January 23, and together they kept the eleven o'clock appointment at MGM. Awaiting them was the studio's management, Arthur Freed, Bernie Hyman, Sam Katz, and Louis B. Mayer himself. They explained that they liked the script, but were not yet sure how to present it. They would decide about this soon, but it must wait until Mr. Mayer was familiar with the scenario. Lillian Messenger, his secretary, would read it to him. Bill was pleased to be able to call his mother and tell her he was calling from Louis B. Mayer's office.

On February 5 he was assigned an office. He found it too spartan, but he was gladdened to find that *The Human Comedy* had been mimeographed, and two copies of the big script had been delivered to his desk. A special meeting with Mayer was scheduled, and while awaiting it Bill got a haircut at the studio barber shop and walked around the lot. Encountering Pandro Berman, he learned that good things were circulating about his story.

Mayer began the meeting by assuring Bill that MGM wanted to employ him for a long time, and they also wanted to acquire his plays. Bill replied that he was interested in all the various plans they had in mind for him, but at the same time he would want to get on with his own work. Future Saroyan creation was important to him in any negotiations. Mayer acknowledged the complexity of this and postponed further talk until the following day.

When the meeting resumed, Mayer proposed that MGM buy Saroyan's *Human Comedy* from him for $50,000. Moreover, they would employ him as writer, producer, or associate producer of the film at a salary of $1,000 a week. Bill was disappointed in the offer, but agreed to consider it. He would respond on Monday.

Over the weekend Bill discussed these terms with Stanley Rose and Chuck Daggett. The ebb and flow of advice about how much he should ask for and what MGM would actually pay for the story finally irritated him. He was particularly annoyed with Stanley for not playing a more authoritative role in the negotiations, leaving that up to him.

When he telephoned home to report on progress to his mother and Cosette, he learned that his San Francisco draft board had classified him 3-A—which, he judged, kept him only temporarily out of the army's grasp.

He had returned to the Knickerbocker, and on Sunday night he sat down in his room there and wrote up a proposal. Among his requirements were a $75,000 initial payment and $1,500 a week until the picture was finished, another $25,000 when shooting began, and another $25,000 when it was released. All creative ideas were to come from, or be approved by, Saroyan. He would report directly to Mr. Mayer and he would retain all rights to *The Human Comedy* other than motion-picture, and these would return to Saroyan after five years. He wanted suitable offices and a technical clerical staff.

The critical meeting did not go exactly as Bill had hoped. In fact, it was very much MGM's original proposal. He would receive $60,000 for *The Human Comedy*, less $10,000, which would go to Stanley Rose for his service as agent. Bill's salary was to be $1,000 a week and would run for a year.

By day's end Bill was reconciled to it. While it was neither bad nor good, it was acceptable to him at this stage of his overall campaign. From the first payment he planned to give his sister Zabe $10,000 and Henry $5,000, leaving him $35,000 plus his salary, which would, in six months, add another $26,000. Remembering that he still owed about $10,000 in back taxes, his Hollywood bonanza no longer seemed a fortune. However, it was enough to stage his next show.

When he phoned his mother to tell her how he would distribute a portion of his windfall among the family, Takoohi had different ideas. She insisted that it be divided thus: $12,500 to his sister Zabe and her husband, Walt; $5,000 to his brother Henry; $5,000 to herself; and $5,000 to his sister Cosette. He agreed to this, though it left him, after taxes, indebtedness, and the balance on the Cadillac he had ordered, with only $10,000.

Once Bill had sent off checks to his family and paid off his taxes and his personal debts, he was ready to go to work on *The Human Comedy*. Arthur Freed explained that they would take some time to select the appropriate director and an experienced writer for the scenario.

Lunching at Chasen's, Bill paused at a table where his friend John Steinbeck sat with his editor, Pascal Covici. Bill was keenly aware that two of Steinbeck's novels, *The Grapes of Wrath* and *Of Mice and Men,* were being made into major films. When conversation turned to the war, Bill mentioned the uncertainty of his new draft status, and he was surprised by Steinbeck's offer of deliverance. John had an army connection. Bill refused this comradely proposal, not because he felt immune from military service, but because any such favor from Steinbeck would carry an obligation, with perhaps some professional loss of face.

Now he learned that Mayer had ordered a battle plan on the production of *The Human Comedy* and it would be revealed in a couple of days. Indeed, Bill met with Benny Thau, Bernie Hyman, and Sam Zimbalist and got the impression he was being granted his way—his own, Saroyan, unit.

There were daily meetings over plans for producing *The Human Comedy.* When King Vidor was proposed as director, Bill put forth himself instead. What appeared to be the final meeting took place on March 10. Eddie Mannix announced that it was decided, King Vidor was to produce and direct the picture. Bill replied that if that were the case, he would be leaving town. Mannix seemed amused by this and argued with increasing heat that Bill lacked the necessary experience to direct the picture himself. Bernie Hyman firmly concurred.

Bill was adamant. He argued fiercely that he was uniquely equipped for the job. To break the stalemate it was proposed that Bill direct a one-reel film on any story he chose and they would reach a decision on the basis of it. He thought that was a fine idea and promised to start work on it at once. He did so, selecting his own story "A Number of the Poor," which concerned the theft of a cantaloupe from a market. From this tale Bill dictated a screenplay for a one-reel film. Harry Cohn, the shorts production man, brought over an artist to discuss the sets. Casting sent him some actors to interview.

Bill decided to ask MGM for an additional sum of $2,000 for the use of "A Number of the Poor." Mannix replied that if he wouldn't donate the story, MGM wouldn't make it. While Bill accepted this, he vowed to get even.

To pianola accompaniment, Bill worked with a scenarist on the screenplay. When the publicity department on the floor above complained about the noise, Bill told them they would simply have to get used to it. He liked music.

For the cast, he chose Horace McNally, an actress named Taliaferro to play the cantaloupe thief, and a pretty redhead to be Maggie. He wanted Harry Bratsburg but couldn't get him. When a favorite actress, Pass Le Noir, turned up, Bill immediately wrote in a part for her.

Bill began filming "A Number of the Poor," now retitled *The Good Job,* on March 18, and he was pleased with his progress. Mayer came by to have

Bill with Victor Fleming and Sam Zimbalist, two of the MGM executives whom Bill
mistakenly believed would support his producing *The Human Comedy*

a look and to tell Bill that he had plenty of hair and could pull it out if need
be. Bill objected to Cohn's managing hand but liked the two cameramen
and decided his outfit was a good one. When he saw the first day's rushes he
deemed them okay, and over the next several days he completed the film.
He decided it was at least pretty good, and more likely great.

He showed a cut of *The Good Job* to Arthur Freed and Jack McGowan
and believed they approved. With the expert help of Jack Ruggiero on the
moviola he edited the picture and found it less effective than he had hoped.
He realized at last that he had much to learn about the camera and its
method of translating ideas into film. Without a clear idea of how to
improve *The Good Job,* he let it go, somewhat short of perfection.

The next day, he showed the picture to Victor Fleming and Sam Zimbalist, and while both reacted favorably, Bill's thoughts were turning elsewhere.
He bought a camel-hair overcoat and a brown pinstriped suit and persuaded
Stanley Rose to join him in a flying visit to Las Vegas. His first night there
he lost $1,250 rolling dice. On Saturday he lost another $825, and on Sunday went all but broke. That night, he dreamed he was back at the orphanage, an experience he had not had in a long time, and woke with a cold and
a sore throat.

His $3,000 Cadillac convertible was delivered in San Francisco, and he paid for it in full, leaving him with $112 in his bank account and a debt of $810 to his bookie, Rudy Pauly. Pauly refused to deal with Bill further and passed him on to another bookie, who set limits on him. Although Bill continued to place daily bets, he wondered if he could ever get even.

At the studio he now heard unfavorable gossip about his film. Ruggiero told him that one studio executive had told another that Saroyan's picture was a disaster. Although these men had flattered him, he recognized he had made enemies here, and *The Good Job* was vulnerable.

He was now convinced of a conspiracy against him. Mannix eluded him, pleading first a cold, then a labor meeting, and Bill began to read rejection signs in every face he encountered. He acknowledged his own arrogance but felt they had all been worse. He wrote Mayer a note saying the time had come for him to quit, be fired, or make a new plan. This brought a call from Mannix, and a meeting with Mayer was arranged for the following day.

The meeting took place in Mayer's office at six in the evening, with Arthur Freed and Eddie Mannix, and it was all that Bill had dreaded. Mayer, with Mannix's support, told him that the verdict was in on *The Good Job*. Everyone agreed that it stank. They could not possibly let him direct any picture. Time was short, and they were busy men.

An angry Bill replied that he would *buy The Good Job* from them, and, when they consented, proposed to buy back *The Human Comedy* as well. Mayer refused, pointing out that even if Bill could make the picture, he certainly could not raise the money. Then, in Bill's view, Mayer exploded in a major theatrical performance. Swearing, weeping, and praying, he leaped about his desk. He would not consider letting go of *The Human Comedy*.

Unable to imagine salvaging his pride—along with his screenplay and entry to the citadel—Bill announced he was quitting MGM. He would send Stanley Rose back the next day to wind up his affairs. He told himself he had gotten some money from the deal, had a fine new car, and had bought bonds for his nieces and nephews, and he had his health. He was ahead of the game.

On the last day of April he packed up his belongings and left his office, leaving Stanley Rose to settle matters. Mayer agreed only to selling Bill *The Good Job* for $15,000. Bill declined his offer.

When he was encouraged by *Daily Variety* to write his side of the story, he submitted a rambling, facetious piece about "The California Shorebird." In a mock-naturalist manner he explained that the creature's life cycle was brief, and it knew its place in the universal scheme. This, he continued, was not true of the MGM executives, who were full of themselves. Nevertheless, he claimed to have made a net profit of one million dollars in his three

Bill's screenplay for *The Human Comedy* won him an Oscar, and the 1943 film—here with Mickey Rooney as Homer Macauley, Frank Morgan as Willie Grogan, and James Craig as Tom Spangler—became a major wartime entertainment. The novel made from the screenplay became a best-seller.

months with the studio. This last was to deflect any notion that his were sour grapes.

Back at his desk on Fifteenth Avenue, he immediately went to work on a play, *Get Away Old Man.* He took the title from the song lyric "For an old man he is old, and an old man he is gray, but a young man's heart is full of love, get away old man get away." The play would open in an office much like Bill's at MGM, complete with a baby-grand player piano. There were to be three principals. Hammer, the egomaniac Jewish studio head, was clearly Mayer. Ben Manheim, his assistant, was Bernie Hyman. The hero, unmistakably the playwright himself, was the irrepressible genius writer Harry Bird, summoned to prepare a palatable version of Hammer's deceitful, predatory life. There would be an aspiring actress to become Hammer's prey. Harry Bird would rebel against Hammer's power and conniving, refuse to write the screenplay, and rescue the victimized actress.

Bill got off to a good start, feeling he could finish the play in a week. He learned from Stanley Rose that while Mayer was angry over the "Shorebird" piece in *Variety*, some conciliatory offer seemed to be in the making. Thus Bill wrote a letter to MGM, offering to sell it his new play, sight unseen, for $250,000, and sent a copy of the letter to *Variety*.

He reached the midpoint of *Get Away Old Man* to find he had lost all taste for it, but as he neared completion he liked it better, and felt it could be rounded into a good play. Sending it off to the typist, he decided it was crass and vulgar, but at the same time redeemed by its wisdom and compassion. He thought it would cause controversy, and make him some new enemies and maybe a few friends. By "friends," he meant partisans of his Hollywood views, for the making of friends continued to be a matter of indifference to Bill Saroyan.

What mattered to him above all else was the course of his steamy ambition. Now, in his mid-thirties, he could look back on three of his impressive assaults on the entertainment world: on publishing, on Broadway theater, and on Hollywood. For each there had been a spectacular debut, shimmering with the promise of a major discovery, followed by an overreaching, then a fizzling disappointment, a falling out with close associates, and final alienation. It was a rocket's trajectory—and a short one.

The common factor in the three experiences was Bill's failure to root and grow in the medium. Apprenticeship was humbling, and he could not learn from the people around him. He believed in his innate superiority as a writer. Virtuosity was complete within him, and he had no need for more. This was the source of the cockiness Whit Burnett had warned him about at the start of his career. It became a pride that dismissed the counsel of the wise editorial voices at Random House and Harcourt Brace, and of the experienced theater managers Harold Clurman and Lawrence Langner. Finally, that pride insensitized him to the expertise surrounding him at Metro Goldwyn Mayer and made him turn his back on a grand opportunity. Confronting the firm's mighty president, Bill revealed not his talent, but a hubris gone wild.

These experienced men were all willing advisors, but since they were not entirely *for* him, he saw them as entirely *against* him, and he closed his mind to them. He not only denied himself the tempering of criticism, but also refused to shoulder some of the blame for failure, to dig deeper into subject, to struggle over his ideas until he understood them, to work on a play until he had it right.

When confronting the wreckage of his novels and the plays that had failed in summer theaters or closed in lonely houses, he thrust the evidence aside. He either denied the failure or sought outside himself for the cause, planting villainy in the most loyal of his supporters.

This ironclad belief in his talent had a corollary in his luck. When he was in San Francisco and his day's work was done, he would treat himself to a drink at one of his favorite bars and then decide he didn't feel like going home to join his mother and his sister in shuffling the bills and worrying about survival. What he wanted to do was raise some hell.

Thus it was on to Joe Bailey's to place a horse bet, to Oscar Gill's for poker and blackjack and, later, dice. As the lust to win mounted, he drank, tipped the dealers, the waiters, and the girl at the piano, and gave money to fellow gamblers. When he did go home, at two in the morning, he would be drunk, but happy in the belief that his luck had been running. When he felt that way, he often did win, and he reminded himself that Dostoevsky too had been drawn to the fast tides of emotion in the gambler's existence.

When the fever was on, he wanted his cousin Ross beside him. Hoping to stem a losing streak in the fall of 1941, Bill summoned Ross from Fresno. Ross came for the weekend excitement, but he did not change Bill's bad luck, which mounted to $4,000. Bill had no funds to cover the loss, but settled with a check, which he somehow would have to make good.

In Monday morning's scurrying to cover the check, he turned first to his friend George Mardikian, proprietor of San Francisco's Omar Khayyam restaurant. Mardikian's reluctant loan only prolonged Bill's pursuit of a big win, and, now in need of $4,500, he appealed to his publisher, Harcourt Brace.

His editor there was now Frank Morley, formerly of his London publisher, Faber and Faber. When Bill's mother intercepted Morley's assent, she poured a powerful rage onto the cousins. In ordering Ross back to Fresno, she frightened him thoroughly, but the gambling binge went on. In a circus of excess, the cousins bought false Groucho noses with moustache and goggles and kept on betting and losing until the money was gone.

After seeing Ross off for Fresno, Bill told himself the situation could be far worse. Besides, every moment of the experience—the losing as much as the winning, the borrowing and giving away of money, having Ross alongside to share in it, scandalizing his mother and his sister with his recklessness—was a delicious excitement, an antidote to his bête noire, boredom.

Boredom afflicted him when he was unable to work, and that had been rare enough. Lately, though, an unwelcome inertia tended to possess him. Creatively he was often at a standstill. A walk to the ocean, which ordinarily exhilarated him, left him feeling ill and depressed enough to recall the Christmas Eve at the orphanage when he thought he was going to die. His right ear was troubling him. It had always been a little deaf, but now it rang and became even more deaf. If he closed his good ear he could hear almost nothing. The right ear seemed to hiss, a constant whispering. He knew that when sick, he could not tolerate himself or the world or its people. His temper was bad, and he was apt to act swiftly and stupidly about any problem.

Even when he felt well, Bill Saroyan was not tempted to reflect on the advice of two of the most perceptive observers of his literary generation. Writing about his plays, Brooks Atkinson had warned Bill about his short-comings, that his strength was in hospitality, not profundity, and that he suffered from a blight of emotion for which, as an artist, he must find a cure.

Edmund Wilson had put it differently. Considering his work as a whole, he saw the Saroyan weakness as a sentimentality, an illusion of human good-ness. Both critics agreed that Saroyan had suffered emotional damage such that he could not deal reliably with the essentials of human behavior.

In Atkinson's view, Saroyan failed to understand that love, which was his main concern, was a sharing. In Wilson's, it was that Saroyan had disguised the truth about his raffish characters in a misguided adulation of simple folk. Within the Saroyan manner of debonair kidding, he detected a grow-ing smugness, a discernible philistinism. He saw these flaws as "born of the courage Saroyan needed to face a hostile environment." He warned him that "no writer leads a charmed life."

As gloom gathered around his prospects, Bill felt less enlightened by his critics than ill used by them. The reception they had given to *Love's Old Sweet Song* was still painful, and it occurred to him that the American intel-lectual community was both formidable and predominantly Jewish. If you knew what was good for you, you were wary of it. It seemed that many crit-ics, not necessarily Jews, had implied that he was ignorant and not well read. In spite of contrary claims, Bill was sensitive about his lack of educa-tion. Also, they had criticized him for avoiding such human concerns as politics and sex, but neither of these subjects appealed to him in a liter-ary way.

He believed that Jewish critics didn't like his writing because they thought him anti-Semitic. He conceded that he had been irritated into imagining that he was anti-Semitic, but he also knew it was as impossible for him to hate Jews as it was to hate himself. To hate anybody steadily was to hate one's self. He assured himself he had no bitter feelings toward any-body in the world.

And yet he questioned why Jews found it impossible to allow people to be unaware of them as people, as others did. He did not deny they had been persecuted, but what made them persecute themselves? Was there some strength for them in it?

And so disappointment *had* stolen under the tough Saroyan skin to cast doubt on his accomplishment, to crimp his surging creative energy, to draw him to the card table and the horse parlor. It had gone beyond that to stir a rancor not only toward helpful friends, but toward Jews, toward his country gone to war and newly patriotic, and toward its patrician president.

Disappointment had not diminished his belief in the empowering gift of his talent. By instinct, he knew mankind, and he had a voice that summoned readers, that reliably charmed and persuaded them. There was, and could be, no match for Saroyan.

VI

THE ONE GIRL

1941–1942

Although Bill Saroyan was short—only five feet eight inches tall—he was a rakishly handsome man, with strong features and luminous, seeking eyes. Thick black hair thrust up from a broad forehead, and a wide, sensual mouth was ever ready for laughter. He was aware of his looks, wore his broad-brimmed fedora cocked, and gave off a faintly sinister air that interested women.

In their bantering correspondence during the fall of 1936, Bennett Cerf, always ready to confide about his own love life, had asked for news of Bill's. Bill had denied any at all, but then admitted to having a swell eighteen-year-old girl who wanted to marry him. He was picking up table manners and other such niceties from her.

Bill's love life was certainly not consuming. He would later admit that he went about his lovemaking in a practical fashion. When he found himself alone with a girl, he would urge her to lift her dress, rid herself of pants so he could have her at once, and then leave him, for he had work to do, and never the time for women to which they always felt entitled.

He managed to find a number of such relationships with women, but on occasion he was more susceptible. As he indicated in the story "Abandoned Bride at the Fern Hotel," he understood how a man might be so taken with a new recruit at a San Francisco whorehouse as to propose she quit the place and come with him to Hollywood. It was the new recruit who had the good sense to decline.

But in Hollywood during the summer of 1936, he did fall in love seriously, with the girl he had mentioned to Bennett Cerf. Pat Winter came to live with him in the Villa Carlotta. She was a dark-haired, good-looking girl whom he saw as slender, lovely, sweet, and good. He would write about her in a number of stories and recollections.

In "Letters from 74 Rue Taitbout," in 1969, he described her as an aspiring actress from York, Pennsylvania. She was pregnant, not by him, but by a boy from home, and she returned there to have the baby and leave it with her mother. Pat did go home to Chambersburg, Pennsylvania, to have a daughter, and wrote him from there in January 1937 that she was ill with longing for him.

During the spring, he wrote "Coffee and Sandwiches at Louie's on Pacific Street" about their affair. Its hero describes to the girl his feeling of wanting her to go away but knowing that if she did he would find out where she was and follow her there. She replies that she knows what women mean when they say they'll die if they don't see their lover.

He explains what will happen if they give in to these feelings: they will marry and have a little house in which they will be around each other all the time, and after six or seven days and nights of it, this will become boring, and possibly even irritating. The girl agrees, and understands his dread of facing up to fatherhood. They both realize that their love has gone as far as it can go.

In July 1937, Bill and Pat Winter met in Reno for a painfully joyous, two-day reprise of their love affair. He was on his way to New York, determined on an advancement of his writing career, but stopped in Reno for their rendezvous. Pat was at the airport waiting for him, and at first sight he knew both that he loved her wholly and that their affair was over. She knew it too as she came to his room at the Golden Hotel to have a drink and talk and make love for the last time. He thought how sad it was that nothing, even such a love as theirs, lasts. Although Pat tried to hold back her tears, she could not, and while Bill felt the sorrow too, he laughed.

In a restaurant Pat asked Bill for a nickel to put in the slot machine. In her innocence and pain she knew she would win, even as she wanted to lose. When the nickels spilled out, she returned sadly to finish her sandwich.

Bill's own luck had left him with only enough money for a ticket to Chicago. He bought one at the station. With an hour to kill before train time they went into the Bank Club, where Bill bet one of his last two dollars on a crap game and won four. He played on, and in five minutes had won enough for a ticket through to New York, and nine dollars besides.

Pat was not only lovely, but she brought him luck. Moreover, she understood what he wanted and had to do, no matter how painful it was to her. They grieved over parting, but it was ended, and there was nothing they could do about that. He hoped he could learn to write about that someday.

They walked together to the station, where a crowd had gathered to see the streamlined train. He embraced her for the last time and got aboard and saw her among the people, smiling and waving. It occurred to him that people know so little about what they want for themselves and how to bring it about. Time and circumstance would do their damage. Yet he felt that in his heart there would be but one smile forever, and it would be Pat Winter's.

When Bill left for New York, Pat went on to Berkeley to enroll at the University of California. Once settled in a pleasant apartment there, she called Bill's sister Cosette for his address in New York. Bill answered some of her letters and often, particularly after an erotic encounter, recalled her beauty and innocence. Occasionally he felt sick about their separation and believed his memory of her was the only beauty in his life. He reminded himself that he was thirty and within this year hoped to marry and have a child. He felt that only with family responsibility could he save himself from despair.

In early November, when Bill was back in San Francisco, Pat telephoned from Berkeley wanting to see him. When they met, in a college bar, she told him she believed she was pregnant from their time together in Reno. She proposed that they marry and divorce once the baby was born, that perhaps he would care for the baby while she finished college. The very thought of it depressed him.

Pat was able to find another solution, and Bill was left in a mournful mood. He walked on the beach, picking up rocks and thinking of Pat. Sadness came and went but was almost always with him.

Presently he telephoned her, and she came to Carl Street for a visit. She had borrowed a car, and when its battery failed they left it to be recharged and had dinner at a Greek restaurant on Haight Street. He found a change had taken place between them. It was as if he didn't know her any longer.

Having cleared his life of Pat Winter, Bill devoted his afternoons and evenings to the pursuit of San Francisco's many pleasures. A typical course included calls at Joe Danysh's gallery and the studios of his artist friends Matthew Barnes, Hilaire Hiler, and the sculptor Beniamino Bufano. He liked the bohemian life that flourished in the bars. In one bar on Market Street he had a sobering mishap. Mistaking a darkened flight of basement stairs for the men's room, he tumbled to the floor below. Although he walked away, his back would bring him pain for years to come.

He bet the horses and played poker into the morning's small hours and sought out good-looking girls wherever he could. In San Francisco's gaudy subculture of art, wealth, and good times, Bill's swaggering style, the boisterous laughter, the slouch hat, and the dark handsomeness became a familiar and welcome sight.

An artistic community centered around the Grabhorns, whose press on Commercial Street was often the scene for literary parties. Bill was a regular at them, offering advice on whom and what to publish and looking over the crowd, generously sprinkled with Berkeley scholars, patrons, and adventurous young women, for opportunity.

Pat Winter, Bill's devoted Hollywood girlfriend. Their romance became the
basis for several of his most poignant stories.

He had lingering relationships with Anita Zabala Howard, the handsome
wife of the owner of the famous racehorse Seabiscuit, and with Alma
Walker, the flamboyant former wife of William Randolph Hearst Jr. Alma
persuaded him to meet her family in Piedmont, but when she argued that
he ought to marry her he was firm in discouraging the idea.

He was enchanted by the tennis champion Helen Wills Moody, finding
her whimsical style unlike that of his usual girlfriends. He persuaded her to
walk with him at his favorite section of beach, "south of Fleishacker's." Her
wisdom and manner so impressed him that he vowed to alter his raffish
behavior. He watched her play at the California Tennis Club and then
lunched with her, remarking that some of her shots had been embarrassingly bad.

Two weeks later, Helen asked him to tea to say she would be leaving San
Francisco in a few days for New York and then Wimbledon. Before she left,
Bill telephoned her, hoping to see her again. Saying good-bye to her, he felt
he had talked foolishly and was further disheartened to learn that she had
been having an affair with a friend of his.

With each of these three women, his energy and swagger was all they
asked for. Each was accomplished, independent. There was no need for him
to feel obligation or responsibility.

Contrarily, Bill's blues put him in a self-appraising frame of mind, in which he decided that a life that offered him only the briefest associations with the most accessible women was no longer suitable. He was ready for marriage and would soon find the right person to be his wife. He hoped for a home, perhaps in the San Joaquin Valley, near Fresno, a simple, well-designed, well-built house, a place where he would live, work, and bring up a family. The arrival of an heir would do him great good.

But the urgency for permanent relationships, stimulated by a nation plunging into war, had no immediate effect on Saroyan's behavior with women. In Hollywood he saw a great deal of an aspiring actress called Joyce Lynn, but he was always adding to his list of screen postulants. In the course of a day he might entertain three different girls in his room.

When his uncle Aram joined him for supper at Musso and Frank's and asked if he was raising hell, Bill replied that he was not, just enjoying an occasional lay to refresh himself. Everything was nifty. When his uncle cautioned against "nifty" becoming "syphty," Bill laughed hugely.

Early in 1942, while Bill was in pursuit of bright prospects at MGM, he encountered a San Francisco acquaintance, the renowned clarinetist and bandleader Artie Shaw. Shaw kept an inventory of Hollywood's most desirable girls and was generous with it.

On February 27, Artie Shaw introduced Bill to a pretty seventeen-year-old girl named Carol Marcus. Shaw gives a fictional account of this critical encounter in his story "Old Friend." Although the story's stunning heroine appears to be an innocent schoolgirl, she surprises the narrator by her precocity. In their first furious embrace the girl warns him that she is a virgin and intends to remain so until marriage, but there are no further prohibitions. The result is an amorous weekend in which the narrator is taught "some tricks I had never heard of."

A few days later, the narrator and the schoolgirl encounter the "old friend," a writer, in an after-hours bar on Sunset, and it is recognizably love at first sight. The narrator encourages the old friend to pursue the girl, and thinks of providing a warning about the girl's determined virginity, but does not.

In February 1942, Carol Marcus was staying with her mother, Rosheen Marcus, at the Sunset Towers. Both Carol and her mother were hoping their Hollywood visit would bring the girl some opportunity in films. Carol had already acted in a Saroyan play, the Princeton production of *Jim Dandy*, so she was well aware of Bill's credentials as a playwright.

Although still a child in years and appearance, Carol's café society schooling had prepared her well for Hollywood parties. Her look of infant innocence was belied by a quick, perceptive wit, and she instinctively attracted men. She had met Artie Shaw at a party of her mother's, and he became her first Hollywood conquest, and later introduced her to Bill Saroyan. On their first date together, Bill took Carol to dinner at the actor John Garfield's, where he found among the guests the Group Theatre's foremost playwright, Clifford Odets. During the after-dinner poker game, Odets, a nonplayer, was attentive to Carol, and she went into the garden with him.

There Odets asked Carol if she was interested in Saroyan. Carol said that she was, and, indeed, had a crush on him. Odets replied that was too bad, since Bill was a disappointed man; he had hoped to be a titan in the theater.

When Odets and Carol returned, Bill was jealous and angry. When he and Carol left the party there was an episode, during a ride to the beach, which Bill deemed unpleasant. He did not plan on seeing her again.

He had recognized Norma Shearer, "first lady of the screen," on the MGM lot and knew her to be the widow of the legendary MGM head Irving Thalberg, the model for Scott Fitzgerald's *Last Tycoon*. Norma Shearer had seen Bill too, and asked Anita Loos to introduce them. When he invited her to listen to his pianola, she promised to do so. That night he went to Ugene's nightclub for a drink and saw Carol Marcus again. She was with a group that included Bill's friend Martha Stephenson, the recent wife of Victor Mature. When Carol saw Bill she came over to say hello and left him newly desirous.

By the time he decided to do something about it, Carol had left. Bill called Martha, who told him that Carol's mother had returned to New York and Carol was now staying with the Vanderbilts—her friend Gloria; Gloria's mother, "Big Gloria"; and her mother's twin sister, Thelma, Lady Furness. With the address Martha provided, Bill arrived at the Vanderbilt house at four o'clock in the morning, and, although the house was dark, rang the bell until it became clear no one was coming to let him in.

A series of strenuous trysts with Hollywood's wondrous creatures had left him resolved to get back to his work, but he found a gift from Carol Marcus awaiting him. It was Harry James's recording of "I Don't Want to Walk Without You," and it led to their going to supper at the Players and on to a club called Swanee.

Carol used a battery of naughty expressions that pretended to be innocent, and he was amused by her playfulness. He was doubtful of her insistence that *he* was the reason she didn't want to leave Hollywood, but back at his hotel room she wept at the thought of returning to New York.

The next day, he decided their relationship made no sense, but when she phoned him he asked her to join him for a drink with Gene Kelly and Betsy Blair. She came with him to his room, where they were playful, then they went to a series of nightclubs—Streets of Paris, Swanee, and Ugene's—where they joined Jackie Gleason. Walking her home, though, Bill decided he was finished with such relationships as this one.

Meanwhile, he had watched Norma Shearer on Stage 26, standing rather bravely before the unforgiving lens of a close-up camera. When he called her and urged her to visit him, the idea seemed to please her. Her laughter sounded adventurous, but his hunch was that she wouldn't come.

One night at the Players, he saw Carol again, and the sight of her touched him in a wholly unexpected way: he felt as if he had fallen in love with her. A few days later, he invited a new girl to his room, where they drank scotch, listened to his records, and went to bed. While they were making love, Bill found himself thinking of Carol and confided this to the girl. She was understandably angry, and as he dressed to take her home, Carol called to say she could see him late that night. When they did meet, he joked and laughed with her, and, deciding he had gotten over his crush, sent her away.

Although his days were now filled with preparations for filming *The Good Job,* his social life became more active than ever. He continued to see Joyce Lynn and make his way through the nightclubs until four in the morning. Norma Shearer invited him to dinner, during which he decided she must be about forty, and noted how her age showed in her hands, in dry skin and old freckles.

He spent the night before he began production of *The Good Job* with Norma Shearer. She read Shelley to him and showed him the passages she and Thalberg had marked together. Bill was not impressed.

He arrived at the studio at eight the next morning after only three hours' sleep, but got off to a good start with his cast and crew. That night he returned to Norma Shearer's for dinner, heard her collection of Eddie Duchin's Gershwin recordings, and spent the night.

However, he had lost all desire for her. He saw an irony in the widespread belief that she was a great beauty and his discovery that her body was strange, somewhat deathly, eagerly hidden. Henceforth it would be the girls and their sweetness, for him.

On Sunday, while he was entertaining his cousin Kirk Minasian, Bill was surprised to find Carol Marcus and a girlfriend at his door. Carol's behavior in front of Kirk struck Bill as provocative, and he was abrupt with her. Although she didn't look it, he suddenly realized she must be Jewish.

He returned to San Francisco in May, with the Hollywood ordeal behind him. Cosette reported that a Carol Marcus was calling from Beverly Hills, and he told her to say he was out of town. Once powerfully attracted to Carol, he now regarded her as a nuisance, a seventeen-year-old Jewish girl who was a subject for gossip within Hollywood's most undesirable circles. After his MGM experience, Bill's response to tribal prejudice was reflex-like. It reinforced a special distrust of women to whom he was drawn.

Even as he watched the convoys setting out across the Pacific from his window, he had no sense of involvement in an ideological struggle. The March of Time's report of a naval victory at Guadalcanal irritated him with what he saw as false heroics. He felt that kind of patriotism was wrongheaded, for it falsified the horrible reality of war.

He was still unclaimed by the draft, but he suspected that this was a temporary state of grace and that if he were to achieve his most audacious dream—a Saroyan repertory theater in New York—he must do so before the war grasped him. So in June he set off for New York in his new Cadillac, the remaining prize of his Hollywood adventure.

On a Colorado straightaway he was pushing the car to the hundred-mile-an-hour mark when it left the road and came to rest in a ditch. Although unharmed, he was shaken, and the car was damaged. In Denver, waiting for repairs, he called home and found that his draft classification had arrived. He was 1-A, subject to immediate induction into the army, and would soon be summoned for physical examination.

He drove on across the plains more cautiously, experiencing a loneliness that reminded him of his 1928 ordeal in New York, when, in the public library on Fifth Avenue, he had felt himself lost and drowning in grief.

He arrived in New York and rented a $275-a-month apartment at the Hampshire House with a splendid view of Central Park and set about renewing his Manhattan acquaintances. He paid a conciliatory call on Hal Matson. He found Eddie Dowling enthusiastic about *Hello Out There* and ready to present it as part of a double bill. He went to the new plays and trouped from one columnist and celebrity table to another, promoting the Saroyan Theatre as he went.

As he began his search for backers, actors, and technicians, the mail brought him a notice from his San Francisco draft board. He was to report for a physical examination in two weeks. He spent that evening with George Jean Nathan at the Stork Club. The music, dancing, and laughter that surrounded him only deepened the dread of a now imminent swallowing by the army.

As he left the nightclub, at three in the morning, he had a poignant glimpse of Carol Marcus. Although he had eluded her in May, much had happened in the last month, and now, on the Stork's dance floor, she seemed more beautiful than ever. The next day, he invited her along for an evening with Nathan and other theater folk. Nathan approved of Carol at once and proposed to take her to an opening. The following day Carol called Bill, and he took her to the Stork and to Fefe's Monte Carlo, where the bandleader, Sonny Kendis, played all their favorite songs.

Thus a second, café society courtship began. Bill would telephone Carol and suggest she join him at "21" or the Golden Horn. They might go on to

Carol Marcus. Her exquisite beauty and playfulness fascinated
Bill Saroyan from the first. Here they are frolicking together
during a 1945 visit to Fresno.

the theater and later "do the joints"—the Penthouse, Fefe's, Cafe Society, or
the ethnic places downtown, and always the Stork. Here they would be welcomed by smiles at the door and by the swingy seductions of the dance
band, and would be led to the celebrity tables presided over by the columnists Walter Winchell or Leonard Lyons.

When Carol asked him to dinner, he brought Nathan along to the
Marcuses' impressive Park Avenue apartment. They were entertained by
Rosheen and Carol's stepfather, Charles, a corporate executive. The dinner
party, which included Carol's sister Elinor and her boyfriend, Lester Loner-
gan, went on to the Stork, where Sherman Billingsley, the proprietor, saw
that they were given no check.

Carol resumed her full-scale pursuit of Bill, telephoning him often during the day and turning up unexpectedly at his door in Hampshire House,
once with her sister Elinor, once alone, a little frightened, uncharacteristi-
cally timid.

He held her off, remembering that earlier impression of Carol as a girl
with a wretched reputation. But in fact, Carol's humor and exquisite
beauty had found the narrow crack in his heart's armor. He loved her sense
of humor, which laced a girlish innocence with naughtiness. When he told
her that he had been warned about her promiscuity—Leonard Lyons had

suggested that Carol's innocent look might be the disguise of venereal infection—she was very hurt, but was soon making comedy out of the word gonorrhea. Bill and Carol became inseparable. They rode the length of Manhattan on a bus top and drove out to Jones Beach in his Cadillac. While she invariably returned with him to his room at the Hampshire House, where they pleasured themselves, Carol's earlier prohibition was still enforced.

In spite of his reservations, Bill admitted that he was enchanted by Carol. She was everything a woman ought not to be, and yet she was very beautiful, alluringly small and soft, eyes gleaming with wild, zany fun. He had learned from her that her real father's name was Henry Stuart, not a Jew, and that Marcus had adopted her legally. This explained the parental tolerance of her behavior. Although an instinctive skeptic, he dismissed all prior conceptions of her origins.

What he had dreaded most about the army had come to pass: it had singled him out just as his own life was brimming with the most exciting possibilities. In addition to the blooming love affair with Carol, there was the promising novelization of *The Human Comedy* and, above all, the emerging Saroyan Theatre.

Oddly, he spurned another offer of draft immunity. Eric Knight, a Hollywood acquaintance, now at work on training films, knew of Bill's draft status and thought Bill might want to join him. They met for a drink, but when Knight described the purpose of the army films as "motivational," Bill refused to participate. He had no taste for persuading Ohio boys to get themselves killed in the war. He would rather wait for the government to decide where to put him to work.

However, he replied to his San Francisco draft board that since he was now living and working in New York he would be unable to keep his appointment for physical examination. A prompt reply reported his transfer to a New York draft board, from which he would soon receive a new appointment.

Bill had originally declined Frank Morley's proposal that he make a novel out of *The Human Comedy*'s screenplay but had urged Morley to find a journeyman to do the job. Morley had done so, and when Bill called at Harcourt he was introduced to a Mrs. Clifford Dowdey, who was completing the task. When he saw her completed manuscript he declared that as a serious novel it was quite hopeless. At the same time he saw possibilities in revision, and, while this required more effort than he was prepared to make, he went to work.

None of these concerns, nor the scarcity of his funds, diverted Bill from the launching of the Saroyan Theatre. He had only $4,000, which Cosette was forwarding from San Francisco, and he was spending a thousand dollars a month simply living in New York. He told himself that producing a show on such a sum would make him famous for the Saroyan shoestring, if for nothing else.

Bill's first step was to hire a staff. He found two Broadway professionals, David Lowe and Cleon Throckmorton, eager to join in the project. He declined to make a contract with them, believing rightly that they would work for him without one. Lowe soon found that the Belasco Theatre was available, and Bill agreed to lease it for rehearsals and performances.

On July 18, Bill announced the opening of the Saroyan Theatre. Its season would begin with a double bill, *Across the Board on Tomorrow Morning* plus the one-act *Talking to You,* a nightmare-like allegory about the war in Europe. Its characters are the world's outcasts—a deaf man, a blind man, a black man, a Mexican, and a midget. As in other Saroyan plays, the characters have found temporary refuge from the world's violence in a basement shelter.

Bill set about his casting in typically unorthodox ways. He assured Carol of a part and decided she would have the modest role of Lois in *Across the Board.* He had found a number of actors he liked, Canada Lee, Maxwell Bodenheim, and a spirited flamenco singer named Jeronimo. He had been quick to fire his several obvious mistakes. Nevertheless, as he began to rehearse in earnest, the company disappointed him.

In the midst of these preparations, Bill had a call from Nathan saying that John Steinbeck was with him at "21" and "homesick" to see Bill. Their California-based writerly fellowship was in no way enhanced by Steinbeck's ascent to a summit of fame, and now, as Bill arrived at the restaurant, he was greeted by Steinbeck's comradely query about whether he was still as full of horseshit as he had been. Bill asked him to repeat this, which Steinbeck did, to the delight of his wife-to-be, Elaine Scott. Steinbeck kidded him further about his publicity, which, he contended, had made him more character than writer.

Offended by Steinbeck's grandly patronizing manner, Bill argued that his life and work were inseparable and challenged Steinbeck about the lack of humor in his own work. At this, Steinbeck became apologetic, not only approving of Bill's antiwar stand but disparaging his own book *Bombs Away, The Story of a Bomber Team,* just done for the army. Indeed he felt he must now join the air force and endanger his own life, as he had urged younger Americans to do.

He wished the Saroyan Theatre well and wrote down his phone number, urging a visit, but Bill was not appeased. He thought Steinbeck was clever to pretend indifference to a Hollywood that regularly filmed his books and

Saroyan Theatre. Bill's dream of a theater perennially presenting
Saroyan plays foundered here in August 1942.

plays. As for John and Elaine's cordiality, he thought it presumptuous. He
felt they were his inferiors, and confirmed this by his own easiness. Steinbeck had seemed a troubled man who looked bad and got drunk quickly.
Later, Nathan agreed that Steinbeck had bullied him, and that Bill was his
literary superior.

Bill had been transferred from the San Francisco draft board to one at the
Delmonico Hotel in New York. Here, a young woman whom he identified

Citizen Saroyan could not ignore the nation's call to arms.

as Jewish told him he should never be in the army, as he would be giving orders to the officers. Nevertheless, at her instruction, he interrupted rehearsal on July 30 to undergo his physical at St. Luke's Hospital. Five interviewing reporters and photographers stood by recording the event for their papers. A Dr. Dowd dismissed Bill's several ailments as no hindrance to army duty and confirmed his 1-A classification. He would soon learn where to report for induction.

On the night of August 4, Bill achieved the "triumph" he had been pursuing with Carol for a long time, but a week later they quarreled. It was serious enough for Bill to decide not to speak to her again, but when Ross Bagdasarian turned up, Bill brought her along for some drinks and they were soon together. He decided again that Carol was great, the very best of girls.

During early rehearsals he found the plays themselves bored him. Cleon Throckmorton's scenery for the show seemed to have filled his stage with a woodpile instead of fantasy. He had not anticipated the cost of getting his amateur actors into Equity and paying his musicians union wages. The blizzard of bills was unrelenting, and he ran out of money entirely. His only hope of survival lay in several weeks of good business at the box office, and he was increasingly pessimistic about that.

He fired David Lowe, who immediately presented him with a $1,500 bill for his services. Bill settled, acrimoniously, for $825 and realized that without more money he could not open the show. For help he went to his publisher, Donald Brace, who obligingly loaned him $5,000.

On the day of the Saroyan Theatre's opening, Monday, August 17, 1942, Bill found his cast, Canada Lee in particular, rebellious. As curtain time approached he left the Belasco and neglected to address the company before the performance. He returned to the theater while the first play, *Across the Board*, was in progress and found Canada, in his role as the waiter, performing with unauthorized abandon.

As a sullen audience filed from the theater, Bill realized *Across the Board* had gone entirely amok, and even though *Talking to You* had gone a little better, he told himself he could expect only the worst. He prepared himself for a loss of about $7,000, but figured he would get even betting the horses. Failing that, he would write a new play for Hollywood. He understood that the Saroyan Theatre had come and gone. The reviews would be murder.

He was exactly right. The reviewers agreed that Saroyan had presented New York with a boring flop. Even though he felt betrayed by incompetent designers, electricians, and actors, he admitted he had no alibi. The fault was all his, and that knowledge ought to do him good.

In the next few days the box office took in only a few hundred dollars a performance, and, on discovering there was a seven-year-old boy in the cast, the Society for Prevention of Cruelty to Children tried to close the show. Within a week, Bill closed it himself. He had put $11,000 into the venture and owed another thousand. He was overdrawn at the bank, in debt to the Hampshire House, and had only a few dollars in his pocket. He would have to sell his Cadillac.

The critics had told him that he could not write and, on top of that, could neither produce nor direct. They had said that the plays were a bore and the cast had failed to understand them. Not even Nathan had raised a voice in his defense. They had knocked him down; by the time he got up, the marquee had gone dark and the theater was empty.

Even as he insisted that the plays were important and would find their place in the literature of the American theater, he was acknowledging that the Saroyan Theatre's collapse put an end to substantive Broadway prospects and made an unpatchable rip in the sail of his assurance.

Laying to rest his hopes for the Saroyan Theatre brought bottoms of depression. Broke and in debt, he took Carol to the movies and new shows, resenting them from their opening moments. He quit a revival of D. W. Griffith's *Intolerance* at its midpoint and deplored Louis Mayer's favorite new release, *Mrs. Miniver*. He gave grudging approval to the two hit musi-

Lauren Bacall, George Jean Nathan, and Bill and Carol at the Stork Club in 1942

cals, Rodgers and Hart's *By Jupiter* and *Let's Face It,* but decided the latter's star, Danny Kaye, was a bore.

Now an accepted member of the Marcus household, Bill took a liking to its head. Charles Marcus was a vice president of Bendix Aviation, and he pleased Bill with an invitation to visit "the plant." Bill also approved of Carol's friend Gloria Vanderbilt di Cicco, finding her a nice girl, rather serious and unlike what he had imagined.

He was less taken with Carol's friend Oona O'Neill, the seventeen-year-old daughter of Eugene O'Neill. Oona was seeing a great deal of the cartoonist Peter Arno at the time, and, when not with their boyfriends, she and Carol were inseparable. They not only shared confidences but a racy manner of speech. When they called on Bill, he noticed how the girls used rowdy language, speaking it very sweetly but it was no less astonishing to cab drivers, elevator operators, and other bystanders. Indeed, the notes Carol wrote and left behind at the Hampshire House were raunchy enough to raise even Bill's eyebrow.

He found some cause for optimism. As he worked away at the revision of *The Human Comedy,* he was liking it, and a placated Pat Duggan had news of an MGM offer for screen rights to *Time of Your Life.* Duggan expected it to be for $60,000, half of which would be Saroyan's.

Bill celebrated his thirty-fourth birthday, on the last day of August, with Carol. She came to visit him with a bottle of Sherman Billingsley's champagne, a fine cake from her sister Elinor, and a gold bracelet, inscribed "William Saroyan" on one side and "Love, Carol, 8/31/42" on the other. They walked in the park before going on to "21" to meet Nathan, who, Bill thought, was growing vague and uncertain.

The mail of September 10 brought Bill the dreaded draft notice. He was instructed to report for induction into the army in five days back in San Francisco. He went at once to the Delmonico Hotel asking his contact there to arrange for him to report here in New York and not until mid-October. This, he explained, would enable him to finish his work on *The Human Comedy*. She agreed to try and indeed soon succeeded in arranging for his induction in New York on Tuesday, October 13.

Carol's eighteenth birthday fell on September 11. His gift to her was a gold chain bracelet with lock and key which he had found at the Armenian jeweler Desteian's. He had no sooner given it to her than he decided their affair was over. She was great fun to be with but too cosy with the nightclub crowd for a serious relationship.

In fact, they were entering a time of frequent emotional cloudbursts. They walked in the park and dined together affectionately. Carol told Bill that Gloria Vanderbilt had told her to marry him, and she was now awaiting his proposal. But then they would quarrel. Their difference might begin over her fear of cats, or a woman who chided her for combing her hair at a restaurant table, or over soldiers and sailors who paused to admire her and give Bill the sign of their approval. But argument was most heated over Carol's habitual flirtatiousness and enjoyment of his jealousy. They would part furiously, vowing never to see each other again, only to enjoy the sweetest of early-morning reconciliations at the Hampshire House.

One angry parting did seem final, and no word passed between the two until the following day, when Bill called Carol to win some sympathy for his plaguing back pain. She soon came by to bring him a hot pad and followed it up with a touching letter. He was surprised by her eloquence. She wrote that he was the only man with whom she had ever had a real relationship and so seemed her only chance for true happiness. Wanting to marry him was the natural outcome. She felt all her joking was simply caution, and it was this, regrettably, which had kept her from sharing her real feelings. She wished him well in whatever he would do now—the army, a new play, and new love.

He called to thank her, but added he had called only because of the pain in his back. Then at two the following morning, she called him, laughing giddily with Oona O'Neill, who was spending the night with her. The next morning, Bill called Carol, and that night they met and talked earnestly for many hours. Bill insisted that if she went out with other men, their relationship was ended. Carol was open to the idea of exclusivity, except that Jules Glaenzer, head of Cartier's, was in love with her and had asked her to lunch and the baseball game. She had accepted and planned to go with him.

The emotional fluctuations of Bill's love affair did not keep him from work on *The Human Comedy*. He finished the revision to his satisfaction and saw the manuscript, with each of its twenty-three chapters headed by a Don Freeman drawing, into Frank Morley's hands at Harcourt on September 25.

It was also cheering for Bill to know that a new Saroyan play was about to rise in the very ashes of the Saroyan Theatre. Eddie Dowling's production of *Hello Out There,* paired with G. K. Chesterton's *Magic,* was trying out in Philadelphia and would open at the Belasco on August 29.

Although Dowling continued to be the most loyal of Saroyan champions on a Broadway that had all but forgotten him, Bill grew curiously resentful. The more Dowling was praised for his adroitness as producer, director, and star of the show, the more Bill saw him as a ham actor, and a man he did not trust. He had felt all along that the Chesterton play was dreary enough to swamp his own sprightly offering, and the out-of-town reviews confirmed this.

With Carol, Bill was on hand for the New York opening of *Hello Out There.* He felt both Julie Haydon and Eddie Dowling gave poor performances, and so the good reviews surprised him. Howard Barnes, in the *Tribune,* was particularly enthusiastic. There would be a respectable run.

Now all that lay ahead for Bill was the army. In spite of the manipulations that would allow him to report in New York, he now decided he would prefer to join with Californians, and notified both draft boards of this intention. He had mended his relations with Matson and Duggan to the point where he could borrow $500 from them to pay his Hampshire House bill and have $150 for the drive home.

He spent most of his last day in New York with Carol. As he walked her home at midnight, he saw that she was weeping at the prospect of their parting. At six the next morning, she called to say that she would come to San Francisco at his bidding, and that Oona O'Neill would be with her. He did not encourage the idea.

Leaving New York, driving west, he was happy to be on his way and opening a new chapter in his life, but he was thinking of Carol Marcus. The weather was fair, and he drove with the car's top down, reaching Pittsburgh that night. In his room at the Schenley Hotel, he was awakened at two a.m. by a call from Carol. She had tried every hotel until she reached him. She said she was sick with love for him and wanted to come now with Oona and join him there.

Oona O'Neill and Charlie Chaplin at the Stork

He was able to discourage this plan, but the following night in Indianapolis Carol reached him again. After telling him that she was being courted by Orson Welles, Carol put her mother on to say that she was concerned about her daughter's emotional state. Bill assured her that his marrying Carol was out of the question.

Rosheen and Carol called him back, and while Bill protested that the most sensible plan was for them both to forget the whole thing, Rosheen disagreed. She was giving Carol her permission to pay Bill a visit in San Francisco. Bill rejected that idea as well, but later called Carol back, proposing that she fly to St. Louis, where they could meet and continue the journey together. Carol vetoed this. She and Oona would be coming to San Francisco, and she was terribly happy now that this was all settled. She couldn't wait to see him.

Bill continued driving west in the deepening loneliness and despair he had felt on his eastward trip. When a tire blew out near Mojave, he felt unable to reach San Francisco alone. He telephoned Ross Bagdasarian, who, though already in the service, was able to meet him in Bakersfield and share the driving. Bill was relieved to arrive at 1821 Fifteenth Avenue and be home with his family at last.

On October 12, he presented himself to his San Francisco draft board, surprising a Miss Mulcrevy there, who believed he was being inducted in New York. Indeed she had telegraphed him that this was now obligatory. After trying unsuccessfully to return him to New York by airplane, the draft board arranged for a special physical examination three days later in San Francisco.

At this late hour, Bill sought the deliverance of a writing appointment. He telegraphed Robert Sherwood and Elmer Davis, the former *New York Times* and CBS correspondent who was director of the Office of War Information, and offered his services. There was no response.

Although Eddie Dowling had a bleak report on the box-office receipts of *Hello Out There,* he was optimistic about getting Bill a deferment and a government writing job. But even as Eddie pulled strings and counseled him, Bill felt uncomfortable with such conniving and tended to let it all slide. He might well be rejected as unfit for service anyway. His response, like that to Steinbeck's offer, was in part a dread of any debt that might unbalance their relationship.

The galleys of *The Human Comedy* arrived from Harcourt, and as Bill read them, he was delighted to find it had become a respectable novel. He thought it would be good to read. He dedicated the book to his mother, explaining to her and the world that since it was for her, he wished it were a better book, the very best, and, while it was short of that, he had tried to make it so.

Then, on a Wednesday morning in mid-October, he crossed the Bay Bridge to meet Carol and Oona at the Oakland station. He drove them to the St. Francis Hotel in San Francisco, where he got a suite for them at $12 a day, then took them on a tour to Half Moon Bay and to dinner at the New Shanghai Low.

At seven-thirty the next morning, he appeared at the induction center and started through a gamut of doctors. The psychiatrist asked if he had had any nervous breakdowns, and Bill assured him that he had often found himself desperate, restless, and unwell. Without hesitation, the psychiatrist approved him for army service.

When another doctor asked if there was anything wrong with him, Bill described his chronic sinus and sacroiliac conditions. Asked if either interfered with his work, he replied that the sacroiliac condition did not, only because he avoided walking, running, exercising, or standing on his feet longer than necessary.

After lunch and an unexplained three-hour wait in the company of twenty diverse Californians, Bill and his fellow inductees were lined up and presented with registration papers. A captain appeared to read them the Articles of War that explained the consequences of desertion and absence

Carol Marcus and Gloria Vanderbilt on their way to Gloria and
Pat di Cicco's wedding, in California, December 16, 1941

without leave. They raised their right arms, took the oath, and were duly
sworn into the U.S. Army. Bill resented the threatening nature of the oath,
that there was no alternative to obeying it. He did have fourteen days before
he must leave for Monterey and basic training. Reminding himself that
Orson Welles was not a private, he thought there must be a way to avoid it
himself.

That afternoon Bill was able to gather Carol and Oona at the St. Francis
and take them to Fisherman's Wharf for a meal, but he did feel silly escort-
ing the two girls, who were behaving in a conspicuously childish way,
through the hotel lobby.

With Hollywood and a probe into the making of *The Human Comedy* in
mind, Bill began a weekend excursion by driving the two girls to Fresno.
Here he arranged a date for Oona with Ross Bagdasarian, who was stationed at nearby Hammer Field. On Sunday they had a memorable, nude,
swimming party off the rocks at Piedra, and on Monday Bill took the girls
to Hollywood and installed them at the Roosevelt Hotel.

While Carol and Oona visited Gloria di Cicco at the Beverly Hills Hotel,

Bill called on Howard Estabrook, author of *The Human Comedy*'s screenplay. He offered to help with revisions, and urged Estabrook to read his books with an eye to finding material for another MGM movie. Visiting the MGM set where *The Human Comedy* was in production, he met and liked Van Johnson, who was playing the role of Marcus Macauley. He was photographed with the director, Clarence Brown.

Enough of the script was available for Bill to find fault with it. In the "Soldiers in the Rain" episode, he detected an element of war propaganda, which he felt Estabrook had added under MGM pressure. Bill vetoed some of this and proposed a new ending, which met with approving, if silent, nods.

Back in Fresno it became clear that a romance had taken root between Oona and Ross, who decided to join the party for the return to San Francisco. While Oona had been careful in displaying her feeling about Bill, she did not like him and had warned Carol about her infatuation. Thus, by the journey's end, Bill had a matching distaste for Oona. He thought the daughter of Eugene O'Neill was empty-headed, slovenly, and preoccupied with sex.

With the two girls installed at the Hotel Bellevue, Bill looked forward to his last three days as a civilian. Saturday-night entertainment ended at the beach and another swimming party. On Sunday, he and Ross went to the girls' room at the Bellevue and began to drink and sing. Ross did his special vaudeville performance, much of which was in Armenian and included obscene references that convulsed the boys.

They telephoned a third cousin, Chesley Saroyan, a student at Stanford. Chesley joined them, bringing his girl Amie Reichert. All but Oona, who drank little, became drunk, and the noise in the room grew so that a complaint was made and a manager arrived. He requested each of them to sign a statement that they were over twenty-one. All did so, although Amie, at nineteen, was the oldest girl. Carol was just eighteen, and Oona was still seventeen.

Bill called George Mardikian for a picnic lunch, which they collected at Mardikian's Omar Khayyam restaurant and drove out to Bill's special place in the cliffs overlooking the sea. There they had their picnic, hugged, and kissed until Chesley had to leave for Stanford. When it grew dark, Bill proposed that they walk down the road to the sea and go for another skinny-dip. Bill was first in, soon followed by Carol and then Ross. Oona declined, saying she had a revulsion for water, even in a bathtub. The waves were high, and the water cold and roaring. Carol would run out into the waves, scaring Bill, and he would run after her to bring her back. Bill would often recall Carol's beauty there, and how holding her naked in the water was so joyous and wonderful. When she asked what he would do if she drowned, he told her he would drown too, and felt it was the truth.

On the Monday morning of his last week as a civilian he felt his writing career was still on the rise. His novel, *The Human Comedy*, would be published at year's end with a good chance at Book-of-the-Month Club selection and magazine serialization. Hal Matson already had a $2,000 offer from *Woman's Home Companion* for an excerpt. The movie, starring Mickey Rooney, would be released in December, and in spite of Hollywood bungling it would be one of the best pictures ever made.

Hello Out There was still playing in New York, and would continue a few more weeks. He believed *Get Away Old Man* would be produced soon and that it would cause enough discomfort to Louis Mayer to even the score between them. He thought the Guild might want *A Decent Birth* and the National Theatre Conference would surely do *Afton Water*. He would be providing Harcourt with the stories for a new collection, *Elegie*.

He told himself that he did want to marry and raise a family, and that he might or might not choose Carol. The times were so jumbled he was still not sure she should be his wife. If she were still with him in December, though, he would hope to have her pregnant. The timing would be such as to have the child born in late August, as he had been. Perhaps the child could be born in Fresno, too.

He was certainly more and more devoted to Carol, and she lived for him. On one of these late October mornings he called for her at her hotel, and while walking her around downtown San Francisco told her that if she became pregnant they would be married quietly, and if she did not they would be happy and go on. This delighted her.

On impulse, he decided to take her home and drove her out to Fifteenth Avenue. Cosette and Takoohi welcomed Carol at once. Cosette helped Bill get a fire started in the fireplace and brought them Turkish coffee. Bill played the pianola and then asked his mother to come down and join them. She did so, bringing along some family photographs. When it was time to go, Carol kissed Bill's mother. When Bill returned home, he talked with Takoohi about Carol, and she approved, saying that she had opened her bible to a passage that urged man to enjoy his bread and wine.

VII

THE BUGLE'S CALL

1941–1942

Saroyan's hatred for war was tortuous and deep, rooted in his conception of self and society. He summarized it in a note for his 1940 play *The Agony of Little Nations,* admitting that war might be inevitable, as the present one certainly had become, yet the self-murder of millions of men was beyond grief's power to understand. The human heart could be touched by the waste of one life, or even a hundred, but was simply stupefied by the destruction of the countless.

In January 1941, when Whit Burnett asked for a contribution to *Story's* tenth-anniversary issue, Bill replied that he could not provide fiction, but Whit was welcome to print the eight-page explanation of why the war made story writing impossible for him. The essence of it was that he had listened to the propaganda on the radio, read it in the papers, read the stories and books about the war, and thought they all stank. He had tried to understand the men who were making the war and found they stank too. He would have nothing to do with the war. Moreover, he felt responsible for it. It was foolish to believe that defeating fascism was the solution, because the force of fascism was in all human beings. He saw crookedness everywhere, and in himself too. He could find nothing to read, nor to write. There was no point.

Whatever definition of fascism Saroyan had in mind—whether it was the new nationalism, the dictatorship of the right, or anti-Semitism—this was an argument that freed him of any broader commitment than that of his own ambition. He showed no awareness of the social contract whose freedoms he so enjoyed and for which others had served and died. In any case, Burnett decided against publishing the Saroyan manifesto.

While other observers saw the war's cause in ideologies, Saroyan fixed the blame squarely on its leaders. He reasoned that Churchill and Roosevelt, as well as Hitler and Mussolini, were human failures who presented a misleading appearance of greatness. However they appeared to the world, they were pathetic. He held them responsible for compelling masses of human beings to murder each other.

He focused his resentment of international bungling on his commander in chief. Occasionally he dreamed of Franklin Roosevelt. In his dream, the president is in a rickshaw asking if he is Saroyan but mistaking his first name as Edwin. Bill corrects him, repeating "William, William."

The Rooseveltian patrician manner, outspoken social concerns, and assertions of noblesse oblige provoked Bill's enmity toward education and the establishment. These were his own dark chasms, his inadequacies, and his fears incarnate.

Thus there was an irony in his being invited to Hyde Park for lunch with the president and Mrs. Roosevelt. It was early summer of 1940, when FDR was about to run for an unprecedented third term against Wendell Willkie. The playwright Sidney Kingsley had asked Bill to come, and so he found himself in the Roosevelt garden along with such notables as the historian Hendrik Willem van Loon, the columnist FPA, and James Thurber.

He would recall in *Sons Come and Go* how two men carried the president to his chair at the head of the luncheon table, how FDR spoke loudly and laughed a great deal over what seemed feeble ideas, and how his manner seemed that of a show-off. Nor did Bill like the president's seating Edna Ferber on one side of him and Katharine Hepburn on the other.

Only two of the guests, himself and the nearly blind Thurber, declined the opportunity to shake Franklin Roosevelt's hand. Bill was also offended by a snub from Katharine Hepburn, who was conspicuously busy with the Roosevelt cause. When she passed him, rattling the contents of a stationery box, Bill asked if she had the answers there, and she replied frostily that what was in the box was none of Mr. Saroyan's business.

But Saroyan's antiwar outrage was theoretical. He didn't take a conscientious objector's stand, but rather let the army do what it would with an infidel, as though *his* sense of righteousness was equal to the military's and he would willingly put his individualism and self-reliance to the test.

He spent most of his last civilian evening, October 29, 1942, with Carol, came home to an enormous Armenian supper with his family, and called Carol to say good night. Reflecting on the militant's oath he had taken, he saw it as a kind of blackmail. He was not cut out for soldiering. Wanting to kill was beyond him. He wondered if all armies were made up of unwilling men and decided all men were unwilling, but not unwilling enough. In a mixture of dismay and irony, he looked to the morning, when he would be Soldier Saroyan, a threat to enemy armies massing around the world.

The next day, armed with briefcase, typewriter, and portable phonograph, he boarded a troop train for the indoctrination center at Monterey. There he joined three thousand other recruits to be innoculated, issued a uniform, given a GI haircut and an aptitude test, shown films about saluting and the dangers of venereal disease, and sermonized by a chaplain about the rewards of a chaste army life. Bill saw wisdom in the view of a fellow soldier named Torpedo, who foresaw much "beating the old root" here.

While most were bound for basic training at what Torpedo called "Little Rocks," Bill found himself destined for Camp Kohler, near Sacramento. He called Carol, telling her to go to Sacramento and wait for him at the Senator Hotel. He arrived at Camp Kohler on November 5 to undertake the army's six-week grounding in military life. Although Carol had followed his instructions and, with Oona O'Neill, had arrived at the Senator Hotel, he learned that he would have no leave at all for two weeks.

Morning calisthenics took place in the dark, and included such tortures as squatting on his heels and jumping up four times for each direction of the compass. Next came the making and remaking of his bunk, to the endless dissatisfaction of his sergeant. He moved to meals with hundreds of other men. He took part in close-order drill, often with a sixty-five-pound pack, at double time, shouting in cadence.

On the firing range he noted the reverence with which the instructors handled a rifle and how they called it "the piece." He fired his rounds quickly, if inaccurately, and thought he would not like pointing it at anyone.

Like most GIs he dreaded KP duty and using the latrine, but while others grew accustomed to these indignities, Bill found them increasingly offensive. A missed drill cost him an extra assignment of cleaning garbage cans. When he sought relief in the base hospital, he learned his whole company was sore at him for shirking his duty.

Unlike most recruits, he had no need for comradeship, no ability for trust or intimacy with others. Military fellowship struck him as false, an exchange of obligation and indulgence. He courted the dislike of equal and superior alike.

When Bill's sergeant found that he was bribing others to do his KP, he warned him to stop. Meeting with Saroyan indifference, the sergeant advised him to recognize his friends and not alienate them. Bill replied that he didn't want any friends.

It was true. He felt sick in body and spirit, outfitted in ill-fitting clothes and surrounded by lesser men. Elsewhere he would have ignored them. He believed the biggest men in the army were his inferiors. As for his comrades, he knew they hated his guts. He welcomed their hatred. He was angered by the need to flatter others to get along here. He certainly could not write in such circumstances.

At the end of his fourth week of indoctrination he judged it the most painful experience of his life, far worse than that of the orphanage when he was three. He had not anticipated that the humiliations of basic training would so damage his sense of self. Having to follow a superior's orders was devastating. It tattered the bright cloak of his fame and threatened to reveal the deprived, despised orphan boy. The nightmare of his infant years, which he had fought so hard to escape, had reclaimed him.

Moreover, he failed to see any connection between the hardship he was enduring and a national purpose. Any patriotic impulse, like that for friendship, eluded him, and he was astute in making the connection with a childhood that had stunned him into self-sufficiency and left him more familiar with Armenian than American history.

At last he did see Carol. He managed to get away from Camp Kohler long enough to meet her for a few hours at the Senator Hotel, and on occasion she came to visit. Once, when he had finished walking guard duty at two a.m., he found her waiting for him at the main gate, and they talked there until four, when a cab came to pick her up.

He learned that on their way to Sacramento, she and Oona had visited Oona's father, Eugene O'Neill, at his new "Tao House," in Danville, California. She described how Oona had spoken to the famous dramatist as if to another man, flirting—but Carol had seen no affection between them.

Among Oona's admirers in New York was a particularly faithful correspondent she spoke of as "Jerry." His letters were eloquent enough for her to share them with Carol, who was so impressed by the literary flourishes that she borrowed some for her own correspondence with Bill. Hopes that these would impress him foundered when he scolded her for them. From a sweet, simple girl like herself, he told her, they sounded false. Fearing Bill would further disapprove of her plagiarism, Carol did not reveal, until years later, that the objectionable phrases were those of Oona's beau, J. D. Salinger.

Bill spent his first weekend leave at home in San Francisco. When he returned to camp, he brought his mother and his sister Cosette to stay through Thanksgiving at the Senator Hotel. Although Carol had not yet left town he did not want to acknowledge her presence, and so he divided his off-duty obligations. Once, on his way to visit his mother, he encountered Carol in the Senator lobby. By previous agreement they did not recognize each other, but when she entered the elevator he spoke to her, pretending to be a stranger. As he left for his mother's room he told her he would see her later, and did.

While he was in the hospital, Bill's spirits had been raised appreciably by a telegram from Hal Matson and Pat Duggan congratulating him on the

Book-of-the-Month Club's selection of *The Human Comedy* as its main selection for February.

At the same time he learned that in a radio broadcast, Walter Winchell had predicted his marriage to Carol. Bill assured himself that it was not likely, and that he would ask Carol to go home soon. When Carol told him that she had had a wistful telegram from Orson Welles, Bill replied that Orson could have her, and he urged her to return to New York. She was amazed at this rejection, but agreed to leave. Since Oona was going to Hollywood, Carol would try to get Martha Stephenson to accompany her on the train, but in the meantime she would wait in Sacramento in hopes of another week of fun with him before she left.

Bill was amused by Carol's sousing herself with perfume samples in a drugstore, and he bought a bottle of champagne with which to bid the girls farewell. Carol and Oona left Sacramento together before the end of November. Thinking of Carol, he half wanted her to be pregnant with his child, one that might be born in late summer, but at the same time he was glad she wasn't. In spite of Carol's deliciousness, his involvement with her radiated bad luck. He would wait for another girl and another year.

During his first week at Camp Kohler, Bill had written letters to Robert Sherwood at the Office of War Information in Washington, to Frank Capra, who was in charge of an army film project, and to George Jean Nathan, pleading to be put where he might serve his country more effectively. Only Eddie Dowling responded to his appeals. Dowling believed he had arranged for Bill's transfer to Robert Breen's unit at Mitchell Field, but Bill saw no evidence of this.

On December 11, Bill heard from Carol in Beverly Hills. She had got off the train in Fresno, she wrote, and on seeing the top of the Hotel Fresno, she had burst into tears and cried the rest of the way to Los Angeles. She wanted to know if he would like her to return to Sacramento for the weekend, suggesting they could drink champagne, hear some music, and kiss a lot. On December 15, he got permission to sleep at the Senator Hotel and was barely settled there when he had a call from Beverly Hills. He told the hotel operator to say he was out and not to call his room before his wake-up call at five in the morning. Carol did reach him to say that she was leaving for New York on Friday and was being pursued by Orson Welles. Bill was relieved that she was in good spirits and not unduly upset on hearing from him that their love affair was finished.

When he was interviewed by a lieutenant from the Signal Corps Unit at Astoria, New York, he guessed he would be sent there, and when his orders arrived, they confirmed it. On the morning of December 18, he boarded a New York–bound troop train in Reno. There were sick and injured soldiers aboard, along with Japanese internees from California. Nevertheless, Bill enjoyed the card games, watching the snow-covered plains of Wyoming and Iowa slide by, and standing between the cars for a breath of the freezing, clear air.

The train arrived in New York's Pennsylvania Station on the evening of December 21. It was twenty minutes after eight, and he took a cab directly to the Barrymore Theatre, on Forty-seventh Street, where Anton Chekhov's *Three Sisters* was opening. He arrived at the theater in time to see Ruth Gordon perform the last moments of the second act and to join the intermission throng.

In the lobby he greeted the critic Howard Barnes, the columnist Leonard Lyons, and his wife, Sylvia. When a voice said "Hello, Bill," he found it was that of his Saroyan Theatre associate David Lowe, and he turned away. But he was pleased to take George Jean Nathan's arm and see the surprise and delight in his face. Julie Haydon was with him, and the three crossed the street for a drink together, Nathan insisting Bill looked better than ever.

Bill returned to Penn Station in time to find the truck that would take his group across the Queensboro Bridge to the Signal Corps base at Astoria in Queens. This was the former Paramount Studio lot at 3511 Thirty-fifth Avenue in Long Island City. It consisted of a large central building that housed the main stage, many adjoining smaller buildings, and open spaces on which formations and drills took place.

Arriving at his new post, Bill was issued bedding and assigned a bunk, in which he slept so soundly that he missed reveille in the morning. This resulted in Bill's first confrontation with a superior, Sergeant Yagalov. Yagalov detected trouble in his new charge, and explained that Bill was in the army now, and rugged individualism was out. The rules must be obeyed.

Bill found many Hollywood acquaintances at the base. He had known and liked Irwin Shaw since their Group Theatre days. Eugene Solow, who had written the screenplay for Steinbeck's *Of Mice and Men,* greeted Bill warmly and spoke of his admiration for Carol. Hunt Stromberg Jr. told of directing *The Beautiful People* at UCLA. Bill thought that George Cukor, the director of such major films as *David Copperfield, Little Women,* and *Camille,* was a likable, overt homosexual who behaved with all the feminineness of a woman.

Assigned to Company D, Bill was subject to classes, a full load of drills, KP, and a six a.m. reveille formation. However, there was no requirement about sleeping on the post, and many soldiers kept their own quarters in the city.

A telegram from Frank Morley requesting his help with *The Human Com-*

edy galleys got him an immediate pass. His first call in New York was at the Matson and Duggan office, where he learned that his book club income would be at least $25,000. With this he would pay off his $8,000 debt to Harcourt and send $10,000 home. Pat Duggan called Frank Case, proprietor of the Algonquin Hotel, and was able to get Bill a suite there. At $155 a month it seemed steep, but he took it and settled in.

Bill picked up the *Human Comedy* galleys, promising Frank Morley that he'd correct and return them by the next day at five. However, as he began to work on them he found himself too depressed to continue. It was the Christmas season, a time that always brought out his loneliness. In search of some cheer he walked the New York streets and found the crowds full of army and navy officers. Passing them, he deliberately turned away so as not to have to salute. In a store on Forty-second Street he bought a garrison cap, liked the way he looked in it, and set out for "21," hoping to find Nathan or Leonard Lyons. They weren't there or at the Stork Club, but both nightclubs were filled with servicemen and their girls having a wonderful time.

When Bill delivered the corrected galleys to Harcourt, Frank Morley presented him with a letter from Henry Seidel Canby, secretary of the National Institute of Arts and Letters, notifying him that he had been elected a member. Bill thought that since Canby was among the Book-of-the-Month Club judges who had made *The Human Comedy* its February choice, he had better accept.

He went on to a party at the theatrical cartoonist Al Hirschfeld's and left it with Dolly Haas (who later became Mrs. Hirschfeld). He took her to the Blue Ribbon restaurant for supper. While dining with her he was overwhelmed with such loneliness that he went to the telephone and called Carol Marcus. Her response was cool. She told him she had returned to New York only yesterday. When asked if she was going out, she said she was, and did not volunteer to change her plans. Even as he told himself that he did not want her, he grew angry that she wasn't eager for him. He wished her a good time, said he had only called because he had promised to, and hung up.

The following day, Christmas Eve, Gloria di Cicco called him at the Algonquin to say that Carol was coming to her house in the country for an overnight visit and urged him to come along. He explained that he must stand reveille in the morning but promised to call her back. Later in the day he called and declined her invitation. Whereupon Carol called, suggesting they go out to Gloria's for supper and return afterward. He agreed, even as he reproached himself for falling back into his previous pattern with Carol.

Carol joined him in the Algonquin lobby, where Bill had been drinking with Nathan, and after some time they decided it was too late to go to Gloria's. They went to his room instead, and, at midnight, to a Mexican restaurant on Forty-seventh Street, where she entertained him with accounts of her beaux. Orson Welles had met her at the station with a gift of jewelry worth $2,000. She had declined it. Clifford Odets was also pursuing her. She had been out the previous evening with Steven Hopkins, the son of Franklin Roosevelt's influential aide Harry Hopkins. With his Washington connections, she felt that "Stevie" would be president some day.

On Christmas morning, Bill stood reveille in Astoria, and although he had had only four hours of sleep he felt strangely charged with seasonal joy. He returned to the city at once and phoned Carol. She agreed to come and visit him as soon as she had looked at her presents.

At ten-thirty she arrived at his room with a gift. It was a picture of herself on gold metal encased in leather. On its back was written, "I love you darling." He was doubtful of the sentiment, but still thought it was beautiful.

On the day after Christmas, Carol came with him to the Algonquin, where they made love and she sang him Christmas carols. Bill rejoiced in all the holiday pleasures. He could not help loving and feeling happy to see Carol—and, he thought, to hell with any good reasons. A day later, as Carol was leaving his room at the Algonquin, he told her that if she ever went out with Stevie Hopkins or anybody else, he would never see her again. But he promptly reversed himself, deciding that if they really did love each other it might be fine for her to see other men occasionally.

When he called Carol on December 30, she told him she had a date with Stevie Hopkins. He angrily told her to get out of it, to never mention the matter again, and to come to him immediately. She did just that.

On New Year's Eve, he set out to welcome 1943 properly. The Marcuses were giving a party in their apartment at 420 Park Avenue, and he began there, sharing a bottle of champagne with Carol and her mother. Promising to return for Carol he went on to Billy Rose's house, at 33 Beekman Place, where a phalanx of Broadway's aristocracy had assembled. With Carol he shuttled between the two parties until dawn, when he said a loving good-bye.

Although he was enjoying all this high life in New York, with its plentiful drink, food, and beautiful girls, he still felt keenly the "outrage" the army had inflicted on him. This was in part the loss of his freedom, but it was equally a stubborn belief that he was surrounded by inferiors. He resolved to endure the ordeal but to write a hard, tough account of it. He would call it "Captured by the Americans."

In the new year he was ordered to take a course in map reading at the army building on Twenty-third Street. He thought his instructor was good, but the information was of no use to him. The classroom experience recalled school days that had alienated him so much that he had quit formal education for good. He dozed throughout the cartography lectures, and when questioned about longitude and latitude, he replied that he had forgotten what they were. He scored 30 on the first test, the lowest of the forty-five privates in his class. He assured himself that he was getting some great ideas for a play.

At the post he quarreled with the barracks orderly, who addressed him with an ironic "Billy Boy," and shunned Sergeant Yagalov's good-natured jibes at him. When he skipped drill because of not feeling well, he was gigged for deliberate disobedience and confined to quarters. George Cukor told him that, without intending to, he challenged people, and no doubt this was why he had had trouble during basic. Bill agreed with him but saw no way to behave otherwise.

The scenario department assigned Bill to revising a script about AWOL and desertion. When team efforts failed to improve it, he volunteered to do the job alone. He turned out a script that reasoned that the act of desertion was bound to prolong the war and so delay going home. When his superiors saw the Saroyan script, their decision was unanimous—it would not do.

One obvious reason for Bill's lackluster performance as a soldier was the New York nightlife. He was sleeping for only a few predawn hours each night, and it showed in new lines under his eyes and an alcoholic flabbiness of jowl. In spite of chronic daytime fatigue, nightfall brought forth a will to enjoy the world.

One morning he woke at six after only three hours of sleep and, realizing he should already be on his way to Astoria, called Sergeant Yagalov to say he was too sick to attend reveille. Yagalov denied this, and, by ignoring him, Bill began a flagrant rebellion against the army. At nine-thirty he was awakened by a captain who said that a medical officer would visit him presently. Irwin Shaw telephoned to warn him about flouting roll calls and to be sure there was no girl in his room when the army doctor arrived. No doctor appeared, but he was told to report to the army infirmary at 39 Whitehall Street.

Bill's commanding officer, Colonel Gillette, was aware of his transgressions and particularly nettled by *Look* magazine's interest in a picture story on Saroyan in the army. When he summoned Bill to his office and explained that publicizing him was not felt to be in the national interest, the colonel kept him at attention. This, more than denying him *Look*'s exposure, annoyed Bill and inflamed his insurgency.

The colonel suggested that Bill apply for officer's training. Bill, recoiling from the likelihood of further classrooms and tests, replied that he wouldn't be an effective officer. His private thought was that if the army wanted him

to be an officer, they had better commission him one, preferably a general—
with four stars.

Meanwhile, his involvement with Carol was deepening. Once, while
describing the writing process to her, he suggested that she write a short
book for kids, and she began at once. When she brought him the first three
chapters, he was surprised to find some segments were wonderful, and he
gave the whole his guarded approval.

Bill was quick to jealousy. He was furious to learn that while they had sat
together at Nathan's table in "21," the author John Gunther had confided to
her that when Bill left her, *he'd* be waiting.

Carol awaited his summons each evening but feared that he meant it
when he threatened not to see her again. She was often sad now when they
were together. They would go downtown to the Village Vanguard for jazz
and Leadbelly's songs or to 160 Allen Street for Turkish and Armenian
music. They would end up at the Cub Room of the Stork Club, where Sherman Billingsley might send over favors of perfume and champagne. At
evening's end they usually quarreled. Her repeated whispering of "Do you
love me?" annoyed him, and he would be unkind. Carol would leave and
get into a cab, only to pick Bill up as he walked toward the Algonquin, and
return there with him.

Toward the end of January, Carol gave a cocktail party for Gloria Vanderbilt. Shortly after arriving, Bill was infuriated by Pat di Cicco, who
hoisted Carol in his arms, holding her aloft for a full minute. Bill got drunk
and went on the make for any girl who caught his eye. He had taken one of
these into Rosheen's enormous bathroom, where he was surprised by
Rosheen herself. She had opened the door to ask what he was up to—and to
put an end to it.

Late in the evening, Carol confided to Bill that she had been to a doctor
that afternoon, and he had confirmed her suspicion: she was pregnant. Bill
accepted the news and continued to drink. Carol's sister Elinor told him he
looked a wreck. Peggy Fairchild demanded to know if he had been seeing
Jean Dalrymple, whom he had met at her house. Although Bill denied it, he
felt sure she knew he was lying. However, he felt remorse over the possibility of hurting Carol in this way. He decided that if she were really pregnant,
he would marry her. He knew she was a rare girl.

When Bill left the party, at two-thirty in the morning, he was very
drunk. Although aware he had offended the Marcuses and Carol was furious with him, he excused himself with the thought that this was simply the
way he was.

At Astoria, Bill heard a rumor that because of his name appearing so frequently in the gossip columns he would soon be shipped to Wright Field in

Ohio. He did not want to go to Ohio under any circumstances, but certainly not with *The Human Comedy*'s debut imminent. The book's publication was just two weeks off, and the movie would open at the Astor Theatre, on Broadway, a week later, on March 3.

The dreaded orders for Wright Field arrived. He would be leaving on February 15. When he inquired, he was told that although the newspaper publicity he had been getting was bad for any soldier, it was allegedly not the cause of his transfer. The commanding officer in Dayton had wanted some "name" writers, and Saroyan was being supplied. In any case, the whole scenario department at Astoria would soon be dissolved, and all able-bodied men would be going to combat duty. Bill was sure that Wright Field was punishment for the publicity he had been getting, but there was nothing to do but accept it.

He felt a similar resignation toward marriage. He knew Carol was his one and only, and that living with her, waiting for the child to be born, was probably the best thing he could do. They had had a lot of fun together, and she was pregnant.

It was settled. Although he was thirty-four and Carol only eighteen, he was going to marry her. Carol was good for him. Occasionally he doubted she was pregnant, for he knew she imagined things and then believed them to be true. But he accepted that the baby was due in October. If it was a boy he would name him Aram. If a girl, maybe Lucy.

He recalled that according to Carol, her real father was Henry Stuart, an Englishman in his late thirties, who was very tall, very rich, and a Don Juan; Carol had never liked him, nor had he liked her, preferring her sister Elinor. Carol had described her mother as Russian and French, but Bill felt Russian and Jewish would be more accurate. That too was acceptable. Carol resembled her mother but was more beguiling. Her hands were a pleasure, her eyes joyful, her speech sweet, and she had a perfect instinct for comedy. No woman had ever pleased him more. She was happy about having his child. He doubted anyone could be more honest and true, and believed she really loved him, missed him when he was not near, was happy when he was.

They were born under the same astrological sign, Virgo. He was jealous when any man looked at her, but he had to accept it, for she always drew attention. She was not a perfect beauty, but her head was well shaped, her mouth large and captivating—a mouth of love. Her teeth were crooked, and she wore braces for straightening them, which delighted him too. Her hair was a heavenly gold. He resolved to be better to her than any other man could be.

It pained him to realize he had done no new work since joining the army. Nevertheless, his literary luck was running as never before. On February 13, when he called on Frank Morley at Harcourt, he learned that the Book-of-the-Month Club distribution of *The Human Comedy* would be 342,000 copies, bringing in $60,000, half of which would be his. The Harcourt first edition would be 50,000 copies, and it was already a "runaway" seller. A single shop in Boston had ordered a thousand copies.

He could pay all his debts, his 1942 taxes, and have plenty left over. He told Morley that his next book for Harcourt would be the three plays, *A Decent Birth, Get Away Old Man,* and *Jim Dandy.* He would provide a general introduction and some notes to go with each play about its origin. Then he would turn to the short-story collection *Elegie,* editing those stories he had already turned in and adding one or two more. He reassured the anxious Morley that he would not press for immediate publication of either the play or story collection, and, moreover, that while any publisher would be glad to have him, he would be staying with Harcourt indefinitely.

He had good reason to believe that three of his plays would be produced shortly. Gilbert Miller and Fefe Ferry were negotiating for *A Decent Birth.* The National Theatre Conference was planning to do *Afton Water.* Also, he was newly confident of a Broadway production of *Get Away Old Man.* Over a table at the Stork Club he had described the play to the producer Mike Todd. Within a day, Todd had read it and proposed they produce it together on a fifty-fifty basis.

Carol had come with Bill to Todd's Alvin Theatre office, and there the agreement was confirmed, with Mike Todd's check for a thousand dollars. They went on to celebrate at Lindy's, where Bill's satisfaction was marred by noticing that Todd was hugging Carol and that she seemed to be loving it.

In the Marcus apartment at 420 Park Avenue, Bill and Carol's marriage was no longer in doubt, but the date remained uncertain. Rosheen believed she could arrange for him to stay on in New York, and Bill urged her to do so, while Carol expressed doubt that her mother had any influence with the army.

On Saturday night, February 13, with Bill's departure for Ohio set for the following Monday morning, Carol was newly anxious and urged Bill to marry her that night. Rosheen suggested that Judge Ferdinand Pecora, a family friend, would marry them immediately. Bill called Judge Pecora, asking if he would do so. Pecora explained that Bill must first provide a license and a blood test for both parties. If the wedding had to wait for the following week, Bill would work out these preliminaries on arriving in Dayton. Carol could follow him within a day or two, and they would be married there.

Bill reached Dayton on February 15 to find the hotels full and offering no hope of accommodations for himself or Carol. He reported to Wright Field,

Bride and groom. Carol and Bill were married in Columbus,
Ohio, February 20, 1943.

some twenty miles outside the city. Here he was given a bunk and the
immediate task of mopping the dayroom floor. When he protested that he
would not be effective in writing training-film scenarios, he was assigned to
revising "Project 1052: Physical Training for Aviation Cadets."

Carol and her mother arrived in Dayton on February 18 and found a
room at the Biltmore. Bill met them there after retreat, explaining that he
had not felt well, and while he had finally found himself a room at the Van
Cleve, he had as yet made no marriage arrangements. He would do so the
next day.

On Saturday, February 20, a doctor came to Bill's room. In spite of
Carol's screams at the blood-test needle, the necessary preliminaries were
soon completed.

Carol, wary of further delays, found a lawyer who set to work, getting a waiver of the five-day waiting period and overcoming the city clerk's objections that, since Carol was under twenty-one, the consent of both parents was needed.

The bridal couple quarreled, and Bill had another attack of doubts. He deplored the time Carol spent looking into the mirror and her smart-alecky responses to imagined hurts by him, but, generally speaking, she was a delight, very young, good to have at hand, and good to love. Doubts were swept aside. At city hall, Bill paid two dollars for a license, and the ceremony took place at nine-thirty that evening in the lawyer's office. A Judge Edwards presided, and Rosheen was the couple's only attendant.

At Judge Edwards's suggestion, Bill held Carol's hand during the ceremony. When this and the ensuing tension came to an end, he kissed her twice, very gently. Rosheen, who had offered her own wedding ring, wondered why it had not been used. Judge Edwards explained he had read a service that omitted the ring, whereupon Bill put the ring on Carol's finger and kissed her again.

During a long wait for the elevator, Bill kissed Rosheen on the cheek. When at last the elevator arrived, the black operator explained that the vacuum cleaner had been making so much noise he had not heard the bell. They all laughed. In the street, Bill saluted four officers, in a burst of charitable feeling.

On the morning after his wedding night, reading the Dayton Sunday papers, Bill decided that the only difference between being married and not lay in being constantly closer together. He felt this called for an understanding. He not only liked solitude, he *needed* it.

He had begun work on the cadet training scenario, prefacing it with the theory that one's natural inclination is to despise calisthenics but the benefits accrue nonetheless. Since aviation cadets were poetic men, eager to get high in the air, drop objects from great heights, and watch what happens, he felt they might find some pleasure in the physical cavorting.

A few days after submitting the introduction and six-page scenario, Bill was snoozing at his desk when he was awakened by his project officer, Major Warlow, and the unit commander. A befuddled Bill was told by the latter that he had enjoyed reading his script and found his "philosophy" interesting, but what he had written was not right for the army's purposes. Bill agreed and promised to get to work on a revision.

However, he found the revising tough. Every morning his creative will was paralyzed. He knew he was not a lazy writer. But he sat at this scenario all day, and at the end he had only a few foolish notes that he knew were useless. He was ashamed of his failure, but he couldn't help it. Exhausted by army routine, all he wanted to do was sleep. He promised Major Warlow he would complete the scenario in two or three days. When he finally delivered the finished script, he realized that the job—which he normally would have accomplished in a few hours—had taken him nearly a month.

When Bill reminded his command that his duty here was temporary, and that he had been assured of a return to New York at the end of a month, he was told that he would be staying at Wright Field indefinitely. This was disheartening news, but he hoped the imminent celebrations of *The Human Comedy* would change all this.

The novel was published on February 25, and the loyal Lewis Gannett praised it in the daily *Herald Tribune,* while in the Sunday edition Bennett Cerf announced that Nathan had been right—if there was anyone remotely resembling a genius in American letters, his name was Saroyan. In the Sunday *Times,* Wallace Stegner called Saroyan a complete romantic whose "conviction that love conquers all makes him difficult to argue with. One can only disagree." Bill had a congratulatory telegram from Irwin Shaw and a letter from the Yale pundit William Lyon Phelps, calling the book a masterpiece.

In *Time,* James Agee described Saroyan's limitation as "chronic ecstasy," which might afford a clear view of God but would show very little of "the devil and the man caught in the middle." The skeptical reviews depressed Bill considerably. Here, at the summit of his success with *The Human Comedy,* they were still getting at him for falseness. Agee's charge of "chronic ecstasy" was similar to Stegner's mocking his belief that "love conquers all." There was a powerful contradiction at the core of it. Selfless love of his fellow man, woman, and country was strange, dangerous behavior in the real world of Bill Saroyan. Yet in the world of his imagination, the love that had eluded him became a miraculous elixir—the cure for all ills but his own.

The advance reviews of the movie in both *Variety* and the *Hollywood Reporter* were enthusiastic, and Bill received a congratulatory telegram from Louis B. Mayer, whom he continued to regard as "the con."

In the midst of this heady news Bill found he was up for KP duty, six hours of dishwashing. An Armenian fellow soldier advised him, in Armenian, to do the work and conceal his resentment, which would only invite more trouble. In the end, his comrade took over the job and refused Bill's offer to pay him for it.

His arranging to have mail brought to him rather than waiting for it at mail call led to a quarrel with the mail-room orderly, who accused him of wanting special privileges. This caused him to reflect on what Cukor had told him, how he challenged people, made them feel his sense of superiority and contempt for them. He exuded arrogance and impatience with the rules. It seemed to others that he did what he pleased and got what he wanted. Bill admitted that a part of this was true, and he had no regret about it.

Although he tried to undertake some new work, he found he couldn't even think about it. The February weather was bleak. Snow covered the Ohio hills. The sky was dark, and he felt a matching despair he had not experienced since coming east. He had lost the cockiness that he knew was essential to his survival. With the fun knocked out of him, he felt hushed and useless.

On February 26, with the $1,500 balance of Bill's advance payment overdue, Mike Todd telephoned to say he was proceeding with plans to produce *Get Away Old Man,* and would come to Dayton to discuss them. Over dinner he told Bill and Carol that he was on his way to Hollywood, where he hoped to persuade Orson Welles to direct the play. He had many ideas for improving it, and Bill just needed to decide on them. Bill arranged a pass and turned up at Mike Todd's room, where several stenographers stood by for dictation.

What Todd had to say about *Get Away Old Man* struck Bill as critical of his play and too "creative." He wanted a producer, not a collaborator. Instead of revisions he was thinking of Carol alone at the Van Cleve and Todd's visit as having no purpose beyond spoiling his pass. Bored and irritable, he told Todd he couldn't work this way and left him, still expecting a contract and the balance of the advance for his play.

A week later he turned the Mike Todd deal over to Hal Matson, telling him that it was not yet off, but might be very soon. He had refused Todd's recent call and would not be able to do much rewriting of the play.

For some months he had been ignoring Stanley Rose and urging Carol not to respond to Stanley's letters to her. On receiving a hurt, though congratulatory, telegram from his old Hollywood pal, Bill dismissed it as self-serving. With the movie released, he thought Stanley was after more easy money.

Bill and Carol were affectionate, and he was teaching her some Armenian phrases. She proved a quick study, learning to say "My name is Carol" and "How are you?" She was particularly taken with the Armenian equivalent of "What's up?" "*Eench ga, chi ga?*" (What is, is not?) Thus, when Bill telephoned home to make the official announcement of his marriage and put Carol on to speak to his mother, Carol was able to ask, "*Eench ga, chi ga?*" Takoohi, as always, urged Bill to send home some money, to which he agreed, and when they spoke of Henry's baby, she added perceptively, "*Dahr-rohss ver-aht*"—You next.

Bill strongly felt that the drama in which he was the hero was taking place without him. A photograph of Scribner's Fifth Avenue window showed it piled with copies of *The Human Comedy* grouped around Don Freeman's portrait of the author and a sign proclaiming the book to be "The most hatred-hating and heart-warming book of an epoch." Also, a huge lighted sign over the Astor Theatre, on Broadway, proclaimed the arrival of *The Human Comedy* in incandescent white, alternating with a red cursive SAROYAN'S.

He wrote Pat Duggan that these promotional spectacles were of primary importance. He urged Duggan to make a Sam Goldwyn deal for *My Name Is Aram*, explaining that the stories could be woven into a pattern rather than a plot, ending in Aram's arrival in New York.

Although the advance reviews of the motion picture were favorable, they made him feel he had failed, for what they praised bore little resemblance to what he had written. Some of his favorite incidents—Homer's dream of trying to keep the angel of death from reaching Ithaca, Ulysses in the trap and Ulysses at church, dreaming during the singing of "Rock of Ages"—had been cut, and he suspected that Howard Estabrook's screenplay and Clarence Brown's direction had distorted his story.

A print of *The Human Comedy*, which would be shown to Columbus audiences, arrived, and Bill arranged to see it in the Wright Field projection room. He arrived at the appointed hour of two-thirty, but there was an hour's wait while the commanding officer explained why he would remain at this base.

At three-thirty Bill saw one twenty-minute reel, then was moved to another projection room to view the second, then back to the first to see the balance of it. As he watched, he wept frequently. He wanted a cigarette in the worst way but was out of them. When it was over, he walked out of the building in a daze and down to the highway, where he hitchhiked to Dayton.

Arriving at the Van Cleve he told a sympathetic Carol that he was miserable. He got into a warm bath while she ordered room service. Later, in bed, he told her he felt betrayed and unable to fight back, to oppose the awful distortion of truth he had just seen. In the night he tossed and turned restlessly, mumbling to himself and getting up to pace.

He decided that he did not like the picture at all. That others did like it was frightening to him. He thought it a miscarriage, an abomination among all films ever made. He would telegraph this to Mayer. He thought Estabrook was not just an incompetent fool but a crook. Were it not for his family and Carol, he would now defy all the forces of corruption, not just MGM but the army and the U.S. government as well.

The worst of it was that although the picture was a display of falsity, it was very moving, and was likely to be a big financial success and to deceive its audiences. They had made his screenplay into sleazy propaganda that sought to persuade Americans to accept the loss of their sons in this war. It was an outrage to its author.

While still in this beleaguered frame of mind, he had a surprising encounter with an old girlfriend. Trying to find a place at Wright Field that would serve him a late lunch, he stood in line in a giant mess hall for civilian employees and heard his name called gently. He turned to find Pat Winter smiling at him. His first impression was of a face that had aged tragically and wore a mask of rouge. Then, as he recognized the woman he had loved so tenderly, he saw her old loyalty as intact, but it had become a quality he regarded as combined courage and stupidity.

She introduced him to her friend Norma, and when he asked Pat what she was doing there, she replied that she was making moving pictures. He suspected this was less than the truth, and when she asked what he was doing there he replied that he was trying to find some lunch. Pat told him that he had to stand in line, to which he replied that he did not and stepped out of it. He paused long enough to ask how long she had been here and to learn that it had been since Christmas. With a "So long," he headed for the street.

On March 18, while trying to adjust to the crushing news that he would be spending another month at Wright Field, he was told of a change in the army's plans. He would be returned to New York at once. The following day, he and Carol joyfully boarded the 3:50 train for New York, and then moved into the Marcus apartment on Park Avenue.

They soon learned that there was marital trouble between the Marcuses and Rosheen was considering a divorce. Rosheen and Elinor were in Florida. Charles, who was leaving for California, welcomed them and urged them to stay as long as they wanted to.

VIII

HOME FRONT

1943–1944

Rosheen Marcus's return to New York sent the newlyweds in search of a place of their own. On March 23, they moved into an apartment at the Lombardy Hotel, on East Fifty-sixth Street. There Bill rose each morning at a quarter to five and took a cab across the Fifty-ninth Street Bridge, a twelve-minute, seventy-five-cent ride, to his post, the Signal Corps Photographic Center in Astoria. He stood reveille at six, then walked three blocks to Pop Alper's restaurant for breakfast and a reading of the papers. He gave particular attention to the obituary page, the racing results, the gossip columns, the editorial page, and pictures of the raging war.

At seven he entered the building where film scenarios were produced and followed his instructions for the day. At a quarter to four he stood a second formation and marched for forty-five minutes, sometimes shouting in cadence. At half past five he was dismissed and took the subway home. Back at the Lombardy he shed his uniform, looked over the hotel bill of fare, and, while Carol ordered up their meal, relaxed with a book. In her pregnancy Carol seemed especially pretty, and she delighted him, making him laugh a lot. Whenever they were about to have a quarrel, she would try to prevent it by saying, "Dear Miss Blake . . . ," presenting their difference to an imaginary counselor.

Bill's next military difficulty arose from an item that appeared in *Newsweek* reporting that he was at work on a training film about going AWOL. The post command saw it as a breach of security, and Bill was summoned to the office of a Colonel Presnell for reprimand. To forestall this unpleasantness, Bill began to describe a plan to make a movie about Hitler. Presnell replied that he should feel free to offer the Hitler idea to the Office of War Information, the agency that dealt with such projects, but that the work of the Signal Corps was making training films.

Bill acknowledged the colonel's warning about careless military remarks, and then asked what plans the Signal Corps had for him. Would he stay on in New York, and should he rent an apartment here?

Presnell thought he should. When Bill complained about KP duty, the colonel expressed surprise that Bill had ignored Colonel Gillette's advice to apply for officer's training. He had been given the application forms and should put them to use. Meanwhile, Presnell would see about getting Bill into Company A, where he would be exempt from KP.

The next day, Bill was again assigned to KP and had to rise before four o'clock in order to report to the mess-hall kitchen by 5:15. Here he was assigned to the cleaning of pots and pans and worked at it until late in the day, when he found a substitute. He arrived back at the Lombardy with hands that reeked of grease.

The following morning, he woke with sacroiliac pain so bad that he could barely stand. Arriving at the post he called at the medical office, where a Captain Davolos playfully accused him of gold-bricking but gave him some pills that lessened the pain and agreed he should go home.

Back at the Lombardy he had an unexpected visit from fellow scenarists Gottfried Reinhardt and Irwin Shaw. Reinhardt explained that he brought a confidential message from Colonel Presnell. Bill was not wanted at the Signal Corps in New York. Someone high up, maybe Gillette, had decided. Bill should apply for officer's training in military intelligence without delay. Although this raised further classroom specters, Bill agreed to do it. The application that he had found tough to fill out was somewhere in the apartment. Reinhardt, who lived at the nearby Gladstone, urged him to bring the form along to the hotel bar at six-thirty. He would help him complete it.

While Carol searched in vain for the application form, Bill sank lower in spirit. He decided that since the army knew who he was, he would let it send him wherever it pleased. He telephoned Gottfried Reinhardt and cancelled their meeting.

The following morning his back pain was worse, and he called Company D, leaving a message that he was sick at home. At ten, Sergeant Yagalov called to say he could not simply stay at home; he had to report to the base or go to an army hospital. Bill replied that he was too sick to get up but was persuaded to report to the army medical office at 39 Whitehall Street early the next day.

In preparation, Bill prepared a letter saying that after five months of trying, he could no longer perform as a private in the army. He could not sleep, and his nervous system was on the verge of collapse.

When he presented himself at the army's medical headquarters on Whitehall Street, an army doctor questioned him about his back pain and gave him a thorough physical examination. The doctor accepted Bill's letter, read it carefully, prescribed some pills, and told him to return on Monday. When he did so, a corpsman advised that the staff neurologist would see him and tell him if anything was the matter with him. He would tell him plenty if there wasn't.

Captain Benjamin Simon was a small man with a round, fat face. Simon urged Bill to dispense with military formalities and tell him from the beginning what seemed to be the matter.

In the belief that he had at last found his man, Bill told him his complaints. Whereupon Captain Simon agreed that he did not belong in the army, that it was probably impossible to adjust his personality to it—but in fact he *was* in the army, and so must proceed according to its rules. He felt that Bill had displayed a marked lack of sympathy and understanding for others and should have made a more dynamic effort to improve his attitude toward the army.

Bill's response was that the army had denied him the recognition to which his work entitled him. He dramatized this perceived injustice in an outburst of hysteria. Simon was unmoved by Bill's display and told him he could write the adjutant general requesting a transfer to Special Services, but this might result in a less than honorable discharge. Bill said that would be acceptable to him.

Other possibilities for escape presented themselves. Hal Matson had arranged an interview with the OWI and another with *Yank,* but neither was of help. Charles Marcus, who had friends at the Pentagon, got Bill an interview with the ranking Signal Corps officers in Washington.

Bill went to the capital on April 1, believing that rescue was at hand. Major General Colton of the Signal Corps, a man Charles Marcus had described as a good guy with a wonderful sense of humor, received him cordially and took him along to the office of Brigadier General Code. Also present was Colonel Darryl F. Zanuck, founder of Twentieth Century–Fox, who greeted Bill warmly.

Colton got the meeting underway by saying that his wife thought Saroyan was a pretty good writer, which made him not so sure. Bill recognized this as clubbable banter—a style established by the chief executive himself—with which Washington abounded, but he was still resentful of it.

General Code showed an understanding of Bill's problem, saying it was plain that Saroyan would be most useful out of the army altogether, but he didn't see any way that could be done. Bill was offended when Code continued Colton's heavy joshing, saying he had heard that Saroyan was the greatest writer in the world. Bill looked at Zanuck, sure he had volunteered the idea, but did not reply, even when Code asked if that were not the case.

Bill was suddenly weary, and furious. He spoke loudly, disrupting the serenity of military authority, alarming both generals while Zanuck tried to intercede. General Code lapsed into a brooding silence, making it clear he wanted an end to the interview. As he said some final words about the Saroyan "genius," Bill cut him short. Grasping the general's hand, he looked him in the eye and said abruptly that he was most grateful for the man's kindness. Without waiting for Code's reply, he strode out of the office.

Bill Saroyan simply couldn't handle the idea of rank. The Pentagon generals had greeted him with good-natured kidding, intending to be comradely. Even though this implied equality, it seemed to belittle Bill's writer's reputation and so was unacceptable to his four-star literary self-importance. Considering them his inferiors, he could accept neither their humor nor their charity. He returned to New York angry at having put up with them.

When Bill showed George Cukor a letter he had written the adjutant general requesting transfer, Cukor cautioned him against sending it and urged him to call on the sympathetic Colonel Munson instead. When he did so, Bill was pleased by the news. Munson told him to keep it under his hat, but in fact the Signal Corps was going to make him an officer and send him to Capra's unit in Hollywood.

But on April 14, he found he could not get out of bed in time for reveille and again telephoned the post to say he was sick. At eight, Yagalov called him at the Lombardy to ask how sick he was. Bill replied that he was too sick to come now but would turn up later.

He now went to Captain Simon on Whitehall Street and told him that his sickness could not be cured by either medicine or psychiatry, because it was army life itself that made him sick. Simon said that he had discussed Bill's case with his superior and found three possible courses of action.

As a psychiatrist, he could present the case to the army that Bill was unable to adapt and was likely to break down. To army men, he explained, this would be an admission of weakness and likely held against him thereafter. He should consider that danger. A second course would be patience; he could await the promised commission. A third option would be to write the adjutant general requesting a transfer, but again, this might leave him worse off.

Bill said he was desperate enough to think of deserting. Simon told him that would be unwise and was relieved by Bill's suggestion that if he had a week's leave, he could get straightened out. Simon agreed to arrange it.

While Bill was downtown, the Signal Corps had been searching for him at the Lombardy. Carol had refused the army calls and told the Lombardy's switchboard operator to say there was a "Do Not Disturb" notice on the apartment's door. Yagalov insisted that whatever signs were on his door, Saroyan should be notified that the army wanted him to answer his phone. Carol fled the apartment before any officials arrived.

When Bill called Astoria the next morning, he tried to explain to his company commander that he was on sick leave and confined to his present quarters, but he was told by this officer that he was not on sick leave but AWOL.

Back at 39 Whitehall Street, Bill persuaded the medical corps to intercede. Captain Simon agreed to telephone the Astoria command on his behalf. He did arrange the furlough, but first Bill had to return to duty. Simon's last cordial suggestion was that he ask for two weeks while he was at it and to drink up some of that sunshine for him.

On May 3, Bill turned to the writing of a series of letters addressed to his arriving son, Aram. Aram would be his own second chance, just as as he had been *his* father's. He called the series *The Merry Mad Month of May*, and he set out to tell Aram about his current life. He described his present sense of illness, how he had found himself shouting at an army psychiatrist and sometimes thought he was going crazy and didn't want to. He was not ashamed of his son knowing this. He would tell his son more about his temporary madness.

He recalled a first sickness in the hospital room at the Fred Finch orphanage. He was five. It was a Sunday, and the smell of apple blossoms and the sound of the church bells came through the window, and he had a glimpse of the other children marching off to Sunday school. Until that moment he had not been aware that he would die and be denied these sweet sensations. He vowed that once he was well he would live fully, and miss nothing. Thirty years later and sick again, he felt the same way.

He told Aram that he smoked three packages of cigarettes a day, and as a result made a terrible noise hawking and spitting; that he was restless but not, as many believed, rude and conceited. He laughed loudly and wildly, like a fool, but he was a sad man and laughed because he did not want to weep. He did not believe, as Thomas Wolfe did, in schools. If you knew the alphabet, if you knew how to talk, if you understood punctuation, what would you want from a college? Some of his critics had laughed at his intelligence, but they were only confused by his earnestness, and the way in which he innately knew things.

But he felt he *was* the great writer of his day. There was no one bigger or nobler in the world, while in this war his inferiors had been made officers. They were clever but lacked decency and truth as they rushed around like heroes. As he reflected on his impending fatherhood he recalled how Molnár's Liliom had been jubilant at the prospect. He felt no such thing. He felt concern and a sense of responsibility about it, but also confusion. He wondered how it would be if some girl other than Carol were bearing his child.

At home there was growing stress. When Carol complained that she stayed in all day waiting for him and needed an occasional lunch out with a

Bill and an expectant Carol in New York, 1943

girlfriend, they quarreled. When Carol playfully tried to lock him into his closet, Bill reacted by threatening to come out and kill her, and her bitter response ended in a threat to go home to her mother. When, waiting in line for a movie, Carol took longer than he thought necessary to buy some candy, he was furious with her. He was irked by her extravagance in clothes. Fury and sulks became daily episodes, but Carol was always ready to apologize for pinching him and talking while he was trying to read, and they made up promptly.

On May 6 he was assigned to the public relations office to work for the "film magazine," the *War*. He looked forward to his first task, narration for a film about the role of union labor in the war effort. Two days later he received the long-awaited transfer to Company A and rejoiced in a 7:45 roll call, and a lessening of GI duties and the dreaded KP.

Bill was in demand among the many Armenian organizations selling war bonds. When he appeared at a rally in New York, the applause would not stop. He managed only a few words in Armenian, saying he was not a speaker. Whereupon a man cried out, "You are a writer!" There was more thunderous applause, and he was mobbed by women and children wanting autographs. In late May he was given a five-day furlough to go to an Armenian war bond rally in Chicago. Wearing a tailor-made Palm Beach uniform, he sat before a large audience and suffered violin solos and many long speeches before he rose to read the short talk he had prepared.

Although he and Carol were honored at an Armenian party in Evanston and given a hero's welcome, Bill was annoyed by the small $250 honorarium. Having spent that much already, he complained about the agonizing travel and the inevitable rooking by the Armenian organizers of such events.

At the end of May, Carol found an attractive apartment at Two Sutton Place South. It was a fine building, at Fifty-seventh Street and the East River. There was a spacious living room, a terrace with a splendid view of the river, two bedrooms, each with a bath, and a compact kitchen. Bill liked it at once, and Carol signed a two-year lease at $250 a month.

But a quarrel began over the furnishing. When Carol announced she would need $3,000 to furnish the place, Bill protested, and he complained further when she revealed that Charles Marcus would put $2,000 into the furnishing fund as a wedding gift. As she defended her ability as decorator, Carol repeatedly looked at herself in a hand mirror, and when Bill asked her why she did this, she told him it was because she liked to.

Bill proposed that she go home for a couple of weeks, and then amended this, proposing she go home for good. Whereupon Carol donned her coat and left, saying she would send for her stuff in the morning. However, she soon called from a drugstore and returned to the Lombardy, where within a few days peace was restored.

She did write him a letter saying she had thought, mistakenly, that furnishing the apartment would be a source of pleasure for them both. Her father's gift would not have been any reflection on Bill's ability to provide for her. She felt that his pride was overwhelming their loving relationship and they must straighten that out.

From that moment, the furnishing of the apartment did become a shared pleasure. With the help of a decorator named Bournetrotter, Carol visited the shops and fabric houses, and although the bills soon stood at $4,000 Bill rejoiced in the progress and took comfort from the thought that he usually lost $10,000 a year gambling and now felt he was permanently cured of it.

They moved into the apartment on June 25 and enjoyed a first supper under the terrace's red-and-white-striped awning, watching the river traffic and hearing its beguiling sounds. Bill was pleased with his stylish, leather-topped desk, bought an exercise bike, and, with Don Freeman's guidance, went shopping for Renoir prints.

He also wrote his mother, suggesting that she and Cosette come east to stay with them for the birth of his child. He would send them the money, and they should plan on traveling in a bedroom on a good train.

With *The Human Comedy* film playing on screens across the country and the book comfortably seated on the best-seller lists, the name Saroyan was hot. No one knew this better than Bill—except, perhaps, Harold Matson. In spite of a chronic resentment of Matson, and a resolve to make his brother Henry his agent, Bill called regularly at Matson's new offices at 30 Rockefeller Plaza.

They expected Harcourt's book sales to earn $100,000 in royalties. Looking ahead, Bill made no secret of his intention to exclude Matson from future Harcourt contracts. Matson objected, but he withheld no effort on Bill's behalf. He had good news about *Get Away Old Man:* Mike Todd had given him a check for $2,500 and was ready to produce the play.

A few days later, when Matson reported that Todd wanted the revisions he had discussed with Bill in Dayton, Bill refused, proposing to return Todd's money. Matson was reluctant to do so and persuaded George Jean Nathan to intercede. Nathan met with Todd that very night and reported that everything Todd had in mind for the play was typically Saroyan, and he approved it. Matson told Bill that he was going ahead with the deal.

While Bill did not object to Matson's rescue efforts, he was not surprised to learn that Todd had lost interest in the play. In fact, he was pleased. He felt that the play's skewering of Hollywood made it a sure Broadway success. Matson now interested Michael Meyerberg, who had just produced Thornton Wilder's *Skin of Our Teeth,* in the play. When Bill called on him, the producer told him he wanted Fredric March to play Hammer, the studio boss, and Clifford Odets to play the writer, Harry Bird. Elia Kazan, presumably Meyerberg's choice for director, joined them to discuss further casting ideas. Bill had known Kazan since Group Theatre days, felt his aloofness, and recalled hearing that "Gadge" had read, and not liked, the play.

When Meyerberg said that he would be unable to produce *Get Away Old Man* until November, Bill pointed out that this was many months off and perhaps he oughtn't do it at all. In the end, Meyerberg agreed. The resourceful Hal Matson next interested the Theatre Guild in the play. The Guild made a $1,250 advance payment, but soon followed the previous producers in losing heart.

Now the dauntless Matson called with the news that George Abbott was enthusiastic about doing it. Bill met the producer in his office at 630 Fifth Avenue on July 1. Abbott was a tall, swift-moving, intense man of close to fifty. He was slightly red-faced, undoubtedly Irish, with a taste for colored shirts and an apparent understanding of the theater. Abbott began by saying that he liked *Get Away Old Man* and would do it in any case but hoped, for Bill's own sake, he would not demand such stiff terms as Matson was asking.

Bill was inflexible, and Abbott agreed to a $2,500 advance and a royalty scale more generous than he had ever granted.

Hal Matson was tireless in enhancing Bill's prospects. During the summer he brought him news of a $75,000 offer for film rights to *My Name Is Aram.* Bill told Matson to ask for twice that, or more. Matson also had what he described as "a warm deal" for movie rights to *Time of Your Life.* Bill said he would accept $100,000 for them and added that, with his income approaching $70,000 for the year, with surely more coming from his stage and motion-picture prospects, his chief problem was taxes. Matson recommended a tax lawyer, Maurice Speiser, who, on looking over the Saroyan accounts, said he could save him $16,000 on his 1942 taxes. Bill hired him.

When at last the furlough promised by Captain Simon came through, it was a generous one, almost the whole month of July. While Bill longed to be in Fresno for the heat and the taste of its ripe fruit, this would mean leaving Carol, and he was, in fact, very content here on Sutton Place. His view of the East River, ominously black in a thunderstorm, was magnificent. He thought the apartment was as good a place to spend a vacation as he could imagine.

He wanted to make a declaration of his love—one he could not later renounce—and drafted a dedication for his new collection *Elegie.* It would be for Carol, his gift of love, with a wish that any future tears would be theirs to share as they shared their jokes and stories and songs. It made Carol very happy.

Carol's gynecologist, Dr. Ricci, was explicit about suspending sexual relations during the final three months of her pregnancy. The Saroyans made love for the "last" time on July 6. Afterward, on the terrace, watching the evening's river traffic, they played games, shaking their bare feet as if shaking hands. Bill imitated Father Fulton Sheen on the radio, joking about his anti-Semitism and making Carol laugh over it. When he asked her feeling about Jews, she said she found them physically unattractive.

Bill felt he was as happy as he had ever been in his life and, for all he knew, as happy as he would ever be. He was delighted by his wife and the child that would arrive in three months, and he thanked God for his life and whatever lay ahead.

They still quarreled. When Carol compromised the secrecy of their telephone number, the seamless privacy Bill sought was pierced by a call from Martha Stephenson. He threatened to put Carol out so she could join Martha and her friends for good. She fled to the bathroom for some weeping, and when he went to apologize she blew up at him. Bill told her to go to the Stork Club and, from there, home, but as she prepared to do so, he embraced her and restored the peace. Later, when she asked if she could telephone Martha, he said yes.

On July 13, as they set out for dinner at the Matsons', Bill said he didn't like her shoes. They had summoned the elevator, but Carol returned to the apartment in a fury. It was only with the greatest tact, and the word "please"—which embarrassed him—that he persuaded her to come with him.

In the taxi, going down to Twelfth Street, she asked if he was angry at her, and although he was, he denied it. She was petulant, saying that she didn't like him anymore, and when she left the cab, she walked in the way he recognized as her angry walk.

Bill's windfall from *The Human Comedy* had brought him a $22,000 tax liability. Speiser, the tax lawyer, proposed to reduce this to $15,000 by spreading it over four years. Bill objected. Since he had written it in a few weeks, it would be a false claim, but it was still too much to pay and he would need Speiser forever to untangle his affairs. Besides, he explained to a doubtful Matson, the army had prevented his doing any new writing, and so he owed it to himself and his dependents—soon to be two—to postpone *any* tax payments until after the war. Thus, Speiser must go.

But Saroyan knew that the army was not preventing his writing now, and when Hal Matson persuaded *Good Housekeeping's* editor, Herb Mayes, to commission a Saroyan Christmas piece, Bill turned to it eagerly, believing it would start his creative flow and be an easy $1,250. But he struggled over the holiday's religious meanings and again over a requested revision. While the article was finally accepted, Saroyan was left with a sense of infirmity. Some affliction had gotten to his writerly spirit.

George Abbott's mounting zeal for *Get Away Old Man* buoyed Bill's sagging confidence. He conferred with Abbott on casting and obediently followed his suggestions in revising the script. He was further heartened to find that Abbott liked *Jim Dandy* and saw grand possibilities there. He wanted to set it to music by Eric Hansen, and to dance it—a ballerina to play Molly—with sets by Salvador Dalí.

Abbott thought that if Bill could clarify *Jim Dandy*, give Jim more influence on the other characters and heighten the Flora-Johnny love affair, it could be made into great theater. (As Abbott spoke, he rid his desk of notes and papers, tossing them into the wastebasket; Bill felt this a practice worth learning.) He agreed to work on the revisions at once, and the next day, confronting the task, he thought he would begin by writing an essay about the play, primarily for himself. But as he looked over his revisions, he was disappointed. The play now seemed to come to nothing and leave a bad taste. He consoled himself with the belief that Abbott could do something with it.

When he turned up at the Biltmore Theatre on August 19 to observe the first readings, he found a contagious excitement among the assembled actors and actresses. Jessie Royce Landis, who had played the lead in *Love's*

Old Sweet Song, embraced him and said this was his best play. Abbott, who approved of Bill's revisions, glowed with confidence. Nevertheless, when Bill heard the play read onstage, he felt depressed about it.

He ended his furlough reluctantly and returned to duty at Astoria, where he learned that Irwin Shaw had gone to Russia with George Stevens. He was surprised to feel some envy and to wish he were with them. But the post gossip was oddly cheerful. He heard that he had been recommended for a commission and would go before an examining board within the month.

Returning to the film magazine, he was pleased to find that a writer whom he admired had been added to the staff—John Cheever, whose *New Yorker* stories Bill regarded as skillful and distinguished works. He felt comfortable enough with Cheever to share writing problems. When he showed him "The Killer," a story about a soldier who loved killing so much that in battle he shot his own men, John conceded that the main character was "interesting." However, he did not like the title *Elegie and Salute* for Bill's next collection, nor did he approve of a twenty-one-line war poem. When Cheever asked what the poem meant, Bill could not say, and, without resentment, he decided it was a foolish poem.

Bill's unique comradeliness with Cheever was strengthened when Cheever was summoned to the hospital by his wife, Mary, for the arrival of their first child. The next day he returned, the proud new parent of a daughter, delighting Bill with the announcement, "It's a seven-pounder."

He was less pleased by the Cheever sense of humor when it devised a running joke about the Armenian plan to take over the world. While Bill knew Cheever meant it in a playful, even admiring, way, he was more irritated than amused.

To help Bill prepare for his appearance before the board of officers considering him for a direct commission, one of the members sent him the "Officer's Guide" for study. Bill flipped through its pages, found it utterly alien in manner and content, and put it aside.

Now he found that Captain Sommers, the company commander, bore him a grudge. At Saturday inspection, "Ma" Sommers paused to ask him why he had been redlined again on the payroll. When Bill explained that he had been on furlough, the captain gigged him for a dirty belt. Bill's impulse was to refuse to write a promised sketch for the company show or to appear at the officers' board meeting.

The officers' board meeting took place on Friday, August 13, and as Bill came before it he told himself he did not care about the outcome, that he might even prefer to complete his whole army episode as a private. As the meeting got underway, several officers, including Captain Davolos, questioned him sympathetically and spoke warmly on his behalf. Although Bill hemmed and hawed in his answers and showed little eagerness for the opportunity being offered him, he believed they intended to approve him.

Indeed, three days later, the colonel's secretary whispered to him, "Don't tell anybody, but you are a second lieutenant." He asked her when. "Right now," she said, and Bill walked off congratulating himself that after ten months in the army he had been given a direct commission.

The next day, when a Sergeant Hommel gigged him for not standing at attention, he asked Hommel if it was on Captain Sommers's orders. Hommel replied tersely that *he* ran the drill. Bill was now surprised to find his name listed on the Company A bulletin board as having been promoted to Private First class and annoyed when the PR office proposed a picture of Carol sewing a single chevron on his sleeve. When he inquired about his commission and upcoming KP duty, he was assured that if his commission did not arrive before his next KP, he would be assigned easy work.

On September 9 he was told to report to the orderly room to see two basic training films, one on the Articles of War, the other on sex hygiene. Since he had seen both films and hoped to go home early, he felt he could be excused, and appealed to a series of superiors reaching to Captain Sommers. Sommers said he had no record of Bill's previous attendance, and he must see them again. He then invited Bill to join him in the mess hall for lunch, and Bill turned him down. Sergeant Hommel made him the same invitation, and Bill turned him down as well. Bill felt he was demonstrating to them a truth about his own integrity.

The next morning, Bill was questioned by Captain Sommers in a lineup. When asked how long he had been in the army, Bill admitted it had been ten months, and was surprised by Sommers's reply, "We've been too nice to you here." Bill responded that he didn't understand the captain's attitude, and Sommers told him to report to him after the formation.

After cooling his heels for an hour and a half in the orderly room, he was told by Sommers that for his misconduct that morning he would serve two days at hard labor. He was to move bricks in the drill field, and, when his task was completed, he was to report back. He had the right to appeal this sentence.

In a climax of self-destructiveness, Bill replied that he would like to do just that, whereupon Sommers told him to wait in the orderly room. Saluting, Bill about-faced and walked away. Presently he was intercepted by Hommel, who led him into a nearby dormitory to explain that he was making a difficult situation worse by appealing Sommers's decision. He proposed that Bill accept his custody for several days' work, which he would assign. Hommel made a number of such proposals, all of which Bill refused.

Hommel reported this to Captain Sommers, who called Bill back to his desk to tell him he could appeal for a court-martial. Bill said that he would like to do that, right now. Sommers told him to return to his group. News of Bill's feud with the company commander spread throughout Company A, and he was summoned to the base command for a warning about his behavior.

In the early afternoon, he was recalled to Sommers's office. The captain told him he had some bad news for him. He handed Bill a letter that said that his application for a direct commission had been turned down.

The next morning, Bill's leg hurt, and he was too tired and angry to leave the apartment. When a corporal telephoned from the post to ask Bill's whereabouts, Carol replied that he was unable to come to the phone. She was told that a doctor would call on him.

No army doctor arrived that day, but the next morning Captain Davolos phoned from the post dispensary warning Bill of serious trouble if he did not appear in Astoria promptly. Bill said he was unable to leave his bed.

Within a few hours, he was collected by army medics and taken to Fort Jay Hospital, on Governor's Island, where a medical farce-drama lasting almost two weeks began. He was subjected to a marathon of examinations, interviews, and x rays of his back by teams of skeptical army doctors and psychiatrists. At one point he was removed to Halloran General Hospital, on Staten Island, where more of the same took place. He did his case no good by claiming that his back injury had resulted from a fall while directing a play in Paris and later amending the story to a fall from a barstool. A Captain Robert Craig ultimately diagnosed him as "egocentric, selfish, conceited, utterly lacking in a sense of humor, and paranoid," a description that would follow Bill throughout his army career, a matter for reflection by future commanders, both those who believed it made him a useless soldier and those who believed it did not excuse him from his patriotic duty.

On Friday, September 24, he was interviewed by a Major George Carpenter, who left him with the heartening impression that he would be given a Civilian Disability Discharge, which was "honorable and a fine thing."

Immediately after this rise in his hopes he learned that Carol's labor had begun, and he was given emergency leave until Sunday evening. He arrived at Doctor's Hospital, at Eighty-seventh Street and East End Avenue, to find Carol with recurring pains, yet more beautiful than ever. When the nurse put him out of Carol's room he ordered two dozen roses sent to her, had two scotches and a steak, went to the Hotel Pennsylvania for a Turkish bath, and then went home to bed. He was awakened at seven in the morning to learn that his son had been born at four o'clock. The nurse had telephoned repeatedly but he had failed to answer until now.

Confronting his son for the first time, Bill's response was that the boy's head was covered with thick, dark hair, and he was obviously an Armenian. His expression resembled his own, serious and sorrowful, but he would also have a great smile. Dr. Ricci assured him that the red blotches and the bump on the side of the child's head would soon disappear. Bill felt that the face was also that of a very old man, that of a life beginning but also of a life at its end, that time in the world would bring the bloom of importance to it. He felt he would be a handsome boy and man.

Carol seemed newly beautiful, with her freckles all out and terribly happy. He did not think he had ever been so happy as on this great day of Aram's birth. He delighted Carol by saying that in eight years, when she would be twenty-eight and he a young forty-four, they would have six children, one every year and a half.

On Monday, when he returned to Halloran Hospital, the news was unbelievably good. Captain Craig said that he was to be discharged. His Form 40 had been sent down. He would be boarded by the following Tuesday and get his CDD six days later, surely by October 15. Bill's joy was now complete.

Yet he felt no less anger toward those who had caught him in their wretched war. He centered the full bitterness of his heart on the army, on all its trappings, its uniforms, regulations, and customs. The sight of airplanes, ambulances, guns, barracks, and groups of marching men turned his stomach.

His critics had told him he was too sentimental. Well, now they would see his hatred, and it would be fearsome. Once out of the army, he would attack all the murderers, the churchmen, the statesmen, the businessmen, and the writers, too. He would keep love to his family and enjoy it there in private.

At Saturday inspection, Captain Craig told him that Captain Baker's report disclosed nothing wrong with his back. Smiling, he added that they would get together and work something out. Although Bill thanked him, he had a vague sense of alarm. Visiting Carol at the hospital, he spoke of his tension; though it appeared he was scheduled for a Civilian Disability Discharge, he was uncertain, sweating it out, hopeless, and feeling defiant enough to fight it out to the point of imprisonment.

On Tuesday, October 5, the day on which Carol and Aram went home from the hospital, Bill was called into Captain Craig's office and told he would go before the board within ten days and be granted a CDD. He would be out of the army within three weeks. He was stunned by this good fortune, and his joy was such that he joined a poker game and within a few hours cheerfully lost $500.

Among the Halloran patients he wanted to keep in mind for future writings about the war was Sergeant Milan Ovesia, a twenty-four-year-old Romanian from Ohio, son of an Air Corps major. He had lost twenty-six of his men in combat and spoke of gouging out German eyeballs. His brother had been killed in the Pacific, and he was full of hatred for his wife, his mother, and sometimes his father, whom he also loved deeply. There was Saccone, son and brother of bootleggers. He was an innocent street boy who had won out at breaking the law. And there was Pete Tartaronis, a Macy's clerk who had twice been blown out of his tank and had a particular hatred for all officers.

Thursday was unexpectedly warm, and the sight of a Red Cross girl made him lustful. They walked together on the hospital grounds, and he learned she was twenty-four, from Boston, and liked writing. Something in his face touched her, she told him. She guessed it was his eyes.

On Friday, October 8, he went before the hospital board convened in the office of a Colonel Packard. Packard explained that the board had been going over Bill's record, which lay open on his desk. Noting its ups and downs, he asked if Bill had found the army pretty tough. Bill replied that he had. Asked about his back, Bill said that his attacks resulted from work he had been assigned. Packard asked if he meant such unpleasant work as latrine duty. Bill admitted that he did, that he had hoped to overcome his distaste for such work but had been unable to.

The colonel noted that millions of men were able to do such work. He hoped that Bill would be able to write a story about it someday and dismissed him. Bill believed he would be out of the army in a week. A post chaplain, Rabbi Dybin, had assured him he would soon be out. Encountering Bill as he left the meeting, the rabbi invited him to the Yom Kippur service at six. Bill thanked him, but decided against going.

Home on a weekend pass, Bill delighted in his new family. Although Aram cried vigorously, Carol had engaged a nurse, who liked the boy at once but found him anxious and willful. Bill was secure in the thought that by next Saturday he would be a civilian and a writer again. It only remained for him to return to Halloran to sign the papers and get his certificate. With the nurse and a maid on the premises the apartment would be crowded, but they would remain there. Meanwhile, he asked the telephone company to change his number so that army people could not reach him.

He set off for Staten Island on Monday thinking it was for the last time. Arriving at Halloran, he was told by the ward nurse he would have his CDD on Wednesday. When he called at the personnel unit he was shown his service record book, terminating after eleven months and twenty-nine days, along with his certificate of discharge, which he signed and imprinted with his thumb.

Then, on Wednesday, the appointed day, a nurse told him that a snag had come up, and he should go to the patient detachment office to inquire. On the way he encountered Captain Craig. With a troubled expression, Craig told him that the adjutant of his post had asked for a review of the Saroyan case, and he was not getting his discharge.

Dismayed, Bill hurried to the Halloran command. A Captain McCullagh produced Bill's record, apologized for the delay, and told him the matter would be resolved within the next few days.

On Friday at five p.m. he appeared before Colonel Douglas Thom, chief of the Neuro-Psychiatry Division of the Second Service Command, in company with Colonel Halloran, and Captains McCullagh and Craig. The interview lasted only ten minutes, and it was clear they had already reached their decision. Private Saroyan would be discharged from the hospital on Monday with a two-week furlough, whereupon he was to return to duty at his post.

Home on a two-day pass, Bill wrote in his journal that he was only beginning to understand the awful outrage done him, and he was determined to fight it out. He wrote a letter to the Halloran board requesting a review of his fitness to serve. He cited his chronic sinus and back conditions, and an emotional make-up that had made him unable to endure a school classroom or any sort of communal life. As a writer he celebrated individuality. His reputation prevented his being a useful soldier, and to impose service would surely impair his writerly skills.

On Monday, Bill presented the letter to Captain Craig, who promised to read it presently. He heard nothing for several days, as the hospital was readying for a visit from Eleanor Roosevelt—the wards were being scrubbed, and the kitchen was busy with a chicken dinner. He was unable to rest and felt he was going insane. When he complained of the hissing in his ear he was sent to Captain Conway, an ear specialist, who found no infection and assured him there was no place in the army for individuals.

Home for the weekend of October 23, Bill's anger simmered. He felt an abhorrence for those who had thwarted him, and thought they had no right to associate with, let alone instruct, him. He quarreled with Carol, telling her that her outbursts of temperament had been such that, were it not for Aram, he would have left her long ago. Listening to Aram's wails, he thought they could not compare to the grief in his own, desolate heart.

He had believed that his literary eminence was daunting enough to protect him from the nation's wartime madness. Instead the juggernaut U.S. Army had overrun that fragile structure and left it rubble in its path.

Bill took some comfort from knowing that *Get Away Old Man* would begin rehearsing on Monday and from Hal Matson's news that the Guild now wanted to do *A Decent Birth*. Sure that he would soon have two plays on Broadway, he told Matson to ask of the Guild the same stiff terms they had gotten from Abbott, or better ones.

On his return to Halloran on Monday, Bill was summoned to the office of the hospital's head, Colonel R. G. DeVoe. The colonel was an affable man, and Bill sized him up as both a fine gentleman and an ally. Bill told him that he wanted to write an American novel, for the army or any part of the war effort.

A few days later, Bill learned that DeVoe had decided favorably on his case. He was being discharged. Once more he returned to Sutton Place persuaded that he was all but a free man. He and Carol agreed it would be impossible for the army again to promise, yet fail, to discharge him. He spoke of a long drive together, of buying a piece of land, a house in the country. There would be money too, $15,000 from Harcourt for a three-book contract, and much more from a long run, and a movie sale, of *Get Away Old Man.*

On Sunday morning Bill was angered to find that a caller named Charles Tekeyan had eluded his defenses in the lobby and, bearing a manuscript, gotten all the way to his apartment door. While Tekeyan tried to explain that he worked for the children's page of *Hairenik,* Bill sternly turned the young man away, telling him he could not intrude this way. Within minutes of Tekeyan's departure a note from him arrived. He wrote that from Saroyan's early writing he knew him to be a humble, sympathetic person, and he had been surprised to find this same man had thrown him out of his house.

All he had wanted was fifteen minutes of Saroyan's time. He had come to Saroyan as an Armenian and found only selfishness. The Saroyan of *The Human Comedy,* of the preface to *Razzle-Dazzle,* was not the Saroyan of Two Sutton Place. He had read all his work except for *Saroyan's Fables,* but now he knew a fable that was greater than any Saroyan could have written. He signed himself, "Sadly, Charles Tekeyan."

Bill wrote the building manager requesting that all employees must henceforth tell any caller that Saroyan had moved.

The next day, Bill was barely back in his bed at Halloran Hospital when Tekeyan appeared alongside it, bearing his manuscript. Bill again accused him of breaking into his apartment the day before and asked him how he had gotten a pass into the hospital. Tekeyan replied that he had no pass. He got in wherever he pleased. Indeed, he had just come from watching a rehearsal of *Get Away Old Man* at the Biltmore Theatre. He had simply walked in there as he had earlier, at the offices of *Story* magazine and Harold Matson. He was seventeen, he said, and would soon be in the army himself.

He had brought a collection of twenty stories for Bill's inspection. Although he complained of Tekeyan's manners, Bill relented. He gave him seven minutes, and in the course of them determined that Tekeyan was mainly interested in talking, that he was tiresome, and, like so many young men who want to write, lacking in every talent but cheek.

Shortly thereafter Bill was summoned to Captain McCullagh's office, where the captain told him that Colonel DeVoe's decision was now to send him back to duty. Bill replied that he could not do it. After five minutes of argument, McCullagh dismissed him.

He went at once to DeVoe's office, and while waiting for him was so overwhelmed by pain and despair that he began to weep. When at last he spoke with DeVoe, the colonel made it clear that someone high up in the Second Service Command and the command at Astoria had insisted he be returned to duty.

On the following day, Tuesday, November 2, Bill arranged a meeting with the officers who might still influence the decision: DeVoe, Major Vassos, and Captains Paolozzi, Davolos, and Craig. For forty minutes he argued with them and was excused for their deliberations. When Colonel DeVoe called him in for the result and spoke of his books and writing, Bill knew the decision had gone against him again. He was tired enough, and in pain enough, to admit that the army machine had destroyed him.

His furlough had been granted from Astoria, so he was delivered there by army car in the custody of a corporal. Once home on Sutton Place, he thought of escape to Mexico or Ireland, and at once he knew this was a symptom of nervous breakdown. He recognized utter, humiliating madness. He was torn by anger and misgiving. He could not return to duty, nor would the month ahead be long enough to cure him. He wondered if he should spend the thirty days of his furlough in a regular hospital.

However, the next few weeks did work a kind of cure. Aram's sobbing, which had further threatened his sanity, was calmed by the attentions of a new nurse, Miss Violet, and by Rosheen's volunteering as babysitter. When Aram wrapped his finger hard around one of Bill's, Bill found a gentle love for, and a pride in, his son, and he thought he was both fine and handsome.

Each night Bill and Carol saw the current plays and did the nightclubs and restaurants with the Matsons. Bill did not like Elmer Rice's *A New Life*, nor *Manhattan Nocturne*, with Eddie Dowling. Even Paul Robeson's *Othello*, with Jose Ferrer as Iago and Uta Hagen as Desdemona, sank him deeper in spirit. No matter who wrote it, he thought it a tiresome play, short on wisdom and wit.

But there were rising prospects for *Get Away Old Man*. On November 4, George Abbott ran off the first two and a half acts for him at the theater, and he thought it was shaping up well. He had some doubts about Abbott's directing—he took few of Bill's suggestions—but believed in the man's keen sense of box office, and felt sure he would deliver a hit three weeks hence.

After a run-through on the twelfth, Hal Matson judged it a good play in good shape, while Bill was not so sure. At Abbott's suggestion Bill didn't go to Baltimore for the opening there on the fifteenth and was not particularly disheartened by a poor review of it in the *Baltimore Sun.*

The next day, Bill, Carol, and Hal and Tommy Matson went to Baltimore to see a matinee performance of the play at the Maryland Theatre. While Bill judged it only fair, Abbott was confident. It only needed some cutting, and Bill agreed to work on this at once. After three hours of work with Abbott on the script, Bill also felt the play was in good shape. Carol said it would easily be a hit, and Bill felt she was right. At the benefit preview, on November 23, however, Bill had a feeling of letdown. The cast seemed amateur and the direction incomplete, yet Abbott was delighted, for Lee Shubert, the mighty theater manager, had proclaimed the show a hit.

The New York opening took place at the Cort Theatre on Wednesday, November 24, and, with Carol beside him in the front row of the second balcony, Bill watched the performance with delight. At intermission old friends came to congratulate him. Nancy Carol blew him kisses from a box, and he was surrounded by dozens of playgoers seeking his autograph. Jean Arthur was reported to be laughing throughout the play, and Charles Marcus loved it. The Armenian boy Charles Tekeyan lurked nearby. As the play unfolded, the audience responded in a way that made Bill feel it was a hit, a *big* hit, an event in the theater.

Bill, Carol, and the Matsons waited for the reviews at the Penthouse, and at three they arrived in Times Square for the news. It was bad. In the *Times,* Lewis Nichols said *"Get Away Old Man . . .* is, to mince no words about the matter, not so good." There were moments of humor but none of Saroyan's "indefinable pathos." He thought it might be that Saroyan had had such a wretched time in Hollywood that he was still angry when he came to tell about it. His Old Man was a vicious caricature of a producer—what was not heel was simply phony.

While Howard Barnes, in the *Tribune,* found some engaging characters and admired Abbott's direction, he found the play's "lampoon is neither incisive nor profound." He felt that Saroyan had never found out much about the movies. Both reviewers agreed that the best character was that of Sam, the Stanley Rose part, played by Glenn Anders. All the other reviews were as bad or worse. Louis Kronenbeger, in *PM,* described the play as "a muddle and a bore." It shuttled "between harsh satire and wild burlesque," flouting the rule that "Bile and buffoonery do not blend well."

Hal and Tommy Matson, Bill and Carol, in after-theater mode

When Bill got to bed at dawn his back was paining him and he slept fitfully, dreaming of Ross Bagdasarian performing for George Abbott and being embarrassingly bad. The following day, Thanksgiving, Bill and Carol went to the Matsons' for a holiday turkey dinner and then to the Cort to see the last two acts of the performance. Backstage, they found George Abbott bewildered by the reviews. He had been certain they had a smash hit.

Bill had snipped short phrases from the reviews that, in an ad, would give a favorable impression of the play, but Abbott felt they needed to have full quotes to be credible.

Home in bed, Bill was in such agony that he couldn't sleep. He and Carol talked until three a.m. Pain skewered his lower back, afflicted his right leg, and occasionally crept into his left leg too, a new development. Hot baths were no help. When he rose he could not stand straight, and his walk was that of a cripple. Hal Matson called to say that Abbott wanted him to come to his office to confer with a composer about *Jim Dandy.* Bill declined, saying their first responsibility was to save *Get Away Old Man.* They could talk about *Dandy* later on.

Matson reported back that Abbott had taken this as a sign of disappointment in him and that perhaps Bill did not want to do another play with him.

On Saturday, George Abbott learned that Lee Shubert had altered his judgment of the play. Since the week's business had fallen short of $10,000, he notified them to vacate the Cort Theatre. Abbott was posting the closing notice for a week hence.

In the *Journal-American,* George Jean Nathan blamed Abbott for poor casting and direction and Bill himself for altering a good play into a poor one. *Time* called the play "narcissistic," while Wolcott Gibbs, in *The New Yorker,* spoke of "William Saroyan's public love affair with William Saroyan." Under the weight of the critical assault, Bill reacted with uncharacteristic self-doubt, admitting that perhaps it *was* a bad play.

What he did not understand—for he would use it again and again—was that spite, the antithesis of the sentimentality that marked his successful work, had curdled rather than propelled *Get Away Old Man.*

By Sunday, however, Bill was feeling better in body and spirit, solacing himself with a native fatalism, a count-your-blessings philosophy that was his ultimate damage control. In one sense, he told himself, the year 1943 was the best yet. His family, home, wife, and son were all brought into being. He still had money and three unproduced plays, and his journal entries had been uninterrupted by the army. And he was *not* all shot from the army ordeal.

His current writing was quite another matter. The Christmas piece, the only new work he had published during the year, had been a failure. The war stories and his new play, produced after a year and a half of reworking, were failures. Indeed, he felt that his whole career, if he could still claim one, had become a failure.

Nonetheless, the Matsons were coming for dinner, there would be scotch before it, and champagne during it, and the house was clean and bright. There was a fine fire blazing in the fireplace. Carol was beautiful, and Aram was asleep in his carriage on the terrace.

His furlough came to an end on Saturday, December 4, and just prior to it, he consulted Dr. Alan de Forest Smith, at Orthopedic Hospital, about his back. Although Dr. Smith found no source of the pain, he provided Bill with a letter intended to influence the army medical corps toward discharge.

As Bill reluctantly reported back to Astoria, the news was of the Big Four Conference at Teheran, where the allied leaders, Roosevelt, Churchill, Stalin, and Chiang Kai-shek, had just agreed to demand Germany's unconditional surrender. Restored to duty, Bill Saroyan displayed no sign of surrender. He failed to salute Captain Sommers, shrugged off the post commander's suggestion he transfer to an artillery unit, and sought out Captain Davolos so as to present him with Dr. Smith's letter about his back.

Davolos returned the letter indifferently, pointing out that the Halloran Hospital report on his back told the story: the man has a pain in his back, but no one can see it. The army doctors who had attended him were agreed that Saroyan was gold-bricking. Henceforth, whenever he had back pain that kept him from duty, he would be sent to a hospital.

Now Davolos went on to explain that he had done Bill a great favor in recalling him to duty, for the hospital had wanted to give him a "Section 8" discharge for psychological unfitness. Bill replied that he didn't care what kind of discharge he got.

At the end of that week, Bill awoke too sick to shut off the alarm, let alone reach Astoria for reveille. At eleven, he telephoned Davolos, who denied him any medical recourse but the promised hospitalization.

When he called the once sympathetic Colonel DeVoe at Halloran Hospital, Bill was surprised by the terse response. To Bill's protests DeVoe suggested he might prefer service in Guadalcanal. Bill agreed that he might, and the colonel further proposed that a man with Bill's fiery temperament would be happier in the middle of the fight. It was fellows like him who won all the medals, once they got into action. At this sarcasm, Bill ended the conversation.

With no further authority to address, Bill called Davolos, who told him to listen to him for his own good. The post officers were laying for him, and unless he straightened out they were going to give him a Section 8. When Bill repeated that was all right by him, Davolos told him he was wrong, he didn't want a Section 8. Furthermore, he was now officially quartered at the post, so that from the army's point of view he was not sick, but AWOL.

Convinced, Bill shaved, dressed, and took a cab to Astoria, where Davolos took his temperature. He found he had a slight one and sent him directly to the hospital at Fort Totten, where he remained for four days. When he returned to duty at Astoria early the following week he was unchastened. In an interview with Davolos, Bill said he was neither a crook nor a politician and could not play the army game as Davolos had urged. Whatever it assigned him, a Section 8 or overseas duty, it was fine with him. In despair, Davolos said he had tried to talk to him man to man, but Bill was impossible; nobody could talk to him. If that's the way he wanted it . . . And it *was* the way he wanted it.

Finally, in mid-December, when he believed he was caught forever in the Astoria trap, the big change came for Private Saroyan. He was "alerted"— told to prepare for duty overseas. This would be a three-month assignment in the European theater with a unit headed by Major Cahoon, a former film cutter at Columbia Pictures. Irwin Shaw had similar orders.

When Bill went to lunch with Shaw, he was annoyed by Shaw's account of his recent travels. Shaw had flown to Africa and gone by train to Palestine, and his newly heroic manner suggested these were wondrous adventures.

In preparation for their new assignment, both Bill and Irwin had to undergo the "infiltration course" at Sea Girt, New Jersey. There they found themselves firing M1 carbines at beach targets and crawling an eighty-yard course under barbed wire and a barrage of live ammunition. As Bill struggled through the ordeal, he was thinking of men moving to senseless and horrible deaths in this manner, and there was terror in his heart.

Driving back to Astoria, Shaw sang happily and cursed at slow drivers, children, and dogs that got in his way. Bill decided that in spite of the likable manner, Shaw was bluffing. He wasn't the tough guy he pretended to be, and on closer acquaintance, he was losing his appeal.

At a Christmas Eve dinner in the Marcuses' Savoy Plaza apartment, Charles told Bill that he had recently tried to pull Washington wires for him, but General Colton had not forgotten the interview. Nevertheless, Charles had discovered that the army's current plan for Bill was a good one. George Stevens, already in London, admired Bill's work and wanted him there. Together with Frank Capra he would be making operational films.

Marcus was also delighted to tell him that a year ago he had confided to Noël Coward that his beautiful daughter was in love with William Saroyan, who did not love her, to which Coward had replied that one way to cure her would be to get her to read one of Saroyan's plays. Bill did not join in the hilarity.

During this same dinner, when the conversation turned to Nazi atrocities, Rosheen volunteered that the Germans were all criminals and ought to be destroyed. Bill thought this was an embarrassing statement and later told Carol that she should tell him if her mother was Jewish or partly so. Carol was upset by the suggestion and explained that her mother spoke out of loyalty to Charles.

A telegram from Henry reported that his mother and Cosette were setting off by train for their visit to him and would be arriving on January 3. Delighted, Bill arranged a six-day pass for himself and decided to make room for their guests by dismissing both Wilhelmina, the maid, and Miss Violet, the nurse.

The day of Takoohi and Cosette's arrival brought the winter's first considerable snow, tying up New York traffic, but Bill was on hand at Grand Central to greet them. Introducing his mother and his sister to Sutton Place, bringing together Bill's diverse past and present, was an anxious rite. However, the initial greetings went well. Carol provided an enthusiastic welcome and was undismayed when Takoohi expressed disappointment in Aram's appearance.

But presently Takoohi had taken over in the kitchen, filling the apartment with the smell of her lamb with string beans and getting better

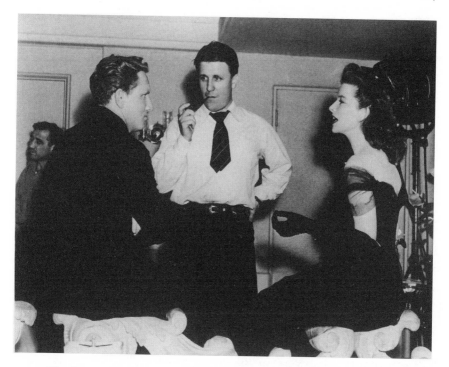

The director George Stevens, here with Spencer Tracy and Katharine Hepburn

acquainted with her grandson. After a fine Armenian supper, which included stuffed cabbage leaves with *madzoon* and garlic, Carol told Bill that his old San Francisco smell, which she had missed, was on him again.

During that first week together, Takoohi praised Carol to her son, finding her not only beautiful but bright, competent, and a skillful mother. When Carol took her to visit Rosheen at the Savoy Plaza, the two outspoken grandmothers got on wonderfully well. Carol was immediately fond of Cosette, who expressed her affection by setting out to knit Carol a bed jacket.

The latest family news concerned Bill's cousin, Chesley Saroyan. At last, Chesley was marrying Amie Reichert, daughter of a rabbi. Bill marveled that Chesley would marry his *first* girl and that the dynamic Uncle Aram had been unable to dissuade his son from marrying a Jewess. Takoohi then reported that a woman writer from *Hairenik* had visited her in San Francisco and told her that the *Hairenik* staff, Ruben Darbinian in particular, had been shocked to learn that William had married a Jewish girl. Rather than point out that Carol was not Jewish, Takoohi had ignored it.

Although his mother was proving remarkably adaptable to the customs of Manhattan's East Side, Bill sensed that Carol was not altogether happy with two women relatives in the house. He often found her in a bad mood over some imagined slight by her mother-in-law. Her voice occasionally took on an ominous lowness, and arguments flared at mealtimes.

At dinner on Saturday night he surprised them all by saying he *wanted* to be shipped. He felt it would do him good to get away from the detestable Astoria army. He was looking forward to the adventure now, the voyage, the change. As for his family's welfare, he cared only for the beginning of another child before he went. This resulted in a maternal row that left them all shaken. In fact, Bill proposed that his mother and his sister move out to a hotel, and they agreed to remain only at Carol's insistence. Takoohi conceded that theirs was a troublemaking tribe—only with difficulty did they get on in the world.

At one meal Bill released a burst of rage at the military service and the war itself and revealed he was writing about it. His new story collection for Harcourt included the army stories "Elegie, Salute," and "The Killer," each of which revealed his loathing for the army. He would also draw an ironic self-portrait, that of a shameless man who does not want to do his duty, a cowardly wretch who does not want to die for America, a dangerous madman who dares to question the absolute authority of the men named by the government to tell him what to do.

When his mother cautioned him, Bill responded angrily. But Takoohi was firm in arguing that he should not publish his army grievances now. In the quarrel's aftermath, he was persuaded to remove them from the new book.

Bill spoke repeatedly of his hope that Carol would soon be pregnant with Aram's sister, Lucy, or his brother, whose name he had decided would be Sweeney. Carol responded on January 10 by announcing she was pregnant. She thought it would be a girl, and Bill rejoiced.

The following day, Bill was notified that he would be departing the country by sea in two weeks' time. He was issued an M1 carbine and a duffel bag, on which he printed his name and serial number. He then went home to arrange for his mother and Cosette to stay on with Carol indefinitely.

His great happiness lay in the belief that Carol was pregnant. He was sure of it. Thus he was shocked by the news that Carol's period had come. He felt as if they had lost someone.

But Carol had never been dearer to him. While she danced to the radio music in their bedroom, Bill was overcome with love for her. He was entranced by the handsome shape of her head and the proud way she held it, by the grace of her movements, her quality of sweetness. Happier than he had felt in years, he told her she was the most beautiful girl in the world.

He bought her a belated wedding ring. It was to be inscribed with the name Saroyan in Armenian on the outside, and inside, in English, "To Carol, Love, always, Bill." He also bought her silver earrings, a necklace, and a gold bracelet with a diamond-set locket to be inscribed with an arrow-pierced heart and the words "Carol, Aram, Bill, 1944."

On January 27, 1944, Bill bade farewell to his family, and Harry, the Marcus chauffeur, drove him to Astoria. Since he had not been able to fit his typewriter into his duffel bag he reluctantly left it with Carol, instructing her to keep up the journal of their life. He expected to return in three months, surely by the first of May, and in the meantime she was to speak to no one outside the family, to tell no one how she felt nor ask for help. He even included Hal Matson in this prohibition.

IX

EUROPEAN CAMPAIGN

1944–1945

Bill arrived in London on February 23, 1944, and reported to the office of the Army Pictorial Service, at 33 Davies Street. He was still suffering from a cold acquired during the weeklong voyage on a swarming troopship, and he was anxious above all else to avoid army barracks.

His commanding officer, a recently promoted lieutenant colonel, was an old friend, George Stevens. Stevens had begun his Hollywood career as a cameraman for Hal Roach comedies. He was part Commanche, and although his face was unusual, with a bulging forehead and crowded features, he was a handsome man. His eyes were warm and intelligent, reflecting his kindliness and keen sense of humor.

On reading a copy of *Get Away Old Man,* Stevens had remarked that he couldn't understand how Bill could write *The Human Comedy* and then something as bad as this, to which Bill had replied that it was because he was so very talented.

The purpose of Stevens's Special Coverage Unit was to film the invasion of Europe. At liberty to choose his script staff, Stevens had singled out Irwin Shaw, Gene Solow, and a twenty-four-year-old Anglo-American, Ivan Moffatt. A long-standing admiration for Saroyan's work had added him to the roster. Bill knew and respected Stevens as a ruggedly independent maker of films with his own, wry mark. Among them were *Penny Serenade, The Talk of the Town,* and *The More the Merrier.* Stevens was sympathetic to Bill's desire for private lodging and gave his permission, but Bill soon found that the hotels that had been recommended in New York—Claridges and the Dorchester—were full.

Irwin Shaw, who had preceded him, did all he could to make Bill feel at home. He shared his office, offered his desk and typewriter until Bill could

Irwin Shaw

get his own, and took Bill to his apartment, at 39 Bedford Street, for a hot bath, a change of clothes, and a drink. He then took him along to join their friend Gene Solow.

Solow, originally Eugenie Solovaitch, had been a fellow soldier at Astoria, but he was now a civilian in the OWI with a rank equivalent to a colonel's, and he shared a penthouse with George Stevens. Gene helped Bill find a temporary room at the Cumberland Hotel in Marble Arch and then took him and Irwin to his club, a place known as Jack's, where wartime celebrities gathered and the food and drink were as good as any in London.

Bustling with uniformed men and pretty girls out for a good time, London was a city under siege. German flying-bombs, the V-1s, rained down upon it every night, leaving scores of dead amid the rubble. As Gene, Irwin, and Bill walked home, the air-raid sirens sounded, and the men took refuge in a crowded station of the Underground.

Shaw offered Bill a more permanent solution to his housing problem by inviting him to move into the Bedford Street apartment he shared with Captain Irving Reis, the former head of the CBS Radio Workshop. Bill gladly accepted. Shaw, who seemed to know everybody in London, took Bill along to the parties. Correspondents, filmmakers, and writers of every sort gathered nightly to trade war stories, girls, theories about Hitler's defeat, and to play poker.

Shaw's current girlfriend was the *Time* correspondent Mary Welsh, a striking blonde from Minnesota, still the wife of Noel Monks, of the *Daily Mail.* Shaw's friend Robert Capa, the *Life* photographer, gave regular parties at his penthouse in Belgrave Square. The Dorchester suite of Charles Wertenbaker, *Time* magazine's chief correspondent, was another poker party locale. Bill thought Wertenbaker was a competent player with a good style, but the best of the lot was Capa, a gambler who loved to play. Winning a pot, he would grin and say that poker was a game of skill. George Stevens was surely the most generous. Usually a winner, he would pick up the IOUs of his own men.

Bill and Irwin were so often together that one of Shaw's ex-girlfriends taunted them as "the Rover Boys." Martha Gellhorn, Ernest Hemingway's wife, described them as the army's two most unmilitary soldiers.

Bill preferred Gene Solow's company. Solow knew the London theater people, and introduced him to Beatrice Lillie and Terrence Rattigan, the RAF tailgunner whose play *While the Sun Shines* had just opened. Solow could get tickets for the most popular shows, and though Bill was not easily impressed by West End offerings, he was glad to go along.

Bill had no sooner moved into the Bedford Street apartment when an order was issued that all enlisted men must live in the barracks. Nothing could have been more humiliating to the two privates, who felt a perverse superiority to the brass with whom they fraternized. Saroyan reacted with typical outrage. If he was to be badgered with the inconvenience and menial duties the move would bring, he would not be able to do the important work for which he had come.

Shaw assured Bill that the difficulty had arisen before, and Stevens had straightened it out. To their delight, Stevens turned up at their door to report that he was mounting a bayonet charge against the bureaucratic enemy, and if they went to barracks, he would go with them.

Stevens prevailed, and they celebrated at Jack's and in an all-night poker game at Bedford Street. This was loud enough to provoke complaints from the neighbors and a warning from the landlord. Indeed, they soon removed to another flat at 14 Pall Mall.

Shaw had been at work on a scenario about the planning for D day, and Bill's first assignment was to study this and discuss it with Stevens. He applied himself to this project with new enthusiasm, but it was soon halted by higher authority. The reason for this baffled even the perceptive Stevens.

Without a project the writers met rarely, and Bill's time was free for endless letters to Carol and poker through the night.

While Bill took to the poker games eagerly, he surprised Shaw by showing little interest in the plentiful supply of attractive women. For a self-proclaimed bum he had grown surprisingly self-righteous about adultery. One of the several reasons was certainly that the young women he saw at the Mayfair parties were often in uniform, and thus monstrous to him, or smart and ambitious, which was no more recommendation. The sound of Irwin's and Mary Welsh's laughter beyond Irwin's closed door particularly annoyed him, and he wrote Carol that the others were making the war into a holiday of wenching.

The army mess was on Orange Street, behind the Ritz. The fare was strictly GI, and the amplified wailing of a black singer filled the hall. As a sour-faced Bill watched Shaw fill his canteen with coffee, Shaw kidded him for not carrying his. In telling Bill he was "a sholdier now," Shaw seemed to imply that his friend was thus failing his patriotic duty.

When Shaw spoke of the German enemy, he told Bill that after the war they would have to be tough with them, men, women, and children. There was no room for any mercy. Bill was shocked, realizing that he was not kidding, as Stevens so often did. Shaw *meant* it.

Like Bill, Shaw had a play, *The Assassin,* for which he sought a producer. Bill had read it and admired it in many ways, but he did not believe it would be successful and told Shaw so. When Warren Munsell of the Theatre Guild dropped into the Davies Street office to inquire about the play, he spoke of his return to New York as reluctant. When Munsell left, Bill remarked on the strangeness of this sentiment. Shaw challenged him again, assuring him that most men were eager to fight this war. Bill was unconvinced.

Even as he shared in the poker-table bravado, playing through the early-morning hours at Capa's or Wertenbaker's, indifferent to the whine and thunder of the buzz-bombs, Bill felt sure they were all bluffing. They saw the war as a holiday in which they put on heroism like a costume over their fear, and ran for cover at any sign of danger.

Still, Shaw's insinuations about the Saroyan courage piqued him, and he was gratified to find that the nightly fireworks, even when the ground trembled beneath his feet, did not bring forth the cowardice he had suspected of himself since childhood. He had no hesitation in making enemies, but he was no brawler, and he shunned rather than confronted them.

One night, as he walked Gene Solow back to the penthouse apartment, they heard the banshee wail of the alert. Once inside the building, Solow rushed to the basement shelter, while Bill and George Stevens watched the spectacle from the rooftop. It was a major raid, lasting for an hour, and there was beauty in it, vivid purple bursts in the sky followed by the enemy's lanterns drifting down. Stevens admitted that their act was foolhardy and that his own fear was considerable.

Hoping for mail from Carol, Bill called daily at the Pictorial Service office, and always found it milling with fellow soldiers. The social center for writers was the French Place, an after-hours club and restaurant on Little St. James Street run for the Free French. Bill thought it was the best place in London. He enjoyed its basement billiard table, where he played snooker with the United Press correspondent Walter Cronkite, and its bar, where he drank with the British novelist Romain Gary and the *New Yorker*'s A. J. Leibling.

When he was introduced to the playwright Robert Sherwood in the club restaurant, Bill recalled that a year and a half before this man had ignored the offer of his writing services. He had sworn not to forgive this slight. But Sherwood greeted him warmly, laughed over a *Time* magazine item about Bill's mistakenly saluting a Red Cross worker, and invited him to visit his office. The permafrost of Saroyan resentment soon thawed.

At the parties as well as the poker games it seemed he was meeting everyone important in London. He drank with the young actor Peter Ustinov and the young poet Dylan Thomas. At Pat Patterson's party for Garson Kanin, he talked with Harold Guinzburg, head of Viking Press, and Arthur Koestler, offending him with the directness of his questions. At the *Horizon* founder Cyril Connolly's, he met the poet Stephen Spender, who was sensitive and courteous; the painter and portraitist Augustus John, who asked if he might sketch Bill; and, finally, Ernest Hemingway, just arrived as the *Collier's* war correspondent.

Greeting Bill, Hemingway called their meeting a long-postponed one. While the famous man was cordial enough, describing his wife Martha's glowing report of him, Bill found Ernest slow-minded and tiresome. He recalled their literary fracas nine years earlier, and how Hemingway's cheeriness had seemed forced. He saw him now as a pretentious swashbuckler, and he had no inclination to embroider their acquaintance.

During the entire spring and early summer of 1944 there was one central thought consuming Bill's thoughts: Carol. Each morning, hope rose that the agonizingly slow mails would bring a letter from her. He wrote her three or four times each day, dense, single-spaced letters telling how terribly he missed her. During his first month in London he had no word from her at all. In describing how this pained him, he pleaded that she find an hour each day to write him. He was lonelier than he had ever been in his life. The pain in his back was murderous, beyond the solace of codeine and hot baths. It kept him from work, from sleep, and even from reading.

Despair, he thought, was shared by every man here, each feeling alone and afraid. What lifted his own heart, though, was remembering the touch of her fingers, the sound of her voice in song, the sight of her dancing, and her sweet delight in him.

He wrote of all the ways he lusted for her now in separation. He longed for her adorable body as if that were all he cared for. He admitted that originally he had thought sexual desire was all that drew him to her, but he had learned a greater truth about what they shared, and it had become the core of his life. Which was not to say his desire was any less.

He dreamed of her as she had been the night they swam naked in the moonlight at Piedra. He dreamed of her as they danced by the living-room fire with the pianola playing *Song of Songs*. As he grabbed her and kissed her, she was radiant and laughing, more beautiful than ever, and it was all so real that the pleasure lasted after he awakened.

He received a first letter from Carol on March 16. It had taken a month to reach him. Henceforth the mail between them was slow but regular. He admitted to being horny and teased her that if he were to sin, it would not be he, but the old devil that got stirred up when on the loose. But he was not tempted. The constant sight of women in uniform was as offensive to him as that of women with hairy faces.

He had hoped that Carol's news would be of a daughter on the way, but this was not the case. He rationalized that it was for the best since she would be beautiful for him on his return. They would drive into the country in his Cadillac, and enjoy the little towns, good food, sunlight, sad cowboy songs, and just being together.

On Easter Sunday, returning from an Armenian service, he thought of them going, as a family, to Armenian church, imagining that Carol would enjoy the ceremony and be able to understand the language of the litany. He wished that she had been with him to smell the incense, hear the old Gregorian chants, see the priest in his golden robe and crown, mumbling, kissing the book, washing his hands. In spite of the ritual's vacuousness, it was simple, beautiful, and touching.

On learning from Steven Hopkins's brother Robert that Steven had been killed, he wrote Carol that he had been close to tears at the news, for the living as well as the dead brother. Poor Stevie Hopkins. He could imagine her feelings.

He had left Carol instructions about "wifely behavior," and her mention, in an early letter, of going out to lunch alarmed him. He wrote her that he didn't like people seeing her, but then he relented and urged her to go ahead but to pick her company carefully. Certainly no men, and no restaurant where men would be apt to join her. He didn't like them to *see* her.

When she wrote that she had to do something to keep from being bored to death and proposed ballet lessons or a job with the OWI, he vetoed both but heartily endorsed her taking lessons in Armenian. He proposed a daily schedule that would divide her time between looking after Aram, housekeeping, taking walks, listening to music, reading, watching movies, and writing to him.

The best of Bill's times in London were Ross Bagdasarian's visits. Ross was stationed in northern England and could arrange occasional two-day passes, which brought him the comforts of Bill's bathtub and scotch. Bill took him to the publisher Victor Weybright's, to the French Place for dinner, and to the theater and the poker games, but mostly they drank, reminisced about Fresno, and laughed.

He wrote Carol that Ross kept him laughing all the time, and how Ross had been amazed at Bill's disinterest in the London girls. Also, when Ross had said he suspected Carol was Jewish, because her mother looked Jewish, Bill had denied it, citing her assurances, thus putting an end to it.

He and Ross spoke the same language, he wrote, and were straight with one another. They sang, told each other stories, and farted together. Ross *was* a true friend, and the mark of that was in the farting. But when Carol asked for Ross's address in order to write him, Bill refused. He had waited for a letter from her for nine days, and now she wanted to write Ross. He was far too jealous for that.

Ross's visits gave Bill a chance to show off his infatuation with London. He had some difficulties with British speech, noting that one had to have the mouth for it. Words were stifled. Several were scrambled into one, or a part of one that would be completed by another speaker. He had sat at many a table trying to participate in the gaiety of a London conversation only to discover there had been no subject at all.

As for the besieged city, though, Bill was enchanted. He loved the sound of the names—Limehouse, Blackfriar's Bridge, Piccadilly, and Charing Cross—and prided himself on a walking knowledge of London's bookshops and back alleys. In a piece for the *Daily Mail* he wrote that as a child he had dreamed of London, and now he was finding it more wondrous than the dream. The immortals of the language remained—King Lear and Oliver Twist, to name two. He saw the British as a noble people, stoical, ever courteous, and with a sure instinct for what was right. They seemed absorbed with detail like children fascinated by an intricate game, yet never disheartened when it didn't work out as planned. The more he knew the English, the better he loved and admired them.

This London tribute, written to defray his gambling debts, was the only piece of writing Bill completed throughout the first half of 1944, but his writerly mind was preparing for better days. He saved the daily papers, with their record of the war's progress, shipping them off to Carol for use in future work, and he kept a careful record of vivid dreams that appeared to be releasing important thematic material to him.

In one he dreamed of a little tiger and how he had to shoot it, through its skull, with his old .22 rifle. As he did so the tiger became human, someone he knew, though not anyone in particular. As it spoke he realized the creature's love for him was great. Nevertheless, he fired a second bullet into its head. As it died in his arms it became a beautiful girl and his tears poured forth.

He also dreamed about a young man in wartime who has managed to avoid the army. Each night he moves to a different hotel, where he writes letters to the leaders of warring nations and drops them from his window. The letters find their way into newspapers and are determined to be wise and the only honest writing in the world.

From the day of his arrival in London, Bill had been looking forward to a visit with George Bernard Shaw. Nine years earlier, Bill had sent him some one-act plays, and the famous playwright had replied, "They are very good, good everyway: character—action—musical talk—modern screenable technique—full range of interest—sound economic and political foundation—all alive-O—make me feel like an ancient classic on the shelf. Go ahead, hard, William: you are IT."

On May 13, Bill wrote Shaw, asking if he could call on him the following week. Shaw agreed and set a date, and Bill prepared himself by reading *Androcles and the Lion* and *The Millionairess.* Setting out on the afternoon of May 24 he armed himself with a copy of his own *The Beautiful People,* and, in light of his host's celebrated vegetarianism, a casaba melon and some mushrooms, string beans, and asparagus he had discovered at Fortnum's.

He was met at the Welwyn Garden City station by Shaw's car and driven to Ayot St. Lawrence. There to greet him was the eighty-eight-year-old playwright, who appeared to be a sweet old gentleman with the manner of a Sunday-school teacher. After a chatty walk Shaw brought him to his living room for tea, and here Bill presented his vegetable offering. Bill had imagined Shaw unwrapping the parcel to marvel at these hothouse wonders and their appearance in wartime. Instead, Shaw remarked that while everyone in America was under the impression he was hungry, he was not. The produce was carried into the hall with the clear implication that it was to go to the housekeeper or less fortunate neighbors.

Shaw performed wittily over the tea, scoffing at the accomplishments of various actors, actresses, and makers of motion pictures. In an eagerness to express admiration for his host, Bill let several opportunities for departure pass by. When Bill tried to press his play upon him, Shaw declined, saying he already had a copy, and he was firm even when Bill explained this was a new, altogether different play. During a moment when Shaw was called from the room, Bill quickly inscribed the book to him and managed to tuck it into a nearby pile before the old man returned to show him out.

Returning to London, he thought what a terrible intrusion he had made upon the Shavian afternoon, cluttering it with his own irrelevance. He had no part of the man's past, present, or future; they had no more in common than that they both occasionally wrote plays.

His disappointment was so great that he could not describe the afternoon to anyone, and when Lester Markel, of the *New York Times* magazine, proposed a piece about his visit to Shaw, Bill put him off by asking five times the $200 offer.

At the *Time* party for Charles Wertenbaker on March 11, Bill found himself with Air Corps Major Spyros Skouras, the new head of Twentieth Century–Fox. Skouras was unusually friendly, telling Bill that his son had told him he must get Saroyan to write a great story for him. Bill was agreeable and suggested that his play *Love's Old Sweet Song* would make a splendid movie. Skouras was not familiar with it, and although Bill sized him up as a nonreader, he agreed to send it to him.

A week later he inscribed a copy of Faber's edition of his *Three Plays*, which included *Love's Old Sweet Song*, and sent it off to Skouras. To his surprise, he was invited to Skouras's office, and there, on April 25, he found the man simmering with expectations. The mogul told Bill he had in mind a project more timely and ambitious than *Love's Old Sweet Song* for the author of *The Human Comedy*. He read from a letter that described the wartime hardships of British civilians, the tragic separations, the daily anxieties, and the food queues, and how these were a testing of a nation's courage that might be a theme for a great picture.

Bill recognized some truth in this national pluck concept—as well as a possibility for a return to New York. He agreed that daily life under siege was unknown in America and that it was a many-sided experience—comic, tragic, and, in the end, ennobling. He felt equal to writing such a story, but how could he, locked as he was in the army's stifling routine?

If he could get Bill a leave of absence, Skouras asked, would he write this story for him? Bill assured him that he would. As Skouras's enthusiasm mounted over what struck Bill as insubstantial stuff, he suspected that Darryl Zanuck had a hand in this, luring him to Fox for the postwar era. Walking him fraternally into the hallway, Skouras confided that he wanted Bill to be with him and his company. No contract was needed, just their word on it.

As they parted, Bill was skeptical, knowing that the zeal of these big studio heads changed with the blowing of each new wind. But on May 3, Skouras reported a plan underway. He had interested Commander Herbert Agar in their project. Agar was assistant to Ambassador Winant and in charge of British-American relations for the OWI. Skouras was arranging a meeting between the two.

At the same time, Robert Sherwood invited him to his office for a visit and a talk about how Bill's writing could be put to better use. Bill thought that between Skouras and Sherwood, he might at least get some leave in Britain, and he wrote Carol, wondering if she could find a way to join him for a month's holiday in the North.

It was widely known that Operation Overlord, the major European invasion, for which the Allied force of 176,000 troops had assembled in Britain, was about to begin. George Stevens's special unit was to accompany the attack, and Bill's name was on the list of those who would go along.

When Bill explained the importance of his writing project for the OWI and his belief that if he were off in France, it would be scuttled, Stevens obliged. He struck Bill's name from the list for France.

A call from Skouras, who was on his way to the States, assured Bill that the plan was set, and all he needed to do was meet with Herbert Agar. Convinced he would soon be home, Bill wrote Carol to tell her how he would arrive. Instead of coming to the apartment, he would take a suite at a fancy hotel and telephone her to meet him there, as if they weren't married but having a wonderful, wild affair.

Herbert Agar was an impressive, statesman-like figure. An Anglophile, Agar spoke of fears for the collapse of Western civilization, raising Bill's suspicions of the academic point of view, but he liked the idea of borrowing Bill from the army and turning him loose to write the British-American story.

Agar's request that Bill be loaned to the OWI for six months was sent to Stevens, who approved it. When Bill asked if anything prevented him from returning to New York to do the writing, Agar was doubtful. Bill could go home *after* he wrote the story.

Bill's uncertainty about his wartime course made Irwin Shaw's patriotic fervor particularly hard to bear. They were at a table together in the French Place when news of Rome's fall came over the radio. Bill was appalled by the ensuing pandemonium and Shaw's lament that if Stevens had let him go he would be walking into Rome now.

Operation Overlord began on June 6, and it was a great disappointment to Stevens that at the last minute his group's departure was delayed. Shaw threw more rowdy parties at 14 Pall Mall, from which Bill withdrew. He could not celebrate any battle; it was simply mass murder.

On D day, Bill learned that his transfer to the OWI was official, and he believed he had found his way to freedom. The exodus from London's hotels sent him in search of the solitude he would now need for work. He found a room at one of London's best, the Savoy, for seven dollars a day, and on June 11, he moved in.

His lovelorn outpourings to Carol continued, regular as mealtimes. He lived for her responses, which came in bunches, several in an Armenian so proficient as to reveal her tutor's hand. The uninterrupted, hopeful flow of this correspondence was his lifeline, but this too proved vulnerable.

On June 17, while dining with Shaw and Gene Solow at the French Place, a soldier named John Krimsky introduced himself to say he had recently had dinner with Carol. He explained that it had been three weeks ago, at Pat and Gloria di Cicco's, on Fifty-seventh Street. Whereupon Krimsky's companion added that he had known Carol since she was a baby, and had reared her. Bill's irritation at this intimacy with his wife was increased as he saw the two men pursuing an available girl in the bar. He wrote Carol on June 18 that the encounter had not only made him question her relationship with the two strangers but also her deceitfulness in failing to tell him about going to Pat and Gloria's for dinner.

He wondered what else she had not told him—not just since he had left New York, but before they had met. Had others known her as he had? She must tell him the truth. If he could not trust her, he did not want her. He had always been alone and was alone again now. He was ready to lose her.

Before she was able to respond to his accusations, the Stevens unit departed for France, in a flourish of gallantry and conquest, and then a delayed batch of affectionate letters from Carol did arrive. Bill was suddenly contrite. He cabled Carol on the twenty-first to disregard his angry letters and remember only that he loved her. He followed up with letters explaining his outburst as a result of his loneliness, saying that his anger was really at himself.

He had changed the title of his forthcoming story collection to *Dear Baby* and dedicated it to Carol as the first of many gifts of his love. As further propitiation he bought Carol a gift, a Persian miniature. It was of a princess feeding her son and featured breasts, which, he admitted, were often on his mind. The next day, however, he had second thoughts about it and took it back to the shop, exchanging it for several old books with pictures, which he felt would appeal to Aram when he was five or six.

He wrote Herbert Agar of his optimism about the book. It would be an act of faith and better than anything he had ever done. He would need six months, and he would need to be in America. After several weeks, Agar invited him for lunch, but before he kept this date, Bill learned that the unpredictable Signal Corps had decided to recall him to Astoria, where the chances were excellent for immediate discharge.

The orders for this long-hoped-for event were actually written, so he apologized to Agar for the collapse of their plan and wrote Carol that he was on his way home. No sooner was this done than he discovered that a cable from the War Department in Washington had changed his orders. Pursuant to Commander Agar's request for him, he was being assigned permanently to London in order to work on a special project.

Bill was dumbfounded at this new twist of ill luck but soon resigned himself to it, placing his faith in Agar. Over lunch, Agar complimented Bill on his London piece, which had just appeared, and convinced him that he had the power to return Bill to New York, once the book was written.

Conventional wisdom had it that Montgomery was ready to finish off the German army and the war was virtually over, but in London there was no letup in the wailing of the sirens and the on-time arrival of the V-2s. The nightly casualty list ran as high as 75 deaths and 375 injuries.

On July 7, a bomb landed on the Thames embankment just behind the Savoy, shattering many of the hotel's windows. Another evening, as Bill entered the hotel dining room, a bomb landed close enough to rain him with broken glass, shake the hotel's foundations, and demolish much of the fourth floor.

Bill decided he would pack his typewriter up to Scotland and work hard there at the book. It would be twenty-one chapters, each of three thousand words, making a total of sixty-three thousand words. He resolved to begin work on August 7 and to finish on his thirty-seventh birthday, August 31, whereupon he would present it to Agar and then go home. He had the OWI reserve him a room at the North British Hotel in Edinburgh.

It would be the story of a good boy with the clear view of a Huck Finn. He would be a conscript who sees the army and its war as the swindle it is, and wants to get even. This boy, like Bill himself—like every man, Bill thought—would be a coward. He had some other characters in mind, including one who constantly falls asleep and awakens to army routine crying out against it. It was to be a love story as well as a hate story, but he was putting aside his bitterness so he could enjoy it and work with the concentration that had generated *Time of Your Life* and *The Human Comedy.*

Bill had visited Edinburgh in 1935, and now, on August 6, 1944, he returned by train. He found that its clatter and bustle were heightened by the war. The North British Hotel was attached to the Central Station on Princess Street, and its reception desk was in the charge of a Scotswoman who did not take to Bill's swaggering style.

She showed him to a tiny, windowless room with neither a bath nor a table. When he told her it would not do, she replied that it was all there was. The Adelphi Hotel, on Cockburn Street, where he had lodged previously, could not accommodate him, nor could any other hotel. He was fully aware that the woman had deliberately given him the worst room in the hotel, but he had no alternative.

In the morning he set up his typewriter on the bureau and tried to get to work, but when the borrowed machine jammed repeatedly he despaired of it. Packing his belongings, he checked out of the hotel and took the first train back to London.

Returning to his room at the Savoy, he located an old L. C. Smith typewriter that pleased him. On August 9, he got down to work in earnest on a novel, or rather two novels: one intended for publication, and another he thought of as for God, which was to say the real book, telling all the awful truths he knew. Both would tell of a world made meaningless and false by war.

He wrote a first chapter, four pages, about a draftee on the day he receives his induction notice. Bill realized that just as Huck Finn had Jim to set free, this boy must have a source for his nobility. It would be his *own* spirit that must be freed. Then the boy himself spoke to his creator, saying his name was Wesley Jackson, and that he was nineteen years old, believed in God, and liked to sing "Valencia."

On the way to Jack's for dinner, Bill found himself whistling a tune, whose words went, "If I had my way dear, you'd never grow old," and he realized it was just what Wesley would whistle when he was sore at some officer.

At the end of three days' work, in which he had completed three chapters, he decided that so far, everything was just right. He had made a beginning that could not fail. It might turn out to be nothing, but it would certainly be an interesting book and probably a readable one and just possibly a great one. By the first week's end he had brought in Wesley's comrades: Victor Tosca, his brother Dominic, Lou Marriacci, Calalokowitz, Joe Foxhall, and Jim Kirby, who would encourage Wesley to write and make a writer of him.

Bill felt he was on his way, writing a chapter a day, and that he would finish on schedule. He was chain-smoking but knew this, like an aching arm, was a part of hard work for him. He would never go against cigarettes, for they were his spirit's companion, the first cigarette of the day bringing it to life.

On August 15, the London papers heralded the new Allied invasion of France, Operation Dragoon, in which the U.S. Seventh Army, under General Patch, landed successfully on the beaches between Marseilles and Nice to begin its drive up the Rhone Valley toward Paris.

When visitors turned up with the latest news from the battle for France, Bill received them grudgingly. One irked him with an account of Ernest

Hemingway's capture of some French wine and a German motorcycle, then summing Hemingway up as a great man and a great writer. Bill conceded Hemingway had an exceptional skill for lean prose, but, as a man, he was no greater than the old Savoy waiter who brought his meals.

Gene Solow, who understood Bill's feelings and shared a few of them, was more welcome. When Solow turned up to tell of George Stevens's skirmishes in filming the recapture of France, Bill was fascinated. Solow believed Stevens's photo unit was the best in France, and that Stevens was getting stuff that was photographically magnificent, and great art. Stevens was happy for the first time since he'd been in the army. He wasn't getting "news," though, and two senior officers, Anatole Litvak and Anthony Veiller, had told him he was being too protective of his boys, not getting the tough stuff. There had been a loud argument between them in the officers' mess.

Bill was glad to give Solow the news of his novel, which he had titled *The Adventures of Wesley Jackson,* to carry back to Stevens.

As Wesley Jackson's story progressed, it followed ever more closely Bill's own army experience: the long train ride across a snow-covered nation to New York; a stay at a hospital on Governor's Island; then time at Halloran Hospital, where he would meet the troops back from Africa, including the sergeant who had lost twenty-one of his twenty-six men in battle, and the Red Cross women looking to get laid; and then he would quarrel there with a high-ranking officer. There would be a girl for Wesley too, perhaps a streetwalker.

On Bill's tenth day of work he read over the just completed chapter thirteen and was unhappy with it. He was tired, too. Looking back over what he had done, he thought it was meaningless nonsense—and worse, he had nothing more to say. He had no sooner admitted this than he reassured himself that it was normal to have such misgivings.

By August 21, the midpoint of the three weeks he had allowed himself, he had written seventeen chapters, seventy-five pages, and was planning ahead. He made Wesley twenty-one and considered an English girlfriend for him. She would be one of the "Piccadilly Commandos." He gave her the name Jill, and Carol's appearance.

He introduced the "letter writer," who addresses the people of the world and mails his notes by dropping them from his hotel window. He envisioned the movie that Skouras would make of the story, thinking that Ross Bagdasarian might play Victor Tosca. He would want George Stevens to direct it and Gene Solow to do the scenario.

In spite of these fancies, he felt the work was going poorly. To make matters worse, he had a frighteningly realistic dream of Carol's infidelity. Coming home, she hurried past him in a way that let him know. She undressed and put on a flimsy nightgown but kept him from their bedroom. He knew that she had been with an interior decorator, and he tried to remember his name so he could go and kill him. Then he and Carol were together weeping at the pain of their loss.

Pacing the Waterloo Bridge in the middle of the night, he felt he couldn't continue with the book. The story seemed hopeless, and as he brooded over what to do, he decided the only option was to start over. He had always believed he could do any sort of writing he chose. Well, clearly he *couldn't.* He could write only his own kind, and that too was unpredictable.

It was by an act of will that he overcame the doubts and accompanying melancholia. Remembering his bargain with Agar, he vowed to keep it. There would be a book, and Skouras could do a movie of it for Twentieth Century–Fox. He would finish on schedule, and he could go home.

When Ross Bagdasarian arrived with a day's leave, they went drinking at Jack's. Major Anthony Veiller, just returned from France, stopped by their table to thank Bill for the loan of a field jacket and to give a good report of the Picture Unit's progress. When he asked how the book was going, Bill told him "fine." He had twenty-two chapters and would be finished in ten days.

As Big Ben tolled the hour of midnight, it seemed to echo Bill's own melancholy in pacing the bridge. With two weeks to go, the writing was slow and painful. He was smoking heavily, and his coughing was chronic. He was lonely and sick enough to question his sanity, wondering if he was more lunatic than genius.

Reading the opening chapters, he found nothing exciting. He hoped his disappointment was simply due to the fact that he was too close to the work. He assured himself that however bad, both books, *Wesley Jackson* and his account of writing it, would be published. They might demonstrate how war makes fools of writers. Anyway, the world would not end if the whole project proved a waste of time.

It occurred to him that he might be on his way to becoming an even bigger fool than he already was. He reflected further that unless a man were a giant among writers, it mattered to no one but himself whether he was a master. He would be thankful for his confidence and his madness. He would remember his wife and son and get on with his work.

Crossing the bridge on the night of his thirty-sixth birthday, he told himself that if the moon, presently obscured by clouds, reappeared by the time he reached the embankment, the book would be okay. He had to slow his pace to inch-long steps, but the moon did emerge, and he took heart from this omen.

Bringing the story to its close, he took Wesley into a German prisoner-of-war camp, there to be reunited with Victor Tosca and to make an escape. As he wrote of Wesley's return to London, Bill found he had finished *The Adventures of Wesley Jackson*. The book was 110,000 words long, and he felt it was certainly readable, and possibly great. Dropping off the first twenty chapters at Agar's office, Bill reported that the job was done, and he learned that, although ill and recuperating in the country, Agar was eager to read the finished manuscript. When he brought in the rest, he learned that Agar had read the first half of the manuscript but as yet had made no comment about it.

Bill sent a copy to Donald Brace, in New York, for Harcourt's immediate publication. He urged Brace to have it retyped expertly and to send this version on to Spyros Skouras for a film. There was to be a companion volume that should be published simultaneously. He sent a third copy to Carol and a fourth, by hand, to George Stevens in France. He was expecting Wesley's adventures to make him some badly needed money in 1945. He thought the magazine serialization might bring him as much as $25,000. He would negotiate that on his own.

Waiting now for Agar's response, he felt a touch of regret for having missed the good times in France—the welcome of the French girls and the carousing—which had illuminated the war stories of returning combatants.

On September 20, Bill was summoned to Agar's office and greeted cordially. In spite of his illness, Agar had finished *The Adventures of Wesley Jackson* and found it not just readable but first-rate. He felt Bill had created a whole new world in its pages. As they talked, Agar did reveal some reservations. The book certainly did raise hell with the army. He felt Bill had occasionally turned from art to journalism in order to assail army people he disliked. Also, he wondered if readers would understand about soldiers living outside of billets.

Bill assured him that they would, and he planned to remove such flaws in rewriting. When he inquired about his return home, Agar said he wanted to do everything he could to bring that about and called a Captain Katzenstein to ask the procedure. Agar was told to address the chief signal officer, General Rumbaugh, in France, and he agreed to do so. Two days later Bill learned that Agar was ill again and had not sent off the letter to General Rumbaugh. There was nothing to do but await his recovery.

Then, on September 25, he called the Dorchester and was surprised to have Agar answer his phone. Bill was assured that the Rumbaugh letter had been sent on Saturday and that all was well. On hearing nothing for four days he called Katzenstein and was told that a request for his transfer had already left Rumbaugh's Paris office for the War Department in Washington. It would take two weeks for a reply.

In early October there was alarming news from another, unexpected quarter. Gene Solow returned from France on October 4 and met Bill in the Savoy bar. He gravely reported that a number of the officers in George Stevens's unit had read *The Adventures of Wesley Jackson,* and they all agreed it was a bad book.

What Bill found most treacherous in Solow's account was that Herbert Agar had given a copy of the book to Major Anthony Veiller for his opinion. Veiller's opinion was explicit. Saroyan's book should not be published until after the war. George Stevens, having read half the book, felt the same way. Solow agreed. He said he was saying this because he liked him. The Wesley Jackson story could not be published, because, if it were, the army would go after him and fix it so he'd *never* get out.

Feeling there was something disingenuous in Solow's delivery of all this gossip, Bill decided Solow was an old woman. Bill should have known it from Solow's poker style. Unable to accept this judgment, he left abruptly. Nevertheless, he had further doubts about *Wesley.* In spite of its truth, the book he had written as a key to his release might be the lock itself. This news from France was so crushing that he felt he could not even write Carol about it. As he went to Jack's for some serious drinking, he guessed he was now in London permanently.

The following day, however, Katzenstein had brighter news. The Agar letter had been approved, and his orders to return to New York would be cut in a matter of days. Bill was jubilant and wrote Carol that he was headed home. No sooner had he done so than Katzenstein reported a hitch. The Adjutant Section of Etousa, European Theatre of Operations, had disapproved, for insufficient reasons, the Agar request that Private Saroyan be returned to the United States. Bill wept with anger and frustration.

He was dining in a Greek restaurant when the waiters burst forth in cheers, and thus he learned that Athens had been liberated. Widespread rejoicing over this event did little to relieve his sense of hopelessness. However, he took some heart from Donald Brace's acknowledgment that a copy of the *Wesley Jackson* manuscript had arrived in New York and that Frank Morley not only liked it but felt it might be his best novel.

While awaiting the result of further appeals to army bureaucracy, Bill had a glimpse of the man he considered his principal enemy. Major Anthony Veiller was seated at a nearby table in Jack's with the British novelist Eric Ambler and his wife. Veiller greeted Bill and told him that Irwin Shaw was in London, staying at the Mayfair. He was "Mister" Shaw now, a warrant officer. Bill did not call Shaw, but he stopped at the French Place and found him surrounded by several returning officers.

Shaw told him of the grand time they had had in France. He had been everywhere, including the Riviera, and there had been only one casualty in the whole of Stevens's unit: Ivan Moffatt had broken his leg in an automobile accident. When one of the group told Shaw, "You've got yourself a million dollars' worth of material," there was a nodding of heads.

Bill did not believe Shaw's exploits had any such value. Battle was so repugnant to him that he could dismiss it as worthless experience. Yet he knew that these adventurers—Shaw in particular—had mined some writerly ore in France while he, in his room at the Savoy, had gotten nothing of the sort.

As if this were not pain enough for Bill, Shaw announced he was leaving for New York in the morning with Veiller and planned to stay there for a couple of months. He would be able to attend to the production of his play. Then, maybe he would go on to China. With Warrant Officer Shaw's departure, Bill continued to await his orders through the end of October and the beginning of November. He learned that the final decision on his future had gone to Shaef, and he knew in his embittered heart that such adversarial officers as Major Veiller would influence this decision, and so it would go against him.

He was so full of anger and hopelessness that he could no longer read or sleep. Unhappiness filled his leg with pain. He realized that in insisting that he wanted no part of the war he had brought this misery on himself.

He was not surprised to learn that Astoria would only reaccept him on a ninety-day temporary basis if Herbert Agar were to justify it and explain why his presence in the States was necessary. Agar was ill again and unavailable, but on November 20 Saroyan wrote him a single-spaced, twelve-page letter, reminding him of the past August's promise that when Bill had completed the book he would be returned to New York.

He noted his eminence as an American writer, his obligation to speak on matters of conscience, and how this was being curbed by an army that wanted conformity and accused him of being unpatriotic. He had been shocked to learn that Major Veiller had received a copy of *The Adventures of Wesley Jackson* and had reported to Agar that its publication should not be permitted. He believed Veiller was unqualified to make such a judgment.

He had been further dismayed to learn that if the book were published the army would "get" him. He saw this as Veiller's threat against him. He recalled that on first hearing of the project, Veiller had asked about the "scheme" he had proposed, thus seeming to prejudge it. This was the same man who had not only questioned Saroyan's need to return home for writing the book but had just bestowed on Irwin Shaw a return to New York so that he could look after the producing of his play.

Bill told Agar how the fall from a barstool had affected his two-and-a-half-year army career, and how, although he had known his injury was incapacitating the army doctors had ignored it at his induction, the rigorous basic training, his subsequent duty at Astoria, and his deportation to Ohio.

He outlined the plot by the Astoria officers against him and how this had put him in the psychoneurotic ward of Halloran Hospital, prevented his discharge, and led to accusations of malingering and disloyalty. Now he was trapped. He had become a man without a station. Astoria would not have him back without Agar's justification, and so he felt that Agar owed it to himself, not to Saroyan, to keep his part of the bargain.

On December 2, he received Agar's response. Addressing him as "Dear Pvt. Saroyan," he stated serenely that he had recommended to the army that it return Saroyan to the United States to revise the manuscript. He hoped it would see fit to do so, but it was up to the army, not himself, to accomplish this.

He went on to point out that whatever assurance he had given about returning Saroyan to the States was based on the belief that he would write the book they had discussed and agreed upon. In the writing, that original purpose had become lost in Saroyan's own concerns. It was Agar's hope that extensive revisions would give the manuscript some resemblance to the original idea and purpose. If he did not think this was possible, Agar could not recommend Saroyan's return to the States to do the work.

In addition, Agar felt it would have been sensible for Saroyan to anticipate that the army might not cooperate enthusiastically in the publication of a book it did not like; and quite apart from the matter of artistic merit, the army did not like his book. He felt the army's reasons for this were as valid as Saroyan's in its defense. He ended by saying that he was doing his best to keep his part of the bargain, as Saroyan had put it, but it had not been made easier by Saroyan's failure to deliver the book they had discussed.

Although Bill had urged Harcourt to get army approval of the *Adventures of Wesley Jackson* manuscript and proceed to publish it, he now wrote Frank Morley that he had decided against submitting the book to censorship. It must remain as he had written it. Rather than publication, he was considering a private printing of a few hundred copies. Would Frank advise him about this?

Just before Christmas he began a novel about the madness of war. He wrote steadily through the holiday, and as he finished chapter three, approved what he had done. But then the writing turned slow and unhappy. He told himself to stick with it, if only to get through the week, but the words failed to come. Chapter four amounted to only two pages. His mind had gone flat.

He believed that if he could write about his plight, wings would come to his spirit and deliver him from his prison. But he could not, and so he remained locked up with no hope of breaking free.

In the early-morning hours of December 31, unable to sleep, Bill was struck with a frightening sense of disaster. Not just the year, but his very *self* had come to an end. His fear and sense of mental breakdown was absolute. He was going mad thinking he had a lot to say and at the same time not knowing what it could be. He rose, turned on the light, and managed to get through the night. During the day, however, the year's last, some of this despair clung to him.

On New Year's Day he was enough recovered from his horrors to write jolly, hopeful letters to Carol, his mother, and Ross Bagdasarian. However, when George Barnes, Agar's assistant at the American embassy, called with reassurances that a copy of *Wesley* had gone to the public relations chief at Etousa and that the censors would decide about it within a few days, Bill responded angrily. It was more deception from the army authorities.

On January 2, George Stevens reappeared in his life. He was just back from Paris for two weeks of work with Carol Reed and Garson Kanin on their British-American film project. He confirmed that he had read only half of the *Wesley* story and had little to say about it except that he felt Bill's troubles could be traced to his relationship with Herbert Agar.

While he had no wish to accept his invitation, Bill was pleased to know that Stevens wanted him back in his unit. As far as he knew, it was the one place in the entire U.S. Army where he was welcome. There would be nothing for him to do there; it was simply a matter of keeping Stevens company.

Over the weekend of January 7, the news of the war in Germany continued to be gloomy. The bloody Battle of the Bulge, in which inadequate and inexperienced U.S. troops had taken the brunt of General von Rundstedt's attack, had at last been turned, but the huge cost in casualties was just becoming known. Bill passed the time in a stupor. While rocket bombs continued to fall near the hotel, he took part in poker games at the army mess.

Then, on January 9, he learned that his orders had finally arrived, and he hurried to pick them up. They were dated December 27 and originated with Etousa, by command of General Eisenhower. Private Saroyan was relieved from detached service with OWI and was to proceed to Supreme HQ Allied Expeditionary Force (Main) APO 757 on detached service with the Public Relations Division to carry out instructions of the theater commander.

Reading his orders over, he continued to hope they would signify a meeting with the censors considering *The Adventures of Wesley Jackson*. From the date, however, he realized they had nothing to do with censors, or with a return to the United States. He showed the orders to George Stevens, who thought it unlikely Bill was being sent to Paris to work on *The Adventures of Wesley Jackson*. Since the APO number was Stevens's own, he guessed Bill had been assigned to his outfit.

While awaiting transportation instructions, Bill was invited to go along with Stevens, Garson Kanin, and Carol Reed to the Pinewood studios in suburban London to see the film on which they were collaborating. It was the one about the invasion of Europe that he and Irwin Shaw had worked on when he had arrived, nearly a year ago. He knew that Garson had taken it over recently and had persuaded Robert Sherwood that it was worthwhile. Watching it from the projection room, Bill decided that, while it showed thousands of human beings involved in a meaningless game, it lacked any breath of life. The project had already cost the government hundreds of thousands of dollars and countless man hours, but it was a disaster, just as he knew it would be. It was not only inhuman, it was antihuman.

On the return drive, Bill gave his opinion bluntly, along with explicit advice on improving the film. Reed seemed attentive, but Kanin appeared indifferent to his views. Whether or not Bill had any effect on the film, which was called *The True Glory*, it would later win the 1945 Academy Award as the best documentary feature film of the year.

On Monday, January 22, Bill was alerted for departure. He packed up and was flown to Paris with orders to report to the army Public Relations Division office on the fifth floor of the American Express Building in the Place de l'Opera.

There he found himself reattached to Stevens's Special Motion Picture Unit, but since Stevens had not yet returned to Paris, he was to report to a Colonel Lawton for daily assignments. Lawton assured him that his new duties had nothing whatever to do with *Wesley Jackson*. Busy with other matters, the War Department was ignoring it.

He was billeted in a tiny room at the Hotel Louis La Grand along with other enlisted men, and, for the present, there was little for him to do. He enjoyed cold, snowy Paris. The women, in their big hats, looked especially smart. He went to a performance of the Folies-Bergère and was pleased at the sight of the clever sets and the chorus girls naked to the waist. Whenever they appeared, he was delighted by a soldier in the audience who howled with the pathos of all the lonely armies.

Bill's own thoughts were only of Carol, and he sent her a box of assorted perfumes. His way to the Louis La Grand took him past a shop displaying a pair of handsome women's shoes. They were size five, and he guessed they were too small for Carol, but he imagined them on her feet. Although they cost 6,500 francs—$130—he ordered a pair in size six.

When he stopped by the shop to pick them up, he found a hat with purple and black feathers and an antelope-skin handbag that were equally irresistible. He added them to the package for Carol and wrote her that if the shoes failed to fit she should accept them as a souvenir.

Saroyan in Paris with Ross Bagdasarian

The correspondents, perhaps three hundred of them, were billeted at the Hotel Scribe, a few doors from the army offices. The Scribe bar was the meeting place, and here Bill found all the old London faces plus some new ones. There was Max Lerner, of *PM,* Charles Collingwood, of the Blue Network, and, of course, Ernest Hemingway, now beardless and surrounded by admirers.

When Bill approached Hemingway's group, one of the correspondents greeted him, calling attention to his arrival, and yet Hemingway seemed not to recognize him and asked where he was. Bill responded by saying that he knew Hemingway even without his beard, and perhaps it was shaving it off that accounted for the memory lapse. Hemingway simply turned away. Presently, Hemingway surprised him by asking how he liked the picture, meaning the victorious march of the Allied armies into Germany. Thinking

A reunion in wartime Paris brought forth Bill's and his
cousin Ross's love of clowning—here with the crew
of a Parisian garbage truck.

Hemingway meant the European-invasion film he had just seen at Pinewood, Bill replied that he didn't like it at all. A puzzled Hemingway got no
further explanation.

Carlos Baker's biography of Hemingway includes an account of a subsequent confrontation at the Hotel George V, where Hemingway and Saroyan
found themselves at neighboring tables and in company with friends.
Noticing Saroyan, Hemingway is reported to have said, "Well, for God's
sake, what's that lousy Armenian son-of-a-bitch doing here?" Saroyan's
companions rallied loyally, and the result was a full-scale brawl that required
a police reinforcement to put the fighters out of the hotel into the Paris
blackout. There was a finale in Hemingway's howl of laughter. On reading
the account years later, Saroyan, never one for combat, denied any such
incident had taken place.

Now Bill was glad to find Ross Bagdasarian at his door. Ross was stationed in a town thirty miles outside Paris and had a pass for the day.
Together they went off to an Armenian pub, where, over glasses of *rakki,*

Ross described his assignment. He was enjoying his work, he told his cousin, and having an affair with a French nurse. She spoke no English, so they were silent together, but she delighted in embarrassing him by unexpectedly turning on the light.

In the course of daily interviews, Colonel Lawton made it clear that there was no chance the army would change its mind about *Wesley Jackson,* and that Bill had better get used to prolonged duty in France with the Special Motion Picture unit. This only stiffened Bill's resolve to see his book published.

He wrote Frank Morley that he now wanted it published as soon as possible and that he was satisfied with the present manuscript. He urged Morley to submit it to the authorities in Washington, telling them that Harcourt was proceeding with its release.

George Stevens returned to Paris to be billeted with other officers at the Crillon, and to confer with Lawton on Bill's future. Lawton was convinced that Bill could, and should, write a great story about the American soldier, one that could become a significant project of the Special Motion Picture Unit.

Bill did not respond to Lawton's enthusiasm. He had an unfavorable opinion of the film unit and trusted no one in the army—neither Lawton nor even George Stevens. He pointed out that in *Wesley Jackson,* he had already written the story of the American soldier, and the army had spurned it.

Bill clung to the idea that when pressed by Harcourt, the army censors would require alterations in *Wesley* and summon him to New York. Although this seemed unlikely to all three, Stevens proposed that Lawton query Morley about it, and, if it were the case, to request Bill be transferred there.

Finally it was determined that Bill would write captions for a picture book on the American soldier. He could go out to the troops with a photographer, interview soldiers, and write brief accounts of them.

The Paris poker games took place much as they had in London. In the course of one high-stakes game with the Hotel Scribe correspondents, Bill lost consistently in a way he hadn't in years, and when it was over he owed Robert Capa $3,000. He gave Capa a note for it and promised to settle the account within a month.

On February 3, he was picked up by the military police and nearly jailed by the station's duty officer for his lack of a pass and his indifference to army regulations. He also learned that Lawton was looking for him. The colonel had decided that they would work together on the American soldier book and that Bill should prepare himself for an exploratory journey.

Bill's coughing and back pain had been such that he doubted he was equal to any travel, but four days later, Bill, Lawton, and a driver set off by jeep on a tour of army units to the east of Paris. They had planned to travel for three days, but as they bumped along the wintry provincial roads, Bill's pain worsened. Reaching Luxembourg on the second day, Bill convinced Lawton to return to Paris so that he could get some treatment.

Although he continued to believe that the conspiracy against him and his crippling back pain were irreversible, at the army's Paris dispensary he found what he had been seeking throughout his enlistment—a sympathetic medical officer. The captain who examined him agreed that his back pain was chronic, permanent, and treatable only with rest and heat. He was willing to certify this and to classify Bill for limited service only.

When Bill shared this report with Lawton, pointing out that it precluded further field trips of the sort that had brought on his pain, Lawton wanted to return to the dispensary with Bill to discuss the matter with the doctor. He was dissuaded only by Bill's protest about interfering with medical procedure.

On that same night, February 11, Bill was admitted to the army's First General Hospital for observation of his back. At last his ailments were taken seriously. Doctors agreed his bar-room fall could have caused a slipped intervertebral disc. Best of all, the medical corps' plan was to return him by air to the States, probably San Francisco, for further diagnosis and possible back surgery.

At last, and by some miraculous reversal of his luck, Saroyan was headed for home. He arrived at Mitchell Field in New York on March 5, 1945, and was able to interrupt his journey here for a joyful reunion with Carol and eighteen-month-old Aram. It was his first glimpse of them in over a year. They agreed that Carol would close the apartment and, with Aram, follow him to California.

His air journey ended in Sacramento, where he was taken by ambulance to DeWitt Hospital, in Auburn, California. At his examination there, he displayed none of the symptoms that in Paris had suggested a need for surgery. He seemed largely recovered and was given a weekend pass.

As planned, Carol had closed the New York apartment and arrived in San Francisco with Aram. There, at 1821 Fifteenth Avenue, Bill was at last reunited with his entire family. Takoohi assumed custody of Aram with firm competence, leaving Bill and Carol to the pleasures of being together. These were such that he failed to report to DeWitt Hospital on Monday morning.

When he appeared on Wednesday he found himself AWOL, but he persuaded the DeWitt authorities that he had telephoned and been granted an extension. While the examining orthopedist and neurologist could find neither acute symptoms nor disabilities that would keep Saroyan from service, it was their opinion that he could no longer render any useful service in the army, and should be discharged. He would be presented to the board with that recommendation.

On April 4, Bill appeared before the board to hear that he was being discharged and his return to civilian life awaited only the surgeon general's approval. Carol was sure Bill was now out of the army, but he clung to a hard-won skepticism. He suspected his bugbear in Washington was not yet ready to relinquish his grasp.

Bill was right. Over the next five months, decision after decision went against his release, and he remained Private Saroyan under the authority of West Coast army hospitals. Someone high up felt him insufficiently incapacitated for discharge and thus deserving of further opportunity to serve his country.

As this epilogue of his army service stretched through the spring and summer of 1945, news came of Germany's surrender and the victorious close of the European war, of President Roosevelt's unexpected death (wringing from Bill a "poor" Roosevelt, to add to the chorus of world grief), of the dropping of the atomic bomb on Hiroshima, of the Japanese surrender, and, finally, of the war's end.

For Bill, the best news of this climactic summer of readjustment was Carol's—she was pregnant. The Saroyans now rejoiced in the belief that a daughter would be born to them the following February.

Also, since Bill was on a perpetually renewing furlough, he and Carol could enjoy their long-awaited holiday together, leaving Aram in the attentive care of his aunt and grandmother. More importantly, Bill could resume his writing career.

Frank Morley advised Bill that with the war's end the army's ruling against *The Adventures of Wesley Jackson* had been lifted. While Bill wanted to revise *Wesley* before it appeared, he felt that could wait until he had reasserted himself with an entirely new book.

He had been looking back over the year 1939, realizing how remarkable it had been for him. It had begun at home on Carl Street but taken him to Mexico, Cuba, London, Dublin, and Paris. And what an exuberance of plays had flowed from his typewriter: *Elmer and Lily, The Hero of the World, Love's Old Sweet Song,* and *Sweeney in the Trees.* And the year had seen the two triumphant Broadway presentations of *My Heart's in the Highlands* and *The Time of Your Life.*

He would write about that year. He gave the book the title *Early Thursday* and planned to finish it by July 31, when he would take Carol to Reno and Fresno for a month's vacation. At the end of May he began, wrote some opening pages, and told Frank Morley to expect the manuscript soon.

Carol also had a project, a story about a family named Hamilcar, which Bill had begun and abandoned years earlier. After she had made up their bedroom she would stay out of his way and busy herself with the Hamilcars. She considered a pen name; when Bill suggested Lucy Flanagan, she rejected it. It made her think of a large Irish woman with a red nose, reeling out of a saloon.

Bill pushed himself to produce a daily chapter of *Early Thursday*, but when he read several, he saw they were a retelling of stories he had written in early 1939. He had written nothing new at all.

Alarmed, he asked God for the grace to do the best work he could. Although he struggled at the dredging of his memory, it was a dream-like confusion, and he could not produce a tangible recollection. Instead of feeling a buoyancy at the outset of writing, he felt irritated, depressed, and hopeless. He lacked the heart to create characters. He resented them, and he suspected it was because the more urgent job was to recreate his own character. The spontaneous, life-loving Saroyan, so sure of the world's follies and his instincts about them that he could not fail, was lost along the path he had come.

Carol, on the other hand, had been busy with the Hamilcar story, and when Bill read it over, he admitted that it was good. She asked him whether he thought it was publishable, and, if it were, whether it would make her famous. He was noncommittal, but Carol told him that she was very eager to be famous.

By the Fourth of July, Bill was sick. He slept poorly. His ear hissed, and he was unable to work at all. He had lost his 1939 book in the wilderness of his pain, and he told himself that he had no need to write a book now.

Instead, he gathered up some old, unpublished stories, thirty-eight in all, to make a collection. Although he found them depressing, he wrote a preface declaring that his hatred for the army was greater than for war itself and equal to what he felt for a censor who had prevented his novel's appearance. He gave it the title *Huckety-Buck*—George Stevens's appeal for luck at the poker table—and sent the manuscript to Frank Morley at Harcourt, hoping he could get it onto the fall list.

He soon heard from Morley that *Huckety-Buck* was unworthy of him and would not do at all for his next Harcourt book. It was one more wound to his confidence. Now his need for a sustaining theme turned him to the past. He would write a sequel to *Time of Your Life*. The scene would still be Nick's bar on Pacific Street, and the characters would be the same, but the time would be the present.

Even as he began a first act, he felt the energy leave him. At nine that same night, he stopped work on the play, admitting he could not go on. Time was passing, and he could produce nothing but alibis.

As he turned to revising the *Adventures of Wesley Jackson* manuscript, he decided that he could write a sequel to it. This would take Wesley, Jill, and their new son through the war's end. He began a first chapter in which Wesley, in his Huck Finn voice, told of his gratitude for Jill's being spared in the bomb blast that had destroyed their house. Although Bill worked on it for several days and the pages multiplied, he recognized the dialogue between Wesley and Jill as mawkish nonsense. Bill's back pain reemerged and kept him from going on. Carol suggested he abandon the project and write something entirely new. He decided she was right.

But in failing to find a persuasive character and situation for yet another play, his irritation took shape in a quarrel with Carol that he felt was the worst they had ever had. At its climax she vowed to go to a hotel, and they were slow to reconcile.

When he told her that he needed the refreshment of a few games of stud at the Menlo Club, she encouraged him. She returned money he had given her so that he could start with a bankroll of $150, and she went to a movie while he gambled. At the end of an hour Bill had lost the $150. He walked to the Omar Khayyam, borrowed $500 from the proprietor, his friend George Mardikian, and returned to lose nearly all of that before his luck changed. By the time he had to meet Carol, he had won back his losses and an additional $65.

Although Bill found time to give Carol a driving lesson and take her to the beach, she was newly contentious. A row over the effects of leaving Aram behind while they traveled lasted until two in the morning and kept Bill from his next day's work. In a subsequent quarrel, Carol revealed her unhappiness at living with his family, losing charge of Aram, and not having a kitchen in which she was free to cook. This dispute too continued into the early hours, and again Bill slept into his work time.

Bill learned that while he and Carol had been away, Aram had missed him to the point of surprising strange servicemen in the park by laying down beside them. He recalled playing a game with Aram in which they would stretch out side by side on the floor and Aram would put his head on his father's arm. He promised Aram more attention.

Looking at his son, he decided Aram's head was the noblest he had ever seen and was delighted when the boy danced to radio music before an audience of his doting aunts. He enjoyed Aram's mispronunciations and his sudden, grinning summons of "Willie!" Realizing how alive and personable Aram had become, he chided himself for not having kept up with him. He recognized that Aram had inherited his own curiosity about things and, like him, would soon be turning it to books, art, music, nature, and himself.

The young Saroyans had barely made themselves at home on Fifteenth Avenue when a spat occurred between Carol and Takoohi over kitchen rights. Bill settled it soon enough but found himself newly despondent. There was no fun for them anymore. The city and the house saddened Carol, and he was not able to cheer her.

When his mother put him to bed, Aram protested angrily, and when Takoohi went to quiet his wails, Carol took it as a rebuke. Bill, who could not bear the sound of his child's unhappiness, was equally distressed.

It occurred to Bill that Aram's unrest and complaining was the result of their neglect. When Aram wanted something, he wanted it at once. When denied, he complained furiously, shaking with anger. When Bill responded to Aram's outcry with his own shouts, the child complained that he was sleepy, his response to the slightest disappointment. Bill saw his son's fury and insistence as ominous, and, while he wanted to be an effective father to Aram, he could only turn away. This abandoning of Aram was because of his need to work, and, also, he knew, his ignorance. He did not know how to put up with, let alone comfort and guide, his twenty-two-month-old son.

Thus, as the world celebrated the victory of democratic nations and the end of a great war, Bill Saroyan confronted himself, the man who had deplored, ignored, and resisted it, to find he was as certain a casualty as those fellow soldiers who lay in the veteran hospitals and hero graves.

His very center, that force of spirit that drove his writing and that he had taken as much for granted as his heartbeat, was missing in action, fallen somewhere on the battlefield where he had taken on the army itself. Without it, he was a hollow man.

Nor was that the end of it, for he had nourished a second purpose, the founding of the William Saroyan family. It was an Old World dream to be realized in the new one, a patriarchy, the heading of a clan that would become his immortality. There was to be a homestead, an adoring wife and mother, and a profusion of happy, healthy children readying for a better life. At last in the role, he found it asking more than he could give.

X

READJUSTMENT

1945–1949

At the end of his summer furlough Bill reported back to Madigan Hospital in Tacoma and there, on September 11, 1945—Carol's twenty-first birthday—Bill was given his discharge from the service. He could hardly believe that after two years and eleven months in the army he was free. That same afternoon, he donned his freshly pressed gabardine suit, and, with Carol beside him, set out for San Francisco. They were overwhelmed with happiness and plans for their future.

Bill thanked God for this new beginning. Lucy would be born early in the new year. He had $20,000 in the Corn Exchange Bank in New York, a sum with which he could do anything, perhaps open his own office there. While his inclination was to return to New York, Carol proposed they look first for a home in California. They decided to dedicate the next few weeks to that search and to reacquainting themselves with Aram.

They considered properties throughout central California, and decided on a lot in San Francisco with a fine view of the bay. It was in Sea Cliff, priced at $11,000, and came with plans for a house that could be built for $16,000. Bill put down $5,000 and found his bank willing to finance the balance and the construction of the house.

Realizing it would be many months before they could move to Sea Cliff, Bill went shopping for a second property, and two days later he bought a recently completed house at 2727 Taraval Street. It contained two five-room flats, a basement garage, and a yard in which Aram could play. The price was $13,720, and he paid for it in full.

Carol was happy with these new prospects. While Bill bought a good stove and, despite their scarcity, located a refrigerator, Carol phoned her mother, asking her to ship out all the furniture and belongings she had stored in New York. As the month ended, Bill and Carol spent much of each day watching the progress of painters, paperhangers, and carpet-layers readying their new quarters. As the first of their belongings arrived from New York and were put in place, Bill and Carol found they liked the two flats so much, they would postpone the building of the Sea Cliff house.

Carol was now in the seventh month of her pregnancy with the child Bill had so confidently named Lucy. Bill was becoming a complete parent to Aram, holding him in his arms, taking him on walks, and inventing games of running and hiding and tossing stones into a can. Sometimes with Carol, sometimes without her, they visited the zoo and the merry-go-round in Golden Gate Park.

Each day Carol and Bill worked on the Taraval house, and it restored their happiness. Carol had chosen the same blue and white floral pattern for their bedroom wallpaper that they had had at Two Sutton Place. As moving day approached, they were in a mood to dance together, and Aram watched them with delight.

Making their formal entry, Bill joked that Carol was too heavy for him to carry across the threshold, so he made do with Aram. Once inside, all three embraced and kissed and toured the premises. The lower floor was to be their living quarters, the upper one Bill's workspace, an office with walls of bright white bookshelves, plus a family room furnished with the baby-grand player piano used in *Get Away Old Man* and a recently acquired organ.

Aram, with the loss of two caretakers, Takoohi and Cosette, was less happy. He balked at taking off his clothes for a bath and when put to bed sobbed so pitifully that Bill gathered him up and tried to comfort him by the fire. Listening to Aram's persistent complaints, Bill was sure he and Carol were not suited for parenting, nor would they be. They must have a nurse, someone permanent.

Money was also a concern. When the last of their furniture arrived from New York Bill gave the mover a check for $1,300. His San Francisco bank account was down to a thousand dollars, and he owed twice that in Taraval Street expenses. The hospital and doctor's bills for Lucy's birth were yet to come, and he felt occasional misgivings about his taxes. He had paid none for 1943 and 1944, nor had he filed any forms. He was going to need an income of at least $10,000 a year.

Their first night at 2727 Taraval brought a further concern. As Carol was first to point out, their new home had not been planned with children in mind. The apartments were two boxes cut up into cells, and the walls muffled no sounds. Moreover, the house was so close to the trolley track and the passage of the cars was so frequent that the house trembled continuously.

Their move had not eased the friction between Carol and Bill's family. She was infuriated by an incident in which Bill, his mother, and his sister had, in her presence, spoken about her in Armenian. She refused thereafter to sit at the table with Takoohi and Cosette and told Bill that the sight of his mother and his sister made her sick. Bill believed that Carol's feeling of exclusion was making her a nag to him and a neglectful mother to Aram.

When Bill called at Fifteenth Avenue to pick up his mail, his mother suggested aspirin for Aram's cold. Returning to Taraval Street, he found Carol on the floor with Aram. When he proposed the aspirin to her, Carol asked if he intended to go home each day and bring her advice. Pained by the tone of her voice and the hatred in her eyes, Bill asked if he were now free not to try to be of help. She told him he was. Upstairs, he found he could not work because of the terrible sound of Aram's crying. He returned to find Carol trying to put the angry child to bed. She was trembling with her confusion over Aram and her resentment of Takoohi and Cosette.

Insisting that it was too early for Aram to be put to bed, Bill lifted him from his crib, carried him to the living room, and lit a fire. In the mail Bill had brought was a carton of chocolate bars sent by his friend Yep Moradian. Bill gave one to his fretful son, watched him unwrap and nibble it, then another. When he took a third, Bill told Aram he could open them all, and dumped the box on the floor.

This intemperate act shattered all restraint between Bill and Carol, and he shouted and cursed at her and she shouted and cursed him back. In the midst of the turmoil Carol paused to swoop Aram up and put him to bed, but then she returned to the fray. They were equally convinced that not only was the house a mistake but their marriage and life together were as well. When at last their fury was spent, Bill sat alone in the kitchen. In his despair he could think only of going out to get drunk or into a poker game or of driving to another town. He stretched out on a bed and slept for a while, waking to find Carol dozing and crying on the davenport.

Thinking how all three of them were demanding and how their life in this clearly unsuitable house now appeared hopeless, Bill thought of moving, but they were broke and could not. Soon Carol did find a children's nurse, a Mrs. Nielson, who would live with them. Even though she talked with a dizzying speed, Bill thought she would be okay. He told himself that it was up to him to see that their life here worked.

Over the next several days, they patched up their quarrel and bought and decorated a Christmas tree. Carol was cheered by the arrival of a mink coat, a gift from her mother. She was equally pleased by a gift from Gloria Vanderbilt and her new husband, the distinguished conductor Leopold Stokowski, a Vertes painting that she hung in their bedroom. Aram's behavior improved markedly, and when Bill brought his mother and sister for a pre-Christmas visit, Carol responded gratefully to Takoohi's compliments on the appearance of her household. Serenity was restored.

Bill had done no writing during the year but felt sure he would begin soon. Harcourt Brace would be striving for a Book-of-the-Month Club selection for *Wesley Jackson,* and even without that it was going to be a big success. He believed that whatever money he needed would always come in. Only two things were important: to be the center of his family and to be a successful writer. He expected the year ahead to be a fruitful one.

On the evening of January 16, 1946, Bill took Carol to Children's Hospital. Lucy, his daughter, was born the following morning. Bill saw her first when she was fifteen minutes old, and he was stunned by the sight. In spite of her long eyelashes and well-shaped head, he thought she was downright ugly. The ears were flat on top, her nostrils were wide like Carol's and her mother's, her mouth was loose and enormous, and her head was covered with red bumps. He thought poor Lucy looked like an old Jew.

Carol, on the other hand, thought her daughter was already beautiful. Bill knew Lucy would grow into her beauty in a month—or a year—and went on to think how funny it was that this *thing* was really a woman, a girl who would soon tear his heart with her loveliness. He hoped her life would be a sweet, fine one, and he saluted her as his darling Lucy, and told her that her papa loved her.

Ten days later, when Bill brought Carol and Lucy home from the hospital, he admired his daughter's blue eyes, noted that her fingers were his, and was convinced that within a month she would be a charmer. Although Bill's own family took Lucy's arrival in stride, Charles and Rosheen Marcus felt she deserved a welcoming visit. They arrived from New York, took a room at the St. Francis, and turned up at Taraval Street to offer help and counsel and to add to the frenzy of the Saroyan household. Aram resumed his sobbing and came down with a flu that needed round-the-clock attention, while Lucy slept peacefully through it all.

Looking at one-month-old Lucy, Bill saw a shy, smiling, absolutely adorable girl, not at all the way Aram had been as an infant. Her mouth had a lovely shape, always in happiness. Her nose was Carol's and already perfect. Her eyelashes were blond, and he thought she would be as fair as her mother.

But there was new trouble. The Marcuses called on Bill's family and returned with a report that Carol had been behaving like an ogre to them. Cosette, whom Rosheen thought looked thin and ill, had announced she would die if not allowed to see Aram once a week. Carol was understandably angry.

Bill was quick to reassure Rosheen that the marriage was fine and that his grandmother adored Carol. It was his mother and his sister who made the discord.

Deciding to have a talk with his family, Bill called at Fifteenth Avenue. While Grandmother Lucy temporized, insisting it was all nonsense, she was no match for Takoohi, who was bursting with fury. In spite of Bill's patience, the discussion was emotional, prolonged, and never wholly resolved.

The conversation did result in an invitation to dinner, and they spent an evening together in which all parties behaved with restraint. When Charles and Rosheen left for New York, Bill conceded that their visit had brought about the healing of several bruised spirits in San Francisco.

The galleys of *Wesley Jackson* arrived from Harcourt. As Bill corrected them, he thought the story read well, and that the book was good, maybe wonderful. But as he reached the end, he was disappointed to find no satisfying climax.

As he returned the *Wesley Jackson* galleys he found that the novel led Harcourt's spring list and would be published on May 16. A letter about it from Frank Morley was, as always, generous. It cheered Bill and strengthened his hunch that *Wesley* would be a Book-of-the-Month Club selection, and a success, in any case. Despite Bill's optimism, Carol was skeptical, and questioned whether in cutting ten thousand words from the book he hadn't lost its essence. But the news from Harcourt was that the Book-of-the-Month Club had made it an "A" book for the March 15 meeting when the committee would make its June selection. If they chose *Wesley*, as he felt they must, it would mean $100,000 for him.

He also wanted to publish the journal he had kept during the writing of *Wesley*, in November, six months after the novel itself. As he worked at journal revisions, he wrote Bob Giroux, his alternate editor at Harcourt, to expect this new manuscript next month, just before he plunged into work on a new, long novel for 1947.

Then, on March 15, a main hope was dashed by a telegram from Frank Morley, which said that the Book-of-the-Month Club had failed to choose *Wesley Jackson* as its next selection. With a taunt about its judgment, Morley was sending a further advance of $5,000, which allowed Bill to pay off some of his debts.

When he called the federal and state tax offices, he was dismayed to learn that he must now file returns for his three agonizing army years and pay the taxes. He guessed he owed about $20,000, and had only $952 in the bank. He would have to appeal once more to Harcourt Brace, and he was no longer so sure that publication of *Wesley Jackson* would solve his money problems.

Nor was there cheer in news from London. The reviews of *Dear Baby*, sent on by Faber, were all poor. Moreover, the newly founded Saroyan Society's appeal for membership in Britain had brought in some testy responses. H. E. Bates proclaimed that "Saroyan is a self-centered writer of no worth," and James Agate said that "Saroyan is an upstart, that his wretched movie and book entitled *The Human Comedy* belittled the name of Balzac and his great work bearing the same title." Finally, a London production of *Time of Your Life* had flopped. Bill was particularly offended by the *Daily Herald* review, which was headed "An Orgy of Self-Pity."

Gambling was the big snake in Bill Saroyan's garden, always waiting for him with its seductive promise of quick riches. It made his blood rush and brought him a feeling of luck and confidence. He rationalized that its heavy losses were really blessings, driving him to his typewriter and starting the flow of his creative powers. Despite the pain and remorse of losing, it delivered, just as winning did, a surge of feeling, and satisfied the craving of a man who, in insulating himself against childhood pain, had numbed his senses.

The disappointments and domestic quarrels of the spring of 1946 brought on a rising tide of gambling. In mid-March Bill became a regular in the poker games at the Menlo Club. He would go off to them with Carol's blessing, a hundred dollars, and a belief that poker would refresh him. His luck was often bad, and he would fortify it with four or five whiskies and then lose all reason and play all night, cashing thousand-dollar checks against an account that barely had funds for the week's household expenses. The following morning brought the reckoning, a frantic search for the soft touches who enabled him to live this way.

As the spring wore on, Bill widened his playing fields. With the counsel of a bookie named Les Cohen, he was betting the baseball games and the horses at Bay Meadows. When he tired of these, he often found his way to the baccarat tables at Russian Mike Bensnehoff's, on Geary Street.

The first touch on Bill's list was his prospering brother-in-law Walter Papazian. Bill would call him to explain his predicament, and, at first, Walt obliged with sums of several thousand dollars. Once, in meeting Walt at the bank, Bill found his sister Zabe had come with him. Accepting Walt's loan, which brought his debt to the Papazians to $5,000, Bill submitted to some sisterly advice about his gambling. Nevertheless, he blamed Walt for admitting Zabe to their confidence. A second touch was his friend George Mardikian, of the Omar Khayyam. In the beginning George too was understanding and could be counted on for sums of $5,000 at a time.

Bill's last recourse was his publisher. After a disastrous Easter Sunday morning's play at Russian Mike's that had cost Bill $2,100 and brought his year's loss to $12,000, he wired Donald Brace and Frank Morley of his urgent need for $20,000. He proposed a loan or an advance for which he was willing to extend his contract to three more books. Harcourt complied, wiring him the money, which allowed him to cover his gambling checks and left a balance of $17,000 for taxes and living expenses.

Bill was indifferent to the damage to his reputation, as if the latter were indestructible. In the army, he had been accused of not caring what others thought of him, and he had agreed that this was true. He was oblivious to the opinion of others. As he would later admit, people were never entirely real to him. He did not see them as having responses like his own; rather, he saw them as persons in a dream, materializing only when they became useful to him.

In early April, the Saroyans had a telephone call from Gloria and Leopold Stokowski that left Carol elated and Bill anxious. "Leopoldo," as Bill called him, confided in Bill that Gloria had suffered a miserable courtroom childhood and even now was being tormented by her fellow Americans, so he was planning to take her to live in a more civilized country, where they could be happy together. Meanwhile, he was bringing her to visit them in San Francisco.

Leopold and Gloria Stokowski arrived on May 2 for a three-day visit, banishing Ellen Erickson, the children's new nurse, to the couch in Lucy's room. Gloria and Carol had a good time cooking together while Leopold prepared a luncheon salad—which Bill thought only fair. Bill did his best to be cordial, but Stokowski was a bona fide star whose prestige seemed to question his own. The Stokowskis struck Bill as a vain, self-indulgent couple, and he was eager for their departure.

A first copy of *The Adventures of Wesley Jackson* had arrived simultaneously with the Stokowskis, and Bill was soon lost in its pages. As always in a first encounter with a bound book of his, he found fault. It seemed to him that his characters talked alike and that they sounded like him.

In spite of promises to Carol, his gambling continued through May. At first he won enough to pay off his debt to George Mardikian and the balance owed on the Sea Cliff lot, but then he began to lose. One night at Russian Mike's, with Carol playing beside him, he lost $3,500 in a few hours.

Adding up the score, he found he had lost $15,000 within the year, and owed his publisher $30,000. He and Carol had only $4,000 to live on indefinitely. He knew her anger at him was justified. He also admitted that he was an incurable gambler, persistently believing in the nonsense that he could get even, that he could win at *any* kind of gambling—poker, dice, horses, baseball, or baccarat—whenever he chose.

After a particularly bitter quarrel, Bill listened as Carol called her mother

for the money to come to New York, but found Rosheen could not provide
it. Clearly Bill was no longer in any condition to write. Even the thought of
it was abhorrent.

Vowing to win real money, he gambled away $20,000 in three days. He
had no income for the foreseeable future, and as he sat at home, a desperate
man, listening to the wailing of both his children, he conceded that it was
not his luck that had betrayed him, but his skill at gambling. He was just no
good at it.

Only one hope remained. *The Adventures of Wesley Jackson* was to be
published on June 3, 1946, now a week off. A few days before, a *Chronicle*
writer he knew appeared at his door. It was Paul Speegle, come to tell Bill
that he had just reviewed *Wesley Jackson* for the newspaper's Sunday book
section. Bill listened as Speegle told him he had liked the stuff about the
army, but did not go for the love story between Jill and Wesley. Speegle's
voice was hardly an influential one, but his praise fell short of what Bill had
anticipated in his hometown paper.

He dismissed Speegle's review in the *Chronicle* as ignorant. Then the *Saturday Review* arrived with a drawing of himself on the cover and, within,
Harrison Smith's review of *Wesley.* Smith summed up the book by saying it
bore little relation to a world in starvation, revolution, and at war, because
Saroyan had no understanding of politics or social schemes. This was a
blow. It was an important review, and Bill felt that bringing up the familiar
charges of narcissism, tearfulness, and fantasy was unfair. He thought of,
then decided against, answering it. He was irritated and disgusted, but he
assured himself that he was neither beaten down nor discouraged.

Anxiety over how Harcourt was taking the news was calmed when Bill
heard from Frank Morley that he was unfazed. (And, although it was in no
way related, Morley was planning to retire from publishing.) Nevertheless,
as Bill awaited other opinions, he wondered if anyone would like it. Talking
it over with Carol, he still felt that *Wesley* was his best book, possibly one of
the best American books ever, and he imagined that if the critics continued
lambasting it, they were going to make fools of themselves.

Late in the week he found the Sunday *Times* review by his friend Irwin
Shaw. "Once more," Irwin wrote, "Saroyan is full of love for the entire
world. He loves the Germans, he loves the Japs, he loves the Bulgarians and
Finns and Roumanians. The only people he can find to hate are the Americans. He forgives the Germans Dachau and Belsen without blinking an eye,
but he cannot forgive the sergeant who assigned him to KP in New York
City." Shaw concluded, "It seems to me that a writer, no matter how far-
fetched and fanciful he may be, should have some compulsion to present
the truth." Bill found Shaw's review the silliest one of all.

Nor was he cheered by Orville Prescott's judgment in Monday's *Times*. Prescott had dismissed *Wesley* as sickening. Bill found the *Newsweek* review severe, but at least it was fair, which the others were not. Convinced the novel would find many friends, he decided to ignore all further criticism of it, continue to prepare the journal of its writing, and publish these reviews and his own introduction along with it.

Throughout this darkening summer of 1946, he clung to the belief that *Wesley Jackson* was a good book that was bound to sell one hundred thousand copies, cancel out his debt to Harcourt, and produce a movie offer, but the news went from bad to worse. The review that irritated him most judged it "the cryingest book of recent memory." Bill was astonished, for he believed it was a *laughing* one.

In early July, *Wesley Jackson* crept onto the *Herald Tribune*'s best-seller list, encouraging Bill to think it was catching on, but it promptly slipped back off. By the end of July, he had to admit the book was a flop. Harcourt had printed fifty thousand copies and managed to get thirty-five thousand into stores. Even if returns were minimal he would earn only $15,000 and still owe his publisher $10,000.

Throughout the summer, Bill told himself that his only recourse to peace of mind was to get started on a new and sustaining work, and he struggled to do so, trying first a novel about a veteran, then another, then a play, but he abandoned each in turn.

Lightheartedly, Carol told him a plot he might use. It concerned a man of forty, just married for the third time, who finds he has made another mistake. His wife is odd, unlike what she had appeared before he married her. He realizes she is trying to get over an affair with another woman. When he discovers that on top of everything else, she is a Jew, he takes an overdose of sleeping pills. Although Bill liked the plot, he did not try to write it.

Carol began to feel responsible for his foundering, and this prompted her to inquire, one night as he left the house, where he was going. When he replied by asking if he were a prisoner, she was hurt as never before. In fact, she no longer trusted him, and when he left without explanation she felt new dread for their future.

But she affirmed her love for him, which had begun when she first saw him and endured to the present. She would rather the marriage end before that love did. She felt their love would outlast their marriage.

Ellen Erickson, the nurse, was losing patience with Aram's persistent crying. When Carol overheard her spanking him for it, she reprimanded her. This set off acrimony between them and then between Carol and Bill. When the consistently serene Lucy could be heard crying, Bill knew that bitterness consumed his household.

The problem with Mrs. Erickson worsened, and when she knocked on their door to complain that their quarreling was keeping her awake, Carol decided to fire her. Once this was done, Carol took a firmer hand with Aram. When he stomped and sobbed for more of their attention, she spanked him. Bill tended to defend Aram, and the result was further arguing.

Mrs. Erickson's departure did little for Aram's serenity. He cried at all hours, prompting Bill to some gentle spankings of his own; Bill also noted that Aram seemed to be a strong-willed boy who used tears as a weapon when denied his way. Lucy, on the other hand, was peaceful, and invariably slept through the night. At six and a half months, she was the sweetest, smilingest, easiest little girl he had ever seen. Even though he paid her scant attention, she looked into his face with delight and clearly loved him.

Bill's disappointment over *Wesley,* his inability to start on a new work, his dwindling funds, and a notice from the IRS that he owed further taxes left him only one recourse: gambling. On August 1, he had some good luck at the Russian Club. He staked his painter friend Manuel Tolegian, took a painting in exchange, and went ahead to win $6,375 of his own. This allowed him to pay off his $5,000 debt to George Mardikian and to renew his plan for New York. They would fly there in a week, put the children into Rosheen's care at the Park Lane, and look for a house.

However, a couple of days later he lost $2,000 at Russian Mike's. On August 8, he drove Carol to the beauty parlor at the St. Francis and promised to wait for her in the Turkish bath upstairs. Instead he went to the Menlo Club and in a stud poker game lost $600 in a single pot. It was all the money he had, and in trying to catch up he not only failed to meet Carol, but lost a further $900.

Driving a furious Carol home, he told her that he had lost the struggle to write absolutely, and there was nothing left for him to do but gamble. He intended to return to Russian Mike's later that night. She was very angry, and assured him that their marriage was finished, that she hated taking care of the children. He could turn them over to his mother and sister. She intended to go home.

By mid-August he had lost another $25,000 and in trying to catch up in the following weeks lost $13,000 more. Another visit to George Mardikian was necessary. He explained to George that in order to get even, he now needed $50,000. If he would loan him this sum, he would put up the motion-picture rights to *Time of Your Life* as collateral.

Mardikian replied that he would give him any amount if he would stop gambling, and then gave him $35,000. With this in hand, Bill bet $6,800 on three baseball teams, all of which he lost. Then, on August 23, he telegraphed Harcourt Brace of his urgent need for a loan or advance of $10,000.

Harcourt telegraphed him the money at once, and he totaled his debts. He owed $30,000 to George Mardikian, $25,000 to Harcourt, and $7,500 to Walt Papazian—$62,500 in all. He had never gotten that "big win" he had counted on, and he had lost $100,000 since Lucy's birth. A full $30,000 had gone through his unlucky fingers just within the last week.

He spoke to Arthur Freed, telling him that he wanted to rent MGM the screen rights to *Time of Your Life* for seven years. Freed sounded agreeable, promising to talk to Louis Mayer and report to him within the next several days.

A letter from Frank Morley urged against publishing the journal about writing *Wesley Jackson*. In agreeing to put it aside, Bill resolved to plunge into work at once. He would write a play a week for the next nine weeks and recoup the money he had lost gambling before November 1.

He began a play about a discharged soldier, whose dreams would be the play's action. There were to be onstage prize fights and bicycle races. Although he finished a first act, he could not go on. He found that he had lost all heart, and no longer believed that what he had to say was worth saying.

On his thirty-eighth birthday, Carol not only gave him a surprise party but let him know that she loved him now more than ever. She felt happy about the year ahead, which might be their best, in which they would have a son named Rock, pay off their debts, and have a big and beautiful house of their own. But her comforting did little to relieve Bill's worries.

After a week, there was still no word from Arthur Freed about MGM interest in *Time of Your Life,* and he wrote it off. He entrusted the sale of the screen rights to the agent Arthur Lyons, but in spite of Lyons's assurances there was no news.

What did cheer Bill was the thought of going east. When Rosheen telephoned that she had found them a fine, white, green-shuttered house on Long Island for $500 a month, he agreed to take it. In early October, Carol would fly east with Aram and Lucy, and he would drive.

Realizing that he would not be able to pay off his debts from any literary income before he left San Francisco, he put his luck to a few further tests. On September 19 he lost a thousand dollars on the horses and went on to the Menlo Club and a poker game in which he lost another four thousand. He left an uncovered check for that amount. He arrived home drunk to report this to Carol and scarcely protested her anger about it.

There was nowhere to turn but to George Mardikian, and he again came to Bill's rescue, with a new loan of $5,000. Bill signed a note agreeing to repay the whole $35,000 debt within the year and securing it with income from all his royalties. Carol and George's wife, Zazenig, were cosigners.

In mid-October 1946, suffering from the evidence that he could not bank on either his creative powers or his gambler's luck, Bill drove off to New York, with his uncle Mihran for company.

His central purpose in transplanting himself and his family was to renew his career as a whole, in books, plays, and movies, but he thought it best to begin by laying out a publication plan at Harcourt Brace. So on arrival in New York, his first act was to take Uncle Mihran to call on his publishers.

Frank Morley, Bob Giroux, and Donald Brace gathered to greet Bill and were receptive to his several projects. His confidence in a Broadway production of *Jim Dandy* brought an assurance that Harcourt would publish the play. When he revealed that Pascal Covici had invited him to provide a "Portable" Saroyan for the Viking series, Morley urged him to let Harcourt do such a book and offered to write its introduction. In parting, Bill assured his publishers he was now ready for work. There would be plenty of new books.

The house the Saroyans had rented for six months was that of E. O. McDonnell, a retired admiral and big-game hunter, in the fashionable Long Island community of Mill Neck. With six bedrooms, servants' quarters, extensive gardener-tended grounds, and a Hungarian cook, it was just the homestead over which Bill had hoped to preside, and just the base from which to lay siege to the entertainment capital.

Carol felt immediately at home. The first children's nurse she hired soon gave notice, but then she found Agnes Caesar, a woman of sixty whose tenure would be a long one. Aram and Lucy liked her and called her Nana. Carol dismissed the Hungarian cook and hired Catherine Sweeney, who had worked for the Nelson Doubledays nearby. Rosheen and Charles Marcus came for dinner and approved.

The move did not lessen Aram's need for attention. Hoping to amuse him, Bill burned some leaves behind the garage. The wind soon spread the fire into the surrounding woods, and Aram was delighted by the spectacle of his father battling the multiplying flames with a spade. Seeing the fire, Carol and Catherine Sweeney summoned the fire department. The wailing of approaching sirens and the arrival of neighbors only increased Aram's enthusiasm and excitement, and an exasperated Bill swept him from the scene.

With Rosheen's guidance, Carol found beauty parlors in Glen Cove and Locust Valley to attend to her hair and planned their launching in North Shore social life. Bill was unenthusiastic. He owed over $60,000, had a bank balance of $600 and not a cent of income, and all his wife could think of was fun. He felt that, like her mother, Carol found this fun in the flattery of all sorts of bogus people.

The news from Ross Bagdasarian was of his marriage to an Armenian girl from Fresno. Her name was Armenonhi, or Armen, and Bill, who had met her, was reminded of his own defiance of the Hay tradition of marrying one's own kind.

But he was delighted by Carol's news that she was pregnant again. According to Dr. Ricci, the child would arrive in July. Sure it would be a boy, Bill named him Rock. He loved rocks. He liked the feel of those he gathered at the seaside. He liked the word's sound and connotation.

Carol had reservations about a third child. She complained that by having children too often she was losing her youth. But Bill discouraged the idea of any delay in their plans for a larger family.

Nevertheless, on December 3, Carol's pregnancy ended in miscarriage. Bill would later maintain that Carol had brought about the event, and would even recall her being closeted with an associate of Dr. Ricci's in her mother's apartment, and subsequently walking Carol around Central Park himself. At the time, however, Bill took the loss philosophically. He thought that Dr. Ricci would see that she was in proper shape, and Carol would soon be pregnant again.

The central brightness in the Saroyans' sky was knowing that Arthur Lyons was making a contract with RKO for the movie rights to *Time of Your Life*. In the midst of these negotiations, Ned Brown of the Lyons office worked out an even better deal with Cagney Productions, the new firm of James and William Cagney. For a seven-year rental of film rights, Bill would receive $50,000 on signing and, a year later, split a second payment of $100,000 with the Theatre Guild.

At the same time, Hal Matson arranged with the Guild to use *Time of Your Life* on the Theatre-Guild-of-the-Air program, but Bill returned the contract unsigned, telling Hal he would sign it only if Matson were representing the Guild and taking his fee from them. Matson's representing him was a thing of the past, he said, creating another lasting huff between himself and his adroit agent.

Christmas would be a happy one, thanks to the Cagneys. Bill was so sure of this income that he wrote and mailed off checks to Harcourt for his debt and to Cosette and Henry for their annual salaries, only to find that the Cagneys had deducted a withholding tax of $10,000 from his check. He was left with a balance of only $100 and had to ask Arthur Lyons for a loan of $1,000.

Nevertheless, he promised the new year would be a wonderful one. At 184 pounds, he was overweight, and he vowed to lose at least 15. There would be no more of the neurotic gambling that had ruined 1946, and he would get to work and write something every day.

But his several attempts at new plays ended in collapse. He did complete some new stories, but they were bitter sketches of desperate men or the whimsical fantasies with which he escaped his own darkness. None worked, and while he sent them out himself, none was accepted.

He revised *Jim Dandy* for Harcourt's publication and sent this new version to several producers, hoping in vain for a sponsor. When he asked Robert Sherwood to read the play, Sherwood appealed to him to join in the boycott of Washington theaters for failing to admit Negroes. Bill replied that Sherwood's cause was a minor one for a time of such major wrongs.

The IRS's growing insistence about his tax delinquency caused Bill to apply for a further extension and to seek the advice of Pincus Berner, of the law firm Ernst, Cane and Berner. He found Berner to be a capable and sympathetic attorney, and their association was to be a long one, in which Berner would often represent his literary work. Berner's first advice was to put eight to ten thousand dollars aside immediately for taxes.

The Saroyans' lease on the Mill Neck house ended in May 1947, and they began a futile home search in Fairfield County, Connecticut. They did find Artie Shaw, who was living in Norwalk and was now married to Kathleen Winsor, author of the best-selling novel *Forever Amber*. With houses on his mind, Bill proposed to Shaw that they collaborate on a musical about moving a mansion from a town's best neighborhood to its slum. Shaw liked the idea.

Failing to find an affordable New York apartment, the Saroyans decided to return to economical Taraval Street. In early May, Bill drove west. Carol joined him in New Orleans, while Nana, now indispensible, flew with the children. En route, Bill and Carol agreed that they loved each other, Aram, and Lucy, and pledged a better life for themselves.

Restored to California, Bill at first spurned fiction for an autobiography. It would deal in some way with the thirty-nine years of his life. Takoohi had often called him *hungnavore*, "wildman" in Armenian, and he thought that might be the book's title. But he settled instead on *My Life I Believe*.

Work on the autobiography was slow, particularly as he wrestled with self-assessment. He had recently found himself described in W. Tasker Witham's book *Panorama of American Literature* as one who "seems to be saying more than he is saying, but when one looks into what he is saying, one cannot make out what it is, and one is not sure he himself knows."

Bill believed his work said clearly that man is basically good and that life should be something to celebrate, yet society makes the achievement almost impossible. But he was not certain that was what he was saying.

Although he had wanted to be a great writer, he knew that he was not—he felt he was nothing. That was okay too. He took some pride in giving that nothingness the illusion of significance. At the same time, he was angered by any slighting reference to his mind. Was he less profound because he did not care about religion, political systems, or traditions of Western culture? His knowledge was instinctive. He understood things without a system of logic.

Dwelling on these uncertainties brought the book to a halt, but in mid-July, still searching for direction, he sat down at his typewriter and wrote some fine stories, surprising evidence that his creative imagination survived.

"The Foreigner" explored the feelings of an Armenian schoolboy who is being discriminated against and his grudging envy of a draft dodger. While the story exploited these two strong, feasible themes, he left them unreconciled, the idea not fully wrought. He made it an Aram Garoghlanian story and coupled it with another, which he wrote in five hours and in just the sort of trance that had brought forth his best work in the past.

This second story, "The Theological Student," was about fourteen-year-old Aram Garoghlanian's pondering the role of the theological student in Russian novels. Researching this in the library leads him on an adventure that mistakenly reports him dead but brings him homely enlightenment. It was another fine, warm, comic story born of his nostalgic recollections of his Fresno boyhood.

This pair of lively stories encouraged Bill to think he could do more, enough for a sequel to *My Name Is Aram,* but after a few magazine rejections, and with no Hal Matson to fall back on, he gave up, sent both to *Hairenik* for publication, and turned to his brightest prospect, the movie version of *The Time of Your Life.*

This was now being made in Hollywood, and the Cagneys had assembled a fine cast. Jim Cagney was to play Joe, and his sister Jeanne would play Kitty. James Barton would play Kit Carson, William Bendix would play Nick, and Paul Draper was cast as Harry the Hoofer. In early August, Bill and Carol drove to Hollywood to assess the making of the film. They were welcomed to the set by Cagney and shown seven reels of the rough cut. Although he was pleased to find them filming the story as he had written it for the stage, Bill found the movie disappointing.

When the Cagneys appealed to him for help with the troublesome ending, he proposed to write them a new one. He promised it would be a work of art and assure the picture's success—but it would cost them $50,000. He did not expect a favorable response, and didn't get one.

The Cagneys sent Bill a revised ending for the picture in which the villainous Blick, killed by Kit Carson in the stage version, is simply beaten up by Cagney's (otherwise passive) Joe. While Bill was scornful of their solution, he felt the prospects for the picture were good. He expected it to raise his esteem in Hollywood and bring him his final payment of $20,000 on the first of January.

While in Hollywood, Bill and Carol had lunched with Charles and Oona

Bill with James Cagney, who would film *The Time of Your Life*

Chaplin in their Beverly Hills garden, and Bill had told Charlie about *Sam Ego's House,* the play he had written as a musical in hopes that Artie Shaw would supply a score. Chaplin suggested Bill send him a copy so that he could urge it on his son Sydney, who was presenting experimental plays at Hollywood's Circle Theatre.

A note from Chaplin approving *Sam Ego's House* was followed by a call from Jerry Epstein, the Circle Players' director. He wanted to produce the play at once, and a delighted Bill told him to do so. The play is a farce about the progress of a house across a California town, with allusions to serious issues, but it simply bewildered its audiences. Although Bill and Carol drove to Pasadena for a performance, even the playwright found no ground for praise.

The year 1947, for which Bill had such extravagant hopes, was becoming one of bereavements. His beloved maternal grandmother, Lucy, died in mid-August. She, above all other members of his family, had taken interest in him. When he was a child, she had scrubbed him. When he was grown, they often sat together after supper to share a cigarette and talk. He had celebrated their relationship in one of his best stories, "The Living and the Dead," and had dedicated *Three Times Three,* the 1936 collection in which it

Charles and Oona Chaplin with Carol and Bill at a rehearsal of *The Son,*
presented by the Circle Players, Hollywood, 1950

appeared, to her. He had given his daughter her name. Despite his dread of
last rites, Bill was a pallbearer at her funeral in Fresno.

His belief that *Jim Dandy* was not only his own best play but one of the
best American plays in fifty years was another fatality. Harcourt published it
in September 1947 to dismissive reviews, and in London, the Old Vic,
which had been considering a *Jim Dandy* production, decided against it.

The play's fate added to a palpable chill at Harcourt. On finding *Wesley
Jackson* excluded from Harcourt's Christmas advertising, Bill had accused
the company of a loss of faith in him, but there was no eluding the problem
that the novel had left his royalty account with a $7,000 debt. Lack of
enthusiasm for Saroyan was such that Pascal Covici, at Viking, had lost
interest in a Saroyan "Portable," and now Harcourt too felt a Saroyan
omnibus would be untimely.

So Bill was ready to quit Harcourt as soon as the present contract, which
included *Jim Dandy* and two additional books, was fulfilled. He would turn
to Doubleday or Harper's, publishers who, he felt, promoted their books
more effectively. For the penniless present, however, he saw no alternative to
loyalty, and asked his publisher for a $15,000 advance on his next three

books. Again, Harcourt was willing to help him out of trouble. Bob Giroux said they would provide the $15,000 he asked—$5,000 as advance against a book, the additional $10,000 as a personal loan, without interest, payable a year hence.

In mid-November 1947, Bill began a long play, *Don't Go Away Mad,* which reflected the darkness of his heart. He placed it in a San Francisco hospital and provided a cast of terminal cancer patients. Among them was a marine veteran who, with a machine gun, had killed the thirty-seven German prisoners of war in his charge.

While he recognized the new play as "talky," more essay than drama, and altogether lacking in Saroyan fun and vaudeville, he continued to work on it throughout the fall, finishing in mid-December. As he mailed it off to the National Theatre Conference and the Circle Players, he thought more kindly of it. Possibly it was the best of all.

His hopes for the year ahead rode on *Don't Go Away Mad,* but the copy he sent to George Jean Nathan brought a discouraging response. Nathan didn't think it came off, and Bill reluctantly accepted that judgment. The critic also advised him against the stiff 10 percent royalty he was asking. Production costs were too high for that.

Bill's brother Henry was now working as George Mardikian's business manager. When invited to his office, Bill anticipated a social visit but found Henry's purpose was to remind him of his $35,000 debt to Mardikian.

Bill promised to settle it and did manage to return $6,000 of it, but he was left to worry about the $29,000 that remained. He could see no practical way of repaying it and admitted to his mother that he owed Mardikian a considerable sum. Her advice was to pay him. When Bill explained it was more money than he had, she offered a memorable alternative—to spit in his eye.

Bill had become so accustomed to quarreling with Carol that a particularly bad day of it, in October 1947, did not at first seem critical. In the late afternoon they went with the two children to a toy store to use up a credit of $2.80. Nothing could be had for that sum, but as they left the store, Aram demanded a fire engine and wept when denied it. In the street, both Aram and Lucy were unruly, and Carol walked away, telling Bill that Aram's offensive behavior was his fault. Carrying Lucy and holding Aram by the hand, Bill called out to Carol to help him with the children, but she declined, and he followed her the two blocks to where they had left the car, with bystanders enjoying the spectacle.

Driving home, Carol continued to defy him, and when he shouted that if she didn't change her attitude he would beat her up, she cringed and wept. Only the children's tears stopped the conflict. Once at home, Aram reverted to sucking his thumb, and Bill persuaded Carol to let him embrace her. Nevertheless, Aram refused his supper.

In an effort to explain his behavior, Bill put the blame on her. He maintained that she was irresponsible toward both children, obsessed by a need to see and be seen by others, and incensed by any denial of it. He felt he should have stopped the car and beaten her or driven her home and left her there. It was up to her whether their marriage was to continue.

This led to further argument over her turning for help to such friends as Gloria Stokowski and her seventy-year-old husband. When Carol told him that she planned to write to Gloria, he leaped at her, shouting that they were finished, and slapped the side of her head.

Protecting herself with a pillow, Carol screamed, sobbed, threw the pillow at him, and said that she too was through. She no longer wanted Bill, or the children, or anyone. Whereupon Bill took her in his arms, comforting her, telling her that he loved her, and in due time they subsided into bed.

Lucy, however, did not sleep. They could hear her rocking in her crib throughout the night. From time to time she cried out, and Carol went to sleep beside her in the living room. Bill was moved to recall the dormitory of the smallest boys at the Fred Finch orphanage, and how some were rockers and some were criers, and how the rockers rocked slowly most of the time, but sometimes they rocked swiftly, making much noise, and one child would bang his head against his crib's headboard. Such thoughts raised Bill's concerns for Lucy, who was forever buzzing with a wild energy that he felt was far beyond her two years.

When Carol summoned a doctor to look at a sty in Lucy's eye, Nana told her it had been unnecessary and quipped that it was because of such overreaction that she didn't like having mothers at hand. Carol was not amused, and Nana proposed that if she were unsatisfied with her, she should get someone else. While Nana had been with them for ten months, proving herself the ideal nurse, Carol told her to pack up and leave. Although the children missed her, Bill did not object to her dismissal, deciding that while an accomplished snob, she was no more than a capable caretaker.

They did not replace Nana, and Bill rejoiced both in the economy and in Carol's taking full charge of the children. She cooked, laundered, and cleaned house while Bill helped with breakfast, straightened the kitchen, and, when he worked late, made and unmade his bed on the living-room couch. They agreed they should have a third child before Lucy was three.

On December 17, Carol heard from her friend Truman Capote that he was in town and agreed that she and Bill would meet him for dinner. As the Saroyans stepped out of the elevator at the Top-of-the-Mark, the small, twenty-three-year-old Capote embraced Carol enthusiastically.

As they drank together, Bill thought Capote's head looked freakish, and saw that he was proudly homosexual. He had worked at *The New Yorker,* and his novel, *Other Voices Other Rooms,* was soon to be published by Random House. He spoke affectionately of Katharine Hepburn, Tennessee Williams, Greta Garbo, and E. M. Forster. When he described a painful love affair, it became clear he was talking about a man.

Capote described stealing out of a poetry reading by Robert Frost. On spotting him, the poet had declared that if *The New Yorker* could not endure his poetry he would read no more of it and, clapping the book shut, had hurled it after Capote. Learning of the incident, Harold Ross, *The New Yorker*'s editor, had asked Capote for a written explanation, and, rather than submit one, he had quit his job.

Although young, Truman Capote radiated the confidence of a literary star, as well read as he was well connected, and this roused some of Bill's enduring resentments. Nor was Capote favorably impressed with Bill. Carol recalled later that while Bill was out of earshot, Capote whispered to her that it was too bad she had produced two children with this man, because the marriage would not last. He was convinced that Bill was insane.

By mid-March 1948, a feeling that Bill was still getting nowhere suggested a move. It always seemed that if only he could find the right place for them to live, their troubles would dissolve and his efforts would be fruitful. Carol admitted to a sadness at the way their marriage was going and at its effect on the children. She felt it was his behavior that caused hers, and she couldn't help that, but she knew that she loved him wholly and hoped they might start anew. So she agreed to sell the Taraval house and buy a farm somewhere near Fresno, where there would be a studio for Bill and the big house they had always wanted.

They went at once to Fresno and soon found a farm for sale on Highway 41, the road to Yosemite. The farm was called Lane's Bridge, and it had twenty-six acres bordering on the San Joaquin River. There was a twenty-five-year-old wooden house on a hilltop and an unfinished guest house nearby. Bill thought the land looked suitable for keeping sheep, cattle, and horses and for a site for a future house, complete with studio, office, library, gym, and the theater he had always wanted. He felt that Aram and Lucy would thrive here. The price was $32,000, and they agreed to buy it.

Carol arranged for her mother to loan them $10,000 to help with the $15,000 cash payment required, and they put the Taraval house up for sale at $22,500. Bill asked Henry to offer George Mardikian the house, furnished, at $30,000. Since Mardikian was in Europe, Henry cabled him the proposal.

As April drew to a close, Bill and Carol engaged a Fresno decorator and made plans to fix up both houses. Bill was aware that his debts now topped $100,000, but felt, in his seesaw fashion, that his talent and good luck would dispose of them.

The hopes he fastened on George Mardikian collapsed. In need of cash, Mardikian was not only unwilling to buy the Taraval house, but wanted an immediate payment of $10,000 on Bill's $29,000 debt. Harcourt, to whom he owed $10,000, was no longer a source of funds, and the news from Hollywood was that while *Time of Your Life* would soon open in New York, there would be no further income from it until the following year.

In early May, Bill drove Carol and the children to Fresno, where he borrowed an additional $10,000 from his uncle Mihran, and then on to see their new home on Highway 41. They arrived to find clouds of dust blowing in from the west and the house oven-like under a spring sun. With diminished enthusiasm, they decided simply to clean the place and move in without the renovations they had planned.

Carol soon felt the dilapidated house was beyond her citified powers of restoration and grew skeptical about her adaptability to farm life. She saw in the Lane's Bridge property only more drudgery for herself and further isolation from a life she might find tolerable.

Rosheen responded to Carol's despair by saying she had made a lot of money in the stock market and would refurnish the Lane's Bridge house, complete with a new kitchen and deep freeze. Further, she would come out at once to help with plans for it. She came to San Francisco, and, two days later, Bill and Carol drove her to Fresno to see the house and grounds, for which they had already paid $15,000 and owed an additional $17,000. Within moments of arrival, Rosheen agreed with Carol that Lane's Bridge had been a terrible mistake. Reluctantly, Bill capitulated and inquired about getting back his money. The agent doubted this was possible.

With some difficulty, Bill managed to insert an unusual ad in the classified section of the *San Francisco Examiner*. It appeared on June 8, under the heading NO LIES IN THIS AD, and described the ranch house as old, lacking telephone, barn, and garage. The equipment it did have was inoperable. The land was arid and without irrigation. Its seclusion was assured. Admitting to having paid $32,000 for it, the owner asked $35,000 and questioned the sanity of anyone interested, but provided the Bagdasarian telephone number in Fresno. While it had the appearance of a gag, he had an idea it would interest somebody and told Armen to expect callers.

Understanding that his real estate ventures had brought him into serious trouble, he turned to his fickle luck for help. In a week's rampage of gambling he lost nearly $20,000. Since he had already borrowed $10,000 from his uncle Mihran, he turned to Walter Papazian to pay his new gambling debt, and was scolded for this by his mother and his weeping sister Zabe. He assured them he would be out of debt and in the money within six months. However, the owner of the Lane's Bridge house was angry about the *Examiner* ad and was suing for the full payment. Over the weekend of June 19, Bill realized that he was overdrawn by $2,500 at his bank, and that his debts and overdue taxes now amounted to $113,000.

His gloom was momentarily brightened by a telephone call from the agent Irving Paul "Swifty" Lazar, saying that he represented such figures as Lillian Hellman, Maxwell Anderson, and Budd Schulberg and that he could make a profitable picture deal for him. Bill encouraged him to do so, and in the meantime set about the task himself.

After seeing a preview of the filmed *Time of Your Life,* he wrote William Cagney his congratulations. He had enjoyed himself so much he had forgotten it was his. Soon afterward he wrote William Cagney admitting that he was broke, in debt, and in need of $75,000. He believed that his play *The Beautiful People* would make a surefire film. He proposed to coproduce and direct it, supervising the script and shooting it within sixty days. He thought Jeanne Cagney could play Agnes Webster, and James Barton, Jonah Webster. He wanted an advance of $25,000 and the balance on completion and release of the film.

At the same time he called Dore Schary, production head at RKO, and interested him in filming a Saroyan play, perhaps *My Heart's in the Highlands.* But in the last days of June, he heard that Schary had lost interest in *Highlands.* The next day Cagney called to apologize for being slow in getting to *The Beautiful People,* but he had read it at last and didn't think it a good scheme commercially.

The filmed *Time of Your Life* was having a bewildering reception. Its fine cast was admired and assured a cluster of Academy Awards, but the picture rambled. It was seen as "a collection of great moments set in a string of lulls." Cagney's feisty portrayal of the melancholy Joe made his rearrangement of Tom and Kitty's lives seem bullying. James Agee called it "a blend of Nehi and sacramental wine," and felt that although this faithful production was the best that could be done on a screen, the work was a play and could exist only on a stage. *Variety* doubted that exhibitors outside the major cities would accept the unfamiliar stage format, and indeed there was trouble over the release and distribution. The result was a critical loss to the Cagney organization, and an embittered James Cagney returned to Warner Brothers.

Bill reluctantly admitted that his big Hollywood deal had never arrived. But that was not the worst of it. On July 3, he had a particularly bitter quarrel with Carol, and, at its peak, she asked when he had fallen out of love with her. He told her it was in 1946, soon after Lucy was born, the night she had called him at the Menlo Club and warned that if he did not come home at once he would find her gone. Returning, he had found her perfumed, painted, and in a transparent negligee, but her lips were thick with spite and her voice raw with hatred. When he had tried to placate her she had mocked him. He would never lose the recollection of a wife who loathed him.

The next morning, Carol told him she was leaving him. She would return to New York with the children and take an apartment there. She would want a nurse for them and would require a thousand dollars a month for her own and their support. As the days of estrangement went on and Bill realized Carol was serious, he decided that divorce was inevitable. They were simply not suited, and in trying to hold the marriage together they would do more damage to themselves and the children.

Carol maintained that the reason she was getting the divorce was because he wanted her to. He thought it was the truth, and it left him nothing to say. He felt they had tried to make a marriage but had failed. He wished her happiness and, for the sake of the children, peace of mind.

Although it occurred to Bill that Carol was playing some sort of game that might at any moment end in reconciliation, she engaged a Montgomery Street lawyer, Albert Picard, and a court appearance was scheduled for Tuesday, July 13. The July 11 weekend newspapers carried accounts of the Saroyan divorce.

The children seemed to him unaffected by the breakup. Lucy, of course, had no idea what it was all about, but Aram appeared reconciled to the idea of life with his mother and his sister in New York.

Ernst, Cane, Berner and Gitlin, his New York lawyers, cautioned him against a fixed monthly alimony of a thousand dollars. With his uncertain earnings as an author he should provide only a percentage of his income.

On the day Carol was to appear in court, she and Bill reconsidered their situation, and then, entrusting the children to Takoohi for a few days, drove off to Reno for a retreat. The outcome was an apparent success. They agreed on their errors and how to correct them. Bill decided that they were at last married and okay.

Now, nearing his fortieth birthday, they would make a fresh start. The Cagney money was due, and one of his plays would surely appeal to a producer for Broadway's fall season. Indeed, Alfred Fischer and Herman Levin were already interested in *Don't Go Away Mad.*

The Saroyans decided on a further change. They would move back to New York. Inquiry there brought the description of a new five-room apartment at 41 West Fifty-eighth Street. It was opposite the Plaza Hotel and had a wood-burning fireplace. They could have a five-year lease at $360 a month and move in on October 1.

Carol planned the furnishing while Bill tried to make some order of his finances. He persuaded George Mardikian to buy the Taraval house for $21,500, thus reducing his debt to $7,500. In leaving Mardikian's office, Bill dropped a $20 bill into the pickle jar of money Mardikian kept on his desk for luck. He proceeded to Les Cohen's for some grand bets on the races at Del Mar, losing $4,000 in the session.

At home and depressed by his bad luck, he called Cohen back and placed a $4,000 bet on a horse called Grim Magic in the last race. Driving with Carol and the children to his mother's, Bill confessed his terrible run of luck, which left him owing $14,000 to his bookie. Carol scolded him and told him that now they would never get to New York, and he took full blame for this, but as they drove past the Cliff House, the results of the last race at Del Mar were announced over KSAN. The winner was Grim Magic, paying $15.50 to win.

Bill stopped the car, hugged Aram for joy, and declared his love for his wife, daughter, son, and everyone in the world. Grim Magic had repaid his debt of $14,000 to Les Cohen and his $8,000 bank loan and given them $4,500 with which to go to New York. He resolved that some day he would write a really good gambling story.

In mid-August 1948, Bill, Carol, and the children arrived in New York by train, checked into a suite at the Plaza Hotel and went to look at their new apartment. Carol decided, and Bill agreed, that the walls would be gray, the ceilings white, and the parquet floors stained dark. At Lord and Taylor's they ordered six studio couches, and, through a decorator, $6,500 worth of custom-made furniture, which included a $750 desk for Bill. At Cartier's, he bought a silver punch bowl for $1,050. It came with a ladle and a dozen goblets, which he judged enough for their anticipated family. Aram was entered at the Walt Whitman School on Seventy-eighth Street.

They caught up with old friends, George Jean Nathan and Julie Haydon, and Al and Dolly Hirschfeld, and saw the new plays. Bill felt *A Streetcar Named Desire* was poorly staged and performed, but acknowledged that Tennessee Williams was the most important playwright to emerge since his own debut. He was equally harsh on the production of his one act *Hello Out There,* at the Cherry Lane in Greenwich Village, but he thoroughly enjoyed taking Aram and Lucy to the ice show. Lucy, at two and a half, clapped enthusiastically and chatted with their neighbors.

But a reckoning was sobering. His debts stood at $32,000. He had only $400 in cash—not enough to pay his current income-tax installment, or even to move into the new apartment.

Carol borrowed $2,000 from her mother, and Bill promised to repay his entire $13,000 debt to Rosheen on January 1, when the Cagneys' $20,000 arrived. In the meantime they moved to the inexpensive Meurice Hotel and took many meals at the Fifty-seventh Street Automat, where, Bill grumbled, beef pie had gone from three to six nickels. For work, Bill took a room at the Great Northern and pinned his primary hopes on Broadway. These were raised by the producers Alfred Fischer and Herman Levin. Although they had cooled toward *Don't Go Away Mad,* they liked *Sam Ego's House* and proposed an advance of $2,500 for it. But this prospect withered in negotiations over a suitable advance, leading Bill to suspect he did need an agent.

Lewis Funke, the *New York Times* drama editor, encouraged Bill to write about the current theater from a playwright's point of view. He promptly got to work on an article that he called *Confessions of a Playwright.* In it he complained that just as the meat pies at Horn and Hardart's had deteriorated as the price doubled, so had the theater. With tickets at six dollars plus tax, he felt bilked. In an increasingly sorehead manner he went on to cite the Dramatists' Guild as more hindrance than help. It had taken his money and given him nothing in return. He had a similar opinion of agents. A good play finds its own producer with no need to pay a commission, he wrote. He was equally disdainful of producers, who were merely businessmen who invest the money of others and profit even if the play fails. An occasional producer mistakenly felt entitled to tell the playwright how to rewrite his last act. As for directors, they were not composers but conductors. Their task was to accomplish the playwright's intent and no more. There were not many directors who understood this principle.

Finally, he felt the critics exerted too great an influence on what survived. Their standards were tuned to Broadway success, and they tended to overlook original new work. Why should theatergoers be sheep following the goats? The opinion of patrons should be sought. In the end, Lewis Funke rejected the piece as too long for him.

An omnibus collection—Bill's best stories drawn from nine books—had now been approved by Harcourt, given the title *The Saroyan Special,* and was prepared for November publication. In spite of hopes that the Book-of-the-Month Club would find it an attractive premium, it had not. The book would have to make its own way.

In late October, Bill, Carol, and the children moved into the new apartment, 3A, at 41 West Fifty-eighth Street, and it had the feel of a new beginning for all. Their social life was busy. They saw John and Belle O'Hara and the John Gunthers, dined with the Michael Arlens, and occasionally turned up at the Stork to join Nathan, who was drinking iced coffee these days instead of alcohol, on doctor's orders.

Bill's own health, as usual, caused him to complain. His right ear rang persistently, and chest congestion was chronic. When he consulted a doctor about his trouble urinating, he learned that his prostate was swollen but not infected.

Carol had found a Scots woman, Miss Carlile, to look after the children.

Aram was a restless but happy boy, smiling and laughing and anxious to report on life at Walt Whitman School, where he was making friends. Lucy was irrepressible. She had a keen awareness of a daughter's rights and was quick to assert them. But she was no less a delight to her father. She reminded him of a little peasant girl in a Renoir painting.

Bill acknowledged that his family had come near to breaking up last July, but that Carol had stood up to some tough times, and now, after six years of marriage, they were ready for a new life together and a new child.

This optimism roused his creative energy from a long sleep. Before the year was out, he was once more turning painful boyhood experience into affirmation and framing it in maturity's wisdom. Within a few months, he produced a dozen stories, and some were fine ones.

It was a short-story renaissance. It included "Third Day After Christmas" and "The Parsley Garden," both drawing on his own childhood bitterness, plus "The Pheasant Hunter," in which the father of a willful eleven-year-old boy grants his son's wish for a shotgun, sits by as the boy's hunting expedition founders, and proves that passiveness and setting an example is all there is to fatherhood.

In "The Cocktail Party," a mature writer, embittered by his own failure and the success of others, drops in on his ex-wife's cocktail party and finds surprising consolation in the literary expectations of his grown son. In "The Poet at Home," he drew a whimsical self-portrait of a failed, one-play playwright, hopelessly in debt. In the wistful resolution, he *does* write a second play, but its acclaim is kept from him by a wife who loves him as a failure.

He was understandably proud that some of these stories found immediate markets. *Cosmopolitan* bought "The Cocktail Party" for $5,000. The *Saturday Evening Post* paid $3,000 for "The Pheasant Hunter," and *Harper's Bazaar* paid $300 for "The Parsley Garden."

The long-delayed Cagney money, $20,000, arrived in January 1949, allowing him to pay his bills and slim his debts to George Mardikian and the Marcuses. Nevertheless, his concern about money persisted. He calculated their monthly expense—for rent, nurse, food, and laundry—at $850, and he had enough money for only two more months.

Then, into this interlude of new beginnings and fresh hopes, came an unexpected provocation. While attending a concert they met a man who spoke of the mother of Carol's friend Sonia Greeniva as Carol's aunt. Carol was clearly upset by this, and the next day Bill inquired further.

On the evening of March 29, Bill asked Carol for an explanation of the mystery, and she told him the truth. She had invented Henry Stuart of Long Island. There was no such person. In a burst of candor, she went on to reveal that she was an illegitimate child, that most likely her father was a William Mandel, a Jew.

To Bill's dismay she revealed that she had lied about her mother too. Rosheen was not of Scottish, French, and Russian extraction as she had said. While she had used such misleading names as Dore, her real one was Ray Brophman, and she was a Jew. Furthermore, Carol's sister Elinor's father was a Sam Schapiro, who had been married briefly to Rosheen. When Charles Marcus had married her, he had adopted both girls and given them his name legally.

Shocked by this news, Bill announced that since she had deceived him, he could no longer live with her. In spite of the hardship it would cause Aram and Lucy, he would leave her.

Carol protested that she was frightened of being alone in the Fifty-eighth Street apartment, so Bill did not leave immediately. Over the next week they argued over the collapse of trust between them, Bill insisting that the fault was Carol's. Although brokenhearted for her and the children, he felt that the marriage had become hopeless. He must start a new life.

On April 5 he moved to a room at the nearby St. Moritz Hotel, and there he received a note from Carol. It proclaimed her love for him, and urged him to respond to it and come home. Bill could not imagine reconciliation. Despair prevented him from thinking clearly, but he knew his son and his daughter were lost to him. He was plagued by a sense that his own mean spirit was being revealed, for his concern was less for the heartbreak and damage he was causing than for his own survival. Nevertheless, he must get on with his life, however foolishly.

He felt that Aram and Lucy had been born in falsehood and thus questioned whether there could be true hope for them. He thought there was not, but that he must pray for them anyway. He asked God to deliver them from the influences of both their mother and their father.

On Saturday, April 9, Carol arranged for Miss Carlile to drop Bill's mail off while taking the children to the park. Bill met them in the lobby of the St. Moritz. On seeing her father, Lucy hugged his legs for a long time. When she asked if he was coming home, he was unable to answer. On Fifty-ninth Street Aram pointed out a blimp in the sky and asked his father about it, then suggested he come with them into the park. Bill pleaded that he had to work. When Aram asked where, he pointed out his room in the hotel. From its window he watched Miss Carlile leading his two children along a path, slowly and, it seemed, happily.

With debts of $13,000, less than $2,000 in the bank, and prospects at zero, his finances were more precarious than ever. Nevertheless, he occupied himself with setting up separate checking accounts, cashing in the bonds he had bought for Aram and Lucy in 1941, and discussing with Melville Cane, Pincus Berner's partner, the details of a separation agreement, a divorce, and alimony. For the present he would leave New York and go to Europe as soon as he could find the necessary money or assignment. He applied for a new passport.

He took to aimless wandering around New York. He rode a tube train to Jersey City, a bus from there to Union City, another back to Manhattan, and wandered on Broadway until late at night. It seemed to him that he must find an Armenian girl to be the mother of any further children.

He was oblivious of any duty to the wife he had chosen, the children he had conceived, or the social fabric in which he lived. All that had been trumped by a tribal self that was now confirming his dreaded cowardice.

On Easter Sunday, April 17, Carol telephoned in the afternoon asking if he wanted to take the children to the park. Aram and Lucy arrived in his room at 2:45 and waited for him to get dressed, and then all three went to the park cafeteria for a picnic that was Bill's breakfast. Bringing them home, he found the once-familiar apartment had become strange to him. He lingered for half an hour, but at the sound of Carol's voice calling his name, he fled, taking the stairs rather than meet her.

The next day, when he discovered that he could fly to Ireland for $317 on TWA, he bought a ticket and left at once for Dublin.

XI

ESCAPE

1949–1950

WHEN TRAVELING eastward along the transatlantic route by which his parents had come to America, Saroyan always felt himself in pursuit of some truth, some Old World revelation that had been denied him. Now, in April 1949, his need was for a perception, an endurable attitude toward the mess his life had become.

But in fact he was pursued by guilts he could not entirely suppress, a love for his wife and his children he could not dismiss any more than he could his prejudice, a vestigial anti-Semitism he was forever muzzling and denying. He was simply in flight, running away from himself in an illusion of escape, and it began to take on the grotesqueness of a nightmare.

After a long sleep in Dublin's Ivanhoe Hotel and a walk around the rainy city, he counted out his funds at $161 and decided against renewing old acquaintances here. Instead, he flew to Paris and took a room at the Scribe Hotel. In his four-year absence France seemed to have become a ruin, abounding in predators of all kinds. He found his way to a private casino, the Opera Club, and there, between two and five in the morning, he lost his remaining $130 at baccarat.

He cabled his New York bank for $550 of the $600 he had left there for Carol and the children. Awaiting it, he called on Kingsbury Smith of the INS to ask for a reporting job. Smith proposed he cover the forthcoming wedding of Rita Hayworth and Aly Khan. Although Bill agreed to submit a sample of his writing, the assignment struck him as contemptible, and he did not pursue it.

Bill's $550 arrived at American Express on April 28, and with it he paid off his $75 hotel bill and proceeded to the Opera Club to lose the rest of it. However, he was now familiar enough for credit and was allowed to cash a

Bill with Mondadori Brothers, his Italian publishers

Bill in Venice

check for $1,000. With this he won back his losses and enough more to proceed with his tour to Italy and Spain. In these two countries he anticipated the charity of his publishers. If he were lucky, he would go on to the Near East.

He was pleased to find his cousin Chesley in Paris and took him and his wife, Amie, to dinner and on to a performance of Edith Piaf. The resourceful Carol discovered his whereabouts and called to say she was anxious about him. Although moved by the sound of her voice and concern, he could not forget her deceit and rejected her appeal as more of the same.

In the belief that he would be able to write as he traveled, Bill had brought along his typewriter, but on the first leg of his journey to Italy there was a change of railway cars that carried off the one on which he had left his typewriter. He was now thwarted in his writing plans and doubtful of the railroad's assurance that the machine would be found and returned to him.

In Milan, his Italian publishers, the Mondadoris, father and son, were as amiable as he had hoped, giving him lunch, posing with him for newspaper photographs, and advancing him funds to go on in the first-class style that comforted him. But as he traveled, Bill's thoughts turned homeward, bringing him the pleading faces of Aram and Lucy as he had last seen them.

After settling himself at the Danielli in Venice, he went for a look at the city and bought a blue cap for Lucy. He had $800 and felt that he would have good luck at the Lido casino. A day of gambling there brought his bankroll to more than $1,000, and in Venice's sumptuous leather shops he treated himself to a belt, a passport case, and a toilet kit.

Arriving in Rome, he was disappointed to find there was no gambling. Although the weather was splendid, the eternal city's beauty was wasted on him. He was lost without his typewriter, and time seemed to have stopped. Sadness continuously overtook him. In his room at the Hassler he woke from a painful dream of his son. Aram's eyes had been full of tears.

He arrived in Monte Carlo at three a.m. on a May morning to find a baccarat game going in the casino; within ten minutes, he had won $100. Returning to the casino the next day, he won more and left Monaco with a profit of $225. He won again at the casino in Aix-en-Provence, and in a Marseilles coin shop he felt flush enough to buy some gold pieces, which had always intrigued him. He paid $90 for a large English one dated 1887.

In Spain, he was received by his publisher, Jose Janes, as warmly as he had been in Italy. He was put up at the Palace Hotel and given 25,000 pesetas, of which half was advance and half a loan.

A letter from Chesley in Paris reported that the lost typewriter, miraculously, had been delivered to him. But Bill's blues still increased. He dreamed of Aram repeatedly, of his son's eyes turning away from him in loss.

Each night he dreamed of Lucy, too, and even Carol. He was making love with Carol when he woke. He was desolate.

There was no longer any appealing destination, but he now lacked the thousand dollars he had promised to Carol by June 1. Knowing there was a famous casino in Estoril, he flew on to Portugal.

He arrived in Lisbon on May 25, found a room at the city's grandest hotel, the Aviz, and was impressed by its palatial structure and grounds. At the Estoril casino he played roulette throughout the evening, losing heavily. At the edge of disaster his luck turned, and he not only recouped his losses but won 10,500 escuderos. The next morning he triumphantly cabled the promised $1,000 to Carol. He followed it with a letter of stern advice to her and postcards to Aram and Lucy. He then revisited the casino, where his luck held for another spectacular gain, followed by a vertiginous loss and a last-minute early-morning rescue.

When Bill discovered that the oil baron Calouste Gulbenkian, an Armenian renowned for his wealth and generosity, was a resident of the Aviz, he made himself known and was invited to lunch. Gulbenkian, a man of perhaps ninety years, struck Bill as a dynamic and altogether delightful man. While his English was perfect, they spoke Armenian, and he took a kindly interest in Bill's life. He was acquainted with "Charley" Marcus.

The following day proved an unlucky one. Bill's gambling at Estoril was uncertain from the start. He felt his luck would turn before the end, but it did not. At closing time, four a.m., he had lost $825 and was absolutely broke. In order to pay his hotel bill, he had to sell the gold coin he had bought in Marseille.

On May 29 he left for Paris by train but was put off at the border town of Villa Fomoro for lack of a Spanish visa. Ill with the flu, a persistent stinging of his prostate, and a heart full of despair, he managed to cross the border on a local train and reach the French resort town of Biarritz. Although he had only a few dollars left from the sale of the gold coin, he took them to the casino, and, in spite of low limits, he managed to run his stake up to 41,000 francs, $125. God, he felt, was looking down on him.

On returning to Paris, he was determined to prove this sponsorship at the Opera Club and managed to inch his capital to $140. But what cheered him most was a newsy letter from Carol in response to his from Lisbon. Lucy had had her tonsils out, and Aram had lost a tooth. Miss Carlile had been replaced by a black girl from Father Divine's flock in Harlem. She was called Positive Ray, and the kids liked her. Carol had included a favorite photograph of Aram and Lucy. All was well.

It was increasingly clear to him that even with his typewriter restored he would get no writing done here, nor would the European casinos provide him with the funds to support him and his family. Thus, on June 22, he boarded the *New Amsterdam* for a return to New York.

He stopped at the Hampshire House, hoping to settle matters with Carol. He found her newly independent. Her friend Leila Hadley was sharing the apartment, while the children were in Westbury, Long Island, staying with Mrs. Burton, Leila Hadley's mother.

Carol insisted that she would need $1,000 a month, as specified in the separation agreement. The Marcuses stoutly backed her up and had hired a lawyer named Schenker to represent her. Bill told Pincus Berner that because the marriage had been based on a deception, he wanted it annulled. Berner strongly advised against the notion of an annulment and any legal reference to the deception. Bill was not persuaded, and he urged his lawyer to proceed with both.

Berner was also functioning as Bill's agent, and he had little good news for his client. Brooks Atkinson, of the *Times,* and Richard Watts Jr., of the *Post,* who had been sent copies of *Don't Go Away Mad,* had agreed that it was a very bad play, and a review of a Boston production of *Jim Dandy* was mainly a tribute to the producer for overcoming its difficulties. Bill took this stoically.

At Harcourt Brace he was reminded that he owed his publishers $19,000, and they were eagerly awaiting the books that would earn it. He promised them three by the year's end: the previously spurned journal of writing *Wesley Jackson,* which he wanted bound with the reissued novel; a play collection led by *Don't Go Away Mad;* and a new volume of short stories.

Harcourt at last agreed to publish *Wesley* with its journal, under the title *The Twin Adventures,* assigning him a pair of editors, Denver Lindley and Eugene Reynal. The short-story collection would have a long introduction, "The Writer on the Writing," in which Bill described the essentials of his craft: the necessity of writing for money while retaining his integrity, and of creating his own character through his work.

The book would include the fine stories of his recent productive periods and lead off with a novelette, *The Assyrian.* It gave the book its title and was based on his encounter with Gulbenkian at the Aviz in Estoril. The narrator is a gambling fool who narrowly survives a heart attack in the hotel lobby.

Although he could find no interest in his plays for stage or film production, Swifty Lazar assured him that he could sell Saroyan work, past and future, to Hollywood. Bill encouraged him to do so, and on July 15 accompanied Lazar to the opening of *Miss Liberty.* He was surprised to see Carol there. She was with Leila Hadley's boss, Al Capp, the creator of the comic strip *Li'l Abner.*

On July 20, he flew home to San Francisco, broke but determined to find the money to pay off debts and provide the monthly thousand dollars that Carol required of him. The sight of Aram's toolbox and Lucy's toy elephant in the garage was a poignant one, and he was glad they were avoiding New York's summer heat at Mrs. Burton's house on Long Island. He wrote them letters and, in a covering note, asked Positive Ray to read them to his children.

In his loneliness and need he went to burlesque shows and dropped in at Sally Stanford's bordello in its new location on Pine Street. He often stayed for hours, talking with the girls. In the aftermath of these visits he would worry over any soreness in his penis, and recall the venereal anxieties that had haunted his bachelor days.

On August 26, he received from Carol a snapshot of Aram playing with Leila Hadley's son Arthur. He also read in a society column of the *New York World–Telegram* that Charles Chaplin and Oona O'Neill had been together at the Champagne Room of El Morocco with Carol Marcus Saroyan and Al Capp. Mrs. Saroyan had said she was determined to make her separation a permanent one.

Bill recalled meeting both Capp and his wife with Leila Hadley at the Stork Club. He remembered Mrs. Capp as rather old, and that they had a number of children. He guessed that Carol and Al Capp were having an affair. It would be a sneaky one, he imagined, and wondered if Mrs. Capp would simply accept it or if there were plans for divorce. In correcting his galleys of *Don't Go Away Mad,* he changed a reference to *Li'l Abner* to *Joe Palooka.*

He was hoping to go to Reno or Las Vegas for six weeks, have a divorce by November 15, and drive to New York to spend Christmas and New Year's with the children. He saw himself sailing for Europe and the Near East in February with plenty of money in his pocket. For the present, however, he was a month behind in the rent at Fifty-eighth Street. The tuition fees for Aram's and Lucy's schools were now due. He would need $2,550 by October 1, and he was broke.

He began a letter to Carol acknowledging the two months' rent he owed and his $3,500 debt to her mother, vowing to pay them. But then frustration with his collapsing marriage and career spilled forth. She had failed to account for money he had already sent. He reviled her again for the seven-year deception about her parentage. He told her that since he had never had a wife he hadn't lost one, but he did fear for her influence on his children. Then, in spite of Rosheen and Charles Marcus's generosity to him, he added them to the conspiracy against him. Finally, he included Pincus Berner, his own lawyer, in the acrimony for failure to deal effectively with his grievance. He wanted an annulment of his marriage, and if Berner could not provide it, he would fire him.

Instead of sending this volatile letter to his wife, he sent a three-page paraphrase of it to Pincus Berner and a copy to Carol.

The following day he did write Carol that as soon as they agreed on a separation agreement he would divorce her. The apartment was to be for the children alone. He intended to visit them there without her presence. He warned her about extravagance and her childish fears of being alone in the apartment. He was particularly concerned about Lucy's anxiety, sleeplessness, and curious restlessness of spirit.

Finally, he told Carol that the children must not be deceived about their race. He wanted assurance that whatever the consequences they be told the truth about their origins and allowed to take pride in it.

Carol's response to his letter to Berner about herself, her mother, and her stepfather was fury. In a surge of contempt she released him from any obligation to support her or their children. She was leaving that conflict to him and his conscience.

But her anger was somewhat appeased by the arrival of his check for the August and September rent. He learned that the children were just back from their summer at Westbury and all was serene.

Literary prospects were less so. Lazar raised old Hollywood hopes by suggesting an original screenplay, for which Bill promptly sent him an outline. The story would be about Paul Smith, who, at fifty, was the age of the century. His joys, sorrows, songs, and achievements would be those of his times.

Lazar soon had favorable studio response to the *Fifty-fifty* idea. At MGM Arthur Freed's enthusiasm was such that Bill decided to develop it as a novel as well as a screenplay. Setting to work, he saw his central figure as the man of the twentieth century. Wary of fictional invention, he sought autobiographical waters, providing Paul with a twin sister, Paula, who would share his childhood in a Presbyterian orphanage. Paul would become a doctor; Paula would become a famous actress.

Now Lazar had an offer. Bill Perlberg of Twentieth Century–Fox would give a $15,000 option on *Fifty-fifty*. If he liked the treatment, there would be an additional $45,000 for Bill to write the screenplay. Bill suggested $25,000 for the option and $50,000 on acceptance, which would apply against 2 percent of the gross. He had no interest in writing the screenplay.

While Perlberg did not welcome his offer, Bill's expectations grew. His opening chapter, which took place on the last day of 1949, had Paul Smith returning home to find his wife in the arms of another man. Bill liked it well enough to write two more chapters and send them off to Herbert Mayes, at *Cosmopolitan,* to Gene Reynal, at Harcourt Brace, and to Lazar. He felt sure that this was his long-sought break.

But Herbert Mayes responded coolly to the three chapters, and Gene Reynal persuaded him that they were unworthy of him. Reading them over he saw they were more synopsis than fully developed fiction, and now the basic scheme itself seemed dubious. He could no longer work on the novel.

A barrage of telegrams from Lazar praising the three chapters of *Fifty-fifty* did little to raise Bill's spirits. The silence from Hollywood became palpable, proving the hollowness of Lazar's promises and Bill's own imprudence in turning down Perlberg's $15,000 offer.

The lively creative flames that had sprung up in the year's early optimism had guttered out. He even wondered if he could turn writing into a second profession and find another by which to earn the $25,000-a-year income he now needed.

He found consolation in the arrival of galleys of *The Assyrian and Other Stories* from Harcourt. The introduction was confident and serene, full of truth he had learned about his profession, and the stories were honest reflections of his experience in life. He decided it was a good book.

Walking to the library on September 22, Bill considered returning to Carol and his children. In spite of the idea's appeal, he soon rejected it. There was no point in deceiving himself; she would never change. He must look for a new wife and make a new family.

But in sending sixth-birthday greetings to Aram, Bill suffered another attack of the blues, and composed a letter to Carol asking if she felt they could start over. Reconsidering, he wrote a second note proposing she write him all about herself. Before sending either he talked to his mother about a possible reconciliation. Takoohi was stoutly opposed, and so he decided to go ahead with the divorce. He was left with a feeling of utter failure—in his family, his profession, and himself.

When Carol sent him catalogs of the childrens' schools, they arrived in a United Features Syndicate envelope that had contained *Li'l Abner* material. She wrote that she had a part-time job working for Jerry Capp, Al Capp's brother. He told himself that Carol had every right to a new personal life, and that it was no business of his, but still he was jealous. It was absurd, but he was pained to think of his wife having an affair with the rich, successful, forty-year-old, married Al Capp.

As the month drew to a close, Berner sent him signed copies of the separation agreement, and Charles Angoff of *American Mercury* bought his ten-year-old, one-act play *Once Around the Block*. The check for $200 that Angoff had enclosed allowed Bill to set out at once for his divorce. He decided against Reno because of its many associations, and went to Las Vegas instead. It was close to Hollywood, in case he had business there.

Bill borrowed $55 from his mother and drove to Las Vegas, arriving on October 1 and moving into the $28-a-week Coronado Court. Although he was without funds, he was confident that a local lawyer would take him on and his money problems would solve themselves in some way or another.

Bill in Las Vegas

Although penniless, the sound of rolling dice was too enticing. On his first night in Las Vegas, he hocked his watch for $5 and ran it to $85 at the crap table before his luck turned. Through a Fresno friend, Vic Hall, he established credit, cashed checks for $1,500 that he did not have, and by one in the morning had lost everything. He sent a desperate wire to Gene Reynal and Donald Brace at Harcourt asking them to increase his debt to $25,000 and send him the balance. Their response was prompt, courteous, and negative.

Sure he would find a way out of his difficulties, Bill hired a Las Vegas lawyer to arrange his divorce, persuaded his friend Vic Hall to hold his checks, moved to a better motel, the El Rancho Vegas, and continued to gamble.

Rescue did come, not from his luck but from his old, though often scorned, friend Stanley Rose. Stanley promised him money from a publisher and then persuaded Howard Cady, Doubleday's West Coast editor, to offer a $12,500 advance for a novel to be delivered by July 1. The $6,250 Bill received on signing the contract enabled him to send Carol $2,250, the sum he owed her for the rest of the year.

He also agreed to write a six-thousand-word piece for *Life* magazine on gambling. He was paid $2,500 at once, promised a second $2,500 on accep-

Al Capp, 1947

tance, and provided with staff photographer Peter Stackpole to record his research at the Golden Nugget. He wrote the piece, but he knew it was a poor one and was not surprised when *Life* rejected it.

By mid-November, when his six weeks' residency in Nevada was complete, he had his divorce, but had lost $15,000 in the casinos. He was weak and ill from the steady drinking and gambling and returned to San Francisco deeper in debt than ever. He owed Pincus Berner a year's fee, $2,500, and federal taxes of $10,000. He did manage to borrow $1,500 from his bookie, Les Cohen, in order to pay the incidental bills Carol had sent him.

Then a man named George Tobin inquired about film rights to *Hello Out There*. He represented James Whale Productions, a Huntington Hartford enterprise. Bill set a price of $25,000, and while Tobin protested it was too much, he called a day later to offer $8,500. While Bill held out for more, he booked a drawing room on a train that would bring him to New York on December 19. He also wrote Carol asking if she would move to her mother's while he spent Christmas week with the children.

Tobin raised his offer to $9,000 plus a percentage of the gross, and Bill accepted it on the condition that he have the money at once. On December 16, with the most pressing of his debts paid, money in his pocket, and a bicycle for Aram in the baggage car, Bill boarded the train for New York.

Traveling east, he assessed 1949 as largely a failure. While he had sold four short stories and earned $10,000, he had written no new plays or novels. *Don't Go Away Mad* had been published on November 17 to a dearth of reviews. *The Assyrian and Other Stories* would be published in January of the following year, and *The Twin Adventures* would appear in April. The only further prospect for royalty income was the song he and Ross had written in the summer of 1939, "Come On to My House." Ross had hopes it would soon be recorded.

In New York, he left his luggage and Aram's bicycle in the lobby of 41 West Fifty-eighth Street and went up to the apartment to find Carol and his children waiting for him. Hugging Aram and Lucy he looked forward to a fine Christmas week, but after a few minutes the telephone rang, and he heard Carol speaking softly into it. Donning a new long mink coat, she said she had to go out for a few minutes and left him with the children.

From a brown envelope Aram proudly took mats of Al Capp's *Li'l Abner* comic strip and tried to entertain his father with them. He was soon aware of Bill's discomfort and put them away. Bill found no picture of himself on display. Positive Ray, the maid, seemed to move about stealthily. After the lapse of a half hour without Carol's return, Bill left, only to find her arriving by taxi in front of the apartment. He confronted her angrily, and together they went into the St. Moritz coffee shop.

Here Carol admitted that the phone call had been from Al Capp. He had asked her to meet him at the train, and she had just done so. She had been having an affair with him for the past eight months. She added that Capp had three children and no intention of divorcing his wife, Catherine, to marry Carol.

Bill understood that she had banished the children to the country in order to use the home he had made for Aram and Lucy as a rendezvous with her lover. Although appalled by this thought, he returned with Carol to take the children for a walk in Central Park. He found them still napping; when he lifted Lucy from her bed, she smiled and said, "I thought you were Al Capp." In the course of the walk in the park she repeated this frequently.

At the walk's end, Bill told Carol he would not be staying at the apartment. She had polluted it. The sight of his children broke his heart. He was going to a hotel, and would spend Christmas alone. That night he moved into the Essex House on Fifty-ninth Street and refused to talk to Carol when she called him.

The next day, he visited Hal Matson to tell him the story. Matson was sympathetic. He invited him home for dinner, and had some good news as well. Maurice Evans was planning a revival of *The Time of Your Life* at the City Center, paying an advance of $1,000 for it. Matson was curious about gossip about the Saroyans. He had corrected those who said Bill's marriage had broken up because of his discovery of Carol's Jewishness.

That afternoon, Carol called to ask if he wanted to see the children. Claiming other engagements, Bill hung up on her but then found she had left him a note. It asked him not to ruin Christmas for the children. She urged him to turn away from anger, since they had much to be happy about—not the least being her love for him, which was still whole.

As his rage ebbed, he conceded that he still loved Carol and felt she was the most desirable woman he had ever known, and he always would. He could not conceive of anyone more right for him than Carol, were it not for her deceitfulness. He saw himself as a generous, comparatively innocent man who had been taken in by her wiles, deluded by her mischievousness and bewitching loveliness.

Deciding that he needed to be a friend, he joined her on December 21 to prepare for the children's Christmas. Watching her trim the tree, he was overcome with desire for her. At twenty-five she was more beautiful than ever. They hugged and kissed until his lips were swollen and her chin and lips were red and sore.

On December 22, he asked that she take him to her mother for an account of her parentage. With Carol and Bill before her, Rosheen told the story. She had been fifteen years old when she had Carol. Carol's father had been twenty-one. He was William (Billy) Mandel, now living in Tucson, Arizona. Charles Marcus arrived as Rosheen finished her story and joined with her and Carol in urging Bill to reunite his family.

The promise of this new understanding was shaken the next day when Carol, who was to meet him at three p.m. to take the children for a drive, failed to appear. When Rosheen returned with the children and no knowledge of Carol's whereabouts, he was sure she was with Capp, and in a rage he looked for them at the Warwick. He failed to find Carol until she returned to the apartment late in the day. He did not believe her when she said she had been with Leila Hadley.

When he asked her if she loved him at all, Carol replied that she did not, at which point Aram put his hands over his eyes and fell sobbing across his father's lap. Carol assured Aram that she had been joking, and gradually he was appeased.

Charles, Rosheen, and Elinor Marcus came by the Fifty-eighth Street apartment to celebrate Christmas Eve with them. Then Chesley and Amie Saroyan, just arrived from Paris, joined them. When they had all gone, Bill and Carol danced until three a.m., hugging and kissing. Carol was radiant with happiness, and both felt reason to rejoice.

Christmas Day had them up early, after only a few hours' sleep, to watch the children open their gifts. Before long, however, a new crisis arose. Carol wanted to see Al Capp on New Year's Eve. Dismayed, Bill wrote to Rosheen to say that her daughter needed psychiatric help. In the course of a long talk with Carol that night, Carol agreed, and encouraged him to interview the psychiatrist Emmanuel Klein, with whom she had had a number of sessions.

During Christmas week, Bill did visit Dr. Klein but was left unsatisfied by the man's cautious opinion that, if Carol were willing, there was a possibility for a change in her pattern of behavior. But now he and Carol saw each other often. They shopped and dined together, and on one night Carol came to Bill's room at the Essex House, where they made love for the first time since mid-March.

They agreed to spend New Year's Eve together with the children, but when he found her gone during the afternoon of the thirty-first he was sure she was with Capp. When she returned at five-thirty, Bill was in a rage. He called Rosheen and Pincus Berner, threatening to go to court to get custody of the children.

After talking to Carol, he was gradually mollified and persuaded that for the children's sake they must remain friends. Carol told him that she wanted a career of her own, preferably in the theater, and he said he would try to help her. With the New Year before them, he resolved to find a nearby apartment for himself and get back to daily writing.

Indeed, throughout this painful holiday season, brooding in his room at the Essex House, he began several works based on his perception of Carol. One play he titled *Adorable Liar,* another, *Queen Lust,* and a novel, *Deceit.* All three depicted a beautiful, false young woman whose ambition makes a fool of the unfortunate man who falls for her. He abandoned all three in agony.

He admitted to a helpless love for Carol and likened it to a disease. Just the sight of her tormented him. But he reasoned against his jealousy. He had to give her the freedom to go her own way and be her friend so they could be good parents to the children.

Then Carol was mysteriously absent from Charles Marcus's sixty-fourth-birthday party on January 4. She turned up in time to go to the Stork Club with Bill, but they quarreled on the way home and again the next day when he found her missing from the apartment. Sure now that she had been with Capp both times, he announced to Rosheen and Pincus Berner that Carol was psychopathic and that he was absolutely through with her.

The next day, Carol was elusive during the afternoon, and when they talked in the evening he found her irrational. She summoned Al and Dolly Hirschfeld to help explain her feelings, and the four talked until four a.m. Bill was convinced that Carol was going back to Al Capp.

On Sunday, January 8, following a sleepless night in which he was sure Carol was with Capp, he wrote the cartoonist a careful letter explaining that his concern was for his son and daughter. They were, as he was, helpless victims of their mother's psychopathic personality.

Perhaps Capp could succeed where Bill had failed. If he planned to marry Carol, he should make this known to all. If not, their affair would disqualify Carol as the mother of Bill's children, and he would take the necessary legal steps.

He showed the letter to Pincus Berner and to Charles and Rosheen Marcus, all three of whom dissuaded Bill from sending it. Instead, he left a note for Carol saying she must keep their home for the children alone and tell them the truth about their origins. Otherwise, she was free to behave in any way she chose—he no longer cared.

At Bill's request and expense, Ross Bagdasarian arrived from California, and together they moved into a larger room at the Hampshire House. Ross stood by him as always, but on hearing Bill's list of complaints against Carol and his belief that she needed therapy, Ross disagreed. Neither Bill nor psychiatry would change Carol. She was gladly what she was.

On Saturday, the fourteenth, they went to call on Carol. After an outburst from Bill they proceeded, a trio, to Caruso's for spaghetti. Later they went to Charles and Rosheen's, where Carol wept continuously. That night, Bill and Ross talked until three a.m. about sexual experience with their wives and other women. Ross explained that it was only after three months of marriage and repeated attempts that he had satisfied his wife, Armen. Bill admitted he had never done so with Carol. He thought he needed to try.

Lucy's fourth birthday was on January 17, and Bill brought her the presents she wanted: a skate key, books, and a charm bracelet. He joined Lucy and her mother for tea at Schrafft's, a cartoon movie, and a candle-trimmed cake.

On January 20, walking along Fifth Avenue, he encountered Carol with Oona Chaplin. Guessing that Carol would be going out with Capp and the Chaplins, he ignored her entirely as he greeted Oona with an embrace. Bill was grateful to Charlie Chaplin. Recently, Sydney Chaplin and his partner, Jerry Epstein, had offered to produce another Saroyan play at their Circle Theatre. They had suggested *A Decent Birth,* with Ross Bagdasarian directing. Bill had proposed an alternative, *The Son,* a revision of a 1939 play *The Hero of the World,* and they had agreed to it. But even as he valued the cordiality and advantage he had enjoyed from Oona, Charlie, and Sydney, and even though Carol had assured him that Charlie was on his side and had urged a return to him, Bill was doubtful. He decided that they were Carol's friends, not his, and that Chaplin, like Capp, was probably derived from the Jewish name Caplin.

Two days later, he had a good talk with Carol. After it, they called on the Chaplins in their room at the Plaza and brought them back to Fifty-eighth Street for a visit with the children. When the Chaplins had gone, Carol asked Bill if he would take her to Europe in the summer, and Bill said yes. They planned to have dinner together, after which she would spend the night with him at Hampshire House.

Afloat in this period of reconciliation, Bill acknowledged that he would rather be with Carol than anybody in the world. They had dinner the following evening at "21" and again went to Bill's room at Hampshire House, where, with Ross's advice in mind, he made love to her as generously as he could. When he took her home, at a quarter to three in the morning, he was planning another such evening and believed they had reached a new understanding.

The next evening, while he was visiting the children and envisioning a reclaimed Carol, she telephoned at seven-thirty to say she would not join him as they had planned. At nine-thirty, she telephoned him at the Hampshire House. She was speaking from Al Capp's hotel room and wanted him to say how many times they had been together physically since his return.

When he replied that it had been three times, Carol put Capp on to speak to him. Capp was friendly and worldly. He was open about his affair with Carol and said he was in love with her. He was going to divorce his wife and marry Carol. His wife would marry again. He ended by saying he felt Bill had taken his girl. He suggested they meet, then decided against it.

Bill wished Carol every happiness and said good-bye. He had lost her. He called Rosheen, who assured him that the Al Capp business was nothing and that Carol would come back to him. This was no consolation. He was thoroughly shattered and unable to sleep. In patrolling Fifty-eighth Street, he saw a light on in 3A and went up to the apartment. In her bathrobe, Carol admitted him, saying that if Al Capp knew she had let him in, he would kill her. He left after five minutes. At two in the morning he called his mother in San Francisco, and her advice was explicit: Let Carol marry Al Capp. She needed a man with money.

From Berner's office he wrote Carol a letter listing his grievances against her and then his intention: he needed to have absolute custody of the children. He sent copies to both Al Capp and the Marcuses. His gravest concern was for Lucy. He wondered how much damage had already been done to the child's soul by her mother. He wanted legal action now, and thought of calling his uncle Aram, asking him to fly to New York and look into his case.

Carol was outraged by Bill's letter and called Pincus Berner to say that she would not dignify Bill's charges against her with a reply. She denied making the telephone call to Bill from Capp's and having an affair with

Capp. She would fight to keep her children and would, in the course of it, reveal aspects of Bill's nature no one knew about.

Berner reported that Carol had a new lawyer, Arnold Krakower, the husband of Artie Shaw's ex-wife. When Berner suggested that they might achieve his ends without expensive court proceedings, Bill was unswayed. There was to be no compromise. He had to have custody of the children and take them home to their family in California. Carol was to have visitation rights only. If necessary, he would call in another lawyer.

On February 7, Bill called his mother. Again she advised him to let the children go, but Uncle Aram, in Fresno, saw no reason for surrender. There was a good case against Carol, but it was important to get concrete evidence. Acting on this advice, Bill interviewed Charley, the Italian elevator operator at 41 West Fifty-eighth Street. He told Bill that Al Capp had been admitted to apartment 3A at least twenty times in recent months. There had been a great many parties. On one occasion, Carol had arrived home by taxi at three a.m., said good-bye to a male companion, gone out again at seven a.m., and returned at three p.m., looking very tired. The past night she had come home with a young man at 12:45 a.m. and gone out again fifteen minutes later. The cab fares were low, so she must have come from nearby, perhaps the Warwick, Capp's hotel. Charley said that all the boys marveled at Mrs. Saroyan's stamina.

Convinced that this was the behavior of a nymphomaniac, Bill told Berner that they must have Carol watched. Reluctantly, Berner put him in touch with the Aetna Detective Bureau. Bill authorized the company to record all conversations at Carol's phone number and to assign two detectives to night and day watch of Carol's comings and goings. He called Ross Bagdasarian, who was at Stanley Rose's in Hollywood, and urged him to return to New York on the next plane.

Instead of Ross, Stanley Rose arrived to act as his comrade. Rose had fortified himself against his chronic fear of flying with an unusual dosage of whiskey, and he was mumbling drunk. The telephone tap had not been permitted, and although the "eyes" had been on duty for several days they had collected no evidence. Indeed, Carol had noted them parked across from the apartment building's entrance and had stood in front of their car to record its license number.

On the afternoon of February 12, Bill decided he needed to see the children on common ground, and he asked Don Freeman and Stanley Rose to help find them during their daily walk in Central Park. Freeman and Rose found them near the zoo and brought them, along with Positive Ray, to meet Bill at the Plaza. Bill hugged and kissed them both, whereupon Aram and Lucy behaved like members of a sympathetic jury, asking him if he was really as bad as their mama had said and if he truly intended to take them away from her.

The next morning, Krakower complained to Berner that Bill and two "gorillas" had tried to kidnap the children in the park. In the evening, Al Hirschfeld came to see Bill at the Hampshire House, hoping to mediate between him and Carol. She would not ask a penny for either herself or the children, he said. She would support them on money she earned or from the generosity of her parents. Bill was unmoved. He told Hirschfeld that Carol was holding the children hostage. He wanted custody and would go to court to get it.

On February 14, Bill called on Berner and told him he was not being aggressive enough, so he was firing him. When Berner pointed out that in view of his service, which had gone far beyond the professional, this was ungracious behavior, Bill agreed.

Nevertheless, he went looking for a new lawyer, preferably Armenian, and found him in Alan Fenner—originally Aram Fenerdjian. In a two-hour session with Fenner, Bill learned what he had been unable to accept from Berner: that he didn't have much of a case against Carol, that the law was entirely on her side. He must continue to pay for her support and that of his children.

He saw himself as the victim, not just of Carol, but of the whole Marcus family. They had won, and they had destroyed him. Hopeless, deciding that he would soon pack up and return to San Francisco to get back to work, he went off to the forty-second-birthday party of Mac Kriendler, one of the proprietors of the "21" Club. There, at ten-thirty, he was called to the telephone and heard his sister Zabe's voice speaking from San Francisco. Their mother had suffered a cerebral hemorrhage and been taken to St. Francis Hospital. He told Zabe he would be home on the next available plane.

Bill arrived in San Francisco on the evening of February 17 and went directly to the hospital. Takoohi, with Mihran at her bedside, was awake and stunned to see Bill. Tenderly, he kissed his mother's cheeks and pressed her hands tightly. She turned to her nurse and asked if she knew who this was, then told her proudly that he was her son—William Saroyan.

XII

THE BIG MUSTACHE

1950–1951

Takoohi's physician, a Dr. Allen, told Bill that the next three days would be critical ones, and during them there must be no more visits. At home on Fifteenth Avenue, Bill thought that his mother would pull through. He telegraphed Positive Ray, asking her to send a get-well message from Aram and Lucy to their grandmother, and wrote Pincus Berner a conciliatory letter, thanking him and his wife for their support.

Although Takoohi's condition seemed to improve, Dr. Allen reported that the ruptured vein had not healed and that there was more blood in her spinal fluid. Then, on the morning of February 23, Bill's sister Zabe, with her daughter Gloria, came to pound on his back door to tell him that their mother was dying. For a day, Takoohi clung to life. Bill was so pleased to find that Carol had written his mother a kind letter that he felt a rush of charity for his wife, reflecting that she, too, was a mother.

As the family gathered for the closing of Takoohi's life, Bill found that even his uncle Zaven Minasian had come, a man he had not forgiven for suing him fifteen years before over the story "Little Caruso." Zaven had claimed, rightly enough, that it had ridiculed his operatic ambitions. The men huddled together for storytelling, vying for an extreme of obscenity, as if it were an antidote to death's approach. They told tales of wild cocksmen fornicating with sheep, cows, knotholes, barrels. His uncle Archie told them, and Bill told them, but his uncle Aram still told them best.

Takoohi Saroyan, born in Bitlis, Armenia, in 1882, died at noon on February 25, 1950, at the age of sixty-eight. The grieving Bill chose her casket at Currivan's Chapel on Sunset and a burial plot with places for four at Cypress Lawn Cemetery, thinking he would have his father's remains brought here from San Jose. The $1,375 he paid for these final necessities drained his bank account, but he was remembering the last words he had heard his mother say, and how proud of him she had been.

Takoohi's funeral took place on the last day of February. After it, Bill and Ross went into town and drank until three in the morning. They found some cheer in prospects for *The Son* and the opportunity it presented for Ross to prove himself as a director.

Bill arrived in Hollywood on March 15 to join Ross at the Circle Theatre, where *The Son* was already in rehearsal. When he had given Ross a sheaf of revisions for the play, the two went with Sydney Chaplin to the Chaplin house on Summit Drive. There, Oona appeared in an evening gown while Charlie came downstairs in old clothes to cook them steaks over a charcoal grill. After dinner, Ross sang the "Come On to My House" song and explained that he had not only arranged for a recording of it but would sing it himself in *The Son*'s vaudeville scene. Charlie liked the "House" song, and told them they should do an Armenian musical.

The Son portrayed events in a multifamily history between the years 1908 and 1939. Its story of love and patriotism gone wrong was fragmentary and often bewildering. Watching a run-through on the nineteenth, Bill recognized that the play was imperfect, but thought Ross was doing a good job of directing.

When Bill found that Ross had added very little of the new material he had given him and seemed anxious to keep Bill from the theater, he grew suspicious of his cousin and thought Ross might be worrying more about himself than the welfare of the play. At the final rehearsal, Bill was dismayed. He thought it was hopeless and abruptly asked to be taken back to his hotel. Ross followed him, and blamed Jerry Epstein's interference. Bill was unappeased. Ross had been too clever, and had not leveled with him when it was important. He decided that his cousin, heretofore his best friend, was stupid.

The opening-night audience, which included the Chaplins, the Edward G. Robinsons, and the full press corps, was assurance that *The Son* was a Hollywood event. Bill brought John Fante and Stanley Rose for support and this time endured the whole play. He deemed it not as bad as the previous performance, but bad enough. He noticed that Ross was avoiding him and dismissed all hopes for the venture.

He told Stanley Rose that *The Son* had been Ross's big opportunity, but he had failed it. All he could do was sing "Come On to My House" in every performance. He was a ham. Nevertheless, when Ross came by with proofs of the "Come On to My House" sheet music and assurances that a recording was imminent, Bill was reconciled enough to agree that *The Son* had been a disappointment to them both.

Bill had a list of Los Angeles–area Armenian girls who were thought to be likely candidates for the new Mrs. Saroyan. He appraised several, noted that one was seventeen, and another, who was studying ballet, had a wonderful figure; all spoke Armenian. After one look, however, he lost interest in each one. He thought of Carol all the time. He suspected that Capp had abandoned her and wondered what she was doing. He also wondered where he would ever find a girl so powerfully appealing to him.

Unable to pay further lodging expense, Bill moved from the Knickerbocker Hotel to Ross and Armen Bagdasarian's house, in Sherman Oaks. It was here that Rosheen called Bill on Easter Sunday to give him some advice about restoring his marriage. She told him that if he made a lot of money, Carol would come back to him.

This was not at all what Bill wanted to hear, and he told Rosheen that under these circumstances Carol should marry Al Capp. Yet the thought of having Carol back possessed him, and charged the love-hate dynamics that attracted them as irresistibly as it parted them. He spent the rest of the day in despair.

On Monday, Carol called. She made it plain that Al Capp was no longer important to her and that nobody was helping her except for Krakower, who had loaned her money. Bill urged her to quit her frivolous life in New York and come home to him. They would begin again, marry again.

While Carol resisted, he felt she was pleased by his wanting her back. She agreed to think about his proposal. Meanwhile, she urged him to speak to Krakower, which he did. The two men had a reasonable conversation. Bill admitted to Carol's urgent need of money and said he would try to supply it.

He thought $60,000 would put him in the clear, and in Hollywood this did not seem an impossible feat. At MGM he urged Arthur Freed to interest Spencer Tracy in *The Assyrian*. At Warner Brothers he pressed Jerry Wald to buy "The Parsley Garden." When Wald was cool to that, Bill outlined an original story called "Come Back to Carthage," which concerned a man in California who is still in love with his beautiful ex-wife and is anxious about their two children.

Although he pursued every likelihood, no proposal brought him the offer he sought, and when he called Carol on April 17, he said he hoped she would understand that he was doing his utmost to get money for her. Carol, preoccupied with moving out of 41 West Fifty-eighth to a new apartment, took his warning against high expectations as a rebuff and said she feared he would use whatever she said to avoid his responsibility or to take custody of the children.

In a burst of anger he abandoned his hopes for reconciliation, called her names, and told her that if she would stop harassing him for money, she could keep the children.

Carol had not given him her new address, but on April 23, he traced her by telephone to the Hotel Volney, at 23 East Seventy-fourth Street. They spoke, and she told him she would be there with the children and Positive Ray until June 1 and that she would not remarry him, because she didn't love him.

When she telegraphed that Aram's school, Allen Stevenson, was demanding the overdue tuition at once, Bill had to scrape the $400 sum together by collecting a debt and borrowing from his uncle Mihran, but he added an extra $20 for Carol to spend on herself.

Listening to Aram Khachaturian's *Masquerade,* he remembered dancing to it, first with Carol, then with Aram. He wept for his loss, stopping when Cosette appeared with his coffee, only to resume when she left. He especially missed Lucy, recalling her words to him when he saw her last in front of the Plaza, and how, when he had called from Hollywood, she had told him to take a taxi and come home.

He thought of Aram's particular gladness, which often burst forth in his own dance. Lately he had taken to ending each day by wishing his son, daughter, and wife a good night and asking God to bless and keep them.

A note from Aram, addressed by Carol, telling Bill that he had only two more weeks of SCA-OOL arrived on May 15, and he recognized the misspelling as a joke between them. He was delighted by his son's firm hand and convinced that Aram too would find writing his life. If he could just get some money soon, he would ask Carol to send him the children for a July visit.

Carol wrote, thanking him for the several checks, which had paid Aram's tuition, but now he needed to pay Lucy's at Miss Hewitt's. There was also a $100 doctor's bill, and both children needed shoes. She knew very well that he was broke, which was why she became severe and self-righteous with him. He had gambled away a fortune while she was trying to provide Aram and Lucy with a decent life. She had no intention of living in a cold-water flat because of his outrageous behavior with money. She assured him that both children were growing up happy. They were incredible children. They kept his picture in their room, and their lives were smooth as they could be without a dime. She wished him well.

A telegram arrived on May 25 reminding Bill of his $2,500 debt to Vic Hall's El Rancho Vegas and his others to Thunderbird and the Last Frontier. The California tax office demanded his arrears of $1,238.52 within the next ten days, and, on June 1, Cosette turned away a process server representing the New York landlord to whom he owed $2,500.

Although certain that his only recourse lay in serious writing, Bill had scant assurance in his recent accomplishments. Despite excellent reviews, *The Assyrian* had sold barely four thousand copies, earning him only $2,000. *The Twin Adventures* had just been published to a chilly reception. In the Sunday *Tribune,* William Zinsser conceded that *Wesley Jackson* was a "pretty good war novel," but that he found the "diary" a bore. In the Sunday *Times,* Nelson Algren was not half so kind.

Among his debts was the novel he owed Doubleday, and now he saw that as his main—and perhaps only—chance. Searching for its theme, he spent several days in self-examination. Still without a plan, he began by typing, knowing that what he typed was aimless but withholding any judgment until he had several chapters.

By the second day, he had a title, *Rock Wagram,* and a main character. Rock, born Arak Vagramian, was thirty-three, just out of the army, a movie actor, and a onetime Fresno bartender. Further characters emerged from recollection. There was Paul Key, born Keesler, a clever, discontented MGM production chief; his bumbling nephew, Sam Schwarz; the seventeen-year-old New York beauty Ann Ford; and Rock's eighty-one-year-old grandmother.

Although aware that he was drawing his two women and the Hollywood moguls from life, Bill did not identify the central figure as himself, nor did he feel the novel's scheme was an apologia for his own pre-war and postwar behavior.

The design for *Rock Wagram* pleased him and restored his belief in himself as a writer, enabling him to work on the book for six-hour stretches. The momentum of getting on with it and the sense of discovery that lay ahead was overcoming the emptiness of his heart.

In addition, he began a series of short stories, which he called *A Torch for Life,* and a third project, a journal of his writing, which he called *More Later.* But his struggle with *Rock Wagram* was painful. Reading over the day's work, he was often troubled by it. There was no sense of gladness with himself. Nearing the story's end he missed the rush of accomplishment. But, typically, he reassured himself that he wasn't obliged to write a *great* book, that if it should fail it would still have been worth doing.

Discouragement only fueled his energies. He promised that nothing would stop him—neither illness nor any other misfortune of heart or spirit. He felt that in ten years' time there would be a great deal more of his work, and it would be ever better. Keeping up with his three projects, he labored around the clock and understood he was on a binge. When at three or four in the morning he did go to bed, he was too exhilarated by the effort, and its accompanying coffee, to sleep.

His cousin and fellow writer Archie Minasian told him he was killing himself with work, thus raising chronic concern about his health. Earlier in the year he had consulted Stanley Rose's Dr. Cutler about his oozing penis. Cutler had thought it was gonorrhea and treated it successfully with sulfa, penicillin, and prostate massage. But aside from occasional pains around his heart, he now felt fine. Looking into the mirror, admiring the enormous, patriarchal moustache he was cultivating, he thought he looked great, just right for a man approaching his forty-second birthday.

He finished the last chapter of *Rock Wagram* in the first week of June. It revealed that the only remains of Rock's marriage are hopes for his son and his daughter. He finds an Armenian girl for his second wife and sees her into a first pregnancy. His faltering film career holds new promise too. Looking at Rock's latest test, Sam Schwarz proclaims him to be never better.

Rock Wagram had taken him thirty-nine days to write, and it amounted to well over one hundred thousand words, his longest writing effort ever. He thought it read well and was often amusing. Sending it off to Doubleday's editor in chief, Ken McCormick, he felt he was a writer reborn.

He expected the money to follow soon. The first came from a story, "Bill McGee's Brother," which he had written during a single night in Hollywood, hoping it would please a studio. *Cosmopolitan* had turned it down brusquely, but Erd Brandt, of the *Saturday Evening Post,* wrote that, in spite of the single-spaced manuscript, he liked the story and was taking it. He sent congratulations and a payment of $3,000. Bill celebrated by writing a check for Lucy's school bill.

There were further boosts to his spirit. Richard Dunham, at the University of Wyoming, invited him to Laramie to put on a Saroyan play of his choice and to speak at the arts celebration there in July. Bill agreed, thinking it might get him to New York, and sent Dunham *Afton Water,* retitled *A Western Awakening.*

His plan was to go to Laramie for the festival and then continue east. He would stay a day or so in New York, long enough to see Aram and Lucy, Ken McCormick, and a rehearsal of an off-Broadway production of *The Son.* He hoped to persuade McCormick to contract for his two additional books.

With Archie Minasian, Bill toured the countryside inspecting new housing developments. He found a site in the San Francisco suburb of San Mateo enticing enough for him to put down a $200 deposit on a yet-to-be-built $23,500 ranch house. He thought it just right for his kids to visit, and as the site of a possible second marriage.

When he wrote Carol about having the children for a few weeks, she declined to send them now, since they were both just over the mumps, but held out the possibility of a later visit. Meanwhile, she was in urgent need of

$1,000. He was about to send it when a letter from Arnold Krakower, Carol's lawyer, advised that he was $5,125 in arrears on his payments to Carol. He was expected to provide her a sum of $750 each month, plus the cost of the children's schools, clothing, and doctors. Moreover, he must pay Krakower's own fee of $2,500. Bill felt newly besieged, and the idea of a family reunion in New York lost all its appeal.

Bill arrived in Laramie on July 2 and was met on the station's lawn by a mounted welcoming party. He was photographed shaking hands with his host, Richard Dunham, and being driven off in an open carriage pulled by two burros.

He enjoyed his reception as distinguished visitor, one of a galaxy that included Paul Engle and Walter van Tilburg Clark, and he was pleased by this introduction to academic life. He gave a lecture, "New Directions in Contemporary Playwriting," to an afternoon audience in the student union. It lasted only twelve minutes, but the questions that followed filled the balance of the allotted hour, and he felt it had gone well.

He watched rehearsals of *A Western Awakening* apprehensively, but the play's one, well-publicized performance took place on July 20, and while it seemed to fall apart at the end, he was surprised at how well it had gone. The large audience applauded enthusiastically and called repeatedly for the author—who, having already left the theater, failed to appear.

His pleasure in being lionized was shaken by news from Cosette that *Cosmopolitan* had rejected *Rock Wagram*. There was no word from Ken McCormick, who had received his copy two weeks before and promised to read it at once. Looking over his own copy, Bill decided it was a terrible mess and McCormick would also reject it.

In response to Bill's query, McCormick called him to say he had indeed read the novel but he wanted Howard Cady's report before responding. Nevertheless, Bill felt McCormick liked *Rock Wagram*. He was now confident he would have the rest of his advance and be able to buy his San Mateo house.

Arriving in New York on July 24, he took a room at the Statler and decided that although he might inquire about Aram and Lucy at their schools he would not try to see them.

When he went to Doubleday, he was aware of people turning to look at his huge mustache and for the first time had misgivings about it, but he was soon caught up in meeting his new publisher. As he settled in Ken McCormick's office, he was relieved to find a $12,500 check, the balance of his advance, awaiting him. McCormick, a slim, soft-spoken, nervous man of his own age, listened attentively as Bill described the two additional books he was offering him, the story collection *A Torch for Life* and the journal, *More Later*.

As for *Rock Wagram,* McCormick felt the title should be shortened to *Rock,* and he had some suggestions for further revision. He wanted more of Ann Ford. He wanted to remove the preambles and ruminations that began each chapter, interrupting the narrative's flow, and he wanted more of an ending. Bill discouraged him about the first two requests but agreed to write a new ending. In parting, McCormick told Bill that *Rock* was a new kind of novel for him. Bill understood this as flattery, induced by his having invested in the book.

On his first night in New York, Bill went uptown and walked along East Seventy-sixth Street until he found number 17. It was a four-story building opposite the Surrey, where Garson Kanin lived. From the street he could see that the top floor was dark, but there were lights on the third floor. He stepped into the vestibule and found the name Saroyan listed for the upper apartment and guessed that Carol, Aram, Lucy, and Miss Ray occupied the top two floors.

He walked four blocks to Lucy's school, Miss Hewitt's Classes, at 68 East Seventy-ninth, then to Allen Stevenson, at 132 East Seventy-eighth. He returned to 17 East Seventy-sixth to find the third-floor lights still on. He walked down to 41 West Fifty-eighth to look up at the windows of the third-floor apartment, now hung with a new tenant's curtains.

The next day, he watched a rehearsal of *The Son,* which was to open at the Circle Theatre on August 15. Although he found himself enjoying it, he guessed it would meet a hostile reception, but he believed that on so small a stage, it would not be damaging to him.

When interviewed about *The Son* by Harvey Breit, of the *New York Times,* Bill listed his accomplishments and then bristled at the journalist's observation that he would have been better off to write one good book rather than so many indifferent ones.

The major event of his New York visit was a dinner with Ken McCormick. He discovered that McCormick, originally a writer, had hitch-hiked to New York from his home in Portland, Oregon, in 1928. Not only were they the same age, but on first arriving here they had both stayed at the Twenty-third Street YMCA.

While McCormick spoke agreeably and generally about publishing the two books Bill had brought along, he wanted him to understand Howard Cady's position as West Coast editor. Cady had brought Saroyan to the Doubleday list, and thus he must see every manuscript first. *Torch* and *More Later* would go off to him in the morning and reach San Francisco before Bill did.

Returning to California, Bill congratulated himself on having seen the place where Carol and the children lived, as well as getting the balance of his Doubleday advance and meeting the people who would be publishing him. He expected generous advances from Doubleday for the other two books.

In San Francisco he found a letter from Carol scolding him for not supporting his children. She had enclosed snapshots of them at Coney Island, and he was moved by the sight of a playful Lucy and a sad-eyed Aram, grinning in spite of his missing tooth. Putting aside $4,000 for his new house, he paid off the $2,250 in back rent at Fifty-eighth Street and wrote Carol, offering her a monthly alimony of $500, if he could have Aram and Lucy during their vacations.

On August 1, he began work on a novel he called *The Laughing Matter.* It would take place in 1911 and portray the Nazarenus family, a father, mother, son, and daughter. Their farm was a sixty-acre vineyard in Clovis. The boy, whom he named Red, was a joyful child who laughed at the sight of grass blowing in the wind.

Simultaneously he began a novelette, a fable about love he called *Tracy's Tiger.* Tracy, whose imagination has provided him with a companionable black panther, finds himself beside a real one, a dangerous escapee from the circus. It was a fanciful narrative that suited his whimsical voice.

These books were barely underway when Howard Cady called to say that the *Torch for Life* and *More Later* manuscripts had arrived from New York. He had read them and was unhappy with the prospect of publishing either as they stood. Perhaps some of the *Torch* sections could be fitted into *Rock Wagram,* which he was now editing, but both new books were so self-exposing as to seem an invasion of privacy. Bill protested that any man could invade his own privacy. If he were a writer, it was obligatory.

When Cady accused him of not caring what he wrote, Bill agreed. He put down everything he cared to. He insisted that he needed the money and must have a contract for these two books. Cady pointed out that Stanley Rose, through whom he had acquired *Rock Wagram,* was feeling left out and perhaps ought not to be. Bill dismissed the suggestion.

The next day Cady arrived at Fifteenth Avenue to dissuade Bill from publishing the two books just submitted. He reminded Bill of his own admission that the poems in *Torch* were dreadful. Cady believed much of the material would be damaging to him. As for the journal, *More Later,* he suggested Bill keep one for all his work and, when he had a stockpile, cull it for a single writer's journal.

Unmoved by Cady's advice, Bill insisted on having $25,000 at once for *Torch* and an additional $25,000 for *More Later,* on the first of the next year. Cady now revealed that Ken McCormick's reader's report on *Torch* was unfavorable. The young woman's opinion was that the book was irresponsible, and its author worse. When Bill questioned the reader's credentials he found she was a friend of Carol's.

Bill assured Cady that Doubleday would want to publish the two books he was now writing, *The Laughing Matter* and *Tracy's Tiger*. As Cady left, Bill was convinced their conference had been unsuccessful, but Cady agreed to telephone Ken McCormick with Bill's demands. Although angered and depressed by the meeting, Bill felt it would not be at all unsuccessful if the contracts went through.

A letter from Carol arrived describing her harassment by bill collectors. Her only friend had been Krakower, to whom she now owed $2,500. She urged Bill to pay this now, and he agreed to send her the money he had put aside for the San Mateo house. Keeping only a dollar in his account, he wrote Carol a check for $4,431.05, all the money he had in the world.

He then called Howard Cady and said that if Doubleday found his demands too stiff, he would consider a counteroffer. If there was no interest in the two books he was writing now, he would offer them to another publisher and they could simply publish *Rock Wagram*. Waiting for a response to this, he felt very vulnerable.

On August 4, Bill was surprised by a call from Rosheen in Beverly Hills. She asked if he was still interested in Carol. Bill replied that it was a question of Carol's not being interested in him. Rosheen disagreed. If he wanted her, Carol would come back to him.

Recalling expectations raised and dashed, Bill accused Rosheen of lying and crookedness of every sort. Unfazed, Rosheen told him she would call Carol, invite her out, and have her come to San Francisco and see him. She went on to say that Carol feared him and thought he would only throw Al Capp in her face again or leave her with more children to care for. Yet when Rosheen told him that Carol was more beautiful than ever and invited him down to stay with her, he was tempted to go, to be there when Carol arrived.

An hour later, Rosheen called back. She had talked to Carol, and it was just as she had said. Carol wanted to come back to him, and had for a long time. Within moments Bill was hearing this from Carol herself. There had been no cooling of Capp's interest in her. He loved her, wanted to marry her, indeed had loaned her $8,000, but she would not marry him. She wanted Bill to come back to her and the children in New York.

When Bill countered that he could not work in New York, she said she understood. She would fly to San Francisco the next day, stay at the Fairmont, and get Rosheen to come up and be with her. Yes, Carol said, she could be a real wife and a real person to him now. Bill said he wanted her to come back to him.

When this was settled, all in an hour, Bill willingly put aside all work for the day. Contemplating a reunion with his family, he thought what a preposterous life this was. Clearly it was a time to celebrate. He called Archie and Mihran to join him for drinks, and when they had arrived he called

Howard Cady. Cady declined to join them, for he was at home with his wife and his children, but he invited them all to his house in Berkeley.

The ensuing party at Cady's was a lusty one, and in the course of it Bill decided Howard was a first-rate fellow. But it lasted until late, and the next morning Bill awoke with a hangover and some qualms.

He had no money at all, and he felt the kind of desperation about it that invariably served as a springboard to his gambling. He understood that Carol provoked this, and he thought perhaps he should not have encouraged her to come out. His jealousy of Capp reawakened, and he recalled that Carol had turned the kids over to Positive Ray so she could be Capp's mistress.

He was so troubled now that when Carol called to say she was unable to leave until tomorrow he told her it was better she not come at all. Carol was dismayed. He told her that in a few months, when he had more money, they could meet and see if they might make a family again. Meanwhile, she should take no more money from Capp, spend the $4,431 now on its way to her, and not bother him further until November.

Furious, Carol accused him of hating women. Her mother, who believed he was romantic, had told her she didn't know Bill. Well, she did, and all too well.

A few days later Carol acknowledged his check tartly; she wrote that he could have it back if he wanted it, and then added that she did not know if he could be her friend, but she was sure that he lacked any understanding or affection for her. Whenever she allowed herself to trust in his concern for her or their children she was left devastated. She would not be so foolish again. However, she would get on with the raising of Aram and Lucy, who were happy and enthusiastic about returning to their New York schools the next month. She was enclosing some snapshots. If he wanted the children to call him, she would arrange it.

Howard Cady's unfavorable opinion of *Torch* and *More Later* was supported by McCormick. Doubleday did not want them. However, they were ready to offer him advances of $12,500 each on the novel and novelette he was completing. Bill agreed, urging Cady to raise the figure to $15,000 but accepting his refusal to do so.

When he called at Cady's office on Market Street to work on *Rock Wagram*, he found himself defending a passage the editor had cut. Cady assured him that the omission was a kindness to the reader, and Bill gave in, reflecting on the nature of readers and why they read all the miserable books they did. Cady had a number of editorial reports on *Rock Wagram*, and Bill was angered to find they shared a tone of intellectual superiority, treating him as a "light" writer. He decided that Doubleday was less a publishing house than a business that tried to turn every book into a best-seller.

Meanwhile, he was working. When he finished *Tracy's Tiger*, Bill sent it off to Howard Cady and Herb Mayes, believing the latter would hesitate over it yet have to take it. He was well along in *The Laughing Matter*, which, with Red's drowning, had become a tragedy. It would run to eighty thousand words and be completed by his birthday at the end of the month.

Doubleday's $12,500 check for *The Laughing Matter* arrived in mid-August. With it, Bill paid his debts to his bookie, Les Cohen, and to the three Las Vegas casinos. He considered the balance of $5,582.96 and then paid off the $5,000 debt to his uncle Mihran. This left him owing Harcourt $12,000, Rosheen $4,000, another $4,000 on his house in San Mateo, and taxes of $13,000.

He decided to send the spurned collection, *Torch for Life*, to Harcourt, directing it to Donald Brace and Alfred Harcourt. He enclosed a letter explaining his new publishing affiliation. In what he described as a gesture of good faith he waived any advance on the book. He asked only for a quick decision and felt confident they would leap to accept it. Donald Brace soon acknowledged receipt of *Torch*, but it was Gene Reynal who delivered the decision: Harcourt was declining the book.

The Son opened in New York on August 15. Bill's old scourge Brooks Atkinson told *New York Times* readers that, although the cast had done its best, *The Son* was "hardly more than a random collection of peevish attitudes signifying nothing but confusion." While there had been a "disarming naivete about his work when he was noisily loving the beautiful people," Saroyan was now "denouncing God for the evil, swindle and treachery of the horrible people." Atkinson concluded, "Mr. Saroyan seems to be taking the world to task for a creative failure within himself and the spectacle is not a pretty one." Howard Barnes, in the *Herald Tribune*, was equally dismissive. A few days later, William Saroyan's *The Son* closed, after five performances.

Bill finished the novel *The Laughing Matter* on August 31, his forty-second birthday. It had been a month's work and came to eighty thousand words. He sent it to McCormick in New York, explaining to Howard Cady that he preferred to deal directly with the editor in chief. He wanted faster service. He wanted to supervise the book's production. When Bill told Cady that he needed the $12,500 advance for the book, Cady pointed out that he had to read the manuscript first. When he did, he assured Bill it needed substantial revision.

There was some good news in the mail. Ken McCormick liked *Tracy's Tiger*. Another $12,500 would soon be coming from Doubleday. The editor was on his way to Reno for a divorce and would be putting in his six weeks of Nevada residence at the Zephyr Cove Inn. Bill decided the time was right for a Reno holiday.

When the two met in the Zephyr Cove lobby, Bill gave the impression

of a confident, debonair gambler. Drinking, telling wonderful stories, pausing at the slot machines long enough to scoop up a pocketful of winnings,
he led McCormick on to a casino at Tahoe City. Once there, Bill's glass-
in-hand swagger caught the management's notice. Presently, his luck
underwent a dramatic change, and before he was through gambling he
had lost $9,000.

Back in San Francisco he tried to turn this course with a bet of $2,000 on
a horse, which lost. He continued betting until Les Cohen stopped his
credit at $22,000. Adding up, Bill found he had lost $33,000 in one week
and brought his debts to a total of $64,000.

Angry and ashamed, he blamed his behavior on the failure of his marriage and the loss of his children. When Carol phoned and put the children
on to speak to him he asked Aram to come and visit him in his new San
Mateo house. Aram said he hoped his mother would let him. When she
agreed to and then proposed that she come out, bringing the children, Bill
refused. He wanted to see only his children, he said, and felt he might never
do so again. In a rage clearly born of self-reproach, he told her to marry
whomever she chose and called her and her mother terrible names.

He soon heard from Krakower, who insisted on monthly $750 payments
and requested that he take out a life insurance policy as well. Aware that his
cousin Suren Saroyan had a reputation as an aggressive lawyer, Bill asked
him to settle the alimony business for him. Suren's advice was that even
$500 a month alimony would be excessive, and Carol's threat of collecting
through the courts was an empty one. He would deal with Krakower. Bill
felt relieved, though he knew he must steer clear of New York now in order
to avoid Carol's clever lawyer and parents.

His concern for Aram and Lucy prompted him to write both their
schools asking about their progress, and on December 16 he was pleased to
hear from the headmistress of Miss Hewitt's that Lucy's attendance record
had been excellent and she was a bright, quick, and cooperative little girl.
Although still in the pre-primary class, she was eager to learn and already
knew her numbers. Courageous, imaginative, and popular with other children, she was a child of whom Bill could be proud. To his question about an
appropriate Christmas present, the headmistress suggested a doll, and in
closing asked if he wished to buy a school bond of either $500 or $1,000,
which he declined to do.

A letter from Allen Stevenson about Aram was equally gratifying and
proposed a bow and arrow or a ukulele as gifts the boy would welcome.
Father's Day would be held at the school on February 22, and he decided to
be on hand, making sure that he did not encounter Carol.

He was promised that the new house in San Mateo would be ready for him sometime in February. Ironically, his first thought for its furnishing was of a family portrait, with Aram, Lucy, Carol, and himself in a group. As he provoked and presided over the dissolution of his family, he yearned to commemorate it in a painting for his hearth. When he learned that a firm in New York, Portraits Inc., could provide one for a thousand dollars, he commissioned it. The painter, Robert Sloan, agreed to render Bill's face from a photograph.

When the galleys of *Rock Wagram* arrived, Bill was further annoyed to find that Cady, with McCormick's approval, had made substantial cuts. He told McCormick that he wanted the novel restored to the one he had submitted, that it should be printed on good paper and look like Hemingway's recent *Across the River and into the Trees*.

In spite of McCormick's objections, Bill repaired the damage he felt had been done to *Rock Wagram*. When the editor saw the extent of this he pointed out that it would require resetting the book, which would be at the author's expense and would postpone its publication until mid-March. He further explained that to "lead" *Rock* as generously as the Hemingway book would add a hundred pages to it.

Keeping the conversation swift and chilly, Bill insisted on having his way. Although Doubleday had advanced him $37,500 on three as-yet-unpublished books and appeared to be his only source of income, he saw no reason for cordiality. He agreed to McCormick's suggestion that they forget their differences and make the book a success, but he was already turning to thoughts of a new publisher.

His $15,000 debt to Harcourt made them an unlikely prospect, but Random House was always appealing, and when Bennett Cerf sent him a book, Bill replied by asking how much he might advance for a new Saroyan novel.

A bemused Cerf confessed surprise at Bill's inquiry, since he understood he had just signed up with Doubleday. In any case, he felt Bill had had his waltz with Random House, and they would be better friends if he were published elsewhere. He could not help recalling the Humpty-Dumpty legend as he wished him good luck. Bill cloaked his disappointment at this brush-off from his former sponsor with indifference.

With the year 1950 drawing to a close, Bill wanted to see Aram and Lucy. He wanted to drive east by way of Mexico and reach New York early in January. With that in mind he had his old Cadillac put in shape and prepared to leave as soon as the new *Rock Wagram* galleys arrived from Doubleday.

It was the holiday season, and San Francisco bustled with parties of old friends, but he found little joy in them. Encountering the *Chronicle* columnist Herb Caen at one party, he was irritated to find that Caen's Doubleday book, *Baghdad by the Bay*, had sold over twenty-five thousand copies, and was maddened further by the columnist's puzzlement over why, with plenty of houses available in Marin, Bill would want to buy one in San Mateo.

There were no galleys from Doubleday by Christmas, but Carol had sent records with the voices of Aram and Lucy wishing him a Merry Christmas. A family dinner at the Papazians was heartening, but when he found that Al Capp's Christmas comic strip bore greetings to Miss Positive Ray, along with the Hirschfelds, Chaplins, Gunthers, and Krakowers, Bill felt wounded.

At home, laying out his eastward course on a map of Mexico, he wept for his loneliness. At 7:15, Cosette woke him from a doze to say that Aram Saroyan was calling from New York. Presently, he heard his son say that he missed his papa very much and wished he would come to visit him. Bill agreed to do so and asked where, to which Aram replied that they had a bed for him.

Lucy came on to say that Aram had given her a pink ballet dress. When Bill learned that his presents had not yet arrived, he assured her they would and that a doll was on its way. She was thrilled. When he asked if there was anyone else who wanted to speak to him, there was a cautious admission that Mommy was also there.

Now Carol spoke, saying she had tried to reach him the day before but there had been no answer, and earlier today there had been a six-hour delay. He found the sound of her voice heartbreaking, so much so that he felt he might burst and could not get beyond the most formal greetings. He was able to thank her for letting the children speak to him on this day. Her good-bye was tender.

In this tide of emotion, he told himself that while he could have Carol back in two seconds he mustn't permit her to make a fool of him again. Returning to the Papazians', he finished a bottle of Walt's scotch and got very drunk.

The next day, although the *Rock Wagram* galleys had still not arrived, he told Ken McCormick to send him an additional set at Stanley Rose's in Hollywood, and with $50 borrowed from Cosette he began his journey. It was essential that he collect a $200 debt from Rose, but on arrival at Rose's apartment in the Chateau des Fleurs he found that Rose was in the veterans' hospital, and broke.

When the *Rock Wagram* galleys arrived, Bill read them at once, liked the new ending, and felt it was a good book. After returning the galleys to Doubleday, Bill looked up his oldest friends, Ross Bagdasarian, the painter Manuel Tolegian, and his wartime comrades Gene Solow and George Stevens.

With Stanley Rose's release from the hospital, his apartment became a carnival scene, horse betting by day and carousing by night. Throughout a farewell lunch at Musso and Frank's, Bill insisted that Rose pay his $200 debt; when a reluctant Stanley agreed to settle with $100, he threw the money at Bill, who threw it back. It was Ross who gathered up the currency and joined Bill for a drive to El Centro and a visit to their prosperous friend Alex Pilibos.

Pilibos welcomed the two cousins and took them to a casino in Imperial, where Bill drank, gambled, and lost, necessitating a telephone appeal to Cosette for the loan of another $500. The next morning, as Ross left for home, Bill learned that his cousin had persuaded their host to loan him $3,000. Driving alone toward Tucson, Bill felt bested. Ross's winning out at the fundraising prompted surprisingly contemptuous thoughts about his cousin and best friend. Rather than the Hollywood big shot he yearned to be, Ross was simply a schemer making a career of borrowing from everybody.

At El Paso, Bill crossed the Rio Grande to Juárez and went on into Mexico. He drove through the countryside and the poverty-stricken towns, noticing how each had its own handsome, whitewashed church. The Indians appeared to thrive amid the filth and hardship. Their faces seemed jolly, especially the children's, and the little girls were very beautiful.

He arrived in Mexico City on January 12, still brooding about failure and Carol. With less than $50, he chose a $6 room at the Hotel Del Prado and reacquainted himself with the city he had visited during his miracle year, 1939. At a café, he picked up a girl, and by evening's end he had blown the rest of his money. However, he managed to establish credit and stayed a week in the Mexican capital, making friends in the Armenian community and going to cockfights and parties.

Once, in his room at the Del Prado, it occurred to him that his new acquaintances in Mexico City saw him as a carefree, happy man, not the hopeless one he was. The role of jaunty, insouciant boulevardier he so readily assumed was another Saroyan contradiction, as was his belief that he could escape his sense of failure in travel. He knew despair was a relentless stalker. Not for a moment, night or day, had he eluded that demon.

He drove north, crossed into Texas at Galveston, and headed eastward. At the St. Charles Hotel in New Orleans he found a choice of *Rock Wagram* jacket designs awaiting him and agreed with Ken McCormick on the best one.

His arrival in Miami was marked by a summons for running a red light, and after he had paid the $10 fine he was left with only $5. Then, cruising Miami Beach, he passed the McFadden-Deauville Hotel at Sixty-seventh Street and remembered that its manager was Warren Freeman, the brother of his friend Don Freeman, illustrator of *The Human Comedy.* Presently

Warren was welcoming him, providing him a room, cashing his $100 check, and promising to get him a date and take him to an undercover gambling joint.

That evening, the accommodating Freeman steered Bill and a blind date into the Riviera Club. There Bill blew the $100 in a crap game, established credit with the management, and proceeded to play roulette and baccarat throughout the night. At six in the morning he found the place was closing and he had lost a staggering $60,000. He left two checks with the cashier, each for $30,000.

When he told the owner, Mr. Aldus Turner, that he had no money, Turner proposed they meet at six that evening at the Sea View Hotel. As this appointment neared, Bill decided he would offer Turner the rights to an unproduced play to clear his debt. Turner awaited him with his wife and was surprisingly cordial, inviting Bill to a fish restaurant for dinner.

From a phone booth, Turner called his syndicate boss, a Mr. Bissell, who was equally understanding of Bill's predicament. He felt it somewhat the fault of the Riviera for extending him too much credit. What could Bill pay? When Bill suggested $10,000, Bissell compromised on $15,000, payable in two installments of $7,500 each, the first due in two weeks, the second two weeks later.

The following morning, a Freddie Fredericks from the Riviera, a man of large size, arrived at Bill's door to collect two postdated checks for $7,500 each.

Although he won a few dollars at Hiahleah race track in the afternoon and picked up a girl at a party after the races, in the evening he was too disheartened for more of Miami's recreation. On January 30, he checked out of the McFadden-Deauville, with Warren Freeman insisting that Bill was his guest. His intention was to drive on to New York or back to California, but instead he paused at a travel agency, bought a round-trip air ticket to Havana, and drove to the airport.

Arriving in Havana with $80, he took a room at the Hotel Nacional, which cashed his check for $250 and directed him to a casino called the Montmartre. There he lost the $80 and moved on to the Tropicana, where he lost the rest and an additional $100 for which he cashed a second check. He fell asleep at dawn, dreaming of Carol and his children.

He repeated this pattern a second day and then flew back to Miami, where he reclaimed his car and started north. He reached the Roosevelt Hotel in Jacksonville on February 2 and called Cosette. She told him that Carol had recently called Ross and talked with both him and Armen about the possibility of a reconciliation.

He asked Cosette to stake him yet another $500 and put it into his account. Next, he called Ross, who confirmed that Carol was eager to come back to him. Then he called Carol and talked to her for an hour. She proposed to join him now, bringing the children. Together they would drive to California.

He did not want to make a mistake, hurt the kids, or her, or himself, anymore. He told her to write him so he could think about it, and she agreed to do so. In the meantime, he added up his debts, the $35,000 he owed the government in 1949 and 1950 taxes, and loans, which brought the total to $100,000, plus the new demands from the Riviera's Freddie Fredericks.

On Saturday morning, Carol telephoned. Aram came on to yodel for him and Lucy to count and sing in French. Carol said she had been unable to write the letter as he had suggested. When she refused to try further, they quarreled. He urged her to leave the children and fly down that night. They could talk and, if it worked out, drive to New York together. Carol declined. She felt it would be wrong. In that case, he said, he would leave for San Francisco in the morning. After he had hung up, however, he reflected that Carol's response had been reasonable enough. Why *should* she fly to Jacksonville?

So Bill set out to drive the thousand miles to New York. He did it in twenty-six hours, pausing only near Wilmington, Delaware, where he was stopped for speeding and fined $20 plus court costs. Arriving, he checked into the Biltmore Hotel and slept until Monday morning, when he went to call on Aram at the Allen Stevenson School. He took Aram to lunch at Hamburg Heaven, and at the boy's request they went on to 17 East Seventy-sixth Street, where Bill was welcomed by Lucy, Carol, and Miss Positive Ray.

Carol told him she wanted to resume their life together. She would be a true wife to him, and they would have more children. But in the unfamiliar apartment, Bill was newly apprehensive. His financial difficulty seemed overwhelming. When Carol dismissed it as mere money, he was not reassured, but when she told him he lacked the patience to live, he thought that was perceptive.

Together they went to "21" for drinks and on to the Golden Horn for dinner. Bill learned that Charles Marcus had left Rosheen for a woman in Florida who was said to be an alcoholic; that Elinor was returning from Switzerland to have her child in this country; and that Gene Reynal, whom Carol had seen at a party, had described the *Torch* book as unpublishable. Although they spoke of their own plans for the future, Bill's old suspicions and grievances quickly reemerged.

The following evening, they dined at the apartment with the children and enjoyed putting them to bed together. Later, Carol complained of the difficulty Suren Saroyan was making for Arnold Krakower in the settlement. Their conversation ended in an ugly argument, but Carol called him at his hotel to make amends, and he offered her all rights to *The Girls,* one of a dozen plays he had written during a productive heat in October. It portrayed a young woman who is an heiress and her friend, who pretends to be one. He told her it had a good role for her as well as the possibility of income.

During the week they had a constructive talk with Arnold Krakower, and Bill confessed his recent gambling disaster to Carol and Rosheen. In spite of Bill's financial plight, Carol suggested he borrow money and take her to Lisbon or Ireland, places that he had found so appealing.

Bill now felt the need of Ross's counsel, and he no sooner asked for it than Ross flew from California to be with him. Bill and Ross took Carol and Rosheen to dinner, and they all felt confident that a reconciliation was working itself out. On the night of February 14, Bill and Carol were together again, so satisfactorily that Carol wanted to join Bill and Ross on the drive west. Bill explained that before she could come to him in California, he needed to settle his debts, buy his house, and make a substantial film deal. He expected to do all three soon, and then a new life could begin.

His other hopes for New York were largely disappointed. Broadway producers shunned the new plays, and Ken McCormick had no encouraging reports about *Rock Wagram.*

When he called at the Portraits Inc. studio to see Sloan's painting of his family, Bill disliked it and refused to accept it. His solution to the Riviera debt was to wire Freddie Fredericks, care of the Mercantile Bank in Miami, that he had been unable to get a loan elsewhere and to request it from them. The bank responded that Mr. Fredericks was unknown there.

Pincus Berner's advice was to forget it, and Bill soon persuaded himself that he was not in serious trouble. The game had been a crooked one, and the government was turning up the heat on casinos. Why else would they settle a $60,000 debt for a quarter of that sum?

Bill and Ross set out for California in the Cadillac. Driving night and day, they arrived in Los Angeles on February 25. Bill moved into the Sunset Tower, determined that this time he would make some kind of killing in motion pictures. He wrote Carol that he had thought of nothing but her during the trip, that he was hopeful about his love for her and their future together. He was doing everything possible now to earn money for it. He asked for her love and trust and help in finding their way.

She replied affectionately, hoping his plan to write an original screenplay would be successful. She admitted that just as he often sensed hysteria in her, she sensed violence in him, but she felt sure they could solve their problems with time, friendship, and generosity.

When a first copy of *Rock Wagram* arrived, he liked how it looked, but he was annoyed by a Doubleday ad that described the novel's hero as "a daring young man who never quite catches up with the facts of life." This had touched Bill's quick as well as the novel's weakness. Its beleaguered hero, Rock, held the author's grievance toward a hostile world.

He asked McCormick if the ad copy meant the hero or the author was a simpleton, and assured him the book was an important, possibly great, novel. He admitted that he was sometimes a difficult author and didn't help matters by wanting to get rich quick, but he felt no need to apologize for his editorial meddling. Later, while a little drunk, he read parts of *Rock Wagram* and thought it might be a mess.

In spite of his every effort, his financial prospects remained discouraging. The Miami Riviera demanded payment in four installments of $3,750, borrowed from his own bank. Cosette reported that the GI loan that he had been counting on for the San Mateo house had been turned down. His debts amounted to $105,000.

In these bleak circumstances, he wrote Carol that he loved her insanely but wanted an accounting of all her past sexual encounters. She should speak fearlessly and pour everything out. He wanted to be sure that she was earnest, that she would be his, and their children's, alone, that she would renounce her past and all of its people. He was requesting Carol's submission to his dominant role in a new marriage.

In the following week, he lunched with Dore Schary and Arthur Freed, and talked to Stanley Kramer about *Highlands* and *Don't Go Away Mad,* but nowhere did he find encouragement. Thus, when Carol called in response to his letter, he had to put her off again, and they had an angry exchange.

He was left with a feeling of such utter aloneness that on the following day he telephoned Carol and, sweeping all conditions aside, asked her to come out at once. She agreed to leave the children in Ray's care and come to California within a few days. Joyous at the prospect of a new life, Bill wired Carol $500.

She arrived on a Wednesday night, and their reunion was as happy and full of promise as he had hoped. Bill had taken grander quarters at the Beverly Carlton, and here they discussed and agreed on a plan for the future. They would remarry, bring the children out, and, for the present, stay in Beverly Hills.

They soon found an available furnished house at 708 North Rodeo Drive. It had pleasant grounds and a tennis court and could be had on a six-month lease for $450 a month. They celebrated their reunion that night and again the next day at the Chaplins. Congratulations arrived from Irwin Shaw, Gottfried Reinhardt, and Irving Lazar. Carol had lunch with Martha Stevenson Goetz and with Oona Chaplin, and there was a party at John and

Joyce Fante's, after which Bill found himself annoyed with Carol but able to quell an outburst.

On Sunday they called New York to tell Aram, Lucy, and Miss Positive Ray that they were to pack up and join them in California. With the family all but reunited, Carol and Bill moved into the new house on March 14, stocked its kitchen, and launched themselves into the fast stream of Hollywood social life.

XIII

SECOND HONEYMOON

1951–1952

With Ross Bagdasarian's help, Bill painted fresh lines on the tennis court, bought sneakers and rackets, and organized daily games. All felt full of promise in the new homestead on North Rodeo Drive, except for the silence that shrouded *Rock Wagram*'s publication day, March 15.

The New York reviews came over the weekend in a dark, wounding volley. In Saturday's *Tribune,* John Hutchens decided that despite the main character's resemblance to the author, Rock Wagram was a ponderous figure, by turn groaning with self-pity and swaggering with self-satisfaction. Far from growing here, as his publisher maintained, Saroyan was simply more somber and portentous.

In Saturday's *Times,* Charles Poore saw this novel as a sequel to the previous *Wesley Jackson,* a book he recalled as a "shrill and cranky *Farewell to Arms.*" The fault of both was their main characters' tendency to forgive all mankind its trespasses except for those committed against himself. The author had become "a middle-aged man on a sighing trapeze."

In Sunday's *Times Book Review,* Nelson Algren made fun of *Rock Wagram*'s story, which pivoted on the hero's marrying "the loose and beauteous 17-year-old in trembling hope she will learn Armenian." He summed up, "Saroyan is a man who says a great deal that washes nothing but his own laundry."

In the *Saturday Review,* John Brooks found the characters superficial, the italicized philosophical interludes tedious, and the writing sloppy. On absorbing the bad news, Bill accepted it with a now habitual fatalism, admitting to depression and yet not giving in to it.

The Sunday *Tribune* review, which came a week later, was the kind he had hoped for. Gene Baro saw *Rock Wagram* as Saroyan's maturest work of fiction. Abandoning his earlier whimsy and naïveté, Saroyan had written a serious book well worth a careful reading. But the review had come too late and alone to make a difference.

Saroyan had given *Rock Wagram* two main themes, that of his hero's disastrous marriage and that of his failing career. For the first theme he had used his own 1942 experience of returning to California for induction to show Rock's misgivings about marrying the amorous seventeen-year-old glamor girl from New York, Ann Ford.

Rock's loyal cousin argues persuasively for the union, as does his wise old grandmother, Lula. On reminding Rock of his obligation to make a family, she shares memories of his departed father and chides Rock for his lack of manly moustache and his qualms about turning his blond girlfriend into a dutiful Armenian wife.

Saroyan's perception of his own collapsing career as a writer is reflected in Rock's as an actor. Rock has been discovered (while tending bar) and made into a star by the opportunistic Hollywood mogul Paul Key. While Key dies at the end of part two, it is his successors, a son and a nephew, who, in part three, confirm Rock's talent, which has survived both the war and the disastrous mistake of his marriage to Ann Ford.

Although Ann never appears in the novel, she must bear the blame for being a liar, a spendthrift, and a shrew who in a momentary denial of love for him sets him free of obligation to her and their children and so causes the family's ruin.

The message of *Rock Wagram* was not a favorable portent for the launching of his and Carol's second marriage. Moreover, the verdict—that the book was a critical and popular failure—was undeniable. Bill had believed that making fiction of his agonizing postwar experience would prove his skill as a novelist. But he had found neither a sympathetic central character nor a persuasive conflict and story. What had shone through was simply grievance. If self-obsession had marred *Wesley Jackson,* it had ruined *Rock Wagram.*

Each of these novels had carried Bill's grandest hopes and their foundering was devastating. He was left on hard ground, the other end of his emotional seesaw. He was nothing, nobody. At the same time he could see that other self, the survivor at the opposite end. That Saroyan was only in eclipse, in need of more time, still the old wizard.

The coming of Aram and Lucy was a compensating joy. They arrived at midnight on March 20 in fine health and exuberant spirits, delighting in the goldfish with which Bill had stocked the tiled pool, the house itself, and the prospects for their new life in California. The next morning, Bill walked both children to the nearby Hawthorne public school, where they enjoyed

Second wedding, 1951. Ross and Armen Bagdasarian, Bill, Archbishop Calfayan,
Carol, and Araks and Manuel Tolegian

the playground. Bill explained to Aram that he would soon enter second
grade there.

Bill's new responsibilities and creative self-doubt made him urgently willing to work for hire, and in late March he found a taker. Charles K. Feldman, the talent agent and friend of the influential Twentieth Century–Fox
head Darryl Zanuck, had a job for him. It was to rewrite the screenplay of
John Steinbeck's 1947 novel *The Wayward Bus.*

Bill would receive $1,250 a week for four weeks, with a bonus of $750 if
Feldman was pleased with the results—a total of $8,000. The influential
Feldman felt he could also sell some Saroyan material for a film. In spite of
a reluctance to work on Steinbeck material, Bill agreed to do so, rented an
office at 1135 South Beverly Drive in Beverly Hills, and started in.

He and Carol drove to Santa Monica to take out a marriage license, and
on Easter Sunday, March 25, 1951, they were married for the second time.
The ceremony took place at St. James Armenian Church with Archbishop
Mompreh Calfayan presiding. Manuel Tolegian was Bill's best man. His
wife, Araks, with Ross and Armen Bagdasarian, were witnesses.

The ring was that of their first marriage, a gold band inscribed on the outside with Saroyan in Armenian, in English within, but Bill promised a much grander one soon.

Since they were tired and hungover from a party the Chaplins had given them the previous night, the wedding celebration was modest, but they phoned the good news to Carol's mother in New York and to Bill's family in San Francisco. Although the wedding day ended in a quarrel, Bill was gratified at this uniting of his family. He estimated that its operating expenses would come to $1,250 a month.

It was a week of fresh hopes. The day after the wedding, Bill took Aram to the Hawthorne school and went on to his office to begin work on the new script for *The Wayward Bus*. Carol did some typing for Bill, and he took her shopping for a ring. At Tobias's, she chose a $1,350 diamond one. There were true Hollywood parties every night. At the Feldmans they sat down to dinner with Walter Wanger and Joan Bennett, Norman Krasna and Ginger Rogers, Jerry and Ann Wald. They went nightclubbing with the Chaplins, the Shaws, and the Goetzes. But mornings were marked by hangovers. By Saturday, Bill and Carol had had a major quarrel. After putting in seven hours of work at his office, Bill returned home, and, although Carol made his supper, he refused to speak to her. He went alone to see Maugham's *Trio*.

After ten days of work on *The Wayward Bus,* he was mired in it, racked by guilt about not earning the $2,000 Feldman had paid him and filled with anxiety that he would not receive the additional money promised. He was relieved to have another $3,000 on April 10, followed by an idea he thought would get the job done. He told Feldman he was sure he would complete it in another week.

The going was slow and painful, but he plugged on. When he delivered scenes to Feldman, the agent made suggestions and asked for some rewrites but made no sign of approval for the work as a whole.

In late April, after five weeks of work, Bill handed Feldman a "final" script. While awaiting Feldman's judgment, he returned gratefully to his own work. This was at Doubleday's urging, a minor revision of *Tracy's Tiger* and then a major one of *The Laughing Matter.*

He told himself that *Rock Wagram*'s failure did not bother him. Moreover, he foresaw that *Tracy's Tiger* and *The Laughing Matter* would fail too, and that he could live with it.

For lack of alternatives, he could only thicken the hide that deflected all criticism and enabled his survival in a hostile world. It cost him sensitivity and polarized him, leaving a confident, jovial, outer self to face the day and an anguished, uncertain, inner one to endure the night. Saroyan the writer wandered between the two.

Now Feldman called to reveal his dissatisfaction with Bill's rewrite of the *Wayward Bus* script and summon him to a conference about it. As a result of their talk, Bill wrote and delivered several new scenes promptly. To his surprise, Feldman was delighted with them and seemed excited about the entire project. Presenting Bill with another $3,000, he asked for further scenes and assured Bill he would direct the film.

Throughout May, Bill worked with Feldman, polishing the *Bus* script and enjoying an income to offset his new expenses. Carol's ring, the $1,500 in debt she had brought from New York, and a visit by Positive Ray to Father Divine's Philadelphia rally brought his expenses to $5,000 for the month.

Of the five Saroyan plays that Bill gave him, Feldman liked *Violin Messiah* and felt he could sell it. But for the big money Bill needed, Feldman proposed he write a screenplay for his client, Greta Garbo. Bill would give it a try.

Meanwhile, Bill's new lease on marriage was becoming much like the old one. There was pleasure in taking the kids to the movies and picnicking with them at the beach, but Carol's behavior was a constant irritation. She went shopping with Oona, nagged him for money, picked silly fights, insisted on having things her way, failed to look after the children, and wore a mask of white skin cream throughout the day in order to appear more gorgeous at night.

For their own parties, Bill grumbled about Carol's preparations and having to spend so much money on liquor and food. A big party would include the Chaplins, the Feldmans, the Reinhardts, the Gunthers, the Shaws, the Goetzes, the Stevenses, the Solows, and even Greta Garbo. They lasted until three or four in the morning, and Bill enjoyed them. But the hangovers and arguing continued. Once, during a morning "scene," Carol announced she wanted a divorce.

Bill's central purpose, a productive writing program, was in trouble. He had called the Garbo screenplay *Gabriela* and struggled to provide something to Feldman, but progress was painful. When he showed Feldman a section of the *Gabriela* script, he was not surprised by the lack of approval. His mood was black, and he blamed it on Carol.

Then, on June 8, there was an unexpected change in his fortunes. Ross burst into Bill's office with the news that the song they had written in 1939, now called "Come On-A My House," was being recorded in New York by four major companies. Mitch Miller at Columbia was boosting it, and there were versions by Kay Armen and Rosemary Clooney. They were going to be rich.

When they heard the Kay Armen record they were pleased, but when they heard Rosemary Clooney's they recognized a stunning performance. Within a few weeks the industry charts fulfilled their glossiest expectations. By mid-June, it was the national best-seller, and they reckoned it would bring them each at least $10,000.

They set out immediately to write three more, drawing on Armenian folk songs. "Zeyback" became "Come and Dance with Me, Love." "Saroi Yerk" became "Heartless Girl," and "Acilan Guler" became "All I Want Is All There Is, and Then Some." As in "House," Bill composed the lyrics while Ross attended to the music. In drawing contracts with several record companies for these new songs, Bill took the advice of his friend Manuel Tolegian and hired a lawyer named Huston Carlyle to represent him. He was Armenian, born Hrant Cartozian.

Ross's good luck was compounded by Feldman, who arranged for Elia Kazan to cast him in his film *Viva Zapata*. At last Ross seemed to be on his way out of debt, while Bill sank ever deeper in it.

Carol's ambition for a film career was encouraged by the Chaplins and her other friends and accounted for what Bill saw as her all-day preparations for a party and, once there, her delight in self-display. He was annoyed by the attention men paid her, by her sleeping late into the morning, and by the consequent neglect of her wifely duties.

Customarily now, Bill ate little or nothing at the parties but drank steadily, so the evenings ended in a quarrel and morning brought the hangover and headache that made writing difficult or impossible. In mid-August, Bill decided he could not continue this way of life. He told Carol that her ambition and the social life it required were bankrupting him as a writer and a man. Henceforth, all his energy would go into his writing and the immediate needs of their family. There were to be no more parties here or anywhere else. He was refusing future invitations and canceling those already accepted. He expected her to share in this change of behavior.

Carol felt this would be an encroachment on her own career. She continued to accept invitations and went alone to parties. Their quarrels were more frequent and heated enough for Carol to threaten Bill with a ruinous divorce.

He learned that Carol had indeed consulted Jerry Giesler, a lawyer well known for his successful criminal cases, about a divorce. When Rosheen Marcus, ever the peacemaker, called to urge Bill toward a compromise, reminding him of the high cost of lawyers, Bill replied that he could not put up with Carol's behavior no matter what the cost of lawyers.

Bill declined an invitation to Rosheen's dinner party and that evening watched Carol set out for it alone. At eleven, Oona Chaplin called him from the party, urging him to come and make up with Carol, for Aram's sake if no one else's. No, he couldn't, Bill told her. Carol had threatened him by going to a lawyer, and a party was no place to surrender.

Invariably he came home at seven to find Carol already out. Although he saw the children for a few minutes, he never asked her whereabouts. He would heat some vegetables for his supper. When he went to bed at ten, Carol was still out. He would rise at five or six in the morning, go to his office, and work there all day. He felt both children loved and needed Carol and Positive Ray too, but there was nothing more he could do for them. This time, he said, Carol would have to decide how much she needed for the children's care before a court.

On October 7, Bill sought an annulment of his marriage and drew up a letter of explanation, which he sent to Jerry Giesler, with copies to both Rosheen and Charles Marcus. He hoped they could all be of help to Carol, Aram, and Lucy. In the letter he maintained that Carol was an incorrigible, helplessly self-destructive liar who was unable to perform as a wife and a mother or to deal with reality. Her need for beauty parlors and expensive clothing was compulsive. Her response to criticism for neglecting the children was hysterical cursing, the hurling of objects, and ordering him from the house. He believed that the children's nurse was actually Carol's.

He also revealed his suspicion that in 1947 Carol had aborted their third child and made herself sterile. He proposed to Giesler that Carol now undergo a physical examination to determine her ability to bear further children. Giesler replied that such an examination would be improper, that neither he nor his client would agree to it without a court order, and that, in view of his accusations, Carol was suing him for divorce.

At an early hour of November 1, while Bill was still asleep, Carol borrowed the key to his office on Beverly Drive and paid it a visit. There she gathered up a file of his current business records and $680 in cash. On delivering these to her attorney, she returned home to admit what she had done and to say these articles would be returned to him when he agreed on certain restraints in forthcoming legal proceedings.

His response was a legal one, an answer and cross-complaint prepared by his lawyer, Suren Saroyan. In this, he sought annulment of the marriage and custody of the children. He charged that Carol had failed as wife and mother, and was a chronic liar who lived only for her own pleasure, as well as a parasite and courtesan who had exploited both Al Capp and himself while abandoning Aram and Lucy to the care of a Father Divine disciple, Positive Ray. He also charged that she had surgically made herself sterile.

To Bill's surprise and annoyance, the lawyer now representing Carol was the same Huston Carlyle, Manuel Tolegian's friend, who had represented him for the recording contracts.

A day or so after delivery of his cross-complaint, Bill returned to the house on North Rodeo to find Carol, the children, and Miss Ray gone, having left no clue to their whereabouts. When he called the Hawthorne school, he found that Carol had withdrawn both children without explanation and left no indication of where they could be found.

Carol soon wrote to say that the children were enrolled at Webster School in Malibu. They were well and happy and sent their love. He could visit them whenever he chose. She explained that she had left him because she could no longer expose Aram and Lucy to his violent, irrational behavior. As for herself, she had been horrified by the vicious and false accusations in the cross-complaint. Thinking of Aram and Lucy, the charges were as tragic as they were ridiculous. She was ashamed for him.

Carol had found a $150-a-month apartment on the Malibu Highway where she could stay until early next year, while Bill moved to a room at the Beverly Carlton. At this remove, their hostility cooled, and by mid-December their lawyers had worked out a memorandum of agreement. Bill agreed to pay Carol $450 a month out of a trust fund made up of one half of his current and future royalties, notably those from "Come On-A My House."

With the divorce now ready to be filed, Bill became a regular visitor in Malibu and in early January 1952 began searching the neighborhood for a house to buy for Carol and the children. He was undaunted by knowing that his bank balance stood at $50 and his financial clouds had never been thicker. He owed $36,000 in gambling debts, $45,000 to friends and relatives, and another $40,000 in back taxes. Warnings by the IRS were followed by a warrant attaching his property.

When the deputy collector from Santa Monica came by to ask some questions, Bill found him an agreeable man, but his visit resulted in a front-page story in the *San Francisco Examiner* reporting the $10,216 federal lien against the playwright William Saroyan for 1950 taxes. The Saroyans' landlord at North Rodeo maintained they had left the house in a filthy and uninhabitable condition, and he was bringing suit for damages of $3,000. Bill's Beverly Drive office landlord demanded unpaid rent of $1,100, and the *Los Angeles Times* gave a full account of the proceedings.

Help from his publishers was no longer at hand. After a long silence from Doubleday about *The Laughing Matter,* Ken McCormick finally wrote that he wanted to make substantial cuts in the manuscript. Bill gave provisional consent. His debt to Harcourt stood at $12,500 and chilled his welcome there.

During his 1951 tenancy at 708 North Rodeo, Bill had written a reflective piece about life as a telegraph messenger in Fresno. It recalled how fast and

Aram shares his father's pride in bicycle ownership.

gracefully he had ridden his broken-down bike, how this style reflected his eagerness for life and became that of his writing. Recently, his eight-year-old son, Aram, had demanded a bike seemingly too big for him, and he had granted his wish reluctantly, but then had enjoyed the fatherly pleasure of their bicycling together.

These two cycling episodes provided the frame for a series of recollections drawn from the years between them. It became a book-length memoir that included his parents' journeys from Bitlis, his misery at the orphanage, dislike of school and teachers, joy in being a newsboy, love of Armenian food, loneliness in New York, and decision to become a writer.

While the book was made of incidentals, the raw material and by-products of his fiction, this exploring of his own formative experience delivered him from the bitterness of present failure to the wishful, childhood world of Aram Garoghlanian, his fictional boyhood self. It was to prove a rich mine and bring about a Saroyan renaissance. He called this collection *The Bicycle Rider in Beverly Hills* and sent it to Scribner's. To his surprise, the publisher accepted it at once, and he agreed without bargaining to an offer of $5,000. He soon heard from Harry Brague, his editor there, that the book would appear in the fall of 1952.

His 1942 Cadillac, which had survived 110,000 miles of hard driving and many repaintings, was ready for retirement. Bill wrote the Ford Motor Company proposing they swap him a new station wagon for six travel pieces for the *Ford Times*. Ford accepted the offer and gave him a 1952 Ranch Wagon.

As the newspapers reported on the progress of the Saroyan divorce, Carol's two lawyers proved Rosheen's prediction true. Jerry Giesler attached Bill's only current income, $6,000 in "Come On-A My House" royalties from Duchess Records. Huston Carlyle not only exacted a $450 monthly payment for Carol in the separation agreement but sued for and collected his own legal fee, of $1,941.

Bill's fury settled on Carlyle, who, as an Armenian and the recommendation of his friend Manuel Tolegian, seemed especially perfidious. Manuel, a painter and musician, had been Bill's devoted drinking and gambling companion for fifteen years and his choice for best man at his recent wedding. Bill not only owned and prized a Tolegian painting, *The Picnickers,* but together they had recorded a dialogue about art that Manuel hoped to use as introduction to his book on painting.

When Bill asked Manuel to get Carlyle to "lay off," the painter refused, saying he was "on Carol's side." Stunned by this breach of loyalty, Bill denied him the use of their dialogue and consigned him to the Saroyan oubliette, where two other betrayers already languished. The first of these was his uncle, Zaven Minasian, because of the 1935 suit over "Little Caruso." The second, surprisingly, was his cousin Ross Bagdasarian. Once his loyal apprentice, Ross was now scoring in the music business and as an actor. Ross had followed his small role in *Viva Zapata* with that of a sailor in *Destination Gobi.* What Bill could neither forgive nor forget was that a year and a half before, during their visit to the generous Alex Pilibos, Ross had gotten his big touch in first. These three men, Bill assured himself, were crooks and betrayers and would never again enjoy his goodwill.

Legal wrangling over their divorce had brought forth terrible resentments between Bill and Carol. His countersuit accusations, his determination to show Carol up as very different from the innocent victim she played, had led to her threat to expose the Section 8 taint of his army discharge. But as they settled into separate lives, this rancor seemed to vanish.

Indeed, they again resolved to be friends, and he visited her and the children most evenings. Braving a flood on the Malibu Highway, Bill appeared for Lucy's sixth-birthday party. While Carol pursued her acting career, now finding small movie and TV roles, Bill shared in the babysitting.

In February, when she had to leave Malibu, Carol found another reasonable apartment, at 9701 Olympic Boulevard in Beverly Hills, and Bill enjoyed helping her and the children with their move.

Then, on March 6, 1952, in Santa Monica court, Martha Stephenson, now Mrs. Hayes Goetz, stood beside Carol and supported her complaints, while John Fante stood as witness to Bill's year of California residency. Carol's divorce and request for separate maintenance of the children were granted.

During the spring of 1952, Bill decided he lacked the serenity in which to work and needed a business manager who would keep his creditors at bay. He encountered a man named Bill Stern, who seemed interested in the job. Bill liked Stern's air of competence, his intelligent questions about the literary life, and his willingness to deal with all its exigencies. Bill hired him and found him just the advocate he wanted. Stern stood up smartly to threats from Carol's Huston Carlyle and the angry Beverly Hills landlord.

Through the William Morris Agency, Stern even discovered the big deal that had eluded Bill for so long. It was a television series to be called *The William Saroyan Playhouse,* for which Bill would provide thirteen half-hour scripts. There would be a corporation, of which Bill would own 60 percent. The agency men, Rodney Amateau, Arthur Desser, and John Beck, would not only promote and produce the shows but pay Bill a substantial salary. Desser agreed to settle Bill's debts, too, make an arrangement with the tax people, and get access to the "Come On-A My House" money that Jerry Giesler had sequestered. This all had the look of a main chance, and Bill signed the corporation agreement. He presented *The Bad Men* as the first of the plays and set out to write a dozen sequels.

Throughout the late spring of 1952, he continued to write scripts for *The Saroyan Playhouse* and by mid-June had completed ten. The corporation members seemed pleased and spoke of interest from NBC. Bill discouraged Rodney Amateau from directing the episodes, for he planned to handle that himself. Desser, who was looking after his debts and taxes, gave him an advance of $1,000 and the promise of a regular salary. Bill felt his luck had turned at last.

But by late June, Bill found himself stuck in the eleventh play and empty of will to go on with the series. Depressed and out of sorts, he focused his irritation on Bill Stern, who had arranged for further loans from the corporation but, as security for them, surrendered the title to Bill's car. In exchange for a $1,500 loan from his uncle Mihran, Bill transferred the car's ownership to him. Deciding that Stern was too "in" with the agency men, Bill demanded an accounting of funds. When Stern provided this, Bill saw that his own debt to the corporation was approaching $10,000 and so far no investor had been found.

He foresaw that, if his plays were produced, he would soon be supporting a retinue of managers. He told Stern that he could handle all these corporate functions himself and would prefer it. He would do no more plays for the corporation and wanted to dissolve it. Dismayed, Stern went off to discuss this with Desser, who, understandably, had no interest in releasing Bill from their contract.

Now Bill found Stern more elusive than ever, and Desser determined to produce the Saroyan plays. Bill took his grievance to Abe Lastfogel, head of the parent organization, the William Morris Agency. Lastfogel arranged to dissolve the corporation if Bill would repay the $5,100 in loans made to him. Thus it was agreed, leaving Bill with a substantial new debt and angry at the outcome.

As Bill saw to the demise of the corporation, settling with it in a payment of $1,100, he learned that Bill Stern's failings and presumed crookedness might be attributed to illness—Stern had suffered a stroke and undergone brain surgery. Another grand plan for a Saroyan Theatre appeared to have gone bust.

Carol's social life was busier than ever. While she was off at cocktail or dinner parties, Bill turned up to cook Armenian rice and burgers for the kids and to demonstrate kite flying in the park. Frequently they gathered their family for meals together or a day at Malibu.

Bill was still powerfully attracted to Carol and occasionally insisted on his conjugal rights. When they were seen together enjoying themselves, gossip held the Saroyans would marry again, and this notion headed a Dorothy Kilgallen column. Bill felt this was Carol's and Rosheen's strategy, neither of whom had expected him to go ahead with the divorce. Carol seemed pleased by the talk.

He knew, because she told him so, that Carol was seeing many men now: the librettist and songwriter Adolph Green; the MGM executive Benny

Bill on his Malibu deck

Thau; Mel Ferrer, who wanted her to join his La Jolla company; Gerry Mayer, Louis B.'s nephew; and, always, Marlon Brando. He told himself he was no longer jealous, concerned only for her welfare and that of the children. They would not live together again.

Bill felt she lacked real talent as an actress and was simply pursuing her fantasies. He held the Chaplins responsible for encouraging her in this foolishness. Charlie surely knew better.

There was some irony in the arrival of a revised Saroyan family portrait. Sloan, the artist, had redone it in watercolors. The result was an improvement, but hardly enough for Bill to welcome the accompanying bill of $1,400.

Malibu Beach had become the locus of Bill's life. All four Saroyans were drawn to it for weekend picnics. Bill walked it with his friend John Fante, discussing their favorite subjects—gambling and writing. It was on one of these walks in early February that he saw a beach cottage for sale. The cottage was on pilings, and at high tide the surf crashed up through them and under its floor. Bill was reminded of both a treehouse and a beached ship, and he was determined to have it.

The price was $15,900, and the cash required $4,000. He made his offer, of a rental with option to buy, and on the last day of February it was accepted. He was overjoyed. He took Aram to see it first and to help him move in some belongings. On Sunday he took Carol to dinner at Jack's fish restaurant at the beach and then to visit the house, building a first driftwood fire in its fireplace.

Mia Agee, who had been Carol's Malibu neighbor, called at the bungalow with messages from her, and Aram and Lucy often sought out the two Agee girls, Didi and Andrea, but Bill kept his distance from the shy and serious James Agee. Bill admired his screenplay for *The African Queen,* but the man was Chaplin's friend and an influential book reviewer for *Time* who had ridiculed *The Human Comedy,* so no writerly camaraderie grew between them.

If Bill ever needed a friend, it was now, and he certainly had one in John Fante. He had known Fante as a fellow writer since his earliest Hollywood ventures and shared with him a boisterous sense of humor and a taste for whiskey and cards. John lived with his wife, Joyce, and his four children, Nick, Dan, Victoria, and James, in a large house on Point Dume which Bill could see from his front window. He thought Joyce was a happy woman and their marriage the same. Sometimes with his boys, sometimes alone, John came by to walk the beach with Bill, to fish or clam or collect driftwood for the cottage fireplace.

They talked about the writing of good movies, the money they would make from them, and the novels they would write when they were rich. With John, Bill could speak of how writing was not just a way of life for him, but a way of staying alive. He presumed that every writer was harassed, as he was, by the suspicion that whatever he was at work on was a project without importance or meaning. It led him to agree with whoever had said that writing was easy but it was a torture getting ready to do it. He also believed that the only thing a writer can do is try, that success came only from a willingness to edge, however slightly, toward a truth.

They shared a contempt for most of their fellow screenwriters, whom they doubted would ever free themselves from captivity in Hollywood. When Fante spoke of his admiration for the Norwegian novelist Knut

Hamsun and the debt he owed him, Bill envied him, and admitted to being a poor reader, lacking the patience to read a book to its end.

Fante's new novel, *Full of Life,* would be published in April, and he was apprehensive about its reception. Bill read it and thought it was a fine book. He told Fante it was an unusual novel with a new kind of hero. When Bill spoke of *Rock Wagram* and its poor treatment at the hands of New York reviewers, John told him that while some of the stuff in italics was very funny, *Rock Wagram* was a bad book. Bill protested that it was a work of genius, that nobody else in five centuries could have achieved it, while Johnny (as Bill called him) cackled with derision and delight.

Whatever the pain of the divorce, there was one major consolation during this period: Bill was getting to know his children. Aram was first to spend the night with his father at the beach house, and he agreed that it was the best place they had ever lived. Together they fished in the surf and went clamming near the Malibu Pier. When Lucy was allowed to come along, she took to the fishing and the beach walks with all the enthusiasm of her brother.

The nearest appropriate school was a Catholic one, and Aram and Lucy seemed to like it at first, but Aram did not like it nearly as well as Webster, where he had begun the year. He found it slow and dull and resented the sisters' expectations that he would pick up after himself.

Poignant recollections of his own days at Emerson made Bill feel that Aram's dislike of school was perfectly natural, that boys want to learn things in their own way. A Father O'Connor joked with Aram, calling him Caesar, but Aram and his friend Brennan had made trouble for one of the teachers, Sister Lena. She had reprimanded him for his manners toward a sister and kept him after school for a sentence of meditation. When Aram described how Sister Lena had shaken him and pulled him up in his seat by the hair, he laughed, but Bill knew Aram had been amazed and hurt, because *he* himself had been in similar situations, years before.

Also, the boy now spoke of concern about his soul, and about Holy Communion, in which, as a non-Catholic, he did not participate. While recuperating from the measles in May, Aram asked his father if it would be better to kill someone or commit suicide. Bill replied that he would prefer killing and added that in school Aram was being taught what Catholics believe. As Protestants, the Saroyans believed something better. Aram corrected him, saying that it was not necessarily better, just different, and his father agreed.

As for Lucy, Bill was finding her a strangely incandescent, wholly delightful child. She often lay awake at night, and she was a jumper. She jumped up and down as though unable to contain her urgent spirit. She did it to protest what she found disagreeable, and to approve happy events or prospects. As a developing storyteller, she jumped for punctuation.

She would plead with Bill to let her see the caged glass bird he had brought her from Barcelona. He would let her hold it but then put it away for fear she would break it. He was sure she was over her apprehension that he did not love her. She knew now that he did. Aram was her behavioral opposite. Ever preoccupied, he moved along reflectively even when pursuing his own fancies, pausing to watch things and think about them.

Although the kids had good times together, they often fought. Once, playing on the kitchen floor, Aram snapped his sister's face with a rubber band. Lucy responded by kicking Aram in the mouth and rejoicing in his tears. As she crowed over this accomplishment, Aram flung himself at her, and Bill had to pry them apart.

When he had heard them out and requested apologies in turn, Aram complied grudgingly, and Lucy indifferently, sipping at her lemonade. Bill understood that Lucy found pleasure in tormenting Aram and recalled there was an Armenian word, *jengch,* for this indulgence. He decided the essential conflict lay in Aram's wish that Lucy be a boy, while Lucy wanted Aram to be a girl.

Although Bill had several talks with Aram about his work and behavior at school, and Aram not only promised to do better but anticipated earning honors, the school year ended with Aram's failing his courses. He could not proceed into the fourth grade. Carol consulted with the sisters and agreed to tutor him in reading over the summer, and Bill spent a painful weekend with Aram making clear his disappointment about the boy's reluctance to study.

Aram was obviously bored with school, and Bill wondered if this wasn't simply his being spoiled by his mother. When he mentioned it to his doctor, the man explained Aram's school failure as the boy's response to rejection, to Bill's having left him, his mother, and his sister. Bill recognized some truth in this diagnosis and was troubled by it.

To Bill's surprise and delight, the work of the defunct Saroyan Theatre Corporation now bore fruit. The interest it had started at NBC was real. On August 20 he received a telegram from Robert Saudek, at the Ford Foundation in New York. Saudek wanted to produce the Saroyan series on the foundation's Omnibus program.

When Ford offered $4,000 each for six of the plays, Bill asked for $6,000 each, a total of $36,000. Within three days Ford had agreed to his terms. Omnibus would present the plays on Sunday evenings from November through May. Bill would appear on the broadcasts and receive a payment of $15,000 on signing and the remaining $21,000 in monthly installments of $1,000.

Thus, on August 31, he celebrated his forty-fourth birthday at the Malibu Beach house in a miraculously happy frame of mind. Aram, Lucy, Carol, her sister Elinor, Elinor's husband, Henri de la Bouillerie, and their son Hubert, were all on hand to share in another bolt of good fortune for Bill, just when there seemed no hope at all.

Within a few weeks, Scribner's would publish *A Bicycle Rider in Beverly Hills,* and some of the seventy-five hundred copies of its first edition were already in stores. Doubleday would bring out *The Laughing Matter* early the following year. Carol had gotten Aram into fourth grade at the Beverly Hills public school on trial. Suren Saroyan was straightening out Bill's tax problems, and a dentist was putting his teeth in shape. Bill was to have his money and his *Saroyan Playhouse.* He was ready to go to work on the six pieces for the *Ford Times* and as many TV plays as possible.

On September 4, he and Carol found an unfinished house in nearby Pacific Palisades which they liked and felt was suitable for her and the children. It was at 1008 Maroney Lane, in a development called Southdown Estates. It was priced at $23,750 and required a $5,000 down payment. With the Ford Foundation's advance of $15,000 and royalties of $2,750 coming from Duchess Records, he felt flush enough to buy the house for Carol.

XIV

THE REVIVAL

1953–1955

As 1952 DREW to a close, Bill found lawyers were his constant scourge. In New York, Pincus Berner's charges mounted as he negotiated Bill's Riviera Club debt. Suren Saroyan's settlement with the Beverly Hills house and office landlords came to a reasonable $2,200, but Suren's bill for recent legal services amounted to $6,000—larger than Giesler's. Suren was his cousin, and Bill felt newly betrayed.

But even as he suffered the daily news of his debts, Bill believed in the brightness of his future. His Omnibus series gave him good reason. The plays were to be short ones, running for twenty minutes or so, and would make a segment of the hour-long Sunday program presided over by Alistair Cooke. Robert Saudek agreed to begin in December with *The Bad Men,* to follow it with *The Christmas Tie,* and, in January 1953, with *The Man in the Cool Cool Moon.* Bill was supposed to appear on every program, but as the time for each of the first three approached, he begged off. Watching them at Carol's, he thought they were poorly done.

Omnibus insisted he come to New York for the fourth play, *Vive,* to be broadcast on Sunday, January 19, 1953, and they sent him $450 for a ticket. He took along four plays—*A Picture for Life, Two or Three Marriages, The Macaroni Secret,* and *The Abracadabra Kid*—all of which he felt sure Omnibus would want for future shows. Arriving in New York on January 12, he checked into the Pierre Hotel and appeared at the studio where *Vive* was in rehearsal. He took an instant dislike to the set and then found that while his play had been cast with two of the theater's foremost comedians, Bert Lahr and Bobby Clark, they were unable to mine the humor he had given it. He spent some time alone with Lahr and Clark trying to direct them, but it was in vain. He wrote the production off as hopeless.

Bill learned that George Jean Nathan wanted to see him, but with neither

Alistair Cooke and Bill Saroyan, regulars on the Omnibus TV program

trophies nor prospects to display to his old Broadway sponsor, Bill did not seek him out. He did find time to call on Hubbell Robinson, at CBS, and to interest him in future Saroyan television plays. He told Robinson that he wanted to be executive producer of his own series for CBS.

Saudek seemed to avoid him. When they encountered each other, it was by accident in the men's room. Bill had a strong impression that while the Omnibus producer was committed to two more Saroyan plays he was cool to the idea of further ones.

The final performance of *Vive* confirmed Bill's earlier judgment: it was a fiasco. As he set out for home, the newspaper reviews agreed.

On January 26, Bill sent Saudek *The Oyster and the Pearl* as his fifth presentation and requested the rest of his money. The Ford Foundation responded that since it was deducting a thousand dollars for each of his three absences from the program and the Bureau of Internal Revenue had attached $15,000 of his account, the balance due him would be far less than he expected.

This led to several months of negotiation and an argument over the final play in April. Bill insisted on *Scalawag's Heaven,* while Saudek refused it. In late March they reached a compromise, which substituted *The Abracadabra*

Kid and satisfied the tax lien so Bill could emerge with a $3,000 payment intact.

He did not return for either the *Oyster and the Pearl* performance, on February 15, or that of *The Abracadabra Kid,* on April 19 (which, incidentally, starred the actor Walter Matthau). Watching the shows from Pacific Palisades, he was less approving than his family, but he admitted they were better than *Vive* and resolved to write more TV plays.

The Laughing Matter, the last of the three books under his Doubleday contract, was to be published on March 5. When the first copy arrived, Bill liked its looks, jacket, format, and type. He read it straight through, hoping to get a sense of how the book would fare. He had no strong feeling about it, but here and there he thought it so "lean" as to seem contrived. It was his honest prediction that it would fail. He didn't believe Doubleday had plans to promote it, and thus it would be another defeat for him.

He was right. In the Sunday *New York Times,* John Brooks was respectful of the body of *The Laughing Matter* but deplored its ending, which forfeited the story's meaning in violence and left the reader cheated. Frederic Morton's review in the *Herald Tribune* was crushing, as were those in the *Saturday Review* and *The New Yorker.* The *Nation's* reviewer said Saroyan should be ashamed of *The Laughing Matter.*

Elizabeth Bowen in *The New Republic* praised the author for his prior rescue of the short story from banality and for giving voice to "the odd man out." But she found *The Laughing Matter'*s story, that of a family holiday shot through with misery and rage, almost unbearable. Too much happened too rapidly. It was not felt. There was no hint of consolation.

Bill accepted that he had another book in the chute to oblivion. He had written *The Laughing Matter* in August 1950. It was the summer in which he had avoided seeing Carol in New York, was persuaded to have her back, but then refused her. It was also the summer in which Doubleday had rejected *Torch* and *More Later* and in which *The Son* had failed so dismally at the Circle.

The Laughing Matter was Bill's Armenian *Othello,* written in revenge for his jealousy, his constant desire for Carol, and his failure to mold her into the subservient Armenian wife he could tolerate. Evan Nazarenus is the author's self-image, an Armenian-American writer with a son, daughter, and a lovely, unstable wife, Swan. In Evan's absence, Swan has had an affair with Milton Schweitzer, whose child she is now carrying. Evan is torn between serious damage to his pride and family responsibility, but Swan, knowing Evan's alienation, opts for an abortion and suicide. This leads to a bloodbath: Evan's shooting and killing of his helpful brother, the suicide of Milton Schweitzer, and Evan's own fatal car crash. It was so bitter a work that even its author would finally reject it.

The Laughing Matter was Bill's third attempt at the big novel that could renew his license as a significant American writer, and it had failed more humiliatingly than *Wesley Jackson* and *Rock Wagram* before it. But here was the score, posted for all to see: as a postwar American novelist, he had struck out. He had failed to achieve even a fraction of the acclaim that had come to him for his stories in *Trapeze* and for *The Time of Your Life*.

This must have confounded him, but he did not ask the questions that might occur to a curious bystander: Was it loss? Had the bright bird of his talent flown away into the war clouds of 1941? Or was it the form? Were the novel's demands for structure, character, and patience too much for his impulsive skills? Or was it the times? Had these earlier triumphs been relatively simple ones—his own youthful concept of self as a heroic, disenfranchised David taking on the Goliath of an inhibiting, misleading, establishment-ridden society?

If being out of step with a misguided army was Wesley's problem, it was neither Rock's nor Evan's. The heroes of these later novels were burdened with wives, women determined to have wills and lives of their own. In neither case had Saroyan the novelist made a fair or interesting contest of it, or even understood its nature. If he had grown in other understandings, he had clung to antiquated, pre–*Doll's House* notions of a woman's role in marriage.

As always, Bill's response to deepening disaster was to start anew. Although he struggled for a month to begin a novel, he produced only a sheaf of introspection. Neither plot nor theme emerged. He had come to hate even the idea of writing. He often felt like throwing it over and turning to something else, yet he always concluded that writing was the only kind of work for which he was suited. He would not quit.

The Ranch Wagon had made frequent journeys to Fresno and San Francisco, acquiring mileage and traffic scars, while the contract for the six pieces he had promised *Ford Times* in exchange went unfulfilled. The magazine's editor, Ed Ware Smith, had surprised Bill by declining a piece about Fresno and three more thereafter. But he liked Bill's fifth effort, "The Return to the Pomegranate Trees," well enough to request some changes and, at last, to publish it. Bill made further fruitless efforts to please *Ford Times,* and finally Smith wrote him that so much labor had been expended on both sides, it was felt he should be relieved of any further obligation for his car. This was one more symptom of a faltering skill and too painful to acknowledge.

Believing in a book market for these retrospective pieces, Bill encouraged the agent Barthold Fles to find a publisher for a collection to be called *Growing Up in America.* Fles contracted with A. A. Wyn for it, with half the $2,500 advance to be paid on signing. Bill now gathered the several travel pieces that *Ford Times* had turned down with six short stories that had not yet found a market, and sent them to Fles, saying this material would complete the book and entitle him to the $1,250 balance of his advance.

After some delay, Wyn admitted his unhappiness with the material and his unwillingness to pay for it until it was satisfactory to the editors. In a spiteful mood toward the whole publishing establishment, Bill pressed Fles to confrontation, saying there would be no book at all unless the balance was paid now. Wyn asked for changes but provided the requested payment.

Bill was called into the Hollywood office of the IRS for an interview. A tax officer named Neblett studied his file and proposed that if he could raise the $35,000 he still owed the government, Neblett would recommend that all penalties be forgiven. Bill knew it was a generous concession but had no way to raise such a sum. He told Neblett that he was pursuing a big deal. If and when he made it, he would take up the offer.

The bonanza promptly announced itself. On May 11, 1953, he opened a telegram from Hubbell Robinson, the CBS television executive on whom he had called in New York. Maintaining that he would yield to no one in adventurous spirit, Robinson offered Bill $25,000 annually for a CBS series, further terms to be agreed upon.

This unexpected good news was confirmed in the trade papers, and a jubilant Bill Saroyan laid plans for his production staff. He would hire his cousins, Archie and Kirk Minasian, as his assistants, and pay them each $400 a month. He would want a private secretary for himself, too, a man with experience in writing for television. He resolved to be tough with CBS when the contract arrived for signature and called Culbertson and Neblett at the tax office to describe this rise in his prospects. He assured them he would be in to deal with his arrears as soon as the "papers" arrived.

He set to work on a pilot, a one-hour Christmas TV play about a department-store Santa Claus, but when the CBS contract appeared it was a disappointment. There was no provision for the supervision of production he had proposed to Hubbell Robinson, only an arrangement whereby CBS would do whatever Saroyan plays it liked. Even as he told himself he had to make this deal in order to survive, he could find no advantage to himself in the CBS terms. Negotiations proceeded fitfully throughout the summer, but no agreement was reached, and in mid-August he wrote Archie Minasian not to count on that job.

The IRS tightened its screws, warning Omnibus to make no further payments to him until its account was settled and putting liens on any Saroyan assets it could find. With $50,000 in arrears, Bill was ordered to report to the appellate court with his forms for the years 1949 through 1951.

When he told the tax officers that an opportunity to buy his Malibu bungalow would occur in the spring and he wanted to take it, he was assured that if he became the property's owner they would seize it. However, a note from tax officer Neblett encouraged Bill to stay on at Malibu, so long as he held only an option on, not an interest in, the property. Cosette, ever his willing banker, now agreed to buy the Malibu house for him in her name. She borrowed the $6,000 down payment and bought the house. Thus the cottage became Saroyan property and beyond the eager revenuers' reach.

During these privations, Robert Saudek offered $1,000 to repeat the previous year's *Christmas Tie*. Bill asked $6,000 for it, and although Omnibus raised its offer to $3,000 the haggling continued until Bill learned that Saudek had taken the play off his schedule and was disinclined to discuss it further.

The telephone and water companies threatened to suspend Bill's service for delinquent payments. Cosette reported that a tax lien had been placed on his share of 1821 Fifteenth Avenue. The IRS had put future income beyond his reach and left him feeling that any work he might turn to was futile.

Although he occasionally found money to make his $400 payments to Carol, there was never enough to dispel anxiety. He was often without cigarettes, gas for the car, and even bread for his table, and he was no longer writing at all. Dwelling on his plight and the suspicion that he could not escape it, he found the neighborhood poker game irresistible. When he lost, as he generally did, he wrote postdated checks against an empty bank account.

By mid-September, four of his checks to players in the game had bounced. One to John Fante for $1,100 troubled him greatly. Although he assured each man that it was a mistake and he would soon make the check good with cash, he knew only one way to do so. He borrowed $1,000 from his uncle Mihran. He also asked George Mardikian for a loan of $10,000 and was happy with the $1,000 he was offered.

He was annoyed to learn from a Hollywood columnist that Bill Saroyan was "down to his last cent," and from Walter Winchell that the $50,000 he had been paid by Omnibus had gone to settle his Las Vegas gambling debts. When Carol called to remind him of $400 in taxes due on the Maroney Lane house, he lost his temper and cursed both her and her mother.

The navy had stationed Bill's nephew, Arnold Papazian, at San Diego, and this brought his sister Zabe's family to the beach cottage for overnight visits. When his three Papazian nieces, Gloria, Barbara, and Jackie, departed, he found a $100 bill in his fruit bowl, and when Jackie returned to hang curtains for him, she left behind a pair of $50 bills. After Walt and Zabe's visit he found both a $10 and a $5 bill in his coat pocket. It felt to him like "soiled currency." It was too painful a reminder of how he had helped the Papazians buy their first house and provided savings bonds for their children, how in the meantime Walt had prospered in business, and how he once, when Bill was in need, had failed to help.

Bill's customary hypochondria worsened. He was drinking, so most mornings he suffered from a hangover, and he was never without pain somewhere in his body. His dentist, Dr. Shiell, had installed an inlay that refused to stay in place, and his jaw ached persistently. From the dental chair he complained to Dr. Shiell about his incompetence, and when Dr. Shiell sued for his $1,200 bill, Bill responded with a threat to countersue for $50,000 in oral damages.

He was still troubled by prostatitis, and Dr. Saul Fox, who treated it with occasional massage, told him it would recur, rather like a cold. Bill was pleased to learn that "a lay" often improved the problem. Unexplained pains multiplied, and he submitted to a four-day examination at the Sansum clinic, in Santa Barbara. The doctors found nothing more grave than a sty and a duodenal ulcer. He was urged to quit smoking and drinking alcohol and coffee.

Bill felt little reason to celebrate his forty-fifth birthday, but he did agree to a family party on August 31, 1953. Arriving, he was greeted by a chorus of Aram, Lucy, and their friend Kip Hadley, singing him "Happy Birthday." Everyone had a gift for him. Aram had made a card, and Lucy had done a drawing. Kip's present was a small box, which he described as a savings bank. Carol's was a carton of scented soap. Although touched, Bill was uncomfortable at the center of these rituals and churlishly resentful that the roast was undercooked and the cake store-bought. To Carol's and the children's disappointment, he left his party early. Home in Malibu, he went to bed and read for several hours.

Having lost heart in his own fiction, it had been galling to find, early that year, that Carol had completed seventy-five pages of *Rooms,* a novel about her mother's deceptions. Moreover, he thought the book was good. He delighted her by saying so and urging her to get on with it. At the end of the year, Bill put a new ribbon in Carol's typewriter for a final draft of what had become *Somebody's Mother,* sent it off for professional typing, and arranged for Hal Matson to read it.

When Matson returned Carol's manuscript with suggestions, Bill guided her toward a revision. Carol proceeded earnestly on this, and so he was surprised to learn in early May that she planned to take the children to Europe for the summer. The Chaplins were in Lausanne, and her sister Elinor was in Geneva. Although he would miss all three greatly, he agreed to provide the summer's monthly payments before they left.

He did some inquiring of his own about travel, pricing a round-the-world air journey and an August cruise. But an invitation from Margo

Jones's Round-Up Theatre, in Dallas, to present his 1950 play *A Lost Child's Fireflies* seemed a more sensible avenue of escape.

In late June, when Carol flew off to Geneva with Aram and Lucy, Bill arranged with his uncle Mihran, just recovered from a serious operation, to join him for the drive to Dallas. The midsummer heat was intense, and by the time they reached Prescott, Arizona, it had thoroughly cooked the usual cordiality between nephew and uncle.

There was a dispute over adjusting a tourist cabin fan and another over Mihran's lingering in the Prescott bank. When it was time to go, Bill did not like to be kept waiting. Mihran, on the other hand, was so offended by Bill's behavior that he refused to speak. Wordless, he returned to Fresno by bus.

Bill proceeded to Dallas, where the Round-Up's Afro-American company presented another of his meandering, multifamily chronicles. This one followed children into adulthood, the tragedies of war, and their own errant hearts. Although *A Lost Child's Fireflies* was well received as a portrayal of small-town life and Bill admired the production, it generated no further interest in the play.

News from Carol was giddy. She and the kids had been with the Chaplins and were now with Elinor and Henri de la Bouillerie, at 12 Chemin de Velours in Geneva. She reported that the house was lovely, that there were *two* maids, one of whom brought her breakfast in bed, and that she had been to a ball. Life here was sweet, fun, and just as she would have it. She exulted further in a plan to leave Lucy with Elinor and Aram with the Chaplins, and go off to Paris for a week.

Carol's next bulletin described her Paris experience as the best of her life. She had gone on to London with her friend Kay Kendall and was now planning a trip with her to the Basque country, this time taking the children. All of France, she told him, was just as Renoir had painted it, and in Paris she had dyed her hair black.

As so often in the past, new hope came to Bill in a phone call from Hal Matson. Matson had interested the producer George Abbott in a Saroyan musical about San Francisco. Matson was confident of terms similar to those he had made with Abbott for his current hit, Richard Bissell's *The Pajama Game*.

There was heady talk of a Rodgers and Hammerstein score, and Bill agreed to a $500 advance, a 2 percent royalty, and an immediate trip to New York for discussions. At his request, a second $500 for travel was promised.

While Bill awaited this money for his ticket to New York, a cable arrived from Carol reporting that Lucy had had an appendix attack and operation. He should cable money for it to Clinica Regina Carmeli, in Chiavari, Italy.

He had thought them headed for the French-Spanish border and could not understand how they had gotten to Italy, but he was concerned about Lucy and asked Matson to cable $150. Whereupon a second cable from Carol arrived asking for an additional $600.

By this time the check for his travel expenses had arrived from George Abbott, and with it Bill set out for New York via Las Vegas, hoping to multiply his meager funds. The stopover resulted in a $350 loss, and he was able to send Carol only half the sum she had asked for.

Arriving in New York on August 17, he was relieved to learn from Matson that Carol had cabled that all was well. Lucy was wonderful. They were returning to Geneva and coming home the first week of September.

Bill had written a first scene for the San Francisco musical on the train, and he offered it confidently to George Abbott. Abbott responded with a series of conferences, which included his assistant, Hal Prince. In these, the producer provided a plotline for what they decided to call *Ah, San Francisco,* and Bill felt he could deliver a satisfactory book for it in a week's time.

The weather was hot and sticky and his ulcer was newly restive, but he settled into his room at the Hampshire House and worked, often until dawn, on the story. At the end of five days he was exhausted. He felt he didn't know what he was doing and thus it was probably bad. He delivered a first act to Abbott and the next day was summoned by the producer. What he had written, Abbott told him, was not a musical but a fantasy and would not do. He proposed to pay Bill a thousand dollars for what he had done and urged him to complete it on his own, and then return in October when there would be time for them to start on an altogether new idea.

Once home in Malibu, Bill wrote further scenes for *Ah, San Francisco,* but Abbott spurned them. He felt Bill had gone astray and advised him to put no further work into the musical.

Bill was at Los Angeles Airport to meet Carol, Aram, and Lucy and shared the children's joy in their homecoming. While they ran to visit neighbors, Carol spoke wistfully of her time abroad. She turned thirty on September 11, and it seemed to Bill that her summer of travel had only intensified her restiveness and will to make some kind of vivid impression on the entertainment world. He accepted this with a new indulgence.

Calling at Maroney Lane, he was likely to encounter Marlon Brando, Adolph Green, or James Agee, but he believed the fires of his jealousy over Carol were so banked that he could suffer the parade of her suitors. He even wished she would marry again. He promised to help with her acting career, suggested some experience with the Round-Up company in Dallas, and wrote Margo Jones recommending Carol.

On October 22, 1954, in the midst of this autumn of drift and purposelessness he learned that Stanley Rose was dead. Archie Minasian called to read him the obituary in the Palo Alto paper, which described Stanley as one of the fabulous characters of Hollywood.

Bill was skeptical of Stanley as such, and thought of him simply as a pitiful old con man, but he felt a chill in his bones and wondered why there had been no mention of Rose's death in the San Francisco papers. Just three months before, Bill had stopped in Rose's birthplace, Matador, Texas, for a look at his mother's house there. Although he hadn't called on her, he had learned she was still alive.

He began a story, which he called "My Lonely Pal." It described a friend who had been a disreputable drunk, and how the news of his death saddened the narrator, and made him suspicious of his sorrow and also truly sorry for the part of himself that had died with the friend. It was a way of saying that he saw others not as autonomous individuals with complex lives like his own, but as characters in a play who had substance only when they entered the flow of his own experience.

A few days later, Bill read that Ernest Hemingway had received the Nobel Prize for literature. He recalled that in January the front pages had reported that the writer and his wife, Mary Welch, had been killed in an African plane crash. He had not been surprised the next day to find that the couple had survived—one more episode in the serial of Hemingway adventures.

He took a consoling thought from this major award to Hemingway. His own career, too, had reached an honorific stage. Mark Schorer, Sinclair Lewis's biographer, was urging Bill to place his correspondence and manuscripts in the safekeeping of the University of California. With the support of Allen Tate and Malcolm Cowley, he was proposing his Stanford mentor, Yvor Winters, for membership in the American Academy of Arts and Letters. Archibald Macleish had invited him to deliver the Spencer Lecture at Harvard.

And as always, he felt a big chance was coming, and might soon announce itself in the ringing of a telephone and perhaps the voice of Hal Matson. On November 22, Matson's voice brought just such news. Jean Dalrymple wanted to revive *The Time of Your Life*, with Franchot Tone in the lead. It was to be a fortnight's run at the City Center in New York, which could lead to a longer one on Broadway. Hal had assurance of $1,000 for Bill's expenses in returning to New York.

Delighted, Bill immediately saw himself as director and urged Hal to arrange it. He also saw the revival as an opportunity for Carol, who had just been spurned by Margo Jones. He wrote Jean Dalrymple about the play and told her how right Carol was for the part of Mary L. At Carol's request, he also suggested that Gloria Stokowski be considered for the part of Elsie Mandelspiegel. He assigned Aram the newsboy role, Lucy that of Anna, and Carol that of Mary L. for a family reading of the play.

On Thanksgiving Day, Jean Dalrymple called to say that Sanford Meisner had already been engaged to direct, but Carol could have the Mary L. role and Gloria, Elsie Mandelspiegel's. They would open in late January, and rehearsals would begin immediately after New Year's. Bill should plan on being in New York before Christmas.

Coaching Carol for the part, he felt she was making good progress. He was persuaded that the fifteen years since the play's writing had left enfeebling marks, but that it could be made into a lively current work. He revised the whole play and sent it off to Jean Dalrymple.

He arrived in New York on December 20. He settled once again at the Great Northern, birthplace of the original *Time of Your Life,* where he could still get a room for $7.50 a day. Jean Dalrymple took him to lunch at "21," and while she was tactful, he could tell there was trouble coming about his revisions. The first gathering of the principals took place at Franchot Tone's apartment in the Warwick Hotel. Sanford Meisner introduced himself cordially, and when the matter of the revised version arose, Tone said he would perform whatever Bill and Meisner decided between them.

But during a second meeting at the Warwick, in which Tone arrived with Gloria Stokowski, Bill's case for staging his revised version of the play met with general grumbling. The next morning, Jean Dalrymple telephoned to say that on reading the revised version, Tone opposed it. Believing this to be "Group Theatre" orthodoxy, Bill was adamant. Meisner and Tone insisted on staging the original 1939 version of the play. While Bill still believed this was a disastrous decision, he saw no alternative and finally agreed to it. He felt now that the revival would be a flop, that reviews would be bad, and there would be no Broadway run. Were it not for his hope of gaining some money from the production, he would have found it funny.

Meanwhile, Meisner had decided that Gloria was hopeless, quite unable to express emotion, and he asked Bill what to expect of Carol. Although Bill felt the same might be said of Carol, he replied that she was much more of an artist.

During the year his feelings of betrayal, particularly by those close to him, multiplied. His Judas List now began with his uncle Aram, who had excluded his brother Henry from a family party. Next came his uncle Mihran, his frequent benefactor, his father's own brother, for turning stubbornly mute during their journey to Texas. Suren Saroyan, his lawyer, was on the list because of a thieving fee and his insistence on collecting it. Another major benefactor, George Mardikian, was included for demanding repayment of the latest $1,000 loan and for trying to repair Bill's broken friendship with Manuel Tolegian. Next came Alex Pilibos, for ignoring a written request for a "business" loan. John Fante, forgiver of debts and once the closest of pals, made Bill's list for unfriendly behavior during a poker game. Arthur Freed was on it for a tardy payment, as was Shiell, his litigious dentist, and, most recently, George Abbott, for his carping at the now dead *Ah, San Francisco*. Finally, there were the old grievances. These included his brother-in-law Walter Papazian, and, although he had recently been polite to him, his cousin Ross Bagdasarian.

The list's length suggested to Bill that he might be at fault in some cases, but he dismissed the notion, comforting himself with the year's several fallings-in. He and Hal Matson had been working together closely throughout the year. Howard Cady, now at Henry Holt, had been cordial about a new book, and some of the old warmth had returned to his friendship with Gene and Betsy Kelly.

Carol arrived in New York on New Year's Eve to stay with Gloria Stokowski at 8 East Sixty-sixth Street. During the week, the newspapers had reported that Gloria was leaving her husband, Leopold Stokowski. At her party that evening, Gloria was with Frank Sinatra, and Bill was told that the two were in love.

On New Year's Day, 1955, Bill started a new play, which he titled *The Cave Dwellers*. It would take place on the stage of an abandoned theater, which would be a kind of womb, peopled by the unborn. They would be dreamers, waking at the entrance of the boss of the wrecking crew that was demolishing the theater.

Time of Your Life rehearsals began on Sunday, January 2, on the City Center's third floor, but Bill did not attend. When asked if he would speak to the cast, he declined. He had nothing to say. His only funds were an allowance of $100 a week from the City Center, and he felt alone and lost. On two consecutive nights he walked to Sardi's, peered at the after-theater crowd within, and turned away.

But he finished *The Cave Dwellers* in a week, and asked Hal Matson to find a producer for it. He then turned to writing pieces about the *Time of Your Life* revival which had been requested by drama editors of both the *Times* and the *Tribune*. He was irked to find that Carol, after a week under Sanford Meisner's direction, believed Meisner to be the Messiah.

On January 12, a week prior to the opening of *Time of Your Life,* Meisner invited Bill to a run-through on the City Center's stage. Bill sat through the three-hour ordeal with mounting misgivings. He thought Meisner's direction was misguided in every way, and Tone's portrayal of Joe was affected and repellent. His play was in the hands of incompetents.

When Jean Dalrymple called to ask what he thought of their prospects, he told her his opinion bluntly and profanely. She was hurt as much by the manner as by the substance of his response. He told Hal Matson that it would be a preposterous fiasco, that the reviews would be fierce, and rightly so.

Bill described the disaster-in-the-making at the City Center to the producer Jed Harris, who agreed to help out. After watching a rehearsal, Harris provided some advice. When this was dismissed by Franchot Tone, Bill and Harris agreed that the play's last chance had been lost. They could not see how the curtain could go up on Wednesday night. Harris suggested that for years Dalrymple had had a crush on Franchot Tone, and only this could explain the calamity.

Carol, preoccupied with rehearsals, was elusive, but Bill was able to see her at Gloria's late one night. Her fans, Adolph Green, George Axelrod, and Marlon Brando, were supportive, but she despaired of her own performance. She was dismayed to find that Bill did not plan to see the preview on the eighteenth, and urged him to change his mind. He told her the play was hopeless, and walked home.

Hal Matson persuaded Bill to attend the preview, and it confirmed all his fears. He thought Gloria Stokowski was embarrassing, Carol terribly misdirected, and the entire production miserable, worse than before. However, it seemed that the play itself had survived the mistreatment.

Bill went to the opening on January 19 with Hal and Tommy Matson. When he encountered Jean Dalrymple, she told him she wished he would not go around town knocking the play. He saw but avoided Rosheen Marcus, who was with a man not her husband. Seeing the Hirschfelds, he remembered that they had believed Carol's theory that he was anti-Semitic and given him a bad time about it, so he ignored them.

He was upset by Gloria's performance. The audience had laughed at her hysterical wail, and when, at her exit, one of the streetwalkers had remarked, "Nick, what the hell kind of joint are you running?" there had been laughter and applause. Carol had done well enough in spite of Tone, but the production itself—lighting, music, directing—had been stupid. Nothing had worked. The play had been hideous and cute, and it had bored him to extremes of agony.

The cast party was at the Gotham Hotel. Although Carol was late arriving, she made a spectacular appearance. Her dress looked expensive enough to make Bill wonder about its source. His voice, particularly while he spoke with Sanford Meisner, grew contentious, loud enough to bring complaints from other guests. At three-thirty, Bill took Carol to Times Square for the early reviews, and they went to Reubens to read them. Carol was disappointed to be roundly ignored by them, and Bill was baffled by them. They parted at five, in a quarrel.

The next morning, Bill read all the reviews and could not believe his eyes. He knew the play was a mess and Gloria monstrous in it, yet the reviewers had only praise for both. If a new play of his had been so badly staged, they would have slaughtered it. Yet the revival was an undeniable smash hit.

Brooks Atkinson described it as "Saroyan's skylarking comedy from 1939" and deemed it better than "the petty popular comedies being written today." He praised the direction and felt Meisner was clearer about the play's theme than its author had been "when he dashed it off fifteen years ago." It was now plain that the play was about "the fundamental decency of ordinary people against the viciousness of authority."

Bill looked in at the Saturday matinee and decided that Carol was not bad anywhere and that Gloria was improving. The Shuberts were interested. There was talk of a musical and a film. When Jean Dalrymple called to ask if he would be willing for a six-week Broadway run and a Victor recording of the play, he said he was and referred her to Hal Matson.

There was a flurry of inquiries about new Saroyan enterprises. What about a musical built around Duke Ellington? He went to Hickory House and talked to Ellington about it, and thought he might come up with a workable idea. He also spent an afternoon with Harold Arlen and Yip Harburg seeking the musical possibilities in *Jim Dandy*. Although Arlen went to his piano and improvised a theme that the play suggested, they could not find a workable story. Bill felt he could provide one and set out to do so, giving it the title *The Bell Chord*.

In Helen Ostrow Jacobson, Matson found a producer for *The Cave Dwellers*. Jacobson was excited about the play and ready to produce it in mid-October. Carol had fresh hopes for Bill's play *The Girls*. Her lawyer Arnold Krakower, among others, was interested in financing it.

On January 26, John and Jane Gunther gave a party for Carol. John O'Hara, Marcia Davenport, Roald Dahl, and his wife, Patricia Neal, Judy Holiday, Jules Styne, and Adolph Green were there. The verdict on *Time of Your Life* was unanimous: seeing it was obligatory. Bill sensed the triumph in the air but felt it was less his than Carol's. She was flourishing on the attention, and he was saddened to hear that she was now determined not to return to California.

For all the good press, the City Center's box office reported slim sales. The Shuberts found no suitable Broadway theater and proposed a road tour instead. Franchot Tone was cool to that idea, and while Eddie Dowling was willing, it seemed likely the revival was all but ended.

At the final performance, on January 29, Franchot Tone asked Bill to come onstage and stand at the bar drinking beer during the opening minutes of the play. He did so and backstage met most of the cast for the first time. At the party afterward, he declared this last one the best performance yet.

Returning Carol to Gloria's at three in the morning, he told her he no longer found any reason to stay in cold New York. It had been fifty days since he had seen Aram and Lucy, so he was going home to Malibu.

XV

IN THE CHUTE

1955–1961

DURING THE SPRING of 1955, Carol's reports from New York were buoyant. She was getting small parts in television and found reason to hope for both a Broadway role and publishing interest in her novel. Bill believed she would soon be discouraged enough on both scores to come home to Palisades.

He was thus unprepared for her call in early March. She was elated with news that Random House had taken her novel, *The Secret in the Daisy.* She was to have an advance of a thousand dollars and fall publication. Although Krakower had decided it was too late to present *The Girls* this season, Jed Harris might do it, and she had a good chance in other plays. So she had no intention of an early return to California. Aram and Lucy could come to her. Bill reminded her that it was he who had gotten her a part in a play, he who had helped her write her book, that the children were happy here in Palisades, and she was not. Why must she drag them after her?

Because, Carol replied, she already had an idea for a second book, and there was a good part waiting for her in George Axelrod's new play. In a major declaration of independence she pleaded for his understanding that she was neither useless nor a case nor entitled to feel only what he wanted her to feel. She would not return to the dishes. She was appalled at the damage he had done to himself and believed it came from his belief that he was a saint in a world of crooks, when the truth was *he* was the crook.

This fall she was going to come into her own. Random House was sure that her book would be a critical success, and she would be in a play at the same time. She would have her own money and her second book written. She planned to live in New York and California *with* her children and make them happy. She ended by reporting that when the black dye was washed from it, her hair had turned red.

Carol decided to wait out the early summer in California. When Bill and the children met her at Burbank Airport her first news was of James Agee. He had died the previous day, bound for his psychiatrist in a New York taxi.

She was excited about *The Secret in the Daisy.* It would be published on August 1, and Bennett Cerf thought highly of it. Gallimard was publishing it in France, and Bantam would probably bring out the paperback edition. She was getting on with her writing career, too. A story she had just written was being considered at *The New Yorker,* and a second novel was already worked out in her head. It was about her last four and a half months in New York, and she had a title for it, *Morning Every Morning.*

As for her stage career, she had put in three months in Sanford Meisner's acting class. She and Gloria, who was now divorced and back in her Gracie Square apartment, had been offered parts in a summer tour of *Picnic.* Gloria had accepted.

Bill grew accustomed to having dinner at Maroney Lane, but shortly after Carol's return he learned that Marlon Brando was also expected, and he left, raging about Carol's turning the house into a circus instead of a home for Aram and Lucy. Brando's blue car parked in front of the Maroney Lane house at all hours became a familiar sight. One night when Bill lingered to watch the car races on the television, Aram confided that Marlon had arrived. He surprised the two at the supper table, whispering like a pair of conspirators. When Bill invited Brando to join in watching the races, the actor simply shook his head.

Carol told him that although Marlon Brando had always wanted to marry her, and had offered to pay her living expenses, they had never had sexual relations. It was simply a friendship, and, as evidence, Carol showed him the praiseful letter Brando had written her. She went on to say that Brando hated actors and acting. He believed his skill was only a trick, and that as soon as it had made him enough money he was going to quit.

Bill wondered about the tongue-tied male role popularized by Brando, if that unwillingness to speak masked homosexuality. He thought Brando's letter looked like one only a homosexual man could write.

When Carol called to say the *Daisy* galleys had arrived and to ask for his help, he urged her to bring them over at once. For three days Bill sat with her, poring over the novel and then making sweeping cuts and revisions. The result, he believed, was good. He went on to compose the author's note, the blurb, and even a letter that would accompany the new material to her editor, David McDowell. Recognizing Bill's hand in the revisions, McDowell objected. Pointing out that they would be too costly, he returned the galleys to Carol for less radical changes.

These intimate and exhausting sessions at Malibu and Maroney brought a confession from Carol. She told him that fear had once pervaded her life.

She used to be scared of him, but no longer. She used to fear becoming like her mother and so she had tried to be a wife to him and mother to the children, but it was impossible. She had to be free.

In New York these last months, she had been wild, out every night, at every party in town. Whatever hour she came in, she would shower and go right out again. She got no sleep. What things she had learned, too. Truman Capote had told her about his unbelievable life. At a party, Marilyn Monroe had taken her aside to confess that her mother and her sister were in an insane asylum and that she was illegitimate. Carol had admitted that she was too.

In the midst of these all-night sessions, when too weary to get on with the editing, Bill and Carol made love. However, Bill's view of Carol was hardening. He anticipated that she would return to New York without the children, that, like her mother, she was a child abandoner, committed to parties and a lot of men.

At the end of June, Carol entrusted the children to her friend Jean Widmark and flew off to New York to read for a part in a new play, *Will Success Spoil Rock Hunter?*, by George Axelrod. Bill learned from Walter Winchell's column that its producer, Jule Styne, had not yet found a lead for the play, and had passed up the likes of Marilyn Monroe for it because he thought they could not act. Carol was flying to New York to solve the problem, he thought wryly. He was willing to bet that Carol hadn't a chance for it, and that the producers knew it.

Carol returned at the end of June to report that she had won a role in *Rock Hunter*. It was not the lead, which had gone to Jayne Mansfield, but a small one, that of the secretary. Rosheen was off to Italy for a year, and Carol was to have her apartment at 970 Park Avenue. She was returning to New York in two weeks, taking the children and entering them in nearby PS 6, the best public school in the city.

With departure imminent, Carol often came to the Malibu cottage after parties and stayed from midnight until dawn, talking about herself and quarreling. He reminded her of the loss of their third child at Mill Neck, the one that was to be their second son, Rock, and how it had wounded him so deeply. While she did not admit that she had aborted the child, she also did not deny it, and he felt it confirmed.

Carol's confessions invariably led them to make love. Once, while lying together in bed listening to a Brahms piece on the radio, they realized it was the same one they had first heard together at the Hampshire House, thirteen years earlier. They were both moved by it.

When Carol asked if Bill loved her, he admitted he did, and when she said that she loved him too, they both laughed.

Bill reflected that although born poor, Carol had the ancient soul of a coquette. She knew how to please men. She chose her long-range involvements with care, rich and famous all. The others served as errand boys. Had he not married her, he would have found her a fascinating character.

He did not begrudge Carol's literary hopes. When she presented him with a copy of *The Secret in the Daisy* inscribed as a first book for her first and sole love, he embraced her and they laughed and read their favorite passages to each other.

He told her the book looked and read well and she had achieved a good thing. He wrote a glowing review of it and sent it to the *Times,* the *Tribune,* and *The Nation,* with no takers. But the critical response to *The Secret in the Daisy* struck him as evasive and mainly bad, and he decided that Carol's book was a flop.

Bill was in the audience for the first New York performance of *Will Success Spoil Rock Hunter,* in October 1955, but he was not favorably impressed. He described Axelrod's play as about familiar Hollywood characters and a girl with big breasts. He judged it to be obscene and despicable. As for the acting, he felt Martin Gabel's was the only creditable performance. Walter Matthau, whom he had admired, disappointed him. Carol, for all her faults, was the best of the three women. He could not believe there would be favorable reviews.

But the reviews were good. *Rock Hunter* was a hit. Ironically, Carol seemed disappointed by the accolades, as if everything she had planned for herself had happened instead to Jayne Mansfield. Nevertheless, her spirit was intact.

While he occasionally took Carol to dinner, and made his habitual sexual demand, he found her listless and full of fantasies about her future and complaints that he really did nothing for his children, that it was her father who supported them. She did agree he could have them in California for the following summer.

Early in 1956, Carol wrote Bill in Malibu that she had taken a long lease on an apartment at 53 East Ninety-third Street. Her story "A Woman's Place" appeared in a March 1956 issue of *Collier's,* and he thought it did her credit, as did the note about her and a photograph from the play.

Since Carol, no other woman had interested him. He liked only those who would come to him at the cottage for an hour or so of sport and put no demands on him.

He learned from Walter Winchell's column that Carol was planning to marry the British critic and playwright Kenneth Tynan, and he presumed it was he who had taken her to Italy during the summer of 1957. By early fall, however, Carol was back in New York, understudy to Ann Baxter in Jose Quintero's production of Carson McCullers's *Square Root of Wonderful.*

Since she had been cast off by Al Capp some seven years ago, Bill believed she had been with Brando, James Agee, Adolph Green, Jones Harris, and, most recently, Tynan. Yet the attraction between them remained. On his recent visit to New York, she had proposed he take her back, but then promptly agreed it would be impossible. The bitterness was too strong.

When he returned to New York in October 1958, Carol was leaving for a pre-Broadway road tour of S. N. Behrman's *The Cold Wind and the Warm,* and he went to Philadelphia to see the play. Her part, that of Myra, the belle of Worcester, was substantial. He thought she played it well enough, but he sensed that both the play's future and her own within it were in doubt. The Philadelphia reviews were not favorable.

Before leaving for Europe in February 1959, Bill dined with Carol and Lucy at Ninety-third Street and was surprised to find Walter Matthau there. Bill was depressed by the evening and attributed it to what he saw as the inconsistency of Carol's having a maid to serve and clean up so she could get on to an insignificant part in a minor play.

But he was mistaken about the cause of his gloom. Carol's course toward independence from him had been completed by Walter Matthau. The two would marry that summer, leaving Bill wholly alone, as a man, a writer, and a father.

The last half of the fifties, those years in which Bill would himself turn fifty, were overcast with his knowing he had not published a book since *The Laughing Matter,* in 1953, nor had a play on Broadway since *Get Away Old Man,* in 1943. Yet he was always launching a promising venture, a novel, a play, or a book of recollection, and Hal Matson continued to be tireless in the Saroyan cause.

During the spring of 1955, Matson sold an article, "Twenty Years of Writing," to the *Atlantic Monthly,* and "The Whole Voyald," a story about the tenuous yet tender relationship between a divorced father and his son, to *Cosmopolitan.* Moreover, he contracted for Broadway productions of two Saroyan plays, *The Girls,* with Arnold Krakower, and *The Cave Dwellers,* with Helen Jacobson.

Bill's aversion to agents, even one as able as Hal Matson, flared again into a quarrel. Indifferent to Hal's ingenuity and hard work, Bill disliked and refused to sign the play contracts. Whereupon the usually patient Hal Matson had finally had enough Saroyan ingratitude, and in mid-March told him to look elsewhere for representation.

Bill now unshelved a novel begun in 1953 and since shunned by four publishers. Like "The Whole Voyald," it was about ten-year-old Aram and himself and drew on fatherly feeling, a rich source of "positive tropism," the

Saroyan transformation of painful experience into pleasure which had marked his Aram Garoghlanian stories. He called the book *My Father Is a Writer,* and in working on it he felt the return of confidence. Since the *Atlantic Monthly* had just run his "Twenty Years of Writing," he sent this revised novel there along with two stories.

A flurry of good news came in response. Edward Weeks, the editor in chief, wrote accepting both stories and the novel. Weeks planned on revising the book and changing its title. Heartened, Bill started a similar novel, for and about Lucy, planning to finish by his forty-seventh birthday, the last day of the month.

Work on the Lucy novel was interrupted by a visit from his cousin Chesley Saroyan, once a close friend and literary protégé. Having left his wife and children and spent eight months in a Seattle mental hospital, Chesley was in serious trouble. Recent outbursts of violence against his father, Bill's uncle Aram, were bringing about his parents' divorce. Bill listened sympathetically to Chesley's painful history but saw no way to help him.

Chesley was accompanied by his brother Eugene, who described recent surgery on his nose performed by a Dr. Joel Pressman. This interested Bill, who considered his own nose in need of improvement, and led him to consult Dr. Pressman and agree to undergo a rhinoplasty.

The Lucy novel, provisionally titled *Mama Girl,* had become his daughter's adventure in New York as Carol's apprentice and pal, pursuing dreams of stage success. At its midpoint, he felt he didn't believe in it. For Lucy's sake he overcame his skepticism and plugged away, completing it as promised on his forty-seventh birthday. Retitling it *The Bouncing Ball* and thinking it might appeal to a woman's magazine, he sent it off to the *Ladies' Home Journal.*

He entered UCLA Hospital on September 13 and emerged ten painful days later with a new nose. Confronting it, he was displeased. It was shorter but tipped up in an unattractive way. He hoped he would like it better when the inside sewing was undone and the swelling subsided.

He was diverted by further cheerful news from New York. Robert Saudek wanted him back on Omnibus. Would he produce a script to be called *The Boyhood of William Saroyan* for airing on October 16? The offer was $6,000 for the writing and more for acting in it. He said he certainly would. Here was more proof of what was wanted from him—affectionate memories of a childhood where ragged Armenian boys laughed, sang, and prevailed. Promising to deliver the script in a week, he assembled it easily from his earliest Fresno recollections, mailed it to Omnibus, and bought a ticket to New York.

Arriving at his dowdy yet beloved Great Northern Hotel on September 29, he called Omnibus to find that both Robert Saudek and his associate

Paul Feigay approved what he had done. They would pay the promised sum, allow him to direct it, and provide an additional $1,500 for each appearance. Pointing out that three quarters of whatever he made would go to back taxes, he insisted on $10,000 for the writing of it, and Saudek agreed.

When he telephoned Carol's apartment he learned from Lucy that Martha Stevenson Goetz had given Aram a World Series ticket, and that they were now at Yankee Stadium watching the game. Bill hurried to 970 Park Avenue and with Lucy watched the final innings on TV. In the following days, he spent as much time as he could with both children, taking them to Child's for pancakes, to the Palace for vaudeville, to Madison Square Garden for the rodeo, to the Met for the ballet, and to the Broadway soft-drink stands to sample orange julius and coconut milk.

Although his nose had all but healed, he liked it no better. Leonard Lyons had an item about it in his column. Carol teased him about it, and Martha Goetz told him he should get Pressman to do it over. Looking at himself in the mirror, he conceded his mistake. It was a bungled job.

He was soon busy at the Omnibus office readying *Ten Scenes from the Boyhood of William Saroyan*. He was pleased by both the casting of sixteen-year-old Sal Mineo in the title role and, as he added a final polishing, his script.

On October 5, Bill returned a phone call from Erd Brandt of the *Saturday Evening Post* and learned that he had been shown *The Bouncing Ball* by the editors of the *Post*'s companion publication, the *Ladies' Home Journal*. Brandt had read and discussed the novel with his coeditors, Ben Hibbs and Stuart Rose, and they wanted it. Bill was further astonished to learn that they planned to run it in five installments, for which they intended to pay him $4,000 a piece, a total of $20,000. Although overwhelmed by this unexpected good fortune, Bill asked for time to think it over.

He sought Saudek's advice, which was that he might get $30,000. Bill called Brandt back and asked him for $36,000. Brandt took forty-eight hours to consider it and then agreed. The *Post* would pay $6,000 at once and the remaining $30,000 in three monthly installments.

Bill was ecstatic. He had found the elusive upward path at last and with a novel he had almost abandoned. The book, finally titled *Mama I Love You*, had been his gift to Lucy, but now it was also her gift to him. He had captured her spellbound voice with its pure love for her divided family and perceptions of a mystifying adult world. Twink, the ten-year-old Lucy's counterpart, tells of her mother's acting fantasy fulfilled in a reflection of *Time of Your Life*'s tortuous path to triumph. The story ends in her being restored to her father, but Twink's adoration of both parents is only frosting to the painful dissolving of her family and offers scant insight into the cause.

Curiously, Bill attributed this good fortune less to joy in his daughter than a will to popularity. He felt that his guide in *Mama I Love You* had been commerce rather than art, and it had turned him from the truth that lay in his embittered heart. In either case, it was the wistful Saroyan mode of an enchanted childhood that had illuminated *My Name Is Aram* and *The Human Comedy.*

Ted Weeks had been working out a Saroyan publishing plan, and as Bill went to meet him, he guessed that the *Atlantic's* editor in chief would be impressed by the *Post's* endorsement. Weeks had invited him to lunch at the Century Club, and Bill's first glimpse revealed him as older than expected. Newly sensitive to noses, Bill was struck by the pronounced hook to his host's. Weeks was indeed impressed with the *Post's* anointing of *Mama I Love You* and amazed that Bill had written it in a single month. He felt it had a good chance for a summer Book-of-the-Month Club selection and wanted to publish it in May, immediately following the serialization.

As for *My Father Is a Writer,* now retitled *Papa You're Crazy,* Weeks now felt it was too episodic. He would put off publication until the following year, giving Bill time to provide it a stronger story line.

Bill had not encountered an editor with Ted Weeks's intellectual certainty, nor did he find the trait endearing. When Weeks warned him against making more than $100 worth of galley corrections, Bill decided he was an old lady from Boston and that already he had had enough of the Atlantic Monthly Press.

Reflecting on *Mama,* he was pleased that it had changed his luck and made him a little fortune, but he understood it was junk. It did not speak at all from the dark, inner truth out of which a big, honest, admirable book would have to come. Nor did he imagine *Papa You're Crazy* was any better. Neither book would enhance his reputation as a novelist, but, for the present, that was okay with him.

The Omnibus presentation on Sunday, October 16, was live, and Sal Mineo was splendid as the young Saroyan. The others did equally well, but Saroyan himself blew his lines. At one point he had to refer to his notes, and at another he inadvertently omitted a part of the introduction. When he reached 970 Park Avenue afterward, Aram, Lucy, and Carol assured him he had done well, that clearly Alistair Cooke and everyone at Omnibus liked him. However, he could not dismiss the memory of his unforgivable fluff.

Robert Saudek too commended Bill and had a further assignment for him. Omnibus was preparing an educational series of twenty-six short films, to be called *Under the Sun,* and he wanted Bill to write and perform introductions for them. He would receive $500 for each.

The visible Saroyan success on Omnibus and in the *Saturday Evening*

Post was not lost on the Internal Revenue Service. On October 7, Culbertson of the Los Angeles office had filed a $20,000 lien against Bill's Omnibus income. Bill's new affluence led him to see it as his opportunity to rid himself of his tax hobble altogether, and he wrote the San Francisco office, proposing to settle his $62,000 debt to the government with a payment of $30,000. He turned to Pincus Berner, asking him to negotiate for him.

Berner did persuade the tax office to a compromise, but he had no sooner done so than Bill had a baffling change of heart. Parting with $30,000 to an institution he had come to regard as his enemy was too distasteful. He preferred the standoff. Later, he would pay off his taxes in full.

Bill's second honeymoon with Omnibus was losing its rapture. He was replaced as director of the year-end production of his own *Best Year in the History of the World*. Then he quarreled with the director of the *Under the Sun* episodes in which he performed. When he saw the rushes he did not like his own appearance before the camera. There was a peculiar hissing to his speech, as if his mouth were dry, and a pomposity of manner that he found unacceptable.

As the year 1956 began, *Mama I Love You* was running in the *Post*, featured as "one of the most engaging novels of the year by the celebrated and unpredictable William Saroyan." Bill felt confident the *Post* would also want a new novel, which he called *The Immigrant's Son*. But the magazine declined it along with *Papa You're Crazy* and a new novelette, *Pointy Shoes*.

In the course of the summer of 1956, the *Post* took a story, "Iceland," and the *Reporter* took a piece on American writing that had been shunned elsewhere. But mostly the mail brought rejections. *The New Yorker*, *Playboy*, *Redbook*, *Argosy*, and the *Lion* all sent his stories back. Each turndown angered him, and he was left not knowing where to send these orphans.

His romance with the big magazines was cooling. It was no consolation that the slicks themselves were in trouble. During the year, two newsstand staples, *Woman's Home Companion* and *American*, had gone out of business. In December *Collier's* would follow them to the grave, without publishing his "Girl with the Most Beautiful Mouth in America," for which it had paid $8,000.

To make matters worse, the IRS office was increasingly vigilant about intercepting the money coming from Omnibus, the *Post*, and the play publisher, Samuel French. All of his $28,000 at the *Post* was liable to the tax collector's reach on January 1, 1957.

Thus, once again, Bill appealed to a surprisingly sympathetic Culbertson in Los Angeles, proposing to settle his $62,000 debt to the collector for $25,000. Awaiting a departmental response, he was irked at the revenuers' willingness to "deal." Recalling that they had threatened to take his house and had invaded his professional relationships, he felt new contempt for them. He put his defiance into "An Open Letter to the Government," and sent it to *Variety,* which published a version of it. Thus, when Bill again turned his tax proposal over to Pincus Berner for negotiation, the lawyer found Culbertson disinclined to compromise.

Mama's publication day was a disappointment. The reviews admired the ten-year-old narrator's voice and found it a funny, touching book, even surpassing his other recent novels, but as a whole they were patronizing. *Time*'s was bad enough to call for an angry letter to the editor.

When Kenneth McKenna called from MGM to inquire about rights to *Mama,* Bill's old grievance over *The Human Comedy* prompted his refusal to sell the rights. He would only lease them. Olin Clark, MGM's story chief in New York, offered to negotiate for *Mama* but balked at Bill's prerequisite, that MGM release *The Human Comedy* to him. Subsequently Bill asked Abe Lastfogel, of William Morris, to inquire if MGM would return the screen rights in exchange for a seven-year lease to the rights of *Mama I Love You.* MGM would not, and there were no further inquiries.

When *Mama I Love You* appeared in England, the reviews were dismissive, scoring the book for its coyness. Bill, who had believed his British audience was unswervingly loyal, blamed hostile critics, but a letter from Faber's explained he was no longer writing the kind of novels his British readers expected of him. It underlined what his conscience told him, that the widening of his readership through the slick magazines—and pleasing that readership—had estranged his book audience.

Lucy sent him a two-page enthusiastic letter about *Mama,* and he judged this a final benefit, that the book had come and gone.

The Whole Voyald, a collection of nostalgic California stories, was published by Atlantic Monthly Press that fall of 1956, but the reviews were scattered and faint in praise. He had seen no ads for it, and the advance sale was only twenty-two hundred copies. *Mama* had reached seven thousand. Bill was ready for a new publisher and recalled that Howard Cady had moved to Putnam.

Bill believed that whatever the current market for his work, his fame was indestructible. It had come to him in 1934 with *Trapeze* and been confirmed in 1939 with *Highlands* and *The Time of Your Life.* Now he vowed that before he was fifty he would write a simple, great, masterly novel. It occurred to him that he might, one day, get the Nobel Prize. He reasoned that nothing had ever stopped him, that he had intelligence, skill, love, and a touch of genius. Madness, too. Why not the Nobel? He would want a big book to coincide with turning fifty.

But he was not working on a book, big or otherwise. Instead, he was betting the horses and playing poker, and with consistent bad luck. Each evening he would mix a pitcher of icy martinis, sip them by himself, then wander up to the inn for company at its bar. Once, seeking his way home, he had been drunk enough to drive by the cottage. The morning hangover was a regular impediment to work.

He was disturbed to find the freckles of age appearing on the backs of his hands. They were similar to, though not as pronounced as, Chaplin's. He was twenty pounds overweight. One by one, his painful teeth were deserting him. When he drank coffee, he felt a burning near his heart, and there were constant reminders from his ulcer.

During the fall of 1956 a dinner-party conversation turned to the matter of taxes, and Bill was impressed by a general agreement that once you got behind the only way to catch up was to establish residence in Europe.

For the first time it occurred to him that living in Europe might be his solution. He had frequent invitations to present his plays there. When he suggested this to Pincus Berner, the lawyer replied that unless he had a major source of income abroad, residence there would do him no good.

Surveying the current Broadway season, he found plays written and directed by such acquaintances as Harold Clurman and Garson Kanin and again resolved to end his galling fourteen-year absence from Broadway. Throughout the winter of 1957 he worked at revising the best of his old plays, *Afton Water, Muscat Vineyard, Violin Messiah, Cave Dwellers,* and *An Imaginary Character Named Saroyan.*

He believed he had greatly enhanced each one, and so it was painful to not find a producer willing to take one on. Then, in early March, Carmen Capalbo inquired about the availability of *The Girls.* Although Capalbo had a current hit in Graham Greene's *The Potting Shed,* Bill did not believe his interest was serious. However, it did cause him to reread his revised plays. He came to the glum conclusion that with the exception of *Saroyan,* they were all slow, dull, and ill-made. It was because he had lost his essential spirit.

Thus, on April 10, he was startled to learn that Stanley Chase and Carmen Capalbo were ready to produce a new Saroyan play. They urged him to come to New York to help with the choice. It appeared to be his long-awaited return to Broadway. His talks with Carmen Capalbo left Bill in some doubt about the man's skill as a director, but the royalty terms were generous. He was pleased that Chase and Capalbo had chosen to do *The Cave Dwellers* and that it would open in early fall. He felt confident of a good Broadway run.

Bill arrived in New York on May 1, recharged with optimism and flush enough to check in to the St. Regis. His first act was to call on Carol and the children at 53 East Ninety-third Street and reassert his fatherly role. He wanted to take both children to Europe for the summer.

The four principals in the *The Cave Dwellers* are a pair of ill, aging actors, known as the King and Queen; the Duke, an ex–boxing champ; and a waiflike girl. The King, a former clown, has bet his shoe he can get a laugh from the demolition crew and, poignantly, has lost. All four are starving, cold, and terrified of the world outside.

In the huddling together of the characters there is ample opportunity for Saroyan musings on war, religion, mankind's nature, and the singular solace of love. They are joined by a family with a trained bear. The Duke seeks milk for all and returns with a milkman's lug of bottles. The pursuing young milkman arrives to look around the needy circle and depart without a word. The waiflike girl has somehow communicated with him, and in the end the Duke brings girl and young milkman together.

Cave, with its fanciful kinship to Thornton Wilder's *Skin of Our Teeth* and Samuel Beckett's recent *Waiting for Godot,* is surely the most spectacular and interesting of Saroyan's postwar plays. After Bill's fourteen years of theatrical famine, it was a main chance. Yet with its opening just four months off, he showed surprisingly little interest in the play's production. He asked for no voice in the casting, no seat in rehearsals, no opportunity to defend what he felt important about his play as it took shape.

He would later reflect that *had* he taken part, he would surely have had violent objections and repossessed his play. He knew what a threat he was to the cooperative efforts of staging a play. Writing it was such a private utterance of himself that it could not be shared. Collaboration was impossible.

On the threshold of *Cave's* realization he sailed off for a European holiday with his children. Returning at the end of July, he made the script changes Capalbo requested but still had no interest in the rest of the preparations for an opening at the Bijou Theatre in October.

Back in Malibu, he marked his forty-ninth birthday by beginning an autobiography that would describe the first half century of his life. He borrowed its title, *Fifty-fifty,* from his aborted 1950 screenplay, and he persuaded himself that *this* self-portrait could be his big book.

The news from New York was hopeful. Although Paul Muni had declined the role of the King in *Cave,* Bobby Clark had accepted it. Eugenie Leontovich was to play the Queen, Wayne Morris, the Duke, and Susan Harrison, the girl. Rehearsals had begun, and Bill believed *The Cave Dwellers* would fare well enough to encourage further productions of his plays.

On September 17, Frank Rhodes, of the San Diego Union, passed along a confidence from the secretary of the Nobel Prize committee: it was considering two California writers, Steinbeck and Saroyan. When Rhodes guessed the Nobel would come to Bill in 1959, Bill agreed and looked into the history of its awards. He found that Sinclair Lewis, at forty-five, was the youngest recipient. O'Neill, Hemingway, and Faulkner had all been in their fifties.

Stanley Chase reported that the rehearsals were going well; Bobby Clark had been replaced by Barry Jones, and Carmen was superb in his directing.

The Cave Dwellers opened at the Bijou Theatre in New York in October
1957 and played ninety-seven performances. Here, Bill with its leads,
Eugenie Leontovich and Wayne Morris

The preview performances were sellouts, and the most recent audience had
stood at the final curtain for a ten-minute ovation. However, in spite of
Chase's promise, opening night, October 19, 1957, came and went without
any word. By the following evening Bill was convinced the critics had
panned his play.

Late on the evening of the twentieth, Chase and Capalbo called with the
reviews. All except Walter Kerr's, in the *Tribune,* which scored the playwright's sentimentality, were favorable. Atkinson, in the *Times,* praised it
and predicted it would run all season. There was a line outside the Bijou's
box office assuring the producers of a twelve-week tenancy, and Bill would
have $1,500 for each week of the run.

Bill decided to go to New York. He would find a place to live in Manhattan and work on *Fifty-fifty,* improve *The Cave Dwellers* for future productions, and shop around for a publisher to do his several available books.

Arriving in New York on November 5, he checked into George Jean
Nathan's hotel, the Royalton, on Forty-fifth Street, and went off to the
Bijou to see *The Cave Dwellers* for himself. There he decided that his simple
play had been made into a shambles, a monstrous miscarriage unworthy of

any praise. It was the typical Saroyan reaction to alien hands on his work. His response to Capalbo's presentation of *Cave* was as outraged as it had been to that of Bobby Lewis's *Time of Your Life,* MGM's *Human Comedy,* and Ross Bagdasarian's *Son.*

After the performance, Bill went to the Blue Ribbon with Capalbo and Chase and told them what he believed to be the truth—they had bungled his play, and it would soon close. They disagreed; they felt the production's only weakness lay in Leontovich's performance, and they planned to fire her. Bill concluded that Capalbo was incompetent, as he had suspected, and that *nobody,* himself excepted, could stage his plays.

Carmen Capalbo told Bill that the cast of *The Cave Dwellers* was disappointed that he had never come backstage to greet its members. He replied that he had planned to give the cast a party but had not yet gotten around to it. Then, on December 17, Capalbo and Chase reported dwindling attendance at the Bijou and asked Bill if, when the weekly gross dipped below $14,000, he would cut his royalty. He would consider it, he said, if they would restage the play. The dispute continued through December, until it was made irrelevant with the news that *The Cave Dwellers* would close on January 11, 1958.

Bill was sure it was time for a change in publisher and, oblivious of the Atlantic's expectations, proposed to Howard Cady at Putnam's that he undertake one or more forthcoming Saroyan books. These included *The Cave Dwellers,* the novel *Immigrant's Son,* some novelettes, a collection of essays, and the autobiography on which Bill was working. At Cady's suggestion, Bill submitted the novel.

Knowing that George Jean Nathan had had a stroke, Bill was reluctant to disturb him. Yet they were together at the Royalton Hotel, and on November 14, he sent a gift. Julie Haydon called to thank him and invite him for a drink. Welcoming him, she led him into a big room cluttered with books, records, and a windup victrola. Nathan, wearing shorts and a shirt, sat in an overstuffed chair smoking a cigar. He seemed to be wasting away, and his face looked damaged around the mouth. When he tried to take Bill's hand, his arm trembled and he spoke with difficulty.

Nevertheless, George described theatrical ideas he was pursuing, and he promised to "lick this thing." Although Bill stayed only a few minutes, he was convinced that Nathan would. Later, Julie phoned again, to ask if he would help George down in the elevator and out for a short walk. When Nathan proposed they work on a play together, Bill agreed. Five weeks later, on Christmas Eve, they had a glass of champagne together in what was to be their last meeting.

For Bill, 1957 came to an end at Pincus Berner's New Year's party, where he was in an unusually bitter mood. Not only did he dislike the guests, but he found himself resenting Berner, with his guffaws and his shoulder-caressing hands. Although Bill had no more loyal friend in New York, Bill thought he was an idiot.

This led him to the astonishing New Year's realization that he knew scarcely anyone he liked, nor did he want to. It was the Saroyan social paradox, a bonhomie that could fill a room with cheer and mask the alienation he would describe in *Not Dying* as a way of ignoring the people surrounding him, keeping them creatures of his imagination, no more substantial than characters encountered in a dream.

Early in January, he returned to Malibu, where, at first, he felt content. Ross Bagdasarian met him, drove him home, and saw him almost daily. Bill was fond of Ross's wife, Armen, and of their three attractive children, Carol, Skipper, and Adam. Ross was the best company for a visit to the track or an evening of poker, and his jokes and high spirits made the occasional patriotic meetings at the Armenian Center endurable.

The two cousins worked up an idea for a musical, *Life in Fresno,* and Bill sketched a story for it. But it was here, at the point of collaboration, that misgivings set in. Ross was the only one of his cousins who had tried to do more than earn a living, but he was a troublemaker. Bill was annoyed to find out that Carol had spent an evening with Ross and Armen at their new house and that she had recorded a song of Ross's called "A Little Beauty." He felt Ross had a loyalty to Carol as well as himself, and he could not share *any* of that.

He believed that Howard Cady, at Putnam's, was ready to publish his novel *The Immigrant's Son* and follow it with his current project, *Fifty-fifty.* However, as he resumed work on this, trying to rekindle enthusiasms of twenty years before, he found it so boring that Malibu poker games took precedence in his thoughts.

Depressed by his quick California deterioration, he sought escape and bought a round-the-world steamship ticket. He hoped to work on *Fifty-fifty* and do some journalism for the James Spadea syndicate as he traveled.

Boarding the *President Wilson* in San Francisco, on April 7, 1958, he posed for photographers and gave the first of many newspaper interviews about his voyage to the Orient. As the ship's principal celebrity, he was seated at the captain's table, but he avoided his fellow passengers and presently asked to be seated alone where he could read.

In mid-Pacific he learned that his steadfast sponsor, George Jean Nathan, had died. His response was that Julie must be grateful for release from her poor old patient. Much as he had memorialized Stanley Rose as a drunk, his epitaph for George was as a dandy. As always, gratitude was alien to Bill—it implied dependency, and dependency was weakness, and both were abhorrent. He did not endure any sense of loss for the man who had singled out *Highlands* for praise, directed the writing and casting of *The Time of Your Life,* orchestrated Bill's amazing success in 1939, and given him counsel ever since.

His journey proceeded to a score of exotic ports, where he shopped and visited the tourist sights but found little to interest him. For the most part he was uncomfortable in Asia's heat and repelled by its ubiquitous beggars.

Each day he had a card table brought to his stateroom, and there he found no difficulty writing reports for the syndicate in which he described shipboard life and excursions ashore. By May 17, when he reached Suez, he had done sixty and sent them off but he had not been able to work on *Fifty-fifty* at all.

Bill returned to New York on June 3 anxious to hear Howard Cady's response to *The Immigrant's Son.* When he inquired, the editor said that, while he was willing to publish the book, he wanted revisions. This seemed a crushing of his publishing hopes, and Bill told Cady to return the manuscript. Their deal was off.

Spadea had found only seventeen newspapers willing to take the round-the-world series, and in accepting a $500 check for his work, Bill lost his enthusiasm for journalism but still felt the pieces would make a salable travel book.

Reminding himself of Rhodes's hint that he was up for the Nobel Prize, and wanting a big book to accompany the honor, he promised to resume work on *Fifty-fifty* and complete it by his imminent fiftieth birthday. He continued to feel that at any moment he might receive a cablegram from Stockholm. He knew this was absurd but also that it *could* happen. The committee had made mistakes in the past, and if anybody deserved it, he certainly did.

He finished *Fifty-fifty* on schedule, all 1,401 pages of it, but reading it over he decided it was too unhappy a book to offer for publication, and he set it aside. But on this half-century birthday a score of Soviet writers saluted him by cable from Moscow, reminding him of his audiences abroad. Finding a way to work there was on his mind, and he had several tempting invitations.

There was to be a Swedish production of *The Cave Dwellers,* and Jean Dalrymple would revive *The Time of Your Life* at the Brussels World's Fair. Most enticing of all, Francis Mason, at the U.S. embassy in Belgrade, alerted him to Yugoslavia's interest in filmmaking. He might make a movie there at Yugoslav expense.

He saw more immediate opportunity in a report that McGraw-Hill was enlivening its trade list. His inquiry to McGraw's editor in chief, Ed Kuhn, about his round-the-world travel book brought an interested reply. So Bill called at McGraw-Hill in September, bringing along his likeliest manuscripts, *The Immigrant's Son,* the around-the-world pieces, and the three novelettes. Ed Kuhn and his assistant, Robert Gutwillig, seemed enthusiastic about publishing him and assured a swift response. A few days later, Kuhn called. He had read all three books and lost interest in publishing them.

It was a disheartening rebuff and centered his hopes on the European journey. When he read that three Soviet publishers were preparing editions of his work, he applied for a Soviet visa and cabled Francis Mason that he was ready, as part owner, to shoot a film in Yugoslavia.

He sailed for Sweden on September 18, taking an immediate liking to the *Gripsholm,* which was equipped with stabilizers and a good chef. As always when at sea, he ate and drank copiously and was unable to sleep, but he was developing a plan for the Yugoslav movie. It would involve two male characters, a very grand old man and a wild young boy, a rebel. He puzzled over a way for them to engage, to become father and son.

At the State Theatre in Malmö he watched a performance of *The Cave Dwellers* that he neither understood since it was in Swedish nor liked, and yet he was moved by it. Summoned to the stage, he made a speech, and went on to a dinner in his honor.

In Moscow he was given a suite at the National Hotel, which he believed had been that of the Armenian poet Yegishe Charentz in 1935. Opposite was the Bucarest, formerly the New Moscow, where he had stayed. With the help of his Intourist interpreter he interviewed the manager there, hoping in vain for some trace of the missing story "Moscow in Tears."

In Belgrade he learned that *Time of Your Life* had been a hit at the Brussels fair. There had been eight curtain calls. Over the next several days he conferred with the managers of Avala Film Brograd, the national agency that was to sponsor him, and reached a general agreement. Thirty percent of the film's profits would go to Saroyan until its costs were recovered, whereupon his share became 50 percent. He would provide the story, to be called *Ya, Yugoslavia,* and would return to cast and direct the picture. The old man had become a locomotive engineer, and the boy would meet him by bringing him a kite to repair. However, when he saw some of Avala's past films and realized the slimness of the budget provided, his doubts rose.

Back in New York, his talks with Berner and Gitlin raised concerns about doing the film in Yugoslavia. Nevertheless, he wrote Avala saying it was up to them whether he returned to Belgrade.

In late December, Cosette came to Malibu to spend the holidays with him. On Christmas Day he suffered such grief that he believed he could no longer work there. He told Cosette he was leaving the States, that she should pack up his stuff and rent both houses. He was going to live in

Switzerland. Whereupon Bill had two troublesome teeth pulled, put his Cadillac up for sale, and set out for New York, telling himself it had been fine, but he was quitting Malibu forever.

When he told his lawyers that the tax collector was sending him abroad, Paul Gitlin's advice was to let the government seize Maroney and so solve his problems, but Bill rejected the idea. Berner said he could establish residence wherever he liked, but that Switzerland was the most expensive country in Europe.

His correspondence with Avala was encouraging, and he sent off his final terms. As he sailed for Venice on the *Saturnia,* he was pleased that the customary squad of reporters was on hand to see him off. In the course of the two-week voyage he tried to type up a scenario for *Ya, Yugoslavia* but managed only a few pages of notes.

He arrived in Belgrade on March 11, settled at the Metropole Hotel, and called at the Avala office to begin work. He met Dragan Yevtic, who was to be his aide and translator. Yevtic explained that a first meeting with *Ya, Yugoslavia*'s sponsors had been arranged for the following day and that he would call for him and escort him to it.

Bill assured this gathering that he had a scenario for the picture fully in mind and was ready to proceed. He was told that approval by Avala's ten-member board of writers would be necessary and that they would need to see something on paper. Bill agreed to provide a scenario within two days. The writers would assemble at noon on the coming Saturday to render their judgment. When the matter of financing arose, a man named Aleksander Pajic surprised Bill by saying he had some twelve million dinards, $12,000, in accrued royalties here.

Next day, a Friday, as Bill struggled to expand his notes, Dragan Yevtic called to ask whether he could be of any help, and to invite him to dinner on Monday. He told Yevtic all was well and went off to be interviewed at Radio Belgrade. On Saturday morning, he taxied to the Navodna Bank and found that his account held not 12 million but 92,000 dinards, or $156. He withdrew it all.

As agreed, he turned up at the Avala office at noon, bearing the one-page treatment he had produced, doubtful it would win the enthusiasm of any committee. He was kept waiting and then told that the ten-man board was conferring. If Bill would leave his treatment, it would be translated for the board, which would return a decision on Monday. Bill was angry but left the treatment, agreeing to return on Monday morning.

He found himself in the situation he dreaded most—having to write in company to some standard other than his own. Those who would interpret him—editors, producers, and studio executives, who felt entitled to advise him about his work, alter it, and instruct him about it—were ever his enemy. A committee of Yugoslavians? What had seemed a creative joyride with himself at the wheel had turned into an inquisition.

On Sunday he learned of a sports car for sale. Presently, Armando Mendoza, first secretary to the Mexican ambassador, came by with a relatively new red Karmann Ghia convertible, for which he asked $1,400. Bill looked at it, was assured it came with an export permit and could be driven wherever he chose, and bought it.

On Monday morning, when Yevtic phoned about their appointment with Avala, Bill told him to forget it for the moment. Then, in a staggering act of self-destruction, he paid his hotel bill and fled. After bashing the Karmann Ghia's fender in the hotel car park, he set off for Zagreb and uncertain points beyond. For twelve hours he drove west across Italy, putting Yugoslavia behind him but without a destination. In Milan he took a sudden dislike to his Yugoslav license plates and, hoping to replace them with Swiss ones, drove on to Domodossola, putting the red roadster onto the car-train for the tunnel ride to Brig.

In Switzerland he drove to Vevey and from a gas station telephoned the Chaplins. Learning that Oona was out and Charlie was in London, he drove on to Geneva, where he tried futilely to get Swiss plates. He decided to proceed to Paris, perhaps do some ISIS lectures, and trade in the little car for a Mercedes-Benz. However, as he drove through Lyons he lost his direction, and encountering a sign for the road to Aix-en-Provence and Marseilles, he followed it. Eight hours later, he arrived in Aix, went straight to the casino, and lost $1,400 at baccarat.

The next day, he drove to Marseilles, looked at a Mercedes 260, then went on to Nice, took a room at the Ruhl Hotel, and won at the casino. He stayed for a week, gambling each night, winning at first and feeling flush enough to inspect a fourteen-room villa priced at $25,000. By Good Friday, March 27, he had lost $6,000—the price of a new Mercedes or a house in Spain.

With $2,000 left he drove through a heavy rain toward Genoa, telling himself he had become lost and had no idea what he was doing. An inner voice cautioned him to think carefully, to stop gambling before he was completely ruined. On Easter Sunday he paused in San Remo long enough to part with what remained of his money at the casino. He cabled both Pollinger and his Italian publisher, Arnaldo Mondadori, for more money and, while waiting for it, borrowed from the hotel. By Friday his gambling loss for the young year had reached $10,000, and he admitted that his moving to Europe had become a fiasco.

Throughout the first half of April he traversed the Riviera, gambling nightly at Monte Carlo, Nice, or Cannes, winning as much as half a million francs in an evening but finally losing it all. He knew that he was his own captive. Cashing a last check on April 11, he recalled his six years of thrift and industry at Malibu for which he now had nothing to show but a huge tax debt. He was crushed by guilt and loneliness.

But even as he managed to quit the Mediterranean and make his way to Paris, the lure of the casinos clung to him like unrequited love. He had no sooner taken a room at the George V than he made for the Cercle Gaillon and lost another 46,000 francs.

In eight weeks, he had lost $12,500 to the cards. Although he slept the days away, he awakened at six each evening to the seductive call of the baccarat tables. He had done no writing, of course, and understood that he was living in a nightmare from which there seemed no waking.

Then he encountered Irwin Shaw, always a favorable omen, in the hotel lobby. Shaw spoke of working on a screenplay for Darryl Zanuck, who was at the neighboring Plaza Athenee. Although Bill had not seen Darryl Zanuck in fifteen years, he gave Shaw a message for him: Could they discuss some business? Zanuck's reply was encouraging. He not only welcomed Bill to his suite at the Plaza Athenee, but listened sympathetically to his account of awesome gambling losses and the need to make money.

Zanuck was a small, energetic man with prominent teeth, a clipped white moustache, and an exquisite air. A gambler too, he told of losing $400,000 the previous year at the casinos. He spoke admiringly of Bill's work and described several projects that could be mutually profitable. He said he would send him one.

The next morning, Zanuck sent him John Fante's script for *The Devil Is a Woman*. Bill liked it and urged Zanuck to bring Fante to Paris to develop the screenplay. Zanuck revealed that it was to be a vehicle for his twenty-seven-year-old French girlfriend, Juliette Greco. She was a beauty, and was known as Jujube. As a child she had been jailed for her work in the Resistance, and she had retained a reckless air. As a protégé, Jujube would be a man's full-time occupation.

Bill asked Zanuck if he wanted an original story for her, and the producer replied that he did. He would pay Bill's living expenses until they could draw up a working arrangement. Although it was well known that Virginia Zanuck confidently awaited her husband's return to Palm Springs, Bill recognized Darryl's infatuation as the lifeline it was. At the Fox studio he saw Greco's performance in *Naked Earth* and drew up an outline for a screenplay he called *The Secret of Lily Dafon* or *The Paris Comedy*.

It would tell a story similar to what he saw as Juliette's, of a young, adventurous Parisienne and her playfully predatory adventure with a rich American. It would begin with a scene in which Lily, a pretty, teenage girl, is being

Darryl Zanuck, chief of Twentieth Century–Fox, and his protégée, Juliette Greco

cross-examined about her love life by her mother, grandmother, and great-grandmother. The morning newspaper describes a rich Texan whose wife's refusal to give him a divorce has brought him to Paris to find a mistress. Although the accompanying photograph shows him with a girl who resembles her, Lily denies it is she. The three older women are too canny to believe her. Both Zanuck and Juliette Greco—to whom he described it while they were gambling—liked the idea and urged Bill to proceed. Bill promised to bring it to Zanuck in play form in nine days.

Bill saw in Darryl Zanuck, a man three years older than himself who was awed by his literary reputation, fathomlessly rich, and foolish over his Jujube, the patron with whom a kindly providence had at last rewarded him. He did not see Zanuck as the kindred result of an agonizing, fatherless childhood who had scaled the summit of Hollywood through shrewdness. Nor did he perceive that, however Zanuck might be deceiving himself with Juliette, he remained potentially formidable as an adversary.

A Zanuck assistant brought the initial terms: $1,000 for hotel expenses through the month of May, and an advance of $7,500 for the play to apply against a $45,000 purchase price if Zanuck wanted it. Bill began to write the play, *Lily Dafon,* imagining Gary Cooper in the role of George Hannaberry of Dallas, richest man in the world, and introducing a French realtor to sell him a chateau that, at the film's end, would fall to Lily.

Bill often dined with Zanuck and Juliette at the San Francisco or Le Petit Baton and then went on with them to gamble at the Aviation Club, a members-only casino on the Champs-Élysées. It was high-ceilinged and opulently furnished, with an excellent restaurant as well as a bar and gaming rooms. Bill's gambling luck was also improving. Playing chemin de fer at the Aviation, he won 200,000 francs, and a week later, as Zanuck lost two million at baccarat, Bill won 75,000.

In mid-May Bill finished and revised the whole of *Lily Dafon,* left it for Zanuck's approval, and for a week waited for some word. At the Aviation he lost 235,000 francs in a single night, and over the next several evenings lost everything. He pawned his watch, and the next day borrowed 20,000 francs from the hotel in order to keep playing. Anxious and broke, he became angry at Zanuck for his silence.

At a party at Irwin and Marian Shaw's, he was impressed by their always luminous circle of friends and envious of their "palace" at 49 rue Boileau. He was determined to have a place of his own, and within a few weeks found an apartment at 171 Victor Hugo that could be leased for the summer.

At last Zanuck was willing to discuss *Lily Dafon.* He liked it, and Bill was invited to the Plaza Athenee to discuss terms. Bill said he wanted to bring over his children for the summer and needed $25,000 now against a total payment of $50,000. He also wanted a percentage of the gross. Zanuck assured him no author ever received a percentage of the gross.

After several days, Bill was invited back to the Plaza Athenee, where Zanuck was ready with his final terms for *Lily Dafon:* he would buy all rights for $50,000. Bill wanted to see it in writing. Zanuck agreed and gave him 500,000 francs as pocket money. With this Bill took John Fante, who had just arrived, to the Aviation Club. There he won another 100,000 francs and went on to show his friend from Malibu a Parisian night on the town.

When the *Lily Dafon* contract arrived, Bill studied it and phoned Pincus Berner in New York. Calculating that he was at the leverage point and must not be bested, he called Zanuck and raised the purchase price to $60,000.

When Zanuck's assistant called on June 4 to reject these terms, Bill told him the deal was off and for the rest of the day refused to answer his phone. A hand-delivered letter from Zanuck expressed disappointment in Bill's behavior. Not only had they already agreed to a $45,000 purchase price, but he had loaned Bill money and paid his hotel bill. He had an obligation. Zanuck urged him to reconsider. Bill wrote in reply that he would repay the loan and the hotel bill but must refuse the terms and any further business between them. The next morning, however, when the assistant phoned, Bill was less adamant. He said he hoped for a new Zanuck offer.

After another loss at the Aviation Club—one of a half-million francs—Bill received a terse telegram from Zanuck saying he would not agree to new terms but would take legal steps to protect his rights in the property.

Bill spent an anxious night and the next day called on Zanuck. The producer wanted some revisions in *Lily Dafon,* and when Bill agreed to provide them, Zanuck conceded to Bill's terms of $60,000. Bill would have $10,000 by check and a deposit of $50,000 to a Swiss bank account.

He congratulated himself that his gambling had once again driven him to work, and that the work had been effective and profitable. He opened an account at the First National City Bank of New York, sent Cosette a check for $1,000 and settled his 100,000 franc bill at the Aviation Club. He was in the clear.

On June 17, he learned from his New York lawyers that the tax collector had disallowed the $12,750 in deductions they had filed for him. Old ire at the repressive governmental system erupted. In spite of their years of loyalty and generosity, Bill angrily wrote Pincus Berner, Melville Cane, and Paul Gitlin that since they were doing him no good, he was quitting them.

Believing that Zanuck was ready to proceed with *Lily Dafon,* he provided him with a five-page letter of instructions on how to make the film. Zanuck replied that Juliette Greco would not be free until November and in the meantime he would be busy with other projects.

In need of fresh work, Bill began an autobiographical account of this Paris summer of 1959, his fiftieth. It involved the current visit of Aram and Lucy along with recollections and reflections of all sorts. He called it *Not Dying,* and while the progress was slow, he finished it at the end of July. Whereupon he turned to a play, *The Moscow Comedy,* which he submitted to Zanuck in late August.

Now his gambling luck went from bad to worse. At two a.m. one August morning, he woke Zanuck from a sound sleep at the Plaza Athenee to ask for another 200,000 franc loan. In sobering daylight, he swore off gambling again and quit the Aviation Club.

Zanuck responded to Saroyan's need by proposing he improve a play in which he was interested. It was *Settled Out of Court,* by Henry Cecil, and concerned a British judge who is confronted in his study by thugs and forced to retry a murder case.

While Bill was indifferent to the play, he wrote Zanuck that it needed much work. He would rewrite it, top to bottom, making a far better play and film. Meanwhile, he had left a million francs' worth of uncovered checks at the casinos and needed $25,000 to cover them. He asked Zanuck to loan him this sum.

The Zanuck reply foretold a change in the weather. He not only declined to make the loan but said he disliked *The Moscow Comedy.* However, he did want a rewrite of *Settled Out of Court* and would advance Bill $10,000 on it with a similar sum on acceptance, *if* the play were produced. Bill would share credit and royalties with Henry Cecil. With no other choice, Bill accepted an initial $5,000 and went to work reluctantly on the Cecil play.

As he struggled with his revision he saw a way to make a radically new play of *Settled Out of Court* and did so. Retitling it *Fair Trial at Gunpoint,* he submitted it to Zanuck.

Bill felt confident enough of the outcome to order a new green Mercedes convertible, priced at $5,545, to be delivered to him in October. It was the best, he reasoned, so why not?

He found a $40-a-day room at the Raphael Hotel on Avenue Kleber and confidently sought Zanuck's opinion of *Trial*—along with the $5,000 balance of the initial payment. He was irritated to find that the producer was busy on location and could not see him now, but he had written a response to *Trial.* Zanuck believed he had improved the play but it needed further work to become satisfactory. And the title must remain *Settled Out of Court.* As for the second half of the advance, Zanuck would be deducting from it the thousand dollars that Bill had borrowed from him.

Bill was furious to find the balance of his payment shrunk. He made some further changes in the script and returned it as a job completed along with a letter complaining about the deduction of his debt from the expected payment. He called Mercedes-Benz to cancel his order for the car.

He tried to reach Zanuck by telephone, and when told he was unavailable, wandered around Paris fuming at him. But ultimately Zanuck, along with Juliette Greco, received him at Twentieth Century–Fox's Boulogne studio. This glimpse of Juliette—inspiration, star, and protectress of *Lily Dafon*—affected him. On impulse, he kissed her hand. He then asked Zanuck what he needed to do to *Settled Out of Court* to make it acceptable. Zanuck assured him he could accomplish it in a few hours, and the final payment would be immediately forthcoming.

After two weeks at the Raphael, Bill's charges had risen to $1,250, and when these were presented to Zanuck's office, Bill learned that there had been no such generous understanding. That night he moved into a $4 room at the nearby La Perouse, leaving the Raphael's bill for Twentieth Century–Fox.

He went home to San Francisco for the holidays and there resolved that the new year would see a new Saroyan book published. From his file he retrieved a novel he had written in 1949, an autobiographical account of a middle-aged writer fighting a losing battle with both his typewriter and his nubile young wife. A rereading convinced him that with some revision it would be a compelling book. He retitled it *Boys and Girls Together.*

In January 1960, he returned to Paris, pausing in London long enough to visit his agents, Murray and Laurence Pollinger, and to seek out Henry Sherek, the producer who would present *Settled Out of Court* in London. In the course of lunch with Sherek he was displeased to learn that while he was to have program credit and earn royalties, the play would be largely Henry Cecil's original version. Later, in giving an interview, Bill observed that his improvements to *Settled Out of Court* had resulted in a far better play than the one Londoners would see.

While in London, he did enjoy Brendan Behan's play *The Hostage,* and he wrote Joan Littlewood, its sponsor, to say so.

Back in Paris, he returned to a bathless room at La Perouse, where he heard from the manager of the Hotel Raphael that $550 of his bill remained unpaid. Bill refused it, saying it belonged to Twentieth Century–Fox. When he reminded the Zanuck office it had neglected his Raphael bill, a Zanuck assistant explained that the bill was his. Bill called on the Raphael's manager and offered to settle by paying half the debt. The manager declined his offer, declaring it a matter for the police. Bill grudgingly paid in full.

He was so angry at Zanuck and the Raphael's manager that he went gambling, determined to win the $550 back. Instead, he lost $3,000. At six-thirty in the morning, as he fell into a drunken sleep, he assured himself he would have that sum ten times over from Twentieth Century–Fox—or somebody. Then Bill found Zanuck newly displeased with him. His unflattering opinion of Cecil's original *Settled Out of Court* and the lament over his scuttled improvements had appeared in a London newspaper. Henry Sherek, ready to open the play, was understandably angry.

This disappointment was followed by a particularly reckless gambling streak that drained all of his income from *Settled Out of Court.* He had lost $10,000 in a year that was barely begun.

The February gloom was brightened by two invitations. The State Theatre in Vienna planned a premiere performance of *The Paris Comedy* on the twenty-seventh of the month and wanted him to attend. Even better, Gerald Raffles, of the Theatre Royal in London, called in response to Bill's letter to Joan Littlewood. He wanted to do a Saroyan play in March and was willing to leave the direction to him.

Raffles welcomed the proposal of *Jim Dandy* and spoke of releasing some of its ideas from the obscurity that had baffled audiences in 1941. Whereupon Bill proposed the clean slate of a new play, *Sam, the Highest Jumper of Them All,* which he had in rough draft. It would be demanding of the cast, but it might clarify that very Saroyan view of humankind on which he had been reflecting since *Jim Dandy.* Raffles agreed.

The opening performance of *Lily Dafon oder Die Parisier Komedie* took place at the five-hundred-seat Akademie Theatre in Vienna, and the applause brought Bill to the stage for five bows. However, he found no signs of interest in extending *Lily's* run. A scornful review of the play in the Rome *American* caused Bill to admit that it was a frivolous portrayal of the Darryl-Juliette love affair, born of his own desire to flatter Zanuck and to spring some of his bottomless affluence. It stiffened his resolve to clear his theatrical conscience with *Sam, the Highest Jumper of Them All.*

In March he flew to London, found a room at his old home, the Savoy, and made ready to stage his first play since the Saroyan Theatre of 1942.

He had set *Sam* in a London bank where its tyrannical president, Mr. Horniman, intimidates his clerk, Sam Hark Harkalark, and exploits his raffish depositors. The first act ends in the bank's robbery and in Sam's clubbing by a bobby in the mistaken belief that he is the thief. Although Sam is declared dead, and his promising career at an end, he is at home practicing the high jump, sure that once he becomes the highest jumper in the world he will be somebody. He does jump to record-breaking heights and explains to an astonished world that he can outperform all others because he is all races and religions and jumps for all people.

Although many believe that the blow to Sam's head has made him crazy, the bank president Horniman is discovered to be guilty of the theft and is led away by a Scotland Yard detective, while Wally Wailer, a rock singer, brings down the curtain with his song "We Were Only Having Fun."

The Theatre Royal, another five-hundred-seat house, was in the East End, an Underground ride from the hotel. On arrival, Bill was welcomed by Gerald Raffles, members of the already selected cast, and eight reporters. Bill told them he was optimistic about the play, and that evening he got busy with revisions.

He cut and rewrote whole scenes and worked long hours with his actors, sometimes having them sit in the orchestra while he spoke from the stage, but at the end of the first week of rehearsal he was tired and unhappy with the play.

By the third week, Bill was still adding to the play and beginning to think it was a good one, a "lark." Some of the new material seemed funny and touching. He felt that in any case he had done his best.

But at a preview performance he was dismayed by the clumsiness of the actors. They were uncertain, and the action faltered. His flourishes seemed arty, and the play's "message" left the charity audience befuddled. Nevertheless, he told the cast that they had done well and that the play would be a hit.

At the opening, on April 6, Bill sat alone in a box and felt the play had come together at last. The actors had given an outstanding performance, and the audience had been with them all the way, bringing them back for three curtain calls. Optimism suffused the cast party, and Bill dismissed such overheard remarks as "What's he after?" and a forecast of bad reviews.

Bill rose at five-thirty the next morning to find the forecast was accurate.

Sam, the Highest Jumper of Them All, which Bill wrote for the East End
Theatre Royal in London. Here, Bill is seen directing its cast.
The play opened in April 1960 to dismissive reviews.

Sam was described by one critic as "drowning in treacle and ooze," and none
had any idea what the play was about. The coup de grâce was delivered by
Time magazine's international edition, which judged the play's zaniness to
be conservative in an age of Brecht and Ionesco and identified its secret as
the playwright's debt to the tax collector and his attempt to earn the price of
a ticket home.

In the play's introduction, Saroyan declares that the meaning is simple
enough: contempt for the phony, even when it is widely accepted as truth.
In any case, there is a discernible Saroyan theme in *Sam.* The hero's accomplishment in jumping is the individual's protest and ultimate triumph over
such conformist institutions as orphanages, schools, banks, armies, and
warring governments. It is a portrayal of the author's belief that any institution that limits the individual will is built of hypocrisy and run by the likes
of Horniman, crooks who are simply out for themselves.

That night Bill told the cast that he did not agree with the critics, and
that they must continue to perform at their best. Again he watched the performance from a box and found that it frequently fell to pieces. Tired, and
no longer sure *Sam* was a good play, he told himself that failure had something to be said for it. When the Sunday papers confirmed that *Sam* was a
total, unredeemed disaster, Bill wrote protesting letters to all fifteen critics
and encouraged the cast to do its best for the sparse audiences it was facing.
On April 15, he returned to Paris.

In a small room at La Perouse he shaved off his mustache and put a want
ad in the Paris *Tribune* for an apartment. He offered three original manu-

scripts in exchange. His only response came from Ed Hagopian, a fellow Armenian from Fresno, who found Bill an apartment in the opera district.

It was a fifth-floor walk-up, four rooms and a terrace at 74 rue Taitbout priced at 5.5 million francs, or $11,000. Bill agreed to buy it, and with Hagopian's help he spent several weeks furnishing it and improving its rudimentary plumbing. Then he invited Lucy and Aram for a summer visit. Hagopian revealed that he too was a writer and became Bill's devoted squire. They collaborated briefly on an around-the-world scenario that they hoped—vainly, as it turned out—would interest Darryl Zanuck.

It was mid-April in Paris, and there were nightly parties at Jim and Gloria Jones' or Art and Ann Buchwald's, where it seemed that all the bright, successful Americans in town gathered. Irwin and Marian Shaw had taken Gertrude Vanderbilt Whitney's house in Neuilly. When Bill went to their party for Pieter Viertel, who was about to marry Deborah Kerr, he could not help recalling his army comrade with his lectures about patriotism and soldierly behavior. Now Zanuck was filming Shaw's screenplay *The Big Gamble,* and his recent novel, *Two Weeks in Another Town,* was being praised and compared with his famous *Young Lions.* Shaw had truly ended up with the spoils of war.

Bill was good at parties. He was able to project a sonorous, storytelling amiability, and he went to gatherings believing that they would cheer him or that he would meet someone interesting or useful. But at the same time, envy tortured him and cast more doubt on his hopes for a productive life in Europe.

Although he told himself that he must heal himself, must make his life in Europe work, he impulsively bought a ticket on the Russian ship *Maria Ulanova* and set out for the Soviet Union. On his seven-week trip, he was shepherded throughout by Intourist guides, who took him through a score of legendary cities. He attended their plays and operas and spoke to Soviet writers assembled at the writers' unions to greet him. In Moscow, he collected 24,000 rubles in royalties, enough for him to travel in style. He celebrated his fifty-second birthday and scolded a cultural attaché for the loss, twenty-five years earlier, of his "Moscow in Tears" manuscript.

Although denied Bitlis by travel restrictions, he did reach the Armenian capital of Yerevan, where Saroyans welcomed him, acquaintances embraced him tearfully, and speeches honored him. A local artist painted two portraits of him.

Returning to Paris on October 8, he found the rue Taitbout apartment chillier than ever, and its bathtub, with its feeble flow and dangerous butane water heater, no comfort to his pleasure-loving flesh nor his chronic aches and colds. All the old problems awaited him too, but they were immediately driven from his mind by a piece in the current *Esquire,* Budd Schulberg's "The Ordeal of William Saroyan."

Surely not malicious in intent, the piece began with Schulberg's admiration for Bill's early stories. He spoke warmly of their fellowship in Hollywood and Bill's triumph—while defying all playwriting rules—in *Time of Your Life.* However, the article did conclude that Saroyan's innocent world and his exceptional promise became a casualty of the war.

Bill was furious. He recalled how old Ben Schulberg had scorned the scripts he had written for him and how Budd had stuttered in trying to defend his father, and later how Budd had tried to indoctrinate him with political concern for the nation's poor. His resentment fastened on Schulberg's laughter, in which he had always heard a Jewish derision toward an Armenian rube from Fresno. Bill called his Paris lawyers, Coudert Freres, and told Gil Carter there he wanted to sue Schulberg and *Esquire* for a million dollars.

Although Zanuck had shunned Bill for months, indicating he had no further interest in his work, he did agree to an audience at his rue du Bac apartment. Juliette had left him, and he was in a somber mood. To Bill's appeal for money, his only suggestion was that he improve *The Paris Comedy.*

In spite of his indifference to political events, Bill found in John F. Kennedy's election a sense of new beginning. By mid-November he had begun an autobiographical account, which he called *Here Comes, There Goes Saroyan.* Although often despairing of it, he worked at this book for the rest of the year and sent it off to Hal Matson, hoping it would appeal to the *Post.*

He ushered in 1961 with a promise to make it the best year of his life. Within a week he had written a radio play, *The Death of Tallstone,* which he sent to Robert Saudek at Omnibus. Then came some very good news from Hal Matson. Herb Alexander, of Simon & Schuster, had offered $25,000 for *Here Comes, There Goes Saroyan.*

Saudek wrote that while he did not care for *Tallstone,* he wanted Bill to come to New York and narrate a program, *Fierce, Funny and Far-Out,* on the new playwrights. It would include Beckett, Ionesco, Albee, and himself. The fee would be $5,000 plus all expenses.

Arriving in New York on February 2, Bill rejoiced in the luxury of the St. Regis, met with Saudek, the director, Michael Ritchie, and the drama critic Walter Kerr, who was to share in the narrating. He took Aram and Lucy to dinner at the hotel and went on to see Edward Albee's *The American Dream,* of which he approved.

For a week he worked at the narration, and by the twelfth he was ready to tape the show, which included scenes from his own work as well as that of Albee, Beckett, and Ionesco. He admired the performances of Myron

McCormick and Barbara Baxley and left New York for San Francisco feeling that he had made a good job of it.

He spent the rest of February in California, where, with Cosette, he chose a black-pearl slab—inscribed "Takoohi Saroyan, Bitlis 1882–San Francisco 1950"—for their mother's grave. He intended to drive his nineteen-year-old Cadillac east but got only as far as Ross and Armen Bagdasarian's "mansion" in Beverly Hills. In trying to reach his cousin earlier, he had learned from his secretary that Ross's "The Chipmunk Song" had sold two and a half million copies, that he had gone to the desert in his new, air-conditioned convertible, that he was buying land in the Imperial Valley, and that he was rich for life.

Bill found that dinner at the Bagdasarians' was now served by two black servants. If that were not humiliation enough, his own car stubbornly refused to leave the Bagdasarian driveway. While getting a push from Ross's Jaguar, Bill decided to give his old Cadillac to John Fante's two sons.

Although he now dreaded Paris, Bill returned to rue Taitbout in late March and urged his Paris lawyers to bring some order to his paralyzing debt and tax problems. Gil Carter began by working out a settlement with the Aviation Club, but the taxes were far more critical. Even if last year's $80,000 income from Zanuck was exempt, he would owe a federal tax of about $27,500. In the course of these discussions, Bill met a new associate of the firm, thirty-two-year-old Harvard Law School graduate Aram Kevorkian. Bill liked and promptly befriended him.

John Crosby's column in the April 3, 1961, Paris *Tribune* dealt with American writers who sought the European refuge from income tax and cited William Saroyan as an example. When *Newsweek* phoned Bill for comment, he responded that he couldn't catch up on his taxes at home but was not catching up in Europe either, so he guessed he'd continue owing them forever. Before the month was out the IRS took due notice of this and announced the end of all such tax havens. Bill suspected that the change, sooner rather than later, would bring him home.

Bucklin Moon, Bill's editor at Simon & Schuster, turned up to take him to dinner and discuss September publication of *Here Comes, There Goes Saroyan*. Bill told him it was "a failure story," and, if nothing else, a departure from expectations. Rereading the book, Bill decided it was very bad and despite the shortness of time had to be revised. For a week he worked at the job and found that his best efforts had still left it a poor book. Moon's response to the revisions was no reprieve. He wrote from New York that they had "taken the guts" out of *Here Comes, There Goes Saroyan*.

On July 3 he read that Hemingway was dead of a gunshot wound in Ketchum, Idaho. His widow, Mary, maintained it was accidental, but Bill

Father and daughter running on Malibu Beach in the spring
of 1952. He was finding her a wholly delightful child.

thought otherwise. He remembered that Mary had been Noel Monks's wife,
then Irwin Shaw's girlfriend. He also recalled that Hemingway's father had
ended his life in the same way, and that it was young Ernest who had found
him. He wondered why Ernest had never written about it. The thought of
Hemingway as a suicide brought Bill an unexpected swell of admiration for
his old adversary.

This era of the late fifties, which had begun with Carol's departure for New
York, had brought Bill closer than ever to his children. Watching Aram at
play on the school grounds he saw him miss a pass, take a hard fall, and
swallow his tears. He worried that his small boy was trying to be a big one
and tried to assure him he needn't excel at sports. He worried about Lucy,

too. She often asked when Carol was coming home. At his evasiveness, she wept that she wanted her mama.

Aram's April 1955 report card shone with As and Bs. Lucy's Bs and Cs were thus doubly distressing to her. Bill took pains to encourage her about school and became an appreciative audience for her dressing up as their neighbor, Miss Farquhar, and serving him tea. They laughed together often, and Bill felt he had been able to assure Lucy that he loved her deeply, a matter about which she had had doubts for years. He suspected these doubts had been encouraged by both Carol and her mother. He certainly found Lucy more relaxed and more beautiful than ever.

As for Aram, there was now a fine understanding between them. He could accept his father's love for his sister. In spite of the sibling quarrels, which were half in fun yet quick and angry, Aram loved Lucy too. It was she who often provoked the conflicts and clearly enjoyed them.

Knowing how he would miss the children when they left for New York, he took them to Disneyland and gave Aram a .22 rifle along with an introductory session in target practice. When he had the good luck to see Aram hit a home run in a school game, he told him truthfully it was one of the great moments of his life. When they left, he was too depressed to work.

While in New York during that fall and winter he saw Aram and Lucy regularly. He took them to the horse show and skating in Central Park, and delighted them by arranging for their appearance as actors in one of his *Under the Sun* introductions. He was pleased to see Lucy dash off a school composition in fifteen minutes and sensed she had a swift talent for writing. Aram was otherwise. He struggled with an assignment on Mayor Wagner and seemed unable to grasp his subject. Bill saw without rancor how devoted both children were to their mother.

He was no part of their life at 970 Park Avenue. Carol, busy with her career, had hired a Scottish woman, Janet Law, to look after them. While Bill approved of Janet Law, he doubted she had brought his children the wanted tranquillity. In her care, Lucy had made a scene much like one of her mother's, and Aram had wept.

Having Thanksgiving dinner alone at the Russian Tea Room, Bill knew that his children were dining at Gloria's and that Carol was there, along with Gloria's new beau, Sidney Lumet. Lumet had played the boy, Johnny, in Bill's first Broadway play, *My Heart's in the Highlands*.

Bill thought of his children constantly, and hoped for their happiness even as they became strangers to him. They called on Christmas Day to say they were going out for dinner, so he prepared his own in his Great Northern kitchenette and dined alone.

He had them for a day during Christmas week. He took them to visit the Statue of Liberty, and saw in Aram a sorrow close to his own. He felt it was

Lucy appeared with her father in the Omnibus
educational project *Under the Sun.*

that sorrow that lit the boy's eyes with intelligence and humor. In the belief
that one day Aram would want to live with him, he told him he could
whenever he chose.

In July 1956, Aram and Lucy, accompanied by Janet Law, came to California to spend the summer with him. Bill and Cosette were at the airport
to meet them. Lucy was first to appear and came bounding from the plane
to leap into her father's arms. Aram and Janet Law were among the last, and
the boy was pale and quiet. He had been sick three times on the flight, and
Janet explained its cause as separation from his mother.

It was good, and a little saddening, to have his kids near again. At
Maroney Lane they enjoyed their neighborhood friends, and Bill did his
best to entertain them, taking them to Disneyland and Tijuana, making an
audience for Lucy's backyard circus, and arranging for Aram to go on a boy
scout trip to Catalina. He found Lucy, who tended to badger her brother,

Father and son enjoy a Yankee victory over the Dodgers in the
opening game of the World Series, Ebbetts Field, October 1956.

the tougher of the two. He worried about Aram's lack of skill in riding his
bike, which led to a bad spill.

Janet Law confided that Aram was a troublesome charge; he alternately
provoked and befriended her. Bill soon took Aram's side against her, and
believed Aram when he said she often spanked him and it was she, not his
mother, who had made him sick on the plane. Bill came to see Janet as a
chronic complainer and let his aversion keep him from Maroney. He told
Aram he must put up with Janet for a while longer but promised that it
would be his father, and not Martha Goetz, who would take him to this
year's World Series.

Bill kept his word, and, thanks to a commission from *Sports Illustrated,*
they were together in the stands to watch the Yankees beat the Dodgers.
During this visit to New York, Aram's paleness, and his doubt and confusion, worried Bill. Aram told his father how he disliked living under the
authority of his mother and his grandmother. Bill recognized his son's want

In June 1957, Bill took Aram and Lucy on a Grand Tour. Here in Venice,
they stayed at the Danielli and went to the Lido to gamble.

of a real home and assured him he could count on his father always. Then
he took Aram to Brooks Brothers for a suit.

When Bill returned to New York in May 1957, confident of a successful
return to Broadway with *The Cave Dwellers,* he visited Lucy's school, took
her and Carol to tea at the Plaza's Palm Court, took both children to see
O'Neill's *Moon for the Misbegotten,* and booked passage for himself and the
children on a Mediterranean cruise.

Bill, Aram, and Lucy sailed from New York on May 20 aboard the Italian
liner *Vulcania.* All three liked the ship, found the food excellent, and
enjoyed the traditional diversions of Ping-Pong, shuffleboard, and horse
races.

It was a stormy crossing, with most passengers seasick, but Aram happily
photographed shipboard life while Lucy painted pictures, made up stories,
and won third prize at the masquerade party. Both children were so excited
by it all they rarely slept before three in the morning.

Once past Gibraltar and into the Mediterranean, the *Vulcania*'s pool was
filled and the ship's orchestra tuned up for dancing. At the ball, Bill danced
with Lucy. On their shore excursions at Palermo, Naples, and the Greek
port of Patras, Aram shot rolls of film and planned a picture book to be
called *Faces of Europe.* Aram and his father argued about photography and
its place in the arts. At Venice, they left the ship for a week and stayed at the

In Monte Carlo, Bill, Lucy, and Aram dined on the terrace
of the Hotel de Paris and played craps, roulette, and
baccarat at the casino.

Hotel Danielli. In the course of it, Bill delivered a graduation speech at an
Armenian college and made daily trips to the Lido casino.

They took the Orient Express to Athens and there embarked for Spain,
where Bill hoped to settle for a month and do some writing. Bill's Spanish
publisher, Jose Janes, met them at Barcelona and drove them to a house in
Sitges which he had taken for them. The Saroyans did not like the house,
and they moved to a Barcelona hotel, where Bill tried to write a play.

Although the sightseeing and entertainments continued, family quarrels
increased. Lucy was content to spend an afternoon reading *Little Women,*
but Aram was moody, by turn elated and despairing. He grew custodial
about his book, retitling it *Kids Are Best.* When Bill offered suggestions,
Aram argued every point and ended by rejecting all his father's ideas.

In Paris, they spent a few days at the George V, time enough for visits to
the Louvre, the Eiffel Tower, and Bill's 1949 gambling haunt, the Opera
Club. Then they sailed for home on July 26, aboard the *Queen Elizabeth.* All
three were happy at the prospect of return, Bill especially, for he had only
enough money left to tip the stewards and pay cab fare from the pier.

As Bill made ready to depart for California, Aram told him he wanted to
leave his mother. Bill urged him to stick it out, and Lucy volunteered to be
helpful to her brother. As Bill boarded his train, it was she who wept.

On his return to New York three months later Bill found Aram newly resentful of his mother. He took both children to a Saturday matinee of *West Side Story.* During it, Aram seemed happy enough, but an hour after parting, the boy called from a drugstore to say he had quarreled with Carol and she had put him out of the house.

Telling Aram to come to the Royalton, Bill called Carol to find she was furious with him for poisoning Aram's mind against her. When he protested that he had said no more than the truth she forbade Bill to enter her house again. Bill took Aram to the evening performance of *The Cave Dwellers* and then sent him home, urging him to love his mother.

The next morning, Aram phoned to say there had been further trouble. Then Carol's lawyer, Arnold Krakower, phoned to propose that Aram, who was too unruly with his mother, live with his father. Bill was cool to the idea, and Krakower said he would speak to Pincus Berner about it. Now Berner called to recommend improvement in Aram's manners toward his mother, that at least he should leave her notes telling her his whereabouts. Bill agreed, but dismissed the idea of taking custody of the boy. He must keep after his work. Later in the week he urged both Berner and Paul Gitlin not to let Krakower push them around.

By the end of November, Aram seemed reconciled to life on Ninety-third Street. He was a reluctant student at Trinity School on West Ninety-first Street but an eager apprentice at the studio of Carol's friend Richard Avedon. He was fascinated by photography and understandably proud of a photo essay of his which was to appear in *Seventeen.*

At Trinity, Aram's principal dreads were algebra and history. He saw no sense to their study, since he could become famous without them. Bill recognized himself in Aram's response to the schoolroom, but he urged him to make good grades and then to quit in February if he could bear no more of it. Aram too felt he should see the school year through.

Lucy, who was doing well at Dalton, was a joy to him. He saw her as beautiful and tough-minded, much as her mother had been. Bill learned that Richard Avedon had photographed eleven-year-old Lucy and selected her, for a feature in *Town & Country,* as one of the eight most beautiful "women" in the world. Lucy told her father that the most desirable boy at Dalton loved her, and she teased Aram about the nude-girl pictures she had found in his schoolbook. Bill observed that it was getting to be the time of sex for them, and gave them his blessing.

As Christmas approached, Bill's concern about Aram grew. When the children visited him at the Royalton, Aram hiccupped and sobbed about the misery of his life, while Lucy passed her father a note saying Aram was like this all the time. Bill took them Christmas shopping, buying Aram the sneakers he wanted and Lucy a camel-hair coat at Saks. Lucy returned six of the twelve dollar bills he gave her, asking him to buy her a surprise. They went on to the theater and a cheerful dinner at the Blue Ribbon.

Since the children were to spend Christmas Day at Gloria Stokowski's, Bill walked through the city. When he spoke to an unhappy Aram, he learned that his mother had given him a bible in hopes it would be useful at school.

It was now Carol's plan that Aram be sent off to a boarding school, and she had consulted Trinity's headmaster, Hugh Riddleberger, about it. Thus, early in 1958, with Bill back in California, Riddleberger wrote him about his concern over Aram's inability to apply himself. His record would make entrance into any good boarding school difficult. He regretted that Bill had not called him when he was in the East.

Bill replied that while it was his own wish that Aram enjoy a sound schooling and go on to a good university, Aram felt otherwise. He believed that schools squashed individuality and turned out a standardized product. Only in Richard Avedon's studio had he found a goal worth pursuing. Bill admitted that quarrelsome parents had been no help to Aram's maturing, but still he must supply his own motivation. As to destinations, he liked Haverford, which had been recommended to him by his friend Christopher Morley.

Riddleberger replied in mid-March that Aram's grades continued to be miserable, that he had no desire to learn, and that most schools would surely turn him down. He had talked further with Carol about him, and it was clear some discipline was needed in the boy's life. He was willing to supply it, but not without both parents agreeing to the details. If they could not present him with a united front he wanted no part in Aram's education. Bill concurred, urging him to help in getting Aram into a good boarding school. Returning from his world tour in June 1958, Bill phoned Ninety-third Street to find that Aram had been admitted to Trinity-Pawling for the fall, and that both children were ready to leave with him for a summer in California.

The train trip with Aram and Lucy was a joy. They played word games and told stories the whole way and on June 10 arrived at Maroney Lane, where Cosette welcomed them to an immaculate house.

Bill delighted Lucy with a new bike and Aram with a driving lesson, but clouds soon arrived in the form of Aram's year-end reports from Trinity. His Civics teacher described him as a sensitive boy who had been granted so much freedom he did not know how to discipline himself nor respond to discipline. He could not direct his attention to anything that failed to appeal to him.

His adviser wrote that Aram was nearly impervious to advice. He would agree about his problems but do nothing about them. He questioned the school's standards and goals, then escaped into a fantasy world. His interest in photography was part of his dream structure. When Bill urged Aram to beware of self-deception, so like his mother's, and to get after the books on his summer reading list so as to make a fresh start at Trinity-Pawling in September, he found his son naggingly argumentative.

In mid-July Bill decided they would all benefit from a trip to San Francisco. They spent several weeks there at Fifteenth Avenue, during which Bill tried in vain to start on a play called *The Animals.*

On the return journey, they made stops at Mihran Saroyan's, in Fresno, and the Bagdasarians', in Selma. Lucy sat with Cosette in the back while Aram shared the front seat with his father. The weather was hot. Aram grew uncomfortable and progressively bored with scenery and conversation, so that his father became angry at him. Bill cursed him furiously, then proceeded to do the same to his mother's friends whom Aram particularly admired—Jones Harris, Jones's mother, Ruth Gordon, Jose Quintero, and, finally, Richard Avedon—people whom he felt had stolen Aram away from his potential and made of him a self-deceiving dilettante. When Bill's anger was spent, the car was silent, and it stayed so until it reached Pacific Palisades, when Aram turned to his father and said that he was afraid he was going to throw up. Bill braked, let Aram out of the car, and watched as Aram threw up at the roadside.

For several days, Bill was ashamed of his own behavior and miserable about its effect on Aram. But as the summer drew to an end, he felt that in spite of its flare-ups and quarrels it had been a fine one. He wanted to see more of his children and felt he should live near them. At the end of October, Bill returned to New York from his first meeting with the Avala Film Agency, in Belgrade. Carol was leaving for tryouts of *The Cold Wind and the Warm,* and in her absence he could stay at the Ninety-third Street apartment.

He was delighted to be parental with Lucy, visiting her at school, nursing her through a cold, taking her to the Bronx Zoo. The news of Aram was astonishing. Headmaster Matthew Dann, at Trinity-Pawling, reported that the boy's work was close to perfect. He had achieved a 95 in General Science and the honor roll in Latin, and stood fourth in a class of forty-four. He had given a good account of himself on the soccer field as well. On a Sunday, Bill and Lucy visited Pawling by train, saw Aram's room, and took him out for a congratulatory lunch.

Bill made the decision to quit California for Europe a few months later, over the Christmas holidays, and so, in mid-January 1959, he was back in New York, able to hear Lucy read her story "Old Posey" in the Dalton Theatre. When Lucy asked why he had not applauded, he told her he had been touched by her performance but didn't think applause fitting. The next day, he delighted her with the gift of a platinum and diamond heart locket.

In spite of his dazzling record at Trinity-Pawling, Aram did not like the school. He thought the teachers were boring second-raters, unsympathetic to his ideas of becoming somebody. He told his father he wanted to return to New York the following year and go to an art and music school. When Bill spoke of moving to Europe, Aram thought he would like a school there.

When Bill proposed Switzerland to Lucy, she said that both Carol and Gloria had urged her against school there, but she quickly added that she didn't want to get involved in the fight between her parents. It was too hard for her to choose. Bill said whatever she did the following year would be fine with him, but he hoped it would be in Europe.

That same summer, in the wake of his Avala and Zanuck adventures, Bill rented an apartment at 171 Victor Hugo in Paris and invited Aram and Lucy for a summer visit. They were to arrive on June 14, but their flight was delayed en route and he grew anxious about them. With no news at three in the morning, he wept with loneliness and frustration.

When they did turn up, a day late, he was overjoyed to see them, and, at Lucy's request, he cheerfully trimmed his great mustache. He bought them sunglasses and a French-English dictionary, and took them walking in the Bois and to see the Jean Arp and Stackpole shows. Irma, the Yugoslav maid, prepared their meals, and in the evenings they went to the movies or played poker.

Bill gave some of each summer day to the children. He took them to the Fourth of July garden party at the U.S. embassy and to the flea market, where he bought Lucy a red velvet music box. They went to see Marcel Marceau and to Prunier's for dinner.

In the art galleries, Aram was a collector, taken first with a Picasso poster at $700 then settling for a $150 drawing by the master. When they went to the races at Le Tremblay Bill lost 100,000 francs while Aram tripled the 8,000 francs his father had given him. Aram, also eager for publication, discovered the *Paris Review* office at 16 rue Vernet and on July 5 hopefully dropped off some drawings and descriptive text. When he stopped by a few days later to be told his drawings were not wanted, he was crushed.

By the end of July, Aram was clearly bored and increasingly troublesome to his father. Both children complained that he was not doing enough to entertain them, and there was growing discord in the household. Irma was openly unhappy with the Americans' behavior, and although Bill tried to fire her she refused to leave. It was Lucy who managed to dismiss Irma and grudgingly undertook her chores of shopping and washing the dishes.

Even his adored Lucy annoyed Bill with her talk of Hollywood and ambition to be famous there. When she trimmed her golden hair to fit these aspirations he was angry with her. When he spoke with both children about returning to him, they told him candidly that they no longer had any interest in living or going to school in Europe.

Midway through their visit, Bill intercepted a telegram to them from Carol, announcing that she and Walter Matthau had married. He was stunned. Lucy would always remember the shock in her father's face and how his body seemed paralyzed by the news. She felt she had seen her father's heart break.

He did accept ruefully that both his children were closer to their mother than they were to him, in spirit and perhaps everything else. Depressed by being broke, unlucky at the cards, and ignored by Zanuck, it seemed just as well.

Early in 1961, after a quarrel with Carol over child support and her borrowing money on the Maroney house, Bill was delighted by a letter from Aram saying that when school was out in June he would like to visit him in Paris.

He sent Aram $500 for his plane ticket and Lucy $1,000 for her summer on a Montana dude ranch. A second letter from Aram told of his writing ambitions and of *The Ride*, a movie he hoped to make about three boys crossing New Mexico in an old car. With brightest hopes for a summer of companionship with Aram, Bill planned their tour of Mediterranean cities and readied the apartment to receive him. He bought a pianola, arranged Aram's art materials, and cleaned and tidied the place thoroughly.

On June 15, Bill joyfully welcomed Aram at Orly and was only slightly disappointed that Aram scarcely noticed his preparations. For a day in Paris, they talked and ate happily together. Bill was less than pleased to hear about Aram's dining with his grandmother and doing errands for his mother and aunt. He was also concerned to find him biting his nails and complaining of constipation. However, Aram was eager for summer adventure, and together they set off enthusiastically in "the red racer."

They drove south toward Bordeaux, visiting the chateaux and cathedrals along their way, and then, through the Basque coast, to Spain. They saw the cave paintings at Altamira, passed through Portugal, dining at fine restaurants, staying at the best hotels, telling jokes, and having fun. In Lisbon, while Bill and Aram waited for a parade to pass, Bill had sought some idea of the nature of his son's anger. He decided it was about everything—youth, sex, parents, school, the world, fear, desire.

Near Cadiz, Bill encouraged Aram to drive the red racer, which he did proudly for forty miles. Then, on June 26, while they were having dinner in Seville, Bill spoke disparagingly of Carol, her new husband, and her insistent demands for money. To his surprise, Aram protested furiously. He told his father that it was he, not his mother, who was at fault. Bill was stricken by this disloyalty. In Aram's swift and savage defense of his mother and Walter Matthau, he found only insult.

Aram was inconsolable for the rest of the night and in the morning told his father that he now wanted to return to New York. They drove in silence to Malaga, where Bill bought him a plane ticket to Madrid and another on TWA the next day to New York. In parting, he gave Aram his watch and a 1907 $20 gold piece for good luck. As Bill drove on alone toward Barcelona, he wept bitterly over one of the saddest days of his life. His eighteen-year-old son had hurt him so deeply with his defense of his mother and showed no concern for Bill's own predicament.

Throughout the rest of his return journey, he repeatedly burst into tears but consoled himself with the thought that he and Aram were much alike, that the difference between them lay in the hardship of his own childhood. He had worked hard since his eighth year. He felt that in time Aram would come to a more balanced concern for him. Meanwhile, he asked God's love and protection for him.

Arriving at rue Taitbout, he looked through his mail for a telegram from Aram, but there was none, and he told himself to accept the fact that the boy preferred being with his mother and her husband. So long as the boy was all right, let him stay away.

When a card from Lucy arrived saying that at first she was surprised at Aram's return but less so in recalling the arguments of two summers ago and how it was she who patched them up, it seemed he had lost them both. They were not Saroyans. Lucy was like her mother and her grandmother in many ways. There was a triviality about her that puzzled him.

A letter from Aram came at last, enclosing snapshots of Lucy, reporting that he was living on West End Avenue, taking typing lessons, and finding the problem of girls difficult. No girl he knew lived up to the promise of perfection which he bestowed on her.

Of course not, Bill agreed, and he wrote Aram in reply that he loved him and if Aram ever needed anything, and he could provide it, he would. In wishing him and Lucy good luck, it occurred to him that this was really all he had to offer.

In April, he had had an irresistible invitation from Purdue University to teach playwriting in the fall semester. He would be paid $5,000 and be able to present a new Saroyan play. Although he was not due there until mid-September, he was sick of Paris and ready to spend the rest of the summer touring the United States. He booked passage for himself and the red racer to Canada and set about cleaning up his affairs. Then, on July 24, he sailed on the *Homeric* for Montreal, with the hope that he could persuade Lucy to leave her Montana ranch a week early and drive on to California with him.

XVI

WHITELANDS HOUSE

1961–1968

As soon as the red racer was unloaded onto the dock at Montreal, Bill set out on the 2,500-mile drive across Canada to see his worrisome but beloved daughter. The report on Lucy's year at Dalton had been excellent, and he believed her only hazard lay in losing interest and in belittling her real abilities.

In spite of hundred-degree heat, he made the trip in four days, arriving at Lucy's M Lazy V Ranch, near Marion, Montana, on August 2, 1961. Lucy came running to meet him and hurtled into his arms. She took him to meet the ranch owners, Norman Hansen and his wife, to the bunkhouse to meet her friends—in particular the nineteen-year-old wrangler Jerry, with whom she confessed to be in love—and, finally, her horse.

When this was done and he saw her so glowing with happiness, there was no question of persuading her to join him, nor could he imagine staying to share in a part of Lucy's life that was so entirely her own. After a visit of only two hours, he resumed his journey toward San Francisco, telling himself that in the time of youth, a father can be a nuisance.

He did not admit that he lacked the flexibility and grace to cast off his own role in order to enter Lucy's diverging one, even though he could do so adroitly in fiction. In *Mama I Love You* and the story "Gaston," he drops his fatherly baggage to enter into a daughterly world, bringing understanding and the cap and bells of his imagination to prove himself at home there.

Bill returned to New York on the day in early September when both Aram and Lucy were starting school, but he made no plan to see them. However, as he walked along Fifth Avenue, his son's startled voice called out to him. He went along with Aram while he bought a paint set for his mother's birthday and then to visit Aram's West End Avenue apartment and to meet his friend Jerry Risley.

When Bill asked Aram to join him for dinner with his friends Zareh and Peter Sourian, he was astonished by Aram's refusal. Aram explained he would rather watch Walter Matthau on television. His father found that unforgivable, but before his departure for Purdue, he took both children to the Brass Rail for a farewell dinner, and they agreed to visit him at the university over their Thanksgiving holidays.

Bill's experience as a university faculty member began on September 17. His sponsor, Ross Smith, met him in Chicago, drove him to Lafayette, Indiana, and saw him to his basement apartment. Smith and his wife, Dorothy, took him on to dinner and a reception at the house of the university president, Fred Hovde.

The next day, he was shown his office, interviewed by the *Lafayette Journal Courier,* and introduced to his fellow instructors. After a staff meeting he delivered a first lecture to theater students and then met his playwriting class. He set his nineteen students to dramatizing "The Prodigal Son" and was pleased with the results. He enjoyed the departmental play productions, the faculty parties at which he was the celebrated guest, and the football pep rallies. He applied for an Indiana driver's license, rented a 1952 Chevrolet, and explored the countryside.

He decided that his play for Purdue would be about learning, the formal education he had rejected forty years earlier. The setting would be the campus and its Wabash riverbank, and it would be outrageous and wild.

Although he had never dealt with racial issues, he chose for a principal character an intelligent black boy. There is a white girl to whom he is attracted and who must choose her way of life. There is also a brilliant science professor. The play would deal with its author's belief that after twenty-one years of schooling, students still knew nothing. He finished it in three days and called it *Trash Along the Wabash.* On hearing that President Hovde disapproved of the title, he changed it to *High Time Along the Wabash.*

At the end of October, he was freed of his classes in order to give all his time to casting and directing *Wabash* for a December 1 opening. He took a dislike to the set design and to his student actors, who tended to turn up late or not at all for rehearsals. Once onstage, they performed so ineptly he suspected a departmental conspiracy against the play. His complaints to Ross Smith brought little improvement. However, he kept on with his preparations through November, rewriting the play and adding a one-act curtain-raiser, *A Nice Day for a Picnic.* By mid-month he felt contempt for both the play and its cast but told himself there would be a performance on opening night.

When Aram and Lucy arrived for Thanksgiving, he met them at Union Station in Chicago. They celebrated the holiday at the Drake Hotel there and saw a matinee of *Bye Bye Birdie* and an evening performance of Ten-

At Purdue in the fall of 1961, Bill wrote, cast, and directed
a play in which he dealt with matters of education
and race. Its final title was *High Time Along the Wabash.*

nessee Williams's *Night of the Iguana.* On Friday, Aram was interviewed for admission to the University of Chicago. Bill bought Lucy a string of cultured pearls at the hotel jewelry shop, and in the afternoon all three drove to Lafayette in Bill's rented Chevrolet. The car's engine startled them with frequent reports like pistol shots.

On Saturday night, the children saw and approved a run-through of both *Wabash* and *A Nice Day for a Picnic.* When they left for New York on Sunday, Bill was lonely without them.

The critical day of December 1 began ominously for Bill, with the appearance in his office door of three men in dark suits. One introduced himself as a U.S. marshal and served him a summons for a $25,000 tax delinquency. He had twenty days in which to reply. That evening, before the Loeb Theatre's curtain rose on *High Time Along the Wabash,* Bill spoke to his cast, telling its members that he expected them to do their best.

The first-night audience of eleven hundred saw the opening riverbank scene of *Wabash,* in which the professor, bound hand and foot, is flogged by the girl. As a bystander, the boy hears the professor's pleas of innocence to some nameless, but clearly sexual, wrongdoing.

In this and successive scenes all three characters talk of male and female roles, the work they will do, the boy's thwarted love for the girl, and, finally, an acceptance of their separate lives. The play is resolved around the belief that this acceptance is a self-fulfillment, and it closes in a parade of animals with Adam, Eve, and their children bringing up the rear.

Thus, Saroyan's solution to the racial conflict he raised so boldly was simply to live with it. The boy resigns himself to being black. Bill had no inclination to explore the possibility that the boy might feel otherwise.

To his surprise, the actors had indeed done their best. It seemed that new magic had taken hold and worked straight through both plays. There had been laughter and applause. There was no question but that *Wabash* was a hit.

Bill celebrated with the cast and crew and, over the next few days, said his good-byes and picked up his last $1,600 check. Departing on December 9, he declared that his fall in Indiana had been a good adventure.

His publisher had persuaded Bill to a change in title and he was now looking forward to the January 1962 appearance of *Here Comes, There Goes You Know Who.* His new optimism came from the belief that he had written a frank confessional. Childhood recollection was there, as was Saroyan whimsy, the ironic cover for his bitterness. Alienation was also there. He admitted to estrangement from his family, his acquaintances, his country, and his times. His central paradox was there, that he felt as great as any man alive, yet knew he was nothing.

He recognized his gambling as a madness but rationalized it as a motivation to write. He had taken to writing to escape from meaninglessness, only to find that there *was* no meaning. He had turned his back on Broadway but wrote new plays that, though not yet produced, performed, or witnessed, were the real American theater. The book was about failure, loss of purpose, and preoccupation with death.

On reading the galleys he thought it a fine, seriocomic book and perhaps a popular one that might tempt the Book-of-the-Month Club. He thought that henceforth he might confine himself to autobiography.

He returned to Paris on January 9, 1962, and it was here he had first news of how the book would fare. In the *Herald Tribune,* Brooks Atkinson described a "grab-bag" of a book written as though the author were shooting dice and unlucky throughout. Saroyan had managed to make his autobiography uninteresting. In the *Times,* Charles Poore alluded to Steinbeck and called the new Saroyan "the Gripes of Wrath."

Time magazine, his constant adversary, mourned the loss of his "wonderfully hammy love for humanity," and noted a new "peevishness." The reviewer granted Saroyan a modest but lasting place in literature in spite of "the I of his boundless ego," and said that "whenever he gets involved with issues or ideas [he] falls flatter than Bagh-arch, the Armenian flat bread." He concluded that "with a lover like this, humanity needs no enemy."

Here Comes, There Goes You Know Who had flopped and left Bill angry, confused, and suffering a major crisis of spirit. He was deeply in debt, not writing, and lonely. He felt estranged from his children. He supposed that they did love him, or at least the image of a father, but it was never in a way that was any use or comfort to him. In a pinch, they were always on their mother's side.

Bill's depression manifested itself in a new paroxysm of gambling. He went each night to the Aviation Club and within two weeks of his return to Paris had lost $7,500. If ever there was a gambling fool, a man addicted to risking his precious serenity and future on the turn of a playing card, it was William Saroyan. Gambling was the sweetest, most dreadful seduction he knew.

When his debt to the Aviation reached $20,000, he turned for help to his new publisher in New York. Hoping for a $15,000 advance on a new book, he phoned Herb Alexander and learned more hard truth: in spite of early enthusiasm for *Here Comes,* it was not selling. Alexander no longer had an interest in publishing its sequel.

This compounded Bill's anger with Hal Matson, whom he held responsible for his investing the $25,000 *Here Comes* advance in Pocket Books only to see it tumble to a fraction of the purchase price. Nevertheless, he phoned Matson for help and found him doubtful he could find anyone willing to advance money on a Saroyan book or play.

Bill urged him to sell half of his Pocket Books shares and send him the money. Awaiting its arrival, he returned to the Aviation, where Peretti, the manager, greeted him with an accusatory rubbing of fingers. Bill responded by losing more. He gambled on through March and April, borrowing from other players, borrowing from the casinos, borrowing from his friend Aram Kevorkian, draining his last-ditch account at Pollinger's, and, finally, humiliatingly, borrowing $10,000 from the prospering Ross Bagdasarian in Beverly Hills.

At fifty-three, on the threshold of the 1960s, that dynamic era of sexual and social revolution, his most recent stage offerings were *Lily Dafon; Sam, the Highest Jumper;* and *High Time Along the Wabash.* Yet he continued to scorn his rivals. He viewed Tennessee Williams as a fellow artist who was simply a better businessman. He added Inge and Albee to his list of competitive playwrights who, as homosexuals, could only pretend knowledge of both sexes.

Saroyan's imagination, his once sure instinct for the common man's plight, and buoyant humor had atrophied. He had failed to grow in understanding of the world or in his craft since his investiture a quarter century earlier.

But he could hear only the voice of his inner imperative urging him on. For the rest of the decade he would launch new plays with a springboard leap that soon beached him. A dozen such failures did not shake his belief that a triumphal return to Broadway was possible and that it would avenge all the slights of an indifferent world.

Nor did disappointment in *Here Comes* alter his commitment to autobiography. Looking backward was what he now did best. He could recall his childhood, even the critical years at the Fred Finch orphanage, with less pain and more honesty than ever before.

As autobiographer he had published *Bicycle Rider* in 1952 and *Here Comes, There Goes You Know Who* in 1961. These would be followed by eight more, autobiographical works all marked by frank insights and the confident, bemused narrative voice, which retained enough of its original spell to seize even an indolent reader's attention. He had known a multitude of major figures in the theater, movie, and writing worlds and delighted in deflating their egos.

But he brought to these works a careless, meandering structure and a garrulousness that had come with age, so each of the ten memoirs was published under new auspices. Nevertheless, they gave him a late-life reputation for reminiscence, and he kept his book audience by becoming what he had tried to escape, an ethnic-American writer.

As for Saroyan the novelist, the year 1962 was particularly gloomy, for he watched the Nobel Prize he coveted go to his once scorned fellow Californian John Steinbeck. Yet he was no less desirous of producing a winner himself. There would be two more Saroyan novels.

Since quitting Ernst, Cane and Berner, Bill had done without a New York attorney, but when Paul Gitlin of that firm called to report the death of Pincus Berner, Bill took the opportunity to ask agenting advice. Gitlin offered to market the two books Bill had ready to show, one of which was the novel *Boys and Girls Together,* the other the memoir *Not Dying.*

While at first Gitlin met wide resistance to publishing Saroyan, in July 1962 he found that William Jovanovich, Harcourt, Brace and World's new head, wanted to see Saroyan return to the Harcourt list. Jovanovich was ready to publish both books, offering an advance of $5,000 and a 15 percent royalty for each.

From Gitlin, Bill learned that Jovanovich was the son of a Montenegrin miner, and had been born in a tent during a long, Colorado mining strike. After twenty-five years as a rising educational salesman and administrator at Harcourt, he had overwhelmed all rivals to make the firm his own. His

William Jovanovich, the dynamic educational publisher,
became head of Harcourt Brace in 1955 and added his
name to those of its founders. He wanted Saroyan back
on the firm's list.

enthusiasm for Saroyan—as much a shared ethnic-Americanness as awareness of Bill's glory days—was surely to be cultivated.

In September, the forty-four-year-old Jovanovich, a tall, authoritative
man, who was to influence Bill as much as any publisher, welcomed him to
his office. The two books were already scheduled for 1963, and he stood
ready for more. He assigned him the editor Julian Muller and took him to
lunch at the Union League Club, where he spoke proudly of his Polish
mother and of his two sons, Stefan and Peter.

Julian Muller decided that the novel, *Boys and Girls Together,* was more
ready and would be the first of the books to appear. It was, in essence, Bill's
bitter recollection of the year 1946, which he had spent with Carol and the
children in the Taraval Street duplex. Its story is that of a middle-aged writer
and gambling man, down on his luck and unhappy with a troublesome
young wife. She complains of her loneliness and the loss of her youth and
beauty in this clerk's house. She wants better clothes, better times. She hates
his family as he does hers. He sees her as ugly, a nag, ignorant, and dirty, and
their drinking and quarreling keeps him from writing. The climax comes at

Bill painted abstractions as swiftly and confidently as he wrote, dating each work and preserving it. Here he stands with one he made in 1969.

a party, when the death of an elderly guest, unmistakably modeled on Leopold Stokowski, scarcely interrupts the revels.

As publication, in March 1963, approached, Bill was pleased that the *Saturday Evening Post* bought four chapters, but he heard little from Harcourt. Virginia Kirkus's gloomy forecast for the book explained the silence. When Bill saw a first copy of the book he shared her pessimism, disliking his jacket photo and his facetious dedication.

The reviews were hostile. They identified its hero as the author himself in a dour, postwar mood and found he had come a long, unhappy way from the gifted, exuberant, daring young man of the 1930s. Most reviewers found that despite redeeming moments, this was trivial, tasteless work, unworthy of the old pro.

The *Atlantic*'s reviewer declared that the book grated like a phonograph record stuck in one groove and noted that the Saroyan genius was for theater and short stories; he had yet to write a satisfactory novel. The British reviews were, if anything, worse. The *London Times* described it as "weary, narcissistic, self-absorbtion," and the *Observer*'s reviewer wrote that the book had made him "want, as Saroyan himself might put it, to upchuck."

Like so many of Bill's representatives, Paul Gitlin was proving resourceful and tireless. In April 1963 he brought Bill together with the Curtis Publishing nabobs for lunch, and he then pressed the *Saturday Evening Post* to make Bill a contract writer. Although Bill failed the test of an assignment on baseball, Gitlin prevailed. The *Post* agreed to take him on as a contributing writer. He would receive an annual $12,000 in monthly installments against the stories and articles he would provide over the year.

This would be especially fortunate, since the guarantee would fall under his European-resident tax exemption. The *Post* editors would propose article subjects and on acceptance pay $2,000 for them.

When Bill saw an early copy of his memoir, *Not Dying*, with twenty-six of his own abstract line drawings, he liked the book and believed that when it appeared in September it would restore his authorial luster. It was an account of his fiftieth summer, that of 1959, when Aram and Lucy had visited him in Paris. The title was his response to an interviewer's question. How had he gotten so old?

Although he had failed to give *Not Dying* a structure, its meandering way touched such critical episodes in his writing life as its boyhood beginning, the influence of Stanley Rose, identification with Dostoevsky through gambling, and his final visit with George Jean Nathan. It also provided his views on marriage, divorce, parenting, art, writing, success, and failure.

The Kirkus forecast saw more vitality in this book than in his recent fiction, and Bill thought the signs were hopeful. But when *Not Dying* was published, in September, the major reviews were unkind. They found Saroyan's thoughts on writing of interest, but the rest was trivial and repetitious. Dore Schary, in the *Tribune*, wished Saroyan hadn't taken his readers for granted, for what the book revealed was "a talented man who is losing his rich zest for living."

Home in San Francisco during the summer of 1963, Bill clung to his fraying hopes of recognition as a novelist. With the approach of his fifty-fifth birthday, he brought out an old reject, the work he had variously titled *The Immigrant's Son*, *Old Nose*, and *California Poppy Field*. In its account of his own professional and marital crises he saw new possibility.

The novel portrayed Bill's experiences in the fall of 1955. He was Yep Muscat, a writer whose success lies behind him; he is trying to pay off his tax indebtedness by manipulating some New York agents and producers. Among the recognizable portraits were those of Aram and Lucy, Carol in her *Rock Hunter* role, George Abbott, and Robert Saudek. Bill set to work revising his novel, renamed it *One Day in the Afternoon of the World*, and sent it off to Harcourt.

The year 1964 began well for him. A piece on Dylan Thomas was taken by the *Post*, and a call to Jovanovich assured him that Harcourt would publish *One Day in the Afternoon of the World* in May and looked forward to a story collection for the fall.

In March, awaiting the novel's appearance, Bill set off for Europe and another try at pilgrimage to his ancestral town of Bitlis. He paused in New York, hoping for good news about the forthcoming novel. There had been no first serial and little trade interest in *One Day in the Afternoon of the World,* so Jovanovich had faint cheer to offer. When Bill proposed that Harcourt publish a Saroyan bibliography, the Jovanovich response was glacial. Nor had he only imagined that Jovanovich's admiration was cooling. Just before sailing, Bill found that Harcourt's offer for his new story collection, *After Thirty Years: The Daring Young Man on the Flying Trapeze,* set a royalty rate of only 7½ percent.

He told Jovanovich that if he were unwilling to pay a straight 15 percent, he should return the manuscript. Jovanovich replied that he would cable his decision to Bill on board the ship. The Jovanovich cable arrived when Bill reached Naples. It was a refusal to alter the royalty, and Bill told himself that was good; he would rather go unpublished than accept cheap terms.

In Istanbul he inquired about reaching Bitlis, applied for the necessary permits, and found three Armenian companions with a car who were willing to make the seven-hundred-mile trip across Turkey. They set off on May 9, driving through steady rain to Ankara, Trabzon, and Erzurum in Armenia.

After a pause at Lake Van they proceeded through occasional hail and snowstorms, arriving in Bitlis on May 16. Bill was exultant. After fifty-five years of imagining it he had reached the mythic city of his origins and found it even grander than in his dream. The town overlooked a harbor of Lake Van and was surrounded by highlands with snowy peaks. Cold streams rushed down to its meadows. Although the people were Turks, they wore bright costumes, and he saw goodness shining from their faces.

With the mayor of Bitlis he visited the sites of former Saroyan houses and the top of Alexander's citadel, where Bill and the mayor sprawled in the noonday sun. He was disappointed to find that Bitlis's only Armenian was an old man who wished to leave. Bill too found no reason to tarry and left after only a few hours.

By the first of June he was back in Paris to be greeted by some favorable reviews of *One Day in the Afternoon of the World.* The book was described as hilarious on the front page of the *Chicago Tribune,* and the fussy *New Yorker* found that when he wrote about Manhattan as he had here, Saroyan was truly himself.

But the naysayers carried the day. They found Yep Muscat's dilemma—his failure at marriage and loss of fame—was not resolved nor even probed but simply lost in an enthusiasm for baseball, vaudeville, and assurances that love is the answer to life's questions. Yep had been denied any self-analysis. Beneath a surface jauntiness lay only his despair. *One Day* was more of Saroyan's grievance against a perfidious world.

After many years of trying, Bill reached his ancestral
town of Bitlis in May 1964.

Now, at fifty-six, Bill Saroyan could reflect on his two late-career novels
and know he had brought them his several undiminished gifts—the ear, the
near-perfect pitch for spoken language, and the bemused, tolerant narrative
voice—yet neither *Boys and Girls* nor *One Day* had become the career-
crowning work of which he had thought himself capable.

He had not dodged the dark, central anguish of his life, which he
believed would be the source of a big novel. He had embraced the twin
essences of his unhappiness. His failure to love a woman, to make a life and
family with her, had been the core of *Boys and Girls,* just as the loss of his
stunning early confidence and triumph as a writer had fueled *One Day in
the Afternoon of the World.*

Both were strong tides, and they might have served him better had he
been able to turn them to some kind of wisdom. The recall of painful experience brought forth only his resentment. The positive tropism that he had
been able to invoke in short fiction failed him in the long. Only bitterness,
loss, and growing old shone through. He would not have that novelist's
crown.

As a short-story writer, it was otherwise. Early in 1964, while Bill was in
San Francisco revising *One Day,* his enthusiasm for short fiction rallied. In a
surge of energy and purpose, he wrote a parade of short stories. As in the

springtime of his career, he could produce one in two hours, and he did this daily for a full month. They included "The Literary Life," "The Celebrated Jumping State of California," "The Dostoevsky Story," "I Don't Get It," "The Brigadier General," and "Don't Laugh Unless It's Funny." Saroyan was born again.

He wrote more than sixty stories in the decade, and they brought him an entirely new readership in the national magazines the *Saturday Evening Post, Ladies' Home Journal, McCall's,* the *Atlantic, Harper's, Playboy,* and *The New Yorker.* His emotional-surge method still functioned dependably, and many of his new stories were as good or better than those that had made his reputation in the 1930s. They *had* benefited from his life experience.

The early stories had lacked plot and any character but his own. They had made up for that lack with an outsider's indignation and an intoxicating joy in being alive. The stories he wrote now, in his fifties, generated energy out of family tensions, and he gave them characters, dramatic situations, even happy endings. He was able to preserve the unique Saroyan voice, so sure of its inherited Old World wisdom and its gift of irony and laughter.

"What a World, Said the Bicycle Rider," which the *Post* published in 1962, portrays a man's jealousy provoked by a young wife and how he tries to preserve the innocent world of their children from her betrayal. It is well told and touching, despite its restoring of the now penitent wife for a final upbeat.

"Cowards," published by *Harper's* in 1974, tells how an Armenian boy who dodges the draft is judged to be more hero than coward. "Madness in the Family," a *Post* story of 1967, told how Bashmanians had always been afflicted with periods of lunacy and how the illness came to the New World in the madness of Vorotan Bashmanian. It is simply that the transplanted family is still above ground. Once old Varujan, the gunsmith, dies and is buried at Ararat, Vorotan is cured.

"Gaston" (1961), "Young Lady from Perth" (1961), "Picnic Time" (1964), "Twenty Is the Greatest" (1964), "Lord Chugger of Cheer" (1964), "How to Choose a Wife" (1964), "The Duel" (1964), and "Cowards" (1966) are all stories in which Saroyan was able to perform the old magic of turning the painful experience of his own childhood, or that of his children, into affirmation.

The poignance of his estrangement from Carol and the resulting divided loyalty of the children powers the best of these stories. If he sentimentalizes it by magically restoring the truant wife in "Bicycle Rider," he certainly does not in "Gaston," where the six-year-old heroine, although bewitched by a loving, irresponsible father, chooses to return to her mother.

And so it was the sudden freshening of creative energy for the short story, when other more ambitious forms were beyond him, that brought an unexpected triumph to the last part of Bill Saroyan's career.

In Paris, during May 1962, Aram Kevorkian performed a diplomatic miracle. He brought Bill together with a U.S. tax agent, and the three worked out a settlement to the decades of warfare. If Bill would pay off his $13,500 debt for 1952, and reduce the approximately $25,000 of additional arrears in monthly installments, the IRS would lift its many liens. Bill felt as if he had been released from twenty years in jail.

His taxes were paid, and he was reasonably solvent, so yearnings for California real estate reemerged. On July 20, 1964, he drove to Fresno to look at property. After a week's prospecting in the countryside, he decided that he wanted an inexpensive new house in town. He found it in some tract housing under construction. The house at 2729 West Griffith Way was priced at $13,750, and on August 1 he bought it, then its neighbor at 2739 as well. On August 19, he moved into 2729 West Griffith Way, celebrating with a tub soak in one of its two bathrooms, a shower in the other, and a steak dinner shared with his cousin Archie Minasian.

Although he did no writing during the summer months of 1964, with Paul Gitlin's help he signed a new one-year contributing-writer contract with the *Post* and reached an agreement with Jovanovich about royalty terms for the story collection *After Thirty Years.* There would be the 15 percent royalty that Jovanovich previously had denied him.

Bill and Jovanovich then had several cordial phone conversations in which the publisher agreed to take out some ads for *Boys and Girls Together,* but when Bill asked about paperback rights for *After Thirty Years,* he was told they would be shared in the traditional fifty-fifty manner. Bill insisted on receiving all paperback income, and Jovanovich refused.

In the midst of this conflict, Paul Gitlin called to explain to Bill that it was certainly extraordinary for an author to demand the entire paperback income from his publisher and that he, not Bill, should be dealing with Jovanovich about it. Bill, in his lust for haggling, told Gitlin that if he were to enter the negotiations now he would surely queer the deal. Bill had had an agent in Hal Matson, and he did not want another. When Gitlin reminded him of his own effective performance over the years, Bill hung up. Then, on the last day of August, Bill's fifty-sixth birthday, Jovanovich agreed to the Saroyan demand.

Annoyance with Paul Gitlin grew into an accusation that he had failed to deal effectively with Carol's several lawyers. Bill had had to engage another attorney to fight Krakower, and nothing had been done in his grievance with MGM over *The Human Comedy.* He wanted dynamic, forceful legal representation, and he wanted to hear whether the firm could provide it.

Gitlin replied on September 23 that he had now recovered the equilibrium of which Bill's letter had deprived him. He reminded Bill that the firm had been representing him loyally and ably for thirty years, that he himself had been looking after Bill's affairs for sixteen of them. He pointed out that in each instance Bill, not he, was "misrepresenting" the facts, and his misfortunes had been brought about by his own neglect. Mel Cane was particularly offended by his lack of appreciation. Paul needed only to know where Bill wanted him to send the funds and manuscripts in his custody. Eugene Winnick would keep him advised in the future. Gitlin's Saroyan material arrived by Railway Express in five cartons with collect charges of $65.69.

Although *After Thirty Years* was published in 1965, this book intended to celebrate the Saroyan short story met a great stillness. In spite of promises to the *Post* that he would soon be sending in new work, all attempts failed, and he produced nothing for the rest of the year. He made two European journeys, one in May, another in September, hoping some project would arise along the way.

But in New York he did call at Harcourt, where Jovanovich invited him to a breakfast that was to have favorable consequences. Jovanovich told him that if he wanted to make real money he needed to write a big novel. So Bill would survive, Jovanovich would give him a job in Harcourt's San Francisco office. Bill gave no thought to the job offer and little more to the novel.

He spent the 1965 holidays with Cosette at 1829 Fifteenth Avenue, and during Christmas week Jovanovich turned up at the St. Francis with his wife, Martha, and their three children. Bill was asked to meet and go walking with them. Afterward, during a quiet talk with his publisher, Bill was unhappy to be told again that he must write a big novel and that while there was a chance to sell reprint rights to both *My Name Is Aram* and *The Human Comedy*, he should not expect a big sum for them.

Then, in early February 1966, Jovanovich phoned with extraordinary news. He had persuaded Dell to bring out both *My Name Is Aram* and *The Human Comedy* and to pay an advance of $100,000. Mindful of Bill's feeling about his share of these rights, he was to have 60 percent, $60,000, at once. Bill was delighted, not only for the money but at the belief that this wide distribution would bring interest to his other books. Indeed, Bantam now offered to bring out a collection of Saroyan plays.

Pollinger had good news from England, too. Cassell's was taking on *One Day* and *Not Dying*. Desmond Flower, who would be his editor there, said he believed Saroyan to be one of the great writers of the century. Bill's response to his new affluence was to invest the money, profitably yet safely.

He sought out a Fresno stockbroker, a man called George Mason, at the firm of Schwabacher. He was an Armenian, born Elmassian, and he was enthusiastic about Trans International Air, now selling at 21 and sure to go to 30 in two months. Bill endorsed his initial $25,000 check from Jovanovich to Mason for the buying of Trans International Air shares and later bought more of his recommendations, Blue Crown Oil and Fairchild Camera. Bill became an assiduous student of the *Fresno Bee*'s financial pages.

In late March, he felt sure he was about to become rich in the rising stock market and decided to invest not only his $60,000 from Dell but an additional $23,000 he was able to gather from other sources, virtually all his funds. During early April he called regularly on George Mason and encouraged him to take every advantage of new prospects. He profited from sales of TIA and Fairchild Camera and bought such high-priced shares as Boeing on margin.

In mid-April, the stock market turned down sharply, and when Mason informed him he must come up with $25,000 to cover his losses, Bill protested angrily. A month later, the market was still falling, and he understood that he had been its victim. His $86,000 had shrunk to $59,000. He was particularly angry with George Mason, whom he decided was another crook. He sold all his shares and brought a halt to this quest for easy riches.

More bad news followed. In June, when he called at the offices of the *Saturday Evening Post,* he was told that he was no longer wanted as a contract writer. The editors felt his future with them would be far happier on a speculative basis. He took the loss stoically.

Hoping to improve his prospects, he spent the fall of 1966 in San Francisco hard at work. He prayed for good luck, that the results would be funny and large in spirit. Although he finished a dozen Bashmanian stories, only three proved marketable. The *Post* took "Madness in the Family" and "Mock Trials," paying $4,000 for each, and *McCall's* bought "Help, Help, Help, the Newsboy Hollered," paying, at Bill's insistence, $3,000 for it.

Early in the new year of 1967, he provided texts for *Look*'s picture book *Look at Us,* and Cowles, its publisher, was confident of a good sale. Bantam was bringing out a collection of five Saroyan plays, and Dell, which had paid so handsomely for the reissue of *Aram* and *The Human Comedy,* was interested in a collection of "super" Saroyan stories.

The summer of 1967 was productive. On July 1 he was back in Paris, writing pieces that he called *Letters from 74 rue Taitbout.* The "letters" were addressed to persons who had influenced his life in some way, including his relatives, Fresnoans, a rich Armenian, Hitler, de Maupassant, and Louis B. Mayer. At the same time, he worked on a pair of long, fragmentary reflections and speculations, one of which he called *August Days* and the other, *God's Autobiography.* Although each day threatened a battle with boredom, gambling episodes, spells of depression, and writer's block, on most he had the resolve to level his easel and stand to it for several hours of work.

He believed the most promising of these projects was *Letters from 74 rue Taitbout,* and at the end of September he sent it to the *Post,* which accepted six of his letters, encouraging thoughts of a generous book advance.

On his return to New York, Bill tried *Taitbout* on his former Harcourt editor Bob Giroux, now at Farrar, Straus and Giroux. Giroux was not interested, nor were Pocket Books and Bantam. In due time, however, Robert Gutwillig, at New American Library, offered a modest advance of $2,500, and Bill accepted it.

The other two collections, *August Days* and *God's Autobiography,* generated no publishing interest, but Francine Klagsbrun, at Cowles, whom Bill had met through *Look at Us,* agreed to do an altogether new collection of retrospective pieces, to be called *I Thought I Had Forever But Now I'm Not So Sure.* William Saroyan the writer was still anticipating publication days.

The family man was enduring incremental pain and alienation. In December 1962, Lucy called her father to report that her mother had given birth to a son. He would be named Charles, after Charles Marcus, and Walter Matthau had flown back from Paris to welcome him.

Then, early in 1964, Carol put an end to Bill's productive writing period with notice that she, as the children's trustee, had put the Maroney house up for sale. Next, her long-threatened legal action became reality. Arnold Krakower brought Carol's suit against Bill for $25,000 in unpaid child support.

Alan Fenner, representing Bill, found that Krakower was willing to settle for $15,000, and Fenner's advice was to do this. Bill, who had neither the money nor the inclination to comply, insisted they go to court. The trial began in April, before Judge Harold Baer of the New York Superior Court. Throughout the morning session, Bill suffered acute stomach pain. He spent the noon recess walking through rain to 102 Warren Street, where in 1928 he had worked for Postal Telegraph.

In the afternoon session, Carol was first to give testimony. Bill followed with his, and then Arnold Krakower objected to the trial procedure. The day ended by Judge Baer's overruling Krakower's objections. The next morning, Judge Baer handed down his decision. It was in Bill's favor. Thanks to Alan Fenner's defense, Krakower's case had collapsed. Bill Saroyan no longer needed to pay Mrs. Matthau any money at all.

But there was no end to the acrimony. Arnold Krakower appealed the decision, and in the summer of 1965 the court reversed its earlier decision. He must now pay Carol $20,800 plus legal costs unless he were to appeal. Bill urged Fenner to do so.

The court ruling that obliged him to support his children was threatening enough for Bill to close his California bank accounts. He sent off $30,000, virtually all his money, to the Swiss Credit Bank in Geneva, believing it would be beyond Carol's reach there. He asked that it be invested in the safest nontaxable securities that would earn him the highest interest.

In October 1966, his sense of vulnerability to Carol led to taking stock. He found his net worth was $39,000. This was what was left of his $60,000 fortune from Dell. He reminded himself that he had earned over a million dollars by his writing and that if he had been inclined to hang onto it, to invest it with expert advice, he would have been a rich man.

His current tax bill was for $8,000, alerting him to the vigilant IRS, which was also poised for a substantial bite of his remaining nest egg. He was convinced that smart people paid no taxes at all.

When he inquired about forming a protective Swiss corporation, Aram Kevorkian explained that it must be a U.S. entity, a nonprofit California corporation for which he would need a California attorney. He recommended his Harvard Law School classmate Richard Harrington, who practiced in San Francisco.

During that fall, Aram Kevorkian, known as Jack, had left Coudert Freres to start his own Paris firm, Kevorkian and Caldwell. Bill approved this step and on October 30 asked Kevorkian to establish the Saroyan Foundation. There would be great advantages. He would provide $15,000 in a scholarship fund for Armenian writers and artists of all kinds. He would be the sole judge of the recipients.

Following Kevorkian's suggestion, Bill conferred with Richard Harrington in San Francisco, and on December 13, 1966, the William Saroyan Foundation was incorporated at 1821 Fifteenth Avenue. It would have himself as president, Cosette as vice president, and Henry as secretary-treasurer. Bill made an initial contribution of $1,000 plus the original manuscripts of *The Human Comedy, My Name Is Aram,* and *The Time of Your Life.*

In addition, he made a contribution of $2,500 to the William Saroyan retirement fund, two $5,000 trusts for Aram and Lucy (they were to receive $200 a month from them), and a similar one for Henry's son Hank's education. He paid Henry a salary of $4,000 and Cosette an advance of $8,000, and earned Kevorkian's everlasting gratitude with a check for $10,000 to apply to past and future legal services. When he had done all this, he had used up nearly all his money and made his tax bill a reasonable one.

A man alone, anxious, and progressing through his sixties, Bill was acutely aware of his failing health: the ulcer, the heart, the prostatitis, the teeth, the esophagus. Returning from Paris on the *Bremen* in June 1962, he had rejoiced in the ship's luxury. In a single meal he partook of lobster, dover sole, palm heart, steak, and blue cheese. He felt deserving of this episode of gluttony. He had come through a very hard time. But the indulgence brought on enough misery for him to consult the ship's doctor, who determined that his ulcer was bleeding and that he should have a thorough examination in New York.

There, a Dr. Holzman examined Bill and assured him that his duodenal ulcer was healing and his health was generally satisfactory. However, as the year progressed, so did his pain, and a second visit to Dr. Holzman confirmed that the ulcer was bleeding again and that he must go on a bland diet.

But when his children joined him for a Christmas dinner at Sardi's, Bill flouted Dr. Holzman's orders and followed a Gibson with cannelloni, lobster, roast beef, and mince pie. He suffered throughout the night.

Recurrent pain and feelings of despair haunted him and made him newly sympathetic to his unhappy forty-seven-year-old cousin Chesley Saroyan. During the spring of 1965 in Fresno, he had found Chesley in a suicidal mood. Chesley told of having slashed his wrists and thoughts of having himself castrated. In March, Bill was not surprised to learn that Chesley had died alone in a car accident. Bill saw Chesley's tragedy as his failure to find what to do with himself, but he also believed he had been schizophrenic all his life.

On his return to Fresno, Bill drove to Piedra and found the scene of the accident, then Chesley's shoes, pieces of burned clothes, and three jacket buttons. He brought them home, along with a thistle he had dug up nearby. In Chesley's memory, he planted the thistle in his yard and kept the bits of clothing, with a ribbon imprinted *Beloved* which he took from Chesley's grave.

Bill was doing no writing at all, and his eyes, his teeth, and his ulcer vied to supply his daily pains. He made several visits to Ararat Cemetery, seeking the tombstones of relatives and examining the imbedded photographs. There were days in which he was overwhelmed with boredom and anger at the imbecility of his existence. On occasion he would shout his rage at the afflictions he saw as fat, age, illness, loneliness, estrangement, madness, and death.

In Paris in the fall of 1965, he found that his ulcer was bleeding again and told himself it was no wonder. On a Saturday morning in November he suffered chest pains that he believed signaled a heart attack. He called Jack Kevorkian and Ed Hagopian, who was first to appear, bringing along Dr. Andre Juvenelle. When Juvenelle insisted Bill come to his clinic, Bill did so reluctantly and was displeased when Juvenelle told him that he looked green. He refused to undergo a series of tests and left. He did go on with Hagopian to a nearby lab for a blood test, but when it required filling out forms, he decided to skip this as well. Although he knew Ed Hagopian was devoted to him and wanted only to help, he could not bear his solicitousness. Even as Hagopian tried to be a friend in need, Bill recoiled, and felt lucky to get away. Hagopian's loyal Sancho Panza friendship could not survive the corrosive, Saroyan scorn. The moment the bridge of charity was extended, Bill's self-sufficiency was threatened. A friend in need? Need itself was unthinkable.

Early 1967 found him in San Francisco, so idle that the widespread praise for Elia Kazan's new novel *The Arrangement* was a goad to both his envy and his ulcer. The latter raged, demanding a bland diet and regular dosing with probanthine. Pausing at Bingo Beach for a set of machine photos, Bill confronted an aging face with an enormous, untidy mustache. He felt that he walked like a sick, old man and wondered if he had cancer, but a three-day examination at the Sansum Clinic, in Santa Barbara, found no fault.

On returning to Paris in July 1967, he still could not work. The nagging ulcer had drained his sense of well-being, and his prostate worried him. The need to urinate a dozen or more times in the course of a night added to his insomnia. When he was examined at the American Hospital in Neuilly, he was relieved to find he had no venereal disease, but his prostate was enlarged and there was evidence of a slipped disc in his spine.

He felt that he was in a bad way. When he walked the streets he looked like a vagrant and not, he told himself with an unimpaired irony, like the great man he knew himself to be. Ever preoccupied with appearance, he was a faithful customer of the machine photo booths. He had sat for his first at Coney Island in 1928, and used it on the jacket of *Trapeze*. On his fifty-ninth birthday, he visited the photo booth at the Gare d'Est, which he had established as the best in the world, and sat for three sets to record his face at fifty-nine.

On December 21, 1967, he read of John Steinbeck's death, in New York. The Nobel laureate had been sixty-six, five years Bill's senior. He found this departure mysteriously coupled with another item in the news, about the rocket carrying astronauts to the moon. He recalled knowing Steinbeck years ago in Los Gatos, drinking wine and singing with him and Carol Henning, his wife at the time. John was dead, as he soon would be, and that finality was fine with him.

It put him in mind of his uncle Mihran's dying of cancer in the summer of 1964 and of Armenak's death half a century earlier. Now he summarized his increasingly morbid thoughts. What scared him about death was not the pain of dying, nor even the becoming absent from life's scene. It was the final nothingness. Even though he had been anticipating this nothingness since his first breath, he was still unprepared for it.

· · ·

If the Saroyan health and career were clouded by doubts and misgivings, fatherhood, asserting himself through love and care for his two adolescent children, lay invitingly open to him.

Certainly the most welcome news of 1962 came from Aram. He had been accepted by the University of Chicago. From Paris, Bill wired him congratulations and wrote about plans to see him and Lucy that summer. Lucy agreed to a vacation in the West with him, but Aram rebuffed him with a tart reminder of their Spanish excursion; he would risk no more than a week with him. On arrival in New York, however, Bill found Aram newly receptive. He had a summer job at the *Atlantic Monthly* and often appeared at the Royalton for walks with his father. Aram was not getting along with Walter Matthau, and after an argument with him would quit the apartment for a night on a cot in his father's room.

In late June, Aram saw his father and his sister off on the Twentieth Century Limited for a holiday together. Their first stop was Chicago, for a visit to Northwestern University at Evanston, Lucy's choice for next year's college. They explored its buildings, watched a play rehearsal, and walked the bordering Lake Michigan shore. When Bill's habitual search for stones turned up a surprising number of coins and a silver creamer, he decided that Northwestern must be a rich kids' college.

Their next destination was the World's Fair in Seattle, and they went by the Great Northern's Empire Builder. It paused long enough in Whitefish, Montana, for Lucy to gather some Montana dirt to mail to her mother. She clung to her memories of the M Lazy V Ranch as her favorite place in the world.

They laughed about Lucy's having to wake Bill in the night to silence the trumpet of his snoring. While they arrived in Seattle with only $32, they had great fun seeing the fair on a low budget. Once headed for San Francisco, they knew they had become companions, sharing the joys and privations of their journey.

As soon as they were settled at 1821 Fifteenth Avenue with Cosette to look after them, Bill set about Lucy's entertainment with a tour of the city, beginning with 2727 Taraval, the scene of her babyhood. They went to the Papazians' in Irvington to see her many aunts, uncles, and cousins, to Cypress Lawn to view her grandmother Takoohi's grave, and to Fresno to visit Ross Bagdasarian's vineyard, Chipmunk Ranch. In Beverly Hills they stayed with Ross and Armen at the Bagdasarian mansion on North Beverly Drive, and Lucy renewed old acquaintance in Pacific Palisades.

As Bill turned to writing a play that might bring him back to Broadway in the fall, Lucy grew restless. When "Butch" Janigan, the son of a distant relative, asked Lucy to an Armenian church social, she went and had such a thoroughly good time she hoped Butch would call with a second invitation.

When he did, Cosette intercepted it and refused on Lucy's behalf. Lucy was furious and called on her father to rectify the matter. He did so by reprimanding Cosette but not in restoring Butch's invitation.

Lucy was forgiving, and she and her father returned to New York, convinced they had had a grand summer together. They found Aram, who was preparing for his freshman year at Chicago, in an unhappy mood. Bill's concern about him increased with a visit to his basement apartment, on Eighty-sixth Street. Aram's roommate, Steve Reichman, had a bed, Aram had a cot, and they shared a two-burner gas range and a broken refrigerator. Bill was appalled that his nineteen-year-old son could live this way.

In September, Bill saw Aram off for his freshman year at Chicago and took great pleasure in Lucy's daily phone calls and visits. She went to dinner and the theater with him, flattered him on his television appearances, and happily shared her concerns about boyfriends.

When he saw Lucy in a play at Dalton School he thought she had very little talent for acting and simply shouldn't be interested in the theater at all—and yet she clearly was. When Lucy spoke of going to the Lincoln Center acting school, an idea that her mother and Bobby Lewis had put in her mind, he discouraged her.

Aram returned for the Thanksgiving holiday buoyant with news that *The Nation* had accepted one of his poems, and he spent his first night in New York on a cot in his father's room at the Royalton. They talked through the night.

As 1962 drew to a close, Bill decided that whatever sense his own living in exile had once made, it was now ridiculous. While he lacked the money to produce a play, he had $20,000 in prospect and wanted a New York residence. He was soon taken with a building under construction at 155 East Fiftieth Street. It was to be completed in February of the following year, and he took a three-year lease on a penthouse apartment. The rent was $565 a month, and in writing out an initial check, he rationalized that he now *had* to make big money.

Lucy climbed the twenty-one floors with him to admire the view. He was also pleased to describe his penthouse to Ross Bagdasarian, who was stopping at the St. Regis and arranging promotion of his entertainment ventures. Bill had found him irritatingly full of prosperous, big-cigar, chipmunk talk.

On December 7, well known as a day of infamy, Bill received a letter from Aram with the dismaying news that he was quitting the University of Chicago. Bill's first response was anger. The boy's decision seemed another eruption of their feud, but he accepted it as final rather than one from which Aram might be dissuaded.

While the fatherly role had a strong appeal, that of stern counselor had always eluded him. His own childhood had lacked any such model. Whatever sense of paternal authority he once had, he surely had relinquished in April 1949 by abandoning his family. Carol had given him regular reminders that it was Charles Marcus who had provided the home for his children.

Aram arrived on December 13 in no way shamed by quitting Chicago. He explained to his father that he was leaving the university because there wasn't enough to interest him there. He had discovered how much he loved New York. Nevertheless, he planned to go to Cambridge, Massachusetts, in January. Whether or not he was admitted to Harvard, he would sit in on classes there.

In spite of disappointment, Bill responded in a conciliatory way. Although it seemed plain that this was another instance of Aram's avoidance of trial and hard work, of his always finding an out and justifying it, he did not argue the point or try to alter Aram's decision. He did reflect that these traits of his son were apparent in his brother Henry, and even in Cosette—which was to say the Armenak side of the Saroyans—but they were certainly unlike his own. And, of course, he saw Aram's sense of entitlement and willingness to twist the truth in argument as a quality of his mother's.

Later, in 1964, Bill used this interview with Aram for one of his finest stories. "Twenty Is the Greatest Time in Any Man's Life" takes place in a New York penthouse where a writer is lecturing his twenty-year-old son about his dismissal from college. The father defends his own, cheeseparing, hardworking behavior and urges the son to make demands on himself so as not to become a pot-smoking zombie. The son is enough crushed by the argument so that his father's final rejoinder—to remember that his is the greatest time of a man's life—is a superb irony.

At the end of February 1963, Bill took a room at the San Carlos Hotel, on Fiftieth Street, directly opposite his new apartment. Aram had neither gone to Cambridge nor found a job, and after quarrels with his mother and his sister he customarily turned up at the San Carlos and became a familiar sight, stretched out, reading, on the sofa of Bill's room.

One Sunday in March, as Bill was reconciling himself to the hostile critical response to *Boys and Girls Together,* Aram delivered his own uncomplimentary opinion of the book and of his father's writing in general. Bill, who took Aram's judgment as contempt for himself as well as his work, turned angry and ordered him from his room. Aram left his father on what they both presumed was a permanent basis, whereupon Bill went for several long, nighttime walks. From Lucy he learned that Aram had moved to

Sloan House, the YMCA on Ninth Avenue. He was okay, and Lucy urged her father *not* to make up with him.

By late March, Bill was wholly occupied with moving into his penthouse, and Lucy turned up daily to help with the cleaning and outfitting. She particularly enjoyed walking barefoot in the stream Bill made in hosing the terrace, and he was touched to see her arranging sheets and towels in the linen closet much as her mother had on Taraval Street.

When she told him that she was trying out for the part of a nine-year-old in Jose Quintero's movie, and believed that a hair ribbon would make her look younger than her seventeen years, he thought this just like her mother. There was no thought of how to excel as an actress; it was only important to know people, and to pretend.

Walter Matthau had given Lucy two tickets for the premiere of *The Ugly American,* and she had invited Steve Resnick, her current favorite, to join her. She would wear an evening gown for the first time, and Marlon Brando would be there. This disclosure brought Bill the unpleasant recollection of Brando's hovering around Carol, and his games. He would phone her at two a.m., pretending to be a detective, or a degenerate talking dirty, or a woman with a grudge, and scare her. Bill had always suspected that in the spring of 1949, soon after confessing she was Jewish, Carol had begun some kind of affair with Brando.

He felt that Lucy bore an impossible burden in her mother's influence. At the same time he loved her and wished her luck. He willingly agreed to Lucy's plan to spend the summer at 74 rue Taitbout with her friend Ellen Abrams and wrote Aram Kevorkian to prepare the apartment for their arrival in July.

Still angry at Aram, Bill felt that his son had brought him only pain since the European visit of 1957. As a father he could become entirely objective about his children, judging them as if they were acquaintances to whom he had no accountability. When they displeased him he would conclude that they lacked first-class natures.

The hopes Bill had held for a new and productive life in his midtown penthouse were not being realized. From March 27, the day he moved in, he met one disappointment after another. Water flowed feebly from the taps yet copiously through the bedroom wall and floorboards. There was constant noise from the plumbing and from the elevator machinery directly overhead. Within a week he was sure the apartment was a mistake and proposed legal action against the landlord.

Lucy was to graduate from Dalton on June 7. When she asked her father if he would sit with her mother during the ceremony, he refused. Bill did attend Lucy's graduation alone, and found her the best-looking of the forty girls in her class. Lucy brought him a copy of her school yearbook, lovingly inscribed to him "Tumbleweed," the nickname he had given her as a headlong, fall-prone child. She also brought an olive branch from her brother. Aram was painting and had asked for the materials he had left with his father.

In sending these, Bill included a note welcoming Aram's call. This came on June 15, soon to be followed by Aram himself. He had grown a mustache and a van Dyck beard, and Bill, noticing that his much-nibbled fingernails had grown, was glad to see him. They talked earnestly for two hours. Aram told his father that he would not return to college for another year. He wanted his own apartment and would find a job. He had arranged an interview with *Sports Illustrated.*

He assured his father he was not asking for money, but then added that if his mother's lawsuit was successful he would have some of her settlement. This cut to the quick of his fatherly discomfort—affection and generosity to his children entwined with vulnerability to the predatory Carol. He wanted Aram's love, but all to himself. Although provoked, Bill contained his annoyance and walked Aram to Forty-seventh Street and Fifth Avenue, where they shook hands.

In late June, Bill and Aram saw Lucy off to Paris, and over the next several weeks father and son were close companions. They had long talks together, and Bill was pleased with Aram's responses and his appearance, which, he decided, was that of the symbolist poet Baudelaire.

Not Dying, with its twenty-six drawings by the author, had just come from Harcourt, and Bill gave Aram a copy. Aram turned up at the apartment with a two-page letter about it, telling his father exactly what he thought of the book, but this time Bill accepted it as a son-to-father letter that was as kind and wonderful as it was mean and angry. When Aram understood that his father was not offended by his letter, they were drawn together as never before. They talked and chain-smoked throughout the night and went out to walk the streets together.

Bill found the penthouse intolerable and moved back to the Royalton. Aram, who had applied for a number of jobs, found one at last as a salesman for Collier's Encyclopedias. He called on his father to demonstrate his first lesson in salesmanship and returned the next day to present a second lesson, admitting that he was skeptical of the training course but needed to earn money.

Just before setting out for San Francisco, Bill learned from a triumphant Aram that, after a day's work in Peekskill, he had sold a set of encyclopedias.

At his father's invitation, Aram agreed to a California visit, if it could be after the civil rights march to Washington on August 28. He arrived cheerfully on September 1, bearing some recent poems. Bill took him to Fresno for a visit with their relatives and was pleased that his son took part in the talk and poker around the family table. Indeed, Aram got on so well with their Armenian family that Bill felt these were two of the happiest days of his life.

The return to New York was by train, with a stopover to see Lucy into her freshman year at Northwestern. On arriving in Chicago, they called on Henry Rago, of *Poetry Review.* Rago not only agreed to consider some of Aram's poems but asked him to review Robert Creeley's novel *The Island* for his magazine. They met Lucy's train and joyously celebrated their reunion over a Chinese dinner. In the morning, Bill and Aram saw Lucy into her room at Willard Hall and felt her well launched on a college education.

Four months later, on his way from Paris to California, Bill stopped off again in Chicago to see his daughter. She came rushing to greet him, took him to her room to meet her friends, and then brought him to lunch in the dining hall. Bill was elated with his lively, happy daughter. But at the end of her first year, she disappointed him by deciding not to return to Northwestern. Like her brother, in the Midwest she had starved for New York. Bill listened sympathetically to her explanation and did not try to change her mind.

Throughout the mid-sixties, Bill was pleased to see his son pursue a literary life. In January 1964, Aram celebrated the appearance of his first book, *Poems,* a collaboration with two other young poets. Bill had found him an apartment on Forty-fifth Street, and he was enjoying his job at Bookmaster's. Six of his poems appeared in the April 1964 issue of *Poetry Review,* along with his praiseful review of Robert Creeley's novel. When Bill invited him to San Francisco for a visit, they enjoyed browsing City Lights Bookstore and then a trip in the red racer to Fresno for an appraisal of Bill's new house, on West Griffith Way.

Aram was less impressed with the house than Bill had hoped. They fell into a familiar argument over Aram's dependence on his mother for both his values and his weekly allowance. But it was Aram's twenty-first year, and by the time of his departure, father and son had made peace. In the following year, Aram was busy with his magazine, *Lines,* and sent his father a copy of *In,* his book of eleven poems. Bill wrote his thanks and learned that Aram would spend the summer in Woodstock, New York, writing a novel.

Carol had sold the Maroney house, and Bill suspected that she had profited greatly from this, with no portion going to the children as he had planned. Lucy confirmed his suspicions, and then, since she was moving to a new apartment, asked her father if he would pay her rent, as he had Aram's. Bill refused, explaining that he had already provided for her. Lucy was unappeased.

Then, in late March 1966, while Bill was in Fresno, Aram called from his mother's in Beverly Hills to say he was being considered for the lead in Mike Nichols's film *The Graduate* and had flown out from New York to read for the part. Bill urged him to come up for the weekend, which Aram did. Bill put him up in the corner house, and they had a fine time together. Aram spoke of seeing a psychiatrist, and he was enthusiastic about his recent photographs and poems. He returned to Los Angeles to read for the part, which would go to Dustin Hoffman.

Lucy was pursuing her own acting career. While in New York, Bill tried to reach her and found her backstage at the Plymouth Theatre, where Walter Matthau was appearing in *The Odd Couple*. She was working as Matthau's dresser. Bill met her there after an evening performance, found her in fine spirits, and visited her one-room apartment, at 1035 Park Avenue. Later she wrote him in Fresno to report that she had enrolled at the Actor's Studio, in New York, and to ask if he would write a short scene for her as an acting exercise. He did, and soon he heard that it was just what she had wanted.

On his way to Paris in early June 1966, Bill made a stopover in New York and found Lucy still working as Matthau's dresser in *The Odd Couple*. After the performance, he took her to El Morocco, where they joined Leonard Lyons. As he walked her home, she spoke of plans to go to London in hopes of a part in a play.

While Bill was in Paris during the summer of 1966, Lucy did take her acting ambitions to London. In July, Bill joined her there, hoping he could be of help. He found her staying with friends on Ebury Street, and took her to the Savoy for dinner. They agreed that while she was making her theatrical way, they should see interesting plays together and find themselves a London home. Bill had 5,600 pounds in his London account, and wanted to invest it in suitable real estate. He took a three-month lease on a furnished flat in Chelsea, at 57 Whitelands House, on King's Road.

Lucy had discovered that her friend Kerry Kelly, Gene Kelly and Betsy Blair's daughter, was also in London. Betsy, who had played the lead in *The Beautiful People* and had always liked Bill, was now married to the director Karel Reisz and living in England's Lane. She made Bill welcome there along with Lucy and her several beaux. It was Lucy too who encountered Charlie and Oona Chaplin in the street and was invited to bring her father along to a party. At this party, Bill encountered an actress named Barbara Steele, a woman whose dark, Irish beauty clearly impressed him.

When Lucy's New York beau, Francois de Menil, an apprentice filmmaker and scion of a Texas-rich, internationally prominent family, turned up, Bill invited Barbara, Lucy, and Francois to dinner and took them gambling at the Pair of Shoes and Crockford's. Although both Francois and Lucy won, Bill lost heavily and had to borrow from the managers. On the

Carol and Walter Matthau had become an enviably devoted couple.

way home, first Francois and then Barbara were dropped off, leaving Lucy to ask her father if he was serious about Barbara. He told her that he was not, and explained that she was neither chaste enough to be the woman he wanted for a wife, nor "bad girl" enough for a one-night stand.

The moment they returned to the apartment, Lucy was astonished to be shoved against the wall by her father. It was the first time in her life that he had been violent toward her, and she was baffled by his rage, even more so when he explained it was over her having taken Francois's money to play at the casino. No decent woman would do such a thing.

His own behavior was surely the more questionable, and the motivation seems far more likely to have been Lucy's caring inquiry about why he avoided a woman so attractive to him as Barbara Steele. Lucy had invaded his fragile, misogynous emotional life. Even from a daughter this had been intolerable, but he had no way to tell her so.

Lucy found it difficult to get a work permit, without which it was virtually impossible to act in London. However, Vincent Guy, the director of the Lunch Hour Theatre, thought he could provide one and present her father's one-act play *Hello Out There*. She began rehearsing the Emily Smith role with Guy, then found her permit had been denied. Whereupon Bill withdrew his permission to present the play. With clouding hopes for a London stage appearance, Lucy went off to Paris with Francois de Menil to visit his mother, Dominique.

When Bill called at his new publisher, Cassell's, Desmond Flower greeted him cordially and took him to lunch. At his steadfast literary agency, all three Pollingers—Laurence, Murray, and Gerald—welcomed him with hopes that Penguin would be taking *One Day in the Afternoon of the World.* He assured them that he would soon be writing here in his London flat.

Indeed, he bought a new Olympia typewriter, set it up on a work table, and promised himself he would complete a good piece of work by his fifty-eighth birthday. He put in several bitter days struggling to get under way, but the result was only a sheaf of notes, no real start on anything. He felt too feeble and confused to work.

He became a regular at London's private gambling clubs and at the poker games sponsored by such stage celebrities as Woody Allen and Frank Sinatra. To pay off his gambling debts, he had to sell some securities and counted the damage so far at $15,000. The London summer was already another financial disaster.

Then he heard from Aram, who had canceled a planned visit to Cosette in San Francisco in order to join his father and his sister in London. Aram arrived on August 18 with his hair hanging to his shoulders. He spoke earnestly of his own writing, his interest in New Wave, "concrete" poetry, and the volume, *Sled Hill Voices,* that he was preparing. He had brought a supply of marijuana, which he smoked conspicuously, and he boasted of experiments with LSD. When Bill went out to buy his Chesterfields, Aram asked him to bring back cigarette papers.

With Lucy and Francois's return from Paris, the apartment was newly lively and crowded. Bill thought Kerry Kelly was the sweetest and brightest of Lucy's friends and was surprised that Aram was not attracted to her. Kerry, in turn, shared Bill's skepticism about the audience for Aram's one-word poems.

Francois left for Stockholm to film the dismantling there of a huge sculpture of a supine woman, and on Bill's birthday, Lucy and Aram flew off to join Francois in Sweden. They returned with colds, and the sight of Aram, sniffling and prostrate, provoked his father's wrath. He decried Aram's poetry, his pot smoking, and the weakling quality of his art and his life. He saw no health nor zest in any of it. As tempers cooled, he explained that he had been trying to provoke Aram to self-awareness, but the boy's surly response had proved it hopeless. Aram protested that his father ordered, rather than asked, him to do things, and, when he did agree to a walk, found himself headed for a browsing of the used Rolls Royce showroom.

In the course of one argument, Aram told his father that the written word was obsolete. Bill pointed out that if this were so, *he* was obsolete, for his whole life was committed to the written word. Aram agreed that he was, whereupon Bill decided Aram was deranged. After consulting with Lucy,

Bill wrote her psychiatrist, Dr. Thorne, about what he saw as Aram's problems. He was angry enough to refuse Aram when he asked to bring the poet and magazine editor Tom Clark to the apartment. Bill had observed that Aram rolled special joints for his meetings with Clark.

Nevertheless, it was Clark who provided Aram with a significant opportunity. He arranged a dual poetry reading at Koch's bookshop. Bill celebrated Aram's birthday, on September 25, with a birthday cake and the gift of a fine black wallet. He was on hand for Aram's reading on the twenty-ninth. He thought Aram did as well as the others on the program and was impressed by his being paid £5 10s. for his twenty-minute appearance.

Now another actor, Marc Farren, called to say he was ready to pick up *Hello Out There* where Vincent Guy had left off. He would present the play with Lucy as Emily Smith, along with *Once Around the Block,* and deal with the problem of her work permit. He could get a small theater, the Garrick Yard, in St. Martin's Lane, for a week's run, opening on October 10. Lucy agreed and began rehearsing with Farren. Although her father had frequent disputes with Lucy, accusing her of being selfish, he was pleased to see her working hard on her part. He gave her and Marc Farren some direction and endured several long rehearsals.

He continued to feel that Lucy, like her mother, was ambitious for theatrical fame yet lacked the talent and grit that good acting required. He suspected she had been a poor student of Sandy Meisner, at the Neighborhood Playhouse, and a London appearance would be a critical boost for her self-esteem.

Bill felt that Aram was mending his ways. After three weeks of incessant pot smoking he had given it up entirely and sworn off any future use of LSD. He had even gotten a haircut, his first in eight months, and emerged a new and different person. On an evening when Lucy was at rehearsal, Bill had a sympathetic talk with Aram about writing. Aram said that he wanted to write a big work about these chaotic times. He planned to go to Cambridge, Massachusetts, where some friends had a house. He would settle down there and write the book. When Aram showed his father five typed pages, his first day's work on the project, Bill was pleased. He told him it was fine, with a free, easy style, and urged him to see it through.

A letter from the poet Ted Berrigan with exciting prospects for their future added to Aram's optimism, and he wrote further pages of the novel. Bill approved them and presented Aram with his own return air ticket, booking passage for himself on the *United States.*

Bill went to the Garrick Yard theater to view a run-through of the two plays and declared them in fine shape. He proudly wrote Leonard Lyons in New York that Lucy was about to appear in two Saroyan plays and that Aram had been reading his poetry to appreciative British audiences.

As planned, Lucy's London stage debut took place at the tiny theater on October 10, and Bill thought she was great. At the supper party Karel and Betsy Reisz gave for Lucy, at the Terrasso restaurant, her father congratulated her on a success. He felt both plays had been presented effectively. At the next two performances he was as disappointed as Lucy to find only a handful of people in the audience.

As he reflected on this interlude with his maturing children, he felt it had been divisive. Indeed, he thought it might be their last prolonged time together. He saw each of them as going off in separate directions, lonely yet hopeful, and admitted anxiousness over what would happen to Aram, to Lucy, and to himself.

Lucy decided to stay in London. She would share Kerry Kelly's flat in the basement of the Reiszes' house. When Bill pointed out that Lucy would become a burden to them, she replied that she had nowhere else to go.

He felt that both children were damaged, and that neither had gotten any help from their mother. He was newly resentful of Carol's thrusting them at him, expecting him to hear, guide, and heal them. He had found it tough going and reflected that he had thought they would be a joy to him. Instead, the experience had been agonizing.

His forecast of their parting ways was surprising, for Whitelands had been his chance at playing the patriarchal role he had sought all his life. He had failed at it, being quite unable to forgive his children for being themselves. Although both were in their twenties and had achieved London debuts, he saw them as professional failures. His feelings toward both children were less sympathetic than competitive. Aram, in his New Wave writing, challenged him professionally, while Lucy, in assuming her mother's ambitions and values, did so emotionally. He could not find the ground from which to comfort or console them.

On establishing the Saroyan Foundation in December of that year, he wrote Lucy from San Francisco, describing how she had benefited from the trust. Lucy responded gratefully and told how she had spent ten days in Rome and, thanks to Karel Reisz, met Fellini and Alberto Moravia, but had found no acting job. Whereupon she had returned to Walter and Carol's in California, but felt unwelcome there.

Although Francois had finished his movie *The Big Woman,* he had no idea what to do with it. She no longer saw him, since she had tired of her nanny's role. She was on the outs with Aram, too, but eager to know if he had gotten the part in *The Graduate,* so she could drown in her jealousy.

When Bill went to New York in June 1967, he found Lucy staying with Maureen Stapleton in her apartment on West Seventieth Street. Bill was made welcome there, and when he took Lucy to dinner he found her still struggling to find the course for her life. Some Richard Avedon portraits of her in a recent issue of *Vogue* had raised her self-esteem, but she wanted to accomplish something creative and had turned to writing stories, dashing them off one a day, as he did. Later that evening, Lucy brought out a stack of them. She read him five, and he told her they were really very good and urged her to keep it up.

On each of the next three evenings, he returned to find Maureen's apartment a literary salon. Bennett Cerf's son Christopher, now an editor at Random House, was there, as were Elia Kazan's twenty-two-year-old son, Nick, and Tennessee Williams.

When Aram came down from Cambridge to visit his father, he allowed Bill to give him a haircut in the hotel room and then to loan him money, which, Bill noted disapprovingly, he used for a taxi visit to his mother.

Then on June 20, just prior to his departure for Paris, Bill learned from a joyous Lucy that Random House wanted to publish a volume of her stories. She was to receive an option payment of $250. Whereupon Aram called from Cambridge with similar tidings. Random House would publish his book next spring. Chris Cerf was responsible for both offers, and Bill rejoiced with his children.

Aram, still in Cambridge, phoned to say that he was fed up with the place. He had no friends, and found Harvard self-sealed and America suicidal. Although he was looking forward to publication of two of his books, he had decided to go to Paris and wanted to stay at 74 rue Taitbout. He would be taking along Gailyn McLanahan, a girl he had met during the summer. He would need money for their airfare. Bill sent Aram a thousand dollars and wrote Kevorkian in Paris to dispossess the tenant, Kevorkian's son Andy, and make the apartment ready for Aram's arrival.

In late November, Aram called from Paris to say that Lucy had turned up to join him and Gailyn, and while they liked the apartment, it was cold. Could they get some proper radiators? Pleased that both children were enjoying the apartment, Bill authorized the radiators. In December, when Kevorkian advised that the bill would be $1,200, Bill cabled his approval.

Aram reported in December that Lucy had been rude and unattractively theatrical. She had responded to his lectures with haughtiness and departed for a hotel. Just after Christmas, Aram phoned his father to complain, not just about the apartment, but about Paris itself. The French were no better than the people in Cambridge.

On January 2, 1968, Bill had a report from Jack Kevorkian. He had found Gailyn fairylike, but Aram was something else. To give Bill the flavor of his son's confrontation with Paris, Kevorkian described how Aram had objected to the French custom of shaking hands with the workmen and how, although the heaters had been properly installed, Aram had quarreled with the contractor, blamed him for a wiring difficulty, and called him a crook. He had ordered a new telephone along with a door, shelves, and a bookcase, all at his father's expense.

On January 5, Aram called collect from the Hotel de Lutece, where he, Gailyn, and their kitten had taken refuge. He thought the French people were animals. Paris itself was finished and out of the question. He had to return to New York and needed a thousand dollars to do so. Dismayed and depressed by Aram's behavior, Bill agreed to cable the sum, but wondered how he could truly help his son.

On January 9, he wrote Aram—now returned to an apartment on Eighty-first Street in New York—a stern letter, urging him to accept the human race as he found it. He reminded Aram that he was in his twenty-fifth year, and it was time to take some responsibility for his thoughts and actions and to put himself out for others. He cautioned him against big talk about money and being an artist, and about phoning him for help. If he couldn't be a writer, he should let it go without alibis.

A month later, he warned Aram further about self-delusion. When he had called so urgently from Cambridge and again from Paris about his need to escape those cities, it was actually himself he was trying to flee. Nor was it the apartment heaters, Lucy, false friends, unaccommodating strangers, editors, or other writers who were failing him, but himself. He was mistaken about the importance of the little work he had done. He would not be a great man until the proof of it was in accomplishment recognized by others. He urged him to analyze his chronic hatred of the people around him. It would be tough to change, but he could do it.

Bill's concern about Aram was heightened by an appeal from Gailyn's father, Grant McClanahan, who was troubled by her recent withdrawal and unfriendliness toward her family. When Bill confided this to Lucy, she was quick to explain Gailyn's behavior by Aram's having introduced her to daily pot smoking and his frequent LSD trips. She thought her brother was becoming a monster and urged her father to stop sending Aram any money at all.

During that spring, Lucy wrote her father frequently, sharing her satisfaction in a restored relationship with Francois and her reservations about Aram's new book. Bill replied that it had failed for want of humor. He wished Aram had made it cocky, for as it was you could only feel sorry for him.

Lucy exulted over landing a part in a movie, *Some Kind of Nut,* directed by Garson Kanin, and another in the touring company of *There's a Girl in My Soup.* Moreover, she had arranged a father-daughter interview about generational differences for a German magazine. The fee was to be $2,000.

In March 1968, Bill set out from Fresno in the venerable red racer for visits to the Fort Lewis School of Agriculture at Durango, Colorado; Oklahoma State University at Stillwater; and Central State College at Edmond, Oklahoma. At each he spoke to writing students, delivered a talk, endured a reception in his honor, and accepted a fee that varied from $500 to $1,000.

At Stillwater he received a first copy of Aram's Random House book of poems, and he wrote him that in spite of an initial, impatient rejection of the unusual use of words and the format, he liked the book. Its sparseness appealed to him.

Yet he questioned what one did with such writing. Where did it go? The book, which cost $2.50, took less than three minutes to read; its intent was less to provide the pleasure of reading than to serve as a revolt against that tradition. He suspected the buyers of such a book would be confined to relatives and fellow revolutionists. If it did have a certain cocktail-party vogue, the writer would find himself even more vulnerable than most writers. Ridicule would suggest creative bankruptcy, the lack of real talent.

He told Aram that on the basis of his longer poems and traditional prose, he felt he was a good, possibly even a great, writer, but he worried about his experiments with hallucinatory drugs. They were not only a fad but a crutch for the mind and spirit, a withdrawal from the kind of struggle with the soul one must do to get it right.

He felt that Aram had not yet found his vocational way. He would recognize this in his own confidence and freedom, not likely to be achieved until he was earning his own bread and, like himself, constantly trying to enlarge and improve his work. He ended by assuring Aram of his concern and love for, and belief in, him.

In mid-April, Bill arrived in New York from his college tour and located Lucy at the de Menilses' at 111 East Seventy-third Street. Bill was invited to dinner there, enjoyed Francois's father, Jan, and thought Lucy and Francois looked happy together. But when Aram and Gailyn visited him, he found his son newly anxious. He seemed to make less sense now than he had eleven years ago. When Aram came to see him alone, he told of how his mother had spoken to him as a child, and told him he was not a man.

Bill did consent to work with Aram on his book of 1957 photos, *Kids Are Best,* and, while lunching with his Cowles editors, proposed they publish it. They agreed immediately to a $5,000 advance and a 15 percent royalty to be divided between father and son, four fifths to Aram. No sooner was this settled than Bill encountered Aram and Gailyn on the street, and there was general rejoicing, but within a few days, Aram was complaining to his father about his troubles. Among these, he had found his new editor, Francine Klagsburn, rude.

As Bill made his way west, the red racer, acquired in Belgrade in March 1959 and with an infinity of kilometers behind it, faltered. As he drove from Reno toward California, the little car stopped altogether, and in Truckee it was declared to have reached the end of its road. With his old Lincoln still available, he did not replace it.

Bill's worries about Aram were reawakened when he learned that a quarrel with Random House threatened the publication of Aram's second book, and arguments with Gailyn threatened their relationship. Aram admitted his need for psychotherapy. In July he wrote that he and Gailyn were benefiting from sessions with Lucy's Dr. Thorne, that he now had a literary agent, had poems in forthcoming issues of *Poetry* and the *Paris Review,* and had patched up relations with his publisher. His *Pages* would be out next spring, and he awaited the text Bill had promised for his book of photographs.

On pondering the *Kids Are Best* photographs, Bill confessed to Aram that he was stumped on how to fashion a valid work of them. Until he saw a theme, it would be no kindness to attempt it. He asked Aram if he were interested enough to put in some more work on the concept.

Bill's response to a poem of Aram's in *Poetry* was short on the praise Aram had wanted, and he wrote his father that he was pained by the constant disapproval of his work. While it was his habit to pretend to be above it, he was not. He was humiliated and angry. He wanted to be accepted and loved for who he was.

This prompted Bill to reaffirm his dislike for concrete poetry. He urged Aram to make his poetry accessible to people who had not taken drug trips. He felt these poems were acceptable only for those who had no other recourse. For everyone else, they were a self-indulgence. He thought Aram's purpose in his art was too precious for most readers, bewildering, and even repellent, to them. He could proceed in any direction he liked, of course, but if he chose to put himself out he could achieve far greater things. Long ago, Bill had understood that a man's accomplishment was preordained, but at the same time there was this truth, that if a man believes he can, and works at it, he can transcend his destiny. Finally, his love for Aram was greater than even he knew, and part of it, he must surely understand by now, took shape as carping and finding fault.

In August, Aram replied that the lack of emotional support from his father had led him to feel threatened by nearly all the men he had known and kept him from close friendships with them.

Exasperated, Bill replied with a plea that he stop being a bore and grow up. He wanted to know if anyone besides Dr. Thorne was trying to help him. His mother? Her lawyer? Her friends? Was anyone else sending him money? How could he help when Aram was both living off him and finding fault with his every word?

He found Aram's letters evasive and contentious. His conception of fatherly love was adulation, and responding was an experience like that with his mother, one that had nearly killed him. Bill wanted to help, but he could not speak less than the truth. Aram's fantasy was that he was already someone important. Instead of letting this become an illness, he should earn himself some kind of greatness.

He felt Aram lacked real talent for writing, as he did for painting. Perhaps he had a flare for business and should turn to advertising. He would not close his letter with the word "love," as people did without meaning it. He was fed up and urged Aram to be straight with him from now on.

Aram replied that he was getting help from no one but his father, but he could not grasp what this had to do with their misunderstanding. He asked when he was coming to New York so they could talk about a new book.

Bill responded on Aram's twenty-fifth birthday, September 24, 1968, telling him that their old book *Kids Are Best* was in some jeopardy, since he still had not found a theme for it, and, worse, its editors had just resigned from their publisher. He felt sure Cowles would abandon plans for the book.

Bill presumed that this new book was much like the previous one and so was not likely to bring Aram the income to continue to turn out such books. Aram had to find a way to earn that income, and if he did, it might solve all his problems. Bill wished him a happy birthday, but he was tired of trying to help him. He needed to get somebody else to do it. Carol still had a $30,000 judgment against him. There was but $150 left in Aram's account, and this would be sent to him but after that he would need to get out and make his way. He signed it simply, "Pop."

Aram telephoned to explain that the book he had in mind was based on Bill's letter of July 31 about the drug culture and writing such as Aram's that spoke for it. He had interested Chris Cerf in the idea. Bill was uninterested and asked Aram to see that the letter, now with Cerf, be restored to him.

Lucy and Francois had moved into a loft at 111 East Seventy-third Street, from where she called her father to "tattle" on Aram that he had asked her to cooperate in getting more money out of their father. Then, on October 9, she reported that Aram and Gailyn had been married at city hall in New York.

Aram called to confirm this and say that the bride and groom were on their way to San Francisco. Bill congratulated Aram and spoke encouragingly until the now customary arguing began, at which point Bill told his son to do anything he liked but not to expect to be carried any further. He could no longer do it. Later, he telegraphed Aram that Cosette was sick. Aram should not go to San Francisco, but rather stay where he could get help. Bill had neither time nor money to give him.

On October 15, he heard from Lucy that she and Francois had broken up. There had been no big fights or scenes, but he had let her know, in his quiet way, of his need for liberty. She had gone to her mother in California, and there was trying to cope with her pain and confusion. She sent her love.

Aram and Gailyn arrived in San Francisco in November and found a place to rent, at 2134 Woolsey, in Berkeley. During December, Aram called his father in Fresno several times and spoke at such length and so bewilderingly that his father hung up and, when Aram called back, unplugged his telephone.

Bill spent the holidays in Fresno, but he called Cosette, who was always sympathetic to Aram, to ask what he might do to help him. Although he declined her suggestion that they celebrate Christmas together, when she called from San Francisco on New Year's Eve and put Aram on the phone, Bill exchanged holiday greetings with his son and wished him the best for 1969. The Whitelands prophecy was fulfilled.

XVII

THE MISANTHROPE

1968–1974

SAROYAN'S HYPOCHONDRIA, his anxiety over an ailing body that outreached its actual deterioration, was a mirror of that over his elusive creativity.

Most creative writers produce their significant work before they reach fifty years of age, and it is certainly rare that they publish a major work when they have passed sixty-five. Although Saroyan would certainly not have subscribed to any such limitation, he feared his multiplying episodes of inertia, and as he moved into his mid-sixties tried to dispel them with ambitious writing programs and the struggle to complete them.

To be a working writer, which had once been the easy part, was now difficult. His ventures in the novel, always thinly disguised autobiography, had shown his imaginative leaps to be stumbles, and his vision dark with resentment. Actual recollection, however, came easily, producing insights and sustaining the bonhomie, the confident, boozy Saroyan voice he had spent a lifetime cultivating. This late afternoon of his life was to provide a gallery of self-portraits portraying a cynical old rascal, the wunderkind battered by an unexpectedly crooked world yet still able to summon a chuckle for his lost innocence and to pay tribute to the everlasting miracle of being alive.

He tended to linger in Fresno three or four months at a time and took comfort in a few devoted Armenian friends and relatives. There was his cousin Archie Minasian, who adored him and shared his attraction to gambling and writing. There was Buck Makasian and his wife, Doris, Bill's first cousin. There were his friends Ralph and Roxie Moradian, and the sculptor Varaz Surmelian.

When work was over for the day he enjoyed riding his bike to the post office for the mail, cleaning his houses, and watering his garden, which he did to such excess that it became a jungle encroaching on the sidewalk. The neighbors complained that the author's yard was an eyesore and a fire hazard.

But in spite of its comforts, his birthplace proved a poor place to write. In the summer of 1968, despairing of his August work, he declared that he could not start new work in Fresno. He liked returning to San Francisco, to his old apartment and workroom in the basement of Fifteenth Avenue. He would make his rounds of the neighborhood and take the N car to the Embarcadero for a look at the changes along Market Street.

However, it was Cosette's house, and their relationship was a perfunctory one, more that of a business traveler and his secretary than brother and sister. He was as alone there with his frustrations as in his room at the Royalton, and felt far more isolated.

Whenever he was asked about renting his Paris apartment, Bill replied it was not possible, as it must always be ready for him. He loved walking familiar routes around his neighborhood, grocery-shopping, picking up the Paris *Tribune* and the American magazines, calling on Jack Kevorkian, and dropping in at Krikor Atamian's tailor shop on rue Lafayette for a cup of tea and the latest gossip of the Armenian community.

Nevertheless, a firm resistance to the French language kept him from feeling he belonged in Paris. Aside from the doubtful Zanuck venture *The Paris Comedy,* the city had provided him scant material, and its casinos were a constant threat to the fragile hopes at his writing table.

Travel was admittedly an escape from the despair of confronting work in which he had lost his way and the suspicion that he had nothing more to say. But travel also had a lure in itself. He enjoyed the steamer journeys, the Russian boats that went from France through the Scandinavian ports to Leningrad, and the transatlantic and Mediterranean liners with their gushing baths and big dining saloons where he would sit alone at table. He loved the American transcontinental trains with their dining cars and vista domes, where he delighted in naming the passing plains and mountains.

His European travels, increasingly aimed toward the Soviet Union, with its unspent royalties and the triumphant Armenian welcome awaiting him, had a powerful appeal. The literary mantle he had enjoyed in New York during the thirties and forties and had lost somewhere between London and Mill Neck could be restored in the land of his ancestors. It was the Soviet version, and therefore suspect, but it was a comfort all the same.

In the spring of 1972, Bill had an invitation from Haigazian College, an Armenian institute in Beirut, to make the commencement address at its June graduation exercises. He had pleasant recollections of Beirut, and the honorarium would be $2,000, so he decided to make a holiday of it.

The principal speaker at commencement exercises at
Haigazian College in Beirut, June 1972

In June he arrived at the St. George Hotel there. It was a fine place in a beautiful, sun-drenched city. His Haigazian College host, John Markarian, swept him off to Aleppo, in Syria, for an Armenian Day, which seemed to be a Saroyan celebration. He was taken in an embassy car, its "long horn" making way for him through the villages. The flags, photographers, food, and drink were all out for him.

The peak of his Lebanese holiday was a visit to an outlying section of Beirut, the former swamp of Ainjar, which, in the thirty-three years since the Turkish massacre of Musa Dagh, had been transformed into a valley of five hundred happy, prosperous Armenians, complete with a Calouste Gulbenkian school.

He found here a crowd of people awaiting him, with music, young men whisking handkerchiefs and dancing, a picnic laid out on the tables, and, above it all, a banner reading "Welcome Great Writer William Saroyan." As he joined these rejoicing fellow countrymen, he saw his tribute completed. Beneath the arch a young man cut the throat of a lamb. It was, Bill wrote, one of the most important days of his life.

The Armenian intellectuals he met, even the children, struck him as exceptional, displaying both a sense of humor about the human experience and an appreciation of the miracle of being alive.

His commencement address, to the Haigazian faculty, graduates, and well-wishers, on June 27, was to be the culmination of this splendid festival, and he did not want to fail it. He had written the speech weeks earlier, but as its hour approached he made frequent revisions to it. Dressing carefully in a white suit and a green shirt, he admitted he could do no more. It would simply have to do. Facing his audience of a thousand and launching into his text, he realized the speech was far too long. He lost his place several times and digressed, hoping in vain to recapture the straying attention of his listeners. Finishing the speech, he found he had run twenty-five minutes over his allotted time.

Accepting congratulation in the schoolyard, he noticed that everyone had formidable bad breath. While it was clear that he had disappointed and bewildered his sympathetic audience, he told himself that was acceptable, even appropriate. In any case, he knew his shortcomings on the platform and felt lucky to have gotten off with his honorarium.

His plan was to circle the world, and he bought an air ticket that would take him to California by way of a dozen Asian cities. In most of these he was met by delegates from the Armenian communities and welcomed at dinners in his honor. In Shiraz, Iran, at a banquet for one hundred people, he listened to a Mr. Vartunian's fiery Tashnak speech and rose to reply with a characteristically digressive one, which, like those of his droll character Trash Bashmanian, drew bewilderment along with the applause.

As for his central purpose—the writing of some triumphant, vindicating masterpiece—he was ever hopeful, nearly certain that it lay just ahead, perhaps in the work he was now undertaking. The advice he had given Aram, that he face up to a creative well gone dry, was unthinkable for himself. There was no alternative to the daily struggle.

Unless he was traveling, he tried to start a play or a fictional memoir at the first of every month, and he believed that he held the key to ultimate success. The subject didn't really matter, for that was always the same for him and possibly for every writer. As he told himself in starting a fresh project, the point was to get to work, any work, and then fight to keep writing.

Plays had brought him to the Broadway summit, and he believed they would do so again. He wrote a score of them during the 1960s and 1970s. For the most part, they lacked a subject, began in conversations that tried and failed to generate situation and story, then turned to protest, whimsy, obscurity, and, finally, the author's boredom and abandonment.

In 1971, Bill completed a two-act play he had long planned as a capstone to his writing for the theater. It was a dramatization of the humiliation and pride known to contemporary Armenians. He called it *The Armenians* and set it in 1921, in a back room of the red brick Fresno church where he had been a reluctant Sunday-school pupil.

The characters were three Armenian clergymen and various parishioners with passionate loyalties to the Armenian towns of their forbears. There was no narrative and little characterization but plenty of heated argument about Armenia, the diaspora, and the pain of being refugees from the homeland. Although such questions as whether to remain Armenian or become American, and whether God has betrayed the Armenians or even exists, were raised, all agreed there were no satisfactory answers.

In 1974, the New York Diocese of the Armenian Church volunteered to present *The Armenians* as part of its April arts festival at the Haig Kavookjian Armenian Arts Center. Although the author did not attend a performance he heard a recording of it and protested that the production was "stupid and all wrong, good God."

Although the performance won some favorable reviews, the play itself is persuasive evidence that Saroyan had not regained his early ability to dramatize ideas. Ignoring the need to find a correlative in character and situation, he had simply gathered characters onstage and let them speak to the audience, so many puppets delivering his casual attitudes about the Church and Armenian nationalism.

In January 1969, the *Saturday Evening Post,* for 150 years as dependable a national institution as the mail, and Bill Saroyan's most receptive market, ceased publication. It had paid for and published the bulk of his best late-life work. It had serialized his novels and memoirs and asked of his stories an accessible narrative form.

The *Post*'s passing marked a diversification in national reading taste and curbed Saroyan expectations of major income from his stories. Yet over the next several years, those of his mid-sixties, the surviving magazines continued to publish him.

He found a particularly welcoming and generous editor in Margaret Cousins, of the *Ladies' Home Journal.* The *Journal* bought four of his best stories, "Getting Along at School," "Picnic Time," "The Last Word Is Love," and "How to Choose a Wife." *The New Yorker* took three, beginning with "A Fresno Fable," a wry dialogue between two Armenian-Americans who don't trust *anybody,* including each other.

The *Atlantic* bought "Snake," "The Dostoevsky Christmas Story," and "The Inscribed Copy of the Kreutzer Sonata," a witty account of love as warfare and the prevailing of Old World wisdom. *McCall's* published "Lord Chugger of Cheer," about a boy's first bicycle and a further defense of spoiling children, while *Harper's* bought "Isn't Today the Day," an ironic portrayal of the writer's daily strife, which Martha Foley chose for her *Best Short Stories of 1974.*

But even as he appeared in these top-notch magazines, he knew the stories came from his past, nearly all of them written in the heat of his 1964 one-a-day campaign. While he could still revise short fiction that had been on his shelf for years, he could no longer conceive a promising story idea, let alone develop it into narrative.

Thus he turned to the welcoming lanes of reminiscence, explored in 1953 with *Bicycle Rider in Beverly Hills* and repeated with variable success in *Here Comes,* in 1961, and *Not Dying,* in 1963. While none brought the embrace of the critics nor enlarged his audience, they allowed him to do what he did best, remember and reclaim the indignation and sweet promise of his youth.

I Used to Believe I Had Forever was more literary scrapbook than memoir, but it was in the retrospective mode. Cowles published it in the fall of 1968, and the critics scored it for ponderous ruminations. One reviewer noted unkindly that while the author's manner suggested wisdom and wit, in fact he had nothing profound nor perceptive to say.

It did contain his tribute to Walt Whitman, whom he saw as the Prometheus of American letters. He believed *Leaves of Grass* to be the beginning of American culture and saw the poet as a bank of the qualities he most admired: self-educated, a loner, an impudent upstart willing to make a fool of himself, belonging to no school and founder of none, but a towering figure. Whitman *was* somebody simply by saying so, and thus was the prototypical American.

Throughout the early months of 1968, Bill had assumed his *Letters from 74 rue Taitbout* was proceeding to publication at New American Library. Then, in April, when Bob Gutwillig sent Bill the galley proofs, the editor asked to change the title to *Don't Go But If You Must, God Love You,* Bill decided to keep the original title. He still had not signed the contract, and, on reading it, he wrote Gutwillig that his share of subsidiary rights was unacceptable. He found the editor's reply evasive and then heard from the *Post,* which was about to publish excerpts from the book, that Gutwillig had said the title was still undecided. Angry at this display of editorial initiative, Bill told the *Post* to tell Gutwillig the title was *Letters from 74 rue Taitbout.*

On finding Gutwillig inaccessible, Bill's irascibility locked in place. He instructed the editor's sweet-natured assistant to return the manuscript and galleys so he could take the book elsewhere, and the *Post* to remove NAL's name from the credit line.

The matter was resolved in mid-August, when Michael Cohn, vice president of World, NAL's parent publisher, phoned to explain that custom entitled a publisher to 50 percent of book club rights. Bill told him to fix the contract to his liking within the week or forget it. The former was done.

Taitbout was a gallery of portraits. There was a derisive one of Louis B. Mayer, admiring ones of Geoffrey Faber and Calouste Gulbenkian, touching ones of his cousin Chesley, and an anonymous Pat Winter. The book was published in early 1969, to critical indifference. "We can see where Saroyan lives," said the *New York Times,* "in the big-eyed Armenian child he was then, back in California fifty years ago."

Bill did reveal an interesting awareness that his buffoon manner, the roaring and telling of funny stories inherited from his maternal side, could be offensive. It was always getting out of hand, but even as he told himself to quiet down, he would reassure the rowdy within that he was a really good writer and that others would excuse his making so much noise.

He had begun *God's Autobiography* and the journal-like *August Days* in 1967, and during the year since their completion they had been rejected by his slate of likely publishers. Late in 1968 he sent both manuscripts to Charlotte Mayerson, at Holt, Rinehart and Winston, and her response to *August Days* encouraged him to complete further sections and send them to her. In February 1969, after several months of silence, he called at her office and was surprised to find her ready to contract for the book. There would be a $4,000 advance against a 15 percent royalty. He could provide the illustration and need share only the paperback rights with his publisher.

Delighted, Bill set to work on the manuscript and a jacket drawing. A few days later, when he called at Mrs. Mayerson's office with an armful of manuscript, he was annoyed to be kept waiting. When he complained, she told him that he had to let her work in her own way. Her own way inflamed the Saroyan indignation, and he insisted on an audience with Tom Wallace, Holt's chief editor. This convinced him he was not adequately appreciated at Holt. Rejecting their offer, he asked for the return of his manuscript.

When he offered it to Dial, the editor, Al Hart, agreed to a $2,500 advance and a 15 percent royalty and scheduled the book for publication the following year. It was the summer of Apollo 11 and Neil Armstrong's spectacular moonwalk, so the title became *Days of Life and Death and Escape to the Moon.*

This small book, published in July 1970, fared better than any of the previous memoirs, indeed better than any of his recent books. It was admired for its sprightliness. While its subject was death, the book displayed the old life-lover's accommodation to its onset. Admitting to his failure, pain, and loss of direction, Saroyan was still showing his style.

During May 1971, Bill rediscovered *Places,* which he had written during his 1969 summer in Paris. It recalled sixty-eight places that had been critical in his life: the Twenty-third Street YMCA; Stanley Rose's bookshop; a Paris hotel room where Zanuck had gypped him; the Mill Neck house, where Carol and Rosheen had misused him; the Hampshire House, where girls had besieged him; and Boston, where he had reversed the disastrous course of *Time of Your Life.*

In his revisions of *Places,* he achieved a disciplined, acerbic tone and a surer sense of who he was as a writer than in any of the previous memoirs. His irony was sometimes hard on women and devastating toward Carol, yet the mood was lighthearted. His youthful innocence, cast off in the realities of war and marriage, was recalled.

He sent it to the new publisher, Praeger. That firm's editor, Bill Weatherby, agreed to an advance of $5,000, a 15 percent royalty, and a 65 percent share of paperback rights. Retitled *Places Where I've Done Time,* it would be published with major promotion in March 1972.

Praeger was determined to give the book a full dress launching in the spring of 1972. The firm's announcement ad in *Publishers Weekly* welcoming Saroyan back annoyed him, since he believed he had never been away. He grudgingly agreed to a publicity tour, which took him to talk shows and book signings in Chicago and Minneapolis before a saturation of the New York interview circuit and a party in his honor. All of this roused his ulcer and left him exhausted and eager for a rest in Paris.

On his return from the trip, he found *Places* well received. It had gone into several printings and was becoming the most successful book of his later life. Praeger warned Bill against rosy expectations. While they had shipped nearly twelve thousand copies, books were not moving out of the stores, and substantial returns were expected. At first there was no interest in a paperback edition, but when Dell made a modest offer of $3,000 for reprint rights, Bill predictably demanded 75 percent of the sum. Pointing out that the terms had not been set and thus he had every right to 100 percent, he overcame Praeger's objections, thereby cooling his relationship with yet another publisher.

While he had hoped to start new work during the summer of 1972, he did none, and felt a significant change. He lacked the desire, the will, to begin a fresh project and asked himself if he were simply lazy or if he had suffered a stroke of the spirit. How had so swift a kid gone idle?

He was in a doldrum that often seemed terminal. In June 1973, his sense of writerly sterility and of growing fat overwhelmed him. Half of the precious year had gone for nothing, and he resolved that by his sixty-fifth birthday he would have lost twenty pounds and be launched on new work.

He started with no plan in mind but to start, telling himself that was how it was always done. He undertook three separate works and on July 1 added an additional novel and a play, expecting to complete all five before he turned sixty-five. He kept to a spartan diet, eating one fine meal in late afternoon but otherwise only cottage cheese, tea, and stewed fruit.

His work period was brief and intense, yet struggling with the day's chore his mind wandered and sometimes stopped altogether. Rather than new vistas and ideas he was arriving at dead ends. Although the program went on, it was the hardest writing he had ever done. He finished the season's ordeal with the five works complete, but he did not believe any was marketable.

What sustained Saroyan and steadily restored his solvency during his sixties was the work of his earliest years. *The Time of Your Life*, now thirty years old, had become an American classic, a perennial candidate for revival and a royalty earner for Samuel French.

In September 1968, Jackie Gleason told Bill that he wanted to do a ninety-minute TV musical of *Time of Your Life*, and that CBS would pay $100,000 for the rights. It did not surprise Bill to find that Hal Matson had been instrumental in this proposal. They were thinking of Orson Welles for director, but when Bill recommended himself for the job there was no objection.

As Bill pessimistically anticipated, TV interest in the play languished, but presently T. Edward Hambleton proposed to revive it in the APA Phoenix Theatre's 1969 season. While awaiting Hambleton's offer, Bill heard from the producer Alfred de Liagre and his associate, Martha Scott, who offered to revive it for four weeks at the ANTA Theatre, proposing a $2,000 advance.

When de Liagre spoke of TV rights as well, Bill put him off, saying he had turned down TV offers of $100,000. Actually, he had taken a dislike to "Delly's" aristocratic manner, and when he received the $2,000 with an agreement for signature, Bill, then in Paris, returned the check and was unavailable to de Liagre's phone calls. On hearing de Liagre's voice, Bill pretended to be a lodger and reported that Saroyan was out of town.

Then, in August 1969, Jules Irving offered to present *Time of Your Life* for eight weeks at Lincoln Center. Bill agreed to an advance of $7,000 and a 5 percent royalty. The play opened at the Vivian Beaumont Theatre on November 6, and in spite of carping reviews from Clive Barnes and Richard Watts, it was well received and did such good business that there was interest in moving it to Broadway. While this did not come to pass, the income from amateur productions increased greatly. Bill's royalties from Samuel French exceeded $18,000 in a single year.

The following summer, 1971, Bill agreed to a national tour of *Time of Your Life* starring Henry Fonda and directed by Gene Kelly. He was to have an advance of $5,000 and 10 percent of the gross receipts. Martha Scott, who was in charge of the tour for Plumstead Management, promised a January opening at the Kennedy Center in Washington, followed by engagements in Chicago, Minneapolis, and Philadelphia, and a finale at the Huntington Hartford Theatre, in Los Angeles.

When Martha Scott reported that business on the road was disappointing and asked him to take a royalty cut for the tour's sake, Bill refused. He saw the show in March at the Studebaker Theatre in Chicago, and, in a fit of now chronic irascibility, judged it a fiasco. His particular objections were Oliver Smith's set, the music, the Arab's failure to play the harmonica, and Fonda's performance. Quitting the theater prematurely, he shared his opinion with bystanders, including the show's publicity agent, who suggested that if he felt so strongly about it he might stomp down the aisle and up onto the stage and make a scene. Bill's response—that Henry Fonda's son should have played the Joe role—appeared in *Newsweek*. Nevertheless, he continued to press for his final four weeks' royalties of $14,000 and appealed to the Dramatists Guild to act for him.

Then, in October 1973, he began a series of grandly ambitious work programs, each with multiple projects, all intended to last into the new year. Even as they failed to generate his interest and were discarded, he told himself he had to keep on working, fighting it out.

Throughout his life, William Saroyan had had a remarkable ambivalence toward money. He had scorned money, squandered a fortune of it, and rationalized its loss as motivation for his writing. Yet he constantly sought it from his work and his gambling, for he knew it was power and, in spite of his every denial, a measure of his worth and consequence.

His gambling had been rooted in the belief that he was charmed and lucky enough to beat the odds. His hard-won wisdom was that somewhere along the line, most likely in 1939, his fabulous streak of luck had run out and was never coming back. Now, in his sixties, he resolved to get rich just as those businessmen, for whom he felt undiminished contempt, did in smart investment. Although his 1969 stock market speculation had left him poorer by $10,000, his royalty income was such that by the summer of 1970 he had salted away $80,000 in bank certificates of deposit and securities.

This affluence was still threatened by Carol's $30,000 judgment against him. Her lawyer had put liens on his income at its several sources. Thus, when he received a royalty payment from Harcourt in May 1969, Bill was puzzled about how it had slipped through the Krakower trapline. He soon discovered the reason from Alan Fenner: Arnold Krakower had died in April. Bill told Fenner that he supposed he ought to feel sorry, but he didn't. The man was evil and had given him a bad time.

Looking up the obituary, he learned that Krakower, once a marine corps sergeant, had died at the age of fifty-three in New York Hospital. No cause was given, so Bill proposed that it was from excessive cleverness and self-importance. Bill recalled how Krakower had accused him of telling his children their mother was Jewish. When Bill had inquired what Krakower

Bill loved bicycles. They appeared in his fiction and memoirs.
Here he is getting around Fresno on his Raleigh, 1976.

would have preferred he tell them, the man had not listened but let Bill know he was the law, and had brought judgment and the lien against him. Bill rejoiced in his death.

Bill's unabashed hatred of Krakower illuminates more of his emotional map. His passionate love for Carol had become an equally charged bitterness. Krakower was her gun, aimed where he was most vulnerable, his new wealth. Accrued in these late years, the money was more than lack of want, more than security and a bank balance. It was his reward, countable evidence of his sixty-five years of a writer's achievement and ultimate good luck. His jealousy of it was a miser's, inflaming hostility to any who threatened it and revealing, behind the old, bemused, avuncular mask, a misanthrope.

In early 1971 the aging Lincoln that Bill had bought in New York for a cross-country trip showed terminal symptoms. Pete, his mechanic, advised that the transmission was going, and that it would be unwise to spend more money on the car. On July 30 it collapsed altogether, and Bill sold it to the

Stadium Garage in San Francisco for $225, calculating that the twenty-five thousand miles he had added to its odometer had cost him a pricey twenty cents a piece. It had been a lemon, sold to him by an Armenian hustler. Now, when he looked at cars in the showrooms on Van Ness, only a Rolls appealed to him, and he thought, *Not yet.*

He recalled the bicycle he had bought Aram years ago in Beverly Hills and the book he had named for it. He would have a new car soon, but in the meantime he bought a three-speed Raleigh bicycle for his Fresno errands.

He looked at Volvos and rode in a borrowed one of Ed Hagopian's; he was loaned a Toyota by his cousin Louis Saroyan and thought it a toy. Buck Minasian drove him in his Datsun, Harold Markarian in his Plymouth, Victoria Saroyan in her Mustang. But he thought they were all flimsy cars, lacking in dignity. When Ralph Moradian told Bill he had read in the newspaper that Bill had sold his car in San Francisco and was riding a bicycle around town, Bill admitted he was taking his time in choosing a new car, but by November he still had not done so. He told himself that he was rich; he had $125,000, and could buy a new car if he chose, but he did not.

He liked to ride his bicycle to the post office for the day's mail and to stop at the Thriftimart for a cup of its free coffee, and he convinced himself that the life he enjoyed here did not require a car. When he went to the horse races at the Fresno Fair, or to the park to watch Varaz Surmelian at work on his patriotic sculpture *David of Sassoun,* he could catch a ride with Archie Minasian or Ed Hagopian.

As 1972 ended he was comforted to know that *this* year he had made a $10,000 profit in the stock market. At last, he was taking on some financial stature. He had $34,000 in CDs, $44,000 in stock, and cash in his New York, Paris, and London accounts that brought his total worth to $150,000.

Bill now resorted to his foundation and its tax-shelter potential. He asked Plumstead to make his royalty payments to it, and since these were several thousand dollars a week, $36,000 of royalties accumulated in the foundation's account. Then, as the play's tour expenses mounted, the payments ceased, and Plumstead Playhouse did not respond to Bill's protest that he was owed $16,000.

He now regretted putting the proceeds from the tour into the Saroyan Foundation and beyond his reach. Next he learned that a new tax law had ruled out any advantage the foundation had previously given him and left him liable to a federal tax on its 1972 income. He told Henry that the plan simply didn't work and that they must now dissolve the foundation and put its funds into his own 1972 income.

Richard Harrington, who had set up the foundation, explained that disbanding it would require permission of the IRS and the California secretary of state, triggering investigations. He urged keeping it alive, if dormant, and making a gift of its manuscripts to the University of California's Bancroft Library. James Hart, its director, would see to the safety and cataloging of all Saroyan material.

Bill protested that the tax collector had made him a penny-pincher if not a miser. The foundation was primarily for the benefit of *this* writer. The $36,000 from the revival must not elude him. With that money, he would buy a building in which to keep his papers, and in his own way.

Harrington reminded Bill that he had advised against putting the royalties into the foundation in the first place but did not believe Bill could now simply take the money back. Such a charitable gift was irrevocable. He warned Bill that in reclaiming the money he could expect a challenge from the California attorney general as well as the IRS.

Bill took a part of Harrington's advice, entrusting certain manuscripts to the Bancroft Library and preserving the Saroyan Foundation. Nevertheless, he insisted that the contribution had been in error and grudgingly paid a federal tax of $16,000 for including it in his own 1972 income.

As always, the obituary page was central to Bill's daily study of the newspaper. It gave him an opportunity to pass judgment on a man's life and led him to think of the obituary as a particularly appealing literary form. Dwelling on death confirmed his belief that the wise accept it from the start yet most people in Western civilizations escape the reality in fantasies of wealth and achievement. It occurred to him that while death for a child is a tragedy, if one lives to a great age, it becomes a triumph, an event most wished for. He remembered that at eleven he had come upon an almanac called *Last Words of the Great* and had been exhilarated at the thought of what his own last words would be.

When he wrote an article about death, "Last Words of the Great," for *The Nation,* he gave it the Saroyan stamp, likening death to the Fresno poker player's outraged response to the game's interruption by a gunman: Couldn't the man see he finally had a decent hand?

On reading of Arnoldo Mondadori's death, in June 1961, he had lamented the passing of the last of the great publishers, and added him to a list of three others: Alfred Harcourt, Donald Brace, and Geoffrey Faber. Although they were not yet ready for final tribute, he also put Frank Morley and Robert Giroux down as fine editors. Ken McCormick was included as a nice guy. He excluded James Laughlin, Bob Gutwillig, Howard Cady, and Bennett Cerf because of their assorted failures.

He took the survivor's cold comfort from the passing of his contemporaries, John Dos Passos and John O'Hara, in 1970, and Edmund Wilson, in 1972. On reading of Bennett Cerf's death, in August 1971, he had no forgiveness for his first publisher. He remembered only that Cerf had once crossed him. Bill thought of him as a Columbia know-it-all and felt it unforgivable that back in 1936, supported by his famous editor Saxe Commins, he had spurned *Little Children,* a book that was later published in a dozen languages.

Bill supposed that many readers believed *he* was dead. They had not heard from Salinger lately either, and he was not dead. Readers now knew only Philip Roth, Malamud, and Saul Bellow. He remembered that one night in Paris he had joined James Jones, Gore Vidal, and Irwin Shaw for dinner in the Bois, and that each of these writers was now a millionaire and regarded as important by the critics. On the one hand, he felt they deserved it, on the other he thought that they were second-raters, clever hacks. His own writing was in another class entirely.

He thought Jones a poseur, a forceful man who wrote plodding fiction; that Vidal, a bisexual with emphasis on the homosexual, wrote brilliant, super-clever gossipy stuff that caused enormous pain to his rival Truman Capote; and that Shaw was a huge man who rushed at his writing and did good, straight narrative about people like himself who were deeply boring and worthless. As for Norman Mailer, he recognized the man's very bright sensibility but remembered that at Mailer's party in Hollywood in 1950 or 1951 he had found him a silly bore, unusually pleased with himself.

He was also aware that these views were a revelation of his nature. Was he jealous? he asked himself. He replied in enthusiastic affirmation.

His brother-in-law Walt Papazian's fatal heart attack, in April 1971, following a three-day examination at Stanford Hospital, added to Bill's own sense of coronary frailty. Unusual effort such as climbing stairs or lifting a rock now put him out of breath, and he was alarmed by several episodes of pain in his chest and upper arm. When he was examined in Fresno, Dr. Robert Duerksen assured him that his heart and blood pressure were in good order, and that his trouble was not the suspected angina but a hiatal hernia, a narrowing at the bottom of his esophagus.

What most annoyed him was the frequent need to piss, sometimes hourly in the course of a night. On the morning of May 13, 1971, he noted with customary irony that he had a broken-down prostate, esophagitis, an ulcer, arthritis, and a toothache, but he felt pretty good.

Anxiety about his prostate was heightened by his study of a medical text on the subject and convinced him of his need for surgery. When he presented himself at the Fresno Community Hospital, Dr. Irwin Barg examined him and assured him that he had only a minor infection, for which he prescribed sulfa pills.

Bill's greatest delight was in the vines and fruit trees of his garden. Nothing restored his spirit like watering them, even as the neighbors complained that he was drowning their own citrus crop. For professional advice, he turned to his friend Yep Moradian, who had made a fortune in agrobusiness. Yep dutifully came by West Griffith Way to do the necessary pruning and spraying.

Yep and Roxie Moradian had just completed their elaborate Japanese-style house adjoining a golf course, and in July 1970 they invited the sculptor Beniamino Bufano down from San Francisco. As an old friend of Bufano's, Bill took part in the welcoming and admired Bufano's gift to the Moradians, a three-foot St. Francis, which he assessed at $30,000.

A month later, Yep called Bill with the news that Bufano was dead, having fallen from a ladder in his San Francisco studio. A heart attack seemed likely. Although saddened, Bill declined Yep's invitation to join him for the funeral.

Learning that he had been named an honorary pallbearer did not change Bill's mind. His final, self-exposing thought for Bufano was that the sculptor had a gift for self-exploitation which had persisted too long.

When he read in the *San Francisco Chronicle*'s account of the Bufano funeral that Roxie Moradian had explained Saroyan's absence by saying he was "too broken up" to appear, Bill was furious. He did not want Roxie and Yep speaking for him about *his* business. He felt they were showing off their intimacy with him. This brought out a resentment toward Yep's cleverness in business. Storing grain at government expense was but one of the ways in which he had made money.

It brought George Mardikian to mind, his old friend whom he hadn't seen in twenty-three years. They were of a kind, he felt, these Armenians who had become rich and phony. While he recalled drinking and dining at Mardikian's Omar Khayyam restaurant, writing a preface to his cookbook, he ignored those generous loans that had rescued him from gambling disaster, his huge debt to the man, and his mother's advice about it. Mardikian's aura of American-style success and fame was too radiant for any Saroyan redemption.

Paying tribute to a friend at the time of his death was always beyond Bill Saroyan. When Chuck Daggett had died, in February 1957, his wife, Frances, had called Bill in Malibu to ask if he would say something about Chuck at the memorial service. Bill had known Daggett for twenty-eight years, as a newspaperman and the center of the Stanley Rose Bookshop gang. With Rose, Daggett had encouraged him through the writing of *The

Human Comedy. Bill regarded him as a good guy but a poor man who had never found himself, if there had been anything there to find. He was forever chasing women and getting into trouble about it. Bill had felt that if he spoke at the funeral he would have to be straight, and it would not be suitable for the occasion. He was sorry Chuck was dead, but he would not go to his funeral. Funerals weren't for him.

As he had begged off, telling Frances he was not good at oratory, he understood he was now a monster to her. Although a little troubled by this, he told himself that when he came to write of those days, Chuck Daggett would take his proper place in them.

When Ross Bagdasarian's son Skipper phoned in June 1971, asking if he could stop for a visit, Bill suspected a parry in the Bagdasarian feud. He recalled that the Bagdasarians had been friendly with Carol during the bad time of the lawyers, and that when the Archie Minasians had visited Ross and Armen recently they were hustled away because Mr. and Mrs. Walter Matthau were coming. Bill told Skipper that he was working and refused him.

The same blood ran in his and Ross's veins. They had been dearest friends since childhood, and Bill had introduced him to the world of theater and film, yet six years ago he had banished him for achieving the success that had switched their roles and made Bill into Ross's debtor.

Late on the afternoon of January 16, 1972, Bill had a shocking call from Cosette. Ross had died of a heart attack that morning in Beverly Hills. Rising first, he had gone downstairs, then come back to his room and fallen silent. Armen had found Ross dead. Lucy, who had this news from her mother, had called Cosette.

Bill was stunned and sorrowful but did not expect any word from the Bagdasarian family and was unsure whether to send his condolences. He was sure that he would not be going to any funeral. The *Fresno Bee* called Bill for comment. He said only that he was ten years older than Ross, and that in 1939, while driving from New York, they had collaborated on a medley of Armenian folk songs, "Come On-A My House."

A title for a story occurred to him: "How Many Rolls Royces Did He Own at the Time of His Death?" That night he dreamed of dying, death, and his cousin. In the dream Ross was well dressed and wore alligator shoes, and when Bill offered him baked eggplant, he ate it and agreed it was pretty good.

The next several days were glum. Sorrow lay over everything. Ross's brother Harry phoned the night of the funeral to curse Bill in Armenian for not coming to the ceremony. He told him that many had come, and that the Matthaus were among them. According to Ross's will, Harry was to manage Ross's winery business, and twenty-four-year-old Skipper was to learn it from him.

Bill recalled that just twenty-six years ago, at the time of Lucy's birth, Ross and he had celebrated it in San Francisco, laughing, loafing, walking the streets together, just as they had in London a few years before. Well, that was beyond Ross's recall now, buried as he was in Beverly Hills. For Bill, Ross was still a farmboy, astray in the wilds of the moneyed world.

When Lucy wrote to share her grief, she told Bill how full of life and laughter Ross had been during the recent holidays. He had given her $200 in addition to a bracelet from the Bagdasarian family. Bill replied that he could not believe Ross was dead. He told Lucy about his dream of Ross and also, curiously, of his theory that anyone who dies betrays his family and friends. Bill dreamed of holding Aram in his arms, and when the boy said that his father was dead, Bill assured him that he was here.

Bill's concern about his own health now centered on his prostate. Calling at the University of California Hospital, he told a Dr. Donald Smith there that he needed to piss every half hour. On examining him, Dr. Smith advised that whether or not surgery was required, he could be treated as well in Fresno. Relieved, Bill returned to West Griffith Way on August 1, ready to pursue a sensible, productive life. While his prostate continued to be worrisome, the doctor pronounced him sound—and fortunate in a 150/90 blood pressure.

Bill's morbid state of mind intensified his loneliness and want of family comfort, and yet his visits with Aram and Lucy were sporadic. Both children needed reassurance and money and regularly turned to him for both, but in spite of occasional passionate reunions, they were ever more alienated.

During February 1969, Aram, in New York, called his father in Fresno to ask a series of questions. He found the paternal answers so hostile that he responded with derisive "uh-huh"s and ended by proposing that Bill go fuck himself, to which Bill replied, with full military irony, "Yes, sir."

A few weeks later, Bill was in New York, and while on a night walk, wandered into the Marboro Bookshop, on Forty-second Street. As he browsed, a clerk touched his arm, and he turned to face his unsmiling son. They did not speak, and Bill left the shop quickly for his hotel.

In November of that year Cosette invited Aram and Gailyn for a San Francisco visit of several weeks, but Bill took no part in it other than a phone call for a brief hello. At the same time he learned that without his consent, Aram had sold their correspondence, 250 father-to-son letters, to the UCLA library. This heightened the wall between them.

Lucy's news was more welcome. She called in a happy state to report that she had a role in *Ah Wilderness* at Ford's Theatre in Washington, and had quit smoking. He had tried to get her a part in a TV production of his play *Making Money*, but couldn't. Then she won a part in the Bucks County Playhouse production of *The Prime of Miss Jean Brodie*.

In the spring of 1970 he heard from Aram that he was working at Academy Typing Service in New York, and a month later that he and the now pregnant Gailyn had moved to Marblehead, Massachusetts, and leased a house for a year. Aram admitted that he now knew he was neither a writer nor a photographer. Nevertheless, he still wanted to make a book out of his father's extraordinary letter to him about their generational differences. Bill's response was a firm and immediate no.

Bill learned he had become a grandfather, from Cosette. On October 20, 1970, in Marblehead, Gailyn had given birth to a six-pound, seven-ounce daughter. Although Bill absorbed this news with charitable thoughts for Aram's new family, he kept them to himself. It was Archie Minasian who told him his first grandchild's name was Strawberry. Bill wondered, with Romeo's irony, if there was any importance in a name.

A month later, at Doubleday's invitation, Bill went to New York for a short-story conference. Aram called him at the Royalton to say that he and Gailyn were staying in Lucy's apartment on Eighty-first Street. Bill heard his granddaughter's voice for the first time and agreed to Aram's suggestion that he come by for a look at her.

Bill's visit to Aram's family lasted two and a half hours. In the course of it Aram photographed his father holding Strawberry awkwardly on his lap and told of plans to leave soon for a year in London. Bill found that because of the child, he could believe in Aram now. Afterward, father and son walked downtown together, as far as Seventieth Street, where they exchanged so longs and embraced. Bill proclaimed the day one of the most memorable of his life.

On a return visit to New York in March 1971, Bill learned from Lucy that Aram and his family had not gone to London but returned to Cambridge, where Aram hoped for a teaching job. Aram wrote in October, describing a poet-in-residence position at New Hampshire College, which paid $10,000 a year, but it was Lucy who reported that the job had fallen through.

Bill spent that Christmas solemn and alone in Fresno. He noted that the holiday was only for kids; they were the only justification for the fuss. On Christmas morning, his phone rang seven or eight times, then again at noon, and again at one. He did not answer and told himself he couldn't be bothered.

On Bill's return from Beirut in July 1972, he had a call from Aram, who was at his mother's in Beverly Hills. He reported that he was now sure of his future, which included settling down in the idyllic seaside community of Bolinas, north of San Francisco. He had found the right house for their home and wanted his father to make the down payment for him. Although Bill tried to hear Aram out patiently he was thinking of the boy's drugs and collapsible grand plans and was soon angry. He told Aram he had chosen his mother's custody, and she would surely want to help him now. When Aram replied that his mother and Walter Matthau could not help, Bill did not believe him.

Bill was appalled to find that Aram and his family had in fact moved to Bolinas. Archie and Helen Minasian had visited the unfurnished house, where the young Saroyans took their rest in sleeping bags and lived on welfare.

During a late-September visit to San Francisco, Bill had a phone call from Aram, who asked if he could come in to see him. Bill agreed, and presently his son appeared to have a cup of tea and tell his news. Gailyn was pregnant again, and Bill predicted that this time it would be a boy. Aram's novel *The Street* was making the rounds of publishers. They were living on $200 a month in unemployment compensation. For $30 he received $90 worth of food stamps. Although Aram complained of a gum ailment, Bill thought he looked well. They walked together, and Bill sent him off on the last bus to Bolinas with a shopping bag full of Fresno fruit and vegetables. He thought Aram had talked more sense than usual—but not much more.

Just before Christmas of 1973, Cosette sent him seven snapshots showing Aram, Gailyn with the newborn Cream in her arms, and Strawberry standing by. Although Cream's face was hidden by her swaddling, he thought they all looked great. Bill spent Christmas alone on Griffith Way, letting the phone ring unanswered several times, entertaining himself with a bicycle ride through familiar Fresno streets, dining on stewed squash and kidneys in wine. He proclaimed it one of the greatest Christmases ever.

In March 1974, Bill decided that after eighteen months in Fresno, it was time to depart for Paris. Pausing in New York, he felt prosperous enough to stop at the St. Regis but was displeased to find that the price of a room had climbed to $46 a day. Settling in, he was surprised by a phone call from Lucy. She had learned from the Celebrity Service sheet that her father was in town and where he could be found.

They had spoken briefly a year ago when he was in New York for the *Places* promotion tour, but they had not had a good talk since March 1971, when they had enjoyed a three-hour tea together. Lucy's present apartment on upper Second Avenue was above a Chinese restaurant, and she proudly showed him its hidden entrance and inventive furnishing. On her bulletin board he found pictures of Lucy and her new cat, Rodeo, himself, her mother, Matthau, and their son, Charlie, Aram, Gailyn, Strawberry, Cream, Anthony Perkins, Maureen Stapleton, and Marlon Brando.

Lucy described touring with Maureen Stapleton in *Gingerbread Lady* and how that stage-wise woman had told her she was a capable actress, that it was up to her. She had earned $16,000 in the last year, doing voice-overs for TV ads.

Lucy now admitted to her father that she had been having an affair with Marlon Brando. He had lived here in this apartment, slept in its big bed. He had wept before her and she believed him a man of special sensitivity and tenderness. He phoned her regularly from Hollywood, and they talked for three hours at a time. Dismayed, Bill noted that Brando was fifty, had been married several times, and was simply fooling with her. Lucy disagreed. No, she did not foresee becoming Brando's wife, nor the mother of his children, even though they did talk about it.

When asked what she *would* do, she suspected that she would eventually marry Francois de Menil. He was her best friend, and customarily loaned her his chauffeur-driven Rolls Royce in which to fetch Brando from the airport. Bill was shaken by Lucy's confession and skeptical of any agreeable outcome, but he told her that he understood her attraction to Brando. He was a talented man with excitement about him.

Although Lucy was aware of her father's wounding at this news, and later believed he had given her an ultimatum to choose between Brando and himself, as always he withheld stern parental advice, believing it would go unheeded. Instead, he urged her to live her life, with Brando particularly, as sensibly as she could.

When they spoke of Aram, Lucy told of her new admiration for him and Gailyn and the loving, if unorthodox, family they had become. Aram had delivered Cream himself, with no more than the advice of neighbors. When Lucy suggested her father might let Aram live in one of his Fresno houses, Bill said it would not be feasible.

Finally, Lucy asked where she and Aram figured in his will. Nowhere, he told her. Neither of them did. They were on their own. Everything in his estate would go to the foundation and be administered by experts. He then asked Lucy why she had asked such a question. Had someone put her up to it? Always fearful that her father might doubt her word, she swore that she had asked for herself alone.

She was broke. Yes, at twenty-one she had received from her mother the $15,000 he had provided, just as Aram had. But she had spent it. Aram's money had gone into his several publications. She also knew that her mother had refused Aram the $40,000 he wanted in order to buy property in Mendocino County. She passed along Aram's opinion that when they bothered their father it made him angry and depressed by bringing back bad memories of their mother. Bill conceded that this was largely true.

Their evening together ended soberly, with Bill carrying her garbage bag downstairs. They parted at an all-night newsstand, where Lucy paid three dollars for two packs of cigarettes, a copy of *Rolling Stone,* and the *Post.* He thought the newsie had overcharged her but said nothing.

In any case, Lucy's confesson made a turning point in their relationship. Bill could accept his daughter's passionate devotion to Brando only as a betrayal and a repudiation of himself. It was unforgivable.

He must have had this 1974 revelation in mind while writing the selection in the 1978 collection *Chance Meetings,* wherein he asked himself if there was anyone who had been a delight to know. Most certainly it was his daughter as a child. She had dazzled him with her lovely simplicity. It was in her looks, her voice, her very breathing. He adored her capacity for outrage at injustice. The sight and sound of her beguiled and astonished him. But then, as she became that reality—a young woman—the magic fell away, as with a flower that has withered.

XVIII

OBITUARIES

1974–1979

A LONDON CRITIC once wrote of Saroyan that any similarly discouraged British writer would have long since conceded the game. But Bill was immune to discouragement. He read the scoffing reviews and survived them by ignoring them. He behaved as if he were always on the threshold of a great, perhaps his greatest, work.

This ironclad self-assurance was also his central flaw. Being able to hear but one voice—his own—had arrested his development and denied him the prominence he felt was his. And yet this very unwillingness to submit to the judgment of others was his life preserver; it kept him writing, believing in the sum of his work, until the very end.

Among the conflicts his confidence had withstood was his concession to writing for money. He revealed his mixed feelings about commercialism in corrosive views of such successful competitors as Hemingway, Steinbeck, and Tennessee Williams. He thought they were simply better businessmen.

He conceded his midlife course change, from making art to making money by his writing. He had declared it in 1957 with *Mama I Love You* and the *Post*'s bonanza for it. He had no regrets, nor did he believe it had done his writing any damage. However, it had given the size of advances and royalty scales an ever greater significance. The sums he was able to command became ends in themselves.

In this ultimate stage of his career, he saw the twin streams of art and income, which had seemed remote from each other in his years of proud success, flowing together into the belief that money in the bank, money that could be counted, measured a man's worth. His own past behavior notwithstanding, he now believed his latter-day advice to Aram—that in a writer, miserliness is a necessary virtue.

What is more difficult to understand in the aging, still proud, Saroyan was a fresh indifference to "quality control." Early on, he had enthusiastic belief in everything he wrote. When he did come to an understanding that he was capable of writing inferior stuff, experience showed that most of it was salvageable in the crucible of revision. But increasingly in these last years, he reckoned with work that fell below his own standard and came to terms with it in a remarkable act of artistic self-amnesty. Whether it was any good or not was not his business. Jettisoning that baggage was the only way to proceed. His business was only to add whatever he could to the monument of his fiction, drama, autobiography, and drawing. It was an appalling surrender and self-deception. For a man so proud of his standards, how could he proceed without them? But so he did—or he tried to.

The primary memoir of this period, *Sons Come and Go, Mothers Hang in Forever,* came about through a novel that he had written in Paris during the summer of 1974. He gave it the title *TRA*—ART spelled backward—and he felt it might be his masterpiece. He urged the agent Scott Meredith to find a generous publisher for it, and Meredith agreed to try, but when Bill called at his office he learned that thirty-five publishers had rejected it. Only one, McGraw-Hill, had made a cautious offer, of $5,000. Bill told himself that he would reject it, and Scott Meredith's representation as well.

Nonetheless, at the agent's insistence he did visit Fred Hills, the interested editor at McGraw-Hill, and liked him well enough to accept this minimal advance and to propose an additional book, a memoir on the order of *Places Where I've Done Time.*

On his return to Fresno, Bill learned from Meredith that McGraw-Hill had cooled toward *TRA* and had withdrawn its offer altogether. He decided that he was finished with McGraw and the Scott Meredith agency. Then, during February 1975, he heard from Fred Hills suggesting a book similar to *Places* about people who had been influential and interesting to him. Bill liked the idea, jotted down a list of subjects, and began to write the book the next day.

It would be a gallery of famous people he had known, illuminated by insights he had drawn from the encounters. He began with Yvor Winters, describing him as his first exposure to a professional writer with values and a flinty intelligence, the like of which he had never seen. The list would include Henry Miller, Marilyn Monroe, Greta Garbo, George Bernard Shaw, Hemingway, and Walter Winchell. In May he sent it off to Fred Hills.

As he was leaving Paris for Fresno, there was splendid news. A cable from Hills said that McGraw wanted to publish the *People* book and showed admirable enthusiasm by offering an advance of $10,000.

In New York, Bill was surprised to find that he liked Fred Hills's editing. The book was becoming more than just a collection. As he put himself into the renderings of each portrait, the whole was growing into a Saroyan testament and confession, not only his opinion of these people but a working out of his thoughts about nothing less than the meaning of his life.

He began with a chapter called "What's It All About?," in which he admitted to a certain egotism and explained he had derived it from Jesus Christ. He was sympathetic to Jesus' insistence that He was God, the Son of God, and the whole human race, but took note of the outrageousness of his claim and its emptiness if it did not apply equally to everyone else. In a human being, the claim was an ultimate egotism, a quality he called "raging selfness" and found in many of the greatest people he had known. He would include portraits of these greats. Sibelius, Mencken, and Diego Rivera would be among them.

In the course of his portraiture, he made no attempts to disguise his lifelong hatreds. He remembered that Henry Miller had praised him as America's foremost writer but had turned out to be a wimpish fellow who had only wanted to borrow money from him. He remembered Louis B. Mayer as a man who had conned him out of the rights for *The Human Comedy* and whose funeral was widely enjoyed. He remembered Hemingway for his bullying piece about *Trapeze* in *Esquire* forty years ago, and for his failure as a Nobel laureate to acknowledge his debts to Sherwood Anderson and Gertrude Stein. Nevertheless, Bill admired his suicide as a deliberate, ingenious exit from his life.

In a selection called "Norman Who?," he displayed his resentment of writers more successful than he and, with a saving honesty, wrote how it annoyed him that these luminaries kept him in their shadow. There was a niche for James Laughlin, the esteemed gentleman proprietor of New Directions, who had irritated him first by his passion for Alpine skiing and then proceeded to the unpardonable—losing a Saroyan story that he had solicited.

In the light of these late years he revised some of his strongest judgments. Stanley Rose, whom he had fired and shunned in midlife, now earned back some approval as one of his best friends. Zanuck, while hated by many writers and sometimes by him, was really a good man. At last he paid his overdue tribute to George Jean Nathan, admitting it was Nathan's liking for *Highlands,* and urgings for a long play, that had led to the writing of *Time of Your Life* and its author's taking his place in theater history. Even so, his gratitude was qualified as he recalled Nathan, habitually surrounded by his girlfriends, dying a recent Catholic convert with a priest beside him. He concluded that Nathan had dressed neatly and gone fearlessly among dangerous people, that his death left Broadway diminished, and that there would not be anyone like him again.

As always, he conceded Charlie Chaplin's genius, but he held that he was a monster and proceeded to justify monsterhood as genius's corollary—and then, with surprising candor, he admitted that he too was a monster. With some pain, he remembered making a recording with not yet five-year-old Lucy in which he was full of himself. He now wished that he had passed that half hour with her quietly, not as a blustering genius but as a simple, earnest, loving father.

One of the final portraits was that of his cousin Chesley. He recalled Chesley as the joy of his parents but also a weeping child who seemed to despair of all humanity. Chesley's suicide, dousing himself with gasoline and driving his little blue car over an embankment, brought Bill full circle. He noted how we all live at the edge of despair, saved only by a balance of joy in life, in the *accident* of being. Thus he rejoiced in himself, in all that self's absurdity, his self-love and hatred for the rest of the human race. He admitted that he really hated himself too, yet somehow loved himself as a part of the essential whole.

Home in Fresno on July 19, he heard from Fred Hills that Scott Meredith, who had sent him to McGraw-Hill, felt entitled to his commission on the book's $10,000 advance and, if need be, would sue Saroyan for it. Bill responded with customary asperity. He urged Meredith to sue him, predicting he would not only make a fool of himself but Bill would ask damages. A few days later, McGraw-Hill's lawyer concurred, and no more was heard of Meredith's threat.

As a title for the *People* book Bill proposed *SOBs Come and Go, Mothers Hang in Forever.* A somewhat baffling example of Saroyan's whimsical nomenclature, the title defined this retrospective view of his life, the parade of lawyers, agents, editors, publishers, producers, directors, army officers, and tax agents who had thwarted his purpose only to pass on and be replaced by others, while only two women had penetrated his soul and never been dispossessed. Both had awed him in performance and were the mothers he had known best.

In the end, he and Fred Hills settled on *Sons Come and Go, Mothers Hang in Forever,* even though it made the title even less accessible. He dedicated the book to his Saroyan family, a list of eighteen that included his grandchildren but not his daughter, Lucy.

In a foreword he credited Fred Hills with proposing the book, as well as cutting and rearranging it. His reason for permitting this, he said, was to find out, since he had never before given such liberty to an editor, the consequences. He thanked him and accepted full responsibility for the book. But Bill did not like Hills's blurb and felt obliged to rewrite it. Moreover, Hills rejected a new Saroyan novel, *Epi and Cam,* and Bill's early enthusiasm for the editor chilled.

Although the book would not be published until the following summer, in 1976, there was already a favorable response from Franklin Publications. The Franklin Mint book series, which provided leather-bound "first editions" by "today's greatest authors" to its list of twenty-five thousand subscribers, had the look of a very good thing. Bill would be sharing the company of Nabokov, Faulkner, Updike, Auchincloss, and Auden. Franklin's offer for *Sons* was $25,000.

On learning from Hills that he was to have only 2½ percent royalty from the Franklin Mint first edition, he wrote to McGraw-Hill's president, Alex Burke Jr., insisting that his share was 5 percent. Burke did not agree, and their testy correspondence over it lasted throughout the year.

Sons Come and Go was to be published on August 31, 1976, Saroyan's sixty-eighth birthday. When a first copy arrived in the mail he was pleased with the book's appearance but appalled at its price, $7.95. It would be $8.50 with the tax, and as a man who bought books only from bargain tables, he thought this price was prohibitive. Early response to the book was equivocal. While the Library Journal liked it, the Kirkus forecast found that in this sixth of his memoirs Saroyan had grown crabbier. He was seen as "snapping at the heels of Norman Mailer and six or seven other writers who have beaten him." Capriciously, Sunday's *San Francisco Chronicle* had let Aram do its review. He found his father had shed past sentimentality to become a more sincere and compassionate writer.

There were disappointingly few reviews, but among them was an especially pleasing one. This was Edward Hoagland's, which told readers of the *New York Times Book Review* that the news from Fresno was excellent. The "bold trapezist of the 30s" was "up near the top of his form," that "he writes for joy," a quality in short supply lately, and it was "high time for a Saroyan revival." This opinion was not shared along publisher's row, where Bill had tried and failed to find a house willing to take on any one of his three available books, the novel *TRA* and two memoirs.

The Franklin Library had a favorable response to its offer of *Sons Come and Go* and now wanted to issue more Saroyan titles. These hand-signed books were priced at $40 each, and there would be some $50,000 to share with his publisher.

Franklin had already turned to Harcourt for the rights to *After Thirty Years* and *The Human Comedy* and had presumed the usual fifty-fifty subsidiary rights split between publisher and author on each. Bill did not. He wrote Franklin in December 1976 that if there were to be Franklin editions of the two books, he wanted the split with Harcourt adjusted to 70 percent for himself.

Predictably, Harcourt objected and explained to him that by the contract he had signed, book club rights were shared fifty-fifty. When Bill insisted they were denying him his rightful share, Harcourt grew silent, and Franklin put off plans for new Saroyan titles. Bill's belief grew that he was being cheated by both Harcourt and Franklin. In May he complained of this to Harcourt in strong language and accused his publisher of an additional conspiracy by preventing a reprint sale with Manor Books for *Boys and Girls Together.*

An answer came on July 25, from an equally aggrieved Harcourt editor and vice president, Julian Muller. He wrote that Bill's reasoning was wrong and self-serving, that his attitude was irresponsible and libelous, that he, personally, did not take kindly to being charged as a cheat and conspirator, and that this made it difficult to propose a congenial solution. He explained that by contract the publisher held all rights to his books, including book club rights, in which they shared equally. Franklin Library was a book club.

Harcourt intended to maintain those rights in *The Human Comedy.* As for *Boys and Girls Together,* it was out of print and the rights had been returned to him, so he could negotiate with Manor Books for a paperback edition. Muller suggested that Manor's decision against reprinting *Boys and Girls* could have resulted from Bill's negotiating style. He concluded by assuring Bill that William Jovanovich was aware of this letter and it was being sent with his approval. Nevertheless, he had directed that rights to *After Thirty Years* be returned to the author. Although Bill counted this a victory, and believed the way was now clear to arrange for a new leather-bound edition of the book, no more was heard from Franklin Library.

But there was surprising good news. He had sent off a brief 1972 memoir, *Chance Meetings,* to Norton, and now he heard from Sherry Huber, an editor there, that they wanted to publish it. Bill did not complain about the modest $1,000 advance she offered and happily supplied a self-effacing blurb. He described it as a minor but very pleasant new book.

Among the recollections in *Chance Meetings* was one of his mother as actress. He believed she had had a gift for mime and that she could impersonate persuasively anyone she had met, delivering the exact bearing, movement, and speech.

When the book appeared, in 1978, in Bill's seventieth year, he was heartened by the early reviews. In the *New York Times,* Joel Oppenheimer found that despite the sentimentality, Saroyan remained a great storyteller. Robert Kirsch, in the *Los Angeles Times,* saw Saroyan's talent undiminished.

It was a small book, with only 135 pages, and later reviews found the content shallow. The *Christian Science Monitor* felt *Chance Meetings* was simplistic, that Saroyan "believes in the innocence and decency of everyone he meets." One thoroughly unsympathetic reviewer, D. Keith Mano, in the

National Review, saw the book as typical of "The Ethnic Naive," minimal, never achieving "story" form, "at worst a muttering, at best . . . narrative shaken from a hearth-drowsy, cantankerous old man." What Bill most resented were the several references to him as old. That was nonsense.

The last of the memoirs to be published in Bill's lifetime originated in his fascination with *Variety*'s annual "Necrology," that periodical's list of prominent figures in the entertainment world who had died in the previous year. While absorbed in that of January 1977 he decided to select those figures on *Variety*'s list whom he had known, or known about, and write his own reflections on them. He worked steadily at this for a month, selecting ten names a day. He had little faith in the project, felt the emerging portraits were wild, wayward, and possibly no good at all, but was determined to finish the job.

He wound up with a 135-page manuscript that dealt whimsically with the nature of death, and rambled and digressed in treating his eighty-eight subjects, Victor Alessandro to Adolf Zukor. Sometimes it was startlingly self-revealing.

Arnold Gingrich's death reminded him that the *Esquire* editor had refused to pay more than $200 for "Summer of the Beautiful White Horse," and this warmed old hatred toward his agents Hal Matson, Pat Duggan, and the publisher Herb Alexander for gyppings of yore.

In a portrait of his mother he recalled her temper, her rages over minor irritations in which she had cursed her children fiercely, and how Bill found even her anger beautiful. She fascinated him, and seemed to challenge him sexually. His awe of her led him to compare his emotions toward his own children. He recalled being enchanted by them but disappointed they were not remarkable enough to compel the awe he had felt for Takoohi Saroyan.

In acknowledging his fellow authors O'Hara and Steinbeck, he felt they lacked two qualities his own work enjoyed. In O'Hara it was largeness; in Steinbeck it was comedy. But he conceded his own failure, admitting that he often felt that the work he was doing was worthless, that he really was a stupid egomaniac, unable to write about anyone but himself. So why didn't he give it up? Because, he explained, he had no alternative, and because he had always felt that way. Had he quit in the beginning, he would not have published forty-four books nor shown the world the essay-story, as he had in "Myself Upon the Earth," "Seventy Thousand Assyrians," and "Sleep in Unheavenly Peace."

His most poignant recollection was of Ross Bagdasarian's death and Ross's advice of twenty years ago to keep cool, since Saroyan's quarrelsome reputation was keeping him from the money. Bill had told Ross, the millionaire, that his passion was not to get rich but to get right. He knew he was difficult. Others had told him so, and he admitted his distrust of the human race and its systems, religious, social, and economic. Shutting himself off from others was necessary to him, and he did not exclude relatives like a son and a daughter from this rule.

Bill decided to try his "Necrology" manuscript on Crowell, and when that house rejected the book, on Aram's advice he wrote Jan Wenner at *Rolling Stone,* asking if he would be interested in seeing it. He was annoyed to have no response from Wenner and sent the "Necrology" off to Bobbs Merrill, which soon spurned it.

Then an inquiry from Barry Gifford, of Creative Arts Book Co., in Berkeley, prompted Bill to send him the "Necrology" manuscript, and Gifford responded enthusiastically. He wanted to publish it under the title *Obituaries.* When Bill inquired about terms he learned that the small house could offer an advance of only $500 but did not object to his keeping all rights. Bill agreed.

By January 1979, Creative Arts was ready to publish *Obituaries,* and when Bill called on Barry Gifford and saw a first copy, he decided it was genuine new writing, and would be an important book. He sensed that Gifford and his partners were equally enthused. The advance reviews were favorable, and the first printing was seventy-five hundred copies. Bill's friend Herbert Gold arranged to do an interview for the *New York Times Book Review,* and on April 9 his three publishers, Barry Gifford, Don Ellis, and Penfield Jensen, along with Herbert Gold, assembled in the Palm Court of the Palace Hotel for lunch.

Bill held forth on many subjects, including lawyers. He said that he not only despised them but felt a profound gloating when he heard that death had done one in. Indeed, he felt the living generally took pleasure in their own survival, and from the failure of the dead to do so.

This brought him to suicide, first Hemingway's, then that of Lew Welch, about whom his son, Aram, had written a book. He felt suicide was a cardinal sin against the great miracle of life. This was what he celebrated in writing, the soul's lifetime dance.

The *Publishers Weekly* forecast described *Obituaries* as "an astonishing book, a profound and even original meditation about death." Bill Hogan's favorable review in the *Chronicle* was equally encouraging, while the *New York Times'* reviewer saw it as a persuasive reflection of a life that was "messy, trivial, spiteful at times," yet "flowing on—defying the darkness all about." For the most part *Obituaries* was treated as the small-press alternative venture it was, and it fell short of restoring its author to prominence. Later in the year, it was nominated for an American Book Award, and this distinction was to be the Saroyan finale.

Looking back over the 1970s, Bill found confirmation of his second-wind career as a short-story writer. In her *Best Short Stories of 1974*, Martha Foley had not only included "Isn't Today the Day," his confessional about a writer's ambition and how it is sapped by weakness of flesh and spirit, but she had dedicated the whole volume to him.

More of his fine stories appeared in the magazines during the mid- and late 1970s. The year 1976 began with the reborn *Saturday Evening Post's* publication of "An Act or Two of Foolish Kindness," soon followed by "Twenty Is the Greatest Time in Any Man's Life." Roger Angell, at *The New Yorker,* took "Fire," celebrating arson as a solution to life's adversity, then "The Duel," a beguiling portrait of Trash Bashmanian, once a swordman searching out a Turk to kill, who performs grand, nonsense oratory that is a reproach to Old World hatreds.

For the most part, these were stories that Bill had written in the 1960s. Revision of them, or of the magazine market, rather than fresh inspiration, had made them acceptable. He yearned to begin a new project that would grow and flourish under his hand, just as in the old days.

He was determined to make a definitive statement about the Armenian diaspora and his particular feelings about being Armenian-American. He had begun this in 1973 with his play *The Armenians,* and, projecting an Armenian trilogy, he started a second play in March 1975. This was *Bitlis Forever and Never,* an account of his 1964 pilgrimage to the mythic city of his family's origin. He had expected to find meaning there, the force of his own strong purpose, but Bitlis had become a Turkish city with its only Armenian an old man eager to leave.

The play itself is a one-act, in which Saroyan and his companions drink tea in a Bitlis restaurant and discuss the day's significance. Although the Turks are seen by Armenians as the enemy, Saroyan has found them friendly and hospitable. He reasons that in spite of the genocide, the murder of so many of his relatives, he cannot bring himself to hate Turks. They are no different from any other people.

Again, he gave the work no conflict or dramatic action. He had lost the power of self-delving that in the past had produced character and episode. All he could do now was argue his own rusty belief in the universal goodness of human nature.

While in Paris during 1979, he was heartened by selling a piece, "The Fresno Season," to the Paris *Tribune,* and then he completed his Armenian trilogy with a play he called *Haratch.* The word meant "forward" in Armenian and was the name of the Paris newspaper that was the scene of the play. Here he gathered his cast of thoughtful Hais, Saroyan himself among them, to discuss what Armenians want.

Some say they want revenge for the Turk's slaughter of two million Armenians; others say they want their country back. All agree that because of the diaspora, Armenians lack a unified voice, but that they do love life and people deeply. Even the bloody-minded are persuaded that revenge is folly, survival the triumph, and death the outcome.

As with the previous segments of his trilogy, Saroyan failed to generate a dramatic structure. *Haratch* reads like the transcript of a conference in which the participants discuss their differences and become amiably reconciled to them. Again he had tried to write a play and brought forth a tract.

Although he denied the loss of his creative power, evidence of this lay all about him, and suspicion grew that everything he was writing was worthless. Even as he told himself that there would be new writing, and it would be good because it had to be, one after another of his multiplying projects foundered. Enthusiasm rose in none. He was immobilized. In fact, William Saroyan's unquenchable flame had at last guttered out. He would spend the rest of his days in hopes of its rekindling.

The most likely site for this was Fresno. It was his own source, and his life there was reassuring. After the morning's work he would bicycle to the Fig Village post office, always hopeful of the mails. Day-old *Christian Science Monitor*s were free from a rack. These, with the five-cent books from the library's sale bins, were just the thing for a man who spent the small hours awaiting sleep. Passing Fresno High School, he could recall his running the 220 low hurdles there. His bicycle tour often included Ararat Cemetery, where he would visit the graves of friends and relations, observing that his cousin Chesley Saroyan lay beside his mother. Arriving home on West Griffith Way, he would turn, in spite of the neighbors' complaints and water department warnings, to a copious soaking of his gardens.

He saw only a handful of loyal relatives and friends. One of these, Buck Makasian, husband of his first cousin Doris, he trusted to look after the West Griffith houses in his absence. When Buck died, in June 1975, Bill found a replacement in a young cousin, Ruben Saroyan, who soon became indispensable as handyman, gardener, chauffeur, and occasional counselor.

Bill showed Ruben his $28.39 electric bill and wondered what it might amount to if he were to turn on his heat. Ruben advised him, for his health's sake, to do just that, but Bill remained cautious with the thermostat. He declined Ruben's 1977 invitation for Christmas dinner, telling him that he preferred to spend the holiday alone, and he did, preparing himself a feast of soup, chicken, and white wine and enjoying a recollection of one Christmas past. It was a Christmas of his early twenties in which he went with friends to the Ellis Street Burlesque. There a stripper, whom he recalled as being small and Jewish, had suddenly flung off everything to reveal herself like a rose. There could be nothing more lovely or innocent.

But Fresno was wanting too. Work went stale here. He grew bored and fled to Paris, where his first days were always joyful and sometimes a stimulus. There would be several projects, a play, a novel, a memoir, and a vow to complete them all in the course of a month or six weeks. He found time for articles, too, and an occasional market for them at the *International Herald Tribune.*

He worked, often standing at his ironing board, letting his telephone go unanswered, putting in an hour or so at each endeavor so that his working day might be complete by noon. He enjoyed his lone walks, making a circle tour of Gare St.-Lazare, Trinité, Opéra, the Scribe, shopping for food bargains at Prisunic and Galeries Lafayette and for cheap books at a store called Eppe's on rue Provence, where they could be had six for a franc. He stopped at Poncelet's—no baker's bread could compare—for a baguette and a first bite on the way home.

When Ed Hagopian was in town, he came by to give Bill a haircut. They walked together, often to the U.S. embassy store, where such staples as peanut butter, mayonnaise, and soap could be had reasonably, and once to Père Lachaise Cemetery, where Bill posed for a snapshot beside General Antranik's monument. They visited the tailor shop of Krikor Atamian at 16 rue Lafayette. Atamian was not only obliging about sewing on a loose button, but his shop was a gathering place for the Parisian Armenian community. There was occasional chamber music and good tea, and the conversation was literary as well as political.

Otherwise he kept largely to himself. When he did go to a farewell party, for Jim Jones, it was no comfort to find that his fellow author was completing *The Whistle,* a novel that would be a sequel to *From Here to Eternity* and was expected to make him hot again.

He went gambling rarely now, but he usually paused in his daily walk at the neighborhood cobbler's to admire the owl and to buy a ticket for the Tierce, the national lottery. He would reflect ruefully on the addicts of chance, how they go right on pursuing the big win. But Paris could depress him too. In 1978, when his flat was broken into and robbed of his gold coins and tape recorder, the police were no help. The *Tribune* returned his pieces unwanted. He saw no one. He was sick and unable to write at all.

Failure to produce new work only increased his appetite for travel. Going somewhere raised hopes that he would discover fresh insights or motivations. He welcomed a 1975 invitation to the Philippines for its Afro-Asian Writers' Symposium and, once he had delivered a required speech, enjoyed himself thoroughly. At the palace dinner he was seated beside the first lady, Imelda R. Marcos, and in spite of an attack of stomach gas, managed a conversation with her. He found her witty and must have pleased her, for she sent him a gift of a tape recorder and invited him aboard her DC-8 for a visit to Leyte. On his return to Paris he wrote a play, *Philippine Sun and Moon,* and sent it off to the Marcoses. His hopes for a Manila performance met no encouraging response.

In the following year, he accepted a first invitation to an Armenian arts festival and hoped that while there he would write a great play about contemporary Armenians. Once in Erevan, however, he found himself viewing a poor Russian-language film of *My Heart's in the Highlands* and stage performances of *The Hungerers* and *Hello Out There,* and delivering a talk to an audience of university students. He hurried from one banquet to another, under attack from his esophagitis and a capricious stomach. Clearly, this was no season for the writing of a play.

In the course of a TV interview, he encountered a large and beautiful woman, the daughter of an old Armenian acquaintance. When he proposed that he might call her to come and get in his bed, she replied that if he promised to hug her she would. That evening, deciding that some sexual mischief with a wild, Armenian woman born of a great man would refresh his soul, he called her. A man answered the phone, but the woman was quick to assure Bill it was her son, not her lover, and she was soon on her way to his hotel.

Once he had her to himself, Bill found that she, like the others he had met, felt sure he could help her, perhaps in education for her children or sanctuary for herself. Realizing his mistake, he called for assistance to get the woman into a taxi and gave the bellboy the rubles necessary to see her safely home. In the aftermath he asked the Lord's everlasting help for wild human beings.

On Bill's second Armenian visit, in 1978, a celebration of 150 years of Russian-Armenian friendship, he took part in a week's tour of the remote lake and mountain districts. The austere accommodations brought on his stomach illness and concern about his heart, so he returned to Erevan for examination at the Cardiology Institute. No problems were found.

He went twice to the International Writers' Congress in Bulgaria. The first, in 1977, required a speech to the assembly and a series of parties which left him with a chronic hangover. He enjoyed the side trips, one to Plovdiv in particular. On discovering the Museum of Satire and Humor, he resolved to write a play about it.

He returned to Bulgaria in 1979 for a second writers' congress and was pleased to find his army comrade John Cheever there with his son, Ben, and daughter-in-law, Linda. The four had a pleasant lunch together, in the course of which Bill spoke of their service in the army's farcical battalion at Astoria. Cheever replied that if he had not been transferred to it from his infantry unit, he was sure he would have been killed.

Bill had known and admired John Cheever since their army days. They were able to reminisce about them in 1979 at the Bulgarian Writers' Conference in Sofia.

Where travel tended to leave Bill more dispirited than ever, he found growing solace in his prosperity. When, in 1976, he took financial inventory, he congratulated himself on having become a rich man. He now had a port-folio of blue-chip stocks, 11,500 pounds in a London account, and $125,000 in two Fresno ones.

In Paris he had seen and been intrigued by a one-kilo gold bar. Promising himself to have one someday, he followed the gold market, and during the summer of 1979, when the price fell to $288 an once, he bought gold certifi-cates and Krugerrands. At the sight of a gold bar priced at $28,000, he bought two ingots, each of 100 ounces.

Completing his choleric behavior pattern he found new possibilities for rancor among his most loyal friends. Even his warm relationship with Jack Kevorkian was vulnerable. One evening at the Kevorkians' during the Paris spring of 1974, Bill was introduced to the French actors Jean de Sailly and Simone Valere, close friends of Jack's French wife, Ev. The actors made a modest offer for a Paris production of *Time of Your Life*. When Bill insisted on far stiffer terms and Kevorkian explained they were unreasonable, Bill reproached him for working for the actors rather than himself. In the week that followed Bill grew angry with his friend and lawyer. Feeling that Jack and Ev had used him for their considerable ambitions, he accused

Kevorkian of taking social advantage of him and at the same time billing
him for his services. This caused a rift in their cordial friendship that did not
heal for half a dozen years.

During the following September, his Paris friend Krikor Atamian turned
up in Fresno at Bill's invitation for a stay in the corner house. A few days of
Atamian's visit with no sign of his departing strained Bill's every hospitable
impulse. When Atamian asked if he had done something wrong, Bill
explained that he was doing difficult new writing and so he must ask him to
restore the house to order and visit somebody else. To Bill's relief, Atamian
did so.

Nor was Richard Harrington, the San Francisco lawyer who had performed so many useful services for Bill, immune. Harrington had set up the
Saroyan Foundation and arranged for the safekeeping of certain precious
manuscripts and private papers at the University of California's Bancroft
Library. He was in part responsible for Bill's triumphal visit to the Berkeley
campus, citadel of California higher education.

In the spring of 1977, James Hart, the director of the Bancroft Library,
invited Bill to be principal speaker at the institution's thirtieth annual meeting, on May 8. Early that Sunday afternoon Richard Harrington and his
wife, Judith, picked Bill up at Fifteenth Avenue and drove him to Berkeley,
where Hart showed them around the Bancroft's archives and reading room.
The ceremonies in the Zellerbach Theatre began with introductions by
Hart and the University of California's president, David Saxon. There was a
premier performance of the Saroyan playlet *The Third Person,* in which a
famous author is interviewed by a Finnish newspaperwoman.

Rejoicing in these honorifics, Bill began with his prepared speech on the
relationship of reading and writing to life itself, but the drollery of his manner soon called for putting the script aside in favor of a ramble through his
past. He recalled the 1919 Sunday in Fresno when his mother boxed his ears
for missing the Mother's Day sermon at church, his wartime interview with
George Bernard Shaw, Stanley Kauffman's lack of understanding him in the
New Republic, and the importance of reading all books, including those
orphans of the Fresno Library which could be had for ten cents. He ended
with a salute to his son, his daughter-in-law, and his grandchildren, who
were in the audience.

Monday's *Chronicle* carried his photograph and an appreciative article
about the talk. He had been impressed by the ceremony, had enjoyed himself, and was pleased about his relationship with James Hart and the Bancroft. Finally, Aram wrote, saying his performance had been like Mark
Twain's, only better because he had been himself.

When the Malibu Beach cottage was damaged by a 1978 storm, Bill quarreled over procedure with Cosette, its owner. Deciding he must share ownership, he turned to Harrington for advice. This was that coownership was unwise. Harrington recommended that Cosette sell the cottage and explained how to do this in installments so as to spread the capital-gains tax over several years.

Bill became angry. In spite of Harrington's accomplishments for him, he recalled only that the attorney had left him vulnerable to a stiff federal tax of $20,000 in 1976, and had failed to collect any payment from publishers and producers with whom he had grievances. Bill felt he was not getting the aggressive lawyering to which he was entitled, and in particular he disliked Harrington's advice to sell Malibu.

He wrote him a sharp letter on May 15, telling him to ignore his own opinion and to expedite Malibu coownership. He chided him for having failed to rouse an offer from Franklin Library and to collect from both Plumstead Management and *Rolling Stone*. Bill would proceed with these elsewhere. Harrington patiently explained that since Bill had sold the cottage to Cosette for $10,000 in 1959, coownership would cost him $7,000 in gift taxes. He urged Bill to be less bullheaded and to handle the sale as he had suggested.

Although Cosette was ready to follow the Harrington advice and sell the Malibu cottage, Bill was still firmly against it. He felt the lawyer had failed him in every one of his purposes and was thus contemptible. The outcome was Bill's decision that they keep Malibu and get rid of Harrington.

While it was hardly customary for Bill to rebuild the bridges of fallen friendship, in early summer of 1978, he did so with Yep and Roxie Moradian in Fresno. Bicycling up the road to their house one afternoon, he found them working in their garden, and he accepted their invitation to come into the house for a visit. He returned the next day with a signed copy of *Chance Meetings*. Yep reappeared at West Griffith Way to advise on garden care, and Bill was once more a frequent guest at the Moradians' table.

There was even a yielding in his historic quarrel with the painter Manuel Tolegian. When he learned that Tolegian had done a portrait of Ross Bagdasarian, he wrote that he wanted it and in exchange would agree to using their art dialogue in a book.

But otherwise, Bill's contentiousness simmered on. In spite of episodes of concern for Aram, and pride in his writing achievements and making of a family, the gulf between them widened. In July 1974, Bill heard from Aram in Bolinas that he and Gailyn loved the house they were renting and would buy it if they could raise $4,000 as downpayment. Bill's first response was annoyance. However, he learned from Harrington that Bolinas was an unusually attractive community by the sea, and that this was a good time to buy property there.

Bill arranged for Kirk Minasian to drive him to Bolinas. With his first glimpse of 380 Hawthorn Road, Bill decided that although it was a funky house and garden it was a work of art and most appropriate as the home of Aram and Gailyn, Strawberry and Cream. Presently Aram arrived in a battered Chevy, and with the family assembled Bill presented gifts to the children. As they drank tea, then shouted and laughed in Armenian fashion, it seemed to Bill that the place was enchanted, just right for their kind of life—and that he loved them.

The real estate agent arrived to confirm that the price of the house was $28,000, and that the mortgage payments would be no more than the rent. Bill left Aram with the belief that he would consider ways of helping him buy the house, but he did nothing about it until the following year.

In 1975, when Aram made a second appeal for help with the Bolinas house, Bill replied that he would buy it for him on two conditions: first, that it be in William Saroyan's name, and second, that his mother's lawyers stop pursuing him. If that were acceptable, Aram and his family could stay there forever.

The following day, Bill heard from Lucy, now in Los Angeles, that she and Aram had persuaded their mother to cancel her judgment against him. Carol had pointed out it was *their* money she would be forgiving their father, and they acknowledged and agreed to it.

Bill wrote Aram that his offer stood. He would buy the house, and Aram could live in it rent-free. On April 29, he did so, paying $24,158.68 for it, along with the first monthly installment of $243.

One morning during this early spring of 1975, Bill awoke from a vivid dream in which he had been delightedly kissing a lovely, unknown girl. Then the girl seemed to become Lucy, and, finally, unmistakably, Lucy's mother.

Although on August 31 he celebrated his sixty-seventh birthday in the way he liked best—alone, quiet, watering his garden—neither of his children let the day pass unnoticed. Lucy called for a long talk, and Aram honored him with an extravagantly praiseful sixty-seventh-birthday poem. It was titled "My Father's Flight," and it found its way into the *San Francisco Examiner*. On reading the clipping that Aram sent him, Bill approved of the sentiment—though not of the poem.

Early in 1976, Aram wrote that Gailyn's parents, Grant and Pauli McClanahan, would be visiting Bolinas in March, and Bill agreed to be on hand to meet them. With Kirk Minasian driving, Bill arrived in Bolinas early on the afternoon of March 1 to find the McClanahans had arrived. This first meeting of the grandparents was a cordial one. Grant's years of duty in the consular service, much of it in the Mideast, had given him and

Pauli an authority and an air of being at home any place. The McClanahans seemed pleased with Bill's gift, an inscribed copy of *Days of Life and Death*.

Bill was impressed with Gailyn as a gardener, admiring her crop of beets, onions, and artichokes. He found Strawberry alert and watchful and Cream a fantastic joy of a child, and learned there was yet another Saroyan on the way. There were photographs in the garden, and a loud three o'clock farewell with much grandfatherly hugging of Aram, Gailyn, Strawberry, and Cream.

When Aram wrote that the Bolinas house was in need of a new roof and a $150 contribution would be welcome, he offered to work for it. Quelling customary irritation with his son's appeals, Bill made him a proposition. He would send Aram and Gailyn $1,000 each, on condition that Aram write a daily passage welcoming the newcomer who was expected in October. He should describe the world in which the child would find itself.

Gailyn was to supply drawings and watercolors on the same schedule, and he added a similar invitation, at $500 each, to both Strawberry and Cream. The young Saroyans accepted gladly. On receiving the first installments, Bill approved them and sent off the promised checks. Returning from Europe early in 1977 he learned from Cosette that he now had a splendid, healthy grandson. Armenak Saroyan had been born in Bolinas a month before.

Bill's first act on returning to Fifteenth Avenue was to persuade Archie Minasian to drive him and Cosette to Bolinas for a look at his grandson. When he arrived at Aram's house, five-year-old Strawberry came to him sweetly and lovingly, while her younger sister, Cream, was standoffish at first but finally came for a grandfatherly hug. Bill thought Gailyn radiant, admired her drawings, and praised Aram's helpfulness to her. He examined his forty-day-old grandson and pronounced his ears neat, his feet good, and his head fine. He approved the whole of Aram's thriving household.

Aram was understandably pleased that a poem of his was appearing in the current *Paris Review.* In sending his father a copy, he included a request for much-needed funds.

Recalling Aram's aspiration to join the selective company of the *Paris Review*'s contributors, not unlike his own break-through experience at *Story,* he recognized this as a triumph for his son. Yet instead of praise he offered him some cautions. He told Aram that he liked the poem. It was the best of his he had seen. However, he saw it as self-protective, having to do with the *pose* of being a writer. He reminded him of their conversation in Barcelona, how he had told him that a writer writes because he must. If not compelled, he isn't a writer.

As for money, he pointed to his own miserliness. It was justifiable in a writer. He felt that Aram failed to see a relation between his own writing and the need to support his family. Deceiving himself in this way suggested either stupidity or dishonesty in his nature. He closed the stern, master-to-apprentice lecture by sending his love and enclosing a check for $300.

When Aram wrote that a neighboring Bolinas property was for sale at $1,500 and that buying it would be good protection and investment, Bill agreed. When it turned out the price was twice that, Bill balked at it but felt so generously toward Aram's family that he presented his son with $3,000 to buy U.S. savings bonds for each of the children. Late that same year, Bill persuaded Kirk Minasian to drive him and Cosette to Bolinas for an afternoon visit. They found Aram proud of having bought the adjoining lot for $3,000. Bill happily joined Aram in a ride to school for Strawberry and then a family tea, which featured carrot cake.

Bill was surprised by the young Saroyans' indifference to the dozens of flies with which they shared their house, and he thought they served very expensive food. Nevertheless, they were clearly all thriving. Armenak, now a little over a year old, was a laughing, healthy boy. Bill felt it was a great visit.

Although Lucy had drifted from her father's thoughts, she had taken an apartment in Beverly Hills and began the new year of 1978 with a letter to him. She had had a small part in a movie and recently appeared in a Chicago production of *Barefoot in the Park.* She enclosed the program, some reviews that mentioned her favorably, and some recent publicity photographs.

These showed the face of a strikingly handsome woman, but in examining them Bill decided that her nostrils flared as if she had been through a torment. Clearly Lucy had sent the photographs in the belief that he would find her beautiful. Instead, he saw a skinny, suffering, unattractive girl. Recalling she was nearly thirty-two, he asked God's love and help for her, as if she were beyond his own.

He had a collection of Gailyn's poems and stories which were inscribed to him with her love. Putting them aside, he conceded that with the addition of Armenak, Aram had created a fine young family, and with an income it would fare well.

During February 1978, while Bill was considering what to do about the storm-damaged Malibu cottage, Aram called, offering to go there and put it to rights. Bill refused Aram's offer bluntly, noting that while he spoke confidently, he lacked construction experience. Rebuffed, Aram accused his father of talking to him as if he were fourteen, not thirty-four, and threatened to no longer write to him. In spite of Cosette's efforts as mediator, the wintry relations between father and son resumed.

Nevertheless, Bill kept track of his son's literary career. He knew that

Although Lucy reported on her progress as an actress,
Bill was not impressed, and he disliked this 1978
publicity photograph of her.

Aram's novel *The Town* had not found a publisher, nor had his book about
Lew Welch and the beat poets, *Genesis Angels*. He also learned that his own
onetime agent, "Swifty" Lazar, had been persuaded by Aram's mother and
Matthau to search out movie interest in the latter.

Then, on May 26, Bill learned from Cosette that Aram had had an accident in Santa Rosa. In trying to avoid a motorcycle he had tipped over his
car, wrecking it, fracturing his ankle, and leaving him on crutches. With a
hospital bill and no insurance, he had turned to Walter Matthau for help.
Borrowing $2,000 from Matthau, Aram had promised in return to write a

screenplay for him. Three weeks later, Aram explained to Bill that although he had avoided asking him for help at the time, he now felt he must. This kind of trouble was a father's responsibility. Bill told him that he should not be driving at all, that he lacked the temperament for negotiating in traffic.

He replied further to Aram on June 19, asking for the details of his fix, fully and truthfully. He wanted to know why that big car had turned over and asked if Aram had been smoking pot at the time. Why hadn't he written him about it instead of letting Cosette bring the news? He recalled that Aram had been rude to him during their February telephone talk about Malibu. This brought forth a fresh tirade about Carol, who was always pointing out his own responsibilities and yet had stolen the Maroney house from her children.

At his angriest, he accused Aram of arrogance and meanness and suspected he would misread this letter, consider him an enemy, and proceed to trick him, as he had in the past—keeping up the weakling way of his Bolinas life. In closing, he said he would consider further help but challenged Aram to justify his behaving like a father to him. It was a letter that ended correspondence between father and son.

There was no longer any doubt about disinheriting his children. That same spring, 1978, he instructed Richard Harrington that if his son and his daughter were to be supported in years to come, it must be from their rich mother. He did not want a loophole in his will. To which Harrington replied that Bill's will, dated January 13, 1975, left everything in trust to his grandchildren except for memorabilia and books to the William Saroyan Foundation. Similarly, Cosette's will left Malibu to the grandchildren. He pointed out that renewal of certain copyrights went to Aram and Lucy by law.

On August 31, 1978, Bill celebrated his seventieth birthday quietly in Paris. He was pleased that in spite of his disintegrating, painful body, he had attained this round number of years. Only Lucy remembered the occasion, with a card from Beverly Hills.

In February 1979, Bill learned from Nona Balakian at the *New York Times* that Aram had found, in William Morrow, a publisher for his short book *Genesis Angels*. When she sent Bill a set of proofs, he admired Aram's accomplishment but thought the book, at $7.95, too expensive. Although he mentioned the book proudly during his *Obituaries* interview for the *Times,* no word about it crossed the ice between father and son.

While Bill was in San Francisco during the fall of 1979, Aram called to ask Cosette if his father was there. Rather than speak to him, Bill told Cosette, so that Aram could overhear, that he awaited an answer to his last letter. In spite of misgivings about thirty-six-year-old Aram, he felt that his son would find his place, and his way, in the world.

Nona Balakian, of the *New York Times'* daily book page,
was a loyal Saroyan fan, and when she came to Paris he
enjoyed showing her the sights.

For years Bill had been plagued by multiple ailments, but during the spring of 1975 his concern centered on his prostate. The need to urinate was constant and kept him from more than an hour's continuous sleep, but Dr. Donald Smith, chief of urology at the University of California Hospital, assured him after a series of tests that no prostate surgery was needed now and perhaps never would be.

The year 1977 had been one of fatalities: fifty-five-year-old James Jones, Groucho Marx, Bing Crosby, and, at forty-two, Elvis Presley. Charlie Chaplin's death, at eighty-eight, that Christmas brought Bill a recollection of a man obsessed with thoughts of Jesus. He seemed to hate as well as love him. He also felt that Chaplin had died long ago, certainly before *A King in New York,* perhaps before *The Great Dictator.*

He remembered that in 1947 Chaplin had written to ask for a play in which his kids could appear, and the result was *Sam Ego's House*. He recalled that Chaplin was tightfisted and had made many enemies, but nonetheless had been the primary motion-picture genius of his time and was not likely to be surpassed.

In January 1979, he arrived at Fifteenth Avenue to find that his sister Zabe was suffering from terminal bone-marrow cancer. She had at most a year or two to live. When he and Cosette went to visit Zabe, Cosette went to Zabe's room and spent a half hour with her before both came down to join in a buffet supper. Bill saw how sick Zabe was, and that she knew it and was putting up a brave front.

Throughout 1978 Bill had been concerned by a racing heartbeat and insomnia that sometimes denied him sleep until dawn. On February 4, he was newly alarmed. After a shower he found his penis was leaking blood. It continued for several days, causing him to wonder if he had prostate cancer. After two weeks, the leaking stopped, but he went to the veterans' hospital for a general examination, which found him in satisfactory health. A Dr. Nightingale told him that prostate infection was common in men of his age, that treatment could produce unpleasant side effects, and that in most cases it cleared up by itself. April brought a recurrence of the leaking, but Dr. Nightingale assured him that his condition was nonspecific and commonplace, and he should simply live with it.

Then, in June, during the Bulgarian Writers' Congress, his sleep was interrupted hourly by the need to urinate, and he discovered that his penis was red with heavy blood. During the summer in Paris his health worsened. On the night of July's full moon, chest pain and heart palpitation joined to worry him, and he was too tired for the daily walk on which he depended for restoring his spirit.

He had no Paris doctor. Since his wartime experience some thirty-five years earlier, he had distrusted all of them. He believed that public ignorance had made the medical profession rich beyond all necessity, that fools ran to doctors and then spent a fortune escaping them. He remembered Ed Hagopian working with his friend Dr. Juvenelle to get him into his private clinic. Had he consented, he was sure they would have murdered him.

On August 14, Henry called from Alameda with the news that their sister Zabe had died in the hospital the night before. A letter from Cosette told of Zabe's suffering at the end, how she had been unable to eat or speak. Although he had known it was coming, the news touched him and prompted him to wonder what went through the mind of someone dying. He supposed it was an amalgam of life's memories and anxieties, like haunted dreaming. It would have to be so.

As for himself, he remembered that their mother had lived only to sixty-six, while Zabe had reached seventy-seven, which was not bad. Now that she was dead, the rest of the family could return to the struggle.

His own struggle was twofold, and he put it bluntly: a rottenness in his body and also in his writing. Turning seventy-one in Paris, he congratulated himself on being still at his work, still hoping to call the world's attention to the fact that William Saroyan was alive, as hungry for acclaim in his seventies as he had been in his thirties, and striving as hard for it. He had turned away from other roles, as husband, father, friend, and citizen, and had none to rely on in these final years.

During that summer, he found that urinating was all but impossible, and that he must soon have the prostate operation. Throughout September there were good days when he felt he was on the mend, when he wrote and sent off a piece to the *International Herald Tribune,* when he walked his favorite streets and looked into the lonely eyes of the workmen and sad girls.

But by the end of September, his prostatitis had become a constant agony, and he flew back to San Francisco, planning to consult Dr. Smith again. On October 1, when he called for an appointment, he learned that Dr. Smith had retired and had been replaced by a Dr. Tankago, an Egyptian. Bill decided to wait until his return to Fresno. Once at home on West Griffith Way, he followed the World Series attentively and went to the fair with Yep Moradian. Although he looked up urologists in the telephone book, he did not consult one for ten days.

Then, on October 18, he called at the office of a Dr. Artin Jibilian, whom he learned was a fine young Armenian. His four children included twin boys, Aram and Arek. Believing he was okay, Bill agreed to undergo the examination as soon as possible. On the morning of October 24, Ruben Saroyan gave Bill a haircut and drove him to Saint Agnes Medical Center for a kidney x ray and Dr. Jibilian's urological probe. At 5:05 that afternoon, Dr. Jibilian delivered him the news he had been dreading: the left side of his prostate was hard, and he believed it was cancerous. The next day, the laboratory confirmed the diagnosis.

That night, with a full bladder and its channel firmly blocked, he was newly depressed, yet he consoled himself that he was learning what he must live with until he died. *This* was life, the way it was.

Relief was on the way. A catheter allowed his bladder to empty without pain, and Dr. Jibilian planned an operation and a biopsy that should restore him to health. For four days he stayed at home, making pictures, suspending speculation until after the surgery, and feeling all was well.

The operation took place at Sierra Hospital on October 30, a day unlike any in his experience. He was given a spinal anesthetic, which left him dreamily aware of the glaring operating room. He thought Dr. Jibilian was slow to start and then realized he was already at his probing. From his hips down, Bill's legs were strangely dead.

The aftermath was an agonizing night of pain, flowing blood, headache, and depression. Convalescence was slowed by blood clots and the need to clear them with a syringe. A transfusion was required. All he could do was cling to his tortured life and acknowledge that his medical care was great.

A priest, Father Gourken Yaralian, called and prayed for Bill's recovery in Armenian, and Bill liked it. When at last he entertained expectations, it seemed that Paris, youth, and indestructibility were as distant as the stars. He was allowed to go home on November 4, and at first he felt fully restored. Within a day, however, he had a painful relapse that returned him to Sierra Hospital and restored the catheter. Antibiotics were prescribed.

A week later, he was home enjoying a jar of chicken soup dropped off by the Moradians and was sure the healing had begun. Dr. Jibilian was confident there would be no further complications. In his dense garden, Bill delighted in a hummingbird drinking at the loquat tree. He sent off a poem, "Love," to *The New Yorker*. His sobering view of death's open throat had not altered his belief that within a week or so he would roll a fresh sheet into his typewriter for a new beginning.

On November 21, he called on Dr. Jibilian, who said that in a month's time he would do a further biopsy. Bill replied that they should certainly take that precaution, but that he knew he didn't have cancer. He was pleased that Dr. Jibilian did not dispute him.

XIX

ARMENIA, ART, AND FIRE

1979–1981

ONE NIGHT during November 1979, Bill had a nightmare in which he found himself arguing with Carol in a motel room. Leaving, walking through the lobby, he remembered that he had left his typewriter behind, but in returning for it he dropped the room key into a lily pond. When a floor manager tried to help retrieve it, he quarreled with him.

During December he had several dreams that were even more bizarre and disturbing. In the first, Takoohi came to his bed and, at his bidding, performed oral sex on him, then regular sex, in the course of which he wilted. Whereupon his mother accused him of taking her ring and looked about her, discovering it on the floor. Then Cosette appeared, busy at housecleaning, to remind him that their mother was dead.

In a second dream, he found Aram among bragging, ineffectual friends, telling them patronizingly that although he admired his father, they were on bad terms. Presently he and Aram were alone in a huge theater. The theater seemed to be Bill's, and although it was in need of repair, Aram soon left him to resume his own life.

Next he was with a twelve-year-old Lucy. She danced around him while he tried to speak with Norman Mailer. When she appeared to offer herself to the writer, Bill explained to him that his daughter was a nymphomaniac. Mailer made no reply.

It occurred to Bill that these dreams had emerged from his deciding to let fate, rather than the medical profession, determine the outcome of his duel with cancer. He was unshaken in that. He would live life's natural course and accept its destiny.

He sought to summarize his achievement, telling himself that he had written swiftly in his youth. Then, at thirty, came a decade of hard times. At forty he had settled down into a steady pace. From the age of sixty he had written as a journeyman, without art. Nevertheless, at seventy-one he believed he was still writing well, that the seven works completed in Paris the previous summer were good and important ones. There was a cachet to being a regular contributor to the *International Herald Tribune,* which had taken three of his pieces, paying 1,500 francs for each.

As December 1979 drew to a close, the veterans' hospital confirmed that his prostate nodule was cancerous, but a blood scan revealed that his bones were free of the disease. Bill entered the holiday season with an acceptance of his illness. He would make the best of it, find out the details, and choose how to proceed.

In January he read up on prostate cancer and found the literature reassuring. It was rarely a cause of death. Nevertheless, the pain in his genitals and constant need to piss brought him back to the veterans' hospital in February for a painful biopsy. According to Drs. Crutchlow and Nightingale, the result was favorable, for the cancer had not spread. However, the powerful antibiotic Bactrim was prescribed. At first it seemed a reprieve, but a week later he was frightened by his loss of appetite. There was pain in his right side, and he felt so weak he could not stand while doing his day's writing.

The frequent, painful, bloody pissing brought Bill back to the veterans' hospital on April 3, where he had another genital probe that left him bleeding, angry, and more blocked than ever. Conferring with Dr. Crutchlow on April 7, Bill learned that his cancer, adeno carcinoma, had spread. It was likely that surgical removal of the prostate would not get it all. Thus a course of linear radiation was recommended.

Bill took a few days to consider this, and on April 17 he called on Dr. Charles Prather, whose prognosis was uncertain. It was possible that after a week of treatment, or even seven weeks, radiation would prove futile. He saw no need to rush to it. This last advice suited Bill. He was ready to surrender.

However ill and doomed he was, there was no shirking his daily task of writing. His one purpose was to continue adding to the body of his work. He assured himself that this alone gave life meaning. Since the beginning of the year he had been busy with another *Obituaries.* The first entry was that for Armenak, his father. Although he suspected these portraits were third-rate, he added two or three each day until May 1, when he retitled the manuscript *Alive, Dying* and declared it complete.

He believed that Creative Arts would sell out its ten thousand copies of *Obituaries,* thereby equaling McGraw's performance with *Sons Come and Go,* his best hardcover sale in twenty years, but he felt no particular loyalty.

Creative Arts had piqued him by assuming he would accept a 10 percent royalty. He had insisted to Gifford and Ellis that he *always* got 15 percent.

California State University at Northridge was preparing an edition of 250 copies of *Two Short Summer-time Plays of 1974,* and when these books arrived Bill sent one off to Edward Albee with a friendly greeting. He turned down a presidential invitation to Washington for a meeting at the Kennedy Center, telling himself that he was opposed to the government's getting arty in its bureaucratic way, and was against that national theater in particular.

On the last day of April, Bill's loyal friend at the *New York Times,* Nona Balakian, called with the exciting news that *Obituaries* had been nominated for the American Book Award, and it was her belief it would win. Bill told her that it would not, which was fine with him, as he had no wish for it.

Summer was at hand, and both in spite of his worsening health and because of it, Bill felt an urge to travel. The opportunity came via the U.S. Information Agency in Washington. The Czech and Polish governments had invited him to their writers' meetings in June.

On May 15, he arrived in Warsaw and was joined by Joyce Carol Oates and Susan Sontag. He took part in the interviews, question-and-answer sessions, and embassy parties, where Poles and Americans drank, ate, and fraternized in high spirits. He visited his several Warsaw publishers to meet editors and translators and to collect his royalties. As usual, he went shopping and found a good tape player for 3,000 zlotys.

There were trips to Lublin and Krakow, and while he tired easily he was untroubled by prostate symptoms throughout the week. Nor did they return during his Czechoslovakian visit, which culminated in a big party for him given by the U.S. cultural attaché, Bruce Koch. In Budapest, where he gave a speech at Ambassador Bergold's dinner for him, his afflictions were still at bay, but at a writers' union luncheon in Bucharest, he had an embarrassing attack of esophagitis. It did not keep him from completing his tour of eastern Europe with a visit to Belgrade and a meeting with Ambassador Lawrence Eagleburger.

Back in Paris on June 14, he found an invitation from Philip Kaiser, U.S. ambassador to Austria, to present a Saroyan play in Vienna. Bill proposed *Play Things,* a revision of a 1975 entertainment, and assured him that he would attend its performance.

After a restorative night's sleep at 74 rue Taitbout he began a new play, *I Have Seen Everything and Nothing Works,* completing it within twelve days under the new title *Warsaw Visitor.* It was his rambling meditation on death, framed by anger at the absurdity of his father's early one, and resignation to his own. There are multiple Saroyans in the cast: Moustache, the famous writer, touring the embassy circuit; Saroyan himself, the dying artist who finds his lifework has been depriving death of its mockery; and the Devil as doppelgänger and cynical guide.

In an early scene, Lucy calls to proclaim her love for him. He dismisses her with advice to renounce her whorish life, to find a man who will have her and bear him children. When Aram calls, he turns him away with the same abruptness. Then, with the Devil's help, he explains his rejection of his children through his belief that they are not truly *his,* that all fathers are so deceived. It is the mothers who possess and make the ruin of children.

The Devil appears as a doctor in order to be accused of getting rich from humanity's illness. When asked if he doesn't hope to be a millionaire in ten years, the Devil-doctor denies this, saying, "Five." In the ensuing scenes, Saroyan's life seems to pass in dream-like recollection. He assesses his present seventy-two-year-old self as a madman afflicted by esophagitis and cancer who refuses to lie down and die.

Indeed, as he finished the play, pain returned, and there was a swelling of his groin. He knew the cancer was growing. He called a Dr. Papazian, a woman he had met in Paris, to inquire about an Armenian urologist. She knew of none.

Ambassador Kaiser was quick to arrange the world premiere of *Play Things.* As agreed, Bill attended its performance, at the English Theatre in Vienna, on June 28. He sat in a box with Mrs. Kaiser, and went along to an embassy party in his honor. He had no quarrel with the production of the play but found himself strangely unmoved by the excitement of the evening and the attention it brought him.

Back in Paris, he resumed his daily walks and tried to start writing tasks, telling himself he must continue the routine while dying, for there was nothing else to do. On July 17 he began a new play, *Tales from the Vienna Streets,* convinced that the daily stint kept him from believing he had lost his essence. While the first scenes seemed promising, he was too sick to go on.

The two plays, *Warsaw Visitor* and the fragmentary *Tales from the Vienna Streets,* written as Bill was dying, are whimsical, flamboyant ramblings through his recollections. He intended them as his eschatology, his summing-up, his destiny and self-judgment. His grandiosity prevails alongside his humility in the face of death. The voice that speaks through all three Saroyans is that of a benign, absolute monarch of his universe, one who cannot share in his reign nor accept any criticism of it. His license lies in his writing, his being a genius at it. His gift is divine, and no one rightly can challenge it.

Warsaw Visitor's vision of himself as his wife and children's victim is a revelation of the poison that was destroying him as surely as the cancer. It is the dying Saroyan's repressed yet mortifying knowledge of his failure as a father.

It is a reminder of what he had learned that fall of 1966 in London, that even without Carol's influence, he could not fulfill his fatherly role. When he had it all his way, both children under his roof and care, he could not tolerate, let alone love, a Lucy or an Aram who did not conform entirely to *his* views of loyalty and artistic performance. Nor could he accept the slightest criticism of his hermit-like isolation, his inability to deal with a woman's love or a man's friendship.

He could live with his failure to be Aram and Lucy's father only by thrusting the blame onto them. It was Lucy's perceived whoredom and Aram's perceived incompetence—both perceived flaws of their mother—that drove his disowning and disinheriting them.

By early August 1980, the prescribed tetracycline was no match for the pain and bloodiness of his urinating. He felt the manufacturers of the pills, which cost fifteen cents a piece, were robbers. Weariness and depression caused him to pack up and leave Paris on August 14, believing he would return in November on his way to a meeting in Erevan.

The sense that his life was closing called for a financial assessment. He was pleased that his two CDs of over $100,000 were earning maximum interest and that he had done well in the gold market. What he had bought at $300 an ounce was now worth $525. His two ingots were stowed in a safety-deposit box.

There was difficulty about the Paris apartment. La Fortune, the company with whom he shared 74 rue Taitbout, was making alterations, and in the course of them had damaged his apartment. He quarreled with the firm and its lawyer, became too dispirited to write, and brought suit.

He refused a $360,000 offer for the storm-damaged Malibu property, believing it was worth more, and called his nephew Hank with a promotional scheme. He proposed ads for *Variety* and the *Hollywood Reporter,* offering the beach cottage for half a million dollars and, for an additional figure, screen rights to *An Imaginary Character Named Saroyan.* When no takers for either offer appeared and the county threatened to demolish what was left of the Malibu house, he urged Hank to get an estimate on making the necessary repairs.

Lucy did not forget her father's seventy-third birthday. Her letter reaffirmed her love for him, and yet it left him untouched. Indeed, he decided it was hypocritical. She had lost him forever in her wantonness. He remembered learning that at twenty she had had an affair with a promising movie actor and believed that Herbert Gold's *Obituaries* interview with him, which had appeared in both the *Chronicle* and the *New York Times,* had implied (from his own description of her wanting "to be an actress or a model or something") her behavior was that of an international call girl.

He had written Aram off as well. He felt his son had been sapped by his mother and her friends, left without the grit and energy to do more than pretend at getting along in the world. In the belief that many of Aram's friends were homosexual, he thanked God that Aram was married now and had three kids.

Commencing his seventy-third year on August 31, Bill suspected he would not complete it. A faintness, a shortness of breath, and a pain in his upper back left him feeling death's touch, and yet he went on as usual. He thought of phoning the doctor, going to the hospital, but he waited. During the first few days of September his penis leaked, his heart symptoms recurred, and his back hurt him, but he was still unwilling to ask for professional help. When he did report in to Drs. Werdeger, Duerksen, and Jibilian, he was offered little encouragement. The back pains were not, as he had hoped, bursitis, but the spreading cancer. Codeine was prescribed for his discomfort.

He did not believe the doctors understood the particular course of his disease, and he felt he struggled alone with it. He had a desperate sense of abandonment, of need for a family's support.

The faithful Ruben Saroyan kept him supplied with five different medicines from the veterans' hospital, but none lessened the appetite of his cancer. He was resigned to the pain, and to the loss of every kind of hope, and was willing to die now. It seemed to him that this Armenian had run through all the good luck to which he was entitled.

A bone scan at the veterans' hospital confirmed that the cancer had spread everywhere. He could eat little but cottage cheese and felt it would be best to go to Moffitt Hospital in San Francisco and die there.

His main concern was the William Saroyan library and estate. He wanted a skilled literary expert as its custodian, someone who would prevent the devastation he anticipated from Aram and Lucy. Their feelings of entitlement loomed as an ever greater threat to the monument of his work.

He called Richard Harrington in San Francisco and shared his anxiety over his unpublished work, most of it stored in seven filing cabinets at 1821 Fifteenth Avenue. Harrington said he would ask James Hart to take the manuscripts into the protective care of the Bancroft Library. If Bill were to make a gift of them, there would be benefits to his estate.

Bill had no wish to donate his life's work to any institution but the William Saroyan Foundation, which he proposed to quarter at his San Francisco house. However, he was relieved by the prospect of Bancroft custody and urged Harrington to proceed.

His estate's greatest value, he told Harrington, was his literary property: fifty books published since 1934 in which he held copyright; fifty works in manuscript awaiting publication and/or presentation; a typed journal covering fifty years; and a large collection of his abstract line drawings, signed and dated for future collections.

There were securities and gold in the California Canadian Bank worth over half a million dollars as well as real estate in San Francisco, Fresno, Bolinas, Paris, and Malibu. He wanted to keep both San Francisco and Fresno houses as museums. Neither were to be sold or rented. No unauthorized persons, such as Aram and Lucy, were to have access. Nor was the Paris apartment, which he valued at $200,000, to be sold until an appropriate time. The damaged house at Malibu, valued at $500,000, was to be sold when a buyer was found.

Bill urged Richard Harrington to make him a new will. He also spoke with Professor Dickran Kouymjian, head of the Armenian Studies program at the University of California at Fresno, about a repository there for Saroyan material. Although he suffered through a night that was the worst in his experience, he rejoiced in settling all the details of safekeeping. When his mind was at rest about them, death itself would be a welcome freedom.

In mid-October he enjoyed a remission and was up at his easel to draw in the sun. He watched the World Series and enjoyed the food Ruben brought him. Harrington provided the new will and reported that he and the movers had seen the seven file cabinets safely into the Bancroft Library at the University of California. He would come to Fresno at the end of the week to work out the details of the will. James Hart phoned to say how glad he was to have the William Saroyan collection.

Bill anticipated October 21 as the Big Day, and Ruben trimmed his hair in preparation. As arranged, Ruben met Richard Harrington at the Fresno airport, and brought him to West Griffith Way for a sandwich lunch and a careful review of the new will.

With the anticipated proceeds from the sale of Malibu plus $150,000, the will set up a trust for the benefit of Cosette, Lucy, Aram, and his three children but payable only when they were determined by the trustee to be without other means of support. This would hamper, if not prevent, any family challenge. The Bolinas property would be held for the use of Aram and his family but could not be sold without the trustee's consent.

The literary estate and its income went to the Saroyan Foundation for charitable and educational purposes. The foundation would lend parts of the collection to the Bancroft Library, which would select a literary executor.

Together they worked out a codicil appointing Henry, Cosette, and Harrington as executors. That afternoon, the Armenian Museum delegation, consisting of Dickran Kouymjian, Leon Peters, the head of the university's

Fresno Foundation, and the university's president, Harold Haak, arrived. They witnessed the signing of the new will and assured Bill of museum custody for all Saroyan materials they were given.

Three days later, Bill drove with Harry Bagdasarian around the Ararat and Belmont Cemeteries and past the Chapel of the Light, and then made inquiry at the Neptune Society. He learned that cremation would cost less than $400, a fraction of the expense of undertaker and burial, and decided the society's procedure was the best possible under the law. In taking out his Neptune Society membership, he asked that Ruben Saroyan be his cosigner.

Halloween night brought a pumpkin flying onto his doorstep, and he was well enough to see both the nutritional value and the humor in stewing its broken pieces and enjoying it over the next several days. He listened to the Carter-Reagan debate and although he favored Carter, he took his rejection at the polls on November 4 with a shrug.

He underwent further tests, and on November 10 discussed the results with a veterans' hospital doctor, Michael Jensen-Akoulian. He learned that the cancer had reached his liver, and that he had no more than six months to live. Castration and chemotherapy were rejected in favor of treatment with the drug Stilbastrol.

He was distressed to learn that the rue Taitbout litigation had been settled in La Fortune's favor. Armen Barseghian, the Paris lawyer he had hired to settle his suit with La Fortune, wrote that he owed them $2,800. Thus Bill turned to an old ally. He asked Richard Harrington to inquire of his former Paris friend and attorney Jack Kevorkian if he would intervene and perhaps resolve the problem. He was greatly cheered by a friendly note from Kevorkian in Paris assuring him that he had paid the disputed balance and settled the rue Taitbout matter satisfactorily.

Although he no longer remembered his two children at Christmas, just prior to the holiday Bill sent off checks of $10,000 to Cosette, $2,000 to Henry, and $3,000 to Hank for use in salvaging Malibu. He also sent $1,500 to Henry's daughter, Lucinda Luengo, for the schooling of her three children.

Cosette's will reflected his own in the disposition of Malibu and San Francisco properties, but differed in making specific bequests to Bill's and Henry's grandchildren. He thought this might interfere with the plan for his own estate and the Saroyan Foundation. Thus he asked Richard Harrington to remake Cosette's will so there would be no obstacle. Harrington was proceeding to do this as the year came to an end.

As the new year of 1981 began, the sickness took more of him each day. He was feeble, dispirited, and angry. He urged Richard Harrington to make sure that neither Aram nor Lucy would have any power over his estate, that anything established at this time would not be vulnerable in the future. He was particularly concerned about Malibu, which was half in Cosette's name and still unsold.

When Harrington called Bill on January 17 to discuss the variation between his and Cosette's wills, and the difficulty this might present, Bill grew puzzled and then annoyed. Although they argued for an hour, Bill could not understand Harrington's reasoning and was furious with him.

The next day, Bill was still possessed by this anger. It drove other thoughts from his mind and seemed to threaten his sanity. Nevertheless, on January 20, while reading the *Variety* "Necrology" for 1980, he decided to begin a new *Obituaries* project, and for the next week, he wrote two chapters a day. He knew they lacked a confident voice, yet it was a wonder he was writing at all. He forged on with *Obituaries III*.

On January 26, the mail brought him a three-dimensional greeting card from Lucy. It was postmarked Marina Del Ray and signed Tumbleweed, but this reminder of happy, affectionate times together did not soften his estrangement.

Two days later, anxiety about his own and Cosette's wills and Harrington's resistance to his sense of urgency induced a new attack of his irascibleness. He was persuaded that Harrington had failed him. After a particularly bad night, he could no longer work on *Obituaries III* and put it aside, believing it was only until he had found a new lawyer. In fact, he had brought to a close a half century of devoted marriage to his typewriter.

Through his accountant, he engaged a Fresno lawyer, Gerald Lee Tashjian. On February 4, he asked Tashjian to cancel the two wills Harrington had written for him and Cosette and to prepare replacements. In addition, he asked him to study the Saroyan Foundation and make sure of its invulnerability. He spoke to Richard Harrington on the telephone, instructing him to forward the existing wills to his new attorney. In midconversation, irritation with Harrington caused him to hang up on him. For the next month and a half Bill ran an erratic course between new and old lawyers. He fired Harrington by letter, fumed at him unceasingly, and urged Tashjian to make haste with the revisions.

On March 2, Bill signed the new, Tashjian will. Feeling that he needed a San Francisco lawyer as well, he called upon Robert Damir, an Armenian attorney who, years earlier, had looked into the stalled Franklin negotiations for him. In sending Damir his new will, Bill asked him to replace Harrington in his dealings with James Hart and the Bancroft Library.

When he heard about this change, Hart, an old friend of Harrington's, expressed regret about it. Bill was so irked to hear Hart's admiration for Dick Harrington that he was tempted to quarrel about it. Cosette learned from Harrington that he had been fired by Bill, and when Bill confirmed it he added that it was surely as great a relief for Harrington as for himself.

On March 20, Bill had a call from Jack Kevorkian. He was in New York, asking if he could come to see him in Fresno. Bill was delighted at the prospect of repairing this damaged relationship and of renewed access to Kevorkian advice. He told him that he had replaced Harrington with Damir and that of course he would see him.

Bill was pleased with Damir and his trustworthy Armenian background. In a March 3 letter to him, he described his 1964 visit to Bitlis and the ruins of the Saroyan family's highland compound there. He felt this related to the importance he placed on the Saroyan Foundation. He went on to explain that Aram had displayed a lack of interest in his father's life and work. While Lucy declared devotion to him, her attitude was the same as her brother's.

He wanted to be sure that neither child would have access to his estate or to the William Saroyan Foundation, for he distrusted them. Each was devoted to their mother, who had repeatedly displayed a ruthlessness toward himself and his work.

For Bill, Wednesday, April 8, 1981, was a celebration day. In late morning, Robert Damir and Jack Kevorkian, having just met for the first time, drove up to his door. Over a restaurant lunch, Bill and Kevorkian recalled that it was just twenty years ago that they had met at Coudert Frères in Paris. Over the next several hours the two lawyers went over the wills, the Malibu deed, the sale of the Paris apartment to the foundation, and the foundation itself. No further need was seen for Tashjian's services.

Bill took his two lawyers for a visit to Malaga Vineyard, site of *The Pomegranate Trees,* presented them with signed copies of *Obituaries,* and, with a sense of great accomplishment, sent them off to the airport. Both lawyers returned on the following Saturday for a signing of the final will, which was witnessed by Damir, Kevorkian, and Harry Bagdasarian. Bill basked in a sense of relief. He marveled at what had been accomplished in three days and again congratulated himself on dismissing Harrington.

Only one matter remained to be settled, that of his literary executor. He had been impressed with Kevin Starr's recent San Francisco novel *Land's End* and knew of his earlier nonfiction book, *Americans and the California Dream 1850–1915.* Starr had taught at Harvard and headed the San Francisco Public Library and seemed an appropriate candidate. Although Bill left a message on Starr's answering machine, there was no immediate response.

Although he knew there had been rumors of his death, he had kept his deteriorating condition as secret as he could. He gave Harry Bagdasarian the house keys and asked him to phone each morning at ten. If on the second call there was no answer, he should come and see why. In early April he considered how and when to break his news. He prepared a final statement to give the AP. It would read that while he was aware that all men must die, he had always believed he would be made an exception.

On April 12, he called Henry in Alameda and told him that he was dying. When Henry wept at the news, Bill told him he should not. It was cause to rejoice. He also told his nephew Hank, who had performed so ably on the Malibu problem, but urged them both to keep his secret, from his son and his daughter in particular.

As her father took these precautions in Fresno, Lucy, in Beverly Hills, learned from Jack Kevorkian that her father was terminally ill. Encouraged by Kevorkian, Lucy spoke to Dr. Jibilian and alerted Aram in Bolinas. She told him that their father was dying, and she planned to visit him.

On April 15, Bill's pain and the drugs with which he numbed it had all but immobilized him. Although he could scarcely breathe, he was aware that it was a particularly fine spring day. At one in the afternoon, he heard Ruben, who was gardening outside, speak to someone, and then heard a knock at his front door. When he asked who it was, he heard Lucy's voice saying anxiously that it was she.

He opened the door on a woman he did not at first recognize. She was holding a basket, and he could smell the scent of her perfume. The sight enraged him, and he demanded to know what she was doing here. When Lucy replied that she was here for *him,* he told her she was lying, that she had come to exploit his death.

Stepping into the house and setting down her basket, Lucy told her father that she had learned of his illness through Jack Kevorkian, who had assured her she would be welcome for an hour's visit. Bill's response was that if he had the physical strength he would kill Kevorkian for telephoning her. His rage at her grew. He told her that her "stink" was killing him faster. He fumed about her affairs with famous people, and that at thirty-five she was neither a wife nor a mother nor famous nor rich. When Lucy protested that she was a good person, he told her that was nothing, that murderers were good persons.

She confessed that she had told Aram, and that he was planning to drive down from Bolinas the next day, to which her father protested she must tell him not to, that Aram would kill him by coming now. He asked Lucy if she thought her brother was a writer. She did, and ignoring his skepticism added that he was also a wonderful father. Bill agreed that being a parent was one thing Aram had over his sister.

Indicating the basket, Lucy said she had brought him some food. When he asked what kind, she told him it was chicken.

In an explosion of anger, her father ordered her to take her chicken and her pot and get out of his house. A shattered Lucy left him, dropping the basket inside the door. She found that his screams had penetrated the neighborhood and frightened Ruben away. Her brief visit had left Bill with new torment.

The next day, Harry Bagdasarian drove Bill to Dr. Jibilian's office so that he could learn what to expect of the time that remained. At the end of Jibilian's bleak prediction he told Bill that Lucy had called and that he expected to hear from Aram. What could he tell them?

That he was okay, was Bill's response.

The next morning, Friday, April 17, Dr. Jibilian reported that Aram had asked if he could come down from Bolinas, bringing the three grandchildren for a visit. Bill replied that he would not see them. Instead, he suggested Aram mail him some snapshots of the children. It would be best to send them special delivery. Aram did so, enclosing an entire album.

That same afternoon, Bill received his nephew Hank and posed with him, Ruben, and Harry Bagdasarian for what he facetiously described as deathbed color pictures.

On Saturday morning, Bill phoned James Hart at home to tell him that the only man he wanted for executor and editor of the Saroyan Collection was Kevin Starr, and to ask if he could persuade him. Hart agreed to try, and presently Kevin Starr telephoned. Bill explained to him that he was his first choice for the executorship but he should understand it would require two decades of hard work. Starr agreed to undertake it, and Bill told him he was honored and thrilled by his decision. While Starr was to hear no more about it for years, Bill rejoiced in another accomplishment. Now, in spite of horrible pain and humiliation, everything was done.

The next morning, Sunday, April 19, just before nine o'clock, he was surprised by Harry Bagdasarian, who had let himself into the house and switched on the bedroom light. He told Bill that he had called in the prescribed manner and that there had been no answer. Bill was left wondering if he could no longer hear his telephone.

Also the album of Aram's photographs arrived. Bill examined it, declared it a great Easter gift, put it back in its envelope, and instructed Ruben to return the album to Aram by regular mail.

He was still buoyed by Kevin Starr's agreeing to be executor, and that night he made the final entry in the diary he had kept so faithfully for forty-six years: All was well. He was thinking of the dry rocks of Armenia, of art, and of fire.

On Tuesday morning, April 21, Harry Bagdasarian again entered the house, and found Bill seated at a table but unconscious. With Ruben's help

Bill was put to bed, and Dr. Jibilian was summoned. That afternoon he was admitted, still unconscious, to the Veterans' Administration Hospital. Later in the day, he surprised his doctors by regaining consciousness. On Thursday, the news of Bill's cancer was in the papers. The story said that Saroyan himself had telephoned the AP bureau to report that he had cancer throughout his body.

On Wednesday, April 29, Aram decided to visit his father, bringing along seven-year-old Cream. They arrived at midday, and Aram urged Cream, bearing a bouquet, to precede him. Aram followed apprehensively. Bill watched Cream's tentative approach in silence. The nurse spoke, urging Cream to give her grandfather a kiss. As she tried to lift Cream up to the bed, Bill raised his arm and warned her not to hurt his granddaughter.

When the nurse, indicating Aram, reminded her patient that this was his son, Bill glared at Aram and said that he would never forget him.

Aram had brought his father a book of Pasternak poems, and while Bill ignored the gift, he asked Aram's help in drinking some cranberry juice. He turned to Cream, complimenting her on her mother's painting and then asking her what her father did. Bill did not understand her reply, and Aram had to explain that she had said he wrote screenplays. Bill made no more of this, and father, son, and granddaughter fell into a kind of meditation that lasted throughout visits of a doctor and a nurse. In the quiet, Bill turned onto his side and took Cream's hand in his, then seemed to sleep. On being urged to kiss her grandpa good-bye, Cream did this, and Bill's eyes opened.

As Aram leaned to kiss his father good-bye, Bill flung out his arm and they embraced. Bill thanked him for coming and told him that he had made this the most beautiful time of his life—and death.

As Aram and Cream left the room, Aram heard his father exclaim how unbelievable this visit had been.

Although Lucy was terrified of a second visit to her father, Aram's report encouraged her to return to Fresno on May 2. When she arrived at the hospital she was told that her father refused to see her. A black nurse intervened, opening the door to her father's room and announcing, "Mr. Saroyan, your daughter's here."

At Bill's first glimpse of Lucy he protested that he was dying and couldn't endure this. Lucy replied that they needn't speak. She wanted only to sit beside him for a few minutes. She did so, reaching through the bars at the edge of his bed to take his hand. Presently, he told her that he was glad she had come.

Emboldened by Lucy's visit, Aram returned to Fresno on May 4, bringing his entire family, and Bill greeted them alertly and cordially. He singled out Armenak to pronounce him a winner. When he had spoken to each of the children, he roared that he was a fool of the worst kind and didn't deserve such a tribute. He added a word of praise for his son.

Aram lingered behind the others to say he was glad that he and Lucy had had a good visit, and Bill replied that he admired her bravery in coming a second time. Then Aram asked a worrisome question. He and his family wanted to be near at hand. Could they use the corner house on West Griffith Way?

Bill agreed, saying in that way they could all be together, and when asked if Lucy could also stay there he approved enthusiastically. Yes, Aram could tell both Lucy and Ruben she was welcome there. Aram could do whatever he wanted.

After his guests had gone, however, Bill had misgivings, and he left it to Ruben to tell Aram about them. Aram had barely returned to Bolinas when Ruben called to say that he should not plan on using the corner house, for it would be against the terms of his father's latest will. This stipulated that the house must remain sealed.

On the evening of May 17, Bill's niece, Zabe's daughter, Jackie Kazarian, called on Bill. He failed to recognize her. He was groggy and complained of not being able to sleep. Shortly, he dozed off, and she stayed in the chair beside his bed throughout the night.

He woke in the morning alert, and although unable to speak, he recognized his niece. She held his hand, gave him a fortune cookie, and read him its message, "Bless you with health and happiness." Jackie went to tell the nurse he was awake. When the two returned, he seemed to have fallen asleep, but in fact, Bill Saroyan had died.

·   ·   ·

So exited a man whose consuming wish—that his reputation as an American writer outlive him—was granted. That wish had grown out of his legacy from an Armenian father, a man who had pursued the New World's promise but had lacked the knowledge, hide, and will to survive it. In his son's hands the brown-paper scraps with their indecipherable lines became a powerful force. Atoning for the great gyp Armenak had suffered from America became Bill's mission.

William Saroyan had been heroic. A young champ of the post-Depression years, he had risen up out of the San Joaquin Valley to inspire a generation of American writers searching for new forms and to bring a yearned-for, intellectual pride to Armenians throughout the world.

The truth about William Saroyan begins in the Fred Finch attic room—where he lay ill, alone, and unloved listening to the voices of other orphans singing a hymn. Emerging from the crisis of his illness he knew not only that he would live but that henceforth he would be self-sufficient. He had found the armor for his heart and had "finished crying, perhaps for the rest of his life."

At Emerson School, he learned that being an Armenian boy was contemptible, and it stiffened the rebel in him. In class he scoffed at his teacher and nursed a student inadequacy that took cover in contempt for "the system," and in the clowning that became a lifetime recourse from intellectual challenge.

Yet his literary parentage was American, acquired in the public libraries of Fresno and San Francisco. There he took for his own the Emersonian belief that the power in each man is divine, that he can know its extent only when he's tried it. Whitman too spoke for him in, "I celebrate myself and sing myself. . . . For every atom belonging to me as good belongs to you."

Saroyan did have a writerly gift, an instinct for lively, persuasive language and for artistic truth and expediency. It had led him to combine fiction and essay into a form that seemed wholly new. In such early examples as "And Man," "Snake," and "Seventeen," he was able to give full power to his need to be heard, and in 1934 it delivered him a spectacular initial success in the literary world.

The Saroyan message, first displayed in *The Daring Young Man on the Flying Trapeze,* derives from a discovery he had made in Maupassant's story "Bell," about a crippled beggar. He recognized the outcast as hero and the force of his response to a society that had rejected him. Here Bill found his voice. As a writer he could perform an affirmation of bitter experience. He could respond with joy for simply being alive on a marvelous earth, instead of dead beneath it.

Theater recognition came in 1939 with *Highlands.* The play was a youthful fantasy of wish fulfillment. It was innocence in which poor, hungry people yearn for poetry and a kindly community subsidizes it, as it had in his own 1934 good fortune. Success crested that same year in the prizewinning *Time of Your Life.* Now on Broadway, he continued to speak for the scorned and rejected. The homeless who gathered in his enchanted saloon were good people, decent in spite of vicious authority.

Then, in Hollywood he achieved a third astounding triumph in the writing of *The Human Comedy* and in the welcome it brought him to the power center of the motion-picture world.

Yet for each of these three wondrous Saroyan ascents there was an equally dramatic fall. Each time he had performed a miracle, changing his self-image from that of a ragged, unschooled newsboy into that of a literary wonder boy and genius. He had also repeated a tragic mistake. He had let

Bill used this dandelion blossom to demonstrate—in this case to some Russian writers—
the principle on which he had based *The Time of Your Life*.

himself believe he had done it all himself. He owed no debt to the people at *Story* and Random House who had discovered, edited, and counseled him. In ignoring and provoking them, he had denied himself the feedback, the criticism by which a writer grows.

Similarly in the theater, the surprising success of *Time of Your Life* persuaded Bill that the play's triumph was *all* his, and that his genius extended to directing. He lacked the humility to learn stagecraft from the great teachers—Bobby Lewis, Harold Clurman, Lawrence Langner, and Brooks Atkinson—who were at his side. His hubris ignored criticism, put the blame for failure elsewhere, and led to an artistic slide, away from character and situation toward absurdity and obscurity. It was a path that began in *Love's Old Sweet Song* and *The Beautiful People* and ended in the ultimate conceits of the Saroyan Theatre and *Sam, the Highest Jumper*.

Finally, in Hollywood, his mounting megalomania blinded him to the experience and wisdom of MGM's executives. A belief that he was their better lost him his prize, a *Human Comedy* that was splendidly the result of his own talent and hard work. With a yearned-for Hollywood future in his grasp, victory turned into defeat.

Then, despite his efforts to condemn and ignore it, World War II gathered him in. Once more a precariously towering self-importance disabled him. He was immune to patriotism, and could neither acknowledge superiors nor tolerate the "buddy system" of the military. His army years destroyed Saroyan in midlife, both as a man and an artist. It was as though he had stood for the portrait of Sir Walter Scott's slacker, "concentered all in self," condemned to die twice and be "unwept, unhonored and unsung."

Bill Saroyan did survive the war to revive youthful hopes, to rejoice in that powerful love that had sustained him in separation, and to make a family with his Carol. But he could not live with or without her. Possessive passion and contempt for her lasted for the rest of his life. Their duplicated marriage and divorce proved the worst of his self-immolations. It left him tattered, on the edge of madness, and creatively bankrupt.

As a writer he then responded to experience in an opposite way, a negative tropism that came forth in unmasked bitterness. It accounted for the failure of his three ambitious novels, *Wesley Jackson, Rock Wagram,* and *The Laughing Matter.*

For a time he quelled his bitterness in affectionate concern for his adolescent children. It enabled a new productive era of his writing and included the novels *Mama* and *Papa,* the eight memoirs, and such admirable, late-life stories as "Bicycle," "Voyald," "Picnic," and "Twenty."

London in the summer of 1966 was the scene of Bill's puzzling disengagement from his children. They had lived together as a family of three, each pursuing his or her ambition. Bill had launched Lucy as an actress in *Hello Out There,* and had approved Aram's plans for a novel, yet as they parted that fall he understood that their intimacy was at an end.

He had thought they would be a joy to him. Instead, he found they were Carol's children, that she had "unreasonably" thrown him responsibility for them, asked *him* to mend them—and he discovered that he could not.

Their needs and expectations challenged both the amiable, invincible, mustachioed outer self and the charlatan-fool he knew within.

In the end, he outlived his ability to write for others. He could not suffer a real world where his plays and stories were shunned and critics scoffed at him, so he withdrew to the hermitage of his illusion, where even his children became part of the conspiracy threatening his immortality.

Of the many flaws in Bill Saroyan's nature, one stands out as critical—an impermeable self-reliance, born of early hardship and widely regarded as a virtue. It armored the outcast's feelings of inadequacy, the immigrant American's sense of powerlessness, and gave him his formidable gift and will as a writer. It also spawned his distrust, misanthropy, and compulsive gambling. It denied him artistic growth and the love and admiration he had sought so desperately from the beginning of his tormented life. It led him at last to the self's abyss. What had been so full of wonders now held nothing at all.

In his last years, he avoided all humans he could not subjugate, and was so obsessed with shoring up the fortress of his future reputation that he passed up a last opportunity for affection with his children. Then a lifetime's fears about his health became the agonizing reality of fatal cancer and a death which, at last, he welcomed.

Notes

and Saroyan, 3/31/34–2/1/39; journal,
8/10–12/37.

55–9 Hal Matson, Pat Duggan relations,
quarrel: Matson correspondence,
11/16/38–12/5/39; journal, 8/9/37.

57–61 *Highlands,* the Group Theatre:
Obituaries, 69; Robert Lewis, *Slings
and Arrows* (Stein & Day, 1984),
103–23; Lawrence Langner, *The Magic
Curtain* (E. P. Dutton, 1951); Theresa
Helburn, *A Wayward Quest* (Little,
Brown, 1960); Duggan correspon-
dence, 3/9, 3/13/39; journal, 9/9–26/38.

61–5 George Jean Nathan and *The Time of
Your Life: Sons Come,* 126; George Jean
Nathan, *The Magic Mirror* (Knopf,
1960); *Liberty* magazine, 10/41.

66 Dublin, London, Paris: *Places; Sons Come;*
Saroyan travel notes.

66–7 Minelli and Harlem: Matson and
Duggan correspondence, 6/17/39.

69–73 *The Time of Your Life:* Lewis, *Slings
and Arrows;* Langner, *The Magic
Curtain;* Celeste Holm interview,
9/17/90; *Places,* 147–9; Helburn, *A
Wayward Quest;* Matson correspondence, 5/15/39.

73–6 *Love's Old Sweet Song* and other plays,
critics: Helburn, *A Wayward Quest;*
Langner, *The Magic Curtain;* journal,
9/27/41.

76–7 Prizes: John Hohenburg, *The Pulitzer
Prizes* (Columbia University Press,
1974); Robert Giroux interview.

V. IN THE MOGUL'S PALACE:
1940–1941

78 Brooks Atkinson: *New York Times,* 9/1/40.

79 *A Native American, My Name Is Aram:*
journal, 8/19/38.

80–1 *Across the Board:* journal, 10/20/41.

81–5 *The Beautiful People:* Betsy Blair Reisz
interview, 10/12/90; journal, 9/10,
10/13, 11/10/41.

84–5 Quarrel with Matson, Duggan; *Variety*
ad, *The Beautiful People:* Matson
correspondence; journal, 8/21–9/13/41;
journal, 8/22–5/41.

85–6 *Jim Dandy:* journal, 9/17–9/41.

86 *Hello Out There:* Jon Whitmore, *William

Saroyan, 41; journal, 8/22–5, 9/12–5,
10/1–4/41.

86–7 Writing *Afton Water:* journal,
11/3–12/41; Nathan correspondence,
11/13, 20/41.

87 Hollywood visit and prospects: journal,
11/13–12/1/41.

88 Stanley Rose as agent at MGM: *Sons
Come,* 71; journal, 11/29/41.

89–90 Mayer and MGM: *Sons Come,* 136;
Taitbout, 156; journal, 1/28–4/30/42;
Nathan correspondence, 11/30/41;
Mayer correspondence, 2/9/42.

91–3 Writing *The Human Comedy:* journal,
12/20–9/41, 1/23/42.

94–8 *The Human Comedy* at MGM: Thornton Delahanty, "The Saga of Saroyan
in Hollywood," *New York Herald
Tribune,* 5/10/42; journal, 2/5–4/30/42.

99–100 Writing *Get Away Old Man:* journal,
5/5–9/42.

101 Gambling with Ross: journal, 10/24–9/41.

102 Edmund Wilson, Brooks Atkinson:
Edmund Wilson, *The Boys in the Back
Room* (Colt Press, 1941).

102–3 Introspection, Jewish critics, anti-
Semitism: journal, 9/9, 20, 10/4/41,
11/4/44.

VI. THE ONE GIRL: 1941–1942

104 Sex: journal, 8/16/37, 9/8/41, 11/28/57.

104–6 Pat Winter, 1936: *Taitbout;* "Match
Girl," 45; *Love, Here Is My Hat,* 1, 43;
journal, 7/28/37, 11/4, 19/37, 8/28/38.

107 Helen Wills Moody: Journal, 3/17, 4/7/38.

108–9 Artie Shaw, and meeting Carol
Marcus: Artie Shaw interview, 7/3/89;
"Old Friend," *I Love You I Hate You
Drop Dead* (Fleet, 1965); *Trio,* 88–90;
Saroyan; Carol Matthau, *Mirabella*
(May 1992); *Porcupines,* 18, 20; Carol
Matthau interviews, 6/19, 6/27,
7/27/90; journal, 2/27–28/42, 3/7/42;
Rosheen Marcus interview, 2/13/90.

109–10 Norma Shearer: journal, 3/2–19/42.

111–13 Carol in New York dating pattern,
feelings for each other: journal,
7/7–10/26/42.

113 Carol's description of her father: journal,
7/22/42, 7/15/43.

116 The "triumph": journal, 8/5/42.

113–17 The Saroyan Theatre, *Across the Board, Talking to You:* Nathan correspondence, 6/18/42; journal, 8/1–28/42.

114–15 Steinbeck at "21": *Obituaries,* 257; *Days,* 124; journal, 7/28/42, 5/2/43.

115–116,119 The draft: journal, 6/17, 7/7, 9/9, 10/15/42.

120 *The Human Comedy* as novel: journal, 7/16, 9/22/42.

120 *Hello Out There* by Dowling at the Belasco: Howard Barnes, "New and Old," *New York Herald Tribune,* 9/30/42; journal, 9/29–30/42.

120–1 Driving west, calls from Carol and Rosheen: journal, 10/1–7/42.

123–5 California holiday with Carol and Oona, journal, Oona's distaste: *Porcupines,* 35; journal, 10/14–26/42.

125 Wanting Carol pregnant: Lucy Saroyan memoir, 4, journal, 10/26/42, confirmed in *Porcupines,* 34, 37.

125 Takoohi's blessing: Journal, 10/26/42.

VII. THE BUGLE'S CALL: 1941–1942

126–7 Hatred for war: letter to Whit Burnett and Martha Foley, 1/31/41.

127 FDR, dream, Hyde Park visit: journal, 9/15/41, 1/21, 23/42, 4/30/43.

128–9 Basic training: Camp Kohler, Carol courtship: journal, 10/30–12/18/42; Aram Saroyan, *William Saroyan,* 76; Nathan correspondence, 12/6/42.

129 Oona and J. D. Salinger: Arthur and Barbara Gelb, *O'Neill* (Harper, 1962), 850; journal, 11/8/42.

130–1 Astoria: journal, 12/22/42–2/15/43.

131–2 *The Human Comedy* as novel: journal, 7/10/42; Morley correspondence, 12/6/42.

132–5 Carol, second courtship, deciding to marry: journal, 12/23/42–2/12/43; Lucy Saroyan memoir.

135–41 Wright Field, Dayton, wedding, Mike Todd: journal, 2/16–3/19/43; *Porcupines,* 38.

142–3 Viewing *The Human Comedy,* encounter with Pat Winter: journal, 3/10/43.

VIII. HOME FRONT: 1943–1944

144–5 Lombardy, Astoria: journal, 3/23–5/3/43.

145–6 Back pain: U.S. Army Medical Department Records; journal, 3/25–31/43.

146–7 Pentagon: journal, 4/1/43.

149–50 War bond rallies: journal, 5/9–11, 5/23/43.

150 Sutton Place, Carol quarrels: journal, 4/4, 5/30/43.

151 Details about *Get Away Old Man:* journal, 4/18, 4/29, 5/5/43.

152 Carol pregnancy, sex relations, anti-Semitic jokes on the terrace, and Carol's response, happiness: journal, 5/2, 6/4, 7/5, 7/9, 7/11–13/43; Carol Matthau phone interview, 7/27/90; *Porcupines,* 40.

155–7 Saroyan's rebellion, "paranoid," psychiatric wards at Fort Jay and Halloran Hospitals: U.S. Army Medical Department records; journal, 7/24–11/3, 9/9, 9/24, 10/15, 11/25–26/43; *Not Dying,* 208.

157 Aram's birth: journal, 9/24/43; *Last Rites,* 59.

159 Discharge thwarted: journal, 10/16–25/43.

160 Charles Tekeyan: journal, 9/31–11/1/43.

162 *Get Away Old Man* opens: journal, 11/16–26/43; Whitmore, *William Saroyan,* 38–41.

165 Captain Davalos's advice, and the Section 8: journal, 12/6/43.

165–6 Alerted, at the Sea Girt with Irwin Shaw: journal, 12/18/43.

166–8 Takoohi and Cosette arrive: journal, 1/3–22/43.

169 Farewell: journal, 1/25/44.

IX. EUROPEAN CAMPAIGN: 1944–1945

170–1 London, George Stevens, Irwin Shaw, Gene Solow: Carol correspondence, 2/25–5/25/44; Michael Schnayerson, *Irwin Shaw* (Putnam, 1989); *Sons Come,* 181; *London Daily Mail,* 7/27/44; journal, 5/24/44–1/10/45.

171–2 Air raids and poker: journal, 7/8, 7/16/44.

177–8 George Bernard Shaw visit, letter: George Bernard Shaw collected letters, 417; "My Visit with George Bernard Shaw," *New Republic* (August 1946); journal, 5/24/44.

178–85 Spyros Skouras, Herbert Agar, and writing *Wesley Jackson: Days*, 92; journal, 5/24/44–1/9/45; Carol correspondence, 5/25/44–1/9/45.

183 Jealousy dream: Carol correspondence, 8/25/44.

187–8 Saroyan case against the army: Agar correspondence, 11/20/44.

190 Pinewood visit: Carol correspondence, 1/14/45; Garson Kanin interview, 1/5/92.

190–1 Paris: Carol correspondence, 1/23–2/22/45.

191–2 Hemingway encounter: Carol correspondence, 1/25/45; *Sons Come*, 204; Carlos Baker, *Hemingway* (Scribner, 1969).

194 Luxembourg mission: Carol correspondence, 2/3–22/45.

194 At last a good doctor—homeward bound: U.S. Army Medical Department Records; Carol correspondence, 2/10/45.

194–5 Army hospitals and the war's end: journal, 4/17–9/13/45.

195 Resuming the writer's life: journal, 6/23–8/7/45.

X. READJUSTMENT: 1945–1949

199–200 New homes, Sea Cliff, Taraval: journal, 10/13, 10/15, 12/8/45.

200–1 Friction between Carol and family, gambling and quarrels: *Porcupines*, 53–4; journal, 11/7, 13/45, 1/29, 3/13/46.

202 Lucy's birth: Lucy Saroyan memoir; *Chance Meetings*, 10; Journal, 1/17–26/46.

205–7 *Wesley Jackson* failure, gambling, borrowing: journal, 6/1–9/27/46.

205 Stokowski visit: journal, 5/2/46.

210–11 Mill Neck, *Time of Your Life* screen rights to Cagneys: *Places*, 45; journal, 10/23/46–3/12/47.

211 Carol's third pregnancy and miscarriage: *Porcupines*, 59; cross-complaint seeking marriage annulment, Los Angeles County, California, Nov. 9, 1951; journal, 11/16, 12/4/46.

212 W. Tasker Witham's assessment, his own: Tasker Williams, *Panorama of American Literature* (Stephen Daye, 1947); journal, 12/11/47.

214 *Sam Ego's House* and Chaplin: journal, 8/20/47.

216–17 Carol quarrels, Lucy's rocking: *Porcupines*, 67; journal, 10/23/47.

217–18 Capote visit: *Porcupines*, 56; journal, 12/18/47.

218–19 Lane's Bridge farm: journal, 4/20–6/8/48.

220 *The Time of Your Life* as film: journal, 6/11, 26, 8/2/47, 1/17, 6/16, 19, 21, 29/48.

221 Divorce plans abandoned, reconciliation: journal, 6/8–7/19, 8/5/48.

222 Grim Magic and the move to New York: journal, 8/5/48.

223 41 West Fifty-eighth St.: journal, 8/13–20/48; Confessions of a Playwright for *New York Times* (unpublished article); journal, 8/13/48.

224 Short-story renaissance: journal, 7/11/47, 1/22/49.

224–5 Carol's stunning revelation: journal, 3/29, 4/6, 8/31/49; Lee and Gifford, *Saroyan*, 153–6; Aram Saroyan, *William Saroyan*, 64–72; *Trio*, 84–6, 106; *Last Rites*, 49–51; *Porcupines*, 5, 6; Lucy Saroyan memoir, 7.

225 Bill quits his family: journal, 4/17/49.

XI. ESCAPE: 1949–1950

227–30 Europe, gambling, Gulbenkian: journal, 4/21–8/30/49.

231–2 Glimpse of Carol with Capp, suspicions: *Porcupines*, 74–6; journal, 7/15, 8/26/49.

233 *Fifty-fifty:* journal, 9/7–21/49.

234 *The Assyrian:* journal, 9/26/49.

234–5 Las Vegas divorce, Doubleday contract: journal, 10/2–11/7/49.

237–43 Christmas in New York, Capp jealousy, conflict with Carol, Ross advice, detectives, kids: *Trio,* 15, 80–2; *Porcupines,* 62–3, 74–5; Lucy Saroyan interview, 8/15/89, 5/31/91; Lucy Saroyan memoir, 7–8; Leila Hadley interview, 1/6/92; Capp correspondence, 11/8/50; divorce proceedings in Los Angeles County Court, 11/7/51; journal 12/20/49–2/16/50.

243 Summons to San Francisco: journal, 2/16–17/50.

XII. THE BIG MUSTACHE: 1950–1952

244 Takoohi's death: journal, 2/21–6/50.

244 Minasian suit, "Little Caruso": journal, 8/18, 9/2/37.

245 Ross and *The Son:* journal, 3/19–4/1/50.

246 Carol overtures: 9/22/49–8/5/50.

248 *Twin Adventures* published: journal, 4/12, 5/1–7/9/50.

248–9 *Rock Wagram* written: journal, 5/3–6/9/50.

249 Laramie and *A Western Awakening* (*Afton Water*): journal, 7/2–8/50.

250–1 New York visit, nightwalk: Ken McCormick interview, 2/18/92; journal, 7/24–6/50.

252 *The Laughing Matter, Tracy's Tiger, Torch for Life, More Later,* and Howard Cady: journal, 7/31–10/30/50.

253 Carol rapprochement: journal, 8/4–12/25/50.

254 Ken McCormick and Doubleday quarrels: journal, 8/20–10/8/50, 11/10–13/50.

257 Cerf's rebuff: journal, 11/18/50.

257–60 Long journey east, Los Angeles, Mexico, Miami, Havana: journal, 12/26/50–2/5/51.

261 Reunion in New York: journal, 2/6–13/51.

263 Reunion in Beverly Hills: journal, 2/3, 3/2, 3/25/51; *Porcupines,* 80–5; Lucy Saroyan memoir, 8.

XIII. SECOND HONEYMOON: 1951–1952

265 *Rock Wagram* published: journal, 3/19–27/51.

266–8 North Rodeo Drive, parties, remarriage: journal, 3/8–10/1/51.

267–9 Working for Feldman: journal, 3/21–6/18/51.

269 "Come On-A My House": journal, 6/8–15/51.

271 Redivorce, letter of explanation for Giesler: Petition for Annulment of Marriage and Answer and Cross-complaint filed in Los Angeles County Court, 11/7/51; *Saroyan,* 254; journal, 8/13/51, 10/7/51–3/6/52.

274 *Bicycle Rider:* journal, 1/22/52.

275 Seeing Carol, Malibu cottage, Fante, the kids: Lucy Saroyan interview, 5; journal, 1/15–3/1/52.

280–1 Omnibus and Maroney Lane: journal, 3/21–9/20/52.

XIV. THE REVIVAL: 1953–1955

282 Omnibus: Journal, 4/21–9/20/52, 1/4–12/2/53.

284 *The Laughing Matter: New York Times Book Review,* 3/8/53; *New Republic,* 3/9/53; journal, 8/22–30/50, 3/29/56.

286–7 IRS liens, CBS deal: journal, 5/1, 6/7, 8/16/53.

287 Poker and Fante: journal, 3/14/52, 8/16, 21, 29, 9/3–11/53, 1/12–27/54.

288 Forty-fifth birthday at Maroney: *Trio,* 70, 71; journal, 9/1/53.

288–9 Carol's book, summer in Europe: Lucy Saroyan memoir, 14; Journal, 6/21, 7/2, 8/7, 17, 8/10/54; *Porcupines,* 115–6.

290 George Abbott and *Ah, San Francisco:* journal, 7/29, 8/5, 12/24–7, 9/16/54.

290 Stanley Rose death: journal, 10/22/54.

291–3 *Time of Your Life* revival: *Porcupines,* 115; *Trio,* 99; journal, 11/22–5, 12/22–8/54, 1/17–9/55.

293 *The Cave Dwellers:* journal, 1/8/55.

XV. IN THE CHUTE: 1955–1961

296–7 *The Secret in the Daisy,* Agee death, Brando: *Trio,* 101, 104; journal, 3/9, 14, 30, 5/19, 21, 6/2, 29, 7/20, 11/25/55.

297–8 Confessing, making love in Malibu, her not denying the abortion: journal, 5/24, 6/29, 7/3/55.

298 *Will Success Spoil Rock Hunter?:* journal, 3/20, 6/29, 7/4, 10/11/55; *Porcupines,* 122–32.

300 Matson quarrel: Matson correspondence; journal, 3/21, 24/55; *Obituaries,* 214, 215.

301 Edward Weeks, *Mama* and *Papa* novels, serialization: journal, 7/12, 10/18/55, 3/4, 7/2, 9/5/56.

301 *Boyhood* on Omnibus: journal, 10/16/55, 9/29, 30/56, 10/2, 3, 5, 14/56.

304 IRS: journal, 8/11, 10/12, 18, 19, 11/25, 12/4, 29/55, 5/7, 6/9, 12/6, 23, 28/56, 1/4, 12/57.

305 Nobel hopes: journal, 9/17/57, 7/28/58; to Steinbeck, 12/14/62.

306 Living in Europe: journal, 1/4, 13/59.

306–9 *The Cave Dwellers:* journal, 4/11, 28, 5/9, 14, 16, 19, 9/6, 10/21, 11/5/57.

309 Visit to ailing George Jean Nathan, death of Nathan: *Not Dying,* 87; journal, 11/14, 15/57; *Sons Come,* 126; journal, 4/17/58.

313 *Ya, Yugoslavia: Not Dying,* 148; journal, 10/11–15/58, 3/11–16/59.

314–15 Riviera rampage: *Not Dying,* 26–7, 148; *Chance Meetings,* 99; journal, 3/11–4/16/59.

315–19 Darryl Zanuck and *Lily Dafon, Settled Out of Court: Places,* 51–2; *Sons Come,* 190–1; Journal, 4/21–6/9/59, 2/10/60.

320–2 *Sam, the Highest Jumper* in London: *Days,* 136; journal, 2/23–4/6/60.

322–3 Buying Paris apartment: journal, 5/11/60.

323 Journey to Armenia: journal, 8/24–9/22/60.

324 Budd Schulberg and "The Ordeal of William Saroyan": journal, 10/17/60.

324 *Here Comes, There Goes Saroyan:* journal, 1/27–2/12/61.

325 Aram "Jack" Kevorkian, setting up own firm in 1966, quarrel over French *Time of Your Life:* journal, 3/1/61; Kevorkian interview, 4/29/93.

328–30 The kids, summer of 1956 in California, 1957, the Mediterranean cruise: *Last Rites,* 47; Lucy Saroyan memoir, 7; journal, 6/3–17/58, 4/11/63.

332 Trinity School, Richard Avedon: journal, 3/17, 10/15/58.

334 Criticizing their mother, Aram's response: Aram Saroyan, *William Saroyan,* 127–8; *Here Comes,* "The Time," 254–7; journal, 7/24/58.

335 Victor Hugo and *Not Dying:* Lucy Saroyan memoir, 24; journal, 6/9–8/21/59.

336 Carol marries Walter Matthau, feelings of rejection by both children: *Trio,* 112; journal, 8/26/59; Lucy Saroyan interview, 5/31/91.

336–7 Spain and Aram's protest: *Last Rites,* 152–4; journal, 6/15–7/2/61, 2/4/62.

XVI. WHITELANDS HOUSE:
1961–1968

338 Lucy at M Lazy V Ranch: journal, 7/16, 8/4/61; Lucy Saroyan interview, 8/89; Lucy Saroyan memoir, 29.

338 Aram encounter: journal, 9/11/61; *The Street,* 21.

339–41 Purdue and *Wabash:* journal, 9/17–12/9/61.

341 *Here Comes, There Goes:* journal, 1/22, 2/15/62.

343 Nobel to Steinbeck: journal, 12/14/62.

343 Gitlin and Jovanovich, Harcourt: journal, 7/13, 26, 28, 9/19–20/62.

344–5 *Boys and Girls Together:* journal, 1/14, 2/18, 3/13–8, 5/6/63; Aram correspondence, 7/5/63.

346 Gitlin and *Saturday Evening Post:* journal, 4/1/63, 7/30/63.

346 *Not Dying:* journal, 3/4, 5/19, 7/3, 7/5, 9/25/63.

346–7 *One Day in the Afternoon of the World,* journey to Bitlis: journal, 1/19, 1/26, 5/16–6/6/64.

350 Settling with the IRS, buying Fresno houses: journal, 5/4/62, 7/20, 30, 8/1/64.

350–1 Quarrel with Paul Gitlin: Gitlin correspondence, 9/19, 23/64; Gitlin interview, 1/7/92; journal, 7/7, 8/14/64.

351–2 Jovanovich sale of *Aram* and *The Human Comedy* to Dell, into the stock market: journal, 2/3, 4/66.

352–3 *Letters from 74 rue Taitbout:* journal, 4/19, 5/27, 9/11/68.

353 Birth of Charlie Matthau, and Carol's suit: journal, 12/11/62, 6/21/65.

354 Kevorkian, Harrington, and the Saroyan Foundation, incorporated 1966: correspondence; journal, 9/2, 13/65, 10/30, 11/10, 22, 12/7, 13/66.

355 Chesley's death: *Last Rites,* 105; *Sons Come,* 207; journal, 3/27, 30, 4/3/65.

355 Hagopian and the Juvenelle clinic: journal, 11/6/65; Hagopian interview, 12/7/93.

356 Steinbeck's death, 1967, Mihran's in 1964: journal, 12/18/62, 8/30/64, 12/12/65, 12/2/68; *Days,* 124.

357 Aram to University of Chicago: journal, 9/15/62.

358 The Fiftieth Street penthouse: journal, 12/1, 28/62, 3/23–8/63.

358 Aram quits Chicago: Aram correspondence, 12/7/72; journal, 12/14–16, 31/62; *The Street,* 76; *Friends,* 15.

359 "Twenty Is the Greatest": *Friends,* 19, 51, 82.

360 Brando reflections: journal, 4/11/63; Lucy Saroyan memoir.

363–5 London, Whitelands House, father and children reunited: journal, 4/11/63, 7/7–10, 15/66; Aram correspondence, 10/66–9/67; Lucy Saroyan memoir, 40–6.

368 Aram and Gailyn to Taitbout: journal, 11/23, 12/4, 8, 27/67, 1/5, 9, 2/1, 4/7, 7/17, 27, 31, 8/26, 9/24/68; Lucy Saroyan memoir; Lucy Saroyan interviews, 1989, 1991; Aram correspondence, 11/67–9/68.

369 Censure of Aram's writing, and alienation: *Friends,* 31, 36, 41–6; Aram correspondence, 10/28, 12/13/66, 9/21/67; *The Street,* 101; journal, 12/17/63.

372 Aram and Gailyn marry: journal, 10/9, 11, 12/2/68.

XVII. THE MISANTHROPE:
1968–1974

375 Haigazian College in Beirut: journal, 6/14–27/72.

377–8 *The Armenians:* journal, 11/30/71, 12/29/73, 1/10/74; Whitmore, *William Saroyan,* 20–1.

378 Stories: journal, 3/29, 8/9, 9/17, 10/18, 11/24, 12/27/71, 9/12/72, 2/18, 5/4/74.

379 *Letters from 74 rue Taitbout:* journal, 4/19, 27, 7/12, 15/68, 12/1/70.

380 *Days of Life and Death:* journal, 10/14/69, 4/21, 7/13/70.

381 *Places Where I've Done Time:* journal, 5/27, 9/30/71, 4/5/72.

382–3 *Time of Your Life* re-revived, the national tour: journal, 3/7–27/72.

383 Krakower's death: journal, 5/6/69; *Obituaries,* 217.

385 Affluence: journal, 9/12/71, 9/23/74.

385 Saroyan Foundation and royalties: journal, 6/8/71, 2/14/72–9/10/73.

386–8 Obituaries, memento mori, death of his publishers, Bufano, the prostate: 8/18/70, 5/13, 17, 27, 6/10, 7/4, 5/71, 3/31, 4/8, 9/73.

389 Ross's death: journal, 1/16–8/72; *Obituaries,* 329, Lucy Saroyan memoir, 2.

390 Aram's provocation of his father and silent confrontation at Marboro's, Aram sells letters to UCLA: journal, 2/17, 10/15, 20/69; *Last Rites,* 88.

391 Cordial visit with Aram's family in New York: journal, 12/3/71.

391–2 Aram tries for job at New Hampshire, Bolinas, and hope for downpayment: journal, 7/29–30/72; *Friends,* 68.

393 Lucy confesses Marlon Brando affair: Lucy Saroyan interviews; Lucy Saroyan memoir; journal, 3/19–23/74.

394 Loss of the child in Lucy: *Chance Meetings,* 29–32.

XVIII. OBITUARIES: 1974–1979

396 *Sons Come and Go:* journal, 10/30/74, 2/24, 6/6/75; Fred Hills interview, 10/2/95.

399–400 Franklin Library, Harcourt quarrel: Harrington correspondence, 3/9, 25/77.

402 *Obituaries:* journal, 1/17, 22, 3/1, 4, 5/77, 5/26/78.

403 Armenian trilogy, *Armenians, Bitlis, Haratch:* journal, 3/16/75, 3/8, 8/25/77; Whitmore, *William Saroyan,* 20–1, 25–6, 44–5.

404–7 Fresno-Paris life and travels: journal, 8/2/73, 7/11–8/14/77.

407–8 Quarrels with Kevorkian, Harrington: Kevorkian interview, 4/29/93; journal, 5/16, 17/74.

408 Bancroft speech: journal, 5/6–7/77.

409–10 Bolinas, buying it for Aram, conditions: journal, 7/28, 29, 30, 8/15/72, 10/10/74, 4/7, 8, 21/75, 11/2/77.

410 McClanahan visit: journal, 3/24/76.

411 Birth of Armenak, Aram poem in *Paris Review: Friends,* 83.

412–13 Aram's offer on Malibu, his books *The Town, Genesis Angels: The Street; Last Rites,* 59, 82–5, 88; journal, 9/25/73; Aram Saroyan letter, 8/8/78.

413 Aram's accident, Santa Rosa: Nona Balakian correspondence, 6/17/78; Aram correspondence, 6/19/78; *Last Rites,* 10.

414 End of correspondence, disinheriting both children: Harrington correspondence, 8/17/74, 7/8/78; Lucy Saroyan interview; 6/89.

414 Morrow to publish *Genesis Angels,* Aram misgivings: journal, 3/15/79.

415–16 Chaplin's death, reflections: *Sons Come,* 198; journal, 7/2, 8/11, 12/25/76, 12/25/77.

416 Zabe's death: journal, 8/74/79.

417–18 Prostatitis anxiety, doctors: journal, 2/4–18, 4/17/79.

XIX. ARMENIA, ART, AND FIRE: 1979–1981

419–420 Bizarre dreams, career summarized: journal, 12/13/79.

420 Cancer confirmed, symptoms and treatment: journal, 7/14, 21, 22, 26, 8/3, 18, 22, 9/4, 18, 10/2, 18, 24, 25, 30, 31, 11/1, 6, 10, 21, 12/20/79, 4/3, 7, 10/1/80, 3/11/81.

421 European tours: journal, 6/7–11, 7/10/79, 5/12–6/12, 6/28–9/80.

421–2 *Warsaw Visitor:* Whitmore, *William Saroyan,* 102–3; journal, 6/27/80.

424–5 Concern for literary estate (Saroyan Library vs. Carol, Aram & Lucy): *Warsaw Visitor* in *The Last Two Plays of William Saroyan* (California State University Press, Fresno, 1991), 476–80; wills; *Last Rites,* 31, 78, 175–6; journal, 10/7, 21/80.

426 Neptune Society and cremation plans: journal, 10/24, 25, 29/80.

427 Harrington quarrel, firing: Richard Harrington correspondence, 5/15, 17, 7/8, 8/11/78, 10/18/79, 12/12, 29/80; Robert Damir correspondence, 3/3, 4/8/81; journal, 12/13/79.

427 Damir hired, Kevorkian reappears, signing final will: journal, 11/5/80, 1/12, 2/21, 3/7, 4/8, 11, 17–18/81.

429 Lucy visit: Lucy Saroyan interview, 5/30/91; Aram Saroyan, *William Saroyan,* 145; *Last Rites,* 13, 21, 22, 27–30, 57, 156; journal, 1/26, 4/15, 19/81.

430 Kevin Starr accepts literary executorship: journal, 11/9/79, 4/12, 18/81.

431–2 Admitted to hospital, Aram and children visit, Aram visits, last days: Aram Saroyan, *William Saroyan,* 145–51; *Last Rites,* 118, 127–76; journal, 4/8–19/81.

432 Death: journal, 4/3, 12, 15, 19/81.

Principal Sources

William Saroyan:

> *The Daring Young Man on the Flying Trapeze* (New York: Random House, 1934)
> *Inhale & Exhale* (New York: Random House, 1936)
> *Three Times Three* (Los Angeles: Conference Press, 1936)
> *Love, Here Is My Hat* (New York: Modern Age, 1938)
> *The Bicycle Rider in Beverly Hills* (New York: Scribner, 1952) (*Bicycle Rider*)
> *Here Comes There Goes You Know Who* (New York: Trident, 1961) (*Here Comes*)
> *Not Dying* (New York: Harcourt Brace Jovanovich, 1963)
> *I Used to Believe I Had Forever* (New York: Cowles, 1968) (*Used to Believe*)
> *Letters from Rue Taitbout* (New York: World, 1969) (*Taitbout*)
> *Days of Life and Death* (New York: Dial, 1970) (*Days*)
> *Places Where I've Done Time* (New York: Praeger, 1972) (*Places*)
> *Sons Come and Go, Mothers Hang in Forever* (New York: McGraw-Hill, 1976)
>   (*Sons Come*)
> *Chance Meetings* (New York: Norton, 1978)
> *Obituaries* (Berkeley: Creative Arts, 1979)
> Journal of William Saroyan (1934–1981) (journal)

Aram Saroyan:

> *The Street* (Lenox, Mass.: Bookstore Press, 1974)
> *Last Rites* (New York: Morrow, 1982)
> *William Saroyan* (New York: Harcourt Brace Jovanovich, 1983)
> *Trio* (New York: Linden, 1985)
> *Friends in the World* (Minneapolis: Coffee House Press, 1992) (*Friends*)

Lucy Saroyan:

> Unpublished memoir

Carol Matthau:

> *Among the Porcupines* (New York: Turtle Bay, 1992) (*Porcupines*)

Jon Whitmore:

> *William Saroyan, A Research and Production Source Book* (Westport, Conn.:
>   Greenwood Press, 1994)

Lawrence Lee and Barry Gifford:

> *Saroyan* (New York: Harper & Row, 1984)

Budd Schulberg:

> *The Four Seasons of Success* (New York: Doubleday, 1972) (*Four Seasons*)

Index

Page numbers in *italics* refer to illustrations.

Photographic Credits

A Note on the Type

This book was set in Adobe Garamond. Designed for the Adobe Corporation by Robert Slimbach, the fonts are based on types first cut by Claude Garamond (c. 1480–1561). Garamond was a pupil of Geoffroy Tory and is believed to have followed the Venetian models, although he introduced a number of important differences, and it is to him that we owe the letter we now know as "old style." He gave to his letters a certain elegance and feeling of movement that won their creator an immediate reputation and the patronage of Francis I of France.

Composed by North Market Street Graphics,
Lancaster, Pennsylvania
Printed and bound by Berryville Graphics,
Berryville, Virginia
Designed by Anthea Lingeman